Athenian Officials
684–321 B.C.

Athenian Officials
684–321 B.C.

ROBERT DEVELIN

DEPARTMENT OF CLASSICS,
UNIVERSITY OF TASMANIA

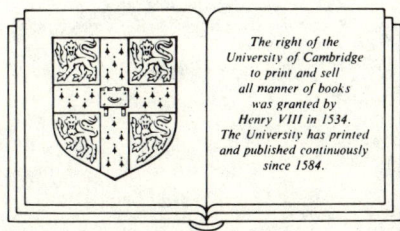

The right of the
University of Cambridge
to print and sell
all manner of books
was granted by
Henry VIII in 1534.
The University has printed
and published continuously
since 1584.

CAMBRIDGE UNIVERSITY PRESS

CAMBRIDGE

NEW YORK   NEW ROCHELLE

MELBOURNE   SYDNEY

Published by the Press Syndicate of the University of Cambridge
The Pitt Building, Trumpington Street, Cambridge CB2 1RP
32 East 57th Street, New York, NY, 10022, USA
10 Stamford Road, Oakleigh, Melbourne 3166, Australia

First published 1989

Printed in Great Britain at the University Press, Cambridge

British Library cataloguing in publication data
Develin, Robert
Athenian officials 684–321 B.C.
1. Greece. Athens. Administration.
Officials B.C. 684–B.C. 321
I. Title
354.3703

Library of Congress cataloguing in publication data
Develin, R.
Athenian officials, 684–321 B.C./Robert Develin.
p.   cm.
Bibliography: p.
Includes indexes.
ISBN 0 521 32880 2
1. Athens (Greece) – Politics and government.
2. Athens (Greece)-Officials and employees – History.
I. Title.
JC73.D45 1989
354.38'500 1 – dc19   88-17765CIP

ISBN 0 521 32880 2

Contents

v

Contents

Preface

Any student of the Roman Republic should be aware of the debt owed to T.R.S. Broughton for making it easier to examine constitutional and political issues. His *The Magistrates of the Roman Republic* not only listed officials year by year, but collected all the relevant source material, summarized known activities and legislation and included some discussion and fundamental bibliography. It seemed that something similar could be done for Athens. In 1980 I secured a research grant from the University of Tasmania to set the project in motion, and from 1981 to 1983 funds were made available from the Australian Research Grants Scheme. Primarily this money paid for the services of a research assistant, and at this point let me record my gratitude to David Betts, who with diligence and accuracy accumulated data for me from literary and epigraphical sources. Hence the store of file cards at the basis of the task of ordering and constant checking. I was fortunate also, while on leave in Princeton in 1981, to have the opportunity to work through the prosopographical files at the Institute for Advanced Study. My thanks, therefore, go to Christian Habicht, also to Steve Bradford and David Whitehead for the coffee and conversation which habitually provided relief from the chore, as well as stimulation, physical and mental. May I also express general thanks to those who have taken an interest and given help, to the readers for Cambridge University Press and to the officers of the Press for seeing matters through.

One debt in particular must be isolated. That is to David Lewis, who has been over the years so generous of his time in debating issues of content and format, for the most part compelling me to admit to necessities, reading and commenting in a forthright manner on developing versions and on so many occasions saving me from error or omission, especially, but by no means only, through his epigraphical

vii

knowledge. The value of this contribution cannot be overestimated in regard to a work where the need for accuracy, clarity, utility and thoroughness is paramount.

Nonetheless, only one name appears as author, that person who must take the responsibility for a work incorporating the results of advice taken or declined. The labour has been hard and sometimes tiresome, but it will be readily appreciated how much has been learned in the process. I have not presumed to anticipate every use that may be made of this volume, but have sought to cover as many lines of utility as I could conceive within the defined compass. There will naturally be disagreements, but although my own opinions have had their part to play, what is here presented will, I hope, provide a point of convenient reference and of departure for future investigations. After 322/1 Athens underwent institutional changes. It was queried at one stage why the work was not extended into the Hellenistic age and perhaps one or more people will take up that challenge. My experience may serve to demonstrate the time and effort needed, but also that there are considerable rewards to be gained by confronting a task which may not be as daunting as it first appears.

Procedures

Each name that is included carries with it, as appropriate, a reference to the number in *PA* and to the page in *NPA* and *APF*; a few have the number in Berve. With members of the council, otherwise mysterious elements may be clarified through the prosopographical index of *Agora* xv. Precise identifications are not always directly attested. Square brackets have been used normally to indicate letters and items of nomenclature restored in inscriptions and also surround epigraphical references which depend upon a sufficient degree of restoration, however likely the result. Real doubt in the restoration is signalled by question marks or direct comment. Where a number of references combine to produce a whole name, the degree of restoration in each reference is not indicated. Round brackets are used for elements of nomenclature which are not certain or not directly attested in the specific evidence, the addition of a question mark signalling doubt. Nonetheless, personal opinion intrudes: where the number of a tribe falls outside such parentheses, this indicates acceptance of the identification; where it is included within them, less certainty.

Texts are cited in approximate chronological order, literary evidence before epigraphical. For the most part citation is intended to be exhaustive; the intention goes beyond the mere establishment of a position for a person. So, for example, references to an archon will provide a conspectus of all specific allusions to the year in question. Then there are the records of the treasurers, where I have also indicated which of a plurality of documents are the actual inventories of the particular year, as these constitute a series (though not unbroken) over a considerable span of time.

Transliteration of Greek names is not consistent and is determined by what I feel comfortable with; hence Corcyra, Cyprus, Corinth, but

Kyrene, Kenchreiai, and I could not bear to spell the historian's name Thoukydides when I do not pronounce it accordingly – the son of Melesias is a different matter. More generally, such variation as occurs should cause no problem.

As for the divisions in the work, Solon, the end of the tyranny, the Persian and Peloponnesian Wars provided demarcation points and after that one had to follow the arrangement of IG.

Chronology

Though there are periods when the chronology of a series of events is debatable, I have for the most part subdued my own discomfort and avoided discussion in favour of more orthodox views, so that the user may find information where it may reasonably be expected to occur. Where possible, I have included remarks under the appropriate year and the placing of some officials follows the chronological scheme indicated under the relevant heading in the ensuing section. I add here only a few brief notes, mainly for bibliographical purposes.

1. *Solon*. His work is included under 594/3 (*q.v.*), though I believe in a *nomothesia* ending in 592/1. For discussion see Rhodes, *Comm.* 120ff., 164, 169f.; add Reeker, *A&A* 1971, 96ff.; Maddoli, *Cronologia* 21ff., 51ff.; Podlecki in *Classica et Iberica* (Festschrift Marique: Worcester, Mass. 1975), 31ff.; Sheppard, *LCM* 1980, 205ff.

2. *The Tyranny*. My belief is that the chronology in *Ath. Pol.* for the ins and outs of Peisistratos is correct, with only the emendation of 'twelfth' at 14.4 to read 'fifth' or 'sixth'. Herein, however, I follow dates to be found in Rhodes, *Comm.* 191ff., placing Peisistratos' three *coups* in 561/60, 557/6 and 546/5. See also Jacoby, *Atthis* 188ff. and notes; Hammond, *Historia* 1955, 381ff.; Heidbüchel, *Philologus* 1957, 70ff., Sumner, *CQ* 1961, 37ff.; Ruebel, *GRBS* 1973, 125ff.; Hind, *CQ* 1974, 1ff.; Maddoli, *Cronologia* 27ff.; Rhodes, *Phoenix* 1976, 219ff.; Schreiner, *SO* 1981, 13ff.; Andrewes, *CAH*[2] iii.3.399ff.

3. *The Pentekontaetia*. Debate still continues and will continue. Fundamental treatments are Gomme, *Comm. Thuc.* i.389ff.; *ATL* iii.158ff.; Deane, *Thuc. Dates*. The latter is in many respects radical, but not a patch on the openly anti-Thucydidean studies of Schreiner in *SO* 1976, 19ff., and 1977, 19ff.; *OAth* 1984, 163ff. One will, of course,

consult Meiggs, *Ath. Empire*, and here is a further selection: P. Salmon, *La politique égyptienne d'Athènes* (Brussels 1965), 100ff.; Podlecki, *Them.* 197ff.; E. Bayer and J. Heideking, *Die Chronologie des perikleischen Zeitalters* (Darmstadt 1975); Milton, *Historia* 1979, 257ff.; Roveri, *RSA* 1980, 27ff., M. Steinbrecher, *Der delisch-attische Seebund und die athenisch-spartanischen Beziehungen der kimonischen Ära (ca. 478/7–462–1)* (Stuttgart 1985), 15ff.; Unz, *CQ* 1986, 68ff. Again I hold heterodox opinions, but here I follow the scheme of Gomme for the most part, though I may deviate by a year.

4. *The Corinthian War.* Works on the period 395/4 – 388/7 are likely to spend time on chronology. The main early treatment was provided by Beloch in *Attische Politik* and *Griechische Geschichte*. See also Aucello, *Helikon* 1964, 29ff.; T.T.B. Ryder, *Koine Eirene* (Oxford 1965), 165ff.; Cawkwell, *CQ* 1976, 271ff.; Hamilton, *Bitter Victories*. In general I follow Funke, *Homonoia* 76ff. and for Cyprus Tuplin, *Philologus* 1983, 170ff.

5. For the years 341–339 see Wankel, *ZPE* 42 (1981), 153ff.

References

Where possible, in the interests of those who might need to use translations, I have used Loeb editions, which can make a difference, for example, in the numeration of Hypereides' speeches or in section references to chapters of Plutarch's biographies. Fragments of orators follow the numeration of Teubner texts. Otherwise standard texts are used, though sometimes it has been necessary to specify the editor. I have generally not felt it necessary to indicate doubts about authorship, so that Dem. and Plut. may mean simply that a work appears in the corpus of the author.

As for secondary references, this is not meant to be a guide to bibliography in any large sense and I have tried to keep this area in reasonable bounds. References to ancient texts on which there are commentaries assume that those commentaries will be consulted. Articles are not included in the bibliography, which is intended to give full details of books and contributions to volumes of essays which are cited in abbreviated form. There follows a list of abbreviations used in the course of the work and the bibliography.

ABBREVIATIONS

Ael(ius) Arist(ides)
Agora XV: *The Athenian Agora* vol. XV: *Inscriptions. The Athenian Councillors* (Princeton 1974)
Agora XVII: *id.* vol. XVII: *Inscriptions. The Funerary Monuments* (Princeton 1974)
Ain(eias) Takt(ikos)
Aisch(ines)
And(okides)
Anth(ologia) Pal(atina)
APF: J.K. Davies, *Athenian Propertied Families 600–300 B.C.* (Oxford 1971)
Ar(istophanes)
Arist(otle)

References

Ath(enaion) Pol(iteia): ? Aristotle, *Constitution of the Athenians*

ATL: B.D. Meritt, H.T. Wade-Gery, M.F. McGregor, *The Athenian Tribute Lists* 4 vols. (Harvard, then Princeton 1939–53)

Berve: H. Berve, *Das Alexanderreich auf prosopographischer Grundlage* vol. II (Munich 1926)

CAH: *Cambridge Ancient History*

CEG: P.A. Hansen, *Carmina Epigraphica Graeca* (Berlin/New York 1983)

Cic(ero)

DAA: A.E. Raubitschek, *Dedications from the Athenian Akropolis* (Cambridge, Mass., 1949)

Dem(osthenes)

Diod(oros of Sicily)

Diog(enes Laertius)

Dion(ysios of Halikarnassos)

FD: *Fouilles de Delphes*

FGH: F. Jacoby, *Die Fragmente der Griechischen Historiker*

Fornara: C.W. Fornara, *Translated Documents of Greece and Rome* vol. I: *Archaic Times to the End of the Peloponnesian War*² (Cambridge 1983)

Front(inus)

Harding: P. Harding, *Translated Documents of Greece and Rome* vol. II: *From the End of the Peloponnesian War to the Battle of Ipsus* (Cambridge 1985)

Hell(enica) Oxy(rhynchia)

Her(odotos)

hyp(othesis)

IG: *Inscriptiones Graecae*

Incs. Bardo: *Inscriptions grecques du Musée de Bardo* (Paris 1936)

Insc. Délos: *Inscriptions de Délos*

Insc. Priene: *Inschriften von Priene* (Berlin 1906)

Isok(rates)

LS: F. Sokolowski, *Lois sacrées des cités grecques* (Paris 1969)

LSS: F. Sokolowski, *Lois sacrées des cités grecques. Supplément* (Paris 1962)

Meritt, *AFD*: B.D. Meritt, *Athenian Financial Documents of the Fifth Century* (Ann Arbor 1932)

Michel, *Recueil*: C. Michel, *Recueil d'inscriptions grecques* (Paris/Brussels 1900–1927)

ML: R. Meiggs and D.M. Lewis, *A Selection of Greek Historical Inscriptions* (Oxford 1969)

MP: Marmor Parium: *FGH* 239

NPA: J. Sundwall, *Nachträge zur Prosopographia Attica* (Helsinki 1910)

Ol(ympiad)

Osborne: M.J. Osborne, *Naturalization in Athens* 4 vols. in 3 (Brussels 1981–3)

PA: J. Kirchner, *Prosopographia Attica* (Berlin 1901–3)

P.Ryl.: *Catalogue of the Greek and Latin Papyri in the John Rylands Library, Manchester* vol. III (Manchester 1938)

Paus(anias)

Plut(arch)

P.Oxy.: *The Oxyrhynchus Papyri*

pryt(any)

Reinmuth: O.W. Reinmuth, *The Ephebic Inscriptions of the Fourth Century B.C.* (Leiden 1971)

References

schol(ion or -ia)
Schwenk: C.J. Schwenk, *Athens in the Age of Alexander. The dated laws and decrees of 'the Lykourgan era' 338–322 B.C.* (Chicago 1985)
SEG: *Supplementum Epigraphicum Graecum*
SIG I³: W. Dittenberger, *Sylloge Inscriptionum Graecarum* vol. I³ (Leipzig 1915) with development by others
Steph(anos) Byz(antinus)
TAM: Tituli Asiae Minores
[Them] (istokles)
Thuc(ydides)
Tod: M.N. Tod, *A Selection of Greek Historical Inscriptions* vol. II (Oxford 1948)
Val(erius) Max(imus)
Walbank: M.B. Walbank, *Athenian Proxenies of the Fifth Century B.C.* (Toronto and Sarasota 1978)
Xen(ophon)

Journal abbreviations follow the system of *L'Année Philologique*

BIBLIOGRAPHY

Accame, S. *La lega ateniese del secolo IV a.C.* Rome 1941
Andrewes, A. *The Greek Tyrants.* London 1956.
   See Gomme, A.W.
Aurenche, O. *Les groupes d'Alcibiade, de Léogoras et de Teucros.* Paris 1974
Balcer, J.M. *The Athenian Regulations for Chalkis.* Historia Einzelschriften 33. Wiesbaden 1978.
Bartolini, G. *Iperide.* Padua 1977.
Beazley, J.D. *Attic Black-Figure Vase-Painters.* Oxford 1956.
   The Development of Attic Black Figure². Berkeley/Los Angeles/London 1964.
Beloch, J. *Die attische Politik seit Perikles.* Leipzig 1884.
Berve, H. *Die Tyrannis bei den Griechen.* Munich 1967.
Bicknell, P.J. *Studies in Athenian Politics and Genealogy.* Historia Einzelschriften 19. Wiesbaden 1972.
Boersma, J.S. *Athenian Building Policy from 561/0 to 405/4 B.C.* Groningen 1970.
Bousquet, J. 'Le compte de l'automne 325 à Delphes', *Mélanges helléniques offerts à Georges Daux* (Paris 1974), 21–32
Bradeen, D.W. and McGregor, M.F. *Studies in Fifth-Century Attic Epigraphy.* Univ. of Cincinnati Classical Studies IV. Norman, Oklahoma, 1973.
Bruce, I.A.F. *An Historical Commentary on the 'Hellenica Oxyrhynchia'.* Cambridge 1967.
Burn, A.R. *Persia and the Greeks.* London 1962.
Cargill, J. *The Second Athenian League.* Berkeley/Los Angeles/London 1981.
Cavanaugh, M.B. *Eleusis and Athens. Documents in Finance, Religion and Politics in the Second Half of the Fifth Century B.C.* Diss. Cornell 1980.
Cawkwell, G. *Philip of Macedon.* London 1978.
Clairmont, C.W. *Patrios Nomos. Public Burial in Athens during the Fifth and Fourth Centuries B.C.* BAR International Series 161. Oxford 1983.
Clinton, K. *The Sacred Officials of the Eleusinian Mysteries.* Transactions of the American Philosophical Society 64.3, 1974.

References

Connor, W.R. *The New Politicians of Fifth-Century Athens.* Princeton 1971.

Davies, J.K. *Wealth and the Power of Wealth in Classical Athens.* New York 1981.

Davis, P.H. 'An Eleusinian building contract', *Classical Studies presented to Edward Capps* (Princeton 1936), 86–9.

Day, J.H. and Chambers, M.H. *Aristotle's History of Athenian Democracy.* Univ. of California Publications in History 73. Berkeley/Los Angeles 1962.

Deane, P. *Thucydides' Dates 465–431 B.C.* Don Mills, Ontario, 1972.

De Laix, R.A. *Probouleusis at Athens.* Univ. of California Publications in History 83. Berkeley/Los Angeles/London 1973.

De Ste Croix, G.E.M. *The Origins of the Peloponnesian War.* London 1972.

De Sanctis, G. *Atthis³.* Florence 1975.

Dover, K.J. See Gomme, A.W.

Dow, S. 'Companionable associates in the Athenian Government', *Essays in Archaeology and the Humanities in memoriam O.J. Brendel* (Mainz 1976), 69–84.

Edmonson, C.N. 'Onesippos' Herm', *Studies in Attic Epigraphy, History and Topography presented to E. Vanderpool* (Hesperia Suppl. 19, 1982), 48–50.

Ehrenberg, V. *Sophocles and Pericles.* Oxford 1954.

Ellis, J.R. *Philip II and Macedonian Imperialism.* London 1976.

Ferguson, W.S. *The Athenian Secretaries.* Cornell Studies in Classical Philology 7. New York 1898.

    The Priests of Asklepios. Univ. of California Publications in Classical Philology 1 no. 5 (1906), 131–73.

    The Treasurers of Athena. Cambridge, Mass., 1932.

Finley, M.I. *Studies in Land and Credit in Ancient Athens, 500–200 B.C.* New Brunswick 1952.

Fornara, C.W. *The Athenian Board of Generals from 501 to 404.* Historia Einzelschriften 16. Wiesbaden 1971.

Freeman, K. *The Work and Life of Solon.* Cardiff 1926.

Frel, J. *Panathenaic Prize Amphoras.* German Archaeological Institute at Athens: Kerameikos Book no. 2, 1973.

French, A. *The Growth of the Athenian Economy.* London 1964.

Frost, F.J. *Plutarch's Themistocles.* Princeton 1980.

Funke, P. *Homonoia und Arché. Athen und die griechische Staatenwelt vom Ende des peloponnesischen Krieges bis zum Königsfrieden (404/3–387/6 v. Chr.).* Historia Einzelschriften 37. Wiesbaden 1980.

Gagarin, M. *Drakon and Early Athenian Homicide Law.* New Haven/London 1981.

Gehrke, H.-J. *Phokion. Studien zur Erfassung seiner historischen Gestalt.* Zetemata 64. Munich 1976.

Ghinatti, F. *I gruppi politici ateniesi fino alle guerre persiane.* Rome 1970.

Gomme, A.W., Andrewes, A. and Dover, K.J. *A Historical Commentary on Thucydides.* Oxford 1945–1981.

Griffith, G.T. See Hammond, N.G.L.

Hamilton, C.D. *Sparta's Bitter Victories.* Ithaca/London 1979.

Hammond, N.G.L. *Studies in Greek History.* Oxford 1973.

    and Griffith, G.T. *A History of Macedonia* vol. II: *550–336.* Oxford 1979.

Hansen, M.H. *The Sovereignty of the People's Court in Athens in the Fourth Century B.C. and the Public Action against Unconstitutional Proposals.* Odense Univ. Classical Studies 4, 1974.

References

Eisangelia. The Sovereignty of the People's Court in Athens in the Fourth Century B.C. and the Impeachment of Generals and Politicians. Odense Univ. Classical Studies 6, 1975.

Apagoge, Endeixis and Ephegesis against Kakourgoi, Atimoi and Pheugontes. Odense Univ. Classical Studies 8, 1976.

The Athenian Ecclesia. Copenhagen 1983.

Henry, A.S. *The Prescripts of Athenian Decrees.* Mnemosyne Suppl. 49. Leiden 1977.

Hignett, C. *A History of the Athenian Constitution.* Oxford 1952.

Xerxes' Invasion of Greece. Oxford 1963.

Hornblower, S. *Mausolus.* Oxford 1982.

Hunter, R.L. *Eubulus: the Fragments.* Cambridge 1983.

Jameson, M.H. 'The leasing of land in Rhamnous', *Studies in Attic Epigraphy, History and Topography presented to E. Vanderpool* (Hesperia Suppl. 19, 1982), 66–74.

Jeffery, L.H. *The Local Scripts of Archaic Greece.* Oxford 1961.

Jordan, B. *The Athenian Navy in the Classical Period.* Univ. of California Publications in Classical Studies 13: Berkeley/Los Angeles/London 1975.

Servants of the Gods. Hypomnemata 55. Göttingen 1979.

Kagan, D.W. *The Outbreak of the Peloponnesian War.* Ithaca 1969.

Knight, D.W. *Some Studies in Athenian Politics in the Fifth Century B.C.* Historia Einzelschriften 13. Wiesbaden 1970.

Kraay, C.M. *Archaic and Classical Greek Coins.* London 1976.

Krentz, P. *The Thirty at Athens.* Ithaca/London 1982.

Labarbe, J. *La loi navale de Thémistocle.* Paris 1957.

Lefkowitz, M.R. *The Lives of the Greek Poets.* London 1981.

Lenardon, R.J. *The Saga of Themistocles.* London 1978.

Lévêque, P. and Vidal-Naquet, P. *Clisthène l'Athénien.* Annales littéraires de l'Université de Besançon 65. Paris 1964 (1973).

Levi, M.A. *Commento storico alla Respublica Atheniensium di Aristotele.* Varese/Milan 1968.

Lewis, D.M. 'The Athenian rationes centesimarum', *Problèmes de la terre en Grèce ancienne* (ed. M.I. Finley: Paris 1973), 187–212.

Sparta and Persia. Cincinnati Classical Studies n.s. 1. Leiden 1977.

Linders, T. *Studies in the Treasure Records of Artemis Brauronia found in Athens.* Acta Instituti Atheniensis Regni Sueciae, series in 4°, 19. Stockholm 1972.

The Treasurers of the Other Gods in Athens and their Functions. Beiträge zur klassischen Philologie 62. Meisenheim am Glan 1975.

MacDowell, D.M. *Andokides. On the Mysteries.* Oxford 1962.

Aristophanes: Wasps. Oxford 1971.

The Law in Classical Athens. London 1978.

McGregor, M.F. See Bradeen, D.W.

'Solon's archonship: the epigraphic evidence', *Polis and Imperium* (Studies in honour of E.T. Salmon: Toronto 1974), 31–4.

'Athens and Hestiaia', *Studies in Attic Epigraphy, History and Topography presented to E. Vanderpool* (Hesperia Suppl. 19, 1982), 101–11.

Maddoli, G. *Cronologia e storia. Studi comparati sull' 'Athenaion Politeia' di Aristotele.* Perugia 1975.

Martina, A. *Solone. Testimonianze sulla vita e l'opera. (Solon. Testimonia veterum).* Rome 1968.

References

Masaracchia, T. *Solone*. Florence 1958.
Mattingly, H.B. 'Periclean Imperialism', *Ancient Society and Institutions* (Studies presented to Victor Ehrenberg on his 75th birthday: Oxford 1966), 193–223.
'The Themistokles decree from Troizen: transmission and status', *Classical Contributions* (Studies in honour of Malcolm Francis McGregor: Locust Valley, New York 1981), 79–87.
Meiggs, R. *The Athenian Empire*. Oxford 1972.
Trees and Timber in the Ancient Mediterranean World. Oxford 1982.
Meister, K. *Die Ungeschichtlichkeit des Kalliasfriedens und deren historische Folgen*. Palingenesia 18. Wiesbaden 1982.
Meritt, B.D. See Pritchett, W.K.
The Athenian Year. Sather lectures 32. Berkeley/Los Angeles 1961.
'The Choiseul Marble: the text of 406 B.C.', *Mélanges helléniques offerts à Georges Daux* (Paris 1974), 255–67.
'Thucydides and the decrees of Kallias', *Studies in Attic Epigraphy, History and Topography presented to E. Vanderpool* (Hesperia Suppl. 19, 1982), 112–21.
Mikalson, J.D. *The Sacred and Civil Calendar of the Athenian Year*. Princeton 1975.
Mitchel, F.W. *Lykourgan Athens: 338–322*. Taft Semple lectures, Univ. of Cincinnati, 1970.
Mosley, D.J. *Envoys and Diplomacy in Ancient Greece*. Historia Einzelschriften 22. Wiesbaden 1973.
Mossé, Cl. *La tyrannie dans la Grèce antique*. Paris 1969.
Mosshammer, A.A. *The Chronicle of Eusebius and Greek Chronographic Tradition*. Lewisburg/London 1979.
Ostwald, M. *Nomos and the Beginnings of the Athenian Democracy*. Oxford 1969.
Page, D.L. *Sappho and Alcaeus*. Oxford 1955.
Patterson, C. *Pericles' Citizenship Law of 451–50 B.C.* New York 1981.
Pečírka, J. *The Formula for the Grant of Enktesis in Attic Inscriptions*. Acta Univ. Carolinae Philosophica et Historica, Monographia 15. Prague 1966.
Peek, W. *Kerameikos* vol. III. Berlin 1941.
Piccirilli, L. *Storie dello storico Tucidide*. Università 18. Genoa 1985.
Pickard-Cambridge, A.W. *The Dramatic Festivals of Athens*[2] (revised by J. Gould and D.M. Lewis). Oxford 1968.
Podlecki, A.J. *The Life of Themistocles*. Montreal/London 1975.
Pritchett, W.K. *The Greek State at War* vol. II. Berkeley/Los Angeles 1974.
and Meritt, B.D. *The Chronology of Hellenistic Athens*. Cambridge, Mass., 1940.
and Neugebauer, O. *The Calendars of Athens*. Cambridge, Mass. 1947.
Quass, F. *Nomos und Psephisma: Untersuchung zum griechischen Staatsrecht*. Zetemata 55. Munich 1971.
Rhodes, P.J. *The Athenian Boule*[2]. Oxford 1985.
A Commentary on the Aristotelian Athenaion Politeia. Oxford 1981.
Roux, G. *L'amphictionie, Delphes et le temple d'Apollon au IVe siècle*. Lyon 1979.
Ruschenbusch, E. *ΣΟΛΩΝΟΣ ΝΟΜΟΙ*. Historia Einzelschriften 9. Wiesbaden 1966.
Salmon, J.B. *Wealthy Corinth*. Oxford 1984.
Samuel, A.E. *Greek and Roman Chronology*. Munich 1972.

References

Sealey, R. *Essays in Greek Politics.* New York [1967].
   A History of the Greek City States 700–338 B.C. Berkeley/Los Angeles/London 1976.
Siewert, P. *Die Trittyen Attikas und die Heeresreform des Kleisthenes.* Vestigia 33. Munich 1982.
Starr, C.G. *The Economic and Social Growth of Early Greece 800–500 B.C.* New York 1977.
Staveley, E.S. 'Voting procedure at the election of strategoi', *Ancient Society and Institutions* (Studies presented to Victor Ehrenberg on his 75th birthday: Oxford 1966), 275–88.
Stroud, R.S. *Drakon's Law on Homicide.* Univ. of California Publications in Classical Studies 3. Berkeley/Los Angeles 1968.
   'State documents in archaic Athens', *Athens Comes of Age. From Solon to Salamis* (Princeton 1978), 20–42.
Sundwall, J. *Epigraphische Beiträge zur sozial-politischen Geschichte Athens im Zeitalter des Demosthenes.* Klio Beiheft 4, 1906.
Thompson, W.E. 'Tot Atheniensibus idem nomen erat', *ΦΟΡΟΣ (Phoros)* (Tribute to B.D. Meritt: Locust Valley, New York 1974), 144–9.
Threatte, L. *The Grammar of Attic Inscriptions* vol. I: *Phonology.* Berlin/New York 1980.
Tracy, S.V. 'Hands in fifth-century B.C. Attic inscriptions', *Studies presented to Sterling Dow on his Eightieth Birthday* (GRBS Suppl. 10, 1984), 277–82.
Tréheux, J. 'Études sur les inventaires attiques', *Études d'archéologie classique* 3 (1965), 1–85.
Usener, K.H. *Epicurea.* Leipzig 1887.
Virgilio, B. *Commento storico al quinto libro delle 'Storie' di Erodoto.* Pisa 1975.
Wade-Gery, H.T. *Essays in Greek History.* Oxford 1958.
Walbank, M.B. 'The decree for Lapyris of Kleonai (*IG* 2².365)', *Classical Contributions* (Studies in honour of Malcolm Francis McGregor: Locust Valley, New York 1981), 171–5.
Wevers, R.F. *Isaeus: Chronology, Prosopography, and Social History.* Studies in Classical Literature 4. The Hague/Paris 1969.
White, M.E. 'Hippias and the Athenian archon list', *Polis and Imperium* (Studies in honour of E.T. Salmon: Toronto 1974), 81–95.
Whitehead, D. *The Ideology of the Athenian Metic.* PCPhS Suppl. 4, 1977.
   The Demes of Attika, 508/7 – ca. 250 B.C.: a Political and Social Study. Princeton 1986.
Wilhelm, A. *Attische Urkunden* vol. v. SAWW 220.5, 1942.

Introduction

THE OFFICIALS

There follow brief remarks on the various officials included in this work. The general criterion for inclusion has been those for whom we have names and who were subject to election, by whatever means, to positions in the service of the state or sections thereof where there is some connexion with the operation of state functions. There will be doubt in some cases, but I have sought justification in the appropriate section below. I have not felt obliged to restrict myself to those positions only which could be termed an *arche* (see Hansen, *GRBS* 1980, 151ff.), but have rather followed what seemed to be (though the term is dangerous) common sense.

There is one area, however, which needs to be dealt with here. I had originally included trierarchs and archetheoroi. This was an issue which provoked debate on both sides of the question. I had thought that trierarchs in particular were of some importance, but of course they were liturgants. If we included them, why should not other liturgants find a place? Systematic lists of those performing the various liturgies could be useful, but the decision was made to exclude trierarchs and with them went any possibility of other liturgants. Consistency has led me to resist an inconsolable plea for archetheoroi, but let me at least include for archetheoroi to Delos a reference to Coupry, *BCH* 1954, 285ff.

Certain assumptions may be held to apply to most, if not all, of the positions included. The state had means of scrutinizing suitability and qualifications for office. A minimum age of 30 may well be ascribed to most officials, but we must not assume that it applied in all cases or that it was necessarily rigid (Develin, *ZPE* 61 (1985), 149ff.).

Specific secondary references will be given in what follows where necessary, but not exhaustive bibliographies in all cases. In general officials may be traced through G. Busolt and H. Swoboda, *Griechische Staatskunde* II (Munich 1926), and U. Kahrstedt, *Untersuchungen zur Magistratur in Athen* (Stuttgart/Berlin 1936). References to *Ath. Pol.* as usual imply Rhodes' commentary.

Archons

The work begins when the archonship became annual. At this stage there were three officials: the archon (eponymous), basileus and polemarchos. At some unidentified point in the seventh century, but before *c.* 630, six subsidiary officers, the thesmothetai, were added (*Ath. Pol.* 3.4). At a later date, by or in connexion with the election reform of 487/6, the college became ten with the addition of a grammateus. At some state each of the three major archons was allowed to choose two paredroi (*Ath. Pol.* 56.1), men to act as advisers, helpers and sometimes substitutes for their archon; these are included as they were important enough to be subject to public scrutiny and accountability (Dow, *Essays Brendel* 8off.).

On archon election see Develin, *AC* 1979, 455ff.; cf. *Athenaeum* 1984, 299, 305ff. At the early date, election was made on criteria of birth and wealth (*Ath. Pol.* 3.6), presumably by a body of electors similarly defined. By the time of Drakon (*Ath. Pol.* 4.2), the qualification was one of wealth and those of hoplite status did the electing. Nine candidates were chosen and the Areiopagos decided who was best suited to each post (*Ath. Pol.* 8.2), a role it may have played earlier too. Solon introduced a system whereby each of the four tribes preselected ten men and the final college was decided by lot, as was probably also at the same time the incumbent of each archonship. This system seems to have been abandoned by 582/1 and seems not to have operated during the tyranny or for some time thereafter. In 487/6, now with ten tribes, tribal preselection and the lot returned, with one member from each tribe represented on the college (*Ath. Pol.* 22.5, 55.1; cf. Bicknell, *AC* 1985, 78ff.). Solon at least made the top census class eligible for the archonship; either then or later it seems the second class was eligible. In 458/7 or 457/6 the zeugitai were granted access.

Our evidence is naturally dominated by eponymous archons. The first possible basileus appears in ?636/5, the first known polemarch in ?557/6. We know of no thesmothetai until 444/3 (given that Drakon was not one). And the first paredros appears under 394/3.

Military

Here I shall list strategoi, then other infantry and cavalry officers, followed by naval personnel and occasional commands.

Strategoi

Fornara, *Generals* 1ff., in the context of his discussion of the reform of 501/0, doubts that there were strategoi before that. Hammond, *Studies* 348ff., accepts that there were. We must indeed do so and the first known general is placed in 607/6. Not only is there evidence for specific generals, they are mentioned in *Ath. Pol.* 4. There we find that a property qualification higher than that of the archons was required, along with other stipulations, and the indication seems to be that one or a number were chosen annually, but this is problematic (Develin, *Athenaeum* 1984, 304f.). They will, I presume, have been elected by the hoplite body and their existence may well be a corollary of the extended franchise. As of 501/0 they were elected one per tribe by the whole demos (as I continue to believe against Fornara and Stanton, *Chiron* 1984, 15f.; see *Ath. Pol.* 22.2, cf. 61.1). As *Ath. Pol.* 61.1 indicates, at some stage the principle of tribal representation was abandoned. The first possible example of a tribe providing two generals comes in 479/8; the evidence on which this is based is not of the best, but thereafter one is not bound to exclude identifications which create double representation. In 441/40 we have indisputable evidence for it and in later years it is hard to avoid the conclusion that more than one tribe could provide two generals. The context of the Persian War seems appropriate for the change, as it would allow the selection of the best military leaders without restriction. In normal circumstances conservatism may have affected results, but again it is no surprise if the onset of the Peloponnesian War sees further loosening in this regard. For debate on the question and electoral procedure see also West, *AJPh* 1924, 141ff.; Wade-Gery, *CPh* 1931, 309ff.; Lenz, *TAPhA* 1941, 226ff.; Ehrenberg, *AJPh* 1945, 113ff.; Hignett, *HAC* 347ff.; Jameson,

3

TAPhA 1955, 63ff.; Dover, *JHS* 1960, 61ff.; Lewis, *JHS* 1961, 118ff.; Staveley, *Anc. Soc. and Inst.* 275ff.; *Greek and Roman Voting and Elections* (London 1972), 87f.; Bicknell, *Studies* 107ff.; Piérart, *BCH* 1974, 125ff.; Ruschenbusch, *Historia* 1975, 112ff.

At the time when *Ath. Pol.* 61.1 was written, generals were elected to specific areas, one ἐπὶ τοὺς ὁπλίτας (in command of the hoplites if they should be led out), one ἐπὶ τὴν χώραν (over the country, to protect it should there be war in Attika), two in charge of Peiraieus, two more of Mounichia, one of Akte, one in charge of symmories, who chose the trierarchs; the others were available for contingencies. Sarikakis, *The Hoplite General in Athens* (Diss. Princeton 1951), 13f., saw this system as coming in after Chaironeia, 338/7; Hammond supposed it originated immediately after the Persian War, but this is surely too early. Information on the activities of generals before 338/7 does not seem to square with having only two available for overseas expeditions, but there was no reason why more could not be relieved of specific duties if it was necessary. Moreover, the system could have come in gradually. Indeed, our first specific evidence provides a general over the country in 350/49, while such a general is mentioned in IG ii² 204.19f. (352/1).

The evidence does not seem to me to support the supposition that more than ten generals were ever in place at the beginning of a year. That this *could* have happened if the need arose is possible, but no such need can be demonstrated.

In 417/16 and 416/15 is the first evidence for possible paredroi.

Taxiarchoi

Ath. Pol. 61.3 mentions the direct election of taxiarchs, one presumes by the demos, one for each tribal contingent. It is clear that they could serve at sea as well as on land. One should suppose that their institution coincided with that of tribally distributed generalships in 501/0. The first known taxiarch appears sometime before 432/1 (appendix to Section IV).

Lochagoi

Ath. Pol. 61.3 says lochagoi were appointed by the taxiarchs. Whether that had always been so, we cannot say, but the first lochagos appears for 479/8 and Bicknell, *Studies* 21 and n.67, supposes they were in charge of trittys contingents.

Hipparchoi

Ath. Pol. 61.4 says that two hipparchs were chosen 'from all'. Each was in charge of five tribal cavalry contingents. However, three hipparchs appear together in the appendix to Section IV, so there could have been change over time. This is our first evidence for such officers, but they are mentioned in *Ath. Pol.* 4.2 and should be accepted as existing then, when they were selected from men of the same wealth category as strategoi (Develin, *Athenaeum* 1984, 304). Cf. Bugh, *TAPhA* 1982, 23ff.

Phylarchoi

Ath. Pol. 61.5 says they were directly elected, one for each tribal contingent. Their history is shadowy. Her. 5.69.2 says that Kleisthenes made the phylarchs ten instead of four. The context can hardly be made military (*pace* Fornara, *Generals* 1, 8), but this does not eliminate the possibility that the phylarchs had a military role to play. Our first known phylarch appears in 430/29. Cf. Bugh, *TAPhA* 1982, 23ff.

Toxarchoi

A single toxarchos appears under 413/12. We are in no position to say more.

Ephebic officers

Contrary to Reinmuth's supposition, the ephebic organization which we view is not visible in 361/60, but is first evidenced in 334/3 (Lewis, *CR* 1973, 254ff.; Dow, *Essays Brendel* 81ff.; Mitchel, *ZPE* 19 (1975), 234ff.). *Ath. Pol.* 42.2ff. gives us a description. Three men from each tribe over the age of 40 were chosen and from these the demos elected one from each tribe to be sophronistes; also elected, from all Athenians, was a kosmetes over all the ephebes. Two paidotribai were elected and didaskaloi, to teach skills to the cadets. For discussion on whether the sophronistai and kosmetai served for one or two years and on other matters see Rhodes, *Comm.* 504ff. The evidence within our period has names under the titles sophronistes, kosmetes, didaskalos, epimeletes, akontistes, gymnasiarch. We also have, in 324/3, a peripolarchos, in charge of patrols conducted by the ephebes; this position in fact arises earlier (411), whether or not it was connected with a similar group. The taxiarchs and lochagoi from the ephebic cadets are not appropriate to this work.

Nauarchoi/archons of the fleet

There are problems of terminology here, as sources could perhaps use 'nauarchos' of a general at sea, while Thucydides can certainly use 'archon' and cognates in referring to strategoi. Our first nauarchos appears in 460/59, but unfortunately through Ktesias. However, the term 'archon of the fleet' is attested epigraphically for 410/9 and it is hard not to equate the two. Also Nepos *Conon* 1.1 is able to separate Konon's exploits as *praetor* and as *praefectus classis*. That there could be at least three such naval officers in a year is indicated by Xen. *Hell.* 1.6.29, where the ten ships of the taxiarchs are followed by the three of the nauarchs. Views on this have been developed by Jordan, *TAPhA* 1970, 229ff. (*Navy* 119ff.). While I am in basic agreement on the existence of such officials, I do not follow his identifications in all instances and indicate my preference in individual cases. I shall also use the designation found in the particular source, though I believe 'archon of the fleet' to have been the actual title.

Pentekontarchoi

See Jordan, *Navy* 147ff. There was evidently one per trireme; the method of appointment we do not know. The first known are found under 405/4, but [Xen.] *Ath. Pol.* 1.2 shows that the position existed earlier.

Kybernetai

See Jordan, *Navy* 138ff. As professionals, helmsmen do not enter our scheme. I mention only one case (407/6) where such a man was given a special charge.

Others

Various other military or partly military positions are evidenced and simply show that *ad hoc* appointments could be made, perhaps by the generals, perhaps by the demos.

1. Phrourarchs could command garrisons as necessary. For the first possible name in this position see the appendix to Section V.
2. An archon at Oropos is placed in 411.
3. An archon at Pylos appears in 410/9.

4. We find an archon at Andros in ?363/2.
5. There is an archon at Arkesine on Amorgos in ?358/7.
6. We have an exetastes in 348/7 who was to inspect mercenaries. He will have been popularly elected (Kahrstedt 241, 272).

Finance

Though many offices had financial aspects, I deal here with those who handled funds, revenues and expenditures or oversaw financial practices. Though they appear late in the piece, I look first at those instances of general financial control which occur.

Theoric commissioners

See J.J. Buchanan, *Theorika* (Locust Valley, New York 1962); Cawkwell, *JHS* 1963, 47ff.; Rhodes, *Boule* 235ff. Control of the theoric fund and thereby of other financial areas seems to have been placed under a new magistracy around 354/3 and continued for the rest of our period. The position was filled by direct election. In its two mentions of it (43.1, 47.2), *Ath. Pol.* clearly indicates that there was a plurality of officials in each year, but whether this was always the case is unclear. Aisch. 3.25 speaks in the plural in regard to the institution of the office, but IG ii² 223 c.6 (*Agora* xv.34) has mention of only a single man ἐπὶ τὸ θεωρικόν in 343/2. However, since the latter is in the company of the prytany secretary and the man in charge of decrees, it seems likely that he is some sort of secretary. The man concerned was, I believe, general in 345/4 and if he was not actually a theoric commissioner, we can remove one objection to the thesis that the commissioners served for a four-year period. At *Ath. Pol.* 43.1 we are told that these officials served from Panathenaia to Panathenaia, which I take to mean a four-year period (*ZPE* 57 (1984), 133ff.). This will have been the case in the 320s, but we cannot be sure that it was so earlier. Though I tend to believe it was, I have not ventured to record known officials in any but the one year the evidence allows.

Financial administrator

Under this title I record Lykourgos and his successors from 336/5 on. See Mitchel, *Lykourgan Athens*; Rhodes, *Boule* 107f. I adopt the date not for the reason given at *APF* 351 (that Lykourgos died liable to euthynai; see the note on 328/7), but because the notice at Plut. *Mor.*

841b–c that Lykourgos was in charge of finances for three penteterides nonetheless ought to take us to the time of his death in 325/4. The term of office was four years and it could be held only once (Develin, *ZPE* 57 (1984), 134).

Tamiai of Athene and the other gods

Our first named tamiai appear in ?550/49 (the next come in 446/5), but they existed at the time of Solon and before (*Ath. Pol.* 4.1, 7.3, 8.1). Before Solon they were directly elected from the same census group as the archons. From Solon on they were chosen by lot from the highest census class (though there may be a suggestion at *Ath. Pol.* 47.1 that this was not always enforced). Perhaps after Solon they were chosen two from each tribe, but later they were certainly one per tribe in the Kleisthenic system. Inscriptions do record named tamiai who total less than ten, but at least this need not indicate that the number elected was constitutionally variable (cf. Develin, *Klio* 1986, 82f.).

In 434/3 was created a second board of ten, the tamiai of the other gods (cf. Develin, *Klio* 1986, 78; in general Linders, *Treasurers*), our first evidence for a name coming in 430/29. They were specifically analogous to the tamiai of Athene. In 406/5 (probably: Ferguson, *Treasurers* 104ff.; Thompson, *Hesperia* 1970, 61ff.; Meritt, *PAPhS* 1978, 292ff.), the two boards were amalgamated, a situation abandoned in 386/5, but resumed by 342/1 (perhaps in 346/5; for references see Linders, *Artemis* 74 n.57).

Both boards, of course, had secretaries. Those of the tamiai of Athene were chosen in reverse tribal order from 443/2 to 429/8, a practice resumed with the joint board until 387/6; it began again in forward order with the reamalgamation, though a form of tribal distribution could have begun with the tamiai of Athene in 356/5 (Alessandri, *ASNP* 1982, 10 n.9). On this see Ferguson, *The Athenian Secretaries* 70ff.; *Treasurers* 8ff.; Tréheux, 'Études' 34.

Hellenotamiai

These were officials of the Athenian league/empire of the fifth century, Athenians from its outset (Thuc. 1.96.2; Woodhead, *JHS* 1959, 149ff.; Meiggs, *Ath. Empire* 44f.). Our evidence on identities begins with a secretary in 453/2. A secretary cycle, in reverse tribal order, is evidenced between 439/8 and 429/8 (*ATL* III.359). The hellenotamiai themselves were elected one per tribe until we find in 410/9 evidence for the doubling of the board (see ML p. 258). I am not persuaded by arguments that iteration was now possible and that equal tribal representation was dropped (see 407/6 and SEG 26.31; 30.22). In 418/17 we have our first evidence for a paredros of the hellenotamiai (Dow, *Essays Brendel* 84). The office naturally ceased with the end of the empire, the last evidence being for 404/3.

Tamias of stratiotic fund

See P. Bruns, *Eisphora-syntaxis-stratiotika* (Paris 1983), 37, 170ff. Dem. 49.12, 16 is evidence that the fund existed by 373 and Dem. 50.10 shows that in 362/1 there were officials concerned with it. The tamias, however, may have come in at the same time as the reorganization which created the theoric commission and the first known incumbent is found in 344/3. He was a single official, and as of the 330s at least the office was held for four years (Develin, *ZPE* 57 (1984), 135). It was filled by direct election (*Ath. Pol.*).

Tamias of dockyards

See Jordan, *Navy* 57f. Our first evidence comes in 377/6, but the office is not mentioned in *Ath. Pol.*, so we cannot be sure as to constancy of existence, title or function and we can only assume a regular election procedure.

Tamias of trireme funds

See Jordan, *Navy* 56f. This official, first evidenced for 363/2, is again not in *Ath. Pol.* A scholiast on Dem. 22.20 attests direct election, though there is some question of the boule having made an irregular appointment (Rhodes, *Boule* 121f.). At some stage tribal rotation may have been used (Rhodes, *Boule* 122 n.1; appendix to Section IX).

Tamias of rigging

Jordan, *Navy* 58f. This official is not in *Ath. Pol.* and appears only in 326/5. Jordan believes he may have been chosen by the curators of the dockyards.

Tamiai of the boule

See Rhodes, *Boule* 141. The first mention of tamiai of the boule is in IG ii² 120.20ff. (probably 353/2) and there are two in our first entry from

343/2. By 335/4 there is only one, as is the case at *Ath. Pol.* 49.4. Election was by lot.

Tamias of dedication
Found in 335/4, he may have taken over part of the duties of the tamiai of the boule (cf. Rhodes, *Boule* 141 n.4).

Tamias of tribe
Also known as tamias of the prytaneis, he is first evidenced in 341/40.

Tamiai of the two goddesses
First known from 329/8, they were two in number. *Contra* Kahrstedt 76, I see no implication that they held office for four years along with the epistatai of Eleusis. IG ii² 1672 simply records different tamiai in 329/8 and 328/7.

Tamias Paralou
The tamiai of the state galleys were directly elected (*Ath. Pol.* 61.7) and that of the Paralos is first found in the appendix to Section VII.

Poletai
Already mentioned in the context of Solon (*Ath. Pol.* 7.3), named poletai do not appear until 402/1 and then only through the secretary. *Ath. Pol.* 47.2 says they were chosen by lot, one per tribe, as will have been the case presumably in the wake of Kleisthenes, though it could have been similar under the previous four tribes.

Logistai
See Rhodes, *Boule* 111. From the middle of the fifth century we know of a board of 30 logistai, but we have no names. *Ath. Pol.* 54.2 records a board of ten chosen by lot. This may already be in place when we have our first names, for 407/6. *Ath. Pol.* does not say so, but they will have been chosen on the tribal principle (schol. Aisch. 3.15). For a different board of logistai see *Ath. Pol.* 48.3.

Taktai
Of these officials of the fifth-century empire we know only of a secretary in 434/3 and possibly Alkibiades in 425/4. If And. 4.11 refers to them, there were ten, perhaps directly elected at need.

Antigrapheus

See Rhodes, *Boule* 238f.; cf. Alessandri, *ASNP* 1982, 36f.
Harpokration *s.v.* ἀντιγραφεύς says that there were two sorts of
antigrapheus, one concerned with financial administration, the other
an official of the boule. For the latter he cites *Ath. Pol.*, Rhodes thinks
wrongly (*Comm.* 601). Aisch. 3.25 says that there was an elected
antigrapheus, a revenue clerk, until the theoric commission took over
the function. When the title reappears later, Rhodes believes that it had
passed to a different official, who had secretarial duties in the boule.
The evidence produces an antigrapheus placed in the appendix to
Section VI as before 377/6. Another appears in 335/4. On Rhodes'
reconstruction they should be of different types. In fact, however, both
appear in bouleutic inscriptions. *Agora* xv.12 is a dedication of the
prytaneis of Pandionis wherein the antigrapheus accompanies the
grammateus of boule and demos; *Agora* xv.43 is a list of bouleutai
culminating with the officials serving the boule. The antigrapheus does
not appear in *Agora* xv.34 of 343/2, which is consistent with Aischines,
who also says that the theoric commission took over the function of the
antigrapheus (and others) until the law of Hegemon came into being.
May it not be, then, that the office was restored after the law of
Hegemon? The duties could still have changed somewhat, but it was
the same office. Pollux 8.98 records a change from direct election to
selection by lot, which may correspond to a change in duties.

The antigrapheus found in 333/2 and 329/8 was probably specially
elected in regard to Eleusis.

Others

In the appendix to Section III is noticed the attribution to
Themistokles and Aristeides of the position of epimeletes of revenues.
The nature of this office will remain unclear, but we are told Aristeides
was re-elected to it.

There could always have been *ad hoc* financial officials, such as those
whom I style eispraktores in 356/5. There are others who appear herein
without title, including Aphobetos in the appendix to Section VIII (ἐπὶ
τὴν κοινὴν διοίκησιν) and Dionysios in the appendix to Section IX (ἐπὶ
τῆς διοικήσεως).

Epimeletai

Here I include all remaining state officials with this title, even though it covers a wide variety. The mysterious epimeletes of revenues has just been mentioned.

Epimeletai of dockyards
This office may have existed in the fifth century, but named epimeletai are not in evidence until 378/7. They are not mentioned in *Ath. Pol.*, but were an annual board of ten, probably chosen by lot, one per tribe. It is possible that during the period 348/7 to 334/3 or thereabouts other officers replaced the epimeletai, as in particular we find an individual chosen from the boule in 346/5. See Rhodes, *Boule* 117ff.; *Comm.* 545f.; Jordan, *Navy* 30ff.

Epimeletes of springs
This official was directly elected and served for four years, at least in the 330s (*Ath. Pol.* 43.1; Develin, *ZPE* 57 (1984), 135f.). For the first known man see 347/6.

Epimeletai of emporion
Ath. Pol. 51.4 says ten such officials were chosen annually by lot. Our single example is a secretary in the appendix to Section VIII. The origin of the office cannot be dated (A.R.W. Harrison, *The Law of Athens* II (Oxford 1971), 27), but the first evidence is *Hesperia* 1974, 158. 21ff., 41 with Stroud's note 180f. (375/4).

Epimeletai of Nikai etc.
See the entry under this title in 334/3 and the epimeletes of pompeia in the appendix to Section IX.

Epimeletai of festivals
1. Epimeletai of the Dionysia are mentioned at *Ath. Pol.* 56.4, where it is said that the board of ten was previously elected directly by the demos, whereas now one per tribe is chosen by lot. Rhodes, *Comm.* 627f., suggests the change came in the Lykourgan period. Our first evidence involving a name records that Meidias failed to be chosen in 349/8 (appendix to Section VIII); otherwise see 343/2.
2. In 329/8 we meet epimeletai of the Amphiaraia at Oropos, a board of

ten not selected on tribal principles.

3. *Ath. Pol.* mentions direct election of four epimeletai of the Eleusinian mysteries, which gives them a place here, even though two are chosen one each from the clans Eumolpidai and Kerykes. This is now confirmed by SEG 30.61.30f., where an age over 30 is restored for those chosen from all Athenians. We know of a pair from 331/30, though earlier Meidias held the position (appendix to Section VIII). It was instituted shortly before the middle of the fourth century. See Rhodes, *Comm.* 636f.

Epistatai

Again this term has varying uses.

Epistatai of public works

For specific public works commissions of epistatai were chosen annually as needed. Names occur from 446/5. For the fifth century we can only assume election by the demos, which seems to have been the case in the fourth century. See Boersma, *Building Policy* 5f.; Rhodes, *Boule* 124f.

Epistatai of Eleusis

Our first evidence comes with a secretary in 422/1 who served for four years. IG i³ 32 provides for the selection of five men, one of whom is to be secretary, annually. So as between this and the evidence for 422/1, etc., there is a change. When we come to 409/8 we are dealing with annual boards and a suggestion that the number of members could change. With 363/2 we would have evidence for an eight-year board, were it not that we seem to be dealing with epistatai for work on the Eleusinion. By the 330s we are faced with a quadrennial board of eight, including the secretary, and some system of tribal representation seems to be included. These matters are dealt with by Cavanaugh, *Eleusis*, who wishes, if hesitantly, to see the board of 363/2 as the normal board of epistatai. However, an eight-year board seems to me beyond the pale. Cavanaugh wants a date for IG i³ 32 in the 430s, perhaps *c.* 432.

Epistatai of Brauroneion

Evidence of names begins in 353/2. Linders, *Artemis* 75f., is of the opinion that the position was instituted at least by the beginning of the fourth century and that it was an annual office, as the evidence indicates. The number of epistatai each year cannot be ascertained.

Epistatai of the mint
One such board, of ten plus secretary, not chosen by strict tribal representation, is found in the appendix to Section VII. Such epistatai are mentioned in *ATL* II D 14 (ML 45) under the fifth-century empire.

Epistates of the navy
Such is Aischines' description of the extraordinary position given to Demosthenes in 340/39.

Epistates of the water supply
Such a position is attributed to Themistokles (appendix to Section III), which was perhaps an *ad hoc* appointment.

Epistates of the Akademy
This otherwise unknown position is found in the appendix to Section IX.

Miscellaneous

In this section I deal with remaining extraordinary and ordinary officials not placed in previous or forthcoming categories. I exclude from direct discussion the positions occupied by Drakon, Solon and Kleisthenes and the sixth-century tyranny, for which see the appropriate years. Tyrants are noticed only in the years they took on the position.

Athlothetai
Ath. Pol. 60.1 says ten athlothetai were chosen by lot, one per tribe. They served for four years and dealt with the quadrennial Great Panathenaia. All this may be retrojected to the fifth century and quadrennial office may have begun in 418/17 (Develin, *ZPE* 57 (1984), 133f., 136f.). The office existed earlier, as Perikles held it (appendix to Section IV), by direct election if we can trust the terminology of Plut. *Per.* 13.6, which we cannot. It has been thought that the men recorded under 566/5 were athlothetai (*q.v.*).

Sitophylakes

Ten were elected by lot, previously five for Peiraieus, five for the city, more recently 15 and 20 respectively (*Ath. Pol.* 51.3). Perhaps the change came with the corn shortage of 330 on (Rhodes, *Comm.* 577). Their history is vague, but they certainly existed in 388/7, where our single individual occurs.

Sitones

So we describe Kallisthenes in 357/6 and Demosthenes so refers to himself being directly elected by the demos in 338/7. The impression is that it was a single position, perhaps *ad hoc*, though later evidence is for a plurality (IG ii^2 744).

Teichopoioi

Our evidence comes solely from 337/6, when tribal assemblies chose men for repair of the walls, though there is a mention in IG i^3 440.127 of 443/2.

The Eleven

These officers were chosen in the time of *Ath. Pol.* (52.1) by lot. They existed at the time of Solon and before (*Ath. Pol.* 7.3). Our first evidence of an individual comes before 411 (appendix to Section V). See Harrison, *Law of Athens* II.17f.

Eisagogeis

Ath. Pol. 52.2 tells us there were five, chosen by lot, each from a combination of two tribes (see Rhodes, *Comm.* 582). We have evidence for a secretary in 425/4, though Harrison, *Law of Athens* II.21 doubts we are dealing with the same eisagogeis.

Synegoroi

MacDowell, *Wasps* 198f., lists the various sorts of synegoroi. There were boards of ten chosen as prosecutors in the matter of magistrates' accounts. See also Rhodes, *Comm.* 597 on *Ath. Pol.* 54.2, where we find they assist the logistai and are chosen by lot. Our first evidence is found in 427/6. The other sorts mentioned by MacDowell are not relevant to our concern. His category C refers to men of the next entry.

Kategoroi

Perikles is said to have been elected one of the kategoroi of Kimon 462/1 (Plut. *Per.* 10.5) and in 324/3 we have another such board. Presumably direct election was employed.

Zetetai

A board of investigators is found in 415/14.

Syndikoi

A board is found in 355/4 as advocates of Leptines' law. There were five and they were directly elected.

Horistai

The Eleusinian hierophant and dadouch were chosen to re-establish boundaries in 350/49.

Probouloi

We have the names of two probouloi in 412/11 (*q.v.*). They were part of a body of ten (though see Pesely, *LCM* 1987, 51), perhaps one per tribe and probably men of considerable age.

Oath-takers

These are listed, as in 422/1, as men in any case chosen, but perhaps also already holding official positions.

Special cases

These concern the phenomena of the late fifth century.
1. In 411 we have a katalogeus to select those who would have full political rights.
2. From 411/10 to 405/4 Nikomachos was anagrapheus to write up the laws of Solon. From 403/2 to 400/399 he and another held a similar position for revision of the laws.
3. Finally, in 404/3 we have the Thirty, the Ten and archons in Peiraieus.

Religion

We have already mentioned some officials concerned with religious matters. The concern here is with others who are evidenced in the general area of state religious business. Some thought has been necessary on criteria of inclusion. In the final analysis the functionaries of Eleusis were not included: see Clinton, *Sacred Officials* 117ff. Priests too have been omitted, as often we cannot be sure of the selection process or the duration of the priesthood; many certainly were lifelong and/or hereditary or confined to certain families: in general see Feaver, *YClS* 1957, 121ff.; Garland, *ABSA* 1984, 75ff. The one exception is noted below.

Hieropoioi

1. *Ath. Pol.* 54.6f. mentions two sorts of hieropoioi, each a board of ten chosen by lot. Only the second concerns us, the yearly hieropoioi who saw to sacrifices and quadrennial festivals other than the Panathenaia. In fact, earlier such hieropoioi did take care of the yearly Panathenaia and such a body is evidenced in the 330s and so was separate (see Rhodes, *Comm.* 606). There were in fact various sorts of hieropoioi, many appointed from the boule (see Rhodes, *Boule* 127ff.). I set out the relevant sorts we find with names in order of appearance.

2. Hieropoioi of Panathenaia. Such, I believe, were the men found under 566/5, who, until later, will have dealt with the Great Panathenaia as well (see above on athlothetai).

3. Hieropoioi of Eleusis. They were probably in charge of most, if not all, matters at Eleusis until the epistatai were created, after which they still continued to exist (see above on the epistatai). Our first name comes from 421/20. On appointment at this time we have no information. In IG ii² 1672.280 we have hieropoioi from the boule and in *Agora* xv.38 the prytaneis of Aigeis praise ten of their number in 341/40 τοὺς ἱεροποιοὺς τοὺς τὰ μυστήρια ἱεροποιήσαντας 'Ελευσῖνι, but I am not convinced that they took the place of the regular hieropoioi.

4. Hieropoioi/syllogeis. See Rhodes, *Boule* 129f., for syllogeis (three per tribe) in the fourth century acting as hieropoioi. For first evidence see 336/5 (perhaps), though syllogeis appear in 341/40.

5. Hieropoioi for the Pythais. They are found in 330/29 to the number

of ten, apparently one per tribe, possibly from the boule, which appointed theoroi to the festival (Dem. 19.128).

6. The suggested hieropoios to Delphi in the appendix to Section IX may be of similar sort.

Delos

1. Amphiktyons. See Rhodes, *Comm.* 693f. The first names occur in 413/12. There seem to have been four amphiktyons and a secretary until we find five and a secretary from 375/4 and an apparently quinquennial office (though not necessarily in strict line with the archon year). The earliest system is unclear. After 367 the evidence demonstrates annual office. It is difficult to be sure whether on a board of five half of the ten tribes should be represented in defined order.

2. Naopoioi to Delos are evidenced in 346/5, specifically an annual position. Two are named with a secretary, but there were more (*Insc. Délos* 104–24.14).

Delphi

A number of officials were sent to Delphi. In general see Roux, *L'amphictionie.*

1. The hieromnemon was the representative to the amphiktyony. He is mentioned in *Ath. Pol.* only among the constitutional provisions at 30.2. Our first possible incumbent is found in 424/3, the evidence (Ar. *Clouds* 623f.) showing that the choice was by lot. It has been suggested that it was a two-year office (Roux 25).

2. There were three pylagorai (or -oi) in a year, chosen by direct election (Dem. 18.149; Aisch. 3.114, 115, 126). Our first evidence may relate to Themistokles (478/7); otherwise we have to wait until 343/2.

3. I have included also the tamias at Delphi of 339/8: see Roux 125.

4. On the naopoioi see Roux 96ff. They seem to have been instituted about 372, although evidence for Athenians begins in 354/3. Here in particular chronological reconstruction is important. I have depended (with gratitude to the author) on P.D. Londey, *Panhellenic Representation at Delphoi in the Fourth Century B.C.* (Diss. Monash Univ., Australia, 1982). See also de la Coste-Messelière, *BCH* 1949, 201ff. and 1960, 467ff.; Bousquet, *Mélanges Daux* 21ff.; Marchetti, *BCH* Suppl. 4 (1977), 67ff.; *BCH* 1979, 151ff.; Londey, *BCH* 1979, 477f.; Roux, *BCH* 1979, 501ff.

Boönai

They were elected directly for the purchase of sacrifices. Our attestation is limited to Meidias (appendix to Section VIII).

Plouton and the Furies

A group of names associated with this cult is found in the appendix to Section IX.

Priest of Asklepios

See Ferguson, *Priests*; Pritchett and Meritt, *Chronology* 74ff., which I follow closely for dates, a sufficient number of which are doubtful; Schlaifer, *HSCPh* 1940, 244ff. There were two centres, in Athens and in the Peiraieus. We cannot be sure that there was a priest for each. Appointment may always have been by lot and surely was annual. Whether or not it was always so from the beginning (the cult was introduced in the year 420: IG ii² 4960), in the fourth century cycles of tribal representation may have been used. From 356/5 (in all probability) the forward tribal order was adopted, corresponding to that of the grammateis of the boule. The first named priests will be found in the appendix to Section VII, the first specifically dated one in 355/4. In one instance the cycle may have been broken (Demon: see 330/29).

Overseas

1. *Ath. Pol.* 62.2 mentions 'all the officials who are sent to Samos, Skyros, Lemnos or Imbros'. When it comes to evidence for our purposes, we fall short. In 329/8 we find generals on Lemnos and Skyros (*q.v.*) and we have a hipparch on Lemnos for three years (appendix to Section IX). In the appendix to Section VIII will be found two epimeletai on Lemnos. Otherwise we seem to be dealing with local officials of klerouchies (Rhodes, *Comm.* 694f.).

2. In 370/69 we have names of two men who led out a klerouchy and in 325/4 the founder of a colony. Presumably this involved some sort of appointment.

Local and sectional

Demarchoi

These seem to have been created under the Kleisthenic reforms (*Ath. Pol.* 21.5). We are told the demarch for Peiraieus was chosen by lot by the whole demos (*Ath. Pol.* 54.8) and the same source says the same about the archon to Salamis, who may be classed with demarchs. First evidence of named demarchs comes in the middle of the fifth century (appendix to Section IV), of the archon to Salamis in 402/1 (cf. appendix to Section VI). Election procedures may have varied: see Damsgaard-Madsen, *C&M* Diss. 9 (1973), 92ff. I include a possible paredros to a demarch in the appendix to Section IX. In general see Whitehead, *Demes*, parts of which I am grateful for seeing before publication.

Epimeletai of tribe

Our first names seem to come from 407/6. There were three per tribe, though one can no longer assume that they were always one from each trittys.

Envoys

On these in general see Mosley, *Envoys*. Three, five and ten were normal numbers. They were chosen by direct popular vote *via* nomination (Aisch. 2.18ff.). Cases which admit of doubt may be found in 596/5 and 508/7, the first clear instance of names being in 480/79. Along with envoys we may class the kataskopoi of 425/4.

Grammateis

The vast majority of public officials were served by secretaries and we find also syngrammateis and hypogrammateis. Some at least of these were all but professionals, drawn from a pool, but not allowed to serve the same magistracy twice. See Rhodes, *Boule* 139, and in general M. Brillant, *Les secrétaires athéniens* (Paris 1911); Ferguson, *Secretaries*. This leads us on to the next section.

Council and people

The annual lists will include any information on bouleutai under the heading 'Council and Assembly'. I discuss the other contents of that category below. Councillors often had special tasks to perform; see, for example, the epimeletai of the dedication in 328/7. We have already had cause to notice some positions associated with the council: tamias of boule, tamias of dedication, tamias of tribe, antigrapheus, epimeletes of dockyards, hieropoioi/syllogeis. Here we are concerned with the secretaries, on which see, besides the works noticed in the preceding section, P. Haggard, *The Secretaries of the Athenian Boule in the Fifth Century B.C.* (Diss. Missouri 1930); Rhodes, *Boule* 134ff.; Alessandri, *ASNP* 1982, 7ff.

Grammateus

The first known secretary to the council is found in the appendix to Section III and could be dated as early as *c.* 500. Whether the office goes back beyond Kleisthenes is unknown. Down to 368/7 the evidence shows that the secretary changed with each prytany in such a way that each tribe was represented and was never from the tribe in prytany. As long as this was the case it is very probable that the secretaries were themselves bouleutai. By 363/2 and probably from 366/5 (Alessandri 11) the grammateus is an annual officer and not a bouleutes (I do not follow Alessandri in the opinion that the prytany secretary and the secretary of the boule were different). *Ath. Pol.* 54.3 says that formerly direct election was employed and they chose men of distinction, whereas now (presumably from the reform of the 360s) the lot is used. Possibly with the reform tribal representation in random order was introduced, but certainly from 356/5, forward tribal order was used.

In charge of laws

The grammateus ἐπὶ τοὺς νόμους was also chosen by lot (*Ath. Pol.* 54.4). He appears in our period only in 324/3.

In charge of decrees

The grammateus ἐπὶ τὰ ψηφίσματα is not mentioned in *Ath. Pol.*, but appears first in 343/2. Election was presumably by lot.

Grammateus of boule and demos

Ath. Pol. 54.5 says this official was directly elected by the demos. He is equated with the grammateus of the polis who appears as early as 414/13 (Thuc. 7.10) as well as much later (Plut. *Mor.* 841f) and with the shortened form 'grammateus of the demos' found in 335/4 and 324/3. The first named such official appears in the appendix to Section VI.

Anagrapheus

This was some sort of secretarial post, first evidenced in 335/4. See Rhodes, *Boule* 138f. He is made assistant to the man in charge of laws by Alessandri, *ASNP* 1982, 35f.

COUNCIL AND ASSEMBLY

Besides recording the officials mentioned in the last section, this category deals with decrees and assembly meetings. All documents tied to a specific year will be noticed and numbered for convenience of reference. The appendix to each section will include all documents which give information on personnel or dating (even if only reference to a prytany), and occasionally some where a specific date has been suggested and so the category begins after Kleisthenes with the earliest documents actually in the appendix to Section III. Earlier measures are noted in a different manner. Very brief descriptions of contents are noted. Proposers are included; if there is more than one, there will be a rider in the document; if the measure is from the boule or is probouleumatic, it will be assumed that the proposer was a bouleutes. The presiding councillor is included as epistates throughout the work, though there was a change. Through the fifth century, the president was simply one of the prytaneis in session. Then there was a change (see Rhodes, *Boule* 25ff). *Ath. Pol.* 44.2f. describes a system wherein each day the epistates of the prytaneis chose by lot one member from each tribe other than his own, identifying one of these as epistates; one could be proedros once in each prytany, epistates once a year. We cannot be sure when this system came in: in 403/2 IG ii² 1.41f. has an epistates from the tribe in prytany; the first evidence for proedroi is now in 379/8 (*q.v.*). From 333/2 the symproedroi are sometimes listed. Epigraphical documents come first, generally in an order which follows the numbers in IG, then any other inscriptional collection, then SEG and *Hesperia*. I have not given great amounts of bibliography, simply, if at all, a recent SEG reference or anything that seemed relevant to the matters in hand. Then come literary references to proposals and to assemblies where these offer anything of substance. After all, most things that happened resulted from an assembly decision. Speakers in the assembly are noted, but not given prominence. Under 403/2 I have included laws with decrees, but thereafter I have a separate heading for nomothetai assuming that this was the means by which laws were created in the fourth century: see MacDowell, *JHS* 1975, 62ff.; Hansen, *Ecclesia* 187 n.15.

Section I
684/3 to 595/4

684/3 (Ol. 24.1)

Archon

KREON *PA* 8781

The name of the first annual archon is preserved by Synkellos (ed. Dindorf
1 p. 400), Kastor of Rhodes (*FGH* 250 F 4) and Velleius 1.8.3, and there is
no reason to doubt it (Cadoux, *JHS* 1948, 88; Jacoby, *Atthis* 172, 348
n.26). The date here given is contrary to those of Cadoux and Samuel,
Chron. 198. *MP* A 32 gives this date; Cadoux says *MP* can make mistakes of
a year or two, but it ought not to be in error in dating the first annual archon
back from the archonship of Diognetos. It seems *a fortiori* probable that
this was the official Athenian version. Too much confidence cannot be
placed in Dionysios *AR* 1.71.5, whose date of 752/1 for the first year of the
decennial archonship renders 682/1 for the first annual one; it is suspicious
because of the synchronization with the founding of Rome, which was
itself a matter of chronological dispute and had been subject to different
synchronization (see Dion. *AR* 1.74). As for other sources, Kastor does not
cause a problem (Jacoby, *Atthis* 346 n.22). Error in Eusebios would not be
unusual and if his date was 682/1 (*Arm.*), it could in any case be no more
than correspondence with Dionysios or the tradition in which he stood.
Eusebios is also tied in with Pausanias in regard to the dating of the
Messenian Wars, on which Pausanias' derived dates for archonships depend. Cadoux's discussion of texts relating to the second war (Paus. 4.15.1,
23.4, 17.2,10, 20.1) concludes that Pausanias is five years out, but I do not
see that this warrants similar emendation in respect of the earlier war. The
chronology of Messenian Wars has been a vexed question since antiquity
(Mosshammer, *Chronicle* 204ff.). We cannot say that even if Pausanias'
chronology is inaccurate, the association of a particular Olympiad year
with a year in a decennial archonship must be accepted. Clearly the dating
of the decennial archonship was not immutably fixed: Synkellos gives two
alternatives, even if neither is acceptable. There could perhaps have been a
contamination of two traditions, one fixing the war by reference to an
Athenian archon year, the other based on one version of the reign of the
Spartan king Theopompos in relation to the twenty-year war.

   Given that Pausanias' implied dates are outside the acceptable param-
eters, *MP* must be given priority. Samuel, however, opts for 683/2 (a date
popular before Cadoux: Jacoby, *Atthis* 346 n.22) and believes that *MP*

27

gives that date and that Dionysios can be made to support it (which is possible). He also accepts that Pausanias is out by one Olympiad. He must, I think, be wrong that *MP* dated this year from 263/2, and indeed he chooses to work from 264/3 for the year of Lysiades.

682/1 (Ol. 24.3)

Archon
LYSIADES *PA* 9332a
On the argument presented under 684/3 there is no reason to reject the evidence of *MP* A 33.

680/79 (Ol. 25.1)

Archon
TLESIAS *PA* 13865
Paus. 4.15.1 with a five-year emendation as argued by Cadoux, *JHS* 1948, 88f. Dating of Kreon to 684/3 leaves this year open. Samuel, *Chron.* 199, prefers 681/80, assuming a four-year error in Pausanias.

671/70 (Ol. 27.2)

Archon
LEOSTRATOS *PA* 9147
Dion. *AR* 3.1.3.

669/8 (Ol. 27.4)

Archon
PEISISTRATOS *PA* 11791; *APF* 445
In the fourth year of an Olympiad (Paus. 2.24.7), restored as the 27th by comparison with the name of the Olympic victor as given by Dion. *AR* 3.1.3 and Eusebios (*Arm.*); Cadoux, *JHS* 1948, 90. Samuel, *Chron.* 199, wonders if Pausanias might not still be out by four years. The man might well be a forebear of the tyrant.

668/7 (Ol. 28.1)

Archon
AUTOSTHENES *PA* 2756a
Accepting Cadoux's argument (*JHS* 1948, 90) that Pausanias' single discrepancy with the victor list in Eusebios is to be explained by a misreading of the name Charmis as Chionis and that Autosthenes can therefore remain in this year (Paus. 4.23.4). Cf. Samuel, *Chron.* 199.

28

664/3 (Ol. 29.1)

Archon

MILTIADES *PA* 10205; *APF* 299

Paus. 4.23.10 with Cadoux (see 668/7). While it cannot be baldly assumed that this man was the same as the archon of 659/8 or that he (or either) was a Philaid, there must be a strong presumption of Philaid attachment; see Cadoux, *JHS* 1948, 90 nn.85, 86; Bradeen, *Hesperia* 1963, 196f. with notes; *APF*. It is difficult to fit a Miltiades of this vintage into the problematic Philaid genealogy given by Pherekydes *FGH* 3 F 2 (cf. Hellanikos *FGH* 4 F 22).

659/8 (Ol. 30.2)

Archon

MILTIADES *PA* 10205; *APF* 299

Paus. 8.39.3. See under 664/3.

645/4 (Ol. 33.4)

Archon

DROPIDES *PA* 4572; *APF* 322

MP A 34.

639/8 (Ol. 35.2)

Archon

DAMASIAS *PA* 3109

Dion. *AR* 3.36.1.

?636/5 (Ol. 36.1)

Basileus

EPAINETOS *PA* 4746

A notorious fragment of one Hippys of Rhegion (*FGH* 554 F 3; Samuel, *Chron.* 200, calls him Hippias, the MS has Hippon) includes the words ἐν Ἀθήναις ἐπὶ βασιλέως Ἐπαινέτου, dating this as Ol. 36, i.e. 636/5 – 633/2, in which Olympiad the stadion victor was Arytamas the Lakonian. No such victor is known: Eusebios has Phrynon of Athens as victor in Ol. 36. The whole citation is problematic and it hardly seems possible to emend one's way out of the difficulty if it involves changing the Olympiad, the name of the victor and the office of Epainetos. Cadoux (*JHS* 1948, 91) with reason advises the admission of ignorance. One might suggest, however, that Arytamas was victor in the diaulon. Pausanias saw an inscription at Sparta recording seven victories of Chionis, three in the diaulon (3.14.3 – perhaps a mistake; see Cadoux 90). We could suppose a misreading of a similar record here. Yet the Athenian archon should not have been confused with a basileus; why should Epainetos be mentioned and not the eponym? Even supposing that the archon died and the basileus took over his duties, the year should still be identified by the eponym. We do have from the end of the fifth century (perhaps) a basileus mentioned in what appears to be a dating formula (IG i^3 1384; i^2 776), which may give us some reason to believe in Epainetos' office, but not with great confidence. Cf. also Jacoby, *Atthis* 307 n.44, and, suggesting that Epainetos replaced Megakles (below 632/1), Miller, *Arethusa* 1969, 81.

?632/1 (Ol. 37.1)

Archon

MEGAKLES *PA* 9688; *APF* 370f.
A much discussed problem. See in general Cadoux, *JHS* 1948, 91; Gomme, *Comm. Thuc.* 1.428f.; Virgilio, *Commento* 98f.; Rhodes, *Comm.* 79ff. On date see also Moulinier, *REA* 1946, 182–202; Jacoby, *Atthis* 366 n.77. On other problems see Freeman, *Solon* 160ff.; Hignett, *HAC* 78, 120ff.; Wüst, *Historia* 1957, 176–91; Wade-Gery, *Essays* 144f.; Lang, *CPh* 1967, 243–9; Levi, *Commento* 9ff.; Jordan, *CSCA* 1970, 154–75; *id. Servants* 56ff.; Ghinatti, *I gruppi* 9ff.; Samuel, *Chron.* 200; de Laix, *Probouleusis* 11; Sealey, *City States* 98f., 105f. n.5; Lévy, *Historia* 1978, 513–21; Andrewes, *CAH*^{2} III.3.368ff.

As to date, both Her. 5.71.1 and Thuc. 1.126.3 assert that Kylon was already an Olympic victor when he attempted his coup and Eusebios places the victory in 640/39. Assuming this latter year is ruled out (though Levi 17 gives it a chance), the possible dates for Kylon's attempt, which was made in an Olympic year, are 636/5, 632/1, 628/7, 624/3, provided that the latter year was not that of Aristaichmos' archonship (see 621/20) and that the attempt should precede Drakon. The date here given merely splits the difference as nearly as possible between Kylon's victory and Drakon's work. While arguments can be produced for other dates (proximity to the victory, proximity to Drakon, etc.), I know of none which tips the balance of probability. A full argument against Lévy's case for 597/6 or 596/5 need not be mounted here; Rhodes, *Comm.* 81f., deals with some points.

Though Herodotos and Thucydides do not mention Megakles as archon (or at all), I cannot share Samuel's pessimism as to the fact. The name is found at Herakleides *Epit.* 2 (hence from *Ath. Pol.*) and Plut. *Solon* 12. Whatever may be thought of the source tradition and of the justice of the Alkmeonid inculpation, it should be accepted that the curse upon the family originated from Megakles' actions as archon in dealing with the Kylonian suppliants. Although Thucydides says that the besiegers went away and entrusted to the archons the task of arranging matters as they saw best as *autokratores*, I cannot place much emphasis on the latter term as used here or on the suggestion that special powers were granted by the voice of the people (Wade-Gery, followed by Hignett); rather was Megakles as archon simply in charge. Other sources are schol. Ar. *Knights* 443; Aristodemos *FGH* 104 F 2.

One should point out that in regard to the Kylonian business, while Thucydides talks about the archons, Herodotos mentions only the prytaneis of the naukraroi. The various attempts to deal with this apparent discrepancy are now discussed by Lambert, *Historia* 1986, 105–12, whose own explanation I find unconvincing. In any event, the Alkmeonid context is shared by both authors (it is unavoidably implicit in Thucydides) and so the case for Megakles' archonship and actions taken therein remains.

621/20 (Ol. 39.4)

Archon
ARISTAICHMOS *PA* 1638
Identified as archon in the year of Drakon's legislation at *Ath. Pol.* 4.1, but without any guide as to date. The date is indicated by a majority of the MSS of Eusebios (*Hieron.*) as Ol. 39.1 (624/3); Ol. 39 recurs in Tatianus *ad Graec.* 41; Clement *Strom.* 1.80.1 and Suda *s.v. Δράκων*. Schol. Aisch. 1.6 cannot be used. 624/3 would be acceptable but for Diod. 9.17, where the figure usually read has Drakon 47 years before Solon; however, it is possible to read 27, which indeed puts us in the correct Olympiad (see esp. Stroud, *Drakon's Law* 66ff.; Rhodes, *Comm.* 109). It seems likely that the interval was between archonships as read from some list and, as Ol. 39 is virtually assured, I accept the emended precision of Diodoros. See also Cadoux, *JHS* 1948, 92; Samuel, *Chron.* 200. Jacoby, *Atthis* 94, 308f. n.58, thought the archon date was invented along with Drakon's constitution around 411; *contra* see Stroud 66f. n.10.

Thesmothetes
DRAKON *PA* 4553
Drakon is indicated as thesmothetes by Paus. 9.36.8 and Clement *Strom.* 1.80.1, and while one cannot be sure whether this was meant to make him one of the six thesmothetai or a specially appointed lawgiver, I favour a special position, whether or not its designation was thesmothetes, a title which would certainly bear the appropriate meaning. See Stroud, *Drakon's Law* 74f.; also Jacoby, *Atthis* 94, 309 n.60, stating that *Ath. Pol.* probably did not know Drakon's precise position (in which case neither did anyone else). If Arist. *Rhet.* 2.23.29 1400b calls him nomothetes, this may be owing to later, natural confusion of *nomos* and *thesmos* (on which see Jacoby 309 n.64; Rhodes, *Comm.* 112, 177, favouring Ostwald, *Nomos* 9ff., 155ff.; cf. Quass, *Nomos* 11ff.). See also Hignett, *HAC* 307; MacDowell, *Law* 42, 44; Ruschenbusch, *Historia* 1960, 148.

On Drakon and his legislation see Stroud, esp. 76ff.; Rhodes, *Comm.* 84ff., 109ff.; Andrewes, *CAH*² III.3.370ff.; Develin, *Athenaeum* 1984, 295–306. I list here laws which have been attributed to Drakon (see Stroud for sources):

1. Homicide: IG i³ 104 (i² 115); Fornara no. 15; Gagarin, *Drakon*.
2. Theft in general.
3. Theft from temples.
4. Idleness and vagrancy.
5. Procedure against attempts at tyranny: Gagarin, *TAPhA* 1981, 71–7.
6. Training and education of children and young men.
7. Proper worship.
8. Special oaths.
9. Debt and land tenure.

Not all of these are to be accepted without question and Drakon did not create a constitution as such.

615/14 (Ol. 41.2)

Archon
HENIOCHIDES *PA* 6427
Dion. *AR* 3.46.1. For the name cf. IG ii² 2823; 7553.

607/6 (Ol. 43.2)

Strategos
PHRYNON *PA* 15029
Strabo 13.1.38f.; Plut. *Mor.* 858a; Diog. 1.74; Polyainos 1.25; Festus 358 L; schol. Aischylos *Eum.* 395; Suda *s.v.* Πιττακός. See Page, *Sappho* 152ff.; French, *JHS* 1957, 238; Wade-Gery, *Essays* 166 n.2; Jeffery, *Local Scripts* 72, 366f.; Berve, *Tyrannis* II.527, 553, 573; Mosshammer, *Chronicle* 246ff.; Frost, *Historia* 1984, 287f.

The tradition makes Phrynon general of the Athenian forces in the war with Mitylene over Achilleion and Sigeion, wherein he was killed in single combat with Pittakos. The date comes from the Eusebian tradition, which also has Phrynon as Olympic victor of Ol. 36 (636), which data are consistent. Her. 5.94f. mentions the struggle between Athens and Mitylene in the context of Peisistratos and, like other sources, includes mention of Alkaios and the arbitration by Periandros – but not Phrynon and Pittakos. Page proposes a solution: Alkaios mentioned Phrynon in his work, thus providing the basis for genuine tradition; Herodotos does not restrict himself to the time of Peisistratos, but freely goes back to an earlier stage of what he says was a protracted struggle. Wade-Gery notes Phrynon as founder of colonies at Sigeion and Elaious, accepting the emendation which produces Phrynon's name at Ps. Skymnos 707f. (cf. *ATL* III.289 n.75); Frost has him as oikistes. Jeffery dates the Sigeion stele to *c.* 575–550 and says it cannot be used to support the tradition of an Athenian colony in the late seventh century – but neither does it deny the possibility. The date, of course, may not be absolutely accurate, but there is no reason to reject Phrynon's military post.

605/4 (Ol. 43.4)

Archon
ARISTOKLES *PA* 1847; *APF* 331f.
MP A 35.

?600/599 (Ol. 45.1)

Archon
KRITIAS (? son of Dropides) *PA* 8789; *APF* 322, 326
MP A 36 places this archon between Aristokles (605/4) and Simon (591/90) and by him dates Sappho's flight from Mitylene. We can date him before 597/6, and if Bradeen, (*Hesperia* 1963, 187) is right that the fourth letter in the name above Kypselos on the archon list (597/6) must be alpha, gamma or mu, then Kritias cannot belong in 598/7. The only other clue is the placing of Sappho's acme in Ol. 45 (600/599–597/6) by the Eusebian tradition. See Cadoux, *JHS* 1948, 92; Page, *Sappho* 224f.; Samuel, *Chron.* 201; Mosshammer, *Chronicle* 250.

Strategos
?SOLON son of Exekestides *PA* 12806; *APF* 322ff.
When Solon, we are told, had secured the repeal of the law which forbade Athens laying claim to Salamis, he was appointed to a generalship in the war against Megara (Plut. *Solon* 8ff.; Aelian *VH* 7.19; see also Polyainos 1.20; cf. Diog. 1.46f.; Justin 2.7.9ff.). For full sources on the Salamis affair see Martina, *Solone* TT 237–55; for discussion French, *JHS* 1957, 241 n.11; Hopper, *ABSA* 1961, 208ff.; Masaracchia, *Solone* 88ff.; Piccirilli, *ASNP* 1978, 1–13; Rhodes, *Comm.* 199f.; Frost, *Historia* 1984, 289. This would seem to fall about the turn of the century. Plutarch appears to put it before Solon's provocation of the Sacred War and his intervention in the affair of the Alkmeonid curse, during which time Athens again lost Nisaia and Salamis to the Megarians, whereupon Epimenides was brought in. If the latter's visit is correctly dated to 596/5, we have an approximate idea of the time, but no more. So the location of the generalship here (and I accept its actuality) is a convenience.

598/7 (Ol. 45.3)

Archon
. . . . A-   or . . . . G-   or . . . . M-
See 600/599.

597/6 (Ol. 45.4)

Archon

[KY]PSELO[S] (son of Agamestor) *PA* 8951; *APF* 295ff.
This and the next archonship depend upon Bradeen's reconstruction of the archon list fragment in *Hesperia* 1963, 193ff.; ML 6a; IG i³ 1031; Fornara no. 23A. Lévy, *Historia* 1978, 519 n.20 (see 632/1), obviously cannot accept this probable restoration.

596/5 (Ol. 46.1)

Archon

[TE]LEKLE[S] or [TE]LEKLE[IDES]
See 597/6.

Envoy?

NIKIAS son of Nikeratos *APF* 403
Diog. 1.110 has him sent to Crete to seek the help of Epimenides, dated to Ol. 46 (596/5–593/2), which agrees with the general date given for Epimenides' visit. This mission is usually supposed to be an invention, but it need not be. See *APF* and Connor, *AJAH* 1976, 61–4. Despite Connor, a Cretan Nikias still seems possible and an inscription of the third century (IG vii 274) produces a tantalizing Nikias son of Epimenides (*PA* 10783).

595/4 (Ol. 46.2)

Archon

PHILOMBROTOS *PA* 14655
Archon the year before Solon (Plut. *Solon* 14.2), now restored in the archon list fragment (see 597/6).

APPENDIX

Ath. Pol. 3.5 refers to EPILYKOS (*PA* 4922; *APF* 296), a polemarch who rebuilt and furnished the Polemarcheion, renamed the Epilykeion. Unfortunately, this pre-Solonian polemarch cannot be simply accepted. He may not have been polemarch and could even belong to the fifth century; Jacoby, *Atthis* 93; *FGH* IIIb (Suppl.) ii.153 n.23; Rhodes, *Comm.* 105. Epilykos' existence is apparently accepted without question by Shapiro, *Hesperia* 1983, 306.

Section II
594/3 to 511/10

594/3 (Ol. 46.3)

Archon

SOLON son of Exekestides *PA* 12806; *APF* 322ff.
Specifically dated to this year by Sosikrates *apud* Diog. 1.62 and a majority
of the MSS of Eusebios (*Hieron.*). Solon's acme is given as Ol. 46 (596/5–
593/2: Tatianus *ad Graec.* 41; Clement *Strom.* 1.65.3), Ol. 47 or 56 (592/1–
589/8 or 566/5–563/2: Suda *s.v. Σόλων*). Demosthenes 19.251 in 343 speaks
of 240 years since Solon. On the chronological problem see Rhodes, *Comm.*
120ff., 164. Though I place all of Solon's activities here, I believe his
archonship saw only the immediate economic measures, with a subsequent
nomothesia stretching to 592/1 (see *LCM* 1984, 155–6).

Plutarch (*Solon* 14.2) records that Solon was chosen ὁμοῦ καὶ διαλλακτὴς
καὶ νομοθέτης, as well as archon. I very much doubt the suggestion that
διαλλακτὴς was on the archon list (Jacoby, *Atthis* 175), but rather see it as
part of the description of his role. Major sources for his activity are *Ath.
Pol.* 5ff. and Plut. *Solon* 12ff.; for full references see Martina, *Solone* TT
260–509. For general bibliography see Rhodes, *Comm.* 125ff.; add
Andrewes, *CAH*²III.3.375ff.; on economic matters Gallant, *ABSA* 1982,
111–24; on coinage Kagan, *AJA* 1982, 343–60; Kroll and Waggoner, *AJA*
1984, 325–40. I list here general heads of Solon's legislation; fragment
references are to Ruschenbusch, *ΣΟΛΩΝΟΣ ΝΟΜΟΙ*; not all measures are
necessarily to be accepted as genuinely Solonian and fragments numbered
from 94 to 152 are in Ruschenbusch's category of items at least doubtful.

1. Cancellation of debts and forbidding of loans on personal security: F
   67.
2. Constitutional arrangements: cf. FF 79–80, 96b, 99, 100, 103–5, 110–
   14, 150.
3. Coinage, weights and measures.
4. Homicide: FF 1–22.
5. Theft: FF 23–5; cf. 111–14, 140, 141.
6. Sexual area: FF 26–31, 74; cf. 115, 124–5.
7. Slander: FF 32–3; cf. 117, 118.
8. Injury: FF 34–5.
9. Legal actions and procedure: FF 36–7, 39–46; cf. 94–8, 106–8, 111–14,
   136–8.
10. Factional strife: F 38.

11. Family, marriage, inheritance: FF 47–59; cf. 104, 111–14, 120, 121, 126, 127, 139, 142, 152.
12. Land and property: FF 60–4, 66, 90, 91.
13. Export: F 65.
14. Debt: FF 68–9.
15. Amnesty: F 70.
16. Sumptuary: FF 71–3; cf. 115–16.
17. Citizen rights for foreigners: F 75.
18. Rights of organizations: F 76.
19. Census registration and livelihood: FF 77–8; cf. 148.
20. Naukraries: FF 79–80.
21. Religion: FF 81–6.
22. Parasitoi: FF 87–9.
23. Capture of wolves: F 92.
24. Protection of laws: F 93; cf. 98.
25. Conduct of speakers: FF 101, 104.
26. Education: F 102.
27. Funerals: F 109; cf. 144–5, 151.
28. Abortion: F 122.
29. Calendar: F 123.
30. Rewards for athletes: F 143.
31. Disabled men: FF 146–7.
32. The content of F 119 remains unclear.

593/2 (Ol. 46.4)

Archon

DROPIDES (? son of Dropides) *PA* 4573; *APF* 322ff.
Said by Philostratos *Soph.* 1.16.2 to have been the one ὃς μετὰ Σόλωνα 'Αθηναίοις ἦρξεν, favoured by Cadoux, *JHS* 1948, 99, because of his identification with the friend of Solon (Plato *Tim.* 20e; on the later tradition that he was Solon's brother see *APF*). Samuel, *Chron.* 201, leaves the matter unresolved. The challenger for the archonship is Phormion, identified by the scholiast on Ar. *Peace* 347 (with a reference to Eupolis' *Demes*) as the fifth of that name, ἀρχαῖος 'Αθηναῖος, μετὰ Σόλωνα ἄρξας. Cadoux suggested a number had dropped out of the text, a view criticized by Bradeen, *Hesperia* 1963, 192, who proposed 546/5 (*q.v.*) for Phormion. The words 'having held office after Solon' are more likely to be vague in a scholiast, especially when in Eupolis' play Solon and Peisistratos appeared. For Phormion in this year see also Maddoli, *Cronologia* 65 n.1; Corbetta, *RIL* 1978, 300.

592/1 (Ol. 47.1)

Archon

EUKRATES *PA* 5742
Sosikrates *apud* Diog. 1.101 places his office in Ol. 47 (592/1–589/8); the

only vacant years are this one and 589/8. His archonship is synchronized with the visit of Anacharsis to Athens, which Plut. *Solon* 5 puts at the time when Solon was drawing up his laws, which for me allows this year (see 594/3).

591/90 (Ol. 47.2)

Archon
SIMON *PA* 12685
MP A 37; Cadoux, *JHS* 1948, 99ff. The alternative Simonides appears in *schol. vet. in Pindari carmina hyp. Pyth. b*, but in *d* he is called Simon: Fornara no. 16D.

Strategos?
ALKMAION son of Megakles *PA* 651; *APF* 371
According to Plut. *Solon* 11.2, Alkmaion was in the records of Delphi as Athenian general in the Sacred War. While it is possible that he held the position for a number of years, the significance of this one is that it marks the capture of Kirrha in the archonship of Simon and in the records (if genuine) Alkmaion's name could have appeared in relation to this event, especially as subsequent mopping up operations were conducted by Thessalian forces. For discussion of difficulties involved in Alkmaion's leadership and its date see Forrest, *BCH* 1956, 49ff.; for recent doubts on the Sacred War see Robertson, *CQ* 1978, 38–73; Lehmann, *Historia* 1980, 242–6; cf. Frost, *Historia* 1984, 289f. The patronymic comes from Her. 6.125.2.

590/89 (Ol. 47.3)

No archon
Ath. Pol. 13.1: the fifth year after Solon's archonship. See Rhodes, *Comm. ad loc.*

588/7 (Ol. 48.1)

Archon
PHILIPPOS *PA* 14364
Clement *Strom.* 1.127.1; Synkellos (ed. Dindorf 1 p. 429).

586/5 (Ol. 48.3)

No archon
Ath. Pol. 13.1: the fifth year after the last *anarchia* (see 590/89).

582/1 (Ol. 49.3)

Archon
DAMASIAS *PA* 3110
MP A 38. The date is also indicated by *Ath. Pol.* 13.2; see Rhodes, *Comm.*
180ff. The scholia on Pindar cited under 591/90, along with *MP*, indicate
that the revived Delphic ἀγὼν στεφανίτης was held in Damasias' archonship
and that can be dated to this year; in the absence of further qualification,
this must be assumed to be the first, legitimate year of Damasias (Cadoux,
JHS 1948, 102f.). The arguments of Samuel, *Chron.* 202, are deficient in
assuming that when *MP* speaks of Damasias τοῦ δευτέρου, he means
Damasias' second year, which cannot be so, as Cadoux showed, and in
supposing that the second *anarchia* of *Ath. Pol.* 13.1 is Damasias' second
year. Damasias is indeed the second of that name to appear as archon (see
639/8).

581/80 (Ol. 49.4)

Archon?
DAMASIAS *PA* 3110
Ath. Pol. 13.2 says that Damasias ἦρξεν for two years and two months. As
Ath. Pol. identifies the archonship as the focal point of *stasis*, perhaps
Damasias continued to call himself archon, but his position was hardly
legitimate and it is possible that his second year at least was signalled as
anarchia (Cadoux, *JHS* 1948, 78 n.9, 102).

580/79 (Ol. 50.1)

Archon?
DAMASIAS *PA* 3110
See on 581/80. After two months he was perhaps replaced by a board of ten
which served for the rest of the year, unless they belong in 579/8. See
Cadoux, *JHS* 1948, 103; Figueira, *Hesperia* 1984, 447–73.

577/6 (Ol. 50.4)

Archon
ARCHESTRATIDES *PA* 2394
Dion. *AR* 4.1.1.

570/69 (Ol. 52.3)

Archon
ARISTOMENES *PA* 1990
Diog. 1.79 (Sosikrates).

566/5 (Ol. 53.3)

Archon

HIPPOKLEIDES son of Teisandros *PA* 7617; *APF* 295f.

His archonship is associated with the beginning of the Great Panathenaia by Pherekydes and Hellanikos (*FGH* 3 F 2, 4 F 22; Fornara no. 26), which must be this year from the tradition of Eusebios: Cadoux, *JHS* 1948, 104; cf. however, Davison, *JHS* 1958, 26ff.; Corbett, *JHS* 1960, 57f. The filiation comes from Her. 6.127.4.

Hieropoioi?

[KR]ATES
[THAS]YKLES
ARISTODIKOS *PA* 1829
BR[YSON]
ANTE[NOR]

Grammateus?

KINESIAS *PA* 8437

IG i³ 507 (i² 463; *CEG* 434; *DAA* 326, pp. 350ff. with discussion). For doubts on date and other matters see Davison, *JHS* 1958, 26ff.; Jordan, *Servants* 118. Three names are totally lost. The occurrence of the word πρῶτοι and the connexion with the Panathenaia point to this year. I think it likely that they were hieropoioi, but for the view that they were athlothetai see Davison and SEG 26.35, restoring ANTE[NORIDES].

?562/1 (Ol. 54.3)

Strategos

PEISISTRATOS son of Hippokrates *PA* 11793; *APF* 444ff.

The idea that Peisistratos' command against Megara was as polemarch has had a long life (de Sanctis, *Atthis* 342; Hignett, *HAC* 113 and n.9; Kinzl, *AJAH* 1979, 32, 42 n.51). There is no warrant for this: Her. 1.59.4 has ἐν τῇ πρὸς Μεγαρέας γενομένῃ στρατηγίῃ, which is confirmed by the use of strategos at *Ath. Pol.* 22.3, this in a technical treatise; Ain. Takt. 4.8 also has Πεισιστράτῳ γὰρ Ἀθηναίων στρατηγοῦντι, while Justin 2.8.2 is vaguer with *dux*. If Peisistratos was polemarch, why was he not so called? His exploits are mentioned at Her. 1.59.4 (followed by *Ath. Pol.* 14.1); Ain. Takt. 4.8ff.; Front. *Strat.* 2.9.9; Justin 2.8.1ff.

As to date, our sources connect the fame won in this war with Peisistratos' ability to seize tyranny in the first instance, so that the generalship should not have been too long before 561/60; I have placed it at the latest possible date, assuming that it was not in 561/60 itself. Berve (*Tyrannis* II.544) says it cannot be before the 560s, while Kinzl (*AJAH* 1979, 32 and 42 n.52, citing Berve) for some reason opts for the early 560s; Bon, in her note on Aineias in the Budé edition (1967), 120, says between

565 and 561. Herodotos, in the context of 561/60, says of the incipient tyrant πρότερον εὐδοκιμήσας; *Ath. Pol.* 22.3 has Πεισίστρατος δημαγωγὸς καὶ στρατηγὸς ὢν τύραννος κατέστη, which could be taken to indicate that Peisistratos was still general when he became tyrant, but at least is evidence for a proximate connexion. So too Justin 2.8.6, though little weight can be placed on this: 'sed Pisistratus, quasi sibi, non patriae vicisset, tyrannidem per dolum occupat'. See also Hopper, *ABSA* 1961, 208ff.; Mossé, *La tyrannie* 63; Rhodes, *Comm.* 199f.; Frost, *Historia* 1984, 290.

561/60 (Ol. 54.4)

Archon
KOMEAS *PA* 8955
MP A 40. Identified as archon in the year of Peisistratos' first seizure of power by *Ath. Pol.* 14.1; Plut. *Solon* 32.3 and *MP*; at least one MS of Eusebios (*Hieron.*) yields this date. See Cadoux, *JHS* 1948, 104ff.; Samuel, *Chron.* 202f.

Tyrannos
PEISISTRATOS *PA* 11793; *APF* 444ff.
On dates see p. xi. For this period see Her. 1.59.5f.; *Ath. Pol.* 14.1ff. For the tyranny as a whole see 546/5. *Ath. Pol.* tells us that the motion granting him a bodyguard was proposed by ARISTION (*PA* 1728 – Ariston in the MSS of Plut. *Solon* 30).

560/59 (Ol. 55.1)

Archon
HEGESTRATOS = *PA* 6309 (cf. p. 408)
Phanias F 21 Wehrli *apud* Plut. *Solon* 32.3 places Solon's death in this archonship, which succeeded that of Komeas: Cadoux, *JHS* 1948, 106ff.

?558/7 (Ol. 55.3)

Hieropoioi?
[DEX]ITHEOS or [MNES]ITHEOS
[ME]LES[IAS]
T--

Grammateus
[KALL]IAS
So *DAA* 327, pp. 353ff., preferring 562/1 or 558/7 for the date, but allowing 554/3 to be possible; *CEG* 435 opts for 562/1, the date also indicated with a query at IG i³ 508. Davison (*JHS* 1958, 29ff.) suggested the men might be athlothetai (cf. 566/5); thus too the restoration reported

at SEG 26.36, whereby the first name above disappears, the secretary Kallias remains, but we have restored

[ALKMEON]

[DEXI]LE[OS]

DAA 328 (IG i³ 509; i² 392) may date after nos. 326 and 327, but cf. Davison for the possibility that it may belong to the *lesser* Panathenaia between nos. 326 and 327. It has a name in relation to the post of grammateus, but it is unclear whether or not it is a patronymic:

PHAIDRI[AS] *PA* 13933.

?557/6 (Ol. 55.4)

Polemarchos

CHARMOS *PA* 15520; *APF* 451

Kleidemos *FGH* 323 F 15 (Fornara no. 30A): καὶ Χάρμου τοῦ πολεμαρχήσαντος θυγατέρα Μυρρίνην ἔλαβεν Ἱππίᾳ..., this of Peisistratos on his return, for the date of which see p. xi. Though the aorist participle may seem troublesome, it was hardly relevant to mention the polemarchy unless Charmos held it in the year of Peisistratos' return. Cf. Dover, *Comm. Thuc.* IV.333.

Tyrannos

PEISISTRATOS son of Hippokrates *PA* 11793; *APF* 444ff.

Her. 1.60.2ff.; *Ath. Pol.* 14.4f. See above on Charmos and for the tyranny as a whole 546/5.

556/5 (Ol. 56.1)

Archon

HEGESIAS *PA* 6309

Ath. Pol. 14.3 says he was archon in the year of Peisistratos' first expulsion, but even if this is not that year, the placing of him in the sixth year after Komeas is likely to be correct. It has been suggested by Cromey (*Historia* 1979, 137) that he may belong to the clan of the Salaminioi, but the name occurs in a number of possible tribes: see 438/7 epistatai; IG i³ 1191 (i² 964); *Agora* XVII.22.95.

555/4 (Ol. 56.2)

Archon

EUTHYDEMOS *PA* 5514

MP A 41; Sosikrates *apud* Diog. 1.68 places him in Ol. 56 (556/5–553/2). Cadoux, *JHS* 1948, 108f.; Samuel, *Chron.* 203; Jacoby, *Atthis* 375 n.112, wanted him in Ol. 56.1.

551/50 (Ol. 57.2)

Archon

K--

IG i³ 1031 (ML 6b; Fornara no. 23B). One might venture an association with one of the two unplaced archons Kritias (necessitated by the description of the archon I have placed in 600/599 as the first Kritias) and Kebris (*PA* 8263), mentioned in Philochoros' third book (*FGH* 328 F 31).

550/49 (Ol. 57.3)

Archon

PHA-- *APF* 269

IG i³ 1031 (ML 6b; Fornara no. 23B). The archon of 490/89 is called Phainippides the second at *MP* A 48; the real name is Phainippos. An earlier Phainippos (or Phainippides) could appropriately be restored here, but cf. Bradeen, *Hesperia* 1963, 190 n.14, and *APF*.

Tamiai?

CHAIRION son of Kle(i)d[ikos] or Kle(i)d[emos] *PA* 15258= ?15254=?15257; *APF* 13

IG i³ 590 (i² 467; *DAA* 330). The date is approximate.

Also IG i³ 510 (i² 393) records the following tamiai about this time (there may well have been eight in all):

ANAXION *PA* 817; *APF* 26

EUDIKOS *PA* 5417; *APF* 189

S-- *APF* 487

ANDOKIDES *PA* 826; *APF* 27

LYSIMACH[OS] *APF* 48

549/8 (Ol. 57.4)

Archon

TE--

IG i³ 1031 (*ML* 6b; Fornara no. 23B).

548/7 (Ol. 58.1)

Archon

ERXIKLEIDES *PA* 5180

The dating of the archon given at Paus. 10.5.13 allows the completion of the name from the first three letters in the archon list fragment IG i³ 1031 (ML 6b; Fornara no. 23B). See Bradeen, *Hesperia* 1963, 190, for unlikely alternatives.

547/6 (Ol. 58.2)

Archon

THES[PIEUS]

IG i³ 1031 (ML 6b; Fornara no. 23B). This is the suggestion of Bradeen, *Hesperia* 1963, 191, for the name on the archon list fragment and it seems preferable to the alternatives which he mentions.

546/5 (Ol. 58.3)

Archon

PHOR[MION] *PA* 14948

See Bradeen, *Hesperia* 1963, 191f., with possible alternatives for IG i³ 1031 (ML 6b; Fornara no. 23B). This will be the Phormion mentioned as archon after Solon by schol. Ar. *Peace* 347 (see under 593/2). The case has been strengthened by McGregor, *Phoenix* 1974, 18–21, and this is not undermined, I think, by Corbetta, *RIL* 1978, 299f. (SEG 28.19). While Bradeen's argument on the supposition that Phormion was archon in the year of Pallene cannot be pressed, that correspondence is allowed on the chronology adopted here.

Tyrannos

PEISISTRATOS son of Hippokrates *PA* 11793; *APF* 444ff.

For the date see p. xi. The final seizure of power and details on subsequent events and general activities under the tyranny are related at Her. 1.60.2ff.; *Ath. Pol.* 15.2ff.; for further sources and the tyranny as a whole see Hignett, *HAC* 108ff.; Andrewes, *Tyrants* 100ff.; French, *Growth* 30ff.; Berve, *Tyrannis* I.47ff., II.543ff.; Mossé, *La tyrannie* 49ff.; Cassola, *PP* 1973, 85f.; Starr, *Economic and Social Growth* 186f.; Rhodes, *Comm.* 189ff.; Andrewes, *CAH²* III.3.402ff.

Peisistratos is credited with helping farmers through loans, though he imposed a five per-cent tax on produce (Thuc. 6.54.5, to be preferred to the other tradition: Rhodes, *Comm.* 215; Dover, *Comm. Thuc.* IV.329f.). He also instituted deme justices (Rhodes, *Comm.* 215f.). We have no reason to believe that he brought in other constitutional measures, but he ensured a crony was archon (Thuc. 6.54.6; Dover, *Comm. Thuc.* IV.330f.). For other measures see Berve 551 and for coinage 550f.; also Kraay, *Coins* 55ff. The tyrants were also active in the field of foreign affairs and in the social, religious and architectural advancement of Athens: Kolb, *JDAI* 1977, 99–138; Frost in *The Craft of the Ancient Historian* (Essays in Honor of Chester G. Starr, ed. J.W. Eadie and J. Ober: Univ. Press of America 1985), 57–78.

?536/5 (Ol. 61.1)

Archon
?[PHRY]NAIOS
MP A 43 indicates the archonship of . . . ναίου τοῦ προτέρου as that in which Thespis first acted and produced drama in Athens, which in the scheme of *MP* must come between the fall of Sardis and the accession of Dareios. Suda *s.v.* Θέσπις says Thespis first acted during Ol. 61 (536/5–533/2); 533/ 2 is occupied and we may as well choose this year. We know of no archon whose name has this termination and the one given is the only one which fits to be found in *APF*; of similar names to be found in *PA*, Athenaios, Arnaios, Eirenaios, Lenaios, Panaios, only the latter might fit this period.

533/2 (Ol. 61.4)

Archon
THERIKLES *PA* 7235
Dion. *AR* 4.41.1; Diod. 10.3.1.

528/7 (Ol. 63.1)

Archon
PHILONEOS *PA* 14677
He was archon when Peisistratos died; computations from *Ath. Pol.* 17.1 and 19.6 and from the archonship of Harpaktides, 511/10, when the tyranny ended, produce this date, which corresponds with one version of Eusebios; 527/6 is now occupied. See Cadoux, *JHS* 1948, 109; Samuel, *Chron.* 204. Jacoby, *Atthis* 371 n.99, on the other hand, considers 529/8 possible, even preferable.

Tyrannos
HIPPIAS son of Peisistratos *PA* 7605; *APF* 446ff.
Thucydides (1.20.2; 6.54.2, 55.1) felt it necessary to insist that Hippias alone was tyrant, though this was clearly held by Herodotos (5.55), as later by *Ath. Pol.* (18.1). However, the latter's general statement (17.3) that after Peisistratos' death 'his *sons* held the rule' will have some relation to reality (cf. Her. 6.39.1, 103.3; Rhodes, *Comm.* 224f.). For sources in general see Berve, *Tyrannis* II.554ff.; on coinage Kraay, *Coins* 6of.; cf. under 546/5.

527/6 (Ol. 63.2)

Archon
[ON]ETO[RIDES] *APF* 421
The names down to 522/1 appear on the archon list fragment IG i³ 1031 (ML 6c; Fornara no. 23c). I follow ML on the restoration here; the alterna-

tive would seem to be Onetor; both are *kalos*-names on vases. That the fragment concerned is from an archon list must be accepted despite the brief flurry involving Alexander, *CJ* 1959, 307–14; Thompson, *CJ* 1959–60, 217–20; Alexander, *CJ* 1959–60, 220–1; Eliot and McGregor, *Phoenix* 1960, 27–35; see also White, *Polis and Imperium* 81–95.

526/5 (Ol. 63.3)

Archon
HIPPIAS (son of Peisistratos) *PA* 7605; *APF* 446ff.
See 527/6. I have followed general opinion in assuming that this was the tyrant, but perhaps the possibility that it was another scion of the tyrant house should be taken more seriously: White, *Polis and Imperium* 89ff.

525/4 (Ol. 63.4)

Archon
[K]LEISTHEN[ES] (son of Megakles) *PA* 8526; *APF* 375
See 527/6; this is the most likely restoration.

524/3 (Ol. 64.1)

Archon
MILTIADES (son of Kimon) *PA* 10212; *APF* 301f.
The first letter is missing on the archon list fragment (see 527/6), but the name, dated to Ol. 64 at Dion. *AR* 7.3.1, enables us to date the fragment: see Cadoux, *JHS* 1948, 110 n.216.

523/2 (Ol. 64.2)

Archon
[KA]LLIADES
The most reasonable restoration on the archon list fragment (see 527/6), the alternatives being Philliades and Telliades; see Cadoux, *JHS* 1948, 111; ML p. 12.

522/1 (Ol. 64.3)

Archon
PEISISTRATOS (son of Hippias) *PA* 11792; *APF* 450f.
See the discussion in *APF*. Peisistratos is named as archon under the tyranny at Thuc. 6.54.6; the archon list fragment (see 527/6) has . . .⁵. . strat[os]. The inscription mentioned by Thucydides is extant (IG i³ 948 (i² 761; ML 11; SEG 31.31; Fornara no. 37)) and there is no bar to dating it to this time. Cf. Cadoux, *JHS* 1948, 111f.

?518/17 (Ol. 65.3)

Archon
?HABRON *PA* 3; *APF* 270

The discussion on the possibility of a Habron in 518/17 by Cadoux (*JHS* 1948, 112) has been superseded by *P.Oxy.* 2438 with commentary by Lobel, published in 1961. The dispute in the tradition was evidently whether Pindar could have been 50 or have died in the archonship of Habron, 458/7. There is the temptation of a Habron on a dedication from the Akropolis (IG i³ 909; i² 742; *DAA* 339) and a candidate for ostracism in the 480s, as well as the existence of a Kal(l)ias son of Habron before the middle of the sixth century (on all of whom see *APF*), and the consequent possibility of a Habron being archon around 520 and so able to be confused with the later archon.

511/10 (Ol. 67.2)

Archon
HARPAKTIDES *PA* 2249

This man was archon when Hippias was expelled in the fourth year before Isagoras' archonship (*Ath. Pol.* 19.2, 19.6, 21.1); Her. 5.55 has the tyranny continue four years after Hipparchos' murder, which must be placed at the Panathenaia of 514/13; Thuc. 6.59.4 says the tyranny went on for three years and ended in the fourth; *MP* A 45 yields this date: Cadoux, *JHS* 1948, 112f.; Samuel, *Chron.* 204. For full details on the murder of Hipparchos, the last years of the tyranny and the expulsion see Berve, *Tyrannis* II.558ff; the major sources are Her. 5.55ff.; Thuc. 6.54ff.; *Ath. Pol.* 18f.; cf. Fornara no. 39.

APPENDIX

There are a number of unplaced archons. For KRITIAS and KEBRIS (*PA* 8263) see under 551/50, where one of them could belong. For PHAINIPPOS or PHAINIPPIDES see 550/49. Finally, Philochoros *FGH* 328 F 202 mentioned an archon LAKRATEIDES (*PA* 8967) who held office during the reign of Dareios (522–486); he might reasonably be assigned to the period 521/20–512/11.

Whether or not And. 1.106 refers in a garbled way to Pallene or in a mysterious way to the events of 511/10 (as seems more likely), there is little warrant for making Leogoras (*PA* 9074) and Charias (*PA* 15322) generals, despite the verb used; see MacDowell, *Mysteries* 212f.; Davies, *APF* 27f.

Section III
510/9–481/80

510/9 (Ol. 67.3)

Archon

SKAMANDRIOS *PA* 12721

The likeliest of the available dates for the archon in office when torture was banned in criminal proceedings: And. 1.43 with MacDowell *ad loc.*; see Cadoux, *JHS* 1948, 113; Samuel, *Chron.* 204; Ostwald, *Nomos* 140f.; Stroud, *Athens Comes of Age* 29.

509/8 (Ol. 67.4)

Archon

LYSAGORAS *PA* 9275a

MP A 46; Cadoux, *JHS* 1948, 113. The suggestion has been made (Knight, *Studies* 18ff.; Bicknell, *Studies* 41 n.158; Pleket, *Talanta* 1972, 74ff.) that this man put Kleisthenes' proposals to the vote, being a possible supporter. This seems to me entirely contrary to *Ath. Pol.* 21.1.

508/7 (Ol. 68.1)

Archon

ISAGORAS son of Teisandros *PA* 7680

Dion. *AR* 1.74.6; *Ath. Pol.* 21.1 gives this as the year of Kleisthenes' proposals; filiation from *Ath. Pol.* 20.1 and Her. 5.66.1. On the basis of Teisandros' name some have supposed a Philaid connexion: Hammond, *CQ* 1956, 127f.; Sealey, *Essays* 25; *contra* Lewis, *Historia* 1963, 25f. Bicknell, *Historia* 1974, 153, again restores the name Kimon son of Isagoras on an ostrakon; at *Studies* 86 he prefers to call Isagoras a Kimoneios. McCargar, *Phoenix* 1974, 275–81, unnecessarily supposes the archon to be distinct from Kleisthenes' opponent. See also Rhodes, *Comm.* 242ff. Isagoras' activities in this year, in which his position as archon could be relevant, are recorded by Her. 5.70ff.; *Ath. Pol.* 20.

Nomothetes?

KLEISTHENES son of Megakles *PA* 8526; *APF* 375

The means by which Kleisthenes carried out his reform is not forthcoming from the sources and has been the subject of debate: Hignett, *HAC* 15,

126f., 130, 393f.; Ostwald, *Nomos* 155ff.; Rhodes, *Comm.* 248. The popular view has been that the measures were put through as decrees of the demos (Wade-Gery, *Essays* 139ff.), though Hignett changed his mind and preferred a legislative commission, following Beloch. I believe that even if Kleisthenes did gain approval from the demos for his proposals, he will have held an administrative post so as to draw up the provisions; he could have headed a commission, but I see no reason why he should not have been appointed nomothetes on his own. Certainly matters as described in *Ath. Pol.* show a distinct parallel with the treatment of Solon. While this may seem paradoxical in the light of Ostwald's theory that Kleisthenes heralded in the era of *nomos* as law decided upon by popular vote, what is here suggested by no means negates that as an intended course for the future.

On the date and in general see Rhodes, *Comm.* on *Ath. Pol.* 21; add Siewert, *Die Trittyen*; Stanton, *Chiron* 1984, 1–41. I persist in holding that the completed reforms were brought in in 505/4 (*q.v.*; *Antichthon* 1977, 18ff.), but I include them here. For the survival of Kleisthenes' laws in documentary form see Rhodes, *Comm.* 241, 375f.; also Bicknell, *Studies* 49f.; against the survival Day and Chambers, *Aristotle's History* 102ff. The chief accounts of Kleisthenes' work are Her. 5.66f.; *Ath. Pol.* 20f.

Kleisthenes instituted ten tribes instead of the previous four, consisting of three trittyes each, one from each of three geographically defined areas, each trittys consisting of one or more demes, each with its own demarch. The council was to be of 500, with 50 from each tribe, each deme having a quota of representatives to the tribal contingent. It may be doubted if Kleisthenes was responsible for the prytany system or the bouleutic calendar (Rhodes, *Boule* 17ff., 224f.). *Ath. Pol.* suggests that the use of deme names was introduced as official practice, but specific evidence does not seem to bear this out. On the demes as replacements for the naukraries and the possible relationship of *Ath. Pol.* on this matter with Kleidemos *FGH* 323 F 8 see U. Cozzoli, *Quinta miscellanea greca e romana* (Rome 1977), 100ff.; Rhodes, *Comm.* 257. Androtion *FGH* 324 F 5 says that Kleisthenes created the apodektai instead of the kolakretai, but the evidence suggests that the two offices existed side by side until (probably) 411; the apodektai are not attested before 418/17: Rhodes, *Boule* 98f. *Ath. Pol.* 22.4, taken with Arist. *Pol.* 3.2 1275b 36, indicates that some non-Athenians, including perhaps metics and people of dependent status (other suggestions include freedmen or their descendants and mercenaries), were made citizens by enrolment in the tribes. Whitehead, *Metic* 143ff., believes the metics as a class were established by Kleisthenes. See also Rhodes, *Comm.* 254ff.

Ath. Pol. 22.1 tells us that the laws of Solon had been obliterated under the tyranny and that Kleisthenes laid down new ones, aiming at the people, including the law on ostracism. I suspect that the laws here are to be seen, as with Solon, as separate from the constitutional enactments and relating to civil procedure (cf. Plut. *Per.* 3.1). This would fit ostracism, which was indeed the creation of Kleisthenes and was the province of the demos (never the boule, despite *Vat. Graecus* 1144; see *Antichthon* 1977, 10–21; 1985, 7–15). Hansen (*JHS* 1980, 91) thinks that eisangalia was now to be to the demos, but see Rhodes, *Comm.* 316f.

Envoys
Bicknell (*Historia* 1974, 118) suggests that Kallias son of Kratios, given medizing descriptions on ostraka, was one of the ambassadors sent to Sardis shortly after the eclipse of Isagoras, but this obviously cannot be pressed. Neither can Raubitschek (*GRBS* 1964, 153) be followed in suggesting that Kleisthenes, Megakles son of Hippokrates of Alopeke and Xanthippos son of Ariphron of Cholargos were on the embassy. On the idea that Kleisthenes disappears from view as a result of his membership of this discredited mission see Cromey, *Historia* 1979, 132f. For the embassy see Her. 5.73.

505/4 (Ol. 68.4)

Archon
?ALKMAION *PA* 647 = ?652; *APF* 382
Pollux 8.110 tells us that the tribes became ten in Alkmaion's archonship; *Ath. Pol.* 22.2 has Hermokreon (see 501/0) in the fifth year after the *katastasis* of Kleisthenes' measures, which, if we do not emend the text, thereby fall in this year. Rhodes, *Comm.* 263, favours 502/1; Bicknell, *AC* 1985, 76ff., produces more argument for the more conventional 507/6. There has been debate on the speed with which the reforms could be carried out (Thompson, *SO* 1971, 72–9; Andrewes, *CQ* 1977, 243–8; Rhodes, *Comm.* 248f.), but there is nothing amounting to proof such as would tell against the plain, credible testimony of *Ath. Pol.*

Cadoux (*JHS* 1948, 114 n.248) suggested he was son of Alkmeonides, but it has been felt more likely that he was son of Aristonymos, the brother of Kleisthenes, and the father of Leobotes, a prosecutor of Themistokles, which would make his deme Agryle (1): as well as *APF* see Lévêque and Vidal-Naquet, *Clisthène* 54 and 115 n.2 with references; Bicknell, *Studies* 54, 75; but see also Barrett, *AncW* 1978, 67–9.

504/3 (Ol. 69.1)

Archon
AKESTORIDES *PA* 470; *APF* 296
Dion. *AR* 5.37.1; Samuel, *Chron.* 205. Possibly a Philaid; the name Akestor is found in the genealogy of the descendants of Philaios at Pherekydes *FGH* 3 F 2.

501/0 (Ol. 69.4)

Archon

HERMOKREON *PA* 5160

Ath. Pol. 22.2 with Rhodes, *Comm.*, for the name and the date. This year saw the introduction of the bouleutic oath and the tribal election of generals.

500/499 (Ol. 70.1)

Archon

SMYROS *PA* 12802

Dion. *AR* 5.50.1. It is generally suspected that the name is corrupt (Cadoux, *JHS* 1948, 116), but it need not be and no suitable alternative has been found; a Myrrhos in the title of a speech by Antiphon is insufficient ground – that name too is unique.

499/8 (Ol. 70.2)

Strategos

MELANTHIOS (son of Phalanthos) *PA* 9764

Her. 5.97.3, 99.1, 100ff. He was in command of the twenty ships sent to aid the Ionians. The patronymic comes from an ostrakon assumed to relate to this Melanthios: *Hesperia* Suppl. 8, 400f. (Vanderpool).

497/6 (Ol. 70.4)

Archon

ARCHIAS

P.Oxy. 2438 places him as fortieth back from Habron (458/7): see Lewis, *CR* 1962, 201.

496/5 (Ol. 71.1)

Archon

HIPPARCHOS (son of Charmos of Kollytos (II) or Cholargos (V)) *PA* 7600; *APF* 451

Dion. *AR* 6.1.1. The identification with the first man ostracized (*Ath. Pol.* 22.4 with Rhodes, *Comm.*) is compulsive: Cadoux, *JHS* 1948, 116. His deme in *Ath. Pol.* is Kollytos, at Plut. *Nik.* 11.6 Cholargos, and though the former seems to be generally accepted, the decision is not easy: Raubitschek, *C&M* 1958, 105.

495/4 (Ol. 71.2)

Archon
PHILIPPOS *PA* 14365
Anon. *vita Soph.* 2; Cadoux, *JHS* 1948, 116.

494/3 (Ol. 71.3)

Archon
PYTHOKRITOS *PA* 12451
MP A 47.

493/2 (Ol. 71.4)

Archon
THEMISTOKLES (son of Neokles of Phrearrhioi) (IV) *PA* 6669; *APF* 212ff.
Dion. *AR* 6.34.1. The archonship is probably referred to at Thuc. 1.93.3;
see Lewis, *Historia* 1973, 757–8, and Dickie, *Historia* 1973, 758–9, against
Fornara, *Historia* 1971, 534–40; subsequently, however, Mosshammer,
Hermes 1975, 222–34; also Podlecki, *Them.* 196. It should be noted that
Thucydides does not say that Themistokles was responsible for the start of
the building of the Peiraieus fortifications, but that a beginning had been
made of it in his archonship. As archon he will probably have had some
hand in the business, even if only of an administrative nature. See Frost,
CSCA 1968, 115; *Plut. Them.* 75f.; Boersma, *Building Policy* 37f.; for other
barely possible aspects of the archonship see Podlecki, *Them*, 6ff., 49.

492/1 (Ol. 72.1)

Archon
DIOGNETOS *PA* 3847
Dion. *AR* 6.49.1.

491/90 (Ol. 72.2)

Archon
HYBRILIDES *PA* 13896
Dion. *AR* 7.1.5; Paus. 6.9.5.

490/89 (Ol. 72.3)

Archon
PHAINIPPOS *PA* 13976; *APF* 269
Ath. Pol. 22.3; *MP* A 48; Plut. *Arist.* 5.7. *MP* calls him Phainippides (the

second; see 550/49); he is also restored in an archon list fragment, as is Aristeides in 489/8: IG i³ 1031 (ML 6d; Fornara no. 23D). Cairns, *RhM* 1971, 131–4, suggests he may have been of the genos Kerykes.

Polemarchos
KALLIMACHOS of Aphidna (IX) *PA* 8008
Her. 6.109.2ff.; Pliny *NH* 35.57 (*dux*); Plut. *Mor.* 305b (strategos), 628e; Polemon 1.5, 2.2; Paus. 1.15.3; Aelian, *de nat. anim.* 7.38; IG i³ 784 (i² 609; *DAA* 13; ML 18). He died at Marathon.

Strategoi
MILTIADES son of Kimon of Lakiadai (VI) *PA* 10212; *APF* 310f.
Her. 6.103.1, 104, 109f., 132ff.; Ktesias *Pers.* 18 (*FGH* 688 F 13); Plato *Gorg.* 576d; Aisch. 3.181,186; Dem. 13.21f., 23.196,198; Ephoros *FGH* 70 F 63; Cic. *Tusc.* 4.19.44; Nepos *Milt.* 4.4ff., 7.1ff.; Diod. 10.27.3; Strabo 9.1.22; Justin 2.9.9ff., 15.18; Val. Max. 5.3 ext. 3; Front. *Strat.* 2.9.8; Pliny *NH* 35.57; Plut. *Them.* 3.3, *Arist.* 5.1, *Mor.* 92c, 184f, 185a, 305b, 343c, 349c, 350e, 552b, 628e, 1098a; Polemon 1.15f., 2.5,20f.; Paus. 1.15.3, 32.4, 2.29.4, 3.4.7, 8.52.1, 10.10.1; Aelian *VH* 2.25; Libanius *Decl.* 9.12; Marcellinus *vita Thuc.* 2; schol. hyp. Ael. Arist. 46 (III.531f. Dindorf); Suda *s.vv.* Ἱππίας, Ἀριστείδης, Μιλτιάδῃ καὶ Ἀριστείδῃ, Θουκυδίδης, Χωρὶς ἱππεῖς.

For sources see Harrison, *AJA* 1972, 353–78. Miltiades was the major figure in the battle of Marathon and subsequently leader of the failed expedition against Paros which led to his condemnation for deceit of the demos (Develin, *AC* 1977, 571–7). Sources mention a decree of his concerning mobilization: Dem. 19.303 and schol.; Arist. *Rhet.* 3.10.7 1411a 10; Plut. *Mor.* 628e; Paus. 7.15.7; schol. Ael. Arist. 46 (III.542 Dindorf). This, however, has been considered spurious: Rhodes, *Boule* 17 n.4; Podlecki, *Them.* 160f.

STESILEOS son of Thrasyleos *PA* 12906
Her. 6.114. He died at Marathon.

ARISTEIDES son of Lysimachos of Alopeke (X) *PA* 1695; *APF* 48ff.
?THEMISTOKLES son of Neokles of Phrearrhioi (IV) *PA* 6669; *APF* 212ff.
Aristeides is made general at Marathon by Plut. *Arist.* 5 (cf. *Comp. Arist. and Cato* 2.1, 5.1) and it is implied that Themistokles was also general. There is good reason for doubt (Fornara, *Generals* 41f.), but a case can be made at least for Aristeides, whose office I accept: Bicknell, *AC* 1970, 433ff.; Badian, *Antichthon* 1971, 7 n.18, 13 n.32; Podlecki, *Them.* 8.

?KYNEGEIROS son of Euphorion of Eleusis (VIII) *PA* 8944
?POLYZELOS *PA* 11957
On both Plut. *Mor.* 305b, 347d; Diog. 1.56. On Kynegeiros Pliny *NH* 35.57; [Them.] Ep. 11 (p. 751 Hercher); Suda *s.v.* Αἰσχύλος; Photios *s.v.* Μαραθώνιον ποίημα. On Polyzelos Suda *s.v.* Ἱππίας.

They have dubiously been made generals at Marathon along with Kallimachos (*sic*) and Miltiades (in full Plut. *Mor.* 305b). Such a position for Kynegeiros, the brother of Aischylos may be a deduction from Her. 6.114 (Bicknell, *AC* 1970, 432); at Justin 2.9.16 he is merely *miles*. Harrison, *AJA* 1972, 358f., opposes his generalship. Polyzelos may be a confusion with the Epizelos son of Kouphagoras mentioned at Her. 6.117.

489/8 (Ol. 72.4)

Archon

ARISTEIDES son of Lysimachos of Alopeke (x) *PA* 1695; *APF* 48ff.
MP A 49; Cadoux, *JHS* 1948, 117. See the discussion at Plut. *Arist.* 1.2,8, 5.7; there is no doubt here as to the identity of the man. See also the archon list fragment IG i³ 1031 (ML 6d; Fornara no. 23D). It has been suggested that another known Aristeides, son of Xenophilos of Alopeke (*PA* 1687; *APF* 52), was this archon and that Aristeides son of Lysimachos held an archonship other than the eponymous between 479/8 and 468/7; the identification of the archon as in Plutarch was merely a deduction from the bare name on the archon list (Badian, *Antichthon* 1971, 11ff.; Bicknell, *RFIC* 1972, 164–72). I prefer to accept Plutarch, where it is clear that his sources (i.e. by the end of the fourth century) thought this was *the* Aristeides. For the unprovable assumption that Aristeides initiated a temple to Athene see Boersma, *Building Policy* 39.

488/7 (Ol. 73.1)

Archon
ANCHISES *PA* 182
Dion. *AR* 8.1.1.

487/6 (Ol. 73.2)

Archon
TELESINOS *PA* 13527
Ath. Pol. 22.5, dating the reform in archon election (Introduction, p. 2). I hesitate to assert a deme, but Kettos (IV) is tempting, given the Telesinos of that deme who appears in IG i³ 728 (i² 650; *DAA* no. 40; *PA* 13533), who may indeed be the same man, as Raubitschek suggested.

485/4 (Ol. 73.4)

Archon
PHILOKRATES *PA* 14568
MP A 50 (Cadoux, *JHS* 1948, 118); IG i³ 4 A.14f., B.26f. (i² 3.16f., 4.26f.; *LS* no.3: on date see SEG 26.1, 30.2; Jordan, *Servants* 51).

COUNCIL AND ASSEMBLY

IG i³ 4 (see above archon) is a decree concerning the duties of the tamiai on the Akropolis.

484/3 (Ol. 74.1)

Archon

LEOSTRATOS *PA* 9148

Dion. *AR* 8.77.1.

483/2 (Ol. 74.2)

Archon

NIKODEMOS *PA* 10973

Dion. *AR* 8.83.1, supported as to name by the Berlin papyrus of *Ath. Pol.* 22.7, so that the Nikomedes of the London papyrus is probably in error: Cadoux, *JHS* 1948, 118 and n.257; Samuel, *Chron.* 205f.; Rhodes, *Comm.* 277. The identification with the son-in-law of Themistokles mentioned at Plut. *Them.* 32.2 (Badian, *Antichthon* 1971, 2f. n.3, 33; Bicknell, *RFIC* 1972, 170) means accepting the name Nikomedes: see Podlecki, *Them.* 206 n.8.

Strategos

?THEMISTOKLES son of Neokles of Phrearrhioi (IV) *PA* 6669; *APF* 212ff. Themistokles may well have been general in a number of years in the 480s, but the reason for this suggestion is the peculiar notice at Nepos *Them.* 2.1: 'primus autem gradus fuit capessendae rei publicae bello Corcyraeo; ad quod gerendum praetor a populo factus . . .'. Nepos goes on to mention the revenue from the mines, which we may thus associate with the archonship of Nikodemos as at *Ath. Pol.* 22.7 and so assume that Aigina must be meant and not Corcyra, there being possibly a confusion with Themistokles' arbitration between Corcyra and Corinth: see Lenardon, *Historia* 1959, 46 n.115; *Them.* 55, 127, 227 n.50, 234 n.200. We are told that Themistokles used the argument of the war with Aigina to secure the use of the revenues for ship-building; it would make sense for him to produce his persuasion and act upon the resolution as general. Sources on this are Her. 7.144.1; Thuc. 1.14.3; *Ath. Pol.* 22.7; Nepos *Them.* 2.2; Justin 2.12.12; Plut. *Them.* 4.1; Ael. Arist. 3.234ff. (Behr); Polyainos 1.30.6; Libanius *Decl.* 9.38, 10.27; Nikolaos of Myra, *Progym.* 8.7 (*Rhet. Gr.* 1.339 Walz). All these are to be found in Labarbe, *La loi navale*; see also Podlecki, *Them.* 11f., 201ff.; Rhodes, *Comm.* 277ff. For the chronology of the war with Aigina see Hammond, *Historia* 1955, 406ff.; Jeffery, *AJPh* 1962, 44–54; Virgilio, *Commento* 108f.; Podlecki, *Historia* 1976, 396–413. See also Piccirilli, *ZPE* 51 (1983), 169–76.

481/80 (Ol. 74.4)

Archon

HYPSICHIDES *PA* 13916

Ath. Pol. 22.8 so dates the recall of the ostracized, but his chronology produces 480/79, which is wrong; see Rhodes, *Comm.* 281. Plutarch (*Arist.* 8.1) retains the correct chronology.

Strategos

THEMISTOKLES son of Neokles of Phrearrhioi (IV) *PA* 6669; *APF* 212ff. Her. 7.173; Diod. 11.2.5f.; Plut. *Them.* 6f. He was sent to Thessaly in the aborted mission to defend at Tempe. Previously he had been involved in the interpretation of the 'wooden walls' oracle: Her. 7.143; Nepos *Them.* 2.7f.; Plut. *Them.* 10.2; Polyainos 1.30.2.

(i)　He is also credited with the decree for the recall of the ostracized (*Ath. Pol.* 22.8; Nepos *Arist.* 1.5; Plut. *Them.* 11.1, *Arist.* 8.1; cf. Philochoros *FGH* 328 F 30; Rhodes, *Comm.* 281f.) and more controversially with the

(ii)　decree for the evacuation of Attika and for mobilization, which may survive in an inscription that also seems to be dealing with the ostracized when it cuts short. The debate has continued; whether or not the inscription is a genuine record, it may go back to genuine material. Texts bearing upon it are Her. 7.144.3, 8.41.1f.; Isok. 15.233; Dem. 19.303; Nepos *Them.* 2.8; Justin 2.12.14ff.; Front. *Strat.* 1.3.6; Quintilian 9.2.92; Plut. *Them.* 7.1, 10.2ff.; *Kimon* 5.2; Ael. Arist. 3.247ff. (*Behr*), 1.154ff. (Lenz); [Them.] *Ep.* 8 (p. 748 Hercher); Libanius *Decl.* 9.38; schol. Bob. *in* Cic. *Sest.* 141; Suda *s.v. ἀνεῖλεν.* For the inscription see Jameson, *Hesperia* 1960, 198–223; *Hesperia* 1962, 310–15; SEG 22.274; ML 23; Fornara no. 55. For the debate see particularly Podlecki, *Them.* 14f., 125f., 147ff.; also conveniently Hignett, *Xerxes* 199, 458ff.; Burn, *Persia and the Greeks* 364ff.; Lenardon, *Them.* 67ff.; Mattingly, *Class. Contrib.* 79ff.; Robertson, *Phoenix* 1982, 1–44; Hammond, *JHS* 1982, 75–93.

(iii)　The decree pronouncing Arthmios of Zeleia an enemy is attributed to Themistokles by Plut. *Them.* 6.3; Ael. Arist. 3.334 (Behr), though a scholiast on Aristides cites Krateros (*FGH* 342 F 14) for Kimon's authorship. For discussion see Meiggs, *Ath. Empire* 508ff.; Podlecki, *Them.* 100f.; Robertson, *Historia* 1980, 293ff., who wants to date it in 407; cf. Walbank no. 2.

APPENDIX

The '[Phry]naios the first' reconstructed as archon for 536/5 implies another of the name who could be one of the missing archons in this period. It is unlikely that an archon was mentioned at all in the decree concerning Salamis (IG i³ 1), let alone that his name can be restored as Boulekles: see ML 14 with bibliography.

Epistates of water supply

THEMISTOKLES son of Neokles of Phrearrhioi (IV) *PA* 6669; *APF* 212ff. So the office at Plut. *Them.* 31.1, in which he collected fines sufficient to have built a bronze statue. We cannot say whether this came before or after his archonship: Podlecki, *Them.* 8. The attribution to him of a position as nauarchos (Plut. *Them.* 18.1) may be referred to a generalship.

Epimeletai of revenues

THEMISTOKLES son of Neokles of Phrearrhioi (IV) *PA* 6669; *APF* 212ff.
ARISTEIDES son of Lysimachos of Alopeke (X) *PA* 1695; *APF* 48ff.
So Plut. *Arist.* 4.2ff. Themistokles' attempts to discredit Aristeides backfired and the latter was re-elected. This ought, one imagines, to date to the early 480s, but we cannot be sure even of that.

COUNCIL AND ASSEMBLY

(i) IG i³ 1 (i² 1; ML 14; SEG 31.1; Fornara no. 44) is a decree placed in the late sixth century concerning Salamis, included here because it is specifically a decree of the demos and seems to mention the boule as it breaks off.

(ii) IG i³ 2 and 3 are put together, though the content of the first (dated *c.* 500)
(iii) is uncertain, while the second (490–480) concerns the Herakleia at Marathon.

(iv) IG i³ 5 (i² 5; *LS* no. 4; SEG 25.5) concerns sacrifices at the Eleusinia, dated in IG to around 500, but a later date is possible. Its preamble as restored makes it a decree of boule and demos:

Grammateus

PARAIBATES *PA* 11609

Section IV
480/79–432/1

480/79 (Ol. 75.1)

Archon

KALLIADES *PA* 7773

Her. 8.51.1; *MP* A 51; Diod. 11.1.2; Dion. *AR* 9.1.1; Diog. 2.5.45
(=Demetrios *FGH* 228 F 2: Kallias; cf. Diog. 2.3.7); *vita Eurip.* 1.3
(Kallias); schol. Aischylos *Prom.* 384; Eusebios Ol. 74.4. There is a poss-
ible confusion with the archon Kallias of 456/5; cf. also Photios *s.v.*
Κάλλειον.

Strategoi

THEMISTOKLES son of Neokles of Phrearrhioi (IV) *PA* 6669; *APF* 212ff.
Her. 8.4.2, 5.1ff., 19.1f., 22.1f., 58.1ff., 75.1ff., 79f., 92.2, 108.2ff.,
123.2ff.; Thuc. 1.74.1; Ktesias *Pers.* 26 (*FGH* 688 F 13); Isok. 4.154, 12.51,
15.233; Kleidemos *FGH* 323 F 21; Dem. 13.21f., 18.104, 23.196,198;
Aisch. 3.181; Nepos *Them.* 3.2ff., 4.1ff.; Diod. 11.12.4ff., 15.4ff., 17f.,
19.5f., 41.1, 57.2; *Anth. Pal.* 7.73, 235, 237; Justin 2.12.1ff., 13.6ff., 14.11;
Front. *Strat.* 2.2.14, 6.8; Plut. *Them.* 7.2ff., 9.1f., 10ff.; *Arist.* 8f.; *Comp.
Arist. and Cato* 5.3; *Mor.* 185b–c, 320f, 345c, 349c,d , 496f, 552b, 869c–f,
871c, 1099e, 1116f; Ael. Arist. 3.316ff. (Behr); Paus. 7.6.3, 8.52.2;
Polyainos 1.30.2ff., 7, 3.11.2; Aelian *VH* 2.28; *Ep.* 13.20; Origen *Cels.*
1.29; [Them.] *Ep.* 9 (p. 750 Hercher), 11 (p. 751 Hercher), 13 (p. 753
Hercher); Aristodemos *FGH* 104 F 1.1, 4, 7; schol. Ar. *Knights* 84; Suda
s.v. ἀνεῖλεν; Photios *Bibl.* p. 371, 32ff. (Bekker).

Athenian commander with the fleet at Artemision and subsequently
responsible for the battle off Salamis. After that he proposed at the
conference of commanders that they break the bridges at the Hellespont
and, when that failed to persuade, that the enemy be allowed to go (cf. also
Podlecki, *Them.* 122). He made demands for money from the islanders.
Plutarch reports Kleidemos' story that he secured money to put men on
ships (cf. Rhodes, *Comm.* 287ff.).

XANTHIPPOS son of Ariphron of Cholargos (V) *PA* 11169; *APF* 455ff.
Her. 8.131.3; Diod. 11.34.2; Suda *s.v.* Περικλῆς; cf. Philochoros *FGH* 328 F
116. Athenian commander to the fleet at Aigina in spring 479.

Note: Aristeides will not have been general in this year: see Fornara,
Generals 42; cf. Mattingly, *Class. Contrib.* 83.

Envoys
KIMON son of Miltiades of Lakiadai (VI) *PA* 8429; *APF* 302ff.
XANTHIPPOS son of Ariphron of Cholargos (v) *PA* 11169; *APF* 455ff.
MYRONIDES son of Kallias *PA* 10509
Plut. *Arist.* 10.8 gives these names on the basis of the decree sponsored by Aristeides, though Idomeneus *FGH* 338 F 6, whom he cites for 10.6ff., has Aristeides himself as envoy. They went to Sparta to rouse the Spartans. Davies (*APF* 302) gives the date as 479/8, probably on the assumption that the envoys were all generals, but Plutarch indicates the year as that of Salamis. For all we know Kimon and Myronides *could* have been generals in 480/79 (cf. Bicknell, *Studies* 103 n.17); the latter at least certainly was in 479/8.

COUNCIL AND ASSEMBLY

Bouleutes and proposer
LYKIDES *PA* 9194
(i) Her. 9.5 records a meeting of the council on Salamis which heard overtures from Mardonios. Lykides proposed that they accept the terms and put them to the demos. He was stoned to death. The story is referred to at
(ii) Lykourgos *Leok.* 124, who mentions a decree against the unnamed victim, while in other versions at Dem. 18.204 and Cic. *de off.* 3.48 the man is named in what is apparently the same episode as Kyrsilos (*PA* 8949), which I suspect to be a derogatory nickname. It must remain open whether there was actually any decree; see Podlecki, *Them.* 161.

Proposer:
ARISTEIDES son of Lysimachos of Alopeke (X) *PA* 1695; *APF* 48ff.
(iii) Plut. *Arist.* 10.4ff. has Aristeides moving a decree giving an answer to
(iv) Spartan envoys, another that the priests should curse any who communi-
(v) cated with the Medes or forsook the Hellenic alliance, and a third establishing the embassy to Sparta (see above).

479/8 (Ol. 75.2)

Archon
XANTHIPPOS *PA* 11159; *APF* 456
MP A 52; Diod. 11.27.1; Plut. *Arist.* 5.7 (Xanthippides). Bicknell (*Studies* 74, 83; *Historia* 1974, 151) has suggested that he might be the son of Hippokrates found on an ostrakon, but Bicknell himself questions the actual existence of the son of Hippokrates.

Strategoi

MYRONIDES son of Kallias *PA* 10509
LEOKRATES son of Stroibos *PA* 9084

Plut. *Arist.* 20.1 would suggest they were at Plataia. The suggestion of Bicknell, *Studies* 101ff., that Leokrates' demotic was Hagnous (v) is vitiated by the findspot of IG i³ 983 (i² 821); see Hansen, *CEG* 312.

ARISTEIDES son of Lysimachos of Alopeke (x) *PA* 1695; *APF* 48ff.
Her. 9.28.6; Nepos *Arist.* 2.1; Diod. 11.29.4, 30.2ff., 33.1; Plut. *Arist.* 11.1, 12, 13.2f., 14.3, 15.2ff., 18.5, 20.1ff., 21.1; *Comp. Arist. and Cato* 2.1, 5.1; *Mor.* 350b, 1098a; Paus. 8.52.2; Aristodemos *FGH* 104 F 2.4; schol. Thuc. 5.18.5.

He was general at Plataia. Herodotos does not mention him by name in the battle, but others add details; he suppressed an anti-democratic plot (Plut. *Arist.* 13.2f.), was involved in giving the prize of valour to the Plataians (Plut. *Arist.* 20.1ff.; Diod. 11.33.1 has him urge the granting of the prize to Sparta) and in proposing the yearly gathering at Plataia, that games be held every fourth year and that forces continue to be levied for the war (Plut. *Arist.* 21.1). These actions seem appropriate to his position as general. Cf. below Council and Assembly.

XANTHIPPOS son of Ariphron of Cholargos (v) *PA* 11169; *APF* 455ff.
Her. 7.33, 9.114.2ff.; Diod. 11.27.3, 34.2, 36.5, 37.1ff.; Plut. *Per.* 3.1; Paus. 1.25.1, 3.7.9, 8.52.3; Aristodemos *FGH* 104 F 3.3; Suda *s.v.* Περικλῆς.

Commander of the Athenian forces at Mykale and later at the successful siege of Sestos.

Lochagos

OLYMPIODOROS son of Lampon *PA* 11389
Her. 9.21.3; Plut. *Arist.* 14.3. He was engaged in a battle at Erythrai (Her. 9.22ff.).

Envoys

THEMISTOKLES son of Neokles of Phrearrhioi (IV) *PA* 6669; *APF* 212ff.
HABRONICHOS son of Lysikles of Lamptrai (I) *PA* 20; *APF* 1
ARISTEIDES son of Lysimachos of Alopeke (x) *PA* 1695; *APF* 48ff.

For all three Thuc. 1.90f.; for Habronichos and Themistokles [Them.] *Ep.* 4 (p. 743 Hercher); for Themistokles Dem. 20.73f.; Nepos *Them.* 6.5ff.; Diod. 11.39.4ff. (478/7); Justin 2.15.1ff.; Front. *Strat.* 1.1.10; Plut. *Them.* 19.1f.; Polyainos 1.30.5; Aristodemos *FGH* 104 F 1.5, 2f.; schol. Ar. *Knights* 811.

Envoys to Sparta in the matter of rebuilding Athens' walls; Themistokles went ahead of the others and effected delays. It has been suggested (Fornara, *Generals* 42; Podlecki, *Them.* 30) that Themistokles and Habronichos were generals, which is possible, but no source says so and Diod. 11.27.3 is directly against it. Diodoros (11.41ff.) continues to describe Themistokles' involvement in the Peiraieus fortifications under 477/6, adding other proposals (see 477/6). If this could be believed, Themistokles *might* be given some official position. See in general Podlecki, *Them.* 30ff.; Lenardon, *Them.* 87ff.; also Meiggs, *Ath. Empire* 414f.

COUNCIL AND ASSEMBLY

Proposers

(i) ?ARISTEIDES son of Lysimachos of Alopeke (x) *PA* 1695; *APF* 48ff.
Plut. *Arist.* 22.1 tells us that when the Athenians returned to the city, Aristeides sponsored a decree that the running of the state be open to all and that the archons be chosen from all Athenians. At the very least this came to nothing and it is a highly questionable report: Hignett, *HAC* 174f.

Plutarch goes on to tell how Themistokles had a secret plan, which the assembly ordained that Aristeides alone should hear; Aristeides reported that the plan, which was to burn the Greek naval establishment, would be profitable, but unjust. So the Athenians told Themistokles to abandon his plan (also Plut. *Them.* 20.1f).

(ii) THEMISTOKLES son of Neokles of Phrearrhioi (IV) *PA* 6669; *APF* 212ff.
Thuc. 1.90 tells how a Spartan embassy proposed that Athens not rebuild her fortifications, but join in pulling down others in Greece. On the proposal of Themistokles, the Athenians replied that they would send an embassy to discuss the points raised. Themistokles then suggested that he be sent ahead of the other envoys (*q.v.*).

478/7 (Ol. 75.3)

Archon
TIMOSTHENES *PA* 13807
Ath. Pol. 23.5; *MP* A 53; Diod. 11.38.1.

Strategoi
ARISTEIDES son of Lysimachos of Alopeke (x) *PA* 1695; *APF* 48ff.
Thuc. 5.18.5f (cf. 1.96.1); And. 4.11; Dem. 23.209; Aisch. 2.23, 3.258 with schol.; *Ath. Pol.* 23.4f.; Nepos *Arist.* 2.2ff.; Diod. 11.44.2,6, 46.4ff.; Justin 2.15.16; Plut. *Arist.* 23f., *Kimon* 6.3, *Mor.* 186b; Anon. Argen. 7f. (*ATL* II D.13; *Hesperia* 1957, 164 (Meritt and Wade-Gery); Meiggs, *Ath. Empire* 515); Paus. 8.52.2; Aelian *VH* 11.9; Philostratos *Soph.* 2.29; *Apoll.* 6.21; schol. Ael. Arist. 46 (III.510f. Dindorf).

He, with Kimon, was involved in the dealings with the allies which led to the transference of leadership from Sparta to Athens and the subsequent reorganization of the alliance and assessment of tribute. The implication of *Ath. Pol.* is that the assessment was completed within 478/7 (accepted at

ATL III.234f.); Diodoros' placing of this under 477/6 is hardly strong evidence against it, although Meiggs (*Ath. Empire* 58ff.) believes that the assessment may have taken some years. The full details may indeed have taken some time to work out and Aristeides may have been in charge without being general, but some arrangement was immediately necessary in 478/7.

KIMON son of Miltiades of Lakiadai (VI) *PA* 8429; *APF* 302ff.
Plut. *Arist.* 23.1f., *Kimon* 6.1ff., 9.2ff., *Comp. Kim. and Luc.* 2.2; Justin 2.15.18; Polyainos 1.34.2.

Though Kimon could have been general in 479/8 (Fornara, *Generals* 42f.), no source says so. This generalship is doubted at *ATL* III.159f. and Rhodes *Comm.* 295. I see no real reason to suppose that he was not sent out with Aristeides and the Athenian contingent to the allied forces against Sestos and Byzantion.

Pylagoras

?THEMISTOKLES son of Neokles of Phrearrhioi (IV) *PA* 6669; *APF* 212ff.
Plut. *Them.* 20.3f. His part in persuading the pylagorai not to approve the Spartan motion to exclude all cities which had not joined in opposing the Persians would suggest that he himself held the office: Roux, *L'amphictionie* 28, 29f.

477/6 (Ol. 75.4)

Archon
ADEIMANTOS *PA* 189
Simonides F 77; *MP* A 54; Diod. 11.41.1; Plut. *Them.* 5.4.

Strategos
?KIMON son of Miltiades of Lakiadai (VI) *PA* 8429; *APF* 302ff.
Her. 7.107.1; Thuc. 1.98.1; Ephoros *FGH* 70 F 191 (Fornara no. 61B(2));
Nepos *Cimon* 2.2; Diod. 11.60.1f; Paus. 8.9.8.

The generalship of Kimon is likely. The capture of Eion is the first action mentioned by Thucydides in his account of the aftermath of the Persian War and Diodoros 11.60.1f. agrees with his priority, though writing under the year 470/69. The scholiast to Aisch. 2.31 gives 476/5 for the fall of the city, though the siege could have begun a year earlier (Fornara, *Generals* 43). The basic problem is the belief that Ephoros ought to put the investment of Eion and the expulsion of Pausanias from Byzantion in the same campaigning season, taken together with Justin 9.1.3, indicating seven years of possession of Byzantion by Pausanias (thus expulsion in 470/69). However, scholars are not loath in other instances to reject the testimony of Justin, whose reference here is retrospective and who may have been guilty of another error if we accept the manuscript reading 'condita [rather than the emendation 'capta'] primo a Pausania'.

And all Ephoros says is that the Athenians sailed out of Byzantion. See Deane, *Thuc. Dates* 94ff. n.10; Meiggs, *Ath. Empire* 73.

COUNCIL AND ASSEMBLY

Proposer

?THEMISTOKLES son of Neokles of Phrearrhioi (IV) *PA* 6669; *APF* 212ff. As noted under 479/8, Themistokles is said to be still involved in Peiraieus fortifications in 477/6 according to Diod. 11.41ff., which also adds that he persuaded the Athenians to supplement their fleet with 20 triremes a year and remove the tax on metics and craftsmen. Neither date nor detail can be accepted without question.

476/5 (Ol. 76.1)

Archon

PHAIDON *PA* 13967

Diod. 11.48.1; Dion. *AR* 9.18.1; Plut. *Thes.* 36.1; schol. Aisch. 2.31 (Fornara no. 62).

Strategoi

KIMON son of Miltiades of Lakiadai (VI) *PA* 8429; *APF* 302ff.

KRATINOS *PA* 8750

LYKOURGOS (? of Boutadai) (VI) *PA* 9246; *APF* 349

LYSISTRATOS *PA* 9591

For Kimon see 477/6; schol. Aisch. 2.31 (Fornara no. 62) gives the other names; it does not say these three were generals, but it seems likely; there is no necessary implication that they were also generals in 477/6. Lykourgos' deme is assigned on the assumption that he was a member of the Eteoboutadai; neither this nor the fact of the generalship can be denied because it creates double representation of tribe VI.

   These generals captured Eion and the latter three subsequently died at the site of Ennea Hodoi. Kimon captured Skyros (Plut. *Kimon* 8; cf. *Thes.* 36.1) and this seems to come soon after Eion, perhaps then also in this year, in which Plutarch dates the oracle telling the Athenians to recover the bones of Theseus (but see Podlecki, *RSA* 1975, 14f.). The sequence in Plut. *Kimon* 8, which goes from Eion to Skyros to the tragic contest of 469/8, cannot be pressed for significance, as it is a thematic chapter with no pretence to close chronological connexion. Neither is the messy Nepos *Cimon* 2 to be used as evidence for a separation of years between Eion and Skyros.

   Kimon may well have been general in a number of subsequent years (perhaps all), for which, however, he is not attested. Diod. 11.60.2ff. has him operate successfully in Karia and Lykia (cf. Polyainos 3.2.5) and then on to a sea victory near Cyprus preceding Eurymedon. Nepos *Cimon* 4 mentions reduction of defecting allies before he includes Skyros, and all this after Eurymedon (which he mistakes as Mykale). For Kimon's dealings with the allies see also Plut. *Kimon* 11. In general see Meiggs, *Ath. Empire* 73ff.

475/4 (Ol. 76.2)

Archon
DROMOKLEIDES *PA* 4564
Diod. 11.50.1.

474/3 (Ol. 76.3)

Archon
AKESTORIDES *PA* 471 = ?472; *APF* 296
Diod. 11.51.1. He could well be a Philaid or a connexion, but that is not enough for deme attribution.

473/2 (Ol. 76.4)

Archon
MENON *PA* 10066
Diod. 11.52.1; hyp. Aischylos *Pers.* 1.12; IG ii² 2318.[1]. A number of men of this name appear on ostraka and one unpublished one apparently refers to conduct in an archonship; this Menon may be the Pharsalian who was given citizenship in the 470s, who may be the son of Menekleides of Gargettos (II) found on ostraka, but I am not confident of this and record the other names on ostraka (which might not belong wholly to separate men): Menon son of Menandrides the Lemnian of Gargettos; Menon son of Neokles; Menon son of Megakles; Menon of Anagyrous (I). For all this see Osborne, *Naturalization* III/IV.20ff.

472/1 (Ol. 77.1)

Archon
CHARES *PA* 15285
MP A 55; Diod. 11.53.1; Dion. *AR* 9.37.1; IG ii² 2318.[12].

471/70 (Ol. 77.2)

Archon
PRAXIERGOS *PA* 12163
Diod. 11.54.1; IG ii² 2318.[23].

470/69 (Ol. 77.3)

Archon
DEMOTION *PA* 3645
Diod. 11.60.1.

469/8 (Ol. 77.4)

Archon
APSEPHION *PA* 2805
So the name in *MP* A 56; Diog. 2.44 (Apollodoros *FGH* 244 F 34); Plut. *Kimon* 8.7; Diod. 11.63.1 has Phaion or Phaidon. He appointed the generals as judges in the tragic competition.

Strategos
KIMON son of Miltiades of Lakiadai (VI) *PA* 8429; *APF* 302ff.
Plut. *Kimon* 8.7. One of the generals who judged the tragic competition in a year when, normally or accidentally, all ten tribes produced a general.

468/7 (Ol. 78.1)

Archon
THEAGENIDES *PA* 6611
MP A 57; Diod. 11.65.1; Dion. *AR* 9.56.1; Plut. *Mor.* 835a (Theogenides); schol. Ar. *Lys.* 1144 (Fornara no. 67A); hyp. Aischylos, *Seven* (Theagenes); *P.Oxy.* 2256 F 2.

467/6 (Ol. 78.2)

Archon
LYSISTRATOS *PA* 9592
Diod. 11.66.1.

466/5 (Ol. 78.3)

Archon
LYSANIAS *PA* 9299
Diod. 11.67.1.

Strategos
KIMON son of Miltiades of Lakiadai (VI) *PA* 8429; *APF* 302ff.
Simonides FF 103, 105; Thuc. 1.100.1; Ephoros *FGH* 70 F 191; Nepos *Cimon* 4.2ff. (Mykale!); Diod. 11.60.5ff. (470/69); Front. *Strat.* 2.9.10; Plut. *Kimon* 12f.; *Mor.* 349d, 496f, 552b; Polyainos 1.34.1; Aristodemos *FGH* 104 F 11.2; Eusebios (*Arm.*) Ol. 79.4 = 461/60; Suda *s.v.* Κίμων.
I take this to be the year of the Eurymedon victory over the Persian fleet,

as well as that in which the revolt of Naxos was put down, which operation may also have involved Kimon. The fullest version, in Plutarch (cf. Diodoros), tells of the winning over of Phaselis, operations in Cyprus and Eurymedon itself, with discussion of the aftermath. The Suda ascribes to Kimon the settlement of territorial limitations on the Persians. See in general Meiggs, *Ath. Empire* 75ff.

465/4 (Ol. 78.4)

Archon
LYSITHEOS *PA* 9398
Diod. 11.69.1; ?schol. Aisch. 2.31 (Lysikrates: see Thompson, *Phoros* 149; Fornara no. 62).

Strategoi
KIMON son of Miltiades of Lakiadai (VI) *PA* 8429; *APF* 302ff.
Nepos *Cimon* 2.5; Plut. *Kimon* 14.1f. Plutarch reports his involvement in the siege of Thasos, preceded by actions against Persians and Thracians and consequent possession of the Chersonese.

LEAGROS son of Glaukon of Kerameis (V) *PA* 9028; *APF* 90f.
SOPHANES son of Eutychides of Dekeleia (VIII) *PA* 13409
Her. 9.75; Paus. 1.29.4f; schol. Aisch. 2.31 (Fornara no. 62: Leagoras). They operated on the mainland of Thrace against the Edonoi in another attempt to found a settlement at Ennea Hodoi; Sophanes at least was killed, but no source says Leagros was: Francis and Vickers, *PCPhS* 207 (1981), 104ff.; see also Thompson, *Phoros* 149 and 453/2.

?EPHIALTES son of Sophonides *PA* 6157
?PERIKLES son of Xanthippos of Cholargos (V) *PA* 11811; *APF* 457ff.
Plut. *Kimon* 13.5 (Kallisthenes *FGH* 124 F 16) indicates that after Eurymedon they sailed beyond the Chelidonian islands, which suggests generalships if true, but only an approximate date. See Rhodes, *Comm.* 334, and for doubts Lewis, *Sparta and Persia* 59f. and n.68.

Envoy
?KALLIAS son of Hipponikos of Alopeke (X) *PA* 7825; *APF* 258ff.
The problem is that of dealings with Persia. Plut. *Kimon* 13.4ff. tells of an arrangement made after Eurymedon, denied by Kallisthenes (*FGH* 124 F 16), but supported by Krateros (*FGH* 342 F 13), naming Kallias. Her. 7.151 has Kallias at Susa at the same time as an Argive embassy, which episode Meiggs (*Ath. Empire* 92f.) wants to put in 461, but this does not convince me. In support of this period for the Peace of Kallias see Walsh, *Chiron* 1981, 31ff.; Meister, *Ungeschichtlichkeit*, has argued that the correct date in the ancient tradition was *c.* 465/4, but that the peace is unhistorical. All I would say is that it is possible that Kallias was used as an ambassador to Persia more than once in the period before and after 450.

464/3 (Ol. 79.1)

Archon
ARCHEDEMIDES *PA* 2314
Diod. 11.70.1; Dion. *AR* 9.61.1; Paus. 4.24.5 (Archimedes); *P.Oxy.* 2256 F
3 Addendum.

Strategos
?KIMON son of Miltiades of Lakiadai (VI) *PA* 8429; *APF* 302ff.
He could have continued in command against Thasos; see 465/4 and 463/2.

463/2 (Ol. 79.2)

Archon
TLEPOLEMOS *PA* 13826
Diod. 11.71.1. The name is known in two demes (*APF* 491), Kephisia and
Euonymon, both of tribe I, but cf. the general of 439/8.

Strategos
KIMON son of Miltiades of Lakiadai (VI) *PA* 8429; *APF* 302ff.
He may have seen out the siege of Thasos (see 465/4). We hear that when he
returned he was prosecuted on a charge of bribery for not invading
Makedonia (Plut. *Kimon* 14.2ff.; cf. *Per.* 10.5; *Ath. Pol.* 27.1). *Ath. Pol.*
says that Perikles accused Kimon as general in the matter of his *euthynai*,
which may well be correct (Rhodes, *Comm.* 335f.). Possibly in the later
stages of this year Kimon led a first expedition to help Sparta; schol. Ar.
Lys. 1144 dates Kimon's expedition to Ithome in 468/7, but this is hard to
accept; yet that Kimon made two expeditions is indicated by Plut. *Kimon*
16.7f., 17.2 (which does not *say* that Kimon led the second expedition).

462/1 (Ol. 79.3)

Archon
KONON *PA* 8699; *APF* 507
Diod. 11.74.1; *Ath. Pol.* 25.2 – the year of Ephialtes' reforms. We cannot
assume (*pace* Raubitschek, *DAA* no. 47, p. 49) that he was the father of the
dedicant Timotheos and so of Anaphlystos (x).

Strategos
KIMON son of Miltiades of Lakiadai (VI) *PA* 8429; *APF* 302ff.
Plut. *Kimon* 15. He may first have gone to Ithome (see 463/2), but he is said
to have gone on a naval expedition, possibly, despite the orthodox dating,
to Cyprus and Egypt, and on his return tried to reverse Ephialtes' legislation. Conventionally, however, this will be the year of Kimon's second or
(i) only expedition to Ithome, for the voting of which he was responsible; his
ostracism is generally placed in spring 461. Sources on the Ithome expedi-

tion are Thuc. 1.102.1f.; Plut. *Kimon* 16.8ff.; Paus. 1.29.8, 4.24.6; cf. Ar. *Lys.* 1138ff. with schol. (Philochoros *FGH* 328 F 117; *FGH* 329 F 4).

COUNCIL AND ASSEMBLY

(ii) **Proposers**
EPHIALTES son of Sophonides *PA* 6157
ARCHESTRATOS
Though other sources associate Perikles with Ephialtes and *Ath. Pol.* 25 talks about Themistokles in this context, *Ath. Pol.* 35.2 mentions the laws of Ephialtes and Archestratos. Other sources pertaining to the reforms are Arist. *Pol.* 2.21 1274a 7–8; Diod. 11.77.6 (460/59); Plut. *Kimon* 15.2, 17.3; *Per.* 9.4, 10.7. The precise content of these measures is uncertain (see Rhodes, *Comm.* 311ff.), but in general they seem to have involved the transfer of judicial functions from the Areiopagos to the demos and the council of 500. Kimon (above) opposed the reforms which had been passed, as earlier Ephialtes is said (Plut. *Kimon* 16.8) to have opposed the expedition to help the Spartans.

461/60 (Ol. 79.4)

Archon
EUTHIPPOS *PA* 5494
MP A 58; Diod. 11.75.1 (Euippos). A friend of Kimon was Euthippos of Anaphlystos (x): *PA* 5496; Plut. *Kimon* 17.4.

460/59 (Ol. 80.1)

Archon
PHRASIKLES or PHRASIKLEIDES *PA* 14978
The first name is in Dion. *AR* 10.1.1 and Plut. *Mor.* 835c; Diod. 11.77.1 offers Philokleides or Phrasikleides, the first alternative perhaps owing to confusion with the archon of 459/8; he probably wrote Phrasikleides, which is restored at IG ii² 2318.30. This sort of name confusion is common (see e.g. under 479/8, 468/7, 464/3, 457/6) and makes a decision difficult. It has been remarked to me that the archon of 371/70 is nowhere called Phrasikleides the second, but I do not think this need carry any weight.

Nauarchos
CHARITIMIDES *PA* 15497
Ktesias *Pers.* 32f. (*FGH* 688 F 14; Fornara no. 72). He was outstanding in Egypt in events which Diod. 11.74.1ff. indicates were in the first year of Athenian involvement, for which this is the orthodox date. Fornara, *Generals* 44, makes him strategos, but I leave his status as it appears in Ktesias; see the Introduction, p. 6.

459/8 (Ol. 80.2)

Archon

PHILOKLES *PA* 14516

Diod. 11.78.1; Plut. *Mor.* 835c, 836a; hyp. Aischylos, *Agam.*; IG ii²
2318.41.

Strategoi

LEOKRATES son of Stroibos *PA* 9084

Thuc. 1.105.2; Diod. 11.78.3f. General in the siege of Aigina. Diod. 11.70
puts the beginning of the Aiginetan 'revolt' in 464/3 and it may have begun
before 459/8, as Thucydides writes 'war having come about against the
Aiginetans.' This does not mean that Leokrates was also general earlier.
Diodoros records the defeat of Aigina under 459/8, Leokrates having been
in the theatre for nine months. This could in fact take us into the archon
year 458/7. Thucydides, however, mentions terms with Aigina at 1.108.4,
between Oinophyta and Tolmides' *periplous*, thus on our chronology in
457/6 or even 456/5. Diodoros has perhaps omitted the siege and assumed
the naval victory brought final success. I will enter Leokrates with a query
in 458/7 and 457/6.

?PH[RYNI]CHOS of tribe I *PA* 15009
?HIPPODAMAS of tribe I *PA* 7611

IG i³ 1147.6, 63 (i² 929; ML 33; Fornara no. 78). Hippodamas, whose name
is in a second hand, may have served alongside Phrynichos or come in the
next archon year or been a replacement. The document is a casualty list of
tribe I. If Phrynichos is the correct name (Daux, *BCH* 1975, 153), we
might make an association with one of that name known from IG ii² 1928.3
(*APF* 558) of the deme Euonymon in tribe I. On Hippodamas cf. Davies,
Wealth 157. Of the choices for the place(s) where these men served, the
eastern theatre and Halieis would seem to be the best possibilities.

?DIKAIOGENES son of Menexenos of Kydathenaion (III) *PA* 3773; *APF*
145

Isaios 5.42 says he died 'serving as general when the battle at Eleusis took
place'. No battle at Eleusis is known, but could be placed in 446, when
(*contra* Davies) tribe III could be doubly represented. However, the
emendation of ἐν Ἐλευσῖνι to ἐν Ἁλιεῦσι remains attractive, and so a generalship in this year.

Note: Clairmont, *Patrios Nomos* 345, records Lysikleides (*PA* 9412) from
IG i³ 1147.48 (i² 929) as phrourarch, but in ML 33 Phrourarchos is a name
and comes after Lysikleides.

458/7 (Ol. 80.3)

Archon

HABRON *PA* 3

Diod. 11.79.1 (Bion); *P.Oxy.* 2438 with commentary; IG ii² 2318.52.

While IG i² 19 restored Ariston (454/3), ML 37 restored Habron, with discussion, and IG i³ 11 opts for Habron in the apparatus. Ariston cannot, at least on other than epigraphical grounds, be ruled out, especially given Diodoros' indication of a war involving Egesta under 454/3 (11.86.2). An update on the epigraphical flurry may be found at SEG 26.8. The case for Antiphon (418/17) has been reiterated and in their view enhanced by Smart, *JHS* 1972, 128–46; Wick, *JHS* 1975, 186–90; *CPh* 1981, 118–21; Mattingly, *Chiron* 1986, 167–70. Habron has found champions in Bradeen and McGregor, *Studies* 75ff.; Meritt, *PAPhS* 1977, 437–47; Madsen and McGregor, *Phoenix* 1979, 238; cf. Henry, *CSCA* 1978, 102. While the armchair epigraphist hardly has a right to pronounce on this, I cannot share Wick's excitement at the revelations of his latest photographs, at least as printed, and feel compelled to take the conservative line. As to Habron's lineage, cf. IG i³ 551 (i² 419).

Strategoi
?LEOKRATES son of Stroibos *PA* 9084
See 459/8.

MYRONIDES son of Kallias *PA* 10509
Thuc. 1.105.4ff.; Lysias 2.52f.; Diod. 11.79.3f.; cf. Eupolis F 128 B.14ff. (Edmonds). Commander of the oldest and youngest to Megara, where there was indecisive fighting with the Corinthians. He was probably in command in Boiotia in spring 457; see 457/6.

COUNCIL AND ASSEMBLY

IG i³ 11 (i² 19; ML 37; Fornara no. 81) is a probouleumatic decree concerning alliance with Egesta (on date see above archon):
Proposers
AR[CHI]A[S]
EUPHEM[OS]

457/6 (Ol. 80.4)

Archon
MNESITHEIDES *PA* 10276
Diod. 11.81.1; schol. Ar. *Acharn.* 10c (Mnesitheos); *Ath. Pol.* 26.2 records him as first archon from the zeugitai.

Strategoi
MYRONIDES son of Kallias *PA* 10509
Thuc. 1.108.2f.; Diod. 11.81.4ff.; Front. *Strat.* 2.4.11, 4.7.21; Plut. *Mor.* 185f, 345d; Polyainos 1.35.1f.; Aristodemos *FGH* 104 F 12.2. He was commander in the defeat at Tanagra and the success at Oinophyta, subsequently took Tanagra by siege and enjoyed successes in Lokris, Phokis and Thessaly, though he could not take Pharsalos (fullest account in Diodoros). Cf. Walters, *AJAH* 1978, 188–91.

TOLMIDES son of Tolmaios (? of Anaphlystos) (x) *PA* 13879; *APF* 74 Aristodemos *FGH* 104 12.2. Made co-general with Myronides at Oinophyta. The demotic is suggested by the identity of patronymic with Autokles, general in 425/4.

?LEOKRATES son of Stroibos *PA* 9084
See 459/8.

Note: That Perikles fought at Tanagra is stated by Plut. *Per.* 10.2. If not general, he may well have have held some position of command. See Fornara, *Generals* 46.

COUNCIL AND ASSEMBLY

IG i³ 9 (i² 26; SEG 10.18; Fornara no. 82) is a decree of alliance with the Delphic Amphiktiony; IG i² dated *c.* 448, as does Roux, *L'amphictionie* 44f., 239ff., SEG has *c.* 450/49, IG i³ gives *c.* 458; Meiggs, *Ath. Empire* 418ff., dates it after Oinophyta, which is here on our chronology; cf. SEG 31.3:
Grammateus
AI . . . .⁷. . .
Bouleutes epistates
MENYLL[OS] *PA* 10061
Proposer
. . .⁵. . IES

456/5 (Ol. 81.1)

Archon
KALLIAS *PA* 7807
MP A 59 (Kalleas); Diod. 11.84.1; Dion. *AR* 10.26.1; schol. Ar. *Acharn.* 10c, *Clouds* 971 (cf. 446/5); schol. Aisch. 2.75 (Fornara no. 84); *vita Eurip.* 1.32, 2.122. Cf. 480/79.

Strategoi
?MYRONIDES son of Kallias *PA* 10509
Could have been in Thessaly (for which see Thuc. 1.111.1) in this year. See 457/6.

TOLMIDES son of Tolmaios (? of Anaphlystos) (x) *PA* 13879; *APF* 74 Thuc. 1.108.5; Aisch. 2.75 and schol. (Fornara no. 84); Diod. 11.84.2ff.; Plut. *Per.* 19.3, *Mor.* 345d; Paus. 1.27.5; Polyainos 3.3. See 457/6. He operated around the Peloponnese, burning the Spartan dockyard and progressing to other exploits, including the capture of Naupaktos, of Chalkis, of the Corinthians, and a defeat of Sikyonians.

455/4 (Ol. 81.2)

Archon
SOSISTRATOS *PA* 13282
Diod. 11.85.1.

Strategoi
PERIKLES son of Xanthippos of Cholargos (v) *PA* 11811 *APF* 457ff.
Thuc. 1.111.2f.; Diod. 11.85. He operated in the Corinthian Gulf, winning
over all the cities in Akarnania except Oiniadai and defeating Sikyon.

TOLMIDES son of Tolmaios (? of Anaphlystos) (x) *PA* 13879; *APF* 74
Diod. 11.85.1. He was busy in Boiotia.

454/3 (Ol. 81.3)

Archon
ARISTON *PA* 2136
Diod. 11.86.1; ?IG i³ [11] (see 458/7); 259 (*ATL* II.8f. List 1; Fornara no.
85).

453/2 (Ol. 81.4)

Archon
LYSIKRATES *PA* 9442
Ath. Pol. 26.3; Diod. 11.88.1; ?schol. Aisch. 2.31 (Fornara no. 62; see
Thompson, *Phoros* 149); restored by some in the Erythrai decree (IG i³ 14 –
no restoration; i² 10 – no restoration; *ATL* II.55 D 10; ML 40 – no
restoration), but there are other possibilities in the 460s and an archon
name need not appear at all. I have sufficient doubt about the date of this
document to relegate it to the appendix.

Strategos
?LEOGORAS *APF* 30
?schol. Aisch. 2.31 (Fornara no. 62). See 465/4. This is the name of the man
involved in a defeat at Ennea Hodoi in the unemended text. He was hardly
the father of the orator Andokides (*PA* 9075); see MacDowell, *RhM* 1959,
376–8, against Raubitschek, *RhM* 1955, 261 n.8. But that he could be a
collateral relative is suggested by Thompson, *Phoros* 149.

Hellenotamiai
  Grammateus
    L[EON]
IG i³ 260 (*ATL* II.8f. List 2; Fornara no. 85).

COUNCIL AND ASSEMBLY

Proposer

?PERIKLES son of Xanthippos of Cholargos (v) *PA* 11811; *APF* 457ff. Kimon's early recall from ostracism is mentioned at And. 3.3; Theopompos *FGH* 115 F 88; Nepos *Cimon* 3.3; and Perikles is identified as the mover at Plut. *Kimon* 17.6, *Per.* 10.3f. The sources tend to place this soon after Tanagra, but as Kimon is said to have made the truce with Sparta here dated to 452/1 on his return, a recall the year before seems more reasonable.

452/1 (Ol. 82.1)

Archon

CHAIREPHANES *PA* 15175

Dion. *AR* 10.53.1; *P.Oxy.* 2438; SEG 10. [12] (IG i³ 13 does not venture Meritt's restoration).

Strategos

?TOLMIDES son of Tolmaios (? of Anaphlystos) (x) *PA* 13879; *APF* 74 And. 3.3; Diod. 11.88.3; Plut. *Per.* 11.5; Paus. 1.27.5. Diodoros mentions actions in Euboia and Naxos under 453/2, but he misses out the archon of 452/1, even though his sequence of Roman consuls is unbroken. Tolmides' actions led to klerouchies and there are considerable problems of dating. Andokides mentions war in Euboia while Athens possesses Megara, Pegai and Troizen. Pausanias goes from Tolmides' periplous (456/5) to Sikyon to the klerouchies to Boiotia to Chaironeia, and elsewhere (5.23.4) mentions the 30-years peace after a *second* revolt of Euboia. In an admittedly vague passage Aristodemos *FGH* 104 F 15 goes from the periplous to the Athenians capturing Euboia *again* to the 30-years peace. And with the new fragment of the quota list IG i³ 259 II 16, we see that in 454 the assessment of Karystos was 12 talents, while in 451 it is 7½ talents (i³ 262 I 23) and 5 talents in 450 (i³ 263 IV 26), so that the Euboian klerouchies may well belong between spring 453 and spring 450. Naxos can then go along with this and also Andros (Meiggs, *Ath. Empire* 123). On these matters see Thompson, *TAPhA* 1967, 483–90; Erxleben, *Klio* 1975, 83–100; Schreiner, *SO* 1976, 26ff.; Gomme, *Comm. Thuc.* 1.376ff.

Hellenotamiai

  Grammateus

    DIO[TI]MOS *PA* 4364

  IG i³ 261 (*ATL* 11.10 List 3).

Envoy

KIMON son of Miltiades of Lakiadai (VI) *PA* 8429; *APF* 302ff.

And. 3.3f.; Theopompos *FGH* 115 F 88; Nepos *Cimon* 3.3; Diod. 11.86.1

(454/3); Plut. *Kimon* 17.6, *Per.* 10.3. On his recall see 453/2. He was involved in negotiations leading to the five-years truce, which is to be put in this year or the next.

451/50 (Ol. 82.2)

Archon
ANTIDOTOS *PA* 1016
Ath. Pol. 26.4; Diod. 11.91.1; IG i³ [17] (i² 32; see i³ for references to debate; Mattingly's date of 418/17 is probably wrong).

Strategoi
KIMON son of Miltiades of Lakiadai (VI) *PA* 8429; *APF* 302ff.
Thuc. 1.112.2f.; Nepos *Cimon* 3.4; Diod. 12.3f.; Plut. *Kimon* 18f., *Comp. Kimon and Luc.* 2.4; Paus. 1.29.13; Aristodemos *FGH* 104 F 13.1; Suda *s.v.* Κίμων.

Diodoros places Kimon's expedition to Cyprus and Egypt, which ended in his death, in 450/49 and 449/8, but his major focus in 11.86–92 has been Sicily. The expedition followed upon the making of the five-years truce (see 452/1). Before his death he enjoyed considerable success in siege and sea battle.

ANAXIKRATES *PA* 805
Diod. 12.3.4. General with Kimon, he lost his life in a battle in Kilikia.

TOLMIDES son of Tolmaios (? of Anaphlystos) (x) *PA* 13879; *APF* 74
This is the probable year of the klerouchies to Euboia, Naxos and Andros; see 452/1.

PERIKLES son of Xanthippos of Cholargos (v) *PA* 11811; *APF* 457ff.
Aelian *VH* 6.10 seems to say that he was general when he proposed his citizenship law. The evidence may have no value, but a generalship remains highly likely.

Hellenotamiai
  Grammateus
   . . . .⁷. . . LES of Halimous (IV)
IG i³ 262 (*ATL* II.11 List 4).

COUNCIL AND ASSEMBLY

(i) IG i³ 17 (i² 32 +) is a decree of pryt. Oineis in praise of the Sigeians:
Grammateus
. . .⁵. . S
Proposer
. .⁴. CHIDES

Proposer

PERIKLES son of Xanthippos of Cholargos (v) *PA* 11811; *APF* 457ff.
Ath. Pol. 26.4; Plut. *Per.* 37.3; Aelian *VH* 6.10; Suda *s.v.* δημοποίητος

(ii) (Fornara no. 86). He moved the law that citizenship be restricted to those whose parents were both citizens. See Rhodes, *Comm.* 331ff.; Patterson, *Pericles' Cit. Law*; Walters, *CA* 1983, 314–36. In addition, Plut. *Per.* 11.5

(iii) says he sent the klerouchies to Naxos and Andros, which may be taken to mean that he made the proposals in the assembly.

450/49 (Ol. 82.3)

Archon

EUTHYNOS *PA* 5654

Diod. 12.3.1 has Euthydemos, but this is a confusion which occurs elsewhere (see 426/5) and the safest guide to name would seem to be IG i³ 21.3, 63, 88 (i² 22; *ATL* 11.58ff. D11; *SEG* 31.6; Fornara no. 92). On the basis of name confusion it has been suggested that the Euthydemos found in the 'Papyrus Decree' is in fact our Euthynos (Meiggs, *Ath. Empire* 517; Fornara no. 94), so dating the beginning of the Propylaia and Parthenon on Perikles' motion; I am not persuaded by this (see 431/30). As to IG i³ 21, its date has been debated; see *SEG* 26.5. In *ABSA* 1970, 146f., Mattingly put it in 426/5 and argued that the archon of 450/49 was Euthydemos; in *Historia* 1981, 113–17, he removes the archon's name altogether from line 3. On date see also Bradeen and McGregor, *Studies* 38, 65ff. Again I follow the conservative line.

Hellenotamiai
  Grammateus
  -- of Halai (II or VII)
  IG i³ 263 (*ATL* 11.12 List 5).

Envoy

?KALLIAS son of Hipponikos of Alopeke (x) *PA* 7825; *APF* 258ff.
Named directly in 449/8 by Diod. 12.4f., though if there was an arrangement with Persia, formal or informal, or even negotiations, they could have been in the previous year. I will not enter the debate on the Peace of Kallias here (see 465/4). See Fornara no. 95; Meiggs, *Ath. Empire* 129ff., 487ff., 598f.; most recently Walsh, *Chiron* 1981, 31ff.; Meister, *Ungeschichtlichkeit*.

Meiggs (146) adds to the embassy Pyrilampes son of Antiphon (*PA* 12493; *APF* 329f.) and Plato *Charm.* 158a certainly assures him of a place as a frequent ambassador to Asia, but I hesitate to be so specific. For other references to Kallias, who may have been fined on his return, see Dem. 19.273; Paus. 1.8.2; Suda *s.v.* Καλλίας.

COUNCIL AND ASSEMBLY

IG i³ 21 (see above archon) is a decree drawn up by syngrapheis concerning arrangements for the Milesians:

Bouleutes epistates
. .⁴. . OR

On the Papyrus Decree see above archon.

449/8 (Ol. 82.4)

Archon
PEDIEUS *PA* 11748
Diod. 12.4.1; ?IG i³ 21.[3] (i² 22 with Bradeen and McGregor, *Studies* 38).

COUNCIL AND ASSEMBLY

(i) IG i³ 1453 (*ATL* 11.61ff. D 14; ML 45; Fornara no. 97) is the decree imposing Athenian coin standard, weights and measures on the allies, which may be dated here if it has any connexion with absence of tribute in

(ii) 448/7 (see Fornara for bibliography; SEG 31.7). It mentions an earlier decree:

Proposer
KLEARCH[OS]

Proposer
?PERIKLES son of Xanthippos of Cholargos (v) *PA* 11811; *APF* 457ff.

(iii) Plut. *Per.* 17 records his decree that all Greeks should be invited to send to a congress at Athens to consider the matters of temples burnt during the Persian War, due sacrifices and peaceful freedom of the sea. Walsh, *Chiron* 1981, 59ff., discusses views that the decree is spurious (also Griffith, *Historia* 1978, 218–19, against Seager, *Historia* 1969, 129–41; Bosworth, *Historia* 1971, 600–16) and concludes that it is genuine, but belongs around 464/3. I accept the decree and retain it in 449/8.

448/7 (Ol. 83.1)

Archon
PHILISKOS *PA* 14419
Diod. 12.5.1; Dion. *AR* 11.1.1; IG ii² 2318.[59].

Strategoi
PERIKLES son of Xanthippos of Cholargos (v) *PA* 11811; *APF* 457ff.
Diod. 11.88.3; Plut. *Per.* 11.5, 21.2. Diodoros places the klerouchy to the Chersonese in 453/2, but it would seem to belong about here on the evidence of the tribute lists (Meiggs, *Ath. Empire* 160); already in 449 a

partial payment is evidenced and there could have been trouble in the area earlier. A casualty list, which cannot be dated internally, shows deaths in the Chersonese, Byzantion and 'the other wars'; a concluding epigram refers to the Hellespont (IG i² 943; ML 48; *CEG* 6; discussion by Clairmont, *Patrios Nomos* 165ff.).

In this year also, I think, Perikles reinstated the Phokians at Delphi and secured for the Athenians the promanteia. Thuc. 1.112.5 has this after the death of Kimon and a Spartan expedition which had handed control to the Delphians. Philochoros *FGH* 328 F 34 has the Athenian expedition in the third year after the Spartan, which would fit dates of 450/49 and 448/7 (I do not believe that Philochoros should be emended to read 'in the third month': Gomme, *Comm. Thuc.* 1.409).

TOLMIDES son of Tolmaios (? of Anaphlystos) (x) *PA* 13879; *APF* 74
Thuc. 1.113; Xen. *Mem.* 3.5.4; Diod. 12.6 (447/6); Plut. *Per.* 18.2f., *Comp. Per. and Fab.* 3.2, *Ages.* 19.2; Paus. 1.27.5; Aristodemos *FGH* 104 F 14.2, 15.1.

He was in Boiotia fighting Boiotian exiles; Chaironeia was taken, but he died after the defeat at Koroneia. Despite Diodoros, I favour an earlier beginning; the confusion could have been caused because these events took place in the summer of 447.

?EPITELES (? son of Soinautes of Pergase (1)) *PA* 4953 = ?4962
IG i³ 1162.4 (i² 943; ML 48). Dated by Meiggs (*HSCPh* 1963, 17) by conjunction with Perikles' operations in the Chersonese (see above). Epiteles died there, but it could have been earlier. The identification is suggested by ML.

Hellenotamiai
  Grammateus
  MENET[IMO]S or MENET[ELE]S of Lamptrai (1) *PA* 10026
IG i³ 264 (*ATL* 11.13 List 7; Fornara no. 95M(1)). On the name see *ATL* 1.176.

COUNCIL AND ASSEMBLY

(i) IG i³ 34 (i² 66; *ATL* 11.50 D 7; ML 46; Fornara no. 98) is a decree of pryt. Oineis concerning the collection of tribute:
Grammateus
[SP]OUDIAS
Bouleutes epistates
. . .⁶. . ON
Proposer
KLEINI[AS] (son of Alkibiades of Skambonidai (IV)) *PA* 8510; *APF* 16
The date used here is that in IG i³, but it is not indisputable. Mattingly

(*BCH* 1968, 485, and *ABSA* 1970, 129ff.) has suggested an association with Spoudias of Phyla (VII), *PA* 12871, hellenotamias in 410/9, and a date of 425/4. See also Meiggs, *Ath. Empire* 599; Henry, *CSCA* 1978, 104. The date and the identity of Kleinias are interdependent.

Proposer

(ii) PERIKLES son of Xanthippos of Cholargos (V) *PA* 11811; *APF* 457ff. He is made responsible for the sending of klerouchies (see above).

447/6 (Ol. 83.2)

Archon

TIMARCHIDES *PA* 13615
Diod. 12.6.1; IG ii² 2318.[71].

Strategoi

TOLMIDES son of Tolmaios (? of Anaphlystos) (X) *PA* 13879; *APF* 74
See 448/7.

PERIKLES son of Xanthippos of Cholargos (V) *PA* 11811; *APF* 457ff.
Thuc. 1.114.1ff.; Ar. *Clouds* 211ff. with schol. *ad* 213 (Philochoros *FGH* 328 F 118); Theopompos *FGH* 115 F 387; Lykourgos F 58; Diod. 12.7, 22.2; Plut. *Per.* 22.1f., 23.

He dealt with revolts of Euboia and Megara, eventually taking over the land of Hestiaia for Athenian settlers.

ANDOKIDES (son of Leogoras of Kydathenaion) (III) *PA* 827; *APF* 29f.
IG i³ 1353.7 (i² 1085; ML 51); cf. Thuc. 1.114; Diod. 12.5. General in the Megara campaign.

Note: See the general Dikaiogenes listed under 459/8.

Hellenotamiai
  Grammateus
  DIOD[ES] of Paionidai (IV)
IG i³ 265 (*ATL* II.14 List 8; Fornara no. 98M(2)). See ML pp. 133, 136, on the dating of the list and the restoration of the name which will depend upon it.

COUNCIL AND ASSEMBLY

IG i³ 37 concerns arrangements with Kolophon:
Grammateus
--os
This is not in IG i² 14/15, but is as read by Bradeen and McGregor, *Studies* 94ff., and incorporated in IG i³. So also the date, as against the suggestion of *c.* 427 made by Mattingly, *Anc. Soc. and Inst.* 210ff.

446/5 (Ol. 83.3)

Archon
KALLIMACHOS *PA* 7992
Diod. 12.7.1, 10.3, IG ii² 2318.[83]. IG i³ 72 is dated 414?, mentioning but
rejecting the restoration of Kallimachos in i² 68; cf. Bradeen and
McGregor, *Studies* 91. Schol. Ar. *Clouds* 971 has the archon Kallias, 456/5,
but the apparatus shows the suggestion of Kallimachos as an emendation
(cf. Davison, *JHS* 1958, 40f.).

Strategoi
PERIKLES son of Xanthippos of Cholargos (V) *PA* 11811; *APF* 457ff.
ANDOKIDES (son of Leogoras of Kydathenaion) (III) *PA* 827; *APF* 29f.
See 447/6.

?DEMOKLEIDES (? of tribe II) *PA* 3474
IG i³ 46.12, 38f. (i² 45; ML 49; Fornara no. 100). He is identified as the one
to found Brea. The use of *autokrator* has no necessary implication, but that
he was general is slightly suggested by the appearance of soldiers at lines
26ff. (the precise reference of this is unclear). Troops may have been
necessary for the operation; compare Hagnon in 437/6. As to date, I accept
in general the arguments followed by ML, but nothing is certain. For the
tribe see 439/8.

Tamiai
  Grammateus
  EXEKESTOS of Athmonon (VII)
IG i³ 437.[45f.], 48f. (i² 340); [453](i² 361); ?454.[4f.](i² 360; see the
apparatus to i³).

Epistatai of Parthenon
STRAT--
SALAM[INOKLES]
KA--
  Grammateus
  E . . . .⁸ . . . of Halai (II or VII)
  Syngrammateus
  ?[ANTIKLES] *PA* 1052
IG i³ 437.33ff. (i² 340; see i³ on line 38 for Antikles).

Envoys
KALLIAS (son of Hipponikos of Alopeke) (X) *PA* 7825; *APF* 258ff.
CHARES *PA* 15286
Diod. 12.7. They negotiated the 30-years peace. Kallias' identity is likely,
but not quite certain, even given his grandson's later trips to Sparta (see
387/6, 375/4).

ANDOKIDES son of Leogoras of Kydathenaion (III) *PA* 827; *APF* 29f.
And. 3.6; Aisch. 2.174; Plut. *Mor.* 834b (Hellanikos *FGH* 323a F 24;
Fornara no. 105). He was one of the ten plenipotentiary envoys to Sparta to
arrange peace.

COUNCIL AND ASSEMBLY

The first secretary of the boule is restored at IG i³ 437.34 (i² 340) and D.M.
Lewis now advises that the second alternative for the name is equally
possible:
Grammateus
[ANT]IDO[ROS] or [ANT]IDO[TOS]

(i) IG i³ 39 (i² 17; Fornara no. 102) is part of a treaty with Eretrians.

(ii) IG i³ 40 (i² 39; ML 52; SEG 26.10; Fornara no. 103; Balcer, *Ath. Reg.
Chalkis*) is a decree of pryt. Antiochis:
Bouleutes epistates
DRAK[ON]TIDES (son of Leogoras of Thorai) (X) *PA* 4551; *APF* 173
Proposers
DIOGNETOS *PA* 3848
ANTIKLES (? of Melite (VII)) *PA* 1051; *APF* 399
ARCHESTRATO[S] (? son of Lykomedes of Phyla (VII)) *PA* 2411; *APF* 346
For the demotics of the last two, by no means certain, see *APF*.

(iii) IG i³ 41 (i² 40/41, 42, 48; SEG 32.3) contains arrangements concerning
Hestiaia.

(iv) IG i³ 46 (i² 45; ML 49; Fornara no. 100) is the decree for the colony to Brea;
the secretary appears at lines 15f. only as dating the syngraphai:
Grammateus
. . . . .⁸. . . . TOS
Proposers
DEMOKL[E]IDES (? of tribe II) *PA* 3474
PHANTOKLES *PA* 14114
For Demokleides and the date see above strategoi.

Appendix: [A]ISCHINES (*PA* 328) is charged with monetary payments in
the Brea decree (IG i³ 46 above); it is hard to know what title to bestow on
him.

445/4 (Ol. 83.4)

Archon
LYSIMACHIDES or LYSIMACHOS *PA* 9475
Philochoros *FGH* 328 F 119; Diod. 12.22.1. For the alternative
Lysimachos see Mattingly, *Historia* 1981, 116.

Strategos
PERIKLES son of Xanthippos of Cholargos (v) *PA* 11811; *APF* 457ff.
Diod. 12.22.2 has the settlers to Histiaia go out this year, which is possible;
see 447/6.

Tamiai
-- of Kerameis (v)
L--
-- of Prasiai (III)
IG i³ 454.6f. (i² 360). I have been tempted into this year rather than the
alternative 447/6 suggested also in IG i³, which see for the restorations.
Perhaps only five were listed (Develin, *Klio* 1986, 82).

Hellenotamiai
Grammateus
EUK--
IG i³ 267 (*ATL* 11.16 List 10).

444/3 (Ol. 84.1)

Archon
PRAXITELES *PA* 12166
Diod. 12.23.1; Plut. *Mor.* 835d.

Thesmothetes
EUCHARIDES son of Euchares (? of Aphidna) (IX) ?*PA* 6144
IG i² 911. Demotic by association with the grammateus of epistatai at IG i³
433.11f., for whom see the appendix to this Section, p. 105.

Strategos
?THOUKYDIDES son of Melesias of Alopeke (X) *PA* 7268; *APF* 230ff.
vita anon. Thuc. 6f. (cf. Fornara no. 108c). The arguments presented by
Fornara, *Generals* 48, for this generalship are not all cogent; see also
Andrewes, *JHS* 1978, 5f.; Piccirilli, *Storie dello storico Tuc.* 178ff. The
colony to Thourioi *may* be ascribable to his initiative.

Tamiai
PH[IL]ONEOS son of Idomeneus of Kephisia (I) *PA* 14683; *APF* 181
ARISTYLLOS son of Hel[lespo]ntios of Erchia (II) *PA* 2132
GLAUK[IAS] son of [Ai]schines of Kydathenaion (III) *PA* 2968
DEMOCHARES son of Si[m]ylos of Potamos (IV) *PA* 3721; *APF* 142
TEISIMA[CH]OS son of Tei[sias] of Kephale (v) *PA* 13487; *APF* 503
CHARISOS son of [? Mela]nthios of Acharnai (VI) *PA* 15492
D[I]ONCHIS son of Xenokles of Phyla (VII) *PA* 3881
DIO[N]YSIOS son of Euklei[des] of Peiraieus (VIII) *PA* 4241
CHAIRELEI[DES] son of Charixenos of Aphidna (IX) *PA* 15135; *APF* 476
[EPICH]ARINOS son of Epichar[es] or Epichar[inos] of tribe x

Grammateus
DEINIA[S] son of Euages of Philaidai (II) *PA* 3173; *APF* 186
IG i³ 455.8ff. (i² 359). They belong to this or the previous year. On the possible identity of Epicharinos see the apparatus to IG i³, which rightly avoids restoration, given that the demotic, unlike any other in the inscription, would have to have been abbreviated if either of the two known possibilities appeared; so we may well be dealing with another man altogether. See also Meritt, *AFD* 31ff.

Hellenotamiai
Grammateus
STROMBICHOS of Cholleidai (IV) *PA* 13023; *APF* 161
IG i³ 268 (*ATL* II.17 List 11); 439.73f. (i² 342.36f.).

COUNCIL AND ASSEMBLY

The first secretary is known from the reading of Lewis reported in *APF* and now ventured in IG i³ 455.5f. (i² 359). He belongs to this or the previous year. This means that Oionichos (cf. *PA* 11371) now disappears.
Grammateus
[HI]PPONIKOS (son of Kallias) of Alopeke (X) *PA* 7658; *APF* 262f.

443/2 (Ol. 84.2)

Archon
LYSANIAS *PA* 9300
Diod. 12.24.1.

Strategos
PERIKLES son of Xanthippos of Cholargos (V) *PA* 11811; *APF* 457ff.
Plut. *Per.* 16.3 says that Perikles was general continuously for 15 years after the ostracism of Thoukydides. The series then ended in 429/8 and Perikles may be entered in every year until then. I do not share the doubts of Kagan, *Outbreak* 160f., on the evidence of Plutarch.

Tamiai
Grammateus
ANDR--
IG i³ 440.123 (i² 343.86).

Hellenotamiai
[S]OPHOKLES (? son of Sophillos) of Kolonos (II) *PA* 12834
Grammateus
[S]OPHIAS of Eleusis (VIII) *PA* 12819
Syngrammateus
SATYROS of Leukonoion (IV) *PA* 12603

IG i³ 269 (*ATL* II.18 List 12); 440.[124f.](Sophias). The restoration of the unique form *Kolonothen* makes the identity of Sophokles with the tragedian; Lewis, *ABSA* 1955, 12ff.; Meritt, *AJPh* 1959, 189. But there is good reason to doubt this: Avery, *Historia* 1973, 509f.

Epistatai of Parthenon
--os of Iphistiadai (v)
Grammateus
TIMOTHE[OS] *APF* 507
Syngrammateus
AN[TIKLES] *PA* 1052
IG i³ 440.112ff. (i² 343.75ff.).

COUNCIL AND ASSEMBLY

The first secretary is found at IG i³ 440.113 (i² 343.76):
Grammateus
--os

442/1 (Ol. 84.3)

Archon
DIPHILOS *PA* 4462
MP A 60; Diod. 12.26.1; Dion. *AR* 11.62.1; Hesychios and Photios *s.v.* Ἐρετρι(α)κὸς κατάλογος.

Strategos
PERIKLES son of Xanthippos of Cholargos (v) *PA* 11811; *APF* 457ff. See 443/2.

Tamiai
. . . .⁸. . . of Kydathenaion (III)
M . . . os of Melite (VII)
LYKOS (? of Koile) (VIII) *PA* 9022 (Laches)
DIERXIS of Marathon (IX) *PA* 3761
ANTIPHI[LOS] of Anaphlystos (X)
[K]LYTIAS of Pergase (I) *PA* 8795 (Kritias)
PETRAI[OS]
THALIARCHOS *PA* 6572; *APF* 211
  Grammateus
  PHILO . . .⁶. . of Aphidna (IX)
IG i³ 457.10ff. (i² 358). Only eight were listed (Develin, *Klio* 1986, 82).

Hellenotamiai
[D]O[R]YPHILOS of Ikarion (II) *PA* 4537
  Grammateus
  [CHAL]KIDEUS of Melite (VII) *PA* 15282; *APF* 568

Syngrammateus
SA[TYROS] of Leokonoion (IV) *PA* 12603
IG i³ 270 (*ATL* II.19 List 13).

Epistatai of statue of Athene
Grammateus
ARRHE[NEI]DES
IG i³ 457.2 (i² 358).

COUNCIL AND ASSEMBLY

The first secretary is found at IG i³ 457.6f. (i² 358). For possibilities of identity see Balcer, *Ath. Reg. Chalkis* 76:
Grammateus
AR[CHEST]RATOS *PA* 2397

Hesychios and Photios *s.v.* 'Ερετρι(α)κὸς κατάλογος record a decree for choosing as hostages from Eretria the sons of the richest men.

441/40 (Ol. 84.4)

Archon
TIMOKLES *PA* 13723
Diod. 12.27.1; schol. Ar. *Wasps* 283; IG i³ 363.[6](i² 293; ML 55); xiv 1097.3.

Strategoi
SOKRATES of Anagyrous (I) *PA* 13102; *APF* 497
SOPHOKLES son of Sophillos of Kolonos (II) *PA* 12834
ANDOKIDES (son of Leogoras) of Kydathenaion (III) *PA* 827; *APF* 29f.
KREON of Skambonidai (IV) *PA* 8785
PERIKLES son of Xanthippos of Cholargos (V) *PA* 11811; *APF* 457ff.
GLAUKON (son of Leagros) of Kerameis (V) *PA* 3027; *APF* 91
KALLISTRATOS of Acharnai (VI) *PA* 8148
XENOPHON (son of Euripides) of Melite (VII) *PA* 11313; *APF* 199f.
LAMPIDES of Peiraieus (VIII)
KLEITOPHON of Thorai (X) *PA* 8548
The full list comes from Androtion *FGH* 324 F 38, eleven names from which I excise Glauketes Athenaios (*PA* 2951); I will not argue this, but at least the passage of Aelius Aristides (3.74 Behr) on which the comment is made which gives us the list says of Perikles δέκατος αὐτὸς στρατηγῶν and the list itself is headed as giving ten generals, so it would be very odd if there were eleven on the list. On this see Lenz, *TAPhA* 1941, 226ff.; Ehrenberg, *AJPh* 1945, 113ff.; Hignett, *HAC* 349, 354ff.; Hammond, *Studies* 376ff.; Jacoby, *FGH* III b ii.136 n.14; Fornara, *Generals* 49; Connor, *Gnomon* 1974, 623.

For Perikles and Sophokles Cic. *de off.* 1.40.144; Strabo 14.1.8; Justin 3.6.12f.; Plut. *Per.* 8.5; Aristodemos *FGH* F 15.4 (wrongly dated). For Sophokles only Ion *FGH* 392 F 6; schol. Ar. *Peace* 681; *vita Soph.* 1.9 (see appendix to this Section, p. 104); Suda *s.v.* Μέλητος. For Perikles only Thuc. 1.116.1ff.; Diod. 12.27.1ff.; Plut. *Them.* 2.3, *Kimon* 13.5 (doubtful: see Fornara, *Generals* 46 n.24), *Per.* 24.1, 25; schol. Ar. *Wasps* 283.

The ten generals were all sent out to the Samian theatre. It could be that all ten did not stay for the whole time and that Perikles and Sophokles were left. Thucydides summarizes the operations; Ion says Sophokles was the one who went to Lesbos (and Chios). Thucydides in fact goes on beyond this year. On the expedition see Meiggs, *Ath. Empire* 188ff.; on the chronology of the war Fornara, *JHS* 1979, 7ff.

Tamiai
[EU]BO[LIDES] of Oion (IV or VIII)
NAUS--
Grammateus
PHYRO[MACHOS] of tribe VIII *PA* 15052
IG i³ 363.9ff. (i² 293; ML 55; Fornara no.113); 442.[177](i² 345.13) (Phyromachos). All ten could hardly have been listed (Develin, *Klio* 1986, 83).

Hellenotamias
. . . S--
IG i³ 271 (*ATL* II.20 List 14).

Epistatai of Parthenon
CHA--
-- of Teithras (II)
Syngrammateus
[ANTIKLES] *PA* 1052
IG i³ 442.170f. (i² 345.6f.).

COUNCIL AND ASSEMBLY

Proposer
PERIKLES son of Xanthippos of Cholargos (V) *PA* 11811; *APF* 457ff.
Plut. *Per.* 24.1, 25.1 says he proposed the expedition against Samos.

440/39 (Ol. 85.1)

Archon
MORYCHIDES (? of Pallene (X)) *PA* 10418 = ?10419
Diod. 12.29.1 (Myrichides or Myriochides); schol. Ar. *Wasps* 283 (Dorychides); *Acharn.* 67 (Fornara no. 111); Suda *s.v.* Εὐθυμένης; IG i³ 363.[6](i² 293; ML 55), xiv 1097.13.

Strategoi

HAGNON son of Nikias of Steiria (III) *PA* 171; *APF* 227f.

PHORMION son of Asopios (of Paiania) (III) *PA* 14958

PERIKLES son of Xanthippos of Cholargos (V) *PA* 11811; *APF* 457ff.

ANTIKLES (of Melite) (VII) *PA* 1051; *APF* 399

THOUKYDIDES (? son of Ariston of Acherdous (VIII)) *PA* 7271; *APF* 54
  or (? son of Pantainetos of Gargettos (II)) *PA* 7272

TLEPOLEMOS of tribe IX *PA* 13863

For all of these see Thuc. 1.117.2f. For Perikles Isok. 15 111; Diod. 12.28; Plut. *Per.* 26ff., *Comp. Per. and Fab.* 2.1, *Mor.* 350e; schol. Ar. *Wasps* 283; Lykourgos F 58.

They were engaged in the Samian theatre; Samos was eventually taken by siege and terms reached in 439/8 (*q.v.*); see also 441/40. For the demotic of Antikles see *APF*; for those of Phormion and Thoukydides and the tribe of Tlepolemos Fornara, *Generals* 49f. On Perikles' movements see Corbetta, *RIL* 1977, 156–66 (the expedition to Cyprus).

Tamiai

KTESION ? *PA* 8903

ST[R]OSIAS *PA* 13027

ANTIPHAT[E]S *PA* 1254

MENANDROS *PA* 9856

TH[YM]OCHARES (? of Sphettos) (V) *PA* 7405; *APF* 524

SMOKOR[D]OS (? of Aphidna (IX)) *PA* 12801

PHEIDELEID[ES] (? of Aphidna (IX)) *PA* 14134

  ### Grammateus

  DEMOSTRATOS of Xypete (VII) *PA* 3625

IG i³ 363.13ff. for Demostratos restored and the demotic of Aphidna (i² 293; ML 55; Fornara no. 113); 458.6ff. (i² 355; ML 54; Fornara no. 114). For the deme of Thymochares see *APF*; for Aphidna as the deme of either Smokordos or Pheideleides see Meritt, *AFD* 48. Only seven were listed in i³ 458 and all ten could hardly fit in 363 (Develin, *Klio* 1986, 82f.).

Hellenotamiai

. . . YLOS of Eleusis (VIII) = *PA* 441

  ### Grammateus

  SOSISTR[AT]OS of Hybadai (IV) *PA* 13297

IG i³ 272 (*ATL* II.21 List 15). *ATL* notes (cf. II.125) that the name Aischylos, tempting given the demotic, has one letter too many to be restored; SEG 10.160 has Hedylos. On the secretary see the note in IG i³.

Epistatai of Parthenon

-- of Xypete (VII)

  ### Grammateus

  -- of Probalinthos (III)

IG i³ 443.202ff. (i² 346).

Epistatai of statue of Athene
  Grammateus
  KICHESIPPOS of Myrrhinous (III) *PA* 8449
IG i³ 458 (i² 355); 459 (i² 355a) (both at Fornara no. 114).

COUNCIL AND ASSEMBLY

The first secretary is found at IG i³ 363.13f. (i² 293; ML 55; Fornara no. 113):
  Grammateus
  [EPICHAR]INOS of Peiraieus (VIII) cf. *PA* 2527
The alternative Archinos is suggested on a file card at the Institute for Advanced Study in Princeton.

Schol. Ar. *Acharn.* 67 records that in this year was passed the decree prohibiting comedy, which was repealed in 437/6 (Fornara no. 111).

439/8 (Ol. 85.2)

Archon
GLAUKINOS *PA* 2975
Diod. 12.30.1 (where the name would be Glaukides from Γλαυκίδου, except that the delta has probably replaced nu); schol. Ar. *Acharn.* 67 (Fornara no. 111); hyp. Euripides *Alk.*; ? IG i³ [208](i² 112).

Strategoi
?[SOKRATES] (of Anagyrous) (I) *PA* 13102; *APF* 497
DEM[OKLEIDES] of tribe II = *PA* 3474
[PHORMION] (son of Asopios of Paiania) (III) *PA* 14958
CH . . . . .¹⁰ . . . ? of tribe IV
[PERIKL]ES (son of Xanthippos of Cholargos) (V) *PA* 11811; *APF* 457ff.
[GLAUKON] (son of Leagros of Kerameis) (V) *PA* 3027; *APF* 91
[KALL]I[STRATOS] (of Acharnai) (VI) *PA* 8148
XE[NOPHON] (son of Euripides of Melite) (VII) *PA* 11313; *APF* 199f.
TLEMP[OLEMOS] of tribe IX *PA* 13863
IG i³ 48.27ff. (i² 50; ML 56; SEG 31.10; Fornara no. 115). The restorations of the names in the treaty with Samos cannot all be regarded as certain; neither can we be sure that CH-- comes from tribe IV. For discussion see ML and Fornara, *Generals* 50; on the inscription see Fornara, *JHS* 1979, 14ff. with Lewis' note; doubts as to names and positions at Bridges, *JHS* 1980, 185–8; also cf. Breslin, *AncW* 1980, 104–6. Perikles is certain (see 443/2). For the short name which should have completed the list see Andrewes and Lewis, *JHS* 1957, 179, suggesting Leon (cf. Thuc. 5.19.2, 24.1); the only alternative which suggests itself is Dion, but it is total reconstruction.

Tamiai
    Grammateus
    . . .⁵. . of Lakiadai (VI)
IG I³ 444.246 (i² 347.12).

Hellenotamiai
    Grammateus
    ERGOPHILOS [of Anaphlystos] (X)
IG I³ 444.247f. (i² 347.13f.); [273] (*ATL* II.22 List 16).

Epistatai of Parthenon
-- of Pergase (I)
    Syngrammateus
    [ANTIKLES] *PA* 1052
IG I³ 444.237,240 (i² 347).

COUNCIL AND ASSEMBLY

IG I³ 48 is the treaty with Samos; the secretary named was first secretary:
Grammateus
    . . . .⁸. . . of Rhamnous (IX)
Proposer
[KALLI]KRATE[S]

438/7 (Ol. 85.3)

Archon
THEODOROS *PA* 6823
Diod. 12.31.1; schol. Ar. *Acharn.* 67 (Fornara no. 111); *Peace* 605
(Philochoros *FGH* 328 F 121; Fornara no. 116A); anon. *de com.* 3.29
(Koster); IG xiv 1097.4.

Strategos
PERIKLES son of Xanthippos of Cholargos (V) *PA* 11811; *APF* 457ff.
See 443/2.

Hellenotamiai
    Grammateus
    -- of Rhamnous (IX)
IG I³ 445.293 (i² 348.59); [274] (*ATL* II.23 List 17).

Epistatai of Parthenon
[HE]GESIAS [of Teithras (II), Tyrmeidai (VI) or Trikorynthos (IX)]   *PA*
6332
--YDES of Halai (II or VII)
    Grammateus
    . . .⁶. . PHILOS

Syngrammateus
[ANTIKLES] *PA* 1052
IG I³ 445.283ff. (i² 348.49ff.).

Epistates of statue of Athene
PERIKLES son of Xanthippos of Cholargos (v) *PA* 11811; *APF* 457ff.
Diod. 12.39.1; Aristodemos *FGH* 104 F 16; schol. Ar. *Peace* 605
(Philochoros *FGH* 328 F 121; Fornara no. 116A); Suda *s.v.* Φειδίας.
Diodoros calls him epimeletes, but if he was anything, he was epistates;
Aristodemos has *ergepistates*, other sources are vague. On the date and
other related matters see below, Council and Assembly.

COUNCIL AND ASSEMBLY

On the date of what follows and further discussion see Frost, *JHS* 1964,
69–72; Mansfeld, *Mnemosyne* 1980, 17–95. Diod. 12.39, in the context of
431/30, talks generally of an assembly at which attacks were made on
Pheidias, leading to a decision to arrest him, and proceeds to similar attacks
on Anaxagoras. Also general is schol. Ar. *Peace* 605 (Philochoros *FGH* 328
F 121); see also above on Perikles as epistates. Plut. *Per.* 31 has more detail:
(i) one Menon was granted immunity by the demos so that he could bring
(ii) information against Pheidias. A subsequent decree granted Menon *ateleia*
and ordered the generals to see to his safety:
Proposer
GLYKON *PA* 3042
(iii) Then at 32.1f. is a decree for *eisangelia* against those who did not observe
religion or taught about the heavens:
Proposer
DIOPEITHES *PA* 4309
(iv) Also a bill that Perikles should deposit his accounts with the prytaneis and
should be judged by jury by special ballot, though an amendment returned
the procedure to a regular jury of 1500:
Proposers
DRAKONTIDES (son of Leogoras of Thorai) (x) *PA* 4551; *APF* 173
HAGNON (son of Nikias of Steiria) (III) *PA* 162 = 171; *APF* 227f.

437/6 (Ol. 85.4)

Archon
EUTHYMENES *PA* 5640
Ar. *Acharn.* 67 and schol. (Fornara no. 111); Philochoros *FGH* 328 F 36
(Fornara no. 118A); Diod. 12.32.1; schol. Aisch. 2.31 (Fornara no. 62);
Suda *s.v.* Εὐθυμένης; IG i³ 446.[314](i² 349.3); 462.[3] (i² 363).

Strategoi
PERIKLES son of Xanthippos of Cholargos (v) *PA* 11811; *APF* 457ff.
See 443/2.

HAGNON son of Nikias of Steiria (III) *PA* 162 = 171; *APF* 227f.
Thuc. 4.102.3; Diod. 12.68.2; Polyainos 6.53; schol. Aisch. 2.31 (Fornara no. 62). He led out the colony to Amphipolis and though only Polyainos calls him general, it is reasonable to suppose that as military operations were involved, a general was sent out as oikistes.

Hellenotamiai
Grammateus
--YLOS
IG I³ 462.15f. (i² 363); [275] (*ATL* II.24 List 18).

Epistatai of Propylaia
[T]IMOGEN[ES] of Ikarion (II) *PA* 13664
D--
EP[I]CHA[RINOS] of Amphitrope (X) *PA* 5004
IG i³ 462.5f (i² 363).

Epistatai of Parthenon
Syngrammateus
ANT[IKLES] *PA* 1052
IG i³ 446.312 (i² 349).

COUNCIL AND ASSEMBLY

In this year the prohibition on comedy (see 440/39) was repealed: schol. Ar. *Acharn.* 67 (Fornara no. 111).
 The first secretary is to be found at IG i³ 446.313 (i² 349.2) and 462 (i² 363):

Grammateus
PEITHIADES

436/5 (Ol. 86.1)

Archon
LYSIMACHOS of Myrrhinous (III) *PA* 9523
Diod. 12.33.1 (Nausimachos); Dion. *Isok.* 1; Plut. *Mor.* 836f; Diog. 3.3; IG i³ 447.[346] (i² 350.35); ii² 2318.[84]; xiv 1097.12.

Strategoi
PERIKLES son of Xanthippos of Cholargos (V) *PA* 11811; *APF* 457ff.
See 443/2. This is probably the date of the Pontic expedition of Perikles (Plut. *Per.* 20.1f.), preceded by Amphipolis and followed by a colony in the area. For a date of 447/6 see Karamoutsou, *Dodone* 1979, 9–36; but for other discussion see Gomme, *Comm. Thuc.* 1.367f.; Meiggs, *Ath. Empire* 197ff.; Meister, *Ungeschichtlichkeit* 37, 108; Clairmont, *Patrios Nomos* 178ff. (with a new fragment changing the evidence).

?LAMACHOS son of Xenophanes of Oe (VI) *PA* 8981
Plut. *Per.* 20.1. He was with Perikles on the Pontic expedition and was left with a force to aid the exiled Sinopians. The generalship is therefore an assumption.

?PHORMION son of Asopios (of Paiania) (III) *PA* 14958
Thuc. 2.68.7 has an undated reference to action in Akarnania, which I do think ought to postdate Samos and antedate other concerns in the area, hence the approximate date. For discussion see Gomme, *Comm. Thuc.* II.202; Meiggs, *Ath. Empire* 204 and n.1; de Ste Croix, *Origins* 85ff.; Salmon, *Corinth* 422f. (by whom I am unpersuaded).

Hellenotamiai
  Grammateus
  -- of Aixone (VII)
IG i³ 463.72 (i² 364.63); [276] (*ATL* II.24 List 19).

Epistatai of Propylaia
-- [? of Leukonoion (IV)]
BL[EPYROS]
IG i³ 463.65 (i² 365.4). Blepyros is suggested on a file card at the Institute for Advanced Study at Princeton.

Epistatai of Parthenon
  Grammateus
  [ANTIKLES] *PA* 1052
IG i³ 447.344 (i² 350.33).

COUNCIL AND ASSEMBLY

Proposer
PERIKLES son of Xanthippos of Cholargos (V) *PA* 11811; *APF* 457ff.
Plut. *Per.* 20.2 says he was responsible for a bill that 600 volunteer Athenians should settle in Sinope, taking the former tyrant's lands. For the date see above on Perikles as strategos.

435/4 (Ol. 86.2)

Archon
ANTIOCHIDES *PA* 1149
Diod. 12.34.1 (with variant Antilochides); IG xiv 1097.1, 6.

Strategoi
PERIKLES son of Xanthippos of Cholargos (V) *PA* 11811; *APF* 457ff.
See 443/2.

?G[LAUKON] (son of Leagros of Kerameis) (V) *PA* 3027; *APF* 91

?[PRO]TEAS (son of Epikles of Aixone) (VII) *PA* 12298
IG i³ 464.105ff. (i² 365.13ff.). The names are probably correct and they
were engaged on expeditions, but we know no more.

Hellenotamiai
DEM[O]CHARES
--ASIPPOS of Phyla (VII)
-- of Kerameis (v)
  Grammateus
  THOINILOS of Acharnai (VI)
For the first two and the secretary IG i³ 464.107ff. (i² 365.15ff.); for the
other hellenotamias and the secretary restored i³ 277 (*ATL* II.25 List 20).

Epistatai of Propylaia
DI--
-- of ? An[aphlystos] (x)
  Grammateus
  EPIKLES of Thorikos (v)
For the first two IG i³ 464.92ff. (i² 365.1ff.); for the secretary i³ 465.120 (i²
366.8; ML 60; Fornara no. 118B).

Epistatai of Parthenon
  Grammateus
  [ANTIKL]ES *PA* 1052
IG i³ 448.366 (i² 351.55).

COUNCIL AND ASSEMBLY

The first secretary is found at IG i³ 448.367 (i² 351.56):
Grammateus
. . . . I . . . OS

434/3 (Ol. 86.3)

Archon
KRATES *PA* 8740
Diod. 12.35.1 (Chares); IG i³ 402.17 (i² 377; ML 62; Fornara no. 121);
449.374 (i² 352.6; ML 59; Fornara no. 120).

Strategoi
PERIKLES son of Xanthippos of Cholargos (v) *PA* 11811; *APF* 457ff.
See 443/2.

Tamiai
. . .⁶. . of Kerameis (v)
  Grammateus
  KRATES son of Naupon of Lamptrai (I) *PA* 8746

IG i³ 364.5f. (i² 295; ML 61); and for Krates i³ 292 (i² 232); 293.18 (i² 233); 317.2f., 7 (i² 256); 318.11 (i² 257); 343.2 (i² 276); 344.19 (i² 277); 449.387f. (i² 352.19f.; ML 59; Fornara no. 120); 465.122 (i² 366.10; ML 60; Fornara no. 118B). IG i³ 292, 317 and 343 are the actual inventories of the year.

Hellenotamiai
? --SIPPOS of Agryle (I)
? TIMOSTHENES
. . .⁵. . M]ACHOS son of Charidemos of Xypete (VII)
Grammateus
PROTONIKOS son of Epichares of Kerameis (V) *PA* 12310
For the first two and the secretary IG i³ 465.123f., 129f. (i² 366.11f., 17f.; ML 60; Fornara no. 118B); for the third man and the secretary i³ 278 (*ATL* II.26 List 21).

Taktai
Grammateus
KR . . . S
IG i³ 281.55 (*ATL* II.29 List 25); 282.[35] (*ATL* II.30 List 26). For the date see *ATL* III.83f.

Epistatai of Propylaia
ARI[STYL]LOS of Melite (VII)
M--
DIKTYS of Koile (VIII)
TIM[OSTRATOS] of Ke--
-- of Thorai (X)
Grammateus
DIOGE[NES] *PA* 3802
IG i³ 465.114ff. (i² 366.2ff.; ML 60; Fornara no. 118B).

Epistatai of Parthenon
Grammateus
ANTIKLES *PA* 1052
IG i³ 449.370 (i² 352.2; ML 59; Fornara no. 120).

COUNCIL AND ASSEMBLY

The first secretary is found at IG i³ 449.372f. (i² 352.4f.; ML 59; Fornara no. 120) and 465.115 (i² 366.3; ML 60; Fornara no. 118B):
Grammateus
METAGENES *PA* 10086

(i) IG i³ 52 (i² 91 and 92; ML 58; Fornara no. 119) comprises two decrees of pryt. Kekropis, one providing for the repayment of monies owed to the
(ii) gods and the institution of the tamiai of the other gods, the other concerning public building and placing restrictions on the money which could be used:

Grammateus
MNESITHEOS *PA* 10281
Bouleutes epistates
EUPEITHES *PA* 5918
Proposer
KALLIAS *PA* 7827
PA has Kallias as the son of Kalliades who was strategos in 432/1; while this is possible, the matter is best left open. As to date, Mattingly (*ABSA* 1967, 14ff.; *BCH* 1968, 450ff.; *ABSA* 1970, 147ff.) has equated the secretary with the Mnesitheos who was hellenotamias in 418/17 from tribe II and tried to date the decrees to 422/1; I am not convinced. Fornara's argument for 418/17 in *GRBS* 1970, 185–96, was countered by Bradeen, *GRBS* 1971, 469–83. See also Linders, *Treasurers* 45, 49, 55ff.; Meritt, *Hesperia* Suppl. 19, 112–21.

433/2 (Ol. 86.4)

Archon
APSEUDES *PA* 2801; *APF* 112
Philochoros *FGH* 328 F 122; Diod. 12.36.1; IG i³ 53.4 (i² 51; ML 63; Fornara no. 124); 54.8 (i² 52; ML 64; Fornara no. 125); [364] (i² 295; ML 61; Fornara no. 126); 402.[?14], 22 (i² 377; ML 62; Fornara no. 121); 450.416 (i² 353.7). For his demotic *APF* might suggest Myrrhinous (III).

Strategoi
DIOTIMOS son of Strombichos of Euonymon (I) *PA* 4386; *APF* 161
PROTEAS son of Epikles of Aixone (VII) *PA* 12298
LAKEDAIMONIOS son of Kimon of Lakiadai (VI) *PA* 8965; *APF* 305f.
Thuc. 1.45.2f.; IG i³ 364.8f. (i² 295; ML 61; Fornara no. 126). For stories of Diotimos see Polyainos 5.22. For Lakedaimonios see Plut. *Per.* 29.2. They were sent to Corcyra with orders not to engage with the Corinthians unless they moved first, but there was action.

GLAUKON son of Leagros of Kerameis (v) *PA* 3027; *APF* 91
DRAKONTI[DES] son of Leogoras of Thorai (x) *PA* 4551; *APF* 173
Thuc. 1.51.4 (though Drakontides appears by emendation from Andokides, which name is repeated at Plut. *Mor.* 834c); IG i³ 364.19ff. (i² 295; ML 61; Fornara no. 126). They brought extra ships to the Corcyrean theatre. Drakontides' name is given as it is restored in the inscription, along with the patronymic in Thucydides and the demotic in *APF*.

[METAG]ENES of Koile (VIII) *PA* 10088
IG i³ 364.20 (i² 295; ML 61; Fornara no. 126). He was another general around Corcyra.

ARCHESTRATOS son of Lykomedes (of Phlya) (VII) *PA* 2411
Thuc. 1.57.6ff. General with a number of others in the north, he took

Poteidaia and other dissident places and then fought in Makedonia. For problems and the deme see Fornara, *Generals* 51, 78. The term strategoi is used at Thuc. 1.59.2 and so nothing else is to be supposed (*contra* Jordan, *TAPhA* 1970, 238 = *Navy* 128).

ARCHENA[UTES] (? of Ikarion (II))
IG i³ 466.145 (i² 367.5). His area of operation is not known. For the deme cf. *PA* 2357; tribe II is at least otherwise unrepresented, for what that is worth.

PERIKLES son of Xanthippos of Cholargos (V) *PA* 11811; *APF* 457ff. See 443/2.

Tamiai
-- of Melite (VII)
IG i³ 466.143 (i² 367.3).
PRONAPES of Erchia (II)
  Grammateus
  EUTHIAS son of Aischron of Anaphlystos (X) *PA* 5484
IG i³ 293.14f., 24f. (i² 233); 318.8f. (i² 257); 344.16f., 31f. (i² 277); 364.16f. (i² 295; ML 61; Fornara no. 126); for Euthias also i³ 292.5 (i² 232); 294.30 (i² 234); 317.3 (i² 256); 319.17 (i² 258); 343.3 (i² 276). IG i³ 293, 318 and 344 are the actual inventories of the year.

Hellenotamiai
[DI]ONYSIOS *PA* 4085
  Grammateus
  PHILE-- son of --ektes or --ektos
IG i³ 279 (*ATL* II.27 List 22).

Epistatai of Parthenon
  Grammateus
  ANTIKLES *PA* 1052
IG i³ 450.411 (i² 353.2).

COUNCIL AND ASSEMBLY

The first secretary, of pryt. Aiantis, is known from IG i³ 53.5 (i² 51; ML 63; Fornara no. 124); 54.9f. (i² 52; ML 64; Fornara no. 125); 364.[2f.], 14 (i² 295; ML 61; Fornara no. 126); 450.414 (i² 353):
Grammateus
KRITIADES son of Phaeinos of Teithras (II) *PA* 8788

(i) IG i³ 53 and 54 (i² 51 and 52; ML 63 and 64; Fornara nos. 124 and 125) are
(ii) decrees of pryt. Akamantis, being alliances with Rhegion and Leontinoi and exhibiting the same people:
Grammateus
CHARIAS *PA* 15323

Bouleutes epistates
TIMOXENOS *PA* 13803
Proposer
KALLIAS *PA* 7827
I do not venture to identify Kallias; see 434/3 proposer and IG i³ 53 note.

Proposer
PERIKLES son of Xanthippos of Cholargos (v) *PA* 11811; *APF* 457ff.
(iii) Thuc. 1.31ff. tells of an assembly addressed by envoys from Corcyra and Corinth and the Athenian decision at a second assembly to make a defensive alliance with Corcyra. According to Plut. *Per.* 29.1 it was Perikles who persuaded the demos to this course. We cannot be entirely sure that this occurred very early in this year, rather than late in the last; see de Ste Croix, *Origins* 318f.
(iv)   For the following matters see Fornara nos. 122 and 123. A decree was passed banning the Megarians from the Athenian agora and the harbours of the empire; sources that ascribe this to Perikles are Ar. *Acharn.* 530ff. and schol.; Plut. *Per.* 30.1ff.; schol. Ar. *Peace* 605 (Philochoros *FGH* 328 F 121), 608; schol. Thuc. 1.67.4; other sources Thuc. 1.139; Diod. 12.39.4. For discussion of the evidence see de Ste Croix, *Origins* 225ff.

Proposer
CHARINOS *PA* 15434
(v) Plut. *Per.* 30.3 (cf. *Mor.* 812c–d) records that after a herald sent to the Megarians was killed, he put a decree of enmity towards the Megarians; this is found also in schol. Ar. *Peace* 246. Connor, *AJPh* 1962, 225–46, wants this to belong to the period 352–349 B.C., but this was countered by Dover, *AJPh* 1966, 203–9. See de Ste Croix, *Origins* 246ff., though I prefer this date to 432/1.

432/1 (Ol. 87.1)

Archon
PYTHODOROS *PA* 12387
Thuc. 2.2.1; *Ath. Pol.* 27.2; Philochoros *FGH* 328 FF 121 (Fornara no. 116), 122, 123; Diod. 12.37.1; hyp. Euripides *Medea*; Suda *s.v.* Μέτων; IG i³ [365] (i² 296); xiv 1097.5.

Strategoi
KALLIAS son of Kalliades *PA* 7827
Thuc. 1.61, 62.4ff.; Diod. 12.37.1; IG i³ 365.[5] (i² 296). He joined operations against Pydna and then enjoyed some success around Poteidaia but was killed. For the date see Fornara, *Generals* 52f., 55; de Ste Croix, *Origins* 319ff. I have not given Kallias a demotic, as the commonness of the name makes that speculative; Fornara, *Generals* 53, opts for Aixone (VII), but one could point out a Kallias son of Kalliades later in Paiania (III) (see Lewis, *JHS* 1961, 118).

PHORMION son of Asopios (of Paiania) (III) *PA* 14958
Thuc. 1.64.2ff.; Isok. 16.29; Diod. 12.37.1; Front. *Strat.* 3.11.1; Polyainos
3.4.1; Athenaios 5.216c; schol. Thuc. 1.64.3; IG i³ 365. [? 13], [? 17], [? 23],
(i² 296). He was sent to replace Kallias, blockaded Poteidaia and laid waste
land in Chalkidike and Bottiaia.

EUKRAT[ES] (of Melite) (VII) *PA* 5759
IG i³ 365.5 (i² 296). General in Makedonia. For the demotic, which I
accept, see Fornara, *Generals* 76f.

PERIKLES son of Xanthippos of Cholargos (V) *PA* 11811; *APF* 457ff.
Thuc. 2.13.1, 21.3, 22.2f.; Diod. 12.39.3, 42.6, 42.8; Plut. *Per.* 33.4ff. He
was in charge of the defence of Attika and, says Plutarch, drove out the
Aiginetans to make way for Athenian klerouchs. This may extend into 431/
30.

KARKINOS son of Xenotimos of Thorikos (V) *PA* 8254; *APF* 283
PROTEAS son of Epikles of Aixone (VII) *PA* 12298
SOKRATES son of Antigenes of Halai (II) *PA* 13099
Thuc. 2.23.2, 25.1ff., 30; Diod. 12.42.7; IG i³ 365.31, 36, 38f. (i² 296). Sent
around the Peloponnese, they caused some damage and attacked fortifications at Methone without success. Then they landed in Elis and subsequently captured Sollion and Astakos and won over Kephallenia.

Tamiai
EUREKTES of Atene (X) *PA* 5759
Grammateus
APOLLODOROS son of Kritias of Aphidna (IX) *PA* 1410
IG i³ 294.28, 35 (i² 234); 319.15, 19f. (i² 258); 345.34f. (i² 278); 365.3f. (i²
296); for Apollodoros alone also i³ 293.16f. (i² 233); 295.41 (i² 235); 318.10
(i² 257); 320.25 (i² 259); 344.18 (i² 277); 346.54f. (i² 279). IG i³ 294, 319 and
345 are the actual inventories of the year.

Hellenotamiai
[PHI]LETAIROS of Ikarion (II) *PA* 14252
PHILOXEN[OS] of tribe III
[HIE]RONYMOS of tribe IV *PA* 7560
[CH]ARIAS of Daidalidai (VII) *PA* 15340
EP-- of tribe VIII
OLYMP[IODOROS] of tribe IX
Grammateus
.. MOCHARES of Myrrhinous (III)
For the hellenotamiai IG i³ 365.7ff., 33f. (i² 296); for Philetairos also and
the secretary i³ 280 (*ATL* II.28 List 23).

COUNCIL AND ASSEMBLY

The first secretary is to be found at IG i³ 365 (i² 296):

Grammateus

-- son of [D]iotimos of Phegaia (II) *PA* 4365

Proposer

PERIKLES son of Xanthippos of Cholargos (V) *PA* 11811; *APF* 457ff.

(i) Thuc. 1.139.1f. mentions the refusal to rescind the Megarian decree; while de Ste Croix, *Origins* 245, is correct to say that Diod. 12.39.4f. and Plut. *Per.* 30f. (and cf. Ar. *Acharn.* 535ff.) only say that Perikles opposed the repeal, it may well be that he put a formal motion.

(ii) Thuc. 1.139.3ff. records an assembly to decide on an answer to Spartan demands at which Perikles spoke and the demos voted as he suggested, that they were willing to have arbitration.

(iii) Thuc. 2.12.2 tells us of a decree passed on Perikles' motion that no herald or envoys of the Spartans should be received when the Spartans had left their own land, by dint of which they refused access to an envoy.

(iv) Thuc. 2.13f. (cf. Diod. 12.40) says that Perikles addressed an assembly to forestall any suspicion stemming from his friendship with Archidamos; he ran through Athenian resources and the demos accepted his advice to bring their property into the city and send their livestock to Euboia and other islands.

APPENDIX

Strategoi

?NIKIAS son of Nikeratos of Kydantidai (II) *PA* 10808; *APF* 403f.

As Fornara (*Generals* 51) remarks, one could easily imagine generalships not otherwise attested for prominent individuals in this period. More specifically, Plut. *Nikias* 2.2 reports that Nikias, whose first datable strategia is 427/6, served as general alongside Perikles while he was alive and held independent command often. 'Often' may be an exaggeration, but one wonders whether one can believe this at all. Might there have been at some point a confusion with Hagnon son of Nikias?

?MENIPPOS *PA* 10033

Again, Plut. *Per.* 13.10 (cf. *Mor.* 812c), in the general context of Pheidias' work on the statue of Athene, mentions Menippos, a friend of Perikles, of whom he uses the verb ὑποστρατηγεῖν; but that this means a strategia for Menippos, let alone more than one (Fornara, *Generals* 50 and n.44), is by no means secure, especially as Plutarch would know ὑποστρατήγος as a Greek term for the Latin *legatus*.

?SOPHOKLES son of Sophillos of Kolonos (II) *PA* 12834
He could have held generalships other than the attested one of 441/40. The
anonymous life of him says he was general with Perikles and Thoukydides;
the latter could be the son of Melesias earlier or the historian in 424/3 (cf.
423/2); section 9 of the life seems to refer to 441/40. This is all problematic,
but a number of strategiai cannot be ruled out. See Ehrenberg, *Soph. and
Per.* 117 n.1; Woodbury, *Phoenix* 1970, 215f.; Lefkowitz, *Lives* 80ff.

?METIOCHOS *PA* 10131; *APF* 308
Also presumably to be fitted into this period, he is evidenced as a crony of
Perikles and, among other things, general at Plut. *Mor.* 811f; Davies, *APF*
wishes to associate him with the Kimonids.

?ERASISTRATOS of Acharnai (VI) *PA* 5024; *APF* 322
A generalship for the father of Phaiax seems to be indicated at Diog. 2.63,
but see *APF*.

?--ODOTOS of tribe VIII
Bradeen, *Hesperia* 1964, 22ff., suggested that he, in no. 5 line 2, may have
been a general and in the year 446; for the name his best suggestion is
Pythodotos. The date may be correct; the strategia is a deduction from the
greater size of the letters in his name.

Strategos or nauarchos
DIOTIMOS son of Strombichos of Euonymon (I) *PA* 4386; *APF* 161
Timaios *FGH* 566 F 98 (with commentary); Polyainos 5.22.3. He is
reported to have gone on a mission to Neapolis, which should fall in the
430s and, if he was nauarchos, before his strategia of 433/2. However,
schol. Tzetzes 733 (*FGH* apparatus) has strategos.

Hipparchoi
PRON[A]P[ES[(son of Pronapides of Prasiai) (III) *PA* 12250; *APF* 471
X[E]NOPHON (son of Euripides of Melite) (VII) *PA* 11313; *APF* 199f.
LAKEDAIMONIOS (son of Kimon of Lakiadai) (VI) *PA* 8965; *APF* 305f.
IG i³ 511 (i² 400; *DAA* 135, pp. 146ff.). The date of the dedication is
disputed and to be deduced from operations in which cavalry can have been
active. Raubitschek opted for Oinophyta in 457, Gomme, *Comm. Thuc.*
II.203, for *c.* 446. The coincidence of names suggests to me that a date in the
early 440s is to be preferred, letter forms being indecisive.

Taxiarchos
KRATINOS son of Kallimedes of tribe VI *PA* 8755
Kratinos T 15 (Kassel-Austin). Gomme, *Comm. Thuc.* II.75, wonders
about 432/1 for the date, but as Kratinos is said to have lived to be 97 and
died during the late stages of the Archidamian War (see TT 3, 10), this is
highly unlikely.

Tamiai
In IG i³ 249 are the remains of names which may refer to two separate boards of tamiai of Athene; I do not record the mere letters.
(a) THEODO--
(b) TIMARCHOS son of Pe- or of the deme Pe--
Grammateus
--STRATOS

?KTESIAS
IG i³ 32.31f. has money being handed over to Ktesias, while at lines 35ff. a rider deals with the count of the money handed over to the tamias by the boule. Is Ktesias the tamias and what sort of treasurer is he? IG follows the dating to 449/8 or 448/7 proposed by Meritt and Wade-Gery, *JHS* 1963, 111ff., but the 430s have been proposed by Cavanaugh (*Eleusis* 140ff.) and the matter is open.

Hellenotamias
?SOSIAS *PA* 13176
Antiphon 5.70; *ATL* 1.570. *ATL* 1.184 has the suggestion that this man may have been hellenotamias in 440/39, but all we know is that he held the office before *c.* 415.

Athlothetes
PERIKLES son of Xanthippos of Cholargos (v) *PA* 11811; *APF* 457ff. The election is reported at Plut. *Per.* 13.6; I avoid dating.

Epistatai
IG i³ 433, 434 and 435 (i² 335, 337, 338) are accounts for public works, of an unknown nature in the first two cases, for the statue of Athene Promachos in the third. They contain the names of epistatai and grammateis, but are dated only to the middle of the century or around 450. I list the cast of characters in order of appearance, representing individual years.
A. IG i³ 433
Grammateus
(a) [?AST]YPHI[LOS]
There are a number of letters which might belong to names of epistatai.
(b) ENLO[GIMOS ?]
--OS
The first name is a suggestion from the files of the Institute for Advanced Study at Princeton.
Grammateus
[E]UCHARI[DES] (? son of Euchares) of Aphidna (IX) ?*PA* 6144
Demotic from the inscription, patronymic suggested by identification with the thesmothetes of 444/3 (q.v.).
(c) --S of Kephisia (I)
Z--

Grammateus
--YNEUS of Thria (VI)
(d) --E.EOS of Kydantidai (II) or Kydathenaion (III)
--ON of Kettos (IV)
DEME--
ARCHILLO[S] of K-- *PA* 2509
Grammateus
PH[IL]ON of Probalinthos (III) *PA* 14871
(e) AM[O]IBICHOS of Lamptrai (I) *PA* 727
O-- of Hestiaia (II)
-- of Myrrhinous (III)
.. THO .. O ...⁵. . of Kettos (IV)
PH . . . LO . . . of ? Th[orikos] (V)
Grammateus
TH[R]ASI[P]POS of Gargettos (II) cf. *PA* 105
(f) After random letters
PYTHODOROS of Phyla (VII) *PA* 12433
-- of Krioa (X)
EP--
Grammateus
N[I]KO . . . . OS of Thorikos (V) *PA* 10876
(g) AUTO[K]LE[S] of Peiraieus (VIII)
STRATO[K]LES *PA* 12926
. . .⁶. . PHI . . . of Erchia (II)
Grammateus
EUTHEMON *PA* 5473

B. IG i³ 434.
Of the preserved letters the only possibility worth mentioning would seem
to be that in line 15 we have either the demotic for Pelekes (IV) for the
grammateus or the name THARREX, which is evidenced a century later in
the deme Lamptrai (I) (*PA* 6584).

C. IG i³ 435; Athene Promachos
The only secretaries of whom traces remain are at lines 36ff. and 94:
(a) **Grammateus**
[K]AL[LIST]RATOS [? of Acharnai] (VI) ?*PA* 8148 (*sic*; it should be 8158)
The deme looks likely and leads to the possibility that this was the general
of 441/40; see Raubitschek, *Hesperia* 1943, 12ff.
(b) **Grammateus**
. . .⁵. . S

Epistatai for work at Eleusis
IG i³ 398 (i² 319) produces a name which seems to be a secretary of the
epistatai:
Grammateus
GLAUKO[N]

Epistates
PERIKLES son of Xanthippos of Cholargos (v) *PA* 11811; *APF* 457ff.
Terminology used in sources indicates that Perikles was epistates of a
number of works, but there is more than doubt that these can be taken
literally (see Boersma, *Building Policy* 73). They are (i) Parthenon: Strabo
9.1.12 (Boersma is wrong to cite Strabo for Perikles' being concerned with
the Telesterion at Eleusis); (ii) Odeion: Plut. *Per.* 13.5; (iii) Harpokration
s.v. Λύκειον reports Theopompos (*FGH* 115 F 136) as ascribing the making
of the Lykeion to Peisistratos, while Philochoros (*FGH* 328 F 37) said
Perikles was epistates of it (cf. Boersma 74).

Demarchoi
IG i³ 248 (ML 53) is dated 450–440 and gives the names of five consecutive
demarchs of Rhamnous (IX):
AUTOKLEIDES
MNESIPTOLEMOS
NAUSIMENES
EUAINETOS
DEMOPHANES *APF* 140

Envoys
PYRILAMPES son of Antiphon *PA* 12493; *APF* 329f.
Plato *Charm.* 158a. He was a frequent ambassador to Asia; see 450/49.

DIOTIMOS son of Strombichos of Euonymon (I) *PA* 4386; *APF* 161
Strabo 1.3.1 (Damastes *FGH* 5 F 8). Ambassador to Susa; see Lewis,
Sparta and Persia 60 n.70.

Uncertain
See IG i³ 399 for the possibility that the remains of a name may be an
epistates at Eleusis or a secretary of epistatai or even of the Amphiktyons to
Delos:
--DES of Hybadai (IV)

COUNCIL AND ASSEMBLY

Grammateis
?PARAIBATES *PA* 11609
See the appendix to Section III (p. 60).

?MECHANIO[N] *PA* 10162
IG i³ 841 (i² 626; *DAA* 383, pp. 410f.). If he could be identified with the
casualty of 459/8 (IG i³ 1147.22; i² 929; ML 33; Fornara no. 78), this would
establish his tribe (I) and a *terminus ante quem* for his office, but I shrink
from the identification.

METROBIOS *PA* 10133
Kratinos F 1 (Kassel-Austin) (Plut. *Kimon* 10.4).

(i) IG i³ 7 (i² 80) is a decree of 460–450 concerning the Praxiergidai:
Grammateus
. . . ⁶ . . s

(ii) IG i³ 8 concerns cults at Sounion and dates about 460–450:
Proposers
KALLIMACHOS
ANTIBIO[S]

(iii) IG i³ 10 (i² 16; ML 31; Fornara no. 68; cf. SEG 28.1) is a decree of pryt.
Akamantis concerning Phaselis:
Grammateus
[O]NASIPPOS *PA* 11439 or [M]NASIPPOS
Bouleutes epistates
NE . . . . DES or E[. . .]EDES
Proposer
LEO[N] *PA* 9099
I use the dating 469–450, though tempted into 465/4; 425/4 is hardly likely.
For the date see ML with bibliography. For the name of the secretary see
the apparatus to IG i³ 10 and i³ 66.4 and Wade-Gery, *Essays* 182 n.1. For
the name of the epistates see IG i³; Wade-Gery suggested Nelonides, but
that the nu is the first letter of the name is uncertain and the alternative
Epimedes has thus been advanced (for the reading which creates only three
missing letters see Bradeen and McGregor, *Studies* 116); a restored
Epimedes of Hagnous in Akamantis was bouleutes in 378/7 (*q.v.*); see also
Fornara, *CQ* 1979, 49 n.1.

(iv) IG i³ 12 (i² 20) is a decree dated in i³ *c.* 433/2, but with a note of other
possibilities; it is an alliance with Halikyai:
Bouleutes epistates
AR--
So I believe he is, rather than an archon.

(v) IG i³ 14 (i² 10; ML 40; Fornara no. 71) and 15 (i² 11, 12, 13; SEG 31.5)
(vi) concern Erythrai; the first seems to have the letter L as the beginning of a
name (? the proposer rather than the archon); I believe the date could be
anything up to about fifteen years before 450.

(vii) IG i³ 18 (i² 23 + 30; Walbank no. 12) is a proxeny decree for certain men of
Parion(?):
Grammateus
DI[OTIMOS?] or DI[ON?]
Proposer
[AR]CHEDEMO[S]
Dated *c.* 450 in IG i³. Walbank calculates that if Dion is restored, which
seems likely, and if the epistates is included, the archon, if named at all,

would have to be that of 458/7, 456/5, 454/3, 450/49 or 449/8, and he wonders seriously about 450/49.

(viii) IG i³ 23 (i² 36; Walbank no. 11) is a proxeny decree for certain Thespiaians of pryt. Aiantis:

Proposer

--ILEOS

The reading is that of Walbank, who dates *c.* 460–440, while IG i³ has *c.* 447.

(ix) IG i³ 27 (i² 27; Walbank no. 13) is a proxeny decree for certain Delphians of pryt. Leontis:

Bouleutes epistates

. . . OSTRATOS

Grammateus

. . . .⁷. . . RATES *PA* 1892 (Aristokrates)

Proposer

. . . .⁷. . . CHOS

Dated in IG i³ to *c.* 450/49, though Mattingly (*BCH* 1968, 481f., 485) wanted it in 422/1, along with IG i³ 28 (next entry). This seems unlikely and Walbank gives *c.* 460–445, pointing out also that there are common names to provide alternatives for the secretary.

(x) IG i³ 28 (i² 143; Walbank no. 17) is a proxeny decree, possibly for certain men of Abydos, of pryt. Leontis:

Grammateus

ARIS[TO]KRATES

Bouleutes epistates

. . .⁶. . R . . . . or . . .⁶. . B . . . S

See the last item. Mattingly's date for this has more chance, but IG i³ puts it 450–440, while Walbank has *c.* 445–435, with 440/39 specifically given a chance. Walbank is also strongly against Mattingly's identification of the secretary as *PA* 1904 or 1925. As for the epistates, the first version is from IG i³, where indeed Nikostratos is restored, the second from Walbank (cf. SEG 32.1).

(xi) IG i³ 30 (i² 31) is a decree described in i³ as praise for a Theraian, but restored by Walbank (no. 16) as a proxeny perhaps for Theramenes and Lakedaimonios:

Grammateus

[E]UKLES

Proposer

--S

These names are based on the readings of Walbank, who wonders whether Eukles could be fitted into IG i³ 21 of 450/49. His date is *c.* 460–445, while IG i³ has *c.* 450.

(xii) IG i³ 31 is a decree of pryt. Antiochis recording a treaty with Hermione:
Grammateus
THEODOROS of Prasiai (III)
Bouleutes epistates
SI . . . ?. .
Proposer
[L]EON
IG dates c. 450, which is preferable to Mattingly's 425/4 (*Historia* 1961, 173ff.; cf. *BCH* 1968, 484).

(xiii) IG i³ 32 is a probouleumatic decree concerning the epistatai of Eleusis:
Proposers
THESPIEUS
[LYSANIAS]
On the date see above on the tamias Ktesias.

(xiv) IG i³ 35 (i² 24; ML 44; SEG 31.9, 32.2) is a probouleumatic decree of pryt. Leontis concerning the priestess and temple of Athene Nike:
Proposers
[GL]AUKOS
HESTIAIOS *PA* 5194
On date see IG i³, SEG and Tracy, *Studies Dow* 281f., who identifies the stonecutter with that of IG i³ 435.

(xv) IG i³ 42 and 43 (i² 34 and 35) are two decrees concerning Kolophon, the
(xvi) second of pryt. Hippothontis. The first is dated c. 445–442, the second c. 435–427, though IG i³ notes Mattingly's suggestion of c. 430 for both.

(xvii) IG i³ 44 is of uncertain import but seems to include the following, dated 450–445:
Proposer
EUA--

(xviii) IG i³ 48 bis is a decree granting privileges to someone:
Grammateus
PROMACHOS
Proposer
MENITES
IG dates 440–430. Two of the men chosen by the honorand, Archestratos and Lakedaimonios, were generals in 433/2.

(xix) IG i³ 49 (i² 54) concerns public water supply:
Proposers
?[HIPP]ONIKO[S]
NIKOMA[CHOS] *PA* 10933
IG i³ dates 440–432, noting Thompson's c. 430.

Appendix

(xx) IG i³ 50 is a probouleumatic decree concerning public works, possibly the Eleusinion, dated *c.* 435:
Bouleutes epistates
PROINAUTES
Proposer
[?KALLIAS]

(xxi) IG i³ 56 (Walbank no. 33) is a proxeny decree:
Grammateus
IA[SON]
Bouleutes epistates
...⁵.. PPOS
Proposers
.....⁹.... S
HIPPOK[RATES]
Walbank follows Meritt's readings, though he does not restore Iason; his date is *c.* 440–425, that in IG is *c.* 430.

(xxii) IG i³ 130 (i² 128) is a decree of pryt. Antiochis concerning perhaps Apollo of Delos and dated to *c.* 432:
Bouleutes epistates
STRATON *PA* 12971
Proposer
LYS[I]KLES ?*PA* 9417

(xxiii) IG i³ 131 (i² 77; SEG 31.11; 32.4) is a decree of pryt. Erechtheis concerning the perpetual right to eat in the Prytaneion:
Bouleutes epistates
--THIPPOS
Proposer
... IKLES
The date given is *c.* 440–432 ? and IG i³ properly avoids the temptation to restore the proposer as Perikles, as there are other names which could fit.

(xxiv) IG i³ 132 (i² 111) is a decree, dated in i³ only to the second half of the century, concerning the building of a temple:
Bouleutes epistates
SMIKYTHO[S] *PA* 12775
Comparison has been made with IG i³ 66, dated 427/6, in which the name Smikythos is restored as epistates.

(xxv) IG i³ 133 (i² 127) is a decree, dated after 434/3, concerning the Anakes:
Bouleutes epistates
AINEAS *PA* 296
Proposer
ELPIA[S]

111

(xxvi) IG i³ 141 (i² 168) is a fragment dated 440–425 of pryt. Antiochis.

(xxvii) IG i³ 145 is a fragment dated 440–430:
Proposer
CHROMON

(xxviii) IG i³ 147 (i² 104) is a fragment:
Grammateus
[AI]SCHYLO[S] *PA* 434
It is correct, I think, to doubt that this is the same Aischylos as the secretary of 412/11, as indeed is the case in *PA*, where the two have separate entries. IG i³ dates 440–420 (?).

(xxix) IG i³ 148 (i² 37) cannot well be dated; it seems to have concerned the Messenians and contains the letters --OKLES Phi, which could refer to a gentleman of Philaidai (II), perhaps a grammateus, but all is uncertain.

(xxx) IG i³ 155 (Walbank no. 24) is a proxeny decree for Krison:
Bouleutes epistates
MELET[OS] or MELET[ON]
Proposer
. . . .⁷. . . N
IG dates *c.* 440–430, Walbank *c.* 435–425, though favouring the late 430s. Walbank also points out that the second name is possible.

(xxxi) IG i³ 156 (i² 56; Walbank no. 22) is a proxeny decree for Leonidas of Halikarnassos of pryt. Antiochis in the second part, as the remains begin with the end of a preceding decree:
Grammateus
CHAROIADES (? son of Euphiletos) *PA* 15528 = ?15529
Bouleutes epistates
HEGESANDROS *PA* 6305
Proposer
CHAIRESTRATOS *PA* 15147
Dated in IG i³ 440–425, by Walbank *c.* 440–435.

(xxxii) IG i³ 184 (i² 163) is the beginning of a decree of pryt. Erechtheis dated *c.* 450.

(xxxiii) IG i³ 185 is the beginning of a decree dated *c.* 440:
Grammateus
--S
Proposer
KIN--

(xxxiv) In the fragment IG i³ 189 (i² 162) there is restored a secretary from Alopeke (X) who may be nothing of the sort. The letters in the line above, HIERO--, could be the beginning of a name. Date 440–405.

(xxxv) IG i³ 207 (i² 139) is the remains of a decree dated 440–420:
Proposer
. E . . . . NDROS

(xxxvi) IG i³ 1454 (xii 1.977; Tod 110) is a decree honouring the Karpathians of pryt. Aigeis or Oineis, now dated to the third quarter of the fifth century (Meiggs, *Trees* 201 and 498 n.36):
Grammateus
TEI[SIAS] *PA* 13471
Bouleutes epistates
ATHENODO[ROS] *PA* 259 = ?260
Proposer
KTESIAS *PA* 8838

Proposers
(xxxvii) For the Arthmios decree and the possibility that it might have been proposed by Kimon in this period see 481/80.

(xxxviii) ARISTEIDES son of Lysimachos of Alopeke (x) *PA* 1695; *APF* 48ff.
Ath. Pol. 24 says Aristeides advised the Athenians to seize the hegemony and leave their fields to live in the city, where there would be sustenance for all. We may not believe this, but it is quite conceivable that Aristeides made proposals in the assembly regarding the empire before his death sometime in the mid 460s.

?ALKIBIADES son of Kleinias of Skambonidai (IV) ?*PA* 597; *APF* 15f.
(xxxix) Dem. 20.115 and Plut. *Arist.* 27.1f. record a decree of an Alkibiades granting land in Euboia and pecuniary benefits to Lysimachos son of Aristeides, presumably in the later 460s. Both the fact and the identity of the Alkibiades are doubtful; see *APF* 51f. Not ascribed to Alkibiades is the
(xl) voting of a dowry to Aristeides' daughter found at Aisch. 3.258; Nepos *Arist.* 3.3; Plut. *Arist.* 27.2ff. (includes Demetrios *FGH* 228 F 45).

PERIKLES son of Xanthippos of Cholargos (v) *PA* 11811; *APF* 457ff.
Plut. *Per.* 8.5 says that the only writing Perikles left was in his decrees. He is specifically credited with the introduction of various sorts of fees for
(xli) service and the like (Plut. *Per.* 9, 34.1; Plato *Gorg.* 515e.2–7). For doubts
(xlii) that he introduced theoric distributions see Rhodes, *Comm.* 514. It is more likely that he introduced pay for service on the juries, for which see also
(xliii) Arist. *Pol.* 2.21 1274a 8–9; *Ath. Pol.* 27.3f.; Rhodes, *Comm.* 338ff. Plut. *Per.* 11.4 mentions the introduction of amusements for the people in the context of the 440s. At *Per.* 12f. Perikles is made generally responsible for a whole building programme, but his precise role cannot be recovered, though some proposals seem to be assumed, as is the case with the corn stoa
(xliv) at Peiraieus mentioned at schol. Ar. *Acharn.* 548. Plut. *Per.* 13.5 specifically mentions Perikles' decree for the Long Wall, which he says Sokrates heard (from Plato *Gorg.* 455e); I refrain from dating this. On the building

(xlv) see Boersma, *Building Policy* 66ff. Plut. *Per.* 13.6 records a decree for the institution of a musical contest at the Panathenaia. According to Plut. *Per.* 14, Perikles came under attack for his expenditure from Thoukydides and his associates and Perikles persuaded an assembly to let him have his way.

?KANNONOS *PA* 8249

(xlvi) A decree of his is mentioned at Ar. *Ekkl.* 1089 with schol. (Krateros *FGH* 342 F 15); Xen. *Hell.* 1.7.20, 34; it could belong to this period. It said that if anyone wronged the demos, he must plead his case in fetters and if convicted, be executed, his property being confiscated and one-tenth going to the goddess. See Hignett, *HAC* 154f., 304f.

Bouleutes

NIKIAS son of Nikeratos of Kydantidai (II) *PA* 10808; *APF* 403f. Plut. *Nik.* 5.1, probably in this period.

Section V
431/30–404/3

431/30 (Ol. 87.2)

Archon

EUTHYDEMOS *PA* 5515

Diod. 12.38.1; Athenaios 5.217a; SEG 10. 226.[11] (see the apparatus at IG i³ 366). I believe he could be the archon mentioned in the 'Papyrus Decree': see 450/49.

Strategoi

SOKRATES son of Antigenes of Halai (II) *PA* 13099
KARKINOS son of Xenotimos of Thorikos (V) *PA* 8254; *APF* 283
PROTEAS son of Epikles of Aixone (VII) *PA* 12298

In autumn 431/30 the forces which they had commanded around the Peloponnese (see 432/1) joined in the invasion of the Megarid (Thuc. 2.31.1) and their generals probably still led them; Fornara, *Generals* 53.

PERIKLES son of Xanthippos of Cholargos (V) *PA* 11811; *APF* 457ff.
Thuc. 2.31.1, 55.2, 56 (cf. 6.31.2); Diod. 12.44.3 (430/29); Plut. *Per.* 34.1ff.; ?Lykourgos F 58. He led the expedition to the Megarid. Sources other than Thucydides say he drove out the Aiginetans and established klerouchs in their place. In summer 430 he led another expedition to the Peloponnese, making landings.

PHORMION son of Asopios (of Paiania) (III) *PA* 14958
Thuc. 2.29.6, 58.2; ?Front. *Strat.* 3.11.1. His activities in the north, joining with Perdikkas against the Chalkideans, may have been curtailed and he may have been involved in the invasion of the Megarid; Fornara, *Generals* 53f.

HAGNON son of Nikias of Steiria (III) *PA* 171; *APF* 227f.
Thuc. 2.58.1, 6.31.2; Diod. 12.46.2 (429/8). With Kleopompos in summer 430 he replaced Phormion and continued with the siege of Poteidaia into 430/29; Fornara, *Generals* 53f.

KLEOPOMPOS son of Kleinias (? of Skambonidai (IV) or Thria (VI)) *PA* 8613; *APF* 16
Thuc. 2.26.1, 58.1; Diod. 12.44.1 (430/29). He was in command of a fleet around Lokris and Euboia in summer 431 and had some success. Later he joined Hagnon at Poteidaia; Fornara, *Generals* 52ff. For the deme see the discussion in *APF*; Thria seems more likely.

Note: At IG i³ 366.6, as will be seen from discussion there, Meritt (SEG 10.226) restored a generalship for

[ARISTO]TELES (son of Timokrates) of Thorai (X) *PA* 2055

There can be no certainty in this at all, but it seems very likely that the man held an office of some kind.

Tamiai of Athene
ANTIMEDES of Kydathenaion (III)

Grammateus
DIOGNIS son of Isandros of Peiraieus (VIII) *PA* 3879

IG i³ 295.38f.,45 (i² 235.35f.,42); 320.22f. (i² 259.20f.); 346.52f.,67 (i² 279); for Antimedes SEG 10.226.9,15 (not restored at IG i³ 366); for Diognis IG i³ 294.29 (i² 234.27); 319.16 (i² 258.15); 345.35f. (i² 278.36f.). The actual inventories of the year are i³ 295, 320 and 346.

COUNCIL AND ASSEMBLY

(i) Taking the name of the archon at face value, the 'Papyrus Decree' (*Strasbourg Papyrus Graeca* 84; Meiggs, *Ath. Empire* 515; Fornara no. 94) will refer to this year in respect of a proposal concerned with money and the building programme (cf. 450/49):

Proposer
PERIKLES son of Xanthippos of Cholargos (v) *PA* 11811; *APF* 457ff.

(ii) The text evidently continues with another decision, that the council should oversee the maintenance of old triremes and see that ten new ones were built each year.

(iii) Plut. *Per.* 34.1 mentions that Perikles kept the people happy with
(iv) distributions of money and specifically that he was responsible for the klerouchy to Aigina.

(v) At 2.24 (cf. 8.15.1) Thucydides reports in terms like a decree the decision to set aside a reserve fund of 1000 talents, not to be used except for defence of the city, and a reserve fleet of 100 triremes each year. One might well suspect that the initiative for this came from Perikles.

(vi) Thuc. 2.29 records first the proxeny for Nymphodoros of Abdera (Walbank no. 30), then mentions that Nymphodoros went to Athens and
(vii) arranged an alliance with Sitalkes of Thrace and had Sitalkes' son Sadokos
(viii) made an Athenian citizen (cf. 2.67.2; Osborne T 4).

430/29 (Ol. 87.3)

Archon
APOLLODOROS *PA* 1375

Diod. 12.43.1; Athenaios 5.217a–b; anon. *de com.* 3.33 (Koster); IG i² 378

(restored by reference to letter traces not visible according to IG i³ 411);
Hesperia Suppl. 8.134 B.[10] (Ferguson; not accepted in IG i³ 136).

Strategoi

HAGNON son of Nikias of Steiria (III) *PA* 171; *APF* 227f.

KLEOPOMPOS son of Kleinias (of ?Skambonidai (IV) or Thria (VI)) *PA* 8613; *APF* 16

Thuc. 2.58.1ff.; Diod. 12.46.2ff. See 431/30 and Fornara, *Generals* 54f. They continued the siege of Poteidaia and then Hagnon returned to Athens.

PERIKLES son of Xanthippos of Cholargos (V) *PA* 11811; *APF* 457ff.

Thuc. 2.59.3, 65.3; Diod. 12.45.3f., Plut. *Per.* 35.4. Diodoros and Plutarch say he was removed from office, but Thucydides only mentions a fine; see Fornara, *Generals* 54f.

PHORMION son of Asopios (of Paiania) (III) *PA* 14958

Thuc. 2.69.1, 80ff.; Diod. 12.47.1, 48 (429/8); Paus. 10.11.6. He blockaded the Corinthian Gulf from winter on and engaged the Peloponnesian fleet with success; this probably continued into 429/8.

MELESANDROS *PA* 9803

Thuc. 2.69.1; Paus 1.29.7; *TAM* 1.44 (see ML 93). Sent to Karia and Lykia to collect money and prevent Peloponnesian obstruction, he was defeated and killed. I reject speculation on the demotic from a fourth-century trierarch (*PA* 9804; *APF* 388) or from a restoration with regard to Euetion, possible general of 414/13 (*q.v.*).

XENOPHON son of Euripides of Melite (VII) *PA* 11313; *APF* 199f.

HESTIODOROS son of Aristokleides *PA* 5207

PHANOMACHOS son of Kallimachos *PA* 14069

KALLIADES

Thuc. 2.70.3, 79; Diod. 12.47.3 (Xenophon and Phanomachos); Plut. *Nik.* 6.3 (Kalliades and Xenophon). They completed the siege of Poteidaia during winter and made an agreement for which they were faulted. They engaged the Chalkideans and Bottiaians in summer 429 and were subsequently killed at Spartolos. Thucydides does not mention Kalliades (he says there were three generals), but on him see Thompson, *CQ* 1969, 160f.

Phylarchos

MENEXENOS son of Dikaiogenes of Kydathenaion (III) *PA* 9976; *APF* 145

Isaios 5.42. He was killed in action at Spartolos.

Tamiai of Athene

? --ENES son of Demok--

Grammateus

THEOLLOS son of Chromades of Phlya (VII) *PA* 6952

IG i³ 411 (i² 378; but see Thompson, *Hesperia* 1965, 148); for Theollos IG i³ 295.40 (i² 235.37); 296.3,4,10 (i² 236.46, 47, 52); 297.16 (i² 237.57); 320.24 (i² 259.22); 321.30,31 (i² 260.27, 28); 322.39 (i² 261.35; SEG 24.28); 346.53f. (i² 279). The actual inventories of the year are i³ 296, 321 and [347].

Tamiai of the other gods
Grammateus
... STRAT[OS]
IG i³ 383.10f. (i² 310.97f.).

Hellenotamiai
[DI]O[NY]SIO[S] of Acharnai (VI) *PA* 4158; *APF* 159
-- of Acherdous (VIII)
AISCHRON of Marathon (IX) *PA* 408
PHILOTADES of Pallene (X)
IG i³ 281 (*ATL* II.29 List 25). For a defence of the dating of Lists 25,26 and 27 see Meiggs, *Ath. Empire* 534ff.; Bradeen and McGregor, *Studies* 20ff.; Mattingly, *CQ* 1978, 83–8, still wishes to reverse this order; see also now Piérart, *BCH* 1984, 172ff.

Envoys
LEARCHOS son of Kallimachos *PA* 9031
AMEINIADES son of Philemon *PA* 666
Thuc. 2.67.2f. Sent to Sitalkes in Thrace, they received as prisoners Peloponnesians who were going to Persia and brought them back to Athens.

COUNCIL AND ASSEMBLY

(i) IG i³ 61 (i² 57; ML 65; Fornara no. 128) includes a decree of pryt. Erechtheis concerning the people of Methone:
Grammateus
SKOPAS
Bouleutes epistates
TIMONIDES
Proposer
D[IOPEI]THES *PA* 4308
For the date see IG i³; ML; Meiggs, *Ath. Empire* 534ff. (cf. 599); but also SEG 31.12.

(ii) Perikles secured a dispensation from his own citizenship law to legitimize Perikles, his son by Aspasia; Osborne T 5.

Thuc. 2.59ff. gives a speech to Perikles at an assembly he is said to have called; as a result they desisted from sending embassies to the Spartans, but no actual motion is mentioned.

429/8 (Ol. 87.4)

Archon
EPAMEINON *PA* 4758
Diod. 12.46.1 (Epaminondas); Athenaios 5.217e; Diog. 3.3 (Ameinias); hyp. Euripides *Hipp.* (Ameinon, Amenon); IG i³ [383](i² 310). For the name confusion cf. 423/2.

Strategoi
PERIKLES son of Xanthippos of Cholargos (V) *PA* 11811; *APF* 457ff.
Thuc. 2.65.4; Diod. 12.45.5, 46.1; Plut. *Per.* 37.1. He was soon dead.

PHORMION son of Asopios (of Paiania) (III) *PA* 14958
Thuc. 2.88.1ff., 102.1f., 103.1; Plut. *Mor.* 345c; Polyainos 3.4.2, 3; schol. Thuc. 2.89.1; schol. Ar. *Peace* 347 (Androtion *FGH* 324 F 8; Fornara no. 130). See 430/29 and Fornara, *Generals* 55. He was engaged in the Corinthian Gulf, landed in Akarnania and made arrangements there; he returned to Naupaktos and in the spring to Athens, where he was fined at his *euthynai*.

KLEIPPIDES son of Deinias of Acharnai (VI) *PA* 8521
Thuc. 3.3.2f., 4.1ff., 5.2ff.; Diod. 12.55.3f. (Kleinippides: 427/6). Sent with two others in summer 428 to deal with Mitylene; an armistice was made, but hostilities resumed. See Fornara, *Generals* 55.

HAGNON son of Nikias of Steiria (III) *PA* 171; *APF* 227f.
Thuc. 2.95.3 with schol. Thucydides mentions him as *hegemon* in the northern theatre and goes on to state the necessity of an Athenian force being in the area against the Chalkideans. It is a fair conclusion that he was general.

Tamiai of Athene
ARCHESTRATOS (? of Phlya (VII)) *PA* 2398
Grammateus
MELESIAS son of Polykles of Oa (III)
IG i³ 297.13,14,21 (i² 237.54,55,62); 322.36,37 (i² 261.32,33); for Melesias i³ 296.5 (i² 236); 298.29f. (i² 238.68f.); 321.31f. (i² 260.28f.); 323.47f. (i² 262.41f.); [348](SEG 24.37.4). The actual inventories of the year are i³ 297, 322 and [348]. I doubt that Archestratos is the same man as the general of 433/2 (*q.v.*).

Tamiai of the other gods
ANTI[PHON ?] [? of Rhamnous (IX)]
ALKIPH[R]ON of Anaphlystos (X) *PA* 644
...?.. TON of Anagyrous (I)
K--
CHARI--

Grammateus
-- of Eleusis (VIII)
IG i³ 383.4ff. (i² 310.91ff.), which is an inventory. Antiphon is restored by Mattingly, *BCH* 1968, 458. Only five were listed.

Hellenotamiai
THEODOROS of Anagyrous (I)
--OS of Sphettos (V)
EPIKR[ATES] *PA* 4863
Grammateus
D[A]MIPPOS of Phyle (VI)
IG i³ 282 (*ATL* II.30 List 26). For the date see 430/29 and for Damippos in particular the following note.

Note: There would seem to be some chance of extracting officials from lines 250ff. of IG i³ 383 (i² 310.1ff.). If the demotic at 254f. is correctly restored we have a *possible* official:
-- of Aphidna (IX)
After that we encounter a reference to hieropoioi and we appear to have the remnants of two names:
--AS
EUTH--
The next reference is to hellenotamiai and this is intriguing, since we already know the names of some who filled that office in 429/8. The major problem is that we cannot be sure that the inscription is in fact confined to this one year, however much we may feel that it is. IG i³ suggests that this side of the stele had a range of 20 to 25 letters, but there seems little to prevent it having been a few letters more. Line 261 had the name of the secretary of the hellenotamiai, which post was filled in this year by Damippos of Phyle; if he is inserted with demotic in line 261, this consumes 28 letters. If the known hellenotamias Theodoros of Anagyrous is restored to lines 267f., line 268 will also contain 28 letters. The other names of which fragments survive could also belong to hellenotamiai:
-- of Melite (VII)
AISCHYL[OS]
--ES of Anaphlystos (X)
LYS--
The third of these *could* be the known Epikrates. For the last man, I would merely ponder a homonym of the hellenotamias of 407/6 (*PA* 9405) Lysitheos of Thymaitadai, which restoration would give line 281 a length of 28 letters.

COUNCIL AND ASSEMBLY

The first secretary appears at IG i³ 383.2 (i² 310):
Grammateus
K[A]LLISTRATO[S] *PA* 8125

428/7 (Ol. 88.1)

Archon
DIOTIMOS *PA* 4366
Diod. 12.49.1; anon. *de com.* 3.38 (Koster).

Strategoi
ASOPIOS son of Phormion (of Paiania) (III) *PA* 2669
Thuc. 3.7.1ff. See Fornara, *Generals* 56, and for the demotic Phormion under 440/39. He went around the Peloponnese in summer 428 and then to Akarnania, where he failed to take Oiniadai. He was killed on the way back from Nerikos.

PACHES son of Epikouros *PA* 11746
Thuc. 3.18.3ff., 28, 33.2ff., 49; Diod. 12.55.5ff. (427/6); Front. *Strat.* 4.7.17; Plut. *Nik.* 6.1f.; *Arist.* 26.3; Polyainos 3.2. From autumn 428 he was in command on Lesbos, where he made terms with the Mitylenians and occupied Antissa. Having operated along the Ionian coast and taken Notion, he returned to Lesbos and further success. He was responsible for acting on the Athenian decrees (see Council and Assembly). Despite his apparent success, he fell on his sword while undergoing *euthynai* on the conduct of his generalship, if we believe what we are told; see Westlake, *Phoenix* 1975, 107–16.

LYSIKLES *PA* 9417
Thuc. 3.19. Sent in winter with four others to collect money, he met his death when he marched into Karia. He may be the proposer of IG i³ 130 (i² 128), but that cannot be firmly dated.

Tamiai of Athene
PANTAK[LES]
  Grammateus
  MEGAKLES son of Megakles of Alopeke (x) *PA* 9697; *APF* 381
IG i³ 298.26,27,35 (i² 238.65,66,74; Thompson, *Hesperia* 1965, 148, 309); 323.44,45,51 (i² 262.38,39,45; SEG 24.29); SEG 24.37.1,2 (i³ 349); for Megakles i³ 297.15 (i² 237.56); 299.42f. (i² 239.79f.); 322.38 (i² 261.34); 324.59 (i² 263.52); 349.58f. (SEG 24.37); 350.65 (SEG 24.38). The actual inventories of the year are i³ 298, 323 and 349.

COUNCIL AND ASSEMBLY

(i) IG i³ 62 (ii² 55b) is a decree concerning the Aphytaians. For a defence of the date see SEG 30.10.

(ii) Thuc. 3.36ff. records the business over Mitylene (cf. Diod. 12.55). An initial decision was to execute prisoners in Athens and also the whole adult male population of Mitylene, women and children being enslaved:

Proposer

KLEON son of Kleainetos of Kydathenaion (III) *PA* 8674; *APF* 318ff.
At a second assembly Kleon spoke again, but his motion was just defeated
(iii) in favour of one proposed by a man who had also spoken at the first
assembly:

Proposer

DIODOTOS son of Eukrates *PA* 3889
Thus the fortifications of Mitylene were destroyed, the land was divided
into klerouchies, for the working of which Lesbians paid rent, and the
Athenians took over the mainland possessions of Mitylene. The prisoners
(iv) in Athens were, nonetheless, put to death on the motion of Kleon.

427/6 (Ol. 88.2)

Archon

EUKLES son of Molon *PA* 5709
Name and patronymic at Arist. *Meteor*. 1.6.8 343b 4; Eukles at Suda and
Photios *s.v.* Σαμίων ὁ δῆμος; schol. Ar. *Wasps* 240; Eukleides at Diod.
12.53.1; schol. Ar. *Knights* 237.

Strategoi

NIKIAS son of Nikeratos of Kydantidai (II) *PA* 10808; *APF* 403f.
Thuc. 3.51; Plut. *Nik*. 6.4; *Comp. Nik. and Crassus* 3.4; ?Athenaios 5.218b.
He was engaged from summer 427 in blockading the Megarians, taking the
island of Minoia. He was later sent to Melos (Thuc. 3.91.1ff.), but this will
at least have extended into 426/5 (*q.v.*). Cf. Thompson, *CQ* 1969, 161f.

NIKOSTRATOS son of Dieitrephes (of Skambonidai) (IV) *PA* 11011
Thuc. 3.75. See Fornara, *Generals* 56f. In summer 427 he went from
Naupaktos to try to settle matters in Corcyra. He was presumably in
command of the Athenians in the naval fighting at Thuc. 3.77f. For the
deme see MacDowell, *CQ* 1965, 41–51.

EURYMEDON son of Thoukles (? of Myrrhinous) (III) *PA* 5973; *APF* 334
Thuc. 3.80.2ff., 85.1. See Fornara, *Generals* 56, 58, 78. He went to Corcyra
with a fleet and sailed away again later. It has been suggested that he was
the father of Speusippos (see *APF*). The association which provides his
deme seems highly likely (but cf. Thompson, *Phoros* 147). Fornara disap-
proves, but see also MacDowell, *CQ* 1965, 44f. n.4. He is likely to be the
general from Myrrhinous in IG i³ 369 of 423/2; Lang and Meritt (*CQ* 1968,
90) have the general in the inscription, but Mattingly (*ABSA* 1970, 137f.)
follows a suggestion of Lewis (*JHS* 1961, 119) that we have an
hellenotamias. See also Gomme, *Comm. Thuc.* III.627f.

LACHES son of Melanopos of Aixone (VII) *PA* 9019
CHAROIADES son of Euphiletos *PA* 15529

Thuc. 3.86.1, 88, 90; Demetrios *FGH* 228 F 31 bis (III B.744) (Laches); *FGH* 577 F 2; Diod. 12.54.4f.; Justin 4.3.6f.; ?SEG 10.226.[7] (IG i² 300; i³ 368 – the text is something of a mess). They were sent out to Sicily where they engaged in operations, Charoiades being killed in battle with the Syracusans. Laches took Mylai and Messina surrendered.

DEMOSTHENES son of Alkisthenes of Aphidna (IX) *PA* 3585; *APF* 112f.
PROKLES son of Theodoros *PA* 12214
Thuc. 3.91.1 with schol., 94ff.; Diod. 12.60.1ff. (425/4); Plut. *Nik.* 6.3. They were sent around the Peloponnese in summer 426 and then ravaged the territory of Leukas and Aitolia, with initial success, but eventual losses, including Prokles (not mentioned by Diodoros). Demosthenes was afraid to return to Athens. On his subsequent status and chronological matters see Fornara, *Generals* 57.

I do not think the chronological attributions used here are seriously undermined by Bloedow (*Chiron* 1981, 65–72), who places Hipponikos in particular in this year. The Athenians will have known when Nikias went to Melos whether he and Hipponikos would be generals in 426/5, but not how long their missions might take.

Tamiai of Athene
[CHAR]MANT[IDES] [of Paiania] (III) *PA* 15501; *APF* 573
 Grammateus
 EUBOULOS son of Philogeiton of Acharnai (VI) *PA* 5354
IG i³ 299.39f.,49f. (i² 239.76f.,86f.); 324.56,57 (i² 263.49,50); 350.62,63,80 (SEG 24.38); for Euboulos i³ 298.28 (i² 238.67); i² 240.91 (not restored at i³ 300.3); i³ 323.46 (i² 262.40). On i² 240.91 see Thompson, *Hesperia* 1965, 148ff. and i³ 300 *ad* 2f. Charmantides' name is nowhere preserved entire, the demotic not at all. The actual inventories of the year are i³ 299, 324 and 350.

Synegoroi
?EUATHLOS *PA* 5238
?KLEONYMOS *PA* 8880
Ar. F 424 (Kassel-Austin); *Acharn.* 710. The sources refer to Euathlos, who seems to have prosecuted Thoukydides son of Melesias shortly before 425, the performance date of the *Acharnians*. Kleonymos comes in through the suggestion of MacDowell on *Wasps* 592.

COUNCIL AND ASSEMBLY

Some of the business over Mitylene recorded under 428/7 may have
(i) extended into this year, in which are placed IG i³ 66 (i² 60) and 67 (i² 53)
(ii) which deal with Mitylene; the second is a treaty, the first a decree of pryt.
Akamantis:
Bouleutes epistates
[SMIKY]THOS

(iii) Dem. 59.104 records the decree making the Plataians Athenian citizens (Osborne D 1):

Proposer

HIPPOKRATES (? son of Ariphron of Cholargos (v)) *PA* 7628 = ?7640; *APF* 456

(iv) According to Diod. 12.53f., the Athenian expedition to Sicily was preceded by an embassy from Leontinoi which included Gorgias and secured an alliance (perhaps rather just help) for that city.

426/5 (Ol. 88.3)

Archon

EUTHYNOS *PA* 5655

The name is guaranteed from IG i³ 369 (i² 324; ML 72; Fornara no. 134); also Philochoros *FGH* 328 F 128; anon. *vita Thuc.* 8; hyp. Ar. *Acharn.* (alternative Euthymenes); Euthydemos is found at Diod. 12.58.1; Athenaios 5.218b (cf. 450/49); other references IG i³ 468.[6] (i² 368); ?[208] (i² 112). Mattingly wants IG i³ 21 (i² 22) here; see 450/49.

Strategoi

NIKIAS son of Nikeratos of Kydantidai (II) *PA* 10808; *APF* 403f.
Thuc. 3.91.1ff.; Diod. 12.65.1ff. (424/3); Athenaios 5.218b. See 427/6 and Fornara, *Generals* 57f. He was sent first to Melos in summer 426, where he could not secure terms, and then went to Boiotia, enjoying success against the Tanagrans. Then he laid waste coastal areas of Lokris.

HIPPONIKOS son of Kallias of Alopeke (x) *PA* 7658; *APF* 262f.
EURYMEDON son of Thoukles (? of Myrrhinous) (III) *PA* 5973; *APF* 334
Thuc. 3.91.4f. and for Eurymedon 115.5, 4.2ff., 8.4, 13.2ff.; Diod. 12.54.6f. (Eurymedon: 427/6), 65.3ff. (Hipponikos: 424/3); Strabo 8.4.2; Athenaios 5.218b (Hipponikos). The two of them led forces into Boiotia and joined with Nikias (*q.v.*). In winter Eurymedon was associated with Sophokles (*q.v.*) in command of forces to go to Sicily and help Corcyra on the way, but they became involved in the capture of Pylos and Sphakteria.

SOPHOKLES son of Sostratides *PA* 12827
Thuc. 3.115.5; 4.2ff., 8.4, 13.2ff.; Philochoros *FGH* 328 F 127; Diod. 12.54.6f. (427/6); Strabo 8.4.2. See under Eurymedon, with whom he was probably associated in the fleet's activity around Pylos (Thuc. 4.15.2, 16.1 mentions 'the generals' in regard to the armistice). On the lack of demotic or tribal affiliation see Whitehead, *JHS* 1980, 210.

LACHES son of Melanopos of Aixone (VII) *PA* 9019
Thuc. 3.103.1ff., 115.6; Philochoros *FGH* 328 F 127. He remained in Sicily, with little success, before being relieved by Pythodoros.

PYTHODOROS son of Isolochos of Phlya (VII) *PA* 12399
Thuc. 3.115.2ff., 4.2.2; Philochoros *FGH* 328 F 127. Sent in winter with the advance force to take over from Laches in Sicily, he was defeated by Lokrians.

SIMONIDES *PA* 12713
Thuc. 4.7. He captured Eion in Thrace in summer 425, but was driven out again.

HIPPOKRATES (son of Ariphron) of Cholargos (v) *PA* 7640; *APF* 456
IG i³ 369.3 (i² 324; ML 72; Fornara no. 134). It is not known where he operated; he is attested in Athens.

Note: Prokles and Demosthenes are not to be included; see Fornara, *Generals* 57, 58; *contra* Lewis, *JHS* 1961, 119f. Neither is Lamachos (Fornara 58) and I cannot see that he need be given any other rank. His generalship mentioned at Ar. *Acharn.* 593ff., will refer to an earlier year. Davies, *Wealth* 151, includes him as taxiarch, citing Ar. *Acharn.* 569 and 1073ff., but I am not persuaded.

Nauarchoi
HIEROPHON son of Antimnestos *PA* 7515
ARISTOTELES son of Timokrates (of Thorai) (x) *PA* 2055
Thuc. 3.105.3, 107.1. They became involved around Akarnania. For the demotic of Aristoteles see Fornara, *Generals* 58, and IG i³ 366.[6] (i² 299; SEG 10.226). For their status, which cannot be regarded as totally secure, see above p. 6; Jordan, *TAPhA* 1970, 238f. = *Navy* 128f.

Tamiai of Athene
ANDROKLES of Phlya (VII) *PA* 873
?[KAL]L[IA]DES of Anakaia (VIII)
   Grammateus
   KEPHISOPHON son of Kephisodoros of Hermos (v) *PA* 8413
For Androkles and Kephisophon IG i³ 300.4f. (i² 240.92f.); for Androkles i³ 369.2,14,15f. (i² 324; ML 72; Fornara no. 134); for Kephisophon i³ 299.41 (i² 239.78); 301.18f. (i² 241.103f.); 324.58 (i² 263.51); 350.64 (SEG 24.38); for Kalliades i³ 468.8 (i² 368), where see the apparatus *ad loc.* for possibilities and for the following lines. An inventory of the year is i³ 300.

Envoys
LEOGO[RAS] *PA* 9072
[PL]EISTIAS
IG i³ 61.51 (i² 57; ML 65; Fornara no. 128). Ambassadors to Perdikkas of Makedon.

?MEGAKLES son of Megakles of Alopeke (x) *PA* 9697; *APF* 381
?LAMACHOS son of Xenophanes of Oe (VI) *PA* 8981
Ar. *Acharn.* 614. Evidently they had been on an embassy soon before the production of *Acharnians*; see *APF*.

?THEOROS *PA* 7223
Ar. *Acharn.* 134ff. with schol. *ad* 134. Aristophanes says he had been sent to Sitalkes, but the reality of the mission cannot be relied upon; cf. MacDowell, *Wasps* 133.

COUNCIL AND ASSEMBLY

(i) IG i³ 61 (i² 57; ML 65; Fornara no. 128; SEG 32.8) includes at lines 32ff. a probouleumatic decree of pryt. Hippothontis concerning the Methonians:
Grammateus
MEGAKLEIDES of Leukonoion (IV) *PA* 9687
Bouleutes epistates
NI[K]OM[ACHOS] or NI[K]OM[EDES]
Proposer
KLEONYMOS
The secretary is also known from IG i³ 369.5 (i² 324; ML 72; Fornara no. 134); 468.3f. (i² 368), and he was first secretary, as we know from IG i³ 369, which also gives us other prytanies of the year: 2. Kekropis; 4. Pandionis; 8. Akamantis; 10. Erechtheis.

(ii) IG i³ 68 (i² 65; Fornara no. 133) is a decree of pryt. Kekropis regulating the collection of tribute:
Grammateus
POLEMARCHOS *PA* 11881
Bouleutes epistates
ONASOS *PA* 11443
Proposers
KLEONYM[OS]
P . . . KRITOS

(iii) A further decree follows at lines 30ff., again of Kekropis with the same secretary largely restored and Kleonymos wholly restored as proposer:
Bouleutes epistates
[H]YGIAINON

(iv) IG i³ 69 (ii² 71; Walbank no. 42) is a proxeny decree, again of pryt. Kekropis and with the secretary restored, along with Hygiainon as epistates and Kleonymos as proposer.

(v) Thuc. 4.17ff. reports an address of Spartan delegates; but they failed to achieve anything, having received a series of demands in reply:
Proposer
KLEON son of Kleainetos of Kydathenaion (III) *PA* 8674; *APF* 318ff.
See also Philochoros *FGH* 328 F 128.

425/4 (Ol. 88.4)

Archon
STRATOKLES *PA* 12927
Diod. 12.60.1; Strabo 8.4.2 (emended); hyp. Ar. *Knights*; schol. Ar. *Clouds*
575; IG i³ 71.56f., 59 (i² 63; ML 69; Fornara no. 136); 369.17 (i² 324; ML
72; Fornara no. 134); ?IG xiv 1097.[14].

Strategoi
NIKIAS son of Nikeratos of Kydantidai (II) *PA* 10808; *APF* 403f.
Thuc. 4.27.5ff., 42ff., 53.1, 54ff.; Diod. 12.65.5ff. (424/3); Plut. *Nik.*
6.4f., 7.3f., *Comp. Nik. and Crassus* 3.4, *Alk.* 14.5, *Mor.* 345d; Polyainos
1.39.1; Diog. 1.72; Suda *s.v. Νικίας*; IG i³ 369.[20f.] (i² 324; ML 72;
Fornara no. 134).

See Fornara, *Generals* 59. He stood down from the command at Pylos in
'favour' of Kleon. Then, with two others, in summer 425 he led a force
against the territory of Corinth with success. He conducted raids in the
north-eastern Peloponnese and returned to Athens. Then, with
Nikostratos and Autokles in summer 424, he took Kythera, ravaged the
coast and sailed north, capturing Thyrea. He took back prisoners.

NIKOSTRATOS son of Dieitrephes of Skambonidai (IV) *PA* 11011
AUTOKLES son of Tolmaios of Anaphlystos (x) *PA* 2724 = ?2717; *APF* 74
Thuc. 4.53ff. See above on Nikias.

DEMOSTHENES son of Alkisthenes of Aphidna (IX) *PA* 3585; *APF* 112f.
Thuc. 4.29ff.; Diod. 12.61f.; Plut. *Nik.* 7.1, *Mor.* 345d, 347a, 349d, 351a–
b; Paus. 1.13.5; Polyainos 3.1.1; schol. Ar. *Knights* 55; IG i³ 369.18 (i² 324;
ML 72; Fornara no. 134).

See Fornara, *Generals* 59. He was in command with Kleon in the
successful operation at Pylos, receiving the surrender of Spartans and
returning to Athens.

ARISTEIDES son of Archippos *PA* 1685
DEMODOKOS of Anagyrous (I) *PA* 3464
LAMACHOS son of Xenophanes of Oe (VI) *PA* 8981
Thuc. 4.50.1 (Aristeides), 75.1; Diod. 12.72.3f. (423/2). They commanded
tribute-collecting ships. Aristeides captured a Persian at Eion. Later they
were all in a troubled Pontos–Hellespont area, where they retook
Antandros.

SOPHOKLES son of Sostratides *PA* 12827
PYTHODOROS son of Isolochos of Phlya (VII) *PA* 12399
EURYMEDON son of Thoukles (? of Myrrhinous) (III) *PA* 5973; *APF* 334
Thuc. 4.46ff., 65.2f.; Timaios *FGH* 566 F 22 (Eurymedon). Engaged
against the exiled party of Corcyra, they incurred discredit in their hand-

ling of prisoners. The Athenian force then sailed to Sicily, where peace was made. Pythodoros and Sophokles were banished, Eurymedon fined on suspicion of bribery to leave Sicily.

?HYPERBOLOS son of Antiphanes of Perithoidai (VI) *PA* 13910; *APF* 517 Ar. *Knights* 1303ff.; schol. Ar. *Acharn.* 846, *Peace* 1319. The passage in *Knights* indicates that Hyperbolos was general in this year, where he is (*pace* Connor, *New Politicians* 146 n.17) placed by Camon, *GIF* 1963, 46ff., though Camon is not entirely sure that he was general (p. 58). The two scholia say that he was, but these might not count for much, were it not that at *Knights* 1313 the word στρατηγῶν is used. This does not seem to be a reference to Hyperbolos' trierarchy (Camon 51ff.), which I decline to date. Scepticism towards evidence on Hyperbolos is especially visible in Baldwin, *AClass* 1971, 151–6.

KLEON son of Kleainetos of Kydathenaion (III) *PA* 8674; *APF* 318ff. Thuc. 4.28.3f., 29ff.; Dem. 40.25; Diod. 12.63.4; Plut. *Nik.* 7.3f., 8.1, *Comp. Nik. and Crassus* 3.4, *Mor.* 345d, 349d; schol. Ar. *Knights* 55, *Clouds* 187, 609; Suda *s.v.* Κλέων.

See Fornara, *Generals* 59, and above on Nikias and Demosthenes. Though other sources call him strategos, Thucydides does not and we should view this as an extraordinary appointment, although we may include it among the generals.

Note: The text at Diod. 12.72.3 has one Symmachos sent out with Aristeides against Mitylenian exiles from Antandros. Thuc. 4.75 is specific that there were three generals in the area and Symmachos is likely to be a confusion with, or corruption of, Lamachos.

Hipparchoi
?SIMON *PA* 12687
?PANAITIOS *PA* 11566
Ar. *Knights* 242f. with schol. I do not think that the context in the play allows us to be certain that they were real hipparchs.

Tamiai of Athene
PHOKIADES of Oion (IV or VIII) *PA* 15066
Grammateus
LYSISTRATOS son of Morychides of Pallene (X) *PA* 9624
IG i³ 300.6 (i² 240.94); 301.16f.,25 (i² 241.101f.,110); for Phokiades i³ 369.[16f.], 23, 24 (i² 324; ML 72; Fornara no. 134); for Lysistratos i³ 302.30f. (i² 242.114f.); *Hesperia* 1970, 59 (Thompson). An inventory of the year is i³ 301.

Hellenotamias
D--
IG i³ 369.26 (i² 324; ML 72; Fornara no. 134).

Taktes

?ALKIBIADES son of Kleinias of Skambonidai (IV) *PA* 600; *APF* 9ff.
And. 4.11; Ael. Arist. 3.119 (Behr) with schol. [Andokides] associates him
with the doubling of tribute. This is vigorously refuted at *ATL* III.350f.,
but I tend to accept it; Develin, *ZPE* 61 (1985), 153, 159.

Eisagogeis
  Grammateus
    KA--
IG i³ 71.60 (i² 63; ML 69; Fornara no. 136).

Kataskopoi
KLEON son of Kleainetos of Kydathenaion (III) *PA* 8674; *APF* 318ff.
THEOGENES of Peiraieus (VIII) *PA* 6703
Thuc. 4.27.3. They were elected for, but did not go on a fact-finding
mission to Pylos. On Theogenes cf. MacDowell, *Wasps* 283f.

COUNCIL AND ASSEMBLY

(i) IG i³ 71 (i² 63; ML 69; SEG 31.13; Fornara no. 136) contains two
(ii) probouleumatic decrees concerning the assessment of tribute, both pro-
posed by the same man:
Proposer
THOUDIPPOS (? of Araphen) (II) *PA* 7251 = ?7252; *APF* 228f.
The first secretary is reconstructed from lines 56 and 59 and IG i³ 369.17 (i²
324; ML 72; Fornara no. 134):
Grammateus
PLEISTIAS *PA* 11864
The first decree is restored to pryt. Leontis (but see SEG 32.9):
Grammateus
. . . . ON
The second, which begins at line 54, is of pryt. Aigeis:
Grammateus
[PHIL]IP[POS]
Bouleutes epistates
. . . .⁷. . . OROS

(iii) IG i³ 61 (i² 57; ML 65; Fornara no. 128) begins at line 56 a decree of pryt.
Kekropis (fifth or sixth prytany) concerning the Methonians:
Grammateus
. . . .⁷. . . ES

Bouleutes epistates
H[I]EROKLEIDES *PA* 7462
Other prytanies are known from IG i³ 369.16ff.; 4. Oineis, 9. Pandionis.

Thuc. 4.27ff. reports how Kleon and Theogenes were chosen kataskopoi

(see above) and how Kleon blamed Nikias for problems at Pylos; Nikias
(iv) suggested Kleon go to deal with it, as he himself stood down. The arrangements for Kleon's expedition were made in the assembly and Demosthenes was chosen to be Kleon's colleague (cf. Plut. *Nik.* 7).

(v) Thuc. 4.41 (cf. Diod. 12.63) records the Athenian decision to keep the Spartan prisoners in jail and kill them if the Peloponnesians invaded. The Athenians also rejected Spartan approaches.

(vi) Thuc. 4.57 records Athenian decisions concerning inhabitants of Kythera, Aiginetan prisoners and Tantalos the Spartan commander.

424/3 (Ol. 89.1)

Archon
ISARCHOS *PA* 7685
Philochoros *FGH* 328 FF 123, 129, 130; Diod. 12.65.1 (alternative Hipparchos); Athenaios 5.218d; schol. Ar. *Clouds* 549; hyp. Ar. *Clouds* A 6; IG i^3 369.[25] (i^2 324; ML 72; Fornara no. 134); ii^2 2318.[96].

Strategoi
HIPPOKRATES son of Ariphron of Cholargos (v) *PA* 7640; *APF* 456
DEMOSTHENES son of Alkisthenes of Aphidna (IX) *PA* 3585; *APF* 112f.
Thuc. 4.66ff., 72.2ff., 74.2, 76f., 89ff., 101.1ff.; Xen. *Mem.* 3.5.4 (Hippokrates); Diod. 12.66, 69f.; Plut. *Nik.* 6.3, *Mor.* 833d (cf. 581d); Paus. 3.6.1, 9.6.3.
    See Fornara, *Generals* 59. They were first involved in summer 424 in the attempt on Megara, which was then lost to Brasidas, the Athenians going home. Attention was then on Boiotia. Demosthenes sailed to Naupaktos to raise an army to take Siphai; he forced certain Akarnanians to join the Athenian alliance, but Siphai could not be taken. Hippokrates led the failure at Delion in winter and lost his life. Demosthenes had a failure at Sikyon.

LAMACHOS son of Xenophanes of Oe (VI) *PA* 8981
Thuc. 4.75.2; Diod. 12.72.4. See Fornara, *Generals* 59f. He lost his ships in the Pontos and marched to Chalkedon in summer 424.

EUKLES *PA* 5704
THUCYDIDES son of Oloros of Halimous (IV) *PA* 7267; *APF* 233ff.
Thuc. 4.104.4ff., 5.26.5; Marcellinus *vita Thuc.* 23, 46; anon. *vita Thuc.* 3; schol. Thuc. 4.104.4. Eukles, defending Amphipolis, during winter sent for Thucydides, who was at Thasos. Amphipolis was lost. Thucydides defended Eion. For his pains he was banished from Athens.

NIKOSTRATOS son of Dieitrephes of Skambonidai (IV) *PA* 11011
NIKIAS son of Nikeratos of Kydantidai (II) *PA* 10808; *APF* 403f.

AUTOKLES son of Tolmaios of Anaphlystos (x) *PA* 2724 = ?2717; *APF* 74
Thuc. 4.119.2. They were signatories to the truce with Sparta.

KLEON son of Kleainetos of Kydathenaion (III) *PA* 8674; *APF* 318ff.
Ar. *Clouds* 581ff. See Fornara, *Generals* 59, 61, for the fact of the generalship. We know of no actions.

Note: For erroneous views on the generals of this year see MacDowell, *CQ*
1965, 41ff.

Officers?
HIPPONIKOS son of Kallias of Alopeke (x) *PA* 7658; *APF* 262f.
LACHES son of Melanopos of Aixone (VII) *PA* 9019
And. 4.13 speaks of the death of Hipponikos as general at Delion, but this is
either confusion (with Hippokrates), falsehood or an elevation of
Hipponikos' actual status. Cic. *de div.* 1.54.123 mentions Laches too as
praetor, but he could have been an officer of some sort. The absence of both
from Thucydides' account seems enough in this instance to deny them
generalships.

Tamiai of Athene
THOUKYDIDES (son of Ariston) of Acherdous (VIII) *PA* 7271; *APF* 54
 Grammateus
 SMIKYTH[OS] or SMIKYTH[ON] *PA* 12773
IG i³ 302.28f.,37 (i² 242.112f., 121); for Thoukydides i³ 369.25,34,35 (i²
324; ML 72; Fornara no. 134); for the secretary i³ 301.17f. (i² 241.102f.);
303.41f. (i² 243.124f.). An inventory of the year is i³ 302. For the patronymic of Thoukydides see Androtion *FGH* 324 F 57 and *APF*. For the
secretary see Thompson, *Hesperia* 1965, 311 n.5.

Hellenotamias
CHAROPIDES of Skambonidai (IV) *PA* 15534
IG i³ 369.27 (i² 324; ML 72; Fornara no. 134).

Hieromnemon
?HYPERBOLOS son of Antiphanes of Perithoidai (VI) *PA* 13910; *APF* 517
Ar. *Clouds* 624. The scholiast to the passage says that there was no record of
Hyperbolos holding the position in this year and Camon, *GIF* 1963, 49ff.,
argues that the reference came in the revised version of *Clouds*; but cf.
Connor, *New Politicians* 114 n.46. For Aristophanes to have written τῆτες
in a revised, non-performed version seems highly unlikely. See also Roux,
L'amphictionie 24.

Envoys
NEON
A--
--OS

AGAK[LES ?]
IG i³ 75.34f. (i² 87). They were to swear to the alliance with Halieis.

ARISTONYMOS
Thuc. 4.122.1ff. He brought the news of armistice to Brasidas in Chalkidike, refusing to include Skione. He reported to Athens. Envoy is the best categorization I can find.

EPILYKOS son of Teisandros *PA* 4925; *APF* 297
And. 3.29. He was ambassador to Persia (cf. Thuc. 4.50). This is the date I prefer, after Andrewes, *Historia* 1961, 1ff.; also Wade-Gery, *Essays* 207ff.; Meiggs, *Ath. Empire* 134ff. For other suggestions see Raubitschek, *GRBS* 1964, 155ff. (just before 415); Thompson, *Klio* 1971, 119–24 (424–418); Murison, *Phoenix* 1971, 24ff. (425/4); Blamire, *Phoenix* 1975, 21–6 (422/1). Meister, *Ungeschichtlichkeit* 79ff., argues that no treaty was made.

COUNCIL AND ASSEMBLY

The name of the first secretary, in pryt. Hippothontis, is known from IG i³ 369.26 (i² 324; ML 72; Fornara no. 134):
Grammateus
[EPI]L[Y]KOS (? son of Teisandros) *PA* 4925; *APF* 297

(i) IG i³ 36 (i² 25; *LS* no. 12; ML 71; Fornara no. 139) is a decree of pryt. Aigeis concerning the priestess of Athene Nike:
Grammateus
NEOKLEIDES *PA* 10631
Bouleutes epistates
HAGNODEMOS *PA* 136
Proposer
KALLIAS *PA* 7810
The secretary also appears in IG i³ 75 and is restored in IG i³ 74 (for which see below). He has been restored also in IG i² 68 (SEG 10.81), but this is not approved at IG i³ 72, which dates the inscription to ?414. This document, with the secretary Phileas that it exhibits, is best placed in the appendix to this Section. Of the more recent literature see Thompson, *Klio* 1971, 122; Bradeen and McGregor, *Studies* 90.

(ii) IG i³ 74 (i² 145; Walbank no. 46) is a decree restored to the prytany of Aigeis (Walbank is somewhat more cautious) giving proxeny to Sotimos of Herakleia or Herakleion.

(iii) IG i³ 75 (i² 87) is another decree of pryt. Aigeis concerning the treaty with Halieis:
Proposer
LACHES (son of Melanopos of Aixone) (VII) *PA* 9019

(iv) IG i³ 61 (i² 57; ML 65; Fornara no. 128) will have been a decree of pryt. Akamantis (eighth prytany; IG i³ 369.32f.) collecting together the decrees concerning Methone:

Grammateus

PHAINIPPOS son of Phrynichos *PA* 13979

Phainippos also appears in IG i³ 73 and Thuc. 4.118.11 (on which see below).

(v) The first part of IG i³ 73 (i² 70; Walbank no. 45) is an undated decree seemingly granting proxeny to Potamodoros, his son and others of Orchomenos:

Proposer

ARCH[ESTRATOS] ?*PA* 2411

In fact, I do not think we can believe with any confidence the identity of this man with the son of Lykomedes, as suggested at *PA*. There follows a

(vi) decree restored to pryt. Akamantis of this year giving further honours, wherein Archestratos proposes a rider:

Bouleutes epistates

AGA . . . ? . . .

Proposer

[HE]RMODOROS

(vii) IG i³ 227 (ii² 8; ML 70; Walbank no. 47) is a probouleumatic decree possibly of pryt. Pandionis granting proxeny to Herakleides of Klazomenai (now made certain by the association with IG ii² 65: Walbank, *ZPE* 51 (1983), 183–4 (SEG 32.10)):

Grammateus

S--

Bouleutes epistates

[N]EOKLEIDES ?*PA* 10631

Proposer

THOUKYDIDE[S] *PA* 7264

The date has been disputed; see the apparatus to IG i³; Henry, *CSCA* 1978, 86; SEG 30.13. We cannot be confident enough to restore the name Simon for the secretary (= *PA* 12686).

Thuc. 4.117ff. deals with the making of an armistice between the Spartans

(viii) and Athenians. This includes an Athenian decree of 14 Elaphebolion and of pryt. Akamantis:

Bouleutes epistates

NIKIADES *PA* 10765

Proposer

LACHES (son of Melanopos of Aixone) (VII) *PA* 9019

Thuc. 4.122 records Athenian reaction to the report of Aristonymos (above
(ix) envoys) which led to a decree to recapture Skione and execute its
inhabitants:
Proposer
KLEON son of Kleainetos of Kydathenaion (III) *PA* 8674; *APF* 318ff.

Erechtheis was sixth or seventh prytany: IG i³ 369.31.

423/2 (Ol. 89.2)

Archon
AMEINIAS *PA* 670
Diod. 12.72.1; Athenaios 5.218d; hyp. Ar. *Clouds* A 6 (Koster); schol. Ar.
Clouds 31c, 549 (Androtion *FGH* 324 F 40); hyp. i Ar. *Wasps*; schol. Lucian
Tim. 30; IG i³ 369.[37], [56] (i² 324; ML 72; Fornara no. 134); ii²
2318.[108].

Strategoi
NIKIAS son of Nikeratos of Kydantidai (II) *PA* 10808; *APF* 403f.
NIKOSTRATOS son of Dieitrephes of Skambonidai (IV) *PA* 11011
Thuc. 4.129.2ff.; Diod. 12.72.8ff.; Plut. *Nik.* 6.4; cf. IG i³ 369. [56f.] with
apparatus (i² 324; ML 72; Fornara no. 134). See Fornara, *Generals* 61. In
summer 423 they were in command against Mende and Skione, the former
being captured, the latter blockaded.

KLEON son of Kleainetos of Kydathenaion (III) *PA* 8674; *APF* 318ff.
Thuc. 5.2f.; Diod. 12.73.2f. (422/1); Suda *s.v.* Κλέων. See Fornara, *Generals* 61f. He was sent out to Chalkidike in summer 422 and took Torone,
whence he set out for Amphipolis. Some of this may have spread into
422/1.

(? EURYMEDON son of Thoukles) of Myrrhinous (III) *PA* 5973; *APF* 334
IG i³ 369.38 (i² 324; ML 72; Fornara no. 134). See Lang, *Hesperia* 1965,
235. The demotic is in the inscription. For the association with
Eurymedon see 427/6.

Note: See also the envoy Amynias and the appendix to this Section on
Sophokles.

Tamiai of Athene
TIMOKLES of Eitea (V) *PA* 13733
  Grammateus
  TELESTES son of Theognis of Hagnous (V) *PA* 13546; *APF* 220
IG i³ 302.29f. (i² 242.113f.); 303.39f., 48 (i² 243.122f., 131); for Timokles i³
369.36, [46f.], 52 (i² 324; ML 72; Fornara no. 134). An inventory of the
year is i³ 303.

Tamias of the other gods
GORGOINOS son of Oineides of Ikarion (II) *PA* 3082
IG i³ 369.55f.,76,77 (i² 324; ML 72; Fornara no. 134).

Envoys
PHAIAX son of Erasistratos of Acharnai (VI) *PA* 13921; *APF* 521f.
Thuc. 5.4f.; cf. And. 4.41. Sent to Sicily and Italy, he won over Kamarina and Akragas to oppose Syracuse, but not Gela. On his way back he conducted negotiations with some cities and made arrangements with Lokrian settlers. On And. 4 see Burn, *CQ* 1954, 138–42.

AMYNIAS son of Pronapes (? of Prasiai) (III) *PA* 737; *APF* 471
Ar. *Wasps* 1271ff. with schol. on 1271 (Eupolis F 209 Edmonds, with schol. Ar. *Clouds* 691). MacDowell, *CQ* 1965, 50 (cf. *Wasps* 139), argues for a generalship; this, though possible, seems unlikely. Amynias was ambassador to Pharsalos in Thessaly. The deme comes from the identification of the father suggested by Raubitschek, *DAA* 207, 463 (with references; cf. *APF*).

Theoroi
?ANDROKLES of Pithos (VII) *PA* 870
?KLEISTHENES son of Sibyrtios *PA* 8525
Ar. *Wasps* 1187 with MacDowell's commentary 284f. However, I am not confident as to the actuality of their sacred embassy.

Note: MacDowell, *Wasps* 138ff., argues that the men mentioned at *Wasps* 74–82 should all be officials of this year. They include Nikostratos and Amynias, who are dealt with above; also a SOSIAS (son of Pythis: *PA* 13177; cf. the unplaced hellenotamias of the name in the appendix to Section IV), although it is suspected that the name is an intrusion, perhaps replacing Nikias; and finally a DERKYLOS (*PA* 3247).
   The credentials for the inclusion of the synegoros -- son of Chaireas (*PA* 15091), on whom see MacDowell, *Wasps* 226f., might depend upon what sort of synegoros he was.

COUNCIL AND ASSEMBLY

The first secretary, of pryt. Akamantis, is found at IG i³ 369.37, [57] (i² 324; ML 72; Fornara no. 134):
Grammateus
DEMETRIOS of Kollytos (II) *PA* 3413

422/1 (Ol. 89.3)

Archon
ALKAIOS *PA* 572

Thuc. 5.19.1, 25.1; Androtion *FGH* 324 F 40; Philochoros *FGH* 328 F 131; Athenaios 5.218b,d; hyp. i Ar. *Peace*; schol. Aisch. 2.31; IG i³ [391] (i² 311); ii² 2318.120; SEG 28.[15] (but see SEG 30.21: 430–426). *ATL* II.33 List 33 has now been shifted to 418/17 (IG i³ 287 after Meritt and McGregor, *Phoenix* 1967, 85f.).

Strategoi

KLEON son of Kleainetos of Kydathenaion (III) *PA* 8674; *APF* 318ff.
Thuc. 5.6ff.; Androtion *FGH* 324 F 40; Diod. 12.74.1f.; Plut. *Nik.* 9.2f.; Paus. 1.29.13; Athenaios 5.215d; anon. *vita Thuc.* 3; schol. Aisch. 2.31; schol. Ar. *Peace* 283, 284; Suda *s.vv.* Βρασίδας, Κλέων.

During summer 422 he conducted diplomatic moves from Eion, failed to take Stagiros, took Galepsos, and then lost his life at the battle around Amphipolis.

NIKIAS son of Nikeratos of Kydantidai (II) *PA* 10808; *APF* 403f.
?LACHES son of Melanopos of Aixone (VII) *PA* 9019
?EUTHYDEMOS son of Eudemos *PA* 5521
Thuc. 5.19.2, 24.1. Nikias and Laches are associated in bringing about the treaty at Thuc. 5.43.2 (see 5.16.1 for Nikias). The three appear together among those who took the oath for peace and alliance, and I share the inference that they were selected from the generals (Andrewes and Lewis, *JHS* 1957, 180), as well as the further conclusion that Lamachos and Demosthenes, being separated from these three, were not chosen *qua* generals (which is not to rule out the possibility that they *could* have been generals). Generalships for Prokles and Pythodoros, who follow this trio in the lists, are possible if (and why not?) the generals were not listed in tribal order, but the explanation of Andrewes and Lewis (see further below) seems preferable. In any event, that Nikias was general is all but certain (cf. also Plut. *Nik.* 9f.).

Tamiai of Athene
Grammateus
PRESBIAS son of Semias of Phegous (I) *PA* 12185; *APF* 66f.
IG i³ 303.40 (i² 243.123); 325.3f., 10f. (i² 264.56f.,63f.); 351.2 (i² 280.71; Fornara no. 141); 352.28f. (i² 281.95f.). Inventories of the year are i³ 325 and 351.

Epistatai of Eleusis
Grammateus
PHILOSTRATOS of Kydathenaion (III) *PA* 14736
IG i³ 391.[2], 9f. (i² 311.3, 10f.).

Oath takers
The following took the oaths for peace and alliance. The reconstruction of Andrewes and Lewis (*JHS* 1957, 177–80) has Lampon and Isthm(i)onikos as religious officials, Nikias, Laches and Euthydemos as generals (*qq.v.*),

then ten chosen commissioners, with Lamachos and Demosthenes added to make up the number. Deme/tribe attributions were made so as to demonstrate tribal order, which could be correct, but other possibilities are noted. The names come from Thuc. 5.19.2, 24.1.

LAMPON *PA* 8996

ISTHM(I)ONIKOS *PA* 7689 = ?7690; *APF* 360

NIKIAS son of Nikeratos of Kydantidai (II) *PA* 10808; *APF* 403f.

LACHES son of Melanopos of Aixone (VII) *PA* 9019

EUTHYDEMOS son of Eudemos *PA* 5521

PROKLES (of ?Euonymon (I) or ?Kephisia (I)) *PA* 12206

PYTHODOROS (? son of Epizelos of Halai (II)) *PA* 12402 = ?12410; *APF* 481

HAGNON son of Nikias of Steiria (III) *PA* 171; *APF* 227f.

MYRTILOS (? son of Lysis) (IV)) *PA* 10497

THRASYKLES (? of tribe V) *PA* 7317

THEOGENES (?THEAGENES) (? of Acharnai (VI)) *PA* 6703

ARISTOKRATES (? son of Skellias ? of Trinemeia (VII)) *PA* 1904; *APF* 56f.

IOLKIOS (? of tribe VIII) *PA* 7739

TIMOKRATES (? of tribe IX) *PA* 13746

LEON (? of tribe X) *PA* 9100 (cf. 439/8 strategos)

LAMACHOS son of Xenophanes of Oe (VI) *PA* 8981

DEMOSTHENES son of Alkisthenes of Aphidna (IX) *PA* 3585; *APF* 112f.

COUNCIL AND ASSEMBLY

(i) IG i³ 391.7 (i² 311.8) tells us who was first secretary (for whom cf. also SEG 25.43b.2). He appears in IG i³ 79 (i² 81), a decree of pryt. Aigeis concerning the building of a bridge near Eleusis:

Grammateus

PREPIS son of Eupheros *PA* 12184

Bouleutes epistates

PATROKLES *PA* 11696

Proposer

THEAIOS *PA* 6642

For the date see Meritt and McGregor, *Phoenix* 1967, 158ff. The deme Xypete (VII) has been suggested for Prepis: Raubitschek, *DAA* 229; Mattingly, *BCH* 1968, 476.

(ii) IG i³76 (i² 90) is the remains of a decree concerning a treaty with the Bottiaians:

Proposer

EUKRATES

(iii) IG i³ 77 (i² 64) is a tribute assessment.

IG i³ 78 will be found in the appendix to this section.

(iv) Thuc. 5.14ff. records the making of peace and alliance, the peace to be effective from 25 Elaphebolion.
See Addenda p. 429.

421/20 (Ol. 89.4)

Archon
ARISTION *PA* 1732
Diod. 12.75.1 (Ariston); Athenaios 5.216d,f, 218d; schol. Aisch. 2.175; IG i³ 80 (i² 82; Walbank no. 49); 82 (i² 84; *LS* 13); 391.8 (i² 311.9); 472.5, 11 (i² 370); 285 (*ATL* 11.33 List 34); ?*Insc. Délos* 91.[14].

Strategos
NIKIAS son of Nikeratos of Kydantidai (II) *PA* 10808; *APF* 403f.
Plut. *Nik.* 10.3ff. Fornara, *Generals* 62, seems correct in arguing for the generalship, though Plutarch does not call him general.

Tamiai of Athene
EUPHEMOS of Kollytos (II) *PA* 6042; *APF* 206
Grammateus
NIKEAS son of Euthykles of Halimous (IV) *PA* 10728
IG i³ 325.4f. (i² 264.57f.); 326.14f.,23f. (i² 265.66f.,75f.); 351.4f. (i² 280.72f.; Fornara no. 141); 352.26f. (i² 281.93f.); for Nikeas i³ 327.28 (i² 266.80); 353.52 (i² 282.109). Inventories of the year are i³ 326 and 352.

Tamiai of the other gods
ST[RATOKL]ES of Kephale (V)
ARISTOPHON of Athmonon (VII)
LYSIMACHOS of Kedoi (I)
THOUDOROS of Gargettos (II)
ANTIMACHOS of Oa (III) *PA* 1131
XENOK[LEIDES] or XENOK[LEITOS] of Phrearrhioi (IV)
ONOMAKLES of Perithoidai (VI)
NIKOBOULOS of Elaious (VIII)
XENOPHON of Rhamnous (IX)
[SO]SISTRATOS or [LY]SISTRATOS of Aigilia (X) *PA* 13290
Grammateus
. . . . .¹¹. . . . . of Halai (II or VII)
IG i³ 472.9ff. (i² 370.7ff.). See Thompson, *Hesperia* 1965, 154f.

Hellenotamiai
-- of Pergase or Agryle (I)
HEDYLOS of Philaidai (II)
PRAXIBOU[L]OS of Paiania (III)
--A]RCHIDES of Kephale (V)
ERGAMENES of Acharnai (VI) *PA* 5046
ARISTOKRATES of Phaleron (IX) *PA* 1925; *APF* 60
ARISTOTELES (? of Thorai) (X)

IG i³ 285 (*ATL* 11.33 List 34; SEG 25.43). Aristoteles' deme is by association with the general of 426/5 (cf. 431/3); perhaps this is a little adventur-
ous, but the tribe will be correct.

Epistatai of statues for the Hephaisteion
APOLEXIS son of Smikythos of Iphistiadai (v)
CHAIREAS son of Epi[gon]os of Hagnous (v) *PA* 15099
PEISANDROS son of Glauketes of Acharnai (VI) *PA* 11770
    Grammateus
    O[IKO]TELES son of Geisias of Lamptrai (I)
IG i³ 472.2ff. (i² 370). For Peisandros see Woodhead, *AJPh* 1954, 133.

Epistatai of Eleusis
    Grammateus
    PHILOSTRATOS of Kydathenaion (III) *PA* 14736
IG i³ 391.9 (i² 311.10). See 422/1.

Hieropoios at Eleusis
THEOXENOS of Kephale (v) *PA* 6992
IG i³ 391.11 (i² 311.12).

COUNCIL AND ASSEMBLY

The first secretary is restored at IG i³ 285 (*ATL* 11.33 List 34; SEG 25.43a)
and found at i³ 472.5 (i² 370):
Grammateus
MENEKLES of Anaphlystos (X)

(i) IG i³ 80 (i² 82; Walbank no. 49) is a proxeny decree of pryt. Hippothontis
for Asteas of Aleia:
Grammateus
PROKLES son of Atarbos of Euonymon (I) *PA* 12226
Bouleutes epistates
TIMIAS *PA* 13657
Proposer
THRASYKLES *PA* 7317

(ii) IG i³ 82 (i² 84; *LS* no. 13) is a probouleumatic decree of the same prytany
concerning the Hephaistia:
Proposer
HYPE[RBOLOS ?] (son of Antiphanes of Perithoidai) (VI) *PA* 13910; *APF*
517
The reason for restoring Hyperbolos is that he was possibly a bouleutes
this year; see IG i³ apparatus and Edmonds on Plato com. F 166–7.

(iii) IG i³ 81 (i² 83; Walbank no. 48) is a proxeny decree for Polystratos (? of
Phleious) and perhaps his brother; it is restored as probouleumatic.

420/19 (Ol. 90.1)

Archon
ASTYPHILOS of Kydantidai (II) *PA* 2661
MP A 61; Diod. 12.77.1 (Aristophilos or Aristophylos); Athenaios 5.218d;
IG i³ 391.14f. (i² 311.15f.); 472.12 (i² 370.10); ii² 2319.[70]; 4960.[12]
(SEG 25.226.19f.).

Strategoi
?NIKIAS son of Nikeratos of Kydantidai (II) *PA* 10808; *APF* 403f.
ALKIBIADES son of Kleinias of Skambonidai (IV) *PA* 600; *APF* 9ff.
Plut. *Nik.* 10.3ff., *Alk.* 15.1. See Fornara, *Generals* 62. If the first passage
of Plutarch implies a generalship for Nikias in 421/20 (*q.v.*), I believe it
must imply one in this year also. Alkibiades created an alliance with Argos,
Mantineia and Elis (see below).

Tamiai of Athene
EUPHILETOS of Kephisia (I) *PA* 6067; *APF* 206
Grammateus
EPIGENES son of Lysandros of Aigilia (X) *PA* 4788
IG i³ 326.15f. (i² 265.67f.); 327.25f. (i² 266.77f.); 352.27f. (i² 281.94f.);
353.49f, (i² 282.106f.); 473.4ff. (i² 379); for Epigenes i³ 328.40 (i² 267.91);
354.73 (i² 283.130). Inventories of the year are i³ 327 and 353.

Tamiai of the other gods
NAUKLES of Melite (VII) *PA* 10523
CHARMIDES of Lamptrai (I) *PA* 15514
. . . . ? . . . . of Kolonai (IV)
CHIONIS of Prospalta (V)
LYSISTRATOS of Kothokidai (VI)
KTESONIDES of Prasiai (III) *PA* 8917
AUTOKLES of Alopeke (X) *PA* 2723
. . . . STRATOS of Halai (II)
BOUTALION of Marathon (IX)
Grammateus
KALLIPPIDES of Euonymon (I)
IG i³ 472.13ff. (i² 370.11ff.). On the deme of the unknown from Kolonai
see Thompson, *Hesperia* 1965, 155. Only nine were listed.

Epistatai of processional vessels
EUK[L]EIDES of Ankyle (II) *PA* 5683
[?ARIST]OKLES of Kerameis (V) *PA* 1866
IG i³ 473.7ff. (i² 379). Aristokles is arbitrary and not in IG i³

Epistatai of Eleusis
Grammateus
PHILOSTRATOS of Kydathenaion (III) *PA* 14736
IG i³ 391.16 (i² 311.17). See 422/1.

Hieropoios at Eleusis
DEMOKRITOS of Alopeke (X) *PA* 3548
IG i³ 391.18 (i² 311.19).

Envoy
NIKIAS son of Nikeratos of Kydantidai (II) *PA* 10808; *APF* 403f.
Thuc. 5.46.2ff. Whether or not he was general, he was one of a number sent to Sparta with requirements and other instructions concerning complaints. At his request the Spartans renewed the oaths.

COUNCIL AND ASSEMBLY

(i) IG i³ 83 is the alliance with Argos, Mantineia and Elis; see above generals and Thuc. 5.42ff.; Plut. *Mor.* 351b. Thucydides tells of the Spartan envoys coming before the council and of subsequent assemblies at which
(ii) Alkibiades and Nikias spoke; the decision was to send the embassy to Sparta:
Proposer
NIKIAS son of Nikeratos of Kydantidai (II) *PA* 10808; *APF* 403f.
See also Plut. *Nik.* 10.3ff., *Alk.* 14f.

419/18 (Ol. 90.2)

Archon
ARCHIAS *PA* 2447
Diod. 12.78.1; IG i³ 391.21f. (i² 311.22f.); 472.[15] (i² 370.13); ii² 2319.77; 4960.13 (SEG 25.226.20); ?i³ [177] (ii² 60; Walbank no. 63); ? *Insc. Délos* 91.[14]

Strategos
ALKIBIADES son of Kleinias of Skambonidai (IV) *PA* 600; *APF* 9ff.
Thuc. 5.52.2, 55.4; Isok, 16.15; Diod. 12.78.1ff.; Plut. *Alk.* 15.3. Some of this could refer to 420/19. In summer 419 he went to the Peloponnese, where he was active, and went home after helping the Argives against Epidauros.

Tamiai of Athene
LYKON of Prasiai (III) *PA* 9274
  Grammateus
  LYSIDIKOS of Gargettos (II) *PA* 9388
IG i³ 327.26f. (i² 266.78f.); 328.37f, (i² 267.88f.); 353.50f. (i² 282.107f.); 354.72 (i² 283.129). The actual inventories of the year are i³ 304, 328 and 354.

Epistatai of Eleusis
  Grammateus
PHILOSTRATOS of Kydathenaion (III) *PA* 14736

IG i³ 391.[23] (i² 311.24).

COUNCIL AND ASSEMBLY

Thuc, 5.56 tells how the Argives complained at Athens of Spartan movements. The Athenians decided to add to the inscription of the treaty 'the Spartans have not kept their oaths':
Proposer
ALKIBIADES son of Kleinias of Skambonidai (IV) *PA* 600; *APF* 9ff.

418/17 (Ol. 90.3)

Archon
ANTIPHON of Skambonidai (IV) *PA* 1277
Diod. 12.80.1; IG i³ 84 (i² 94; *LS* no. 14); 85.12 (i² 95; SEG 12.32); [287] (*ATL* II.33 List 33; Fornara no. 142; cf. Meritt and McGregor, *Phoenix* 1967, 85f.; ML 75); [370] (i² 302; ML 77; Fornara no. 144); 472.16 (i² 370.14); ii² 2319.84; 4960.16f. (SEG 25.226.23f.). See also under the archons of 458/7 and 451/50.

Strategoi
LACHES son of Melanopos of Aixone (VII) *PA* 9019
NIKOSTRATOS son of Dieitrephes of Skambonidai (IV) *PA* 11011
Thuc. 5.61f.,65f.,69ff.; Androtion *FGH* 324 F 41; Diod. 12.79 (419/18); cf. Eupolis F 110B (Edmonds). In summer 418 they went to the Peloponnese, joined in the successful siege of Orchomenos in Arkadia and then lost their lives in the battle of Mantineia.

DEMOSTHENES son of Alkisthenes of Aphidna (IX) *PA* 3585; *APF* 112f.
Thuc. 5.80.3; IG i³ 370.6 (i² 302; ML 77; Fornara no. 144). He was sent in winter to oversee the withdrawal from Epidauros.

NIKIAS son of Nikeratos of Kydantidai (II) *PA* 10808; *APF* 403f.
Diod. 12.80.5; IG i³ 370.20f. (i² 302.19f.; ML 77; Fornara no. 144). Diodoros mentions capture of Kythera and Nisaia, but is not to be trusted.

EUTHYDEMOS son of Eudemos *PA* 5521
IG i³ 370.9 (i² 302; ML 77; Fornara no. 144). General to Thrace.

[?ALKIBIADES (son of Kleinias) of Skambonidai] (IV) *PA* 600; *APF* 9ff.
AUTOKLES (son of Tolmaios) of Anaphlystos (X) *PA* 2724 = ?2717; *APF* 74
KAL[LISTR]ATOS son of Empedos of Oe (VI) *PA* 8142 = ?8125
K[LEOMEDES] (son of Lykomedes of Phlya) (VII) *PA* 8598; *APF* 347
IG i³ 370.17,21 (i² 302.16,20; ML 77; Fornara no. 144). See Fornara, *Generals* 62f. ML will not be committed to restoring Alkibiades and he is

144

only in the apparatus to IG i³; I do not believe that Thuc. 5.61.2 and Diod. 12.79.1 are a conclusive bar to it (cf. Gomme-Andrewes-Dover, *Comm. Thuc.* IV.88). Kallistratos is much safer (see the secretary of 429/8). He is associated with Nikias in preparations for an expedition to the north (see *Comm. Thuc.* IV.154). That the third general was Kleomedes is ventured in ML (cf. *APF*).

Tamiai of Athene
PYTHODOROS (son of Epizelos) of Halai (II) *PA* 12402 = 12410; *APF* 481
CHARINOS son of Aleximachos of Pelekes (IV) *PA* 15435 = 15455
Grammateus
PHORMION son of Aristion of Kydathenaion (III) *PA* 14956
For Pythodoros and the secretary IG i³ 305.3f. (i² 244.134f.) ; 329.2f. (i² 268.102f.; ML 76; Fornara no. 143); 370.3f.,8 (i² 302; ML 77; Fornara no. 144); for Charinos and the secretary i³ 328.38f. (i² 267. 89f.); 354.72f. (i² 283.129f.); for Phormion i³ 306.26 (i² 245.156); 330.19 (i² 269.119). See Thompson, *Hesperia* 1970, 59f.; Develin, *Klio* 1986, 73f. Inventories of the year are i³ 305 and 329.

Tamiai of the other gods
[PH]ILYLLOS of Eleusis (VIII) *PA* 14797
ANTIPHANIDES of Euonymon (I) *PA* 1251
. . .⁶. . . ES of Kydantidai (II)
EUTHYKRATES of Kydathenaion (III)
TEISIKRATES of Potamos (IV)
[S]OSICHIOS of Hagnous (V) *PA* 13301
PASIMENES of Ptelea or Perithoidai (VI) *PA* 11664
-- of Phlya (VII)
DIOPHANTOS of Aphidna (IX)
CHAIRI[KLE]S of Pallene (X)
Grammateus
[E]UBOULOS of Erchia (II) *PA* 5357
IG i³ 472.17ff. (i² 370.15ff.). For restorations see Thompson, *Hesperia* 1965, 155f. But for Pasimenes IG i³ (Thompson again) now reads pi as the first letter of the deme, which leaves only the possibilities mentioned.

Hellenotamiai
-- of Pergase (I)
MNESITHEO[S] (? of Araphen) (II)
-- of Eupyridai (IV)
AISCHINES of Perithoidai (VI)
-- of Aixone (VII)
. . . .⁸. . . . of Thymaitadai (VIII)
[ER]GOKLES son of Aristeides of Besa (X) *PA* 5055
Grammateus
ANT--

Paredros

[HI]EROKLES son of Archestratos of Athmonon (VII) *PA* 7485
IG i³ 287 (*ATL* II.33 List 33; ML 75; Fornara no. 142; for date Meritt and
McGregor, *Phoenix* 1967, 85f.); for Ergokles and the paredros i³ 370.[4f.],
11f., 19f. (i² 302; ML 77; Fornara no. 144), this also for the deme Aixone.

Envoy

ALKIBIADES son of Kleinias of Skambonidai (IV) *PA* 600; *APF* 9ff.
Thuc. 5.61.2; Diod. 12.79.1. Present as such at Argos (cf. strategoi). He
won over allies and is found at Argos again at Thuc. 5.76.3.

COUNCIL AND ASSEMBLY

The first secretary is found at IG i³ 287 (*ATL* II.33 List 33; ML 75;
Fornara no. 142; see above for date); 472.16 (i² 370.14):
Grammateus
. . . ? . . . of Aphidna (IX)

(i) IG i³ 84 (i² 94; *LS* no. 14) is a probouleumatic decree of pryt. Pandionis
concerning the precinct of Neleus, Basile and Kodros:
Grammateus
ARISTOXENOS *PA* 2042
Bouleutes epistates
ANTIOCHIDES *PA* 1150
Proposer
ADOUSIOS *PA* 207
Pandionis was ninth prytany and Aigeis tenth; see i³ 84.19 and the note to
line 2.

(ii) IG i³ 85 (i² 95) seems to have been an honorary decree, seemingly also in the
ninth prytany (but see SEG 29.14):
Proposer
HYPERBOLOS (son of Antiphanes of Perithoidai) (VI) *PA* 13910; *APF* 517

417/16 (Ol. 90.4)

Archon
EUPHEMOS *PA* 6034
Diod. 12.81.1; Athenaios 5.216f–217b; IG i³ 86 (i² 96); 370.[24] (i² 302.23;
ML 77; Fornara no. 144); 472.[20] (i² 370.18); ii² 4960.[18] (SEG
25.226.25).

Strategoi
NIKIAS son of Nikeratos of Kydantidai (II) *PA* 10808; *APF* 403f.
Thuc. 5.83.4. He was set to command an expedition to Chalkidike and
Amphipolis which had to be abandoned.

ALKIBIADES son of Kleinias of Skambonidai (IV) *PA* 600; *APF* 9ff.
Thuc. 5.84.1; Diod. 12.81.2f.; Plut. *Alk.* 15.2f. He went in summer 416 to
Argos to expel pro-Spartans.

KLEOMEDES son of Lykomedes of Phlya (VII) *PA* 8598; *APF* 347
TEISIAS son of Teisimachos of Kephale (V) *PA* 13479; *APF* 501ff.
Thuc. 5.84.3, 114; IG i³ 370.29f., [32] (i² 302; ML 77; Fornara no. 144).
Generals against Melos in summer 416. When the Melians would not
submit, they blockaded the place and went home with the bulk of the
forces.

Paredros?
RHINON son of Charikles of Paiania (III) *PA* 12532; *APF* 67
IG i³ 370.26f. (i² 302; ML 77; Fornara no. 144). See Fornara, *Generals* 63. A
generalship is possible, but unlikely, I think, given the run of the
inscription. For the suggestion of paredros cf. the apparatus to IG i³.

Tamiai of Athene
ANAXIKRATES of Lamptrai (I) *PA* 811
Grammateus
EUXENOS son of Euphanes of Prospalta (V) *PA* 5899
IG i³ 305.5f. (i² 244.136f.); 306.22f. (i² 245.152f.); 329.4f. (i² 268.104f.; ML
76; Fornara no. 143); 330.16f. (i² 269.116f.); 370.25f. (i² 302; ML 77;
Fornara no. 144); for Euxenos i³ 307.46f. (i² 246.175f.); 331.34 (i² 270.134).
Inventories of the year are i³ 306 and 330.

Hellenotamiai
--os of Auridai (VIII)
TIMARCHOS of Pallene (X) *PA* 13633
IG i³ 370.31f. (i² 302; ML 77; Fornara no. 144).

COUNCIL AND ASSEMBLY

IG i³ 86 (i² 96) is a decree of pryt. Aiantis concerning the treaty with Argos:
Grammateus
. .ODOROS [? of Acharnai (VI) or ? Amphitrope (X)]
For the deme see Meritt, *Hesperia* 1945, 123. There is no proposer, unless
the letters SY- began a name; the restoration in IG i³ is not of a name and the
bill could originate from syngrapheis; see the apparatus in i³.

416/15 (Ol. 91.1)

Archon
ARIMNESTOS *PA* 1618
Isaios 6.14; Diod. 12.82.1 (Aristomnetos; Aristomnestos); hyp. ii Ar.

Birds; Hesychios *s.v.* ʿΕρμοκοπίδαι; IG i³ [289] (*ATL* II.36 List 39); 370.[36] (i² 302; ML 77; Fornara no. 144); 472.[20] (i² 370.18); ii² 4960 apparatus *supra* 20; *?Insc. Délos* 91.[14]. See the apparatus of IG i³ 12 against restoration in that text.

Strategoi
KLEOMEDES son of Lykomedes of Phlya (VII) *PA* 8598; *APF* 347
TEISIAS son of Teisimachos of Kephale (V) *PA* 13479; *APF* 501ff.
Thuc. 5.114. See 416/15 and Fornara, *Generals* 63; Gomme-Andrewes-Dover, *Comm. Thuc.* IV.189. That they remained generals at Melos is further strengthened by the arguments rehearsed in *APF*.

PHILOKRATES son of Demeas *PA* 14585
Thuc. 5.116.3f. He brought another force to Melos in winter and the surrender was secured. Thucydides does not call him general, but the implication is likely.

ALKIBIADES son of Kleinias of Skambonidai (IV) *PA* 600; *APF* 9ff.
NIKIAS son of Nikeratos of Kydantidai (II) *PA* 10808; *APF* 403f.
LAMACHOS son of Xenophanes of Oe (VI) *PA* 8981
Thuc. 6.8.2ff., 42ff.; Isok. 16.7 (Alkibiades); Diod. 12.84.3; Justin 4.4.3; Plut. *Nik.* 12.3f., 14.1, *Alk.* 18.1f.; schol. Ar. *Acharn.* 258; schol. Thuc. 6.9.1 (Nikias); IG i³ 370.49ff. (Alkibiades and Lamachos restored; i² 302; ML 77; Fornara no. 144).
   See Fornara, *Generals* 63f. Generals to Sicily, they travelled via Corcyra to Rhegion. That they were generals in this year is made certain by the inscription. They were made *autokratores*, but as they were evidently chosen for Sicily after the elections for 415/14, they were not in this year or the next apart from the regularly elected generals. Whether they were so separated in the next years will be considered under 414/13.

Paredros ?
ANTIMACHOS of Hermos (V) *PA* 1123; *APF* 37
IG i³ 370.53,55,57 (i² 302.41,43,45,47; ML 77; Fornara no. 144). The inscription does not specify the position, but this suggestion seems likely.

Tamiai of Athene
DEXITHEOS of Phlya (VII) or Thria (VI) *PA* 3221
Grammateus
LYSIKLES son of Drakontides of Bate (II) *PA* 9432; *APF* 170
IG i³ 306.24f. (i² 245.154f.); 307.43f. (i² 246.172f.); 330.18 (i² 269.118); 331.31f. (i² 270.131f.); 370.37f. (i² 302; ML 77; Fornara no. 144); for Lysikles i³ 308.67 (i² 247.195); 332.49 (i² 271.149). See Thompson, *Hesperia* 1965, 154, 309. Inventories of the year are i³ 307 and 331.

Hellenotamiai
-- son of --es of Anagyrous (I)
-- son of --os of Skambonidai (IV)

-- of Xypete (VII)
-- of Eroiadai (X)
Grammateus
. . .NIO--
IG i³ 289 (*ATL* II.36 List 39 and p. 125).

COUNCIL AND ASSEMBLY

The first secretary is found at IG i³ 289 (*ATL* II.36 List 39) and restored at i³ 370.36 (i² 302; ML 77; Fornara no. 144):
Grammateus
AR . . .⁶. . .
The secretary Archikles (i³ 91; 92) would fit, but see the appendix to this Section.

(i) Thuc. 6.6 tells of the arguments of the Egestaians and their supporters in assemblies which led to a decision to send an embassy to Egesta.

The debate on the Sicilian expedition is recorded by Thuc. 6.8ff.; Plut.
(ii) *Nik*.12, *Alk*. 17f. On receipt of information from Egesta, the force and generals were voted. Five days later another assembly further considered the forces and supplies and was addressed by Nikias and Alkibiades. Nikias spoke again and unexpectedly found the Athenians convinced that a larger force was necessary. Nikias was then forced to be more specific and the
(iii) Athenians voted full powers to the generals to arrange the expedition; Plutarch names the proposer:
Proposer
DEMOSTRATOS *PA* 3611; *APF* 105f.
See *APF* for possible demes.

(iv) Connected with this could well be the decrees regarding the Sicilian expedition found at IG i³ 93 (i² 98/99; ML 78; Fornara no. 146).

The affair of the Hermokopidai, which involved Alkibiades, entailed speeches in the assembly: Thuc. 6.28; Plut. *Alk*. 19. And. 1.11 mentions an assembly just before the generals left for Sicily at which there spoke Pythonikos.

415/14 (Ol. 91.2)

Archon
CHARIAS *PA* 15324
Philochoros *FGH* 328 F 134 (Chabrias; Fornara no. 147C); Diod. 13.2.1 (Chabrias); hyp. i, ii Ar. *Birds* (Chabrias); schol. Ar. *Ploutos* 179 (Chabrias); IG i³ 95 (Walbank no. 69); 370.[61] (i² 302.51; ML 77; Fornara no. 144); i² 770 a.3; ii² 4960.[21] (SEG 25.226.32); ?i³ [177] (ii² 60; Walbank no. 63).

Strategoi

NIKIAS son of Nikeratos of Kydantidai (II) *PA* 10808; *APF* 403f.
ALKIBIADES son of Kleinias of Skambonidai (IV) *PA* 600; *APF* 9ff.
LAMACHOS son of Xenophanes of Oe (VI) *PA* 8981
Thuc. 6.46.5ff., 61, 62ff., 74, 88.3ff., 94, 96ff.; And. 1.11; Isok. 6.15
(Alkibiades); Nepos *Alc.* 3.1; Diod. 13.2ff., 14.5.5; Front. *Strat.* 3.2.6, 6.6
(Alkibiades); Plut. *Nik.* 14ff., *Aik.* 20ff., *Comp. Nik. and Crassus* 3.5, *Mor.*
802d; Justin 4.4.3ff.; Polyainos 1.39.2 (Nikias), 40.4ff. (Alkibiades); Suda
s.vv. 'Ἀλκιβιάδης, Νικίας, Πάραλος ἢ Σαλαμινία, Πάραλοι (Alkibiades),
Παραφρυκτωρόμενος, Φρυκτός (Lamachos); Photios *s.v.* Πάραλοι
(Alkibiades).

See Fornara, *Generals* 64; for their status see 416/15. In Sicily Alkibiades
won the strategic debate and sought support of Sicilian towns and
reconnoitred. After he escaped to avoid return to Athens and prosecution,
other diplomatic and military efforts were mounted, a success being
recorded before Syracuse and later Epipolai being taken.

TELEPHONOS
IG i³ 370.63 (i² 302.53; ML 77; Fornara no. 144). His assignment is
unknown.

Tamiai of Athene

LEOCHAR[ES ? of Alopeke (X)] *PA* 9166

Grammateus

TELEAS son of Telenikos of Pergase (I) *PA* 13500
IG i³ 307.45f. (i² 246.174f.); 308.64f. (i² 247.192f.); 331.32f. (i² 270.132f.);
332.46f. (i²271.146f.); 370.62 (i² 302.52; ML 77; Fornara no. 144).
Inventories of the year are i³ 308 and 332.

Hellenotamiai

ARISTOKRATES of Euonymon (I) *PA* 1911
PHEREKLEIDES of Peiraieus (VIII) *PA* 14186
PHILOMELOS of Marathon (IX) *PA* 14667; *APF* 548
IG i³ 370.63ff. (i² 302.53ff.; ML 77; Fornara no 144). See SEG 28.16. The
latter two could be paredroi.

Athlothetes

AMEMPTO[S] *PA* 713
IG i³ 370.67 (i² 302.57; ML 77; Fornara no. 144).

Zetetai

DIOGNETOS (? son of Nikeratos of Kydantidai (II)) *PA* 3850 = ?3863; *APF*
405
PEISANDROS son of Glauketes of Acharnai (VI) *PA* 11770
CHARIKLES son of Apollodoros (? of tribe VI) *PA* 15407; *APF* 502f.
And. 1.14, 36. Investigators in the affair of the mutilation of the Herms and
so on. Diognetos' identification is hardly secure; see *APF* and MacDowell,

Mysteries 72, 74f. On whether they were in service in 416/15 see Mac-Dowell 73, 87.

Envoy
EUPHEMOS *PA* 6035
Thuc. 6.81ff. Sent to Kamarina, where he put the Athenian position.

COUNCIL AND ASSEMBLY

The first secretary is found at IG i³ 370.61 (i² 302.51; ML 77; Fornara no. 144):
Grammateus
. . ⁵ . . IDES

(i) IG i³ 95 (Walbank no. 69) is a proxeny decree of pryt. Antiochis, possibly for an Ephesian and his sons:
Grammateus
[KLE]OPHRADES
Bouleutes epistates
. . ⁵ . . ADES
Proposer
[K]ALLISTHENES ? = *PA* 8088
Prytanies of the year are known from IG i³ 370.64ff.: 2. Erechtheis; 3. Aiantis; 4. Kekropis; 8. Antiochis.

The following information comes from Andokides 1, *On the Mysteries*.
(ii) The council voted immunity to Teukros (c. 15). A proposal was made in
(iii) the council for handing over those indicated on a list to the court, which was challenged as illegal (cc. 17, 22f.):
Proposer
SPEUSIPPOS *PA* 12845
(iv) C. 27 mentions two decrees offering money for information:
(v) **Proposers**
KLEONYMOS
PEISANDROS son of Glauketes of Acharnai (VI) *PA* 11770
The demos decided that the information should be assessed by those of the
(vi) thesmothetai who were initiates (c. 28). The rewards were voted. C. 43
(vii) identifies two members of the council:
Bouleutai
MANTITHEOS *PA* 9670
APSEPHION *PA* 2806
I do not feel confident enough to follow the attribution to Mantitheos of the
(viii) deme Teithras (II): see Aurenche, *Les groupes* 95. There was a proposal in the council that the law against torture be suspended:
Proposer
PEISANDROS son of Glauketes of Acharnai (VI) *PA* 11770

It seems likely that he, and therefore the other zetetai (see above), were
(ix) members of the council; see MacDowell, *Mysteries* 87. Further activities of
the council are detailed. At c. 46 we find the following:
Bouleutes epistates
PHILOKRATES *PA* 14572
(x) At c. 71 (cf. 8; Lysias 6.9, 24) we find a decree excluding from sacred areas
those who had admitted impiety:
Proposer
ISOTIMIDES *PA* 7721
(xi) At And. 2.23f. we have a decree granting immunity to Andokides:
Proposer
MENIPPOS *PA* 10034

414/13 (Ol. 91.3)

Archon
TEISANDROS *PA* 13455
Diod. 13.7.1 (Pisandros or Peisandros); IG i³ [371] (i² 297); ii² 4960.23f.
(SEG 25.226.34f.); 6217.2.

Strategoi
NIKIAS son of Nikeratos of Kydantidai (II) *PA* 10808; *APF* 403f.
LAMACHOS son of Xenophanes of Oe (VI) *PA* 8981
Thuc. 6.98ff., 7.1ff., 22ff.; Diod. 13.7ff.; Plut. *Nik.* 17ff.; Polyainos 1.39.3
(Nikias); schol. Thuc. 6.101.6 (Lamachos); schol. Ar. *Thesm.* 841; IG i³
371.[11](cf. line 7).
As with 415/14, the precise division of actions between years cannot be
made. They proceeded to build fortifications around Syracuse and fought
engagements by land and sea. Things began to go badly and Nikias sent an
urgent letter to Athens. Lamachos died and Nikias fell ill.
The position favoured by Fornara, *Generals* 64f., is that the *autokratores*
were apart from the ten elected generals, which would help him to explain
that he has a total of eleven generals for the year. This is properly to omit
Euthydemos and Menandros, who were chosen *in addition* (προσείλοντο:
Thuc. 7.16.1) from those in Sicily to serve until the replacements should
arrive; they were strategoi, but chosen extraordinarily. There are ways to
prevent a list of eleven elected generals being evidenced. A replacement
could have been chosen for Lamachos if needed (Demosthenes and
Eurymedon were regularly elected generals). Alternatively, Pythodoros
Laispodias and Demaratos, whom Thuc. 6.105.2 calls *archontes*, could be
nauarchs, though I doubt that; Konon is more reasonably eliminated. At
all events, I see no reason to believe that Nikias and Lamachos were not
members of the regular college.

MENANDROS *PA* 9857
EUTHYDEMOS son of Eudemos *PA* 5521

Thuc. 7.16.1; Plut. *Nik.* 20.1, 4. See Fornara, *Generals* 65. They were chosen extraordinarily from those in Sicily (see above). They may be included below also as officers before their elevation.

EURYMEDON son of Thoukles (? of Myrrhinous) (III) *PA* 5973; *APF* 334
Thuc. 7.16.2; Diod. 13.8.7; Plut. *Nik.* 20.1; Justin 4.4.11; IG i³ 371.[7] (cf. line 9). Chosen, surely from among the existing generals (see above), along with Demosthenes, for Sicily, whither he went at once.

DEMOSTHENES son of Alkisthenes of Aphidna (IX) *PA* 3585; *APF* 112f.
Thuc. 7.16.2f., 20.2f., 26; Justin 4.4.11; Paus. 1.23.3, 29.13; Suda *s.v.* Νικίας; IG i³ 371.12f. Elected for Sicily with Eurymedon, he stayed in Athens to organize forces. He joined Charikles in raids on the Peloponnese before heading for Sicily.

PYTHODOROS (? son of Epizelos of Halai) (II) *PA* 12402 = 12410; *APF* 481
LAISPODIAS son of Andronymis (? of Koile) (VIII) *PA* 8963
DEMARATOS *PA* 3283
Thuc. 6.105. See Fornara, *Generals* 65. They were active in summer 414 in ravaging the Peloponnese. Although Thucydides does not call them generals, the inference here seems unescapable. On Laispodias see Develin, *JHS* 1986, 184.

EUETION (? of Kephisia (I) or Sphettos (v)) *PA* 5460; *APF* 190
Thuc. 7.9. In summer 414 he could not take, but blockaded Amphipolis. IG i³ 371.3 does not print Meritt's restoration of Euetion with the patronymic 'son of Melesandros' and, there being no other evidence for this and as there is apparently another Melesandros available, Thompson (*Hesperia* 1967, 105f.) restored a general Melesandros with good reason.

? [MEL]ES[A]NDR[OS]
IG i³ 371.[3]. See the last entry and *TAM* 1.44; ML 93. If Thompson is correct, he will have operated in Asia Minor.

CHARIKLES son of Apollodoros *PA* 15407; *APF* 502f.
Thuc. 7.20.1; Diod. 13.9.2. He was in command around the Peloponnese in spring 413, making raids in concert with Demosthenes. He went home after establishing a fortified post in Lakonia. Jordan, *TAPhA* 1970, 223 (*Navy* 124), makes him nauarch. I have assigned no tribe; see 404/3.

DIEITREPHES (? son of Nikostratos of Skambonidai) (IV) *PA* 3755
Thuc. 7.29. See Fornara, *Generals* 65. Instructed to take Thracians back home, he operated in Boiotia in summer 413, taking Mykalessos, which was then lost. The filiation is highly likely.

?KONON son of Timotheos of Anaphlystos (X) *PA* 8707; *APF* 506ff.
Thuc. 7.31.4f. Thucydides says ἦρχε Ναυπάκτου and he may not have been general – or not in this year. He could have been nauarch (Jordan, *TAPhA* 1970, 233 (*Navy* 123)). Nepos *Conon* 1.1 says as *praetor* he commanded

infantry and as *praefectus classis* he performed great exploits at sea, but this cannot be pressed to solve this problem. If he held the generalship, I would be inclined to ascribe it to this year though the next is a possibility. But see also Diphilos in 413/12.

Officers (taxiarchoi?)
?MENANDROS *PA* 9857
?EUTHYDEMOS son of Eudemos *PA* 5521
See above on them as generals. It seems they must have held some position of command for them to be chosen as extraordinary generals. See Jordan, *TAPhA* 1970, 237 (*Navy* 128), calling them *archontes*.

Tamiai of Athene
TEISAMENOS of Paiania (III) *PA* 13447
MELE[S]IAS of Oe (VI)
  Grammateus
  POLYMEDES son of Kephision of Atene (X) *PA* 12036
For Teisamenos and the secretary IG i³ 309.2f. (i² 248.211f.); 333.2f. (i² 272.152f.); 355.2f. (i² 286.150f.); 371.[2f.] (i² 297); for Melesias i³ 308.66 (i² 247.194); 332.48; for Polymedes i³ 310.21 (i² 249.230); 356.31 (i² 287.179). The actual inventories of the year are i³ 309, 333 and 355.

Hellenotamias
-- of Kephale (V)
IG i³ 371.4.

COUNCIL AND ASSEMBLY

Schol. Ar. *Birds* 1297, including Phrynichos F 26 (Edmonds), mentions a decree which should be of this year forbidding anyone to be satirized by name in comedy, though see Sommerstein, *CQ* 1986, 101–8, on the contents and Halliwell, *CQ* 1984, 87, for doubts about the law:
Proposer
SYRAKOSIOS *PA* 13041

Thuc. 7.10ff. tells of the reading of Nikias' letter to the assembly, which resulted in the appointment of Menandros and Euthydemos and the voting of another force.

It is known from IG i³ 371.11f. that Erechtheis held the seventh prytany; cf. 430.5, which thereby will belong to this year and show (line 31) that Antiochis held a later prytany.

413/12 (Ol. 91.4)

Archon
KLEOKRITOS *PA* 8569

Diod. 13.9.1; Plut. *Mor.* 835d (Klearchos), e; hyp. Ar. *Lys.*; IG i³ [136] (Bingen, *RBPh* 1959, 31ff.; *LSS* no. 6; cf. Henry, *Chiron* 1979, 25f.); [405] (SEG 21.72); ii² 1498.[22]; 2318.[129]; 4960.27f., 34f. (SEG 25.226.38f.); ?*Insc. Délos* 91.[15].

Strategoi

NIKIAS son of Nikeratos of Kydantidai (II) *PA* 10808; *APF* 403f.
DEMOSTHENES son of Alkisthenes of Aphidna (IX) *PA* 3585; *APF* 112f.
EURYMEDON son of Thoukles (? of Myrrhinous) (III) *PA* 5973; *APF* 334
Thuc. 7.31ff., 35ff.; Diod. 13.9ff.; Plut. *Nik.* 20ff., *Mor.* 169a; Paus. 1.29.12; Justin 4.5; Polyainos 1.39.4 (Nikias); schol. Thuc. 7.52 (Eurymedon), 61.1 (Nikias), 86.2 (Nikias and Demosthenes); Suda *s.v. Νικίας.*

Demosthenes, after further engagement, met with Eurymedon in Akarnania; they organized forces and then made their way to Sicily, conducting diplomacy and joining Nikias to oversee the Athenian defeats by sea and land. Eurymedon was killed in a naval encounter. The fleet was then commanded by Demosthenes, Menandros and Euthydemos. In the attempt to retreat and escape all lost their lives; Demosthenes and his troops surrendered and then Nikias was forced to do so too; both were subsequently put to death (but cf. Plut. *Nik.* 28.4f.).

MENANDROS *PA* 9857
EUTHYDEMOS son of Eudemos *PA* 5521
Thuc. 7.43.2ff. (Menandros), 69.4ff.; Diod. 13.13.2ff. See above and Fornara, *Generals* 65 n.113. There can be little doubt that they were now regularly elected generals, which is as they appear before Thuc. 7.69.4, though not *autokratores*. It is only at Thuc. 7.69.4 that they are called strategoi, but Fornara's conclusion from the predicative position of the word that they were temporarily given the role by the other generals is vitiated not only by the earlier references (cf. Diodoros), but also by the fact that the phrase οὗτοι γὰρ ἐπὶ τὰς ναῦς τῶν Ἀθηναίων στρατηγοὶ ἐπέβησαν will include Demosthenes, who has also been named.

?DIPHILOS *PA* 4464
Thuc. 7.34. He engaged in an inconclusive naval action in summer 413. The natural conclusion may seem to be that he succeeded Konon (see 414/13) in command at Naupaktos, but he could have been nauarch (Jordan, *TAPhA* 1970, 233 (*Navy* 123f.)).

ARISTOKRATES (? son of Skellias of ?Trinemeia (VII)) *PA* 1904; *APF* 56f.
Thuc. 8.9.2: ?Ar. F 591.70f. (Kassel-Austin). He was sent to Chios to deal with dissension in spring 412. For the identification see Gomme-Andrewes-Dover, *Comm. Thuc.* V.22.

?HIPPOKLES son of Menippos *PA* 7620
Thuc. 8.13. He engaged Peloponnesian ships off Leukas. See Fornara,

Generals 65f. There is a chance that he was nauarch; see Gomme-Andrewes-Dover, *Comm. Thuc.* v.32f., who favour a date of 412/11, with which I disagree.

?STROMBICHIDES son of Diotimos of Euonymon (I) *PA* 13016; *APF* 161 Thuc. 8.15.1. See Fornara, *Generals* 65f. (whence the date). He was to go to Chios. Cf. Jordan, *TAPhA* 1970, 238f. (*Navy* 129).

Hipparchos
?KALLISTRATOS (? son of Empedos of Oe) (VI) *PA* 8142
Paus. 7.16.4ff. The source suggests he was hipparch in this year. A hipparchy is mentioned at Plut. *Mor.* 844b for the orator Kallistratos and there may be confusion with another of that name. Our man is said to have died.

Taxiarchos
EUKLEIDES of tribe IX
SEG 19.42 b col. iii.1. I assume this date for the list (cf. Clairmont, *Patrios Nomos* 193ff.).

Toxarchos
ISODIKOS of tribe IX
SEG 19.42 b col. iii.2.

Tamiai of Athene
POLYXENIDES of Acharnai (VI) *PA* 12057
Grammateus
LEUKAIOS son of Komarchos of Aphidna (IX) *PA* 9051
IG i³ 309.4 (i² 248.213); 310.18f. (i² 249.227f.); 333.3f. (i² 272.153f.); 334.16f. (i² 273.166f.); 355.4 (i² 286.152); 356.28f. (i² 287.176f.); for Leukaios i³ 311.37f. (i² 250.246f.); 357.57 (i² 288.205). The actual inventories of the year are i³ 310, 334 and 356.

Amphiktyons to Delos
Insc. Délos 91 and 92 record names tentatively ascribed to the years around 413/12 and 412/11, names all of which I record here:
-- of Alopeke (X)
CHARTADES of Sounion (IV) *PA* 15538
DIOXIS of Kephisia (I) *PA* 4531
[THOU]DOSIOS (? of Alopeke (X) or Epieikidai (VII))

COUNCIL AND ASSEMBLY
(i) IG i³ 136 (Bingen, *RBPh* 1959, 31ff.; *LSS* no. 66) is probably of this year. It is a decree concerning the cult of Bendis:
Grammateus
[P]ASIPHON of Phrearrhioi (IV) *PA* 11668

Bouleutes epistates
. . .KLES

(ii) Thuc. 8.15 records the decision to release for use the 1000 talent reserve fund.

412/11 (Ol. 92.1)

Archon
KALLIAS of Skambonidai (IV) *PA* 7887
Ath. Pol. 32.1f.; Philochoros *FGH* 328 F 138; Diod. 13.34.1; Dion. *Lysias* 1; Plut. *Mor.* 835d, e; hyp. i Ar. *Lys.*; IG i³ 97 (i² 103; Walbank no. 73); ?[147] (i² 104); ?[177] (ii² 60; Walbank no. 63); 405.15 (SEG 21.72); ii² 4960.[38f.] (SEF 25.226.42f.); 7404; ?*Insc. Délos* 91.[15]. Cf. Henry, *Chiron* 1979, 26, 28 on IG i² 101.

Strategoi
STROMBICHIDES son of Diotimos of Euonymon (I) *PA* 13016; *APF* 161
Thuc. 8.15.1, 16f., 30, 62f., 79.3f. Cf. 413/12. He and Thrasykles are unlikely to have been nauarchs; Strombichides is called general.

THRASYKLES *PA* 7317
Thuc. 8.17.3. See above on Strombichides.

DIOMEDON *PA* 4065
Thuc. 8.19., 20.2, 23f., 54.3, 55.1, 73.4ff. Jordan, *TAPhA* 1970, 236f. (*Navy* 126f.), has him and Leon as initially nauarchs. That they later replaced Phrynichos and Skironides does not show that they were not generals earlier.

LEON *PA* 9100
Thuc. 8.23f., 54.3, 55.1, 73.4ff.; Lysias 20.29. See above on Diomedon and Andrewes and Lewis, *JHS* 1957, 179 n.10.

PHRYNICHOS son of Stratonides of Deiradiotai (IV) *PA* 15011
Thuc. 8.25ff., 48.4ff., 54.3; Krateros *FGH* 342 F 17; Plut. *Alk.* 25.5ff.; Polyainos 3.6; schol. Ar. *Thesm.* 804; Suda and Hesychios *s.v.* Φρυνίχου πάλαισμα.

ONOMAKLES *PA* 11476
Thuc. 8.25ff., 30.2.

SKIRONIDES *PA* 12730
Thuc. 8.25ff., 54.3. For doubts about the name see Gomme-Andrewes-Dover, *Comm. Thuc.* v.60.

CHARMINOS *PA* 15517
Thuc. 8.30, 41.3ff., 73.3; schol. Ar. *Thesm.* 804

EUKTEMON (? of Kephisia (I)) *PA* 5782
Thuc. 8.30. The deme of Euktemon is conjectured by association with *PA* 5798 (*APF* 562), born about 460.

I have given an initial list of generals because of the complex activities of the year. Strombichides was driven into Samos; Thrasykles came to join him and they pursued a force to Miletos. Thuc. 8.30ff. deals with operations against Chios and forces out of Samos in winter. Strombichides returned to this theatre with Charminos and Euktemon and with Euktemon and Onomakles operated against Chios (Thuc. 8.38ff.). Earlier Phrynichos, Onomakles and Skironides had enjoyed success around Miletos before retiring. Diomedon had enjoyed success against Chians and made an agreement with Teos. Then with Leon he recovered Lesbos and Klazomenai and had more success at Chios. These two also attacked Rhodes. Lysias says Leon was at the Hellespont. In that arena Strombichides took Lampsakos and failed at Abydos. Charminos had earlier been defeated at Syme.

Thuc. 8.47ff. tells how the leading lights at Samos determined to overthrow the Athenian democracy. In this Phrynichos took a leading role and he and Skironides were eventually deposed. Diomedon and Leon were reluctant to support oligarchy and cooperated with the Samians for their protection. Charminos was responsible for putting Hyperbolos to death.

EUKRATES son of Nikeratos of Kydantidai (II) *PA* 5757; *APF* 404f.
Ar. *Lys.* 103 with schol.; Suda *s.v.* Ἄπεστιν. He was suspected of bribery and treason.

Phylarchos
PYTHODOROS of tribe VIII *PA* 12405
IG i² 950.180.

Tamiai of Athene
KALLAISCHROS of Eupyridai (IV) *PA* 7760; *APF* 327f.
  Grammateus
  AUTOKLEIDES son of Sostratos of Phrearrhioi (IV) *PA* 2713
IG i³ 310.19f. (i² 249.228f.); 311.35f. (i² 250.244f.); 334.17f. (i² 273.166f.; SEG 22.31; 24.32); 335.30f. (SEG 22.32; 24.33); 356.29f. (i² 287.177f.); 357.54f. (i² 288.202f.). The actual inventories of the year are i³ 311, 335 and 357.

Probouloi
HAGNON son of Nikias of Steiria (III) *PA* 171; *APF* 227f.
Lysias 12.65.

SOPHOKLES (? son of Sophillos of Kolonos) (II) *PA* 12834
Arist. *Rhet.* 3.18.6 1419a.25.

On these probouloi see Gomme-Andrewes-Dover, *Comm. Thuc.* v.6f.; on Sophokles Avery, *Historia* 1973, 511ff.

Envoy
PEISANDROS son of Glauketes of Acharnai (VI) *PA* 11770
Thuc. 8.49, 53f., 56.1, 63.3, 64.1, 65.1, 67.1, 73.2; Plut. *Alk.* 26.1. He was
sent from Samos to Athens, where he was chosen with ten others to go to
Tissaphernes and Alkibiades. Thence he went to Samos, then being sent to
Athens with half the other envoys, with instructions to instal oligarchies in
the subject states he came to on the way. At least his embassy to
Tissaphernes can be called official. Nepos *Alc.* 5.3 calls him general
(*praetor*), but this seems in error, *pace* Connor, *New Politicians* 146 n.18,
and (with a query) Davies, *Wealth* 160.

COUNCIL AND ASSEMBLY

 (i) IG i³ 96 (i² 101) is a decree of pryt. Akamantis concerning the Samians. See
also SEG 31.15.

 (ii) IG i³ 97 (i² 103; Walbank no. 73) is a proxeny decree of pryt. Hippothontis
for Eurytion of Orchomenos and his father Potamodoros:
Grammateus
AISCHYLOS *PA* 435
Bouleutes epistates
KEPHISODOROS *PA* 8356
Proposer
MENETELES *PA* 10022; *APF* 390
APF suggests Meneteles might be the father of the secretary of 399/8 (IG
ii² 1391.3), who was from Phrearrhioi (IV). I am not prepared to put IG i³
147 in this year because of coincidence of secretary's name; it will be found
in the appendix to this Section.

 (iii) Thuc. 8.21 mentions a decree giving the Samians their independence,
which may be associated with IG i³ 96, though that seems to have dealt with
a wider number of areas.

Thuc. 8.53f. tells how Peisandros and others sent from Samos spoke in the
assembly, there was debate and opposition to changing the constitution
 (iv) and the other proposals, but the people came round and voted Peisandros'
embassy (see above) and the replacement of Phrynichos and Skironides as
generals.

Thuc. 8.65ff. tells us of events in Athens to do with the change of
 (v) constitution, of assemblies and proposals. The present arrangements were
suspended and the 400 were to be selected:
Proposer
PEISANDROS son of Glauketes of Acharnai (VI) *PA* 11770
The 400 took over from the existing council.
 (vi) We may place beside this *Ath. Pol.* 29ff., where we find a decree constitut-
ing syngrapheis to bring proposals for the good of the city, with a rider that

Kleisthenes' laws should be sought out; I do not share the doubts on Pythodoros' decree of Sordi, *GFF* 1981, 3–12; Pesely, *LCM* 1987, 51:
Proposers
PYTHODOROS son of Polyzelos of Anaphlystos (x) *PA* 12412
KLEITOPHON son of Aristonymos *PA* 8546
We then hear of the proposals of the syngrapheis, which were approved. A
(vii) programme for the future was drawn up and provisions for the present, the latter being ratified by the people:
Bouleutes epistates
ARISTOMACHOS *PA* 1956

411 (Ol. 92.2)

I use this designation, as distinct from 412/11 and 411/10, for the period of the oligarchy and include here those evidenced during that period. Generals not connected with the oligarchy are listed under 411/10.

Archon
MNASILOCHOS *PA* 10324
Ath. Pol. 33.1; IG i³ [373] (i² 298; ML 81; Fornara no. 150). He was archon for two months.

Strategoi
DIEITREPHES (? son of Nikostratos of Skambonidai) (IV) *PA* 3755
Thuc. 8.64.2. See Fornara, *Generals* 66f. Appointed to the Thracian area in summer 411, he dissolved democracy at Thasos. I do not follow Jordan, *TAPhA* 1970, 234 (*Navy* 124), in making him archon to Thrace.

ALEXIKLES *PA* 535
Thuc. 8.92.4ff. He was arrested by the hoplites in Peiraieus and later released.

THERAMENES son of Hagnon of Steiria (III) *PA* 7234; *APF* 228
Thuc. 8.89.2, 92.6ff.; Lysias 12.65. He confronted the hoplites at Peiraieus.

THYMOCHARES (? of Sphettos) (v) *PA* 7406; *APF* 524f.
Thuc. 8.95.2ff. Sent to Eretria, he lost a naval engagement. For the deme see *APF*.

ARISTARCHOS (? of Dekeleia) (VIII) *PA* 1663; *APF* 48
Eupolis F 43 (Edmonds); Thuc. 8.98.1ff.; Xen. *Hell.* 2.3.46 (cf. Thuc. 8.90.1). On the deposition of the 400, he marched to Oinoe, where he tricked the garrison into losing possession. Xenophon associates him with Aristoteles and Melanthios in building a fort at Eëtioneia. *APF* will not be committed to the association which renders the demotic.

ARISTOTELES son of Timokrates of Thorai (x) *PA* 2055
MELANTHIOS *PA* 9768
Xen. *Hell.* 2.3.46. See above on Aristarchos.

?ANTIPHON (? son of Lysonides) *PA* 1283; *APF* 327f.
Xen. *Hell.* 2.3.40 and Plut. *Mor.* 832f both would attest a trierarchy, but the generalship of Plutarch may be doubted, unless Antiphon gained promotion to that office; Xenophon indicates the contrary by not specifying the strategia. The *Moralia* passage does point to the period of the 400, but the character is rather the man mentioned by Xenophon than the orator (son of Sophilos of Rhamnous (IX) *PA* 1304). See *APF* for discussion.

Taxiarchos
ARISTOKRATES son of Skellias of Trinemeia (VII) *PA* 1904; *APF* 56f.
Thuc. 8.89.2, 92.4. He commanded his tribal contingent at Peiraieus and accompanied Theramenes (*q.v.*).

Peripolarchos
HERMON *PA* 5170
Thuc. 8.92.5. He was commander of the *peripoloi* at Mounichia who helped in the arrest of Alexikles.

Officer?
POLYSTRATOS of Deiradiotai (IV) *PA* 12076; *APF* 467
Lysias 20.14. 16f. *APF* calls him garrison-commander, but a trierarchy may be more likely, or at least some form of naval command. Cf. Gomme-Andrewes-Dover, *Comm. Thuc.* v.202.

Archon at Oropos
POLYSTRATOS of Deiradiotai (IV) *PA* 12076; *APF* 467
Lysias 20.6. I prefer this dating, before his naval exploits, given the context of the Lysias passage.

Tamiai of Athene
ASOPODOROS of Kydathenaion (III) *PA* 2672
Grammateus
EUANDROS son of E[ri]thalion of Euonymon (I) *PA* 5271 = 5267; *APF* 187f.
IG i³ 312.52f. (i² 251.261f.); 335.31f. (SEG 22.32; 24.33); 336.44f. (SEG 22.33; 24.34); 357.55f. (i² 288.203f.); 373.5ff. (i² 298; ML 81; Fornara no. 150); for Euandros i³ 311.36f. (i² 250.245f). See Gomme-Andrewes-Dover, *Comm. Thuc.* v.194ff. The actual inventories of the year are i³ 312. 336 and (?) 358.

Hellenotamias
ANTISTHENES of Hermos (V) *PA* 1190
IG i³ 373.12f. (i² 298; ML 81; Fornara no. 150).

Katalogeus
POLYSTRATOS of Deiradiotai (IV) *PA* 12076; *APF* 467
Lysias 20.13f. Selected to choose the 5000, he was unwilling to do so and constructed a list of 9000. See Gomme-Andrewes-Dover, *Comm. Thuc.* v.202ff.

Envoys
LAISPODIAS son of Andronymis (? of Koile) (VIII) *PA* 8963
ARISTOPHON *PA* 2102
MELESIAS (son of Thoukydides of Alopeke) (x) *PA* 9813; *APF* 232f.
Thuc. 8.86.9. They were sent to Sparta, but the crew of the Paralos handed them over to the Argives. On Aristophon see Gomme-Andrewes-Dover, *Comm. Thuc.* v.289, where there is reluctance to accept the identification of Melesias.

ANTIPHON (? son of Lysonides) *PA* 1283; *APF* 327f.
PHRYNICHOS son of Stratonides of Deiradiotai (IV) *PA* 15011
ONOMAKLES *PA* 11476
ARCHEPTOLEMOS son of Hippodamos of Agryle (I) *PA* 2384
For the first two Thuc. 8.90.2, 91.1, 92.2; for Antiphon and the others Plut. *Mor.* 832f–833a, 833e–834a. Thucydides seems to indicate an embassy of twelve, but more likely he should be taken to mean ten. They were sent to Sparta to make peace, but were unsuccessful. Antiphon and Archeptolemos were condemned as traitors after the overthrow of the 400. That Antiphon here is the orator is accepted at *PA* 1304.

COUNCIL AND ASSEMBLY

The consensus seems to be that IG i³ 98 honouring Pythophanes is to be placed in this period (or at least 411/10), but I cannot accept this, so that the document appears in the appendix to this Section.

Thuc. 8.97.1 records the assembly at which the 400 were terminated and matters handed over to the 5000.

411/10 (Ol. 92.2)

Archon
THEOPOMPOS *PA* 7011
Lysias 21.1; *Ath. Pol.* 33.1; Philochoros *FGH* 328 F 139; Diod. 13.38.1; Plut. *Mor.* 833d; ?IG xiv.1097.[8]. He served for the remaining 10 months.

Strategoi
Generals were chosen by the forces in Samos and others were elected in the city. For the eventual merger of the two sets see Fornara, *Generals* 68.

THRASYBOULOS son of Lykos of Steiria (III) *PA* 7310; *APF* 240
THRASYLLOS *PA* 7333
Thuc. 8.76.2. 81 (Thrasyboulos), 100, 103.2ff.; Xen. *Hell.* 1.1.8ff.; Nepos *Alc.* 5.4 (Thrasyboulos); Diod. 13.38.3ff., 45.7ff., 49.3ff. (the latter two 410/9); Plut. *Alk.* 29.1f. (Thrasyllos; but see 410/9); Polyainos 1.40.9 (Thrasyboulos).
   They were not regular generals but survived the replacements by the

forces at Samos. Thrasyboulos persuaded the soldiers in the matter of Alkibiades' recall and sailed to Tissaphernes to get him. The two were active in the eastern theatre and won the battle at Kynossema in summer 411. Kyzikos was taken in the winter. Xenophon says Thrasyllos returned to Athens to report and request troops and ships. On chronology see Sealey, *CSCA* 1975, 273ff.

ALKIBIADES son of Kleinias of Skambonidai (IV) *PA* 600; *APF* 9ff.
Thuc. 8.82, 85.4, 86.4ff., 88, 108.1f.; Xen. *Hell.* 1.1.5ff.; Lysias 19.52; Nepos *Alc.* 5.4ff.; Diod. 13.42.1ff., 46.2ff., 49.3ff. (the latter two 410/9); Front. *Strat.* 2.5.44, 7.6; 3.9.6; Plut. *Alk.* 26ff., *Mor.* 345d; Polyainos 1.40.9; Athenaios 12.535c.

See Fornara, *Generals* 67. Chosen as an additional general by the forces at Samos, he undertook to go to Tissaphernes, after which he prevented the forces sailing against Athens. Then he went again to Tissaphernes. He was active at Halikarnassos and Kos and shared in operations in the Hellespontine area in summer 411; he managed to escape from Tissaphernes and joined forces with Theramenes and Thrasyboulos in success at Kyzikos.

EUMACHOS (? of Euonymon) (I) *PA* 5342
Xen. *Hell.* 1.1.22. He was left at Chrysopolis with Theramenes. For the deme see Fornara, *Generals* 68, under 410/9 (*q.v.* for the reading of IG i³ 375.35f.).

CHAIREAS son of Archestratos (? of Phlya (VII)) *PA* 15093; *APF* 346
Diod. 13.49.6, 50.7, 51.2ff. (410/9). In command of land forces at Kyzikos. *APF* is wrong to call him tamias Paralou in 412/11; see Gomme-Andrewes-Dover, *Comm. Thuc.* v.266. The demotic is hardly certain.

KONON son of Timotheos of Anaphlystos (X) *PA* 8707; *APF* 506ff.
Diod. 13.48.6 (410/9). One of the city generals, he took help to Corcyra.

THERAMENES son of Hagnon of Steiria (III) *PA* 7234; *APF* 228
Xen. *Hell.* 1.1.12ff.; Nepos *Alc.* 5.4ff.; Diod. 13.47.6ff., 49.3ff. (410/9); Polyainos 1.40.9. A city general, he was active around Euboia and Paros in winter, subsequently with Thrasyboulos in Thrace, joining in the success at Kyzikos.

THYMOCHARES (? of Sphettos) (V) *PA* 7406; *APF* 524f.
Xen. *Hell.* 1.1.1. Sent from Athens in summer 411, he lost a naval engagement in the Hellespont.

SIMICHOS *PA* 13030 or SYMBICHOS or STROMBICHIDES *PA* 13016; *APF* 161
The MS of *Hell. Oxy.* 7.4 reads σιχιον, while at schol. Aisch. 2.31 we have σιμμιχου or συμβιχου. Strombichides appears as an attempt to resolve this; Thompson, *Hesperia* 1967, 106f. I incline to Simichos. He was defeated around Amphipolis.

Tamias of Athene
AMEINIAD[ES] *PA* 662
IG i³ 313.72 (i² 253.265); 337.60 (SEG 22.34; 24.35). The actual inventories of the year are i³ 313, 337 and ?358.

Hellenotamiai
KALLIMACHOS of Hagnous (V) *PA* 8002
PHRASITELIDES of Ikarion (II) *PA* 14987
IG i³ 375.4 (i² 304 A; ML 84; Fornara no. 154). See ML for the date adduced by Meritt and reiterated by him in *PAPhS* 1971, 106; 1978, 290; *contra* Pritchett, *Historia* 1977, 295ff.; also SEG 31.25.

Anagrapheus
NIKOMACHOS *PA* 10934
Lysias 30.2ff. Chosen to write up the laws of Solon, he continued for six years rather than the initial four months. See Dow, *Historia* 1960, 271.

Amphiktyon to Delos
THEANGELOS of Phegaia (II)
Insc. Délos 93.12f. (IG i² p.299.31).

COUNCIL AND ASSEMBLY

(i) Thuc. 8.97 tells of assemblies in the time of the 5000 to deal with the constitution and of the vote to recall Alkibiades; the latter is also at Plut. *Alk.* 33.1:
Proposer
KRITIAS son of Kallaischros *PA* 8792; *APF* 326f.
I give him no tribe; see 404/3.

(ii) Plut. *Mor.* 833 d-834b (Fornara no. 151) retains a decree passed under the 5000 concerning the arrest and trial of Archeptolemos, Onomakles and Antiphon and dated to the twenty-first day of the prytany (of Antiochis):
Grammateus
DEMONIKOS of Alopeke (X) *PA* 3562
Bouleutes epistates
PHILOSTRATOS of Pallene (X) *PA* 14742
Proposer
ANDRON (son of Androtion of Gargettos) (II) *PA* 921; *APF* 34

(iii) Lykourgos 1.113ff. records a decree regarding the trial of the dead Phrynichos for treason:
Proposer
KRITIAS son of Kallaischros *PA* 8792; *APF* 326f.

(iv) They also decreed punishment for any that defended Phrynichos.

Philochoros *FGH* 328 F 139 records a Spartan embassy for peace in this year, and Diod. 13.52f. includes a speech of the Spartan Endios to the assembly. Both identify the chief opponent of peace as Kleophon; see Rhodes, *Comm.* 424f.

410/9 (Ol. 92.3)

Archon

GLAUKIPPOS *PA* 2979

Lysias 21.1; Philochoros *FGH* 328 F 140; Diod. 13.43.1; Dion. *Lys.* 21; hyp. ii Sophokles *Phil.*; IG i³ 99(i² 109); 101 (i² 108; ML 89; Fornara no. 156); [102] (i² 110; ML 85; Osborne D 2; Fornara no. 155); 103 (i² 110a; ii² 142); 375 (i² 304 A; ML 84; Fornara no. 154; SEG 31.25); ii² 1498.[7], [9f.]; ? xiv.1097.[8]; *Insc. Délos* 93.8f. (IG i² p.299.29). The reading at IG i³ 208 seems to rule out the restoration at i² 112.

Strategoi

(THRASYBOULOS son of Lykos of Steiria (III)) *PA* 7310; *APF* 240

(THERAMENES son of Hagnon of Steiria (III)) *PA* 7234; *APF* 228

(ALKIBIADES son of Kleinias of Skambonidai (IV)) *PA* 600; *APF* 9ff.

Lysias 19.52 (Alkibiades); Xen. *Hell.* 1.2.15ff. (409/8; Alkibiades); Nepos *Alc.* 5.4ff.; Diod. 13.64.1ff. (409/8); Plut. *Alk.* 29.2f. (Alkibiades). See Fornara, *Generals* 68f. Andrewes, *JHS* 1953, 1–9, has shown that these three were not official generals from 410/9 to 408/7 (hence the parentheses). Thrasyboulos' defeat at Ephesos (Diod.) is to be ascribed to Thrasyllos (so Xenophon; see below). Theramenes besieged Chalkedon and Byzantion, Alkibiades operating in the land held by Pharnabazos. Xenophon has Alkibiades at Lampsakos and attacking Abydos (cf. Plut.). Andrewes (p. 7) shows Thrasyboulos in the Thraceward area from May 410 to late 407.

THRASYLLOS *PA* 7333

Lysias 32.7; Xen. *Hell.* 1.1.33f., 2.1ff. (409/8; cf. Diod. 13.64.1ff.); Dion. *Lys.* 21; Plut. *Alk.* 29.1f., *Mor.* 345d; Koenen, *Stud. Pap.* 1976, 55ff., 70ff. (text also at Lehmann, *ZPE* 26 (1977), 189f.).

While at Athens, he led out forces, causing Agis to retreat. Then he sailed east, operated against Pygela and suffered defeat at Ephesos. He was more successful against Syracusan ships off Lesbos, then joined Alkibiades at Lampsakos.

EUKLEIDES *PA* 5672 = 5680

DEXIKRATES of Aigilia (X) *PA* 3226

PASIPHON of Phrearrhioi (IV) *PA* 11668

ARISTOKRA[TES] (son of Skellias of Trinemeia) (VII) *PA* 1904; *APF* 56f.

?E[UMACHOS] of Euonymon (I) *PA* 5342

IG i³ 375.17, 35f. (i² 304 A; ML 84; Fornara no. 154; SEG 31.25). For Eumachos, unrestored in IG i³ and denied by Andrewes, *JHS* 1953, 4 n.13, see Fornara, *Generals* 68. The inscription has Eukleides in Eretria, the others at Samos. Bradeen, *Hesperia* 1964, 49f., suggested the latter might

not be official, connecting Pasiphon with the naval archon in his no. 15
(*Agora* XVII.23.107); the deme squares with the tribe under which
Pasiphon is listed as a casualty. I prefer, however, to record him as archon
of the fleet in the next year (*q.v.*). Hence I do not count the Theoros in that
list as general, but as archon of the fleet in this year (*q.v.*). See Jordan,
TAPhA 1970, 229f., 234f. (*Navy* 119f., 124f.).

OINOBIOS of Dekeleia (VIII) *PA* 11357
IG i³ 101.47 (i² 108.38; ML 89; Fornara no. 156). He was general in
Thrace.

Archon at Pylos
HERMON *PA* 5170
IG i³ 375.10 (i² 304 A; ML 84; Fornara no. 154; SEG 31.25). See Jordan,
TAPhA 1970, 234 (*Navy* 125).

Officers
MENANDROS ?*PA* 9857
Xen. *Hell.* 1.2.16. He commanded 120 hoplites in pursuit of Pharnabazos.
The exact position is hard to determine and even a generalship is possible.

PASION
Koenen, *Stud. Pap.* 1976, 57, 60, 70 (line 7) (Lehmann, *ZPE* 26 (1977),
189f.). He was under Thrasyllos at Ephesos. Lewis, *Sparta and Persia* 1
n.1, is tempted to emend him to Pasiphon, but as Pasion is a perfectly good
name, I should resist the temptation.

I come now to the casualty list which is now *Agora* XVII.23, dated to this
year or at least 409, which may take us into the next archon-year. I shall
record here all the data on officers to be found therein, except for the case of
Pasiphon, for which see above on strategoi and 409/8. The tribes correspond to columns in the document.

A. Tribe II: these may be taxiarchs or trierarchs:
   . . .⁷. . . ON
   . . .⁶. . . MOS

B. Tribe IV:
   Archon of the fleet
   THEOROS ?*PA* 7223
   See above on Pasiphon as strategos.
   Taxiarchoi
   AMPHILOCHOS
   PYTHON
   To list them together is a convenience, as they could have served in
   consecutive years; but Bradeen, *Hesperia* 1964, 51, raised the possibility
   that one succeeded the other in this year.

C. Tribe VI: these may again be taxiarchs or trierarchs:
...?... s
...?... MOS

Tamias of Athene

KALLISTRATOS of Marathon (IX) *PA* 8174
IG i³ 313.74 (i² 253.267); 337.62 (SEG 22.34; 24.35); 375.2, 40 (i² 304 A;
ML 84; Fornara no. 154; SEG 31.25). Inventories of the year are i³ 338 and
?359.

Hellenotamiai

PERIKLES (son of Perikles) of Cholargos (V) *PA* 11812; *APF* 458
DIONYSIOS of Kydathenaion.(III) *PA* 4198
THRASON of Boutadai (VI)
PROXENOS (son of Harmodios) of Aphidna (IX) *PA* 12267; *APF* 476f.
SPOUDIAS of Phlya (VII) *PA* 12871
ANAITIOS of Sphettos (V) *PA* 800
PHALANTHOS of Alopeke (X) *PA* 13995
EUPOLIS of Aphidna (IX)
KALLIAS of Euonymon (I)

Paredros

POLYARATOS of Cholargos (V) *PA* 11907; *APF* 461
IG i³ 375.8ff. (i² 304 A; ML 84; Fornara no. 154; SEG 31.25).

Athlothetes

PHILON of Kydathenaion (III) *PA* 14851
IG i³ 375.6 (i² 304 A; ML 84; Fornara no. 154; SEG 31.25).

Hieropoios

DIYLLOS of Erchia (II) *PA* 4450
IG i³ 375.6f. (i² 304 A; ML 84; Fornara no. 154; SEG 31.25).

Anagrapheus

NIKOMACHOS *PA* 10934
See 411/10.

Amphiktyons to Delos

THEODOTOS son of Neoi[k]os
APSEPHION son of Apsithyllos
D[E]MOKRITOS son of [Ph]anias
OL[Y]MPIODOROS son of Telesias *PA* 11391
Insc. Délos 93.4ff. (IG i² p. 299.27ff.)

COUNCIL AND ASSEMBLY

(i) The first secretary is found at IG i³ 375 (i² 304 A; ML 84; Fornara no. 154; SEG 31.25) and in the law quoted at And. 1.96 and referred to at Dem.

20.159 and Lyk. 1.127 protecting the democracy against overthrow:
Grammateus
KLEIGENES of Halai (II or VII) *PA* 8488
Bouleutes epistates
BOETHOS *PA* 2883
Syngrapheus
DIOPHANTOS
The first prytany was of Aiantis and all are found in IG i³ 375: 2. Aigeis; 3. Oineis; 4. Akamantis; 5. Kekropis; 6. Leontis; 7. Antiochis; 8. Hippothontis; 9. Erechtheis; 10. Pandionis.

(ii) IG i³ 99 (i² 109) is a measure of pryt. Oineis emanating from syngrapheis and concerning sacred funds (see Henry, *Prescripts* 13):
Grammateus
[PH]ILIPPOS son of [? Phil]eas of D[eiradiotai ?] (IV) *PA* 14407
Bouleutes epistates
CHARIAS *PA* 15331

(iii) IG i³ 100 is a tribute assessment, though the date is hardly certain.

(iv) IG i³ 101 (i² 108; ML 89; Fornara no. 156) is a decree of pryt. Leontis concerning the Neapolitans:
Grammateus
SIBYRTIADE[S] *PA* 12645
Bouleutes epistates
CHAIRIMENES *PA* 15232
Proposer
. .⁴. . THEOS
IG i³ 229 will be found in the appendix, but Lewis (*ABSA* 1954, 35f.) wondered about restoring there the secretary above.

(v) IG i³ 102 (i² 110; ML 85; Osborne D 2; Fornara no. 155) is a probouleumatic decree of pryt. Hippothontis honouring the killers of Phrynichos:
Grammateus
LOBON of Kedoi (I) *PA* 9184
Bouleutes epistates
PHILISTIDE[S] *PA* 14440
Proposers
ERASINIDES *PA* 5021
DIOKLES *PA* 3983
EUDIKOS *PA* 5419

(vi) IG i³ 103 (i² 110a) is a decree of pryt. Erechtheis honouring the Halikarnassians:
Grammateus
?[AM]YTH[E]ON or ?[EUE]TH[I]ON *APF* 93

The first suggestion is in IG i³, where the upsilon is read with a dot, the second on a file card at the Institute for Advanced Study at Princeton.

Ath. Pol. 28.3 speaks of

KLEOPHON (son of Kleippides of Acharnai) (VI) *PA* 8638

(vii) as the one ὃς καὶ τὴν διωβελίαν ἐπόρισε πρῶτος. To some this has suggested an office as poristes, but I would take the passage to mean that he was responsible for the introduction of the *diobelia*. What the *diobelia* was is uncertain, but payments for it first appear in this year in IG i³ 375. On Kleophon and this matter see Rhodes, *Comm.* 354ff.

409/8 (Ol. 92.4)

Archon
DIOKLES *PA* 3984
Lysias 21.2; Philochoros *FGH* 328 F 139; Diod. 13.54.1; schol. Ar. *Plout.* 179; IG i³ 104 (i² 115; ML 86); 474.5f. (i² 372); ii² 1498.8, 11; cf. the apparatus to i³ 376.65.

Strategoi
For the status of Alkibiades, Thrasyboulos and Theramenes see 410/9.

(ALKIBIADES son of Kleinias of Skambonidai (IV)) *PA* 600; *APF* 9ff.
Lysias 19.52; Xen. *Hell.* 1.3.3ff. (408/7); Nepos *Alc.* 5.4ff.; Diod. 13.66f.; Front. *Strat.* 3.11.3; Plut. *Alk.* 30f.; Justin 5.4.6. He was active at Chalkedon and Byzantion, collected money after Chalkedon and joined with other generals in subsequent negotiations.

(THRASYBOULOS son of Lykos of Steiria (III)) *PA* 7310; *APF* 240
THRASYLLOS *PA* 7333
For sources and confusion of the two see 410/9. Add Xen. *Hell.* 1.3.6ff.; Diod. 13.66.1f.; Polyainos 1.47.2. Thrasyllos (so Xenophon) was active with Alkibiades around Chalkedon.

(THERAMENES son of Hagnon of Steiria (III)) *PA* 7234; *APF* 228
Nepos *Alc.* 5.4ff.; Diod. 13.66.1ff. He was at Chalkedon and Byzantion.

ANYTOS son of Anthemion of Euonymon (I) *PA* 1324; *APF* 40f.
Diod. 13.64.6. He was sent to Pylos, but could not reach there; he was prosecuted unsuccessfully.

LEOTROPHIDES *PA* 9159
TIMARCHOS *PA* 13623
Diod. 13.65.1f. They were sent to Nisaia, where they won a battle. On Leotrophides see Davies, *Wealth* 161.

?PERI[KLES] (son of Perikles) [of Cholargos] (V) *PA* 11812; *APF* 458
IG i² 301.22f. was so filled out at SEG 10.233, but IG i³ 376 does not even print a capital pi and is unsure about the date.

Archon of the fleet
PASIPHON of Phrearrhioi (IV) *PA* 11668
Agora XVII.23 col. IV.107ff. For the date see 410/9 strategoi.

Tamiai of Athene
PHI[L--] of Paiania (III)
Grammateus
[PRESB]YCH[A]RES son of --ochares of Eleusis (VIII)
IG i³ 314.1f. (i² 254.280f.); 339.4 (i² 274.169); 340.22f. (i² 275.187f.). For
the names see Thompson, *Hesperia* 1970, 54ff., who for the tamias ponders
Phileas or Philios. The actual inventories of the year are i³ 314, 339 and
? 359.

Hellenotamiai
--IOS of Alopeke (X)
EPIKOUROS of Kopros (VIII)
-- of Phyle (VI)
[KE]PHISODOTOS
POLY--
AISCHYLOS of Ankyle (II)
IG i³ 376.12ff. (i² 301). There are doubts about the date.

Anagrapheus
NIKOMACHOS *PA* 10934
See 411/10.

Epistatai of Erechtheion
BROSYN[ID]ES of Kephisia (I) *PA* 2929
CHARIADES (son of Charias) of Agryle (I) *PA* 15310; *APF* 569
DIODES of Kephisia (I) *PA* 3882a
Grammateus
ETEARCHOS of Kydathenaion (III) *PA* 5215
IG i³ 474.1ff. (i² 372).

Epistatai of Eleusis
EUPHILETOS of Kephisia (I) *PA* 6067; *APF* 206
Grammateus
KTESOS of Sypalettos (VII) *PA* 8904
IG i³ 386.3f. (i² 313).

Envoys
DOROTHEOS *PA* 4589
PHILOKYDES
THEOGENES *PA* 6688
EURYPTOLEMOS (? son of Peisianax ? of Sounion) (IV) *PA* 5981 = 5985;
APF 377
MANTITHEOS *PA* 9670
Xen. *Hell.* 1.3.13. Ambassadors to the Persians.

COUNCIL AND ASSEMBLY

The first secretary, of pryt. Kekropis, is known from IG i³ 474.7(i² 372; cf. the apparatus to i³ 376.65):

Grammateus
NIKOPHANES of Marathon (IX) *PA* 11065

IG i³ 104 (i² 115; ML 86) is a decree of pryt. Akamantis concerning the re-inscription of Drakon's homicide code:

Grammateus
DIOGNETOS of Phrearrhioi (IV) *PA* 3875
Bouleutes epistates
EUTHYDIKOS *PA* 5555
Proposer
. .E . . .ANES

408/7 (Ol. 93.1)

Archon
EUKTEMON of ? Kydathenaion (III) or Kytherros (II) *PA* 5799 + Add. Xen. *Hell.* 1.2.1; Androtion *FGH* 324 F 44 (Fornara no. 157); *MP* A 62; Diod. 13.68.1; IG i³ 110 (i² 118; ML 90; Walbank no. 87; Fornara no. 160); 111.[3], [6] (i² 120); ?112 (i² 121); 386.2, 174 (i² 313); [476] (i² 374); *Agora* xv.1 (i² 398; *DAA* no. 167); IG ii² 1498.20; *Insc. Délos* 94.[6]. The demotic is constructed from κυρηναῖος, which appears in the scholion which reproduces Androtion.

Strategoi
For the status of Alkibiades, Thrasyboulos and Theramenes see 410/9.

(ALKIBIADES son of Kleinias of Skambonidai (IV)) *PA* 600; *APF* 9ff.
(THRASYBOULOS son of Lykos of Steiria (III)) *PA* 7310; *APF* 240
THRASYLLOS *PA* 7333
(THERAMENES son of Hagnon of Steiria (III)) *PA* 7234; *APF* 228
Lysias 19.52 (Alkibiades); Xen. *Hell.* 1.4.8ff.; Dem. 20.59f.; Diod. 13.68.1ff; Plut. *Alk.* 32 (Alkibiades). Alkibiades eventually sailed to Athens. Thrasyboulos operated off Thrace, reducing a number of places, including Thasos. Thrasyllos sailed to Athens (this in 409/8 still according to Robertson, *Historia* 1980, 289), as would the others according to Diodoros.

Officers
DIODOROS *PA* 3916
MANTITHEOS *PA* 9670
Diod. 13.68.2. They were left in charge at the Hellespont.

Tamiai of Athene
ARE[S]AICH[MOS] of Agryle (I) *PA* 1592

CHAIRE--
Grammateus
DOROTHEOS *PA* 4590
For Aresaichmos IG i³ 314.3 (i² 254.282); 339.5 (SEG 10.199.170);
476.68f. (i² 374.117f.); for him and the secretary i³ 340.20 (SEG
10.199.185); for Chaire-- and the secretary i³ 476.430f. (SEG 10.295); for
Dorotheos i³ 386.175 (i² 313). See Thompson, *Hesperia* 1970, 54. The
actual inventories of the year are i³ 315, 340 and ?360.

Anagrapheus
NIKOMACHOS *PA* 10934
See 411/10.

Epistatai of Erechtheion
Hypogrammateus
PYRGION of Otryne (II) *PA* 12489
IG i³ 476.62, 268 (i² 374.111, 258).

Epistatai of Eleusis
. . . . ? . . . . TOS of Peiraieus (VIII) *PA* 15171
MENEKLES of Hippotomadai (VI) *PA* 9922
Grammateus
AMPHISTHENES of Potamos (IV) *PA* 786
IG i³ 386.2f. (i² 313).

Amphiktyons to Delos
?A . . ⁵ . . of Kydathenaion (III)
--YSI-- of Alopeke (X)
Insc. Délos 94.2f.

COUNCIL AND ASSEMBLY

(i) IG i³ 110 (i² 118; ML 90; Walbank no. 87; Fornara no. 160) is a
probouleumatic decree of pryt. Antiochis granting proxeny to Oiniades of
Palaiskiathos:
Grammateus
EUKLEIDES *PA* 5673
Bouleutes epistates
HIEROKLES *PA* 7482
Proposers
DIEITREPHES (? son of Nikostratos of Skambonidai) (IV) *PA* 3755
ANTICHARES *PA* 1309
For the possibility that Antiochis was first prytany cf. IG i³ p. 359. It
depends on the deduction that the prytanies were in reverse tribal order,
since we know from i³ 476 the following: 5. Oineis; 7. Leontis; 8. Pandionis;
9. Aigeis. On the other hand, Antiochis is one possible restoration for the
tenth prytany and this matter extends into interpretation of IG i³ 377,

which I deal with under 407/6. I am not persuaded that the evidence is sufficient to deduce reverse tribal order here.

(ii) IG i³ 111 (i² 120) is a prescript only:
Grammateus
DOR[OTHEOS?]
The name may be correct, but the man can hardly be the same as the secretary of the tamiai. Cf. Henry, *CSCA* 1978, 86f.

(iii) IG i³ 112 (i² 121) is a mere fragment, restored to produce
Grammateus
[?KLE]ARCHOS
Caution must be sounded, but Klearchos is the name of a councillor of this year (see below).

While the decree which is the second part of IG i³ 118 (i² 116; ML 87; Walbank no. 86; SEG 31.19; Fornara no. 162) seems to belong in 407/6, the earlier part records a settlement with Selymbria made in this year.

I will retain IG i³ 123 (i² 47) in 407/6, but for this year see Vattuone, *Epigraphica* 39 (1977), 41–50.

Alkibiades' return to Athens is described by Xen. *Hell*. 1.4.18ff.; Diod. 13.69.1ff.; Plut. *Alk*. 33f. All tell of him addressing the assembly and that
(iv) he was chosen strategos *autokrator*; the latter two mention decrees for the
(v) return of his property and the lifting of curses upon him.
(vi)

At *Agora* xv.1 (IG i² 398; *DAA* no.167; IG i³ 515) we have a list of bouleutai of tribe 1 Erechtheis:
Lamptrai
TIMOKLE[S] son of [Ti]mok--
--S
--S
Agryle upper
ENDIOS
THOUKLEIDES
Agryle lower
KLEARCHOS
Kedoi
THYMOTELES
[P]ANTEL[ID]ES
Euonymon
[E]LP[I]NES
CHAIR--?
Kephisia
ERYXIS
?KEPHISES

407/6 (Ol. 93.2)

Archon

ANTIGENES *PA* 983

Hellanikos *FGH* 323a FF 25, 26; Xen. *Hell.* 1.3.1; Androtion *FGH* 324 F 45 (Fornara no. 159); Philochoros *FGH* 328 F 141; *MP* A 63; Diod. 13. 76.1; Dion. *AR* 7.1.5; hyp. i, iii Ar. *Frogs*; schol. Ar. *Frogs* 33 (Antinos); IG i³ [114] (i² 119; Walbank no. 89); 115 (i² 123); [117] (i² 105; ML 91; Walbank no. 90; Fornara no. 161; cf. Henry, *Chiron* 1979, 27); 316.[60] (i² 255.323); 342.18 (ii² 1382.17); ii² Add. 1386.[21]; 1388.[48]; 1389.[7]; 1390.[8]; 1400.[22]; 1401.3; 1415.17; 1421.[86]; 1423.13; Add. 1424a.250; 1425.196; 1498.6.

Strategoi

ALKIBIADES son of Kleinias of Skambonidai (IV) *PA* 600; *APF* 9ff. Lysias 19.52, 21.6f.; Xen. *Hell.* 1.4.10,21ff., 5.11ff.; Nepos *Alc.* 7.1ff.; Diod. 13.69, 71, 73.3ff. (408/7); Plut. *Alk.* 33ff., *Lys.* 5.1f.; Paus. 9.32.6; Justin 5.5.2ff.

Chosen general at Athens and made *hapanton hegemon autokrator* (see 408/7), he was successful against Andros and other places. He then operated out of Samos, sharing the blame for the defeat at Notion (on which see *Hell. Oxy.* 4 with Bruce, *Comm.* 35ff.). He went into exile. Nepos and Plut. *Lys.* say he was deposed from office.

THRASYBOULOS son of Lykos of Steiria (III) *PA* 7310; *APF* 240

Xen. *Hell.* 1.4.10, 5.11; Nepos *Alc.* 7.1; Diod. 13.69.3,5, 72.1f. (408/7). He was chosen general at Athens. Xenophon later has him besieging Phokaia. Diodoros says Alkibiades left him at Andros and then has him sail to Thasos and Abdera.

KONON son of Timotheos of Anaphlystos (x) *PA* 8707; *APF* 506ff.

Xen. *Hell.* 1.4.10, 5.18,20; Justin 5.5.4, 6.1ff. He was evidently at Andros before going east to replace Alkibiades.

ADEIMANTOS son of Leukolophides of Skambonidai (IV) *PA* 202
ARISTOKRATES son of Skellias of Trinemeia (VII) *PA* 1904; *APF* 56f.

Xen. *Hell.* 1.4.21; Nepos *Alc.* 7.1; Diod. 13.69.3 (408/7). While the two later sources pair Adeimantos with Thrasyboulos, Xenophon associates him with Aristokrates as land commanders. They accompanied Alkibiades to Andros and thence to Asia.

?PHANOSTHENES *PA* 14083

Xen. *Hell.* 1.5.18; Plato *Ion* 541d. Sent to Andros to replace Konon, he captured two Thourian ships. Jordan, *TAPhA* 1970, 232 (*Navy* 122), makes him nauarch in 406/5. Plato mentions foreigners elected to generalships and other offices, but is specific enough to prove a strategia for Phanosthenes, which seems more likely than any other office, especially since it is being said that Ion can aspire to the generalship.

?P[ERIKLES] (son of Perikles of Cholargos) (v) *PA* 11812; *APF* 458
IG i³ 117.[5f.] (ML 91; Walbank no. 90). The name is restored from the
initial letter, as it was not at IG i² 105.

Kybernetes
ANTIOCHOS *PA* 1153
Hell. Oxy. 4.1f.; Xen. *Hell.* 1.5.11ff.; Androtion *FGH* 324 F 45; Diod.
13.71.1ff.; Plut. *Alk.* 35.4ff., *Lys.* 5.1f., cf. *Alk.* 10.1; Paus. 9.32.6. He is
included because he was left in charge by Alkibiades with disastrous
consequences at Notion.

Tamiai
KALLI--
PHILIPPOS son of Philesias of Prospalta (v) *PA* 14415
--[? of Acharnai] (VI)
MENESTRATOS son of Menes[tratos] (? of Phlya (VII) or Pithos (VII)) *PA*
10000
--of Eleusis (VIII)
ANTIPHON son of Antiphon (? of Krioa) (x) *PA* 1285
?PHILION
Grammateus
[?THRASYLLOS] son of [Gn]athios of Leukonoion (IV)
IG i³ 316.6off. (i² 255; only six listed); for the secretary 340.21 (i² 275); for
Philion Meritt, *AE* 1978, 98.90 (IG i³ 377.25; i² 304 B; Fornara no. 158).
   Inventories of the year are i³ 316 and ? 361. For the now amalgamated
board see the Introduction, p. 8. For the date see also the references at
Thompson, *Hesperia* 1970, 54. The readings have advanced much since
IG i² and we may not have heard the last of the matter. The name Philion
and the fact that he is a tamias of this year are new discoveries by Meritt and
may have to be judged in the context of the debate on IG i³ 377, for which
see under hellenotamiai. For the secretary see Meritt, *AJPh* 1968, 107.

Hellenotamiai
There has been a continuing debate on the inscription which is now IG i³
377 (i² 304; Fornara no. 158; SEG 31.25). Pritchett (*Historia* 1977, 295–
306, and *BCH* 1977, 7–42) maintains that it is a record of two years, thus
providing evidence for iteration in the college, and has provided new
readings. Some of these have been accepted by Meritt (*AE* 1978, 95-108;
cf. *PAPhS* 1978, 288f.), but he still holds that the inscription refers only to
this year, providing readings of his own. This extends to the logistai and
epimeletai as well. In the absence of other evidence for iteration, I am loath
to accept Pritchett's position. In what follows I list the readings of Meritt
and then record variants.
--ON of Kollytos (II)
ERASISTRATOS
LYSITHEOS of Thymaitadai (VIII) *PA* 9405; *APF* 355

ATHENODOROS of Melite (VII) *PA* 274; *APF* 221
THA[RRHY]NON of Kopros (VIII)
PROTARCHOS of Probalinthos (III) *PA* 12295
--TOS of Phaleron (IX)
THRASYLOCHOS of Thorikos (V) *PA* 7348
CHARIADES son of Charias of Agryle (I) *PA* 15310; *APF* 569
Chariades comes from IG i³ 316.65f. (i² 255.328f.) and Meritt (*AE* 1978, 107, with the name as Charikles) places him in this year, while Phal . . . os is assigned to 406/5 (*q.v.*). The readings of IG i³ 377 and Pritchett are more conservative than Meritt's latest, but there are no variants as such; Tharrhynon, however, is completely Meritt's, while at i³ 377.9f. we find .E . . . .ON and at lines 2of. --ON, both actually in the dative.

Logistai
NOUMENIOS of Marathon (IX) *PA* 11140
ARCHEDEMOS of Paionidai (IV)
DE[ME]TRIOS of Hamaxanteia (VIII)
[A]NTIOCHIDES of Alopeke (X)
PHAINIPPOS of Paionidai (IV) *PA* 13983
ARCHEDEMOS of Marathon (IX)
IG i³ 377.1ff. (i² 304.67ff.; Fornara no. 158; SEG 31.25). For the restorations see above on hellenotamiai. Meritt agrees with Pritchett (the text of IG i³ retains the old reading) in not having Noumenios as a patronymic (iota having to be added). Where Meritt sees Demetrios, Pritchett reads MELAN[TH]IOS and for Antiochides will read only . .OCHIDES.

Anagrapheus
NIKOMACHOS *PA* 10934
See 411/10.

Epistatai of Eleusis
EUBIOS of Aithalidai (IV) *PA* 5293
CHA--
Grammateus
SMIKYTHION of Halai (II or VII) *PA* 12769
IG i³ 387 (i² 314).

Epimeletai of tribe IX Aiantis
AM[PH]IAS
EUA[NG]ELOS
AMPHIKEDES
IG i³ 377.21f. (Fornara no. 158) as read by Meritt (*AE* 1978, 98.86f., 103f.; cf. *Mélanges Daux* 262f.). See above on hellenotamiai. IG i³ shows no sign of Amphias and for the second name has EUAITELOS with no dotted letters (but see the apparatus). Meritt is also responsible for the identification of the office.

407/6 (Ol. 93.2)

COUNCIL AND ASSEMBLY

From IG i³ 377 we can see at least that Aigeis held ninth prytany, Antiochis tenth. Were it the case that the later parts of the inscription actually belong to the beginning of this year, we would have Hippothontis (or Antiochis according to Pritchett) as first prytany and Erechtheis as second, but I prefer to accept that these belong to 406/5. See IG i³ p. 359 for discussion and above on hellenotamiai.

(i) IG i³ 101.48ff. (i² 108; ML 89; Fornara no. 156) is a second, probouleumatic, decree concerning the Neopolitans (cf. 410/9), assigned with a query to this year:
Proposer
AXIOCHOS (son of Alkibiades of Skambonidai) (IV) *PA* 1329 = 1330; *APF* 16f.

(ii) IG i³ 114 (i² 119; Walbank no. 89), possibly a proxeny decree for a man possibly of Abdera, is restored to this year in IG i³; Walbank is not averse to this, but is cautious with *c.* 425–405:
Grammateus
-- son of --ilos
Bouleutes epistates
EUKTEMO[N] (Walbank) EUKTE-- (IG i³)
It remains possible that Euktemon is the archon of 408/7. For the secretary cf. the next entry.

(iii) IG i³ 115 (i² 123) is a prescript:
Grammateus
[L]YSIKLES son of E-- *PA* 9418
Bouleutes epistates
--s
Woodhead, *apud* Walbank no. 89, suggested that in that document, compared with this, we might *exempli gratia* think about Lysikles son of Ergophilos of Kydathenaion (III).

(iv) IG i³ 117 (i² 105; ML 91; Walbank no. 90; Fornara 161), probably of this year, is a proxeny decree of pryt. Akamantis in honour of [Archelaos of Makedon]:
Grammateus
[?PHEL]LEUS
Bouleutes epistates
[SIB]YRTIO[S] *PA* 12646
The proposer is totally restored in IG i³ as Alkibiades (approved, but not restored by Walbank). I find this too conjectural to record in any more definite form.

(v) The ratification of arrangements with Selymbria in IG i³ 118 (i² 116; ML 87; Walbank no. 86; SEG 31.19; Fornara no. 162) seems to belong to this year (cf. 408/7); it includes a proxeny for Apollodoros and another:
Proposer
[AL]KIB[IAD]ES (son of Kleinias of Skambonidai) (IV) *PA* 600; *APF* 9ff.

(vi) IG i³ 119 (i² 117; ML 88; Fornara no. 163) will probably also belong in this year; it is a decree concerning the Klazomenians holding Daphnous:
Grammateus
KRATE[S] *PA* 8741
Bouleutes epistates
[EPIGEN]ES *PA* 4779
Proposer
ALKIBIADES (son of Kleinias of Skambonidai) (IV) *PA* 600; *APF* 9ff.

(vii) IG i³ 120 is a fragment dated to this year through the proposer:
Proposer
ALKI[BIADES] (son of Kleinias of Skambonidai) (IV) *PA* 600; *APF* 9ff.

(viii) IG i³ 123 (i² 47; ML 92; Fornara no. 165) probably belongs here (cf. 408/7); it is restored as probouleumatic and records a treaty with Carthage:
Grammateus
. . .⁶. . . s of Aphidna (IX)

Plut. *Alk*. 36 tells how Alkibiades was attacked in the assembly by Thrasyboulos son of Thrason; this led to the replacement of Alkibiades.

For the suggestion that the Arthmios decree belongs here see 481/80.

406/5 (Ol. 93.3)

Archon
KALLIAS of Angele (III) *PA* 7841
And. 1.77; Xen. *Hell*. 1.6.1; *Ath. Pol*. 34.1; *MP* A 64; Diod. 13.80.1; Dion. *AR* 7.1.5; Athenaios 5.218a; hyp. ii Sophokles *O.C.*; hyp. i, iii Ar. *Frogs*; schol. Ar. *Frogs* 405 (Arist. F 630), 694 (Fornara no. 164A), 725; IG i³ 124 (i² 124); 316.66 (i² 255.329); 405.[24].

Strategoi
KONON son of Timotheos of Anaphlystos (X) *PA* 8707; *APF* 506ff.
DIOMEDON *PA* 4065
LYSIAS *PA* 9351
PERIKLES son of Perikles of Cholargos (V) *PA* 11812; *APF* 458
ERASINIDES *PA* 5021
ARISTOKRATES son of Skellias of Trinemeia (VII) *PA* 1904; *APF* 56f.
ARCHESTRATOS of Phrearrhioi (IV) *PA* 2430
PROTOMACHOS *PA* 12318

THRASYLLOS *PA* 7333
ARISTOGENES *PA* 1781
For the full list Xen. *Hell.* 1.5.16; Diod. 13.74.1. Xenophon here and at
1.6.16 has Leon for Lysias (Rhodes, *Comm.* 423, calls Lysias suffect), while
Diodoros here and at 13.97.6 has Thrasyboulos for Thrasyllos; also at
13.101.5 he has Kalliades as general, clearly in error. Other sources Xen.
Hell. 1.6.15ff.; Diod. 13.76ff. (407/6), 97ff.; Lysias 21.8; Ar. *Frogs* 1196
with schol. (Philochoros *FGH* 328 F 142); Xen. *Mem.* 1.1.18 (Erasinides
and Thrasyllos); Plut. *Per.* 37.5 (Perikles); Paus. 6.7.7 (Thrasyllos:
Androtion *FGH* 324 T 15); Polyainos 1.48.2, 4 (Konon); Athenaios 5.218a
(Erasinides).

See Fornara, *Generals* 70. They were all active in the east, particularly
Konon at Mitylene, but only Lysias informs us that Archestratos was there
and that he died. And they were at Arginousai, after which Protomachos
and Aristogenes became exiles, the others, apart from Konon, being
condemned to death. Cf. *Ath. Pol.* 34.1 with Rhodes, *Comm.*

ADEIMANTOS son of Leukolophides of Skambonidai (IV) *PA* 202
PHILOKLES *PA* 14517
Xen. *Hell.* 1.7.1; Diod. 13.104.1f. (Philokles: 405/4). See Fornara, *Generals* 70. They were chosen as replacements to be colleagues to Konon.

Tamias
? -- of Probalinthos (III)
IG i³ 477.5f. (ii² 1655). For the date, which could be this or the next year,
see IG i³ with references. Inventories of the year may be i³ 341 and 362.

Hellenotamias
PHAL. . .OS of Thymaitadai (VIII)
Meritt's consistent reading at IG i³ 377.26 (i² 304 B.91; Fornara no. 158),
now dated by him to this year (*AE* 1978, 107; cf. 407/6 hellenotamiai).

Athlothetai
PROK[L]ES of Kephisia (I) *PA* 12228
? -- of Phaleron (IX)
?PATRO[K]L[ES] (? son of Chairedemos) of Alopeke (X) *PA* 11697
IG i³ 378.15f. (i² 305.8f.). The office for the latter two can only be an
assumption.

Logistes?
ARCHEDEMOS (? of Pelekes) (IV) *PA* 2326
Xen. *Hell.* 1.7.2 says he was in charge of the *diobelia* and Meritt (*Mélanges
Daux* 263f.) makes him logistes, Pritchett (*Anc. Soc.* 1977, 42 n.30) one of a
board of epimeletai.

Anagrapheus
NIKOMACHOS *PA* 10934
See 411/10.

COUNCIL AND ASSEMBLY

(i) IG i³ 124 (i² 124) is the heading of a decree which concerned Kios:
Grammateus
[ER]OTION of Eleusis (VIII)
Now read instead of the previous Sotion (*PA* 13402).

If IG i³ 477 belongs in this year, the fourth prytany was held by Pandionis.

Ath. Pol. 34.1 reports Spartan overtures for peace after Arginousai, which were rejected under the influence of Kleophon; see Rhodes, *Comm.*

(ii) The treatment of the generals after Arginousai is reported particularly by Xen. *Hell.* 1.7 and Diod. 13.101ff. For our purposes we gain most information from Xenophon. The generals spoke in the boule and a motion was passed for their trial by the assembly:
Bouleutes and proposer
TIMOKRATES *PA* 13748

(iii) At the assembly Theramenes spoke against the generals. The council was told to bring in a probouleuma and this concerned the method of trial:
Bouleutes and proposer
KALLIXE(I)NOS *PA* 8042

(iv) (Diod. 13.103.2; Athenaios 5.218a). This was indicted as illegal, but was eventually adopted. Before that we hear of a motion against those who had challenged Kallixeinos' proposal:
Proposer
LYKISKOS *PA* 9213
The prytaneis were cowed into putting the matter to the vote, except one:
Bouleutes
SOKRATES son of Sophroniskos of Alopeke (X) *PA* 13101
(Xen. *Mem.* 1.1.8, 4.4.2; Plato *Gorg.* 473e; *Apol.* 32b; Athenaios 5.217f.). The assembly was addressed by Euryptolemos. In this whole tale Diodoros adds only that an assembly was addressed by the general Diomedon.

405/4 (Ol. 93.4)

Archon
ALEXIAS *PA* 528
Lysias 21.3; Xen. *Hell.* 2.1.10; *Ath. Pol.* 34.2; Diod. 13.104.1; IG i³ 125 (ii² 174; *Hesperia* 1970, 111 (Meritt)); 126 (i² 125; Walbank no. 91); 127 (i² 126; ii² 1; ML 94; Osborne D 4; Fornara no. 166); ?[179] (ii² 73; Walbank no. 92); 405.[30] (SEG 10.220). See IG i³ p.481 against the restoration in ii² 1654.28 by Schweigert, *Hesperia* 1938, 269.

Strategoi
MENANDROS *PA* 9857
TYDEUS son of Lamachos of Oe (VI) *PA* 13884

KEPHISODOTOS *PA* 8312
Xen. *Hell.* 2.1.16ff.; Diod. 13.105f.; Plut. *Alk.* 36.4, *Lys.* 10.5; Paus. 10.9.11 (Tydeus). Chosen as additional generals, they operated from Samos and followed Lysandros. They were at Aigospotamoi with Konon, Philokles and Adeimantos.

KONON son of Timotheos of Anaphlystos (x) *PA* 8707; *APF* 506ff.
Xen. *Hell.* 2.1.28ff.; Isok. 5.61; Dem. 19.191; Nepos *Conon* 1.2; Diod. 13.106.6; Plut. *Alk.* 37.2, *Lys.* 11.3; Justin 5.6.10. See above. He escaped capture, but became an exile.

PHILOKLES *PA* 14517
ADEIMANTOS son of Leukolophides of Skambonidai (IV) *PA* 202
Lysias 14.38 (Adeimantos); Xen. *Hell.* 2.1.30f.; Dem. 19.191 (Adeimantos); Nepos *Alc.* 8.1,4 (Philokles); Diod. 13.106 (Philokles); Plut. *Alk.* 36.4 (Adeimantos), *Lys.* 9.5, 13.1 (Philokles); Paus. 9.32.9 (Philokles), 10.9.11 (Adeimantos).
See above. They were captured with other generals and Philokles was put to death.

EUKRATES son of Nikeratos of Kydantidai (II) *PA* 5757; *APF* 404f.
Lysias 18.4. He was chosen after Aigospotamoi.

Taxiarchoi?
STROMBICHIDES son of Diotimos of Euonymon (I) *PA* 13016; *APF* 161
DIONYSODOROS *PA* 4278
KALLIADES *PA* 7776
Lysias 13.13; 30.14. The first passage mentions the first two among the generals and taxiarchs who came forward in defence of democracy, the second associates Kalliades with Strombichides. They were executed. They may, of course, have been generals. Cf. Davies, *Wealth* 152.

Note: The implication drawn at *APF* 463 from *P. Ryl.* 3.489 col. IV. 100ff. that Eryximachos might have been a general at Aigospotamoi seems to me fallacious, for what is said can be taken to mean that he obtained the release of one of his fellow trierarchs (and he was trierarch).

Pentekontarchoi
-- OS of Phaleron (IX)
ANTIPHATES of Kytherros (III) *PA* 1260 = 1261; *APF* 38
. . .[6]. . . LES of Paiania (III)
IG i^3 1032.38, 99, 337 (ii^2 1951). For the date (pre-403) see SEG 29.149.

Hellenotamiai?
HIPPOK--
--OSTRATOS of Aphidna (IX)
-- of Acherdous (VIII)
IG i^3 379.11ff. (i^2 303.6ff.). The office is inferred. Also in this inscription is restored at lines 42f.

[PHA]INIPPOS son of Ka[llippos] cf. *PA* 13978
who could be an hellenotamias if a connexion can be made with the end of
line 41. Others in the inscription (respectively lines 46f., 47 and 92f.) who
may be officials, even hellenotamiai, are
SIBY[RTI--
--OS of Melite (VII)
[AR]ISTOPHON of Aithalidai (IV) *PA* 2109

Anagrapheus
NIKOMACHOS *PA* 10934
See 411/10.

Envoy
THERAMENES son of Hagnon of Steiria (III) *PA* 7234; *APF* 228
Lysias 12.68ff., 13.9ff.; Xen. *Hell.* 2.2.16ff.; *Pap. Mich.* inv. 5982 (Youtie
and Merkelbach, *ZPE* 2 (1968), 161–9; Henrichs, *ZPE* 3 (1968), 101–8).
He was envoy to Lysandros and then, with nine others, to Sparta, whence
terms were brought back.

COUNCIL AND ASSEMBLY

(i) IG i³ 125 (ii² 174; Meritt, *Hesperia* 1970, 111) is a probouleumatic decree in
honour of Epikerdes of Kyrene, which gives a name only for the rider:
Proposer
ARCHE . .⁴. .

(ii) IG i³ 126 (i² 125; Walbank no. 91) is a proxeny decree for Polypos of
Gortyna or Gortys restored to pryt. Aigeis (see the epistates):
Grammateus
[PO]LYARATOS of Cholargos (V) *PA* 11907; *NPA* 144; *APF* 461
Bouleutes epistates
. . . .⁸. . . . of Araphen

(iii) IG i³ 127 (i² 126; ii² 1; ML 94; Osborne D 4; Fornara no. 166) is a decree
concerning the Samians of pryt. Kekropis, which originated from a pro-
posal of the prytaneis:
Grammateus
POLYMNIS of Euonymon (I) *PA* 12052
Bouleutes epistates
NIKOPHON of Athmonon *PA* 11078
Bouleutes
KLESOPHOS

(iv) And. 1. 73ff. includes a decree for the re-enfranchisement of those who had
lost citizen rights (cf. Xen. *Hell.* 2.2.11):
Proposer
PATROKLEIDES *PA* 11685

(v) At Xen. *Hell.* 2.1.31f. we learn that a decree had been passed that if the Athenians won the sea battle, the right hand of all captives should be cut off. This had been opposed by Adeimantos the general.

(vi) Xen. *Hell.* 2.2.4 mentions the convening of an assembly which voted arrangements to have the city ready for a siege.

There are various sources which talk about the negotiations with Sparta which led to a peace settlement. On the chronology see Rhodes, *Comm.* 436f.; also and in general Krentz, *Thirty* chs. 1 and 2. I begin with Xen.

(vii) *Hell.* 2.2.11ff. We hear of various assemblies and of a proposal in the council that Spartan terms be accepted, which led to the imprisonment of the proposer and the forbidding of any such proposal:

Bouleutes/proposer
ARCHESTRATOS *PA* 2402

Theramenes persuaded the assembly to send him on his embassy (see above), reported back and was sent out again. On his return, he announced the Spartan terms, which were accepted. The sailing of Lysander into the Peiraieus which ends this account may be set beside Plut. *Lys.* 15.1, which dates his possession of the Athenian ships to 16 Mounichion. As Plutarch continues, however, Lysander is evidently out of Athens again and I leave the rest of the story for the next year.

Lysias 12.8ff. adds to this Kleophon's opposition to the terms of peace before Theramenes' embassy (he was subsequently tried and executed).

(viii) We hear of a decree of the council for Agoratos' arrest. Other decrees and procedures are mentioned.

Then Lysias 30.10ff. tells us that Kleophon attacked the boule and we learn the names of two councillors, the first of whom persuaded the council to arrest Kleophon:

Bouleutai
SATYROS of Kephisia (1) *PA* 12598; cf. *APF* 566
CHREMON *PA* 15570

404/3 (Ol. 94.1)

Archon
PYTHODOROS *PA* 12389
ANARCHIA
Xen. *Hell.* 2.3.1 – the year was regarded as anarchia because Pythodoros was the oligarchic choice; Diod. 14.3.1 signals anarchia, as does Plut. *Mor.* 835f; Lysias 7.9 names the archon, as does *Ath. Pol.* 35.1, 41.1; IG i³ [380] (SEG 21.80; cf. 28.47, 29.19); ii² 1498.[21]. See Rhodes, *Comm.* 436f.

Basileus
PATROKLES *PA* 11691
Isok. 18.5.

The Thirty

POLYCHARES *PA* 12099
KRITIAS son of Kallaischros *PA* 8792; *APF* 326f.
MELOBIOS *PA* 10102
HIPPOLOCHOS *PA* 7646
EUKLEIDES *PA* 5680 = ?5689
HIERON *PA* 7525
MNESILOCHOS *PA* 10324
CHREMON *PA* 15570
THERAMENES son of Hagnon of Steiria (III) *PA* 7234; *APF* 228
ARESIAS *PA* 1596
DIOKLES *PA* 4006
PHAIDRIAS *PA* 13937
CHAIRELEOS *PA* 15137; *APF* 85
ANAITIOS (? of Sphettos) (v) ? *PA* 800
PEISON (? of Kerameis (v)) *PA* 11791
SOPHOKLES (? son of Sostratides) *PA* 12827
ERATOSTHENES *PA* 5035; *APF* 184f.
CHARIKLES son of Apollodoros *PA* 15407; *APF* 502f.
ONOMAKLES *PA* 11476
THEOGNIS (or ? THEOMENES of Xypete (VII)) *PA* 6736
AISCHINES *PA* 341
THEOGENES *PA* 6692
KLEOMEDES *PA* 8596
ERASISTRATOS *PA* 5028
PHEIDON *PA* 14179
DRAKONTIDES of Aphidna (IX) *PA* 4546
EUMATHES (? of Phaleron) (IX) *PA* 5807
ARISTOTELES (? son of Timokrates of Thorai) (x) *PA* 2057 = ?2055
HIPPOMACHOS *PA* 7650
MNESITHEIDES *PA* 10277

The full list is at Xen. *Hell.* 2.3.2 and for their activities see Lysias 12, 13, 25; Isok. 18; Xen. *Hell.* 2.3f.; *Ath. Pol.* 34.3ff.; Diod. 14.3ff., 32ff. (401/0); Justin 5.8.5ff.; on Kritias Xen. *Mem.* 1.2.31; Dem. 24.90; Aisch. 1.173; Nepos *Alc.* 10.1; *Thras.* 2.7; on Chremon Lysias 30.12, 14; on Theramenes Plut. *Mor.* 105b; Suda *s.v.* Εὐμεταβολώτερος κοθόρνου; on Phaidrias Dem. 19.196 (Phaidimos); on Charikles Xen. *Mem.* 1.2.31; Arist. *Pol.* 5.6 1305b 26.

For details and sources see Rhodes, *Comm.* 415ff., esp. 427ff.; Krentz, *Thirty*. I have been careful not to ascribe identities, on which see Rhodes 435 and especially Whitehead, *JHS* 1980, 208–13, than whom I believe I am even more cautious. Also on demotics see Walbank, *Hesperia* 1982, 78ff. (Eumathes, Anaitios, Peison, Theomenes (doubtful)), 92f. n.44, 93. When Theramenes was killed, his place was offered to Thrasyboulos

(Diod. 14.32.5; Justin 5.9.13; Orosius 2.17.11), but he refused; if Lysias 30.12 is not careless in saying that Satyros was one of the Thirty, it may be that he took Theramenes' place (Krentz 64). I will not detail the establishment and repeal of regulations during this regime.

Note: I do not accept that the ephoroi of Lysias 12.43, 46, said to be chosen by 'the so-called hetairoi', were in any way state officials.

Archons in Peiraieus
MOLPIS *PA* 10407
CHARMIDES son of Glaukon *PA* 15512; *APF* 330f.
Xen. *Hell.* 2.4.19 (Charmides); Androtion *FGH* 324 F 11 (Molpis; Fornara no. 170B). Cf. Rhodes, *Comm.* 438f.

The Eleven
SATYROS of Kephisia (I) *PA* 12598; cf. *APF* 566
Xen. *Hell.* 2.3.54ff.; Lysias 30.12, 14. Cf. Rhodes, *Comm.* 430, 439.

? --BOLOS of Oion (IV)
Walbank, *Hesperia* 1982, 83f., 93, 94 (SEG 32.161)

The Ten
PHEIDON *PA* 14179
HIPPOKLES *PA* 7619
EPICHARES of Lamptrai (I) *PA* 4991
RHINON (? son of Charikles of Paiania) (III) *PA* 12532; *APF* 67
PHAYLLOS of Acherdous (VIII) *PA* 14125; *APF* 53f.
For the first three Lysias 12.55ff.; for the others *Ath. Pol.* 38.3f.; for Rhinon Isok. 18.6, 8. They were chosen to supersede the Thirty. On the activities of the Ten see Rhodes, *Comm.* 456ff. and 459f., against a second board of ten. For this second board see Walbank, *Hesperia* 1982, 93f. n.47; at 93 n.46 Walbank adds Eratosthenes, but this seems unwarranted.

Hipparchos
LYSIMACHOS *PA* 9486
Xen. *Hell.* 2.4.8, 26. He was with the Thirty.

Tamiai
CHARIADES son of Charias of Agryle (I) *PA* 15310; *APF* 569
-- of Xypete (VII)
MENEKRATES of Oinoe (VIII or IX)
IG i³ 380.2f. (SEG 21.80; 24.45; 29.19). All ten could hardly have been listed; perhaps seven or eight were.
Grammateus
DROMOKLEIDES
Krentz, *Hesperia* 1979, 59 restored him at line 4 of SEG 21.80, where the demotic alone survives, but this means that he has to deny that πρῶτος ἐγραμμάτευε has its natural reference to the first secretary of the council; his contention is that Dromokleides was a tamias and the members of that

board took turns as secretary. This is unacceptable in every way. Dromokleides appears in the conjuction of IG ii² 1370 and 1371 which is SEG 23.81 as secretary to the tamiai. So he ought to remain, without demotic, while the demotic of Prasiai may be left without a name for the first secretary, as it is at IG i³ 380.

Hellenotamiai
CHAIRE--
--CHOS of Peiraieus (VIII)
ATHEMION (? of Rhamnous) (IX)
-- of Anakaia (VIII)
ONESIPHON
IG i³ 380.6f., 12 (see the references under tamiai).

Envoys
KEPHISOPHON (? of Paiania) (III) *PA* 8400 = ?8401 = ?8415 = ?8416; *APF* 148
MELETOS *PA* 9825
Xen. *Hell*. 2.4.36. They were sent as 'private individuals from those in the city' to Sparta to persuade Lysandros to send a garrison.

COUNCIL AND ASSEMBLY

The first secretary is found at IG i³ 380 (see above on tamiai):
Grammateus
-- of Prasiai (III)

Our sources on the time of the Thirty tell of activities of council and demos, but mainly in regard to judicial matters. I have already said that I will not detail the provisions of the Thirty, but we may single out some elements.

(i)   First the acceptance that the democracy be dissolved and the Thirty chosen, opposed initially, according to Diod. 14.3, by Theramenes. The proposer of the decree to establish oligarchy is named at Lysias 12.73; *Ath. Pol.* 34.3; schol. Ar. *Wasps* 157:
Proposer
DRAKONTIDES of Aphidna (IX) *PA* 4546
I may mention too the proceedings in the council concerning the fate of Theramenes, at which he and Kritias spoke (Xen. *Hell*. 2.3.23ff.; Diod. 14.4.5ff.).

(ii) Paus. 1.23.9 tells of the decree to recall Thucydides:
Proposer
OINOBIOS (? of Dekeleia) (VIII) *PA* 11357

We know of three councillors specifically:
Bouleutai
EPICHARES *PA* 4991
And. 1.95. Despite *PA*, he was probably not the same man as the member

of the Ten: see Krentz, *Thirty* 92.

TEISIAS *PA* 13470
Isok. 16.43.

EUANDROS (? son of Erithalion of Euonymon) (I) *PA* 5267 = ?5271; *APF* 187f.
Lysias 26.10.

APPENDIX

Basileus
?PHYROMACHOS *PA* 15053
IG i³ 1384 (i² 776) dated to the late fifth century.

Strategoi
?LAMACHOS son of Xenophanes of Oe (VI) *PA* 8981
See 426/5.

SOPHOKLES son of Sophillos of Kolonos (II) *PA* 12834
Plut. *Nik.* 15.2 has him as general at a time when Nikias also held the position. Westlake (*Hermes* 1956, 110–16; cf. Sealey, *Essays* 110) argues for 423/2, but the argument is weak and based upon a supposition of general-ship representation to which I do not subscribe, as is in part Woodbury, *Phoenix* 1970, 211ff. Ehrenberg, *Soph. and Per.* 117 n.1, though dubious, suggests 421–415. Cf. Fornara, *Generals* 61 n.97.

LYSIKRATES *PA* 9443
Schol. Ar. *Birds* 513. This will date before 415/14.

ANTIPHON (? son of Lysonides) *PA* 1283; *APF* 327
Plut. *Mor.* 832f; Philostratos *Lives* 1.15. Plutarch mentions generalship, which ought to be ascribed to this Antiphon and not his subject, and Philostratos says he was often general. See also 411.

KLEOPHON son of Kleippides of Acharnai (VI) *PA* 8638
While Fornara, *Generals* 70 is correct to say that Ar. *Frogs* with schol. and Lysias 13.12 do not prove a generalship for Kleophon in 406/5 or 405/4, the scholiast does call him general and he may have been so earlier. Cf. Connor, *New Politicians* 146; Lewis, *JHS* 1961, 123.

Note: Theramenes was elected general for 405/4, but was rejected at the dokimasia (Lysias 13.10).

Hipparchoi
[PYTHODORO]S son of Epizelos (of Halai) (II) *PA* 12402 = 12410; *APF* 481
IG i³ 999 (i² 816). Davies, *Wealth* 154, has *c.* 420.

DIEITREPHES (? son of Nikostratos of Skambonidai) (IV) *PA* 3755
Ar. *Birds* 799. Hipparch after being phylarch at a date before 415/14.

Phylarchos
DIEITREPHES (? son of Nikostratos of Skambonidai) (IV) *PA* 3755
See above hipparchoi.

Taxiarchos
THORYKION *PA* 7419
Schol. Ar. *Frogs* 362. Such at some time during the war.

Phrourarchos?
GYLON of Kerameis (V) *PA* 3098
Aisch. 3.171. He could have held some such position when he betrayed
Nymphaion to the enemy.

Note: Clairmont, *Patrios Nomos* 197f., identifies a phrourarch Smikrias in
Agora XVII.22.123 (IG i³ 1192), but in that publication Phrourarchos is
(correctly) a name.

Hellenotamiai
?SOSIAS *PA* 13176
Antiphon 5.70. See the appendix to Section IV.

-- of Kydathenaion (III)
IG i³ 367.2f. (i² 309). Dated only to 430–426; Lewis, *ZPE* 37 (1980), 106f.

DEMODOKOS of Anagyrous (I) *PA* 3464
Plato *Theages* 127e. See *ATL* I.570.

ARISTODEMOS of Bate (II) *PA* 1812
Plut. *Mor.* 841b. The text may be unclear and *ATL* II.125 presumes the
reference is to Lykourgos son of Lykomedes of Boutadai (VI) (*PA* 9249;
APF 349f.). But the run of the passage makes it clear that Aristodemos was
the hellenotamias and the time should be near the end of this period.

The Eleven
DIOGNETOS (? son of Nikeratos of Kydantidai) (II) *PA* 3850 = ?3863; *APF*
405
Eupolis F 122B *b* 15f. (Edmonds). This must be before his banishment in
411 (assuming the identification), for which see Lysias 18.9.

Officials at Eleusis
I include these men under this heading, as it is not always clear what their
exact position is.
A. IG i³ 392: *c.* 420
Hieropoioi
-- of Alopeke (X)
D--
Others
AISCHYLIDES
E-- (? epistates)

B. IG i³ 393: *c.* 420
   Hieropoios
   -- of Xypete (VII)
   Other
   NIKOMA[CHOS] (for whom see also IG i³ 394.5)

C. IG i³ 394 (i² 318): *c.* 420
   Others
   RH--
   AR--

Epistatai
IG i³ 408, dated *c.* 412–405 ?, is conjectured to be related to works on the Tholos. There appears in it what seems to be the beginning of a name:
PHORYS--
This could be that of an epistates or of the grammateus, depending on whether the letters --os in the next line be taken as the ending of the secretary's name or of a patronymic.

The following were epistatai of the golden Nike around 407/6; they come from IG i³ 469.27f. (i² 369.7f.):
THEOTIMOS of Cholargos (V)
SKOPAS of Pithos (VII) *PA* 12735
ANTI--
   Grammateus
   --OS son of Diogeiton of Acharnai (VI) *PA* 3793

Hypogrammateis
NIKOMACHOS *PA* 10934
TEISAMENOS son of Mechanion *PA* 13443
Lysias 30.28 says 'you [have chosen as lawgivers] Teisamenos son of Mechanion and Nikomachos and other men ὑπογραμματέας'. It is not certain that this should be taken literally (Dow, *Historia* 1960, 271 n.1), but at the end of *c.* 27 Lysias has ἀντὶ δὲ ὑπογραμματέως νομοθέτης.

Miscellaneous
IG i³ 411 (i² 378) is included as an account or inventory from the second half of the fifth century. In it appear the remains of an official (?tamias) and secretary. Thompson (*Hesperia* 1965, 148) was not encouraged to identify these remains with the tamiai of 430/29, where I have noticed i³ 411. Given the unwillingness of i³ to be committed to this view, I hope this repetition was justified.

IG i³ 148 (i² 37) contains what appear to be the remains of a name:
--OKLES-- Phi--
The last element could be patronymic or demotic. For speculation on restoration and date see i³; appendix to Section IV decree xxix.

DEMODOKOS of Anagyrous (I) *PA* 3464
He is said at Plato *Theages* 127e to have held many high offices, which should mean others beside those noted elsewhere.

POLYSTRATOS of Deiradiotai (IV) *PA* 12076; *APF* 467
Lysias 20.5 says he held many offices.

A final word on the mass (mess) of detail attached to Antiphon at Plut. *Mor.* 832f and following. There is a story that Antiphon (who is supposedly the son of Sophilos of Rhamnous (IX): *PA* 1304) went as an envoy to Syracuse at the height of the tyranny of Dionysios, which cost him his life. The truth of this must be as doubtful as the activities of any given Antiphon.

COUNCIL AND ASSEMBLY

Documents noticed in the appendix to Section IV which may belong in this period are IG i³ 43, 48 bis, 56, 132, 133, 141, 145, 147, 155, 156, 189, 207, 1454; also the decree of Kannonos (xlvi).

(i)
(ii) IG i³ 59 (i² 75) contains two decrees which seem to concern financial matters:
Grammateus
[PH]ANTOKLE[S] *PA* 14114
IG dates *c*. 430. It would seem to be not later than 422/1. Mattingly, *CQ* 1966, 187 brings in IG i² 37a (i³ 148) and dates to 426/5.

(iii) IG i³ 63 (i² 58) is a decree concerning the Aphytaians dated *c*. 426:
Proposers
PATROKLEIDES *PA* 11685
S[KOPAS?]

(iv) IG i³ 65 (i² 59; Walbank no. 39) is a probouleumatic proxeny decree for Apollonophanes of Kolophon with a rider, dated in IG *c*. 427/6, by Walbank *c*. 435–25:
Proposer
ANTIKL[ES?] ? *PA* 1051

(v) IG i³ 70 (Walbank no. 19) is restored as a probouleumatic decree with a rider granting proxeny, in the view of Walbank, who has the more definite readings, to Chion and his sons; IG dates 430–420, Walbank *c*. 445–430:
Proposer
KLEONYMOS

(vi)
(vii) IG i³ 72 (i² 68 + 69) has two decrees concerning the Boiotians, the first of pryt. Aigeis:
Grammateus
PHIL[EAS] son of Lykos

IG dates 414?, but this must remain open. Cf. Bradeen and McGregor, *Studies* 90.

(viii) IG i³ 78 (i² 76; *LS* no. 5; ML 73; Fornara no. 140) is a decree of pryt. Kekropis originating from syngrapheis, with a rider, and concerning the Eleusinian *aparchai*:
Grammateus
TIMOTEL[E]S of Acharnai (VI) *PA* 13827
Bouleutes epistates
KYKNEAS *PA* 8940
Proposer
LAMPON *PA* 8996

(ix) IG i³ 89 (i² 71) concerns arrangements with Perdikkas of Makedon; it
(x) begins with a rider to a probouleuma and at line 55 begins a separate measure passed in pryt. Aiantis on the proposal of the generals. IG dates 417–413?; for the suggestion of 415 see SEG 31.14.

(xi) IG i³ 91 (i² 144; Walbank no. 64) is a proxeny decree of pryt. Akamantis for Proxenides of Knidos:
Grammateus
ARCHIKLE[S] of Halai (II or VII) *PA* 2495
Bouleutes epistates
[ANTIKRATES] *PA* 1076
Proposer
DEMOS[TRATOS]
Antikrates is restored from IG i³ 92 (see below) and the two are dated *c.* 416/15 in IG, *c.* 430–415 by Walbank; Mattingly last favoured 425/4 (*Phoros* 92f.), 'vix recte' says IG i³. See Addenda p. 429.

(xii) IG i³ 92 (ii² 27; Walbank no. 65) dates to the same prytany as the last entry, with the same secretary and the epistates unrestored; it is a proxeny decree for Kallippos of Thessaly proposed by the generals. Now dated to 422/1; see Addenda p. 429.

(xiii) IG i³ 98 (ii² 12; ML 80; Walbank no. 75) is a proxeny decree in honour of Pythophanes:
Grammateus
--ATES of Ikarion (II)
Bouleutes epistates?
..⁴.. S
Proposer
[HI]PPOMENES *PA* 7554
This inscription is usually dated to 411, but I am sufficiently unconvinced not to have entered it under that year even with a query. The argument for 411 depends very much upon identifying the five individuals mentioned in the prescript (if such it is: Henry, *Prescripts* 14f.) with proedroi of the

oligarchy. It is, however, open to serious doubt that there were men called proedroi doing the work of the epistates during that period; the case is put succinctly, but firmly, by Rhodes, *Comm.* 397f. Walbank, in the 1970 dissertation which became his book, found the name Antikrates in Ikarion (*PA* 1084); Polykrates was another suggestion. He was looking for a man with oligarchic sympathies. Menekrates (*PA* 9949) also appears in the deme, but I would point out that the Amphikrates of IG i³ 177 (see below) would exactly fit the space at the beginning of line 3 of i³ 98. If we could get over the dating of i³ 98 to 411, we could then put both of these documents in the same prytany of the same year. I will not speculate here on the actual nature of the five men mentioned.

(xiv) There is the matter of what may be a proxeny decree for three exiles from the Hellespont. IG i³ 106 (i² 106) and 186 are still associated at Walbank no. 85; IG dates 106 to 409/8, with no date for 186, while Walbank dates the combination *c.* 410–405, with a propensity for 409/8. The following is from i³ 186:

Grammateus

NAUPO[N] (? son of Krates of Lamptrai) (I)

For the relationships see Walbank p. 427.

(xv) IG i³ 107 (i² 106a; Walbank no. 93) is a proxeny decree dated *c.* 409 in IG,
(xvi) *c.* 420–400 by Walbank. It mentions a previous decree, with regard to which we have

Proposer

. . ⁵ . . POS

(xvii) IG i³ 113 (i² 113; SEG 26.23; Osborne D 3) is restored as a probouleumatic decree honouring Euagoras of Salamis, dated *c.* 410 in IG, early 407 by Osborne (cf. Lewis in SEG). The first name might be that of a proposer, the second concerns the rider:

Proposers

[PHR]ASIDEM[OS]

KLEO. . .

I have not ventured to restore the latter as Kleophon.

(xviii) IG i³ 121 (Walbank no. 84) is part of a proxeny decree dated 410–405 in IG, *c.* 430–405 by Walbank; it may be of pryt. Hippothontis, but that depends on the demotic of the man who might be epistates. For the secretary, I record the readings of IG and Walbank:

Grammateus?

AIN--

--AIK--

Bouleutes epistates?

-- of Anakaia (VIII)

(xix) IG i³ 137 (i² 78; LSS no. 8) is a decree concerning the worship of Apollo, dated *c.* 422–416:

Grammateus
ANTIKRATIDES
Bouleutes epistates
--OS
Proposer
PHILOXENOS
For suggestions on the identity of the latter see the commentary of i³.

(xx) IG i³ 158 (i² 160; Osborne x 28) is an honorary decree of pryt. Oineis for Korinthios dated *c*. 430:
Bouleutes epistates
LY--

(xxi) IG i³ 159 (i² 169; Walbank no. 37) is a proxeny decree of pryt. Kekropis or Hippothontis, dated *c*. 430 in IG, *c*. 430–420 by Walbank; I refrain from restoration:
Grammateus
. .⁴. . OS or . . .⁷. . . OS
Proposer
A . . .⁶. . . or AR . . .⁶. . .

(xxii) IG i³ 160 (i² 62; Walbank no. 40) is part of a proxeny decree mentioning Sicily, dated in IG *c*. 435–420, by Walbank *c*. 435–415, though the latter shows that a date around 427 is preferable. Walbank shows a restoration of proposer which I do not follow.

(xxiii) IG i³ 164 (i² 152 and 154; Walbank no. 55) in the second part is a proxeny
(xxiv) decree, dated by Walbank to *c*. 430–410. The whole thing is dated in IG 440–425 and in the first part we find:
Proposer
DEMOKLEIDES *PA* 3475
This part is probouleumatic.

(xxv) IG i³ 165 (i² 85; Walbank no. 35) is a proxeny decree dated *c*. 430–420:
Proposer
T . . .⁶. . . or T . . . .⁹. . . .

(xxvi) IG i³ 167 (i² 149; Walbank no. 43) is a proxeny decree, possibly for Euphemos and sons, dated *c*. 430–415:
Grammateus
--S

(xxvii) I find Walbank's restoration of a proposer in his no. 58 (IG i³ 169) too hypothetical.

(xxviii) IG i³ 170 (i² 150; Walbank no. 54) is possibly a proxeny decree, dated 430–405 in IG, *c*. 430–410 by Walbank:
Proposer
E-- or ECH . . .⁷. . .

(xxix) IG i³ 173 (i² 148; Walbank no. 28) is perhaps a proxeny decree, probouleumatic, dated 430–405 in IG, c. 435–420 by Walbank:
Proposer
AN . . ⁵ . . or AL . . ⁵ . .

(xxx) IG i³ 174 and 175 (i² 93; Walbank nos. 50 and 51) are possibly copies of the
(xxxi) same proxeny decree; the first at least is for Lykon of Achaia and both are dated 425–410 in IG, c. 430–410 by Walbank. The first provides data:
Grammateus
[?THE]AIOS *PA* Add. 6642
Bouleutes epistates
[ARI]S[T]AINETOS or . .LE.AINETOS
Proposer
PEISANDROS (? son of Glauketes of Acharnai) (VI) *PA* 11770

(xxxii) IG i³ 177 (ii² 60; Walbank no. 63) is a proxeny decree of pryt. Oineis (Walbank) for Xanthippos (Walbank) dated 420–405 in IG, c. 420–410 by Walbank:
Grammateus
AMPHIKRATES *PA* 768
Bouleutes epistates
PISTOKLES
Proposer
EUXITHEOS ?*PA* 5901
See above on IG i³ 98. On the basis of Walbank's arguments I am drawn towards 415/14.

(xxxiii) IG i³ 179 (ii² 73; Walbank no. 92) is a proxeny decree dated 415–405 in IG, c. 430–405 by Walbank, though he properly argues for a date close to, if not in, 405/4; the offices belonging to the names must remain uncertain:
Grammateus?
KALLIK--
Bouleutes epistates or proposer?
THEOPH--
(xxxiv) On Walbank's reconstruction, there is also mentioned a previous decree:
Proposer
[T]EISAMENOS (? son of Mechanion) ?*PA* 13443

(xxxv) IG i³ 180 (i² 67; Walbank no. 88) is what seems to be a proxeny decree with a rider, dated c. 415–410 in IG, c. 425–405 by Walbank:
Proposer
. . . ⁷ . . . IAS

(xxxvi) IG i³ 190 (ii² 164) is a problematic piece:
Grammateus
-- son of [Eu]rytimos

(xxxvii) IG i³ 192 (i² 164) has

Appendix

Grammateus?
?[AM]EINOK[LES] or ?[D]EINOK[RATES]

(xxxviii) IG i³ 228 (ii² 32; Walbank no. 66) is a decree of 385/4 which republishes a proxeny for Archonides and Demon the Sikels dated by Walbank to c. 435–415; it is probouleumatic and has a rider:
Proposer
PHRASMON *PA* 14988

(xxxix) SEG 32.16 is the heading of an honorary decree of the late fifth century of pryt. Hippothontis.

(xl) D. M. Lewis (*ZPE* 60 (1985), 108) has discovered elements of an Athenian inscription in *Insc. Délos* 80; the name of the proposer reminds one of the busy orator of 426/5:
Grammateus
EUTHIPPOS
Proposer
[KL]EONYM[O]S

(xli) Athenaios 6.234e records a decree concerning Herakles at Kynosarges:
Grammateus
STEPHANOS son of Thoukydides of Alopeke (X) *PA* 12884; *APF* 233
Proposer
ALKIBIADES son of Kleinias of Skambonidai (IV) *PA* 600; *APF* 9ff.
One might compare IG i³ 134.

(xlii) Isok. 8.82 mentions a decree that tribute should be brought into the orchestra at the Dionysia. Raubitschek (*TAPhA* 1941, 356ff.) brings in Ar. *Knights* 313 and schol. and suggests Kleon may have been responsible in 427/6 or 428/7. A time around 430 would seem vaguely right (cf. Unz. *GRBS* 1985, 40f.).

(xliii) We hear of a decree reducing the payments to comic poets; Ar. *Frogs* 367 with schol. produces the first name of the proposer, schol. *Ekkl.* 102 the second. I record both; Rhodes, *Comm.* 431, manages to have the two working in concert. The measure must date before 405/4.
Proposers
ARCHINOS of Koile (VIII) *PA* 2526
AGYRRHIOS of Kollytos (II) *PA* 179; *APF* 278f.

We have one councillor to add:
Bouleutes
KLEON son of Kleainetos of Kydathenaion (III) *PA* 8674; *APF* 318ff. Ar. *Knights* 774 suggests he was so before 425/4; does *Acharn.* 379–81 suggest 427/6? There may be some connexion with the eisphora of 428 (Thuc. 3.19.1), but what is suggested in *Acharnians* could be in the wake of that rather than exactly at that time.

Section VI
403/2 to 378/7

403/2 (Ol. 94.2)

Archon

EUKLEIDES *PA* 5674

And. 1.87ff., 93f., 99; Lysias 21.4; Isaios 6.47, 8.43; Dem. 24.42 with schol., 133f., 43.51, 57.30; Aisch. 1.39 with schol.; *Ath. Pol.* 39.1; Diod. 14.12.1; Plut. *Arist.* 1.6, *Mor.* 835f; Lucian *Hermot.* 76; *Catapl.* 5; Athenaios 7.329c, 13.577b; *P.Oxy.* 2537, 34,38; Suda and Photios *s.v.* Σαμίων ὁ δῆμος (Harding no. 6); IG ii² 1.[42], 57 (Tod 97; Osborne D 4 + 5; Harding no. 5), 2.[7f.] (but see SEG 32.38); 1138.10, 1370.3; SEG 28.45.[78f.] (SEG 31.56; Harding no. 7).

Strategos

RHINON (? son of Charikles of Paiania) (III) *PA* 12532; *APF* 67
Ath. Pol. 38.4 with Rhodes' commentary.

Tamiai

LYSIK--
THEOGENES of Thria (VI) *PA* 6710
ANTIPHANES *PA* 1209

Grammateus

[MISGO]LAS of Kollytos (II)
IG ii² 1370.3ff. + 1371; Add. p.797 (West and Woodward, *JHS* 1938, 78ff.; Tréheux, 'Études', 41ff. (SEG 23.81)). Only three were listed in what was an inventory for the year.

Anagrapheis or nomothetai

TEISAMENOS son of Mechanion *PA* 13443
NIKOMACHOS *PA* 10934
Lysias 30. They held office for the revision of the laws for four years; see Dow, *Historia* 1960, 271f.

Envoy

PHILON of Koile (VIII) *PA* 14847
Isok. 18.22. He was indicted for malversation on an embassy, but not tried.

COUNCIL AND ASSEMBLY

IG ii² 1 (Tod 97; Osborne D 4 + 5; Harding no. 5) begins with a re-inscription of the citizenship decree for the Samians of 405/4 (IG i³ 127; i²

126; ML 94) and continues with two probouleumatic decrees reaffirming
(i) and amplifying this. The first is of pryt. Pandionis:
Grammateus
AGYRRHIOS of Kollytos (II) *PA* 179; *APF* 278f.
Bouleutes epistates
[KA]LLIAS of Oa (III)
Proposer
KEPHISOPHON (? of Paiania) (III) *PA* 8401 = ?8400 = ?8415 = ?8416; *APF*
148

(ii) The second is of pryt. Erechtheis:
Grammateus
KEPHISOPHON of Paiania (III) *PA* 8416 = ?8400 = ?8401 = ?8415; *APF*
148
Bouleutes epistates
PYTHON of Kedoi (I) *PA* 12471
Proposer
EU . . . .⁸ . . . .

For IG ii² 2 see the appendix to this Section.

(iii) SEG 28.45 (31.56; Harding no. 7) is a decree honouring the heroes of
Phyle, which may be restored with reference to Aisch. 3.187 and the
assumption that Kephisophon was epistates, which should give the
prytany of Pandionis and Agyrrhios again as secretary:
Bouleutes epistates
KEPH[ISOPHON of Paiania] (III) = *PA* 8416 = ?8400 = ?8401 = ?8415; *APF*
148
Proposer
ARCHINOS of Koile (VIII) *PA* 2526

(iv) SEG 28.46 (32.37) is a decree of pryt. Antiochis concerning orphans,
seemingly the one which was indicted as unconstitutional (Hansen, *Sover-
eignty* no.5):
Grammateus
. . . . .⁸ . . . . S
Bouleutes epistates
KALLISTHENES
Proposer
[THEO]ZOTIDES *PA* 6913 = 6914; *APF* 222f.

(v) Suda and Photios *s.v.* Σαμίων ὁ δῆμος (Theopompos *FGH* 115 F 155;
Harding no. 6) record the decision to adopt the Ionic alphabet, in which the
'persuader' appears by emendation:
Proposer
ARCHINOS of Koile (VIII) *PA* 2526

(vi) Archinos was also responsible for a law on legal procedure (Isok. 18.2;
schol. Aisch. 1.163). He features in *Ath. Pol.* 40, urging the execution

without trial of one who did not respect the amnesty in the boule and
(vii) indicting as illegal a proposal to give citizenship to all those who returned
from Peiraieus (also Aisch. 3.195; Plut. *Mor.* 835f–836a; Hansen, *Sovereignty* no. 4):
Proposer
THRASYBOULOS son of Lykos of Steiria (III) *PA* 7310; *APF* 240

A number of measures are ascribed to
Proposer
ARISTOPHON son of Aristophanes of Azenia (VIII) *PA* 2108; *APF* 64ff.
(viii) First is the law that those not born of a citizen mother should be held as
(ix) illegitimate (Athenaios 13.577b), which looks very similar to a decree
mentioned at schol. Aisch. 1.39:
Proposer
NIKOMENES *PA* 10968
(x) Second for Aristophon is a re-enactment of Solon's law forbidding
foreigners to do business in the agora without paying the tax (Dem.
(xi) 57.31ff.). Third is the repayment of five talents to Gelarchos (Dem.
20.149).

(xii) And. 1.82ff. records a decree for the revision of the laws:
Proposer
TEISAMENOS son of Mechanion *PA* 13443

(xiii) Dion. *Lysias* 32ff. records a speech (Lysias 34) against a proposal to restrict
citizen rights to those with landed property:
Proposer
PHORMISIOS *PA* 14945

402/1 (Ol. 94.3)

Archon
MIKON *PA* 10199
MP A 65; Diod. 14.17.1; hyp. ii Sophokles *OC*; IG ii² 1370 + 1371.[9]
(SEG 23.81); 1372.[2] (SEG 23.82); 1407.[27]; SEG 32.161.3.

Tamiai
-- of Teithras (II)
--KLES of Aixone (VII)
RHIN[ON] (? son of Charikles of Paiania (III)) ?*PA* 12532; *APF* 67
    Grammateus
    KLEISOPHOS of Euonymon (I) *PA* 8529
IG ii² 1371.2ff. (SEG 23.81.9ff.); 1372.2ff. (SEG 23.82). I am not confident of the identification of Rhinon with the general of 403/2. IG ii²
1372 + 1402 + SEG 17.39 (SEG 23.82) is an inventory of epeteia.

Anagrapheis or nomothetai
TEISAMENOS son of Mechanion *PA* 13443

NIKOMACHOS *PA* 10934
See 403/2.

In *Hesperia* 1982, 75ff. (SEG 32.161) Walbank has published a number of stelai (poletai records) to be dated in or at least around 402/1, on which may be identified the following officials (for whom see Walbank's commentary):

A.   **Grammateus**
   EUTHYMACH[O]S ? son of Alk[imachos of Agryle] (I)
   One presumes this is secretary to the council. The prytany is the seventh, of Aigeis.
   Poletai
   Grammateus
   --ATOS or -- son of --ates of Plotheia (II)
   Demarchoi
   [M]ENIPPOS of Phaleron (IX)
   . . . . ? . . . . of Sphettos (V)
   . . . . ? . . . . of Kerameis (V)

B. **Demarchos**
   . . . ? . . . of Agryle (I)
   Archon of Salamis?
   LEUKOLOPHOS
   I do not accept the argument that because he has no demotic he cannot be taken as an Athenian citizen; it is his status with regard to Salamis that is relevant in the context of the inscription.

C. **Demarchos**
   NOTHIPPOS of Oion (IV or VIII)

D. **Archons or thesmothetai**
   . . . . ? . . . . S
   CHARISIOS
   Demarchoi
   PLATON of Aphidna (IX)
   ARCHEDEMOS [? of Skambonidai] (IV)

E. **Archon or thesmothetes?**
   --OUT--

   Archon or thesmothetes?
   B--

401/0 (Ol. 94.4)

Archon
XENAINETOS *PA* 11174
Lysias 17.3; *Ath. Pol.* 40.4; Diod. 14.19.1 (Exainetos); Diog. 2.6.55; IG ii²

10.[2] (Tod 100; Osborne D 6 with commentary against the dating of Krentz, *Phoenix* 1980, 298–306 (403/2; cf. SEG 28.47, but see also now the change in Krentz, *ZPE* 62 (1986), 201–4); Harding no. 3); [1372] (SEG 23.82); 1374.[9]; 1375.[13]; 2318.[141].

Tamiai
-- of Kephisia (I)
POLYEUKTOS of Erchia (II) *NPA* 144
ANDOKIDES son of Leogoras of Kydathenaion (III) *PA* 828; *APF* 29ff.
-- of Oe (VI)
DIODO[TOS ?] of tribe VII or VIII *NPA* 54
-- of Aigilia (X)
And. 1.132 (Andokides); IG ii² 1372 (SEG 23.82). Probably only seven were listed.

Anagrapheis or nomothetai
TEISAMENOS son of Mechanion *PA* 13443
NIKOMACHOS *PA* 10934
See 403/2.

COUNCIL AND ASSEMBLY

IG ii² 10 (Tod 100; Osborne D 6; Harding no. 3; Krentz, *ZPE* 62 (1986), 201–4), on the date of which see above under archon, is a citizenship decree for the heroes of Phyle, restored to pryt. Hippothontis:
Grammateus
LYSIADES *PA* 9333
Bouleutes epistates
DEMOPHILOS *PA* 3661
Proposer
[THRASYBOULOS] (son of Lykos of Steiria) (III) *PA* 7310; *APF* 240

400/399 (Ol. 95.1)

Archon
LACHES *PA* 9011
MP A 66; Diod. 14.35.1; Ael. Arist. 3.578 (Behr); hyp. Isok. 11; IG ii² 11; [1374]; [1375]; 1377.7; 1378.[10]; 2318.[153]; Add. 1378 + 1398; SEG 19.126.

Tamiai
MEIDON of Euonymon (I) *PA* 9739
SOPHOKLES (son of Iophon of Kolonos) (II) *PA* 12833
[AL]KIDEMOS of Myrrhinous (III) *PA* 607
PE-- of tribe IV
[D]ERKYLOS of Poros (V) *PA* 3250; *APF* 98
POLY-- of tribe VI

-- of Pithos (VII)

AR[IST]OMEDES (son of Aristophanes) of Azenia (VIII) *PA* 2011; *APF* 65

. . . . .[11]. . . . .   of Rhamnous (IX)

HEGELEOS of Alopeke (X) *PA* 6277

Grammateus

THERSILOCHOS of Oinoe (IX) *PA* 7195

IG ii² 1374.3ff.; 1375.3ff.; for Meidon and the secretary 1377.8f.; 1378.10f. Inventories of the year are ii² 1374 and 1375.

Anagrapheis or nomothetai

TEISAMENOS son of Mechanion *PA* 13443

NIKOMACHOS *PA* 10934

See 403/2.

COUNCIL AND ASSEMBLY

IG ii² 11 is but a fragment:

Grammateus

-- of Halai (II or VII)

399/8 (Ol. 95.2)

Archon

ARISTOKRATES *PA* 1894

MP A 67; Diod. 14.38.1; IG ii² 12.29 (i³ 98); 13; 1375.[20]; [1377]; 1378; 1388.[13f.]; 1392.13f.; 2318.[165]; SEG 19.126.

Tamiai

SOKRATES of Lamptrai (I) *PA* 13116

PHILIPPOS of tribe II *PA* 14370

--DOROS of Oa (III)

THORYKION of tribe IV *PA* 7420

DION of tribe V or VI

LAMPROKLES of Phlya (VII) *PA* 8994

EPIKRATES of tribe VIII

DEMOKRATES of Rhamnous (IX) *PA* 3537

. . . . .[11]. . . . .   of Aigilia (X)

Grammateus

CHAIRION of Eleusis (VIII) *PA* 15263

IG ii² 1375.21ff.; 1377; 1378; for Sokrates and the secretary 1388.14f.; 1392.14f. Only nine were listed and inventories of the year are ii² 1377 and 1378.

COUNCIL AND ASSEMBLY

(i) IG ii² 12 is a decree probably with further honours for Pythophanes (IG i³ 98) of pryt. Kekropis:

Bouleutes epistates
. . .⁷. . . S

(ii) IG ii² 13 is a proxeny decree of pryt. Pandionis for Aristeas:
Grammateus
LYSIMACHOS of Kolonai (IV or X) *PA* 9518
Bouleutes epistates
KLEON *PA* 8663
Proposer
. . .⁶. . . ON

398/7 (Ol. 95.3)

Archon
EUTHYKLES *PA* 5575
Diod. 14.44.1 (Ithykles); IG ii² [1388] (Harding no 10); [1391]; 1392;
1407.27 (removed, however: see SEG 16.115).

Tamiai
EPICHARES of Euonymon (I) *PA* 4986
PROTOKLES of Ikarion (II) *PA* 12315
KEPHISOPHON of Paiania (III) *PA* 8416 = 8415 = ?8400 = ?8401; *APF* 148
CHARIAS of Pelekes (IV) *PA* 15358
DEMOKLES of Kephale (V) *PA* 3499
DIOGEITON of Acharnai (VI) *PA* 3794
DIOMEDES (? son of Lykomedes) of Phlya (VII) *PA* 4072; *APF* 347
ARISTOKLES of Hamaxanteia (VIII) *PA* 1858; *APF* 55
PHILOKRATES of Aphidna (IX) *PA* 14603; *NPA* 166
ANTHEMION of Anaphlystos (X) *PA* 939
  Grammateus
  MNESIERGOS of Athmonon (VII) *PA* 10275
IG ii² 1388 (Harding no. 10); 1391.6ff.; 1392.4ff. These inscriptions are
the inventories of the year; to 1388 add 1403, 1405, 1408, EM 6790 (SEG
23.83).

397/6 (Ol. 95.4)

Archon
SOUNIADES of Acharnai (VI) *PA* 12817
Lysias 7.11; Philochoros *FGH* 328 F 144–5 (Harding no. 12B); Diod.
14.47.1 (Lysiades); IG ii² 1388.8 (Harding no. 10); 1392.[9].

Tamiai
. . . .⁸. . . . ATOS of Euonymon (I)
CHARIAS of Araphen (II) *PA* 15338
DI-- of tribe III
EUBIOS of Aithalidai (IV) *PA* 5293

EUATHLOS of Kerameis (V) *PA* 5239
-- of Acharnai (VI) or Aixone (VII) or Athmonon (VII)
PHILOTADES of Dekeleia (VIII) *PA* 14923
--XENOS of Anaphlystos (X)
Grammateus
MORYCHOS of Boutadai (VI) *PA* 10422
IG ii² 1388.9ff. (Harding no. 10); 1392.9ff. Only eight were listed.

Envoys
--KRATES
HAGNIAS (? son of Polemon of Oion (IV)) *PA* 133; *APF* 82f.
TELESEGOROS (? of Kollytos) (II) ?*PA* 13512
Hell. Oxy. 7.1f.; ?Isaios 11.8 (Hagnias); Androtion *FGH* 324 F
18 = Philochoros *FGH* 328 F 147 (Harding no. 11C). They and others were
sent to Persia, but were captured and executed at Sparta. For date and
discussion see Bruce, *Historia* 1966, 272, 276; Hamilton, *Bitter Victories*
177f.; cf. Seager, *JHS* 1967, 96 n.6. The identity of Hagnias is made very
doubtful by Humphreys, *CPh* 1983, 219ff.; see the appendix to Section
VII.

COUNCIL AND ASSEMBLY

A man who is presumably first secretary heads IG ii² 1391 and I place him
here because in that inscription the tamiai of 397/6 will have been mentioned; the secretary may be mentioned because the paradosis took place
before the boule (*Ath. Pol.* 47.1), but the heading is unique:
Grammateus
. . ⁵ . . os son of Meneteles of Phrearrhioi (IV) *NPA* 126

396/5 (Ol. 96.1)

Archon
PHORMION *PA* 14949
Diod. 14.54.1; IG ii² 1237.10, 45 (*LS* no. 19); 1395.9f.; 1540.50f.

Strategoi
?DEMAINETOS (? son of Demeas of Paiania) (III) *PA* 3265 = ?3276; *APF*
104f.
Hell. Oxy. 6.1ff. (Harding no. 11); cf. Aisch. 2.78. *Pace* Bruce, *Comm.* 51,
the fact that he is said to have made private arrangements with the boule
does not rule out an official position; his ship was state property. Kirchner
suggested the identification, but *APF* is properly cautious. He went to aid
Konon, but was disowned at Athens. This is dated to the end of 397/6 by
Bruce 72; Hamilton, *Bitter Victories* 178 n.45; see also Funke, *Homonoia*
66. If the Milon of *Hell. Oxy.* is the Cheilon of Aischines, the sources will
be associated and there will be an engagement with this Spartan. I am

inclined to think this is the case, but see Cawkwell, *CQ* 1976, 272f. n.14; Hansen, *GRBS* 1983, 163, dates the event of the Aischines passage to before 388.

?KLEOBOULOS son of Glaukos of Acharnai (VI) *PA* 8558; *APF* 544
Aisch. 2.78. Associated with Demainetos; see above. In reference to him *APF* dates this to 388.

Tamias
[HEU]RETES of Alopeke (X) *PA* 5943
IG ii² 1395.8f., which is an inventory.

COUNCIL AND ASSEMBLY

Hell. Oxy. 6.2f. tells of uproar in Athens after Demainetos' departure which resulted in an assembly at which it seems Thrasyboulos, Aisimos and Anytos spoke.

395/4 (Ol. 96.2)

Archon
DIOPHANTOS *PA* 4417
Diod. 14.82.1; Paus. 8.45.4; ?Zenobios *Paroim.* 3.37; ?Hesychios *s.v.* δραχμὴ χαλαζῶσα; IG ii² 1395; 1654.[24] (but see *Hesperia* 1938, 269 (Schweigert), for 405/4 and IG i³ p. 481 for 380–370 for the document); 1656 (Tod 107 A; Harding no. 17); xiv 1097.10.

Strategoi
?KTESIKLES *PA* 8861
Lysias 9.6. The date is the earliest possible. See Beloch, *Att. Pol.* 315; Hansen, *GRBS* 1983, 171, has 393/2 (?).

THRASYBOULOS son of Lykos of Steiria (III) *PA* 7310; *APF* 240f.
Plut. *Lys.* 29.1; Paus. 3.5.4f.; cf. Dem. 57.42. He was sent to Boiotia and was in command at Haliartos.

?HIERONYMOS *PA* 7552
Ephoros *FGH* 70 F 73; cf. Diod. 14.81.4. Diodoros has him with Konon (under 396/5) along with Nikodemos (=Nikophemos: *Hell. Oxy.* 15.1 (Harding no. 12C); Bruce, *Comm.* 99). He may not be an Athenian strategos, though Harpokration, who cites Ephoros, says so.

Hipparchos
PAMPHILOS of Keiriadai (VIII) *PA* 11545; *APF* 365
Lysias 15.5. He is more likely to have been hipparch than phylarch, as a phylarch is subsequently alluded to by Lysias.

Hipparchos or Phylarchos
ORTHOBOULOS of Kerameis (V) *PA* 11489; *APF* 364f.

Lysias 16.13. The mention of Haliartos dates him to this year more firmly than Pamphilos (above). On the role of the hipparchs and phylarchs in this context see Bugh, *TAPhA* 1982, 24.

Tamiai
--RIDES of Ionidai (II)
--IPPOS
--DEMOS
IG ii² 1395.3ff.

COUNCIL AND ASSEMBLY

(i) IG ii² 14 (Tod 101; Harding no. 14) will be the alliance with the Boiotians mentioned at Xen. *Hell.* 3.5.16; Lysias 16.13; And. 3.25.

(ii) IG ii² 15 (Tod 102; Harding no. 16) is an alliance with Lokrians which may be placed in the same context.

Xen. *Hell.* 3.5.7ff. tells of Theban envoys addressing the assembly and the Athenian vote to help; Thrasyboulos' words may have been in the assembly; Hansen, *GRBS* 1983, 169, has him propose the aid, but the text cannot bear this (for an analogy see Dem. 7.20). Cf. also Ar. *Ekkl.* 195f.

394/3 (Ol. 96.3)

Archon
EUBOULIDES son of Epikleides of Eleusis (VIII) *PA* 5325 + Add. = 5317
Lysias 19.28 (Euboulos); Diod. 14.85.1; Ael. Arist. 3.578 (Behr); IG ii² 16
a.5 (Tod 103; Harding no. 2; against the dating of Krentz, *AJPh* 1979, 398–400, see Knoepfler, *AJPh* 1980, 462f. n.2, though Krentz comes back at *Thirty* 85 n.59); 17.14 (Walbank no. 78; Osborne D 8); 18 (Tod 108; Harding no. 20); 19a (Osborne D 7); [20] (SEG 29.86 with Funke, *ZPE* 53 (1983), 152ff.); 1395.[8]; 1407.28; Add. 1424 a.349; 1425.287; 1657 (Tod 107 B; Harding no. 17); 1658; ?[1659]; 2811; 6217 (Tod 105; Harding no. 19C).

Paredros
DIKTYS son of Epikleides of Eleusis (VIII)
Grammateus
PROKLES son of Iophon of Kydathenaion (III)
IG ii² 2811.

Strategoi
THRASYBOULOS son of Lykos of Steiria (III) *PA* 7310; *APF* 240f.
Lysias 16.15. This is presuming that he is 'the fine chap from Steiria' and that he was general in the adverse battle at Nemeia and not a subordinate. On the matter of his generalship at Koroneia see Seager, *JHS* 1967, 99 n.33; Funke, *Homonoia* 113 n.32.

MNESIKL[ES] of tribe VI
[THO]UKLE[IDES] of tribe IX
IG ii² 5221 (Clairmont, *Patrios Nomos* 209ff.; Harding no. 19, which gives a false impression of the text).

?POLYSTRATOS *PA* 12070
Dem. 4.24; Harpokration *s.v.* Πολύστρατος. Supposedly in command of the mercenary force at Corinth; the date is uncertain and Didymos, says Harpokration, found no record of him; see the speculation of Thompson, *GRBS* 1985, 55 n.23. Perhaps he was the first in a chain of commanders, if such it is, as mentioned by Demosthenes, who says citizens were serving. It cannot be regarded as certain from Dem. 20.84 that he was rewarded with citizenship.

Phylarchos
ANTIPHANES of tribe V *PA* 1221
IG ii² 5222 (Clairmont, *Patrios Nomos* 212ff.; Harding no. 19B).

Taxiarchos
LACHES (? of Aixone) (VII) *PA* 9012
Lysias 3.45. He was at Corinth. For the deme see Davies, *Wealth* 151.

Envoys
?EPIKRATES of Kephisia (I) *PA* 4859; *APF* 181
?PHORMISIOS *PA* 14945
Plato com. F 119 (Edmonds); Plut. *Per.* 30.7; Athenaios 6.251a. The date is not certain for their embassy to Persia. For discussion see Bruce, *Historia* 1966, 272, 274ff., 277f.; Seager, *JHS* 1967, 103 n.77; Funke, *Homonoia* 106 and n.12.

?ARISTOPHANES son of Nikophemos *PA* 2082; *APF* 201f.
?EUNOMOS *PA* 5861
Lysias 19.19f. They were envoys to Dionysios of Syracuse, whom they persuaded not to send ships to help Sparta. The date could be 393/2, but perhaps the embassy followed quickly upon IG ii² 18, dated to the sixth prytany of 394/3. Cf. Funke, *Homonoia* 130f.

?EURIPPIDES (? son of Adeimantos of Myrrhinous) (III) *PA* 5955 = ?5949 = ?5956; *APF* 202ff.
Arist. *Rhet.* 2.6.20 1384b.15 and schol. Probably he was on the same embassy as Aristophanes and Eunomos.

COUNCIL AND ASSEMBLY

(i) IG ii² 16 (Tod 103; Harding no.2), on the date of which see above under archon, is a decree of pryt. Akamantis from the boule concerning alliance with Eretria:

Grammateus
CHELONION son of Theog-- *PA* 15546
Proposer
GNATHIO[S] *PA* 3043

(ii) IG ii² 17 (Walbank no. 78; Osborne D 8) contains two decrees of pryt. Aigeis from the boule granting citizenship to Sthorys of Thasos:
Grammateus
[ARI]STOKRATES son of Aischines of Kephale (v) *PA* 1913 = 1895
Bouleutes epistates
AMEIPS[IAS] *PA* 709

(iii) IG ii² 18 (Tod 108; Harding no. 20) is a decree of sixth pryt. of Pandionis from the boule honouring Dionysios of Syracuse:
Grammateus
PLATON son of Nikochares of Phlya (VII) *PA* 11860
Proposer
KINESIAS (? son of Meles) *PA* 8438

(iv) IG ii² 19 (Osborne D 7) is a probouleumatic decree of pryt. Leontis or Aiantis granting citizenship to a Rhodian:
Proposer
SOPH[I]L[OS] *PA* 13414

(v) IG ii² 20 is now augmented at SEG 29.86 and the secretary could be placed in ii² 19 (Funke, *ZPE* 53 (1983), 152ff.); it is a decree in honour of Euagoras of Salamis:
Grammateus?
ARISTOKL[ES] (? of Myrrhinous) (III) = ?*PA* 1850 or 1851
Proposer
SOPHILOS *PA* 13414
The prytany is again Leontis or Aiantis. It remains possible that the date is 393/2.

393/2 (Ol. 96.4)

Archon
DEMOSTRATOS of Kerameis *PA* 3612
Diod. 14.90.1; IG ii² Add. 1424a.352; 1425.291; 1660; 1661 (SEG 19.141); 1664.12; *Agora* xv.2 (SEG 19.150); *Insc. Délos* 97.[1], 6, [20f.] (IG ii² 1634); 97 *bis*.3. On the reconstruction of *Insc. Délos* this Demostratos and not the archon of 390/89 must possess the demotic.

Strategos
?IPHIKRATES son of Timotheos of Rhamnous (IX) *PA* 7737; *APF* 248ff. Xen. *Hell.* 4.4.9,15f.; Dem. 4.24; Nepos *Iph.* 2.1f.; Diod. 14.86.3, 91.2f., 92.2; Justin 6.5.2 (Harding no. 22c); Front. *Strat.* 2.1.6, 3.12.2; Polyainos

3.9.10,45,49,52,54; Orosius 3.1.21; Harpokration, Suda and Photios *s.v.* Ξενικὸν ἐν Κορίνθῳ (Harding no. 22A).

There are problems of chronology with Xenophon and Diodoros, but my assumption will be that Iphikrates remained in command of the force at Corinth until 390/89. A second question is whether he was a strategos of the Athenians or merely a mercenary commander; see Sealey, *Essays* 138 and n.54, Pritchett, *Greek State at War* 2.62f.; Thompson, *GRBS* 1985, 55f. There are indications that he was an official general. On Dem. 4.24 see 394/3 under the strategos (?) Polystratos. Frontinus calls Iphikrates 'dux Atheniensium' and Diodoros 14.92.2 speaks of him laying down his *arche* and the Athenians replacing him with the strategos Chabrias (this should be 390/89, *q.v.*; cf. Xen. *Hell.* 4.8.34). I am inclined to accept that he was strategos, despite the tradition of Justin and Orosius that he was only 20 years old at the time; we cannot say that an age limit was set for the strategia or that it could not be waived if it did exist. See Rhodes, *Comm.* 510; Develin, *ZPE* 61 (1985), 154f.

In this year Iphikrates was successful around Corinth and went into the territory of Phleious. The plundering and attacking of towns in Arkadia may belong here or in 392/1.

Amphiktyons to Delos
PANTARETOS son of Antiphilos of Alopeke (x) *PA* 11606
PAT--
THRASYBOULOS son of Thrason of Kollytos (II) *PA* 7305; *APF* 238ff.
Grammateus
ANT--
Insc. Délos 97; 97 *bis* (IG ii² 1634). In the reconstruction of *Insc. Délos* they served until 389/8.

Envoys
KONON son of Timotheos of Anaphlystos (x) *PA* 8707; *APF* 506ff.
HERMOGENES *PA* 5119; *APF* 269f.
DION (? of Lamptrai) (I) *PA* 4491 = ?4508
KALLISTHENES *PA* 8088
KALLIMEDON *PA* 8030; *APF* 279
Xen. *Hell.* 4.8.13ff.; IG ii² 1424a.350; 1425.289. They were sent to Tiribazos to counter the Spartan mission; see Bruce, *Historia* 1966, 272, 278. I avoid the prosopographical speculation of Sealey, *Essays* 138, but the suggestion for Dion comes from the lambda which follows his name in IG ii² 1425. That inscription has not received the attention due to it (though see Hansen, *GRBS* 1983, 166, indicating on this basis a separate embassy for Dion in 394/3(?)). If we could accept that the dates provided in the inscription were those of the registration of the crowns, we could be sure that the embassy was in this archon year, but I have been warned that registrations could well be in a year subsequent to the award, so that the context of 393/2 in which the crown to the ambassadors appears may be

illusory and their crown may be alongside others, all oɪ which were recorded by the treasurers of 392/1. In any event, I believe that the embassy did go in this year; *contra* Hamilton, *Bitter Victories* 244f.; Funke, *Homonoia* 86 and n.48; *pro* Tuplin, *CQ* 1982, 77, opposed by Whitby, *Historia* 1984, 299.

The presence of Konon, who was at the time in Persian service, seems a problem; yet if he is removed, we will be left with an unparalleled four-man embassy, while five is a normal number. See Jacoby *FGH* on Philochoros 328 F 149; Mosley, *Envoys* 55ff., who (p. 56) is suspicious of this embassy.

392/1 (Ol. 97.1)

Archon
PHILOKLES of Anaphlystos (x) *PA* 14518
Philochoros *FGH* 328 F 149a (Harding no. 23A); Diod. 14.94.1; schol. Ar. *Ploutos* 179 (Diokles); IG ii² 1662; 1663.7; 1664.16; *Insc. Délos* 97.[10]. [18f.], 21; 97 *bis*.[8] (IG ii² 1634); SEG 32.165. Panathenaic amphora: Beazley, *Development* 96f., 118 n.61.

Strategos
?IPHIKRATES son of Timotheos of Rhamnous (IX) *PA* 7737; *APF* 248ff. See 393/2 and add perhaps Polyainos 3.9.43. He was still active around Corinth and possibly in Arkadia.

Amphiktyons to Delos
PANTARETOS son of Antiphilos of Alopeke (x) *PA* 11606
PAT--
THRASYBOULOS son of Thrason of Kollytos (II) *PA* 7305; *APF* 238ff.
  ### Grammateus
  ANT--
See 393/2.

Envoys
ANDOKIDES son of Leogoras of Kydathenaion (III) *PA* 828; *APF* 31
EPIKRATES of Kephisia (I) *PA* 4859; *APF* 181
KRATINOS (? of Sphettos) (v) *PA* Add. 8757a
EUBOULIDES son of Epikleides of Eleusis (VIII) *PA* 5325 + Add. = 5317
And. 3 (Andokides); Dem. 19.277 (Epikrates); Philochoros *FGH* 328 F 149 (Harding no. 23); Plut. *Mor.* 835a (Andokides); schol. Ael. Arist. *Pan.* 172.15 (III.277 Dindorf) (Epikrates).

They were envoys to Sparta on the matter of peace, their willingness to accept which won them exile. On the problem of Philochoros see Funke, *Homonoia* 88 n.56, 143 n.35, against Bruce, *Historia* 1966, 273, 278ff.; Hamilton, *Bitter Victories* 234ff. Kratinos' demotic is an emendation of the close papyrus reading which cites Philochoros; *PA* indicates a restoration of Anaphlystos (x).

COUNCIL AND ASSEMBLY

And. 3 is evidently Andokides' speech in support of peace with Sparta, which was rejected; see Philochoros *FGH* 328 F 149b.

391/90 (Ol. 97.2)

Archon
NIKOTELES *PA* 11060
Diod. 14.97.1; IG ii² 1400.[5]; xiv 1097.11; *Insc. Délos* 97.[10], 21; 97 *bis*.[8]
(IG ii² 1634).

Strategoi
?IPHIKRATES son of Timotheos of Rhamnous (IX) *PA* 7737; *APF* 248ff.
Lysias FF 11–15; Xen. *Hell.* 4.5.3,13ff.,19, 8.34; Dem. 13.22, 23.198;
Aisch. 2.243; Androtion *FGH* 324 F 48 = Philochoros *FGH* 328 F 150;
Deinarchos 1.75; Arist. *Rhet.* 2.23.6 1397b; Nepos *Iph.* 2.3; Plut. *Ages.*
22.2, *Mor.* 350f; Paus. 3.10.1; Polyainos 3.9.24; schol. Ael. Arist. *Pan.*
171.20, 172.1 (III.274 Dindorf); Harpokration, Suda and Photios *s.v.*
Ξενικὸν ἐν Κορίνθῳ (Harding no. 22A).
See 393/2. He was in command of the peltasts, while Kallias commanded the Athenian hoplites, when defeat was inflicted on a Spartan regiment at Lechaion. Subsequently he captured other places.

KALLIAS son of Hipponikos of Alopeke (X) *PA* 7826; *APF* 259ff.
Xen. *Hell*, 4.5.13ff.; Androtion *FGH* 324 F 48 = Philochoros *FGH* 328 F
150; Harpokration, Suda and Photios *s.v.* Ξενικὸν ἐν Κορίνθῳ (variants
Kallikles and Kalliades: Harding no. 22A). See above on Iphikrates.

Tamias
....⁹.... ES or ....⁸.... ON of Rhamnous (IX)
IG ii² 1400.5f.

Amphiktyons to Delos
PANTARETOS son of Antiphilos of Alopeke (X) *PA* 11606
PAT--
THRASYBOULOS son of Thrason of Kollytos (II) *PA* 7305; *APF* 238ff.
Grammateus
ANT--
See 393/2.

390/89 (Ol. 97.3)

Archon
DEMOSTRATOS *PA* 3620
Diod. 14.99.1; IG ii² [1400]; 1407.[28]; *Insc. Délos* 97.[10], [21], 25; 97
bis.[8] (IG ii² 1634). Cf. 393/2.

Strategoi

?IPHIKRATES son of Timotheos of Rhamnous (IX) *PA* 7737; *APF* 248ff.
See 393/2, 391/90.

CHABRIAS son of Ktesippos of Aixone (VII) *PA* 15086; *APF* 560f.
Dem. 4.24; Diod. 14.92.2; ?Polyainos 3.11.6, 15; schol.Ael. Arist. *Pan.*
172.3, 4 (III.274, 275 Dindorf); Harpokration, Suda and Photios *s.v.*
Ξενικὸν ἐν Κορίνθῳ (Harding no. 22A); cf. Xen. *Hell.* 4.8.34; IG ii² 21.2, 21f.,
22 (but see SEG 30.56).
   Sent to Corinth to replace Iphikrates (see 393/2), he seems also to have
been active in the Thracian area, perhaps aiding Thrasyboulos, but this is
problematic. Perhaps he attacked Lakonia (Polyainos 3.11.15 – or 370/
69?). In general see Thompson, *GRBS* 1985, 51–7.

PHILOKRATES son of Ephialtes *PA* 14586
Xen. *Hell.* 4.8.24; Dem. 23.116. He was intercepted on his way to help
Euagoras in Cyprus by the Spartan Teleutias.

THRASYBOULOS son of Lykos of Steiria (III) *PA* 7310; *APF* 240f.
Lysias 28.5, 29.7; Xen. *Hell.* 4.8.25ff.; Dem. 20.59f.; Nepos *Thras.* 4.4;
Diod. 14.94.2ff., 99.4; schol. Ael.Arist. *Pan.* 172.2,5,6 (III.275 Dindorf),
112.2 (III.85); IG ii² 24a.6; 28.7f. (Tod 114; Harding no. 25).
   Abandoning an expedition to Rhodes, he went to the Hellespont and the
Thracian coast, reconciled Amedokos and Seuthes and made arrange-
ments at Byzantion. Thence he went to success at Lesbos and to operations
in Ionia, where he collected money. Then he went south towards the
Eurymedon, where he died at the hands of disgruntled Aspendians. I have
included the sources here, but I will put his death in 389/8.

ERGOKLES *PA* 5052; *APF* 542
Lysias 28; Dem. 19.180; Harpokration and Suda *s.v.* ’Εργοκλῆς; Photios
s.v. ’Εργοκλῆς καὶ ’Εργόφιλος. He was associated with Thrasyboulos and
was indicted for embezzlement of funds, along with his tamias Philokrates.

?DIOTIMOS *PA* 4370; *APF* 162f.
Schol. Ael. Arist. *Pan.* 172.3, 4 (III.274, 275 Dindorf). He replaced
Chabrias at Corinth, perhaps in this year; so *APF*, where also there is
speculation on his lineage, which I do not venture to assert. I presume he
continued at Corinth into the next year. See also Thompson, *GRBS* 1985,
55f.

Tamiai

PARALIOS son of Demodokos of Anagyrous (I) *PA* 11611
PHILOKRATES of Kolonos (II) *PA* 14613
PHILOCH-- of tribe III
-- of Eiresidai (V)
MENON of Oe (VI) *PA* 10081

PATAIKOS of Pithos (VII) *PA* 11680
HAGNODEMOS of Dekeleia (VIII) *PA* 140
KAL-- of tribe IX or X
Grammateus
--RES of Aphidna (IX)
IG ii² 1400.2ff., an inventory.

Amphiktyons to Delos
PANTARETOS son of Antiphilos of Alopeke (X) *PA* 11606
PAT--
THRASYBOULOS son of Thrason of Kollytos (II) *PA* 7305; *APF* 238ff.
Grammateus
ANT--
See 393/2.

Envoy
ARISTOPHANES son of Nikophemos *PA* 2082; *APF* 201f.
Lysias 19.7, 23. He was envoy to Cyprus, but was executed with his father, whether or not he was recalled; Pritchett, *Greek State at War* 2.25; Tuplin, *Philologus* 1983, 173ff.

COUNCIL AND ASSEMBLY

SEG 30.56 retains in this year IG ii² 22, but suggests 388/7 for ii² 21; I will,
(i) however, deal with both here. IG ii² 21 is a treaty with Seuthes, evidently of
(ii) pryt. Erechtheis; ii² 22 concerns Medokos; the fragments of the latter are now separated (SEG 32.44).

389/8 (Ol. 97.4)

Archon
ANTIPATROS *PA* 1162
Diod. 14.103.1; hyp. iv Ar. *Ploutos*; schol. Ar. *Ploutos* 173; IG ii² 2318.[177]; *Insc. Délos* 97.2, [10], [21], 25; 97 *bis*.[8] (IG ii² 1634).

Strategoi
THRASYBOULOS son of Lykos of Steiria (III) *PA* 7310; *APF* 240f.
See 390/89. He died.

AGYRRHIOS of Kollytos (II) *PA* 179; *APF* 278f.
Xen. *Hell.* 4.8.31; Diod. 14.99.5; Plut. *Mor.* 801a (Plato com. F 185 (Edmonds)); schol. Ar. *Ekkl.* 102. He was sent out to replace Thrasyboulos. The scholiast says he served on Lemnos.

?IPHIKRATES son of Timotheos of Rhamnous (IX) *PA* 7737; *APF* 248ff.
Xen. *Hell.* 4.8.33ff.; Front. *Strat.* 1.4.7, 2.5.42, 4.7.23; Plut. *Mor.* 219c; Polyainos 3.9.23,33,58. He was sent out to the Chersonese to counter Anaxibios (Bias in Plutarch), whom he ambushed at Abydos. Again there

may be doubt as to whether he was strategos, but not much: Develin, *ZPE* 61 (1985), 154f.

PAMPHILOS of Keiriadai (VIII) *PA* 11545; *APF* 365
Xen. *Hell.* 5.1.2, 5; Ar. *Ploutos* 174 with schol.; Plato com. F 14 (Edmonds). Sent to Aigina, he clashed with Teleutias the Spartan. When besieged, he was recalled and evidently prosecuted for embezzlement.

?DIOTIMOS *PA* 4370; *APF* 162f.
See 390/89.

Nauarchos
EUNOMOS *PA* 5861
Xen. *Hell.* 5.1.5,7ff. I am content to leave him with the title which Xenophon gives him, rather than make him general. He was sent against Gorgopas, by whom he was defeated off Cape Zoster in Attika.

Tamiai
DOROTHEOS of Anagyrous (I) *PA* 4605; *APF* 174
A-- of tribe II
-- of Halimous (IV)
POLYMNESTOS of Prospalta (V) *PA* 12049
PHANOKRITOS of Acharnai (VI) *PA* 14062
SATYROS of Daidalidai (VII) *PA* 12593; *APF* 273
SMIKROS of Alopeke (X) *PA* 12757
IG ii² 1400.6ff.

Amphiktyons to Delos
PANTARETOS son of Antiphilos of Alopeke (X) *PA* 11606
PAT--
THRASYBOULOS son of Thrason of Kollytos (II) *PA* 7305; *APF* 238ff.
   Grammateus
   ANT--
See 393/2.

388/7 (Ol. 98.1)

Archon
PYRGION *PA* 12485
Diod. 14.107.1 (Pyrrhion); Dion. *AR* 1.74.4; IG ii² 23.5; 2318.[189].

Strategoi
?IPHIKRATES son of Timotheos of Rhamnous (IX) *PA* 7737; *APF* 248ff.
Xen. *Hell.* 5.1.25; Polyainos 2.24; cf. 389/8. He was blockading Nikolochos at Abydos along with Diotimos. Polyainos has a siege of the Chalkedonians.

DIOTIMOS *PA* 4370; *APF* 162f.
Xen. *Hell.* 5.1.25; Lysias 19.50f. See above on Iphikrates. I presume he

was not nauarchos or the like, as he was at some stage according to Polyainos 5.22.3 and Harpokration *s.v. Διότιμος*. He was unjustly accused of embezzlement.

CHABRIAS son of Ktesippos of Aixone (VII) *PA* 15086; *APF* 56of.
DEMAINETOS (? son of Demeas of Paiania) (III) *PA* 3265 = ?3276; *APF* 104f.
Xen. *Hell.* 5.1.10ff.; for Chabrias Dem. 20.76, 78, 82, 83; Nepos *Chab.* 2.1f.; Front. *Strat.* 1.4.14; Polyainos 3.11.9,10,12; for Demainetos ?Aisch. 2.78 (cf. 396/5).

On his way to Cyprus, Chabrias put in at Aigina, where he combined successfully with Demainetos' hoplites against the Spartans and Aiginetans. He then seems to have gone to Cyprus and engaged in Egypt.

?KLEOBOULOS son of Glaukos of Acharnai (VI) *PA* 8558; *APF* 544
See 396/5.

Sitophylax in Peiraieus
ANYTOS *PA* 1322; *APF* 41
Lysias 22.8f.

COUNCIL AND ASSEMBLY

IG ii² 23 is a proxeny decree for a Chian of pryt. Oineis or Aigeis. The surviving final letters of the secretary's demotic allow the demes Iphistiadai (V), Lakiadai (VI), Eroiadai (VIII or X), Keiriadai (VIII).

387/6 (Ol. 98.2)

Archon
THEODOTOS *PA* 6773
Diod. 14.110.1; Ael. Arist. 3.578 (Behr); IG ii² 28 (Tod 114; SEG 31.59; Harding no. 26); 2318.201; *Hesperia* 1971, 163ff. (23) (Stroud: IG ii² 30).

Strategoi
?IPHIKRATES son of Timotheos of Rhamnous (IX) *PA* 7737; *APF* 248ff.
DIOTIMOS *PA* 4370; *APF* 162f.
Xen. *Hell.* 5.1.25f. See 388/7.

DEMAINETOS (? son of Demeas of Paiania) (III) *PA* 3265 = ?3276; *APF* 104f.
DIONYSIOS *PA* 4092
LEONTICHOS *PA* 9036
PHANIAS *PA* 14009
Xen. *Hell.* 5.1.26; Dem. 19.180 (Dionysios); Harpokration, Suda and Photios *s.v. Φανίας* (Phanias); IG ii² 28.[20] (Tod 114; SEG 31.59; Harding no. 26: Dionysios or Leontichos).

217

They followed Antalkidas towards Prokonnesos, but sailed past him. Dionysios was condemned.

?THRASYBOULOS son of Thrason of Kollytos (II) *PA* 7305; *APF* 238ff. Xen. *Hell.* 5.1.26f.; Lysias 26.23f.; Dem. 57.38. He sailed from Thrace and was unsuccessful against Antalkidas. He could have been nauarch. He was said to have practised extortion.

Envoy
?KALLIAS son of Hipponikos of Alopeke (X) *PA* 7826; *APF* 263ff. At Xen. *Hell.* 6.3.4 he is made to say that he went twice to Sparta to make peace and this is likely to be one of those occasions; see Cawkwell, *CQ* 1976, 276 n. 25.

COUNCIL AND ASSEMBLY

(i) IG ii² 28 (Tod 114; SEG 31.59; Harding no. 26) is a decree of pryt. Kekropis honouring Klazomenai:
Grammateus
PARAMYTHOS son of Philagros of Erchia (II) *PA* 11629
Bouleutes epistates
DAIPHRON *PA* 3105
Proposer
POLIAGROS *PA* 11893

(ii) IG ii² 29 (Tod 116) is dated to this year and is a probouleumatic decree, the rider to which grants proxeny to Phanokritos the Parian:
Proposer
KEPHALOS (? of Kollytos) (II) *PA* 8277

(iii) IG ii² 30 is now supplemented at *Hesperia* 1971, 163ff. (23) (Stroud); it concerns klerouchs to Lemnos:
Grammateus
.RI . . . *c.5*

386/5 (Ol. 98.3)

Archon
MYSTICHIDES *PA* 10516
Diod. 15.2.1; IG ii² 31 (Tod 117; Harding no. 29; Osborne PT 130); 1140; 1407.[28].

COUNCIL AND ASSEMBLY

IG ii² 31 (Tod 117; Harding no. 29; Osborne PT 130) is a decree in honour of Hebryzelmis, King of the Odrysians:
Grammateus
NEON of Halai (II or VII) *PA* 10660
Bouleutes epistates
[CH]EILON of Kephisia (I)

Proposer
[EUA]N[DR]OS

385/4 (Ol. 98.4)

Archon
DEXITHEOS *PA* 3215
Diod. 15.8.1; Plut. *Mor.* 845d; IG i³ 228 (ii² 32; Walbank no. 66); ii² 1407.2.

Tamiai of Athene
--TES of Kephale (v)
NIKOMACHOS of Acharnai (VI) *PA* 10944
?LI . . AL-- of tribe VII
IG ii² 1407.3, which with 1414 comprises an inventory (SEG 16.115). The name of the last tamias could begin DI--.

COUNCIL AND ASSEMBLY

IG i³ 228 (ii² 32; Walbank no. 66) is a decree for the re-inscription of a proxeny decree (for which see the appendix to Section V); it is restored to pryt. Hippothontis:
Grammateus
PHILOXENOS son of [D]emainetos of Thorikos (v) *PA* 14696

384/3 (Ol. 99.1)

Archon
DIEITREPHES *PA* 3756
Philochoros *FGH* F 223; Diod. 15.14.1; Dion. *ad Amm.* 5 (Apollodoros *FGH* 244 F 38b); IG ii² 34e.1ff. (Tod 118; Harding no. 31); [36] (Tod 119; but see Lewis, *ABSA* 1954, 33 n.14; 376/5); 1407.4; 3064; SEG 18.69; *Hesperia* 1971, 149f. ([3]) (Stroud).

Tamiai of Athene
THERSIPPOS of Kothokidai (VI) *PA* 7201
?A[PH]AR[EUS] of Pithos (VII) *PA* 2770
DE[X]ITHE[OS] of tribe VIII *PA* 3217
IG ii² 1407.5 (+1414; SEG 16.115).

Envoys
KEPHALOS of Kollytos (II) *PA* 8277; *NPA* 109
--of Alopeke (X)
AISIMO[S] *PA* 311; *NPA* 8
--s of Phrearrhioi (IV)
DEMOKLEIDES *PA* 3476
IG ii² 34.35ff. (Tod 118.39ff.; Harding no. 31). They were sent to Chios to take the oaths of alliance.

N[IK]OSTRATOS of Thorai (X) *PA* 11029
PHAI[N]IPPOS of Azenia (VIII) *PA* 13980
THRASYKLES of Pallene (X) *PA* 7328
HER[M]IPPOS of Poros (V) *PA* 5116
ATHENION of Araphen (II) *PA* 240
IG ii² 36.4ff. (Tod 119). They were chosen to administer oaths of alliance with the Chalkidians, on the date of which see below.

COUNCIL AND ASSEMBLY

(i) IG ii² 34 (Tod 118; Harding no. 31) is from the first prytany, restored as Hippothontis, and is an alliance with Chios:
Grammateus
. . . . ? . . . . son of [? Steph]anos of Oion (IV)
IG ii² 35 is a copy of this.

(ii) IG ii² 36 (Tod 119), the alliance with the Chalkideans, may remain in this year if *Hesperia* 1971, 149f. (3) (Stroud), is a copy of it and is correctly restored by reference to it:
Grammateus
[K]ALLIADES *PA* 7777
Bouleutes epistates
--of Euonymon (I)

383/2 (Ol. 99.2)

Archon
PHANOSTRATOS *PA* 14095
Diod. 15.15.1; Ptolemy *Almag.* 4.11; IG ii² 1930; [1931]; xiv 1098.[4].

COUNCIL AND ASSEMBLY

Grammateus
KLEIDEMOS son of Aines-- *PA* 8495
IG ii² 1930; [1931].

382/1 (Ol. 99.3)

Archon
EUANDROS (? son of Erithalion of Euonymon) (I) *PA* 5267 = ?5271; *APF* 187f.
Lysias 26; Dem. 24.138; Diod. 15.20.1; Ptolemy *Almag.* 4.11. The identification is made in *APF*. He was chosen when Leodamas had failed his dokimasia.

COUNCIL AND ASSEMBLY

At Dem. 24.138 we learn that the proposer of a law had been put death because the law was improper:
Proposer
EUDEMOS of Kydathenaion (III) *PA* 5401

381/80 (Ol. 99.4)

Archon
DEMOPHILOS *PA* 3662
Diod. 15.22.1; *Agora* xv.[6](SEG 24.164); SEG 32.171(c).

COUNCIL AND ASSEMBLY

Agora xv.6 gives us bouleutai of tribe I Erechtheis:
Anagyrous
DEMOPHON
NAUKLES
. . . ISTRATOS
[ATHE]NODOROS
. .⁴. . IMACHOS
. .⁴. . MACHOS
Euonymon
. . .⁶. . . ON
. . . .⁸. . . . S
Other
ARIS--
ANT--
EUTH--

380/79 (Ol. 100.1)

Archon
PYTHEAS *PA* 12340
MP A 69; Diod. 15.23.1; IG ii² 1126 (*LS* no. 78; SEG 28.100, 29.128); SEG 32.171(c).

COUNCIL AND ASSEMBLY

IG ii² 1126 (*LS* no. 78; SEG 28.100) is of the third prytany, of Hippothontis, and Roux, *L'amphictionie* 44, shows it is an Athenian decree incorporating a measure of the Delphic amphiktyony, which thus becomes a part of Athenian law.

379/8 (Ol. 100.2)

Archon
NIKON *PA* 11093
Diod. 15.24.1; Dion. *Lys.* 12; IG ii² 39.8; SEG 32.50.5.

Strategoi
?CHABRIAS son of Ktesippos of Aixone (VII) *PA* 15086; *APF* 560f.
Xen. *Hell.* 5.4.14; schol. Ael. Arist. *Pan.* 172.10 (III.276 Dindorf). He was in command of Athenian peltasts guarding the road through Eleutherai. He may not have been general, but I believe he was. Cf. Cawkwell, *CQ* 1973, 57f.

DEMOPHON *PA* 3693
Diod. 15.26.2f. (378/7); ?schol. Ael. Arist. *Pan.* 173.11, 13 (III.281 Dindorf: Demades or Demeas). Diodoros says he led out a force to help Thebes; the scholiast on Aristides pairs him with Chabrias, provided the emendation is accepted. See Cawkwell, *CQ* 1973, 56ff.

COUNCIL AND ASSEMBLY

(i) IG ii² 39 is a proxeny decree for Larissans.

(ii) SEG 32.50 is a probouleumatic proxeny decree for Euryphon (the first evidence for proedroi):
Grammateus
. . . ? . . . OTOS son of Ch--
Bouleutes epistates
. . . GNETOS son of Ar--?

(iii) There was a decree to aid the Theban exiles (Deinarchos 1.38f.), for the date of which see Cawkwell, *CQ* 1973, 57:
Proposer
KEPHALOS (of Kollytos) (II) *PA* 8277
Cf. Diod. 15.25f. (378/7).

378/7 (Ol. 100.3)

Archon
NAUSINIKOS of Kephale (v) *PA* 10584
Dem. 22.44 and schol.; 59.65; Philochoros *FGH* 328 F 41 (Harding no. 39C) Diod. 15.25.1; Dion. *Lys.* 12; IG ii² 43 (Tod. 123; SEG 31.61; Harding no. 35); 44 (Tod 124; Harding no. 38); [45]; ?155.[3] (*Hesperia* 1938, 626 (1) (Schweigert)); Add. 1424a.35; 1425.30; 1436.11; 1438.[1]; 1622.408, 495; 1741 (*Agora* xv.8); 2318.[210].

Strategoi

TIMOTHEOS son of Konon of Anaphlystos (x) *PA* 13700; *APF* 507ff.
CHABRIAS son of Ktesippos of Aixone (VII) *PA* 15086; *APF* 560f.
KALLISTRATOS son of Kallikrates of Aphidna (IX) *PA* 8157; *APF* 277ff.
Diod. 15.29.7 (377/6); for Timotheos ?Plut. *Mor.* 350f; for Chabrias Xen.
Hell. 5.4.54; Dem. 20.76 (cf. 78, 82f.); Nepos *Chab.* 1.1f.; Diod. 15.32.5,
33.4; Polyainos 2.1.2; ?schol. Ael. Arist. *Pan.* 173.11, 13 (III.281 Dindorf).
Plutarch puts Timotheos in Euboia. Chabrias operated in Boiotia. For
date see Sealey, *Essays* 141; Cawkwell, *CQ* 1973, 56.

Epimeletai of dockyards

?DIOKL[ES] of Pambotadai (I)
IG ii² 1604.1, which I date before 377/6 because of the appearance in it as
trierarch of Philinos, who was tamias in 377/6.

LYKON of Kephisia (I) *PA* 9272
THEOGNIS of Boutadai (VI) *PA* 6741
IG ii² 1622.406, 493.

Envoys

ORTHOBOULOS of Kerameis (V) *PA* 11489
EXEKESTIDES of Pallene (X) *PA* 4721
XENODOKOS of Acharnai (VI) *PA* 11192
PYRRHANDROS of Anaphlystos (X) *PA* 12496
ALKIMACHOS (son of Kephisios) of Angele (III) *PA* 615
IG ii² 41.17ff. (Tod 121; Harding no. 34). Envoys to Byzantion in the
matter of alliance.

?AI[SI]MOS *PA* 311; *NPA* 8
IG ii² 42.19f. (Tod 122; Harding no. 37). It is hard to know exactly how he
is to be seen; he is in the company of synhedroi (of the alliance). For date see
Cawkwell, *CQ* 1973, 50f.

ARISTOTELES of Marathon (IX) *PA* 2065
PYRRHANDROS of Anaphlystos (X) *PA* 12496
THRASYBOULOS (son of Thrason) of Kollytos (II) *PA* 7305; *APF* 238ff.
IG ii² 43.76f. (Tod 123; Harding no. 35); for Thrasyboulos and
Pyrrhandros Aisch. 3.138f. They were envoys to Thebes.

--ON or --AS
THEOPOMPOS *PA* 7016
IG ii² 40.7 (Harding no. 33); ?Aisch. 3.138f.; cf. Deinarchos 1.38.
Theopompos is named in the inscription, which must refer to Athenian
ambassadors (they are called to δεῖπνον in the Prytaneion, not ξένια). For the
rest there is only the accusative ending -ντα and one may speculate about
Aristophon and Leodamas, who, along with Thrason, are mentioned by
Aischines as having been envoys to Thebes. Sealey, *Essays* 175, suggested

371 for Leodamas. On the nationality of the envoys see Cawkwell, *CQ* 1973, 49 nn.3, 5; Cargill, *League* 52ff.

Unknown
Lewis, *Gnomon* 1975, 718f., suggests this date for a document published as a photograph in *AD* 25 B.I (1970), pl.56; in it a payment is made to a secretary of some sort:
Grammateus
[CH]AIRENEOS of Lamptrai (I)

COUNCIL AND ASSEMBLY

(i) IG ii² 40 (SEG 31.62; Harding no. 33) concerns Thebes and Mitylene: it is probouleumatic with a rider:
Proposer
[ST]EPHANOS
He probably ought to stand, rather than Kephalos (*PA* 8277).

(ii) IG ii² 41 (Tod 121; Harding no. 34) is a treaty with Byzantion.

(iii) IG ii² 42 (Tod 122; Harding no. 37) is a treaty with Methymna:
Grammateus
KAL[L . . . ? . . .] of Alopeke (X)
Bouleutes epistates
SIMON *PA* 12698
Proposer
ASTYPHILOS *PA* 2662

(iv) IG ii² 43 (Tod 123; SEG 31.61; 32.53; Harding no. 35) is of the seventh prytany, of Hippothontis, and concerns the Athenian alliance (cf. Diod. 15.28):
Grammateus
KALLIBIOS son of Kephisophon of Paiania (III) *PA* 7900; *APF* 148f.
Bouleutes epistates
CHARINOS of Athmonon (VII) *PA* 15443
Proposer
ARISTOTELES (of Marathon) (IX) *PA* 2065

(v) IG ii² 44 (Tod 124; Harding no. 38) is a decree of pryt. Leontis concerning alliance with Chalkis:
Grammateus
ARISTOTELES son of Euphiletos of Acharnai (VI) *PA* 2061
Bouleutes epistates
PANTARETO[S] *PA* 11605
Proposer
PYRRHANDROS (? of Anaphlystos) (X) *PA* 12496

Schweigert, *Hesperia* 1938, 626 (1), restored ii² 155 as a duplicate of this (denied by Accame, *La lega* 71f.) and later thought 203 was a copy of 155 (*Hesperia* 1941, 339).

(vi) IG ii² 45 appears to be a law concerning public debts.

Agora xv.8 gives us bouleutai of tribe v Akamantis:
Thorikos
--son of Exekestides *PA* 4713
--LES son of I[o]n
--son of Theodosios *PA* 6752
Hagnous
AR[I]STION son of Ari-- *PA* 1738
E[P]IMEDES son of An-- *PA* 4936
MENETIMOS son of O-- *PA* 10025
LAKONIDES *PA* 8976

APPENDIX

Basileus
ONESIPPOS son of Aitios of Kephisia (1)
Hesperia 1971, 256 (4) (Shear) (SEG 32.239). Dated to the fourth century by Shear, the outer termini being 412 and 388. Edmonson (*Hesperia* Suppl. 19.48–50) argues for 403, but I am not sufficiently convinced.

Strategoi
HERAKLEIDES of Klazomenai *PA* 6489
APOLLODOROS of Kyzikos *PA* 1458
Plato *Ion* 541d. If Herakleides only gained citizenship in 399/8 (see now Walbank, *ZPE* 51 (1983), 183f.), then we may presume his strategia was after that and we may put Apollodoros in the same period.

ARCHINOS of Koile (VIII) *PA* 2526
Dem. 24.135 says he was general often.

Notes: Konon during this period was not an elected general of the Athenians: Seager, *JHS* 1967, 101; Funke, *Homonoia* 129 n. 72.

Similarly, the adventures of Iphikrates in Thrace were not as Athenian strategos.

Beloch (*Att. Pol.* 111 and n. 3) believed Thrasyboulos, Anytos and Archinos were generals in the years 403/2 to 395/4, which is possible (and Archinos is included above), but lacking in evidence as to specific years. The statement at Plato *Meno* 90b, which is evidence that they chose Anytos for the highest offices, is hardly enough even to attribute a queried generalship to him in 403/2 (so Hansen, *GRBS* 1983, 160).

Nauarchos
DIOTIMOS *PA* 4370; *APF* 162f.
Polyainos 5.22; Harpokration *s.v.* Διότιμος. See under him as general in 388/7.

Lochagos and Taxiarchos
NIKOMACHIDES *PA* 10931
Xen. *Mem.* 3.4.1. He held both positions many times, but failed to be elected strategos. That election, won by Antisthenes, will be noted in the appendix to the next section, but Nikomachides' service can easily be included in this. Only the theory of tribal representation in the strategia will allow him to be put in tribe III, by association with the tribe of Antisthenes which results from his identification; there is nothing in Xenophon to support it.

Financial officials
The following were discovered by Woodward, *Hesperia* 1956, 86 (4), 92ff. (9c) (SEG 15.22, 25c):
A. PAUS--
PHORYS or PHORYS[KIDES] or PHORYS[KOS]
   Grammateus
   --OS
B. [BOI]OTO[S]
--STRATOS of A--
--KRATES of Ko--

Cf. SEG 15.25a, where the surviving letters may belong to names.

Demarchos
LYSIPPIDES of Thorikos (V)
Thorikos VIII (1972/76 [1984]), 175ff. no. 75; Whitehead, *ZPE* 62 (1986), 213ff. The date is late fifth or early fourth century.

Archon of Salamis
PHILOMELOS
IG ii² 3093.5, dated to the beginning of the century.

Envoys
ARISTOPHON son of Aristophanes of Azenia (VIII) *PA* 2108; *APF* 64ff.
THRASON of Erchia (II) *PA* 7384; *APF* 239
LEODAMAS (? son of Erasistratos) of Acharnai (VI) *PA* 9077; *APF* 523
ARCHEDEMOS of Pelekes (IV) *PA* 2326
Aisch. 3.138f. For the first three see 378/7. They were envoys to Thebes.

?DEMOS son of Pyrilampes *PA* 3573; *APF* 330
Deduced by MacDowell, *Wasps* 144, from the fact that he received a gold cup from the Persian king (Lysias 19.25).

COUNCIL AND ASSEMBLY

(i) IG ii² 2 has been eliminated from 403/2 by Walbank, *Classical Views* 26 n.s. 1 (1982), 259–74; he favours a date of 382/1, but the restoration of the archon leaves open 398/7 or even 408/7; Lewis (SEG 32.38) still wants it in 403/2. Walbank also thinks that fr. a may be separate from fr. b; the first at least is a proxeny decree of pryt. Pandionis for a Boiotian:

Grammateus
. . .⁶. . . os of Kollytos (II)
Proposer
PHILAGROS *PA* 14203

(ii) IG ii² 3 is a proxeny decree of pryt. Aiantis dated *c*. 403/2 (cf. IG i³ p. 196):
Bouleutes epistates
AP[E]MANTOKLES (? of Trikorynthos (IX)) *PA* 1344
Proposer
. . . .?. . . . os
For Apemantokles' demotic see Lewis, *ABSA* 1954, 33.

(iii) IG ii² 5, dated around 400, is reconstructed at SEG 14.36 as a proxeny decree:
Proposer
THEOZOTID[ES] *PA* 6913 + 6914; *APF* 222f.

(iv) IG ii² 6 (Tod 98; Walbank no. 61) is a decree from the boule of pryt. Oineis, dated *c*. 403/2, reinscribing the proxeny for the sons of Apemantos of Thasos:
Grammateus
DEXITHEOS *PA* 3214
Bouleutes epistates
DEMOKLES *PA* 3484
Proposer
MONIPPIDES *PA* 10414

(v) The prytany, secretary and proposer of IG ii² 6 are restored to ii² 7, which honours Kleonymidas:
Bouleutes epistates
. . . MOS

(vi) IG ii² 25 (SEG 15.86; Osborne D 9) gives citizenship to the Thasians Archippos and Hipparchos; Osborne dates *c*. 388:
Grammateus
. . .?. . . s of Peiraieus (VIII)

(vii) IG ii² 26, for the date of which cf. IG i³ p. 196, is a decree of pryt. Hippothontis dated 394–387 honouring Iphitos of Pharsalos:

Grammateus
CHARIDEMOS son of Theoteles of Lamptrai (I) *PA* 15386
Bouleutes epistates
[THR]ASYMEDES *PA* 7359
Proposer
ATHENODORO[S] *PA* 259

(viii) IG ii² 49 is a decree of the boule of pryt. Erechtheis, dated there at the beginning of the century, to the early 370s by Burnett and Edmonson, *Hesperia* 1961, 84 n.28, though *AE* 1957, 84ff., dates the relief to the 380s; it grants proxeny to some Abydenes:
Grammateus
KYDENOR son of Kydenor of Alopeke (X) *PA* 8921

(ix) IG ii² 50 is a fragment from pryt. Erechtheis dated to the beginning of the century, honouring a Samian (for date cf. IG i³ p. 196):
Grammateus
--of Paionidai (IV)
Bouleutes epistates
--of Agryle (I)

(x) IG ii² 51 (Lewis, *ABSA* 1954, 33; Henry, *Chiron* 1982, 104) is a decree of pryt. Aiantis, dated before 387/6, granting proxeny to a Delphian:
Grammateus
[HYPER]BOLOS *PA* 13907
Bouleutes epistates
. . .⁶. . . OS

(xi) IG ii² 58 (for date cf. IG i³ p. 196) is a decree of the boule of pryt. Pandionis honouring an Eresian (?):
Grammateus
EUDRAMON of Acherdous (VIII) *PA* 5442
Bouleutes epistates
EUXITHE[OS] *PA* 5901

(xii) IG ii² 59 is a fragment of pryt. Kekropis:
Grammateus
[PO]LYKLE[S] of Philaidai (II) *PA* 12001

(xiii) IG ii² 61 is a decree honouring a Sicilian:
Grammateus
AMEINIAS of Sphettos (V) *PA* 685
Bouleutes epistates
ANDROTION (? son of Andron) of Gargettos (II) *PA* 915 = 913; *APF* 33f.

(xiv) Lewis, *ABSA* 1954, 34 pondered a date of 373/2. Ameinias is also restored in ii² 62.

(xv) IG ii² 63 (Walbank no. 80; Lewis, *ABSA* 1954, 33) is a decree of the boule of pryt. Erechtheis granting proxeny to Echembrotos of Kleonai:

Grammateus
P[I]STOXENOS *PA* 11836
Bouleutes epistates
[CHA]IREDEMOS *PA* 15117

(xvi) IG ii² 69 is the end of a proxeny decree dated to the beginning of the century:
Grammateus
THEOPROPOS

(xvii) IG ii² 70 + Add. (Lewis, *ABSA* 1954, 34) is dated between 390 and 378 by Henry, *Chiron* 1982, 117 and n.109; it honours three Athenians who have been granted Phokian citizenship:
Grammateus
. . . .¹⁰. . . . . s son of Demoph[i]los of Phegous (I) or Phegaia (II) *PA* 3690
Bouleutes epistates
CH[AR]M[IDES of Lamptrai] (I)
Proposer
O . . .⁷. . .

(xviii) IG ii² 72 is an honorific decree:
Grammateus
. .⁵. . s of Eroiadai (VIII)
Proposer?
ARIST[ION] *PA* 1734

(xix) IG ii² 76 (Lewis, *ABSA* 1954, 33), which Henry (*Chiron* 1982, 108) dates *c.* 378/7, is a decree of pryt. Oineis granting proxeny to Philinos of Byzantion:
Grammateus
NAUSIAS of Atene (X)
Bouleutes epistates
PHE[REKLES of Thria or Phyle] (VI)
If Nausias could be restored in ii² 158, he would be son of [Gl]aukippos.

(xx) IG ii² 77 + Add. (for date cf. IG i³ p. 196) is a decree of pryt. Hippothontis granting proxeny to Komaios of Abdera; it is passed by the boule according to a decree of the demos:
Grammateus
SMIKYTHOS son of Cha[r]inos of Acharnai (VI) *PA* 12788; *APF* 542
Bouleutes epistates
S[T]RATIOS
Proposer
XE[NOTI]MOS

(xxi) There follows a similar measure of pryt. Aiantis (probably earlier than (xx))
Proposer
PY[THON]I[KOS]

(xxii) IG ii² 80 is a probouleumatic proxeny decree for Epichares with a rider; for the reading see SEG 24.78:
Proposer
. . . ? . . . CHOS

(xxiii) IG ii² 81 honours a Megarian:
Proposer
--DOROS

(xxiv) IG ii² 84 is a probouleumatic decree honouring Polychartides and Alkibiades with a rider:
Proposer
KALLISTRATOS (? son of Kallikrates of Aphidna) (IX) *PA* 8157; *APF* 277ff.

(xxv) IG ii² 85 has the following (Wilhelm, *Att. Urk.* V.129ff., argued for 375/4 or 371/70):
Grammateus
--DROKLI--
Bouleutes epistates
? --S
Proposer
--ON

(xxvi) IG ii² 86 is dated to the early years of the century at SEG 24.76 and is a proxeny decree of pryt. Hippothontis:
Grammateus
DOR--
Bouleutes epistates
MY--

(xxvii) IG ii² 145 (Lewis, *ABSA* 1954, 36f.; Osborne T 20) grants honours, possibly citizenship, to Eukles the herald; it is dated 402–399 by Lewis, (?) 402/1 – 401/0 by Osborne (cf. also Rhodes, *Boule* 84f.); it is restored as a decree of the boule, but Rhodes wants it to be of the demos; it comes from pryt. Erechtheis:
Bouleutes epistates
SIMI--
Proposer
EURIPPIDE[S] (? son of Adeimantos of Myrrhinous) (III) *PA* 5955 = ?5949 = ?5956; *APF* 202ff.

(xxviii) SEG 17.16 is a fragment of pryt Erechtheis:
Proposer
GNATHON (of Lakiadai) (VI)
For the deme see *Hesperia* 1983, 106.

(xxix) *Hesperia* 1938, 91 (11) (Meritt), is a fragment of a proxeny decree from the boule of pryt. Kekropis:
Grammateus
. . ⁵. . KLEIDES
Bouleutes epistates
. . . ⁶. . . EMOS

(xxx) *Ath. Pol.* 41.3 tells of the introduction of assembly pay and its augmenta-
(xxxi) tion by two further measures, which must be before 392:
(xxxii) **Proposers**
AGYRRHIOS of Kollytos (II) *PA* 179; *APF* 278f.
HERAKLEIDES of Klazomenai *PA* 6489
(xxxiii) Harpokration *s.v.* θεωρικά (Philochoros *FGH* 328 F 33) makes Agyrrhios responsible for the introduction of theoric distributions.

(xxxiv) Before 393 a measure on eisphora was passed (Ar. *Ekkl.* 823ff. and schol.):
Proposer
EURIP(P)IDES (? son of Adeimantos of Myrrhinous) (III) *PA* 5949 = ?5955 = ?5956; *APF* 202ff.

(xxxv) Between 400 and 380 a decree of unknown content brought an indictment for illegal motion (Lysias F 143; Hansen, *Sovereignty* no. 6):
Proposer
PHANIAS *PA* 14010

(xxxvi) Istros *FGH* 334 F 32 records that the same man moved the decrees which sent Xenophon into exile and brought him back; the first will fall in this period:
Proposer
EUBOULOS (? son of Spintharos of Probalinthos (III)) *PA* 5369
It is, of course, possible that it was not the same man.

(xxxvii) **Proposer**
KEPHALOS of Kollytos (II) *PA* 8277; *NPA* 109
He is said to have proposed numerous decrees (Aisch. 3.194).

Three known to have spoken in the assembly are Theomnestos in the period 394–384 (Lysias 10.1), Mantitheos about 400 (Lysias 16.20) and Philepsios early in the century (Harpokration, Suda and Photios *s.v.* Φιλέψιος; cf. Dem. 24.134).

Nomothetai
(xxxviii) IG ii² 140.8f. mentions a law to do with the Eleusinian cult, which is now dated in or after 403/2 (Rhodes, *Boule* 94f. and 95 n.1):
Proposer
CHAIREMONIDES

(xxxix) About 400 a law was proposed concerning the coming into force of nomoi (Dem. 24.42; MacDowell, *JHS* 1975, 62):
Proposer
DIOKLES *PA* 3989

Agora XV.9 gives us a bouleutes of tribe VIII Hippothontis:
Thymaitadai
ECH[OS]

Agora XV.12 gives us bouleutai of tribe III Pandionis, followed by a secretary of the council and demos and an antigrapheus; it is dated 400–350, but I favour this period:
Myrrhinous
--LIGES
--OKRATES
-- ? (ELIESOO is the transcription)
--N--
--ENE[S]
--ODOROS
--OIO--
Angele
--PIOS
--TES
--RATOS
Prasiai
--K[I]ADES
--S--
--STRATOS ? son of E--
Steiria
--ES
--ODOROS
--AS
Kydathenaion
KALESIAS *PA* 7748
P--ILAS
ARISTOPHANES (? son of Philippos) *PA* 2090
--ETES
--EOS--
PHIL--S ? son of L--
--E--
--MA--
Probalinthos
RH--S
Paiania upper
DEMOKED[ES[(? son of Archekomos) *PA* 3471
HIERON (?--) ?*PA* 7542

[CH]ARISANDROS *PA* 15482

MELESIP[POS] *PA* 9823

POLYARKES *PA* 11910

[T]ELEPHANE[S] *PA* 13573

DIODO[T]O[S]?

CHARIADES *PA* 15318

ARCHANDROS *PA* 2297

ALKIMACHOS *PA* 624

PHILIPPIDES *PA* 14360 or 14361; *APF* 548.

Paiania lower

[?DI]ODOROS cf. *APF* 156

Konthyle

[HE]LIODOROS *PA* 6416

Oa

SOSISTRATOS *PA* 13299

--THION

[A]MPHISTHENES *PA* 788

PAUSANIAS (? son of Pausanias) ?*PA* 11721

Grammateus

--LEIDES son of Philotheros of Oion (IV or VIII) *PA* 14503

Antigrapheus

[ARIS]TION son of Aristonymos of Pallene (X) *PA* 2198

Section VII
377/6–353/2

377/6 (Ol. 100.4)

Archon
KALLEAS *PA* 7766

MP A 70; Diod. 15.28.1 (Kallias); IG ii² [95]; 216.10 (= [217]; SEG 14.47); [1410]; 1411.5; 1424.[17]; 1425.328; 1426.[7]; 1622.[437]; 1635.2, 9, 118, 122 (Tod 125; *Insc. Délos* 98); 2318.[222].

Strategos
CHABRIAS son of Ktesippos of Aixone (VII) *PA* 15086; *APF* 560f.
Diod. 15.30.5. In Euboia he ravaged the land of Hestiaia and left a garrison. Then he won over Peparethos and Skiathos and other islands in the Kyklades.

Tamiai of Athene
CHARIAS son of Chariades of Sybridai (I) *PA* 15361
KLEON son of Thoudi[ppos] of Araphen (II) *PA* 8669; *APF* 229
PATROKLES son of Pasikles of tribe III, IV or V *PA* 11695
[ARI]STOPHON son of Naukles of Lakiadai (VI) *PA* 2115; *APF* 66
PHILINOS son of Gniphon of Phlya (VII) *PA* 14339; *APF* 537
[N]IKESIAS son of Nikesidikos of Phaleron (IX) *PA* 10748
TA-- of tribe X
IG ii² 1410.1ff.; 1411.5ff. The actual inventory of the year was ii² 1410 and probably eight names were listed.

Epimeletai of dockyards
K[A]L[LIAS] ? of Oa (III)
D[I]OGEITON of Acharnai (VI) *PA* 3794
IG ii² 1604.2f. I place them here as a result of the tentative ascription of 1604 to the epimeletai of 378/7 (*q.v.*), thus not following Sundwall, *Epig. Beitr.* 36, who has 376/5 and ventures, without evident justification, to restore epimeletai from Diomeia (II), Potamos (IV) and the spurious Kyrteidai (supposedly V).

Tamias of dockyards
[M]ANT[IAS] (son of Mantitheos) [of Thorikos] (V) *PA* 9667; *APF* 364ff.
IG ii² 1622.435f.

Amphiktyons to Delos
SOSIGENES son of Sosiades of Xypete (VII) *PA* 13214

EPIGENES son of Metagenes of Koile (VIII) *PA* 4805
ANTIMACHOS son of Euthynomos of Marathon (IX) *PA* 1129
EPIKRATES son of Menestratos of Pallene (X) *PA* 4909; *APF* 182f.
   Grammateus
   DIODOROS son of Olympiodoros of Skambonidai (IV) *PA* 3961
Insc. Délos 98.6ff., 59f. (IG ii² 1635; Tod 125); 100.[11](Diodoros).
Sosigenes served only for this year, Epigenes, Antimachos and Epikrates,
along with the secretary, into 374/3.

COUNCIL AND ASSEMBLY

IG ii² 95 is a proxeny decree of the boule in honour of Apollonides:
Grammateus
EUCHARES

376/5 (Ol. 101.1)

Archon
CHARISANDROS *PA* 15471
Diod. 15.36.1 (Chariandros); IG ii² ?173.[8f.](Henry, *Chiron* 1982, 109,
111); 1141.5 (*Hesperia* 1941, 263 (67) (Pritchett)); 1410.[4]; 1411.[1];
1424.19; Add. 1424a.367; 1425.314; 1426.[8]; 1445.[1]; 1635.6f., 27,
[100f.], 118, 122f., 134 (Tod 125; *Insc. Délos* 98); 2318.[234]; xiv 1098.5.

Strategoi
CHABRIAS son of Ktesippos of Aixone (VII) *PA* 15086; *APF* 560f.
Xen. *Hell.* 5.4.61; Ephoros *FGH* 70 F 80; Dem. 13.22, 20.77 (cf. 78, 82, 83),
23.198, 24.180; Aisch. 3.222, 243; Deinarchos 1.75; Diod. 15.34.4ff.; Plut.
Phok. 6.2f., 7.1, *Cam.* 19.3, *Mor.* 349f, 350f; Polyainos 3.11.2, ?3,11; schol.
Aisch. 3.222; schol. Ael. Arist. *Pan.* 173.16 (III.282 Dindorf); IG ii²
1606.78f.,82f.; 1607.[20f.], 115, 126, [145f.]; *Hesperia* 1961, 74ff.
   On the Chabrias monument and the actions of the year see Burnett and
Edmonson in *Hesperia*. Chabrias began a siege of Naxos and won a victory
against the Spartan Pollis off the island on 16 Boedromion (date in Plut.
Phok. 6.3 and Polyainos 3.11.2). Later he drove the Triballoi away from
Abdera and left a garrison. He evidently operated also among the islands.
Diodoros prematurely kills him off and calls him nauarchos; he was
certainly general.

TIMOTHEOS son of Konon of Anaphlystos (X) *PA* 13700; *APF* 507ff.
Xen. *Hell.* 5.4.63ff. (cf. 6.2.2); Isok. 15.108f.; Dem. 13.22, 23.198; Aisch.
3.243; Deinarchos 1.14,75,3.17; Arist, *Oik.* 2.2.23, 1350a.31ff.; Nepos
Tim. 2.1f.; Diod. 15.36.5f.; Front. *Strat.* 1.12.11, 2.5.47; Polyainos
3.10.4,6,12,13,16,17; Ael. Arist. 1.313 (Lenz); schol. Ael. Arist. *Pan.*
173.17 (III.282 Dindorf); IG ii² 1606.[11f.], [25], [29f.], 70, [75], 87;
1607.20, 139f., 143, 153f.

Pace Diodoros, he was general and was not successor to Chabrias. At the request of Thebes, he was sent around the Peloponnese. He brought Corcyra under his control and defeated the Spartan Nikolochos at Alyzeia near Leukas. Diodoros says he won over the cities of Kephallenia and Akarnania, made a friend of Alketas king of the Molossi and gained control of the territory of the cities in those regions. Nepos says he took on as allies the Epirotes, the Athamanians, the Chaonians and all the coastal tribes of the area. The precise relations are unclear; see Tuplin, *Athenaeum* 1984, 549ff.

Officers

KEDON *PA* 8280

Diod. 15.34.5 is probably correct in having him in command of the left wing at Naxos, but there is no warrant to make him general with Beloch, *Att. Pol.* 316, and Hansen, *GRBS* 1983, 170. He was killed. See the next entry.

PHOKION son of Phokos *PA* 15076; *APF* 559

Plut. *Phok.* 6.2, 7.1, *Mor.* 805f. He is given command of the left wing at Naxos, probably in error (see above on Kedon). Gehrke (*Phokion* 2, 3f. and n. 23) and Hansen (*GRBS* 1980, 168) reasonably make him trierarch, but the fact that he was later sent by Chabrias to collect syntaxeis, if accepted, may indicate a position of higher authority; see Develin, *ZPE* 61 (1985), 155.

Phrourarchoi

PHILISKOS

DIOTIMOS ?*PA* 4370; *APF* 162f.

Hesperia 1961, 79 (Burnett and Edmonson). Philiskos was at Abydos, Diotimos at Syros. See Cargill, *League* 153.

Tamiai of Athene

TIMON son of Timokrates of Kytherros (III) *PA* 13846; *APF* 338

-- son of --ratos of Eroiadai (X)

AMEIPSIAS son of Lykomedes of Thorikos (V) *PA* 710

--ES son of Telesarchos of Aphidna (IX) *PA* 13508

D. . . .⁸. . . . son of Dorkis of Dekeleia (VIII) *PA* 4534

Grammateus

EUTHIAS son of Peisias of Kettos (IV) *PA* 5486

IG ii² 1410.4ff.; 1411.1ff. The actual inventory of the year is 1411 and probably six names were listed.

Tamiai of the other gods

. . .?. . . OS son of Meixikles of Anagyrous (I) *PA* 9758

-- son of --ophiles of Phrearrhioi (IV)

. .PHILOS

--S son of Mnesistratos [of Acharnai] (VI)

TIM--

--OBIOS son of Smikythos of Keiriadai (VIII) *PA* 12790
E--
IG ii² 1445.1ff., which is the inventory of the year with perhaps only eight names listed. The deme of the son of Mnesistratos is all but certain; cf. *PA* 10337, 10368, 10369.

Amphiktyons to Delos
IDIOTES son of Theogenes of Acharnai (VI) *PA* 7445
EPIGENES son of Metagenes of Koile (VIII) *PA* 4805
ANTIMACHOS son of Euthynomos of Marathon (IX) *PA* 1129
EPIKRATES son of Menestratos of Pallene (X) *PA* 4909; *APF* 182f.
   Grammateus
   DIODOROS son of Olympiodoros of Skambonidai (IV) *PA* 3961
Insc. Délos 98.6ff. (IG ii² 1635; Tod 125). See 377/6.

COUNCIL AND ASSEMBLY

(i) IG ii² 173 is an honorary decree which may belong here; Henry, *Chiron* 1982, 109, 111.

(ii) An unknown individual proposed an honorary decree for Chabrias after his victory at Naxos; it was unsuccessfully challenged as illegal by Leodamas; Dem. 20.75,79,84,86,146, 23.198, 24.180; Aisch. 3.243; Hansen, *Sovereignty* no. 7.

On IG ii² 36 see 384/3.

375/4 (Ol. 101.2)

Archon
HIPPODAMAS *PA* 7610
Diod. 15.38.1; IG ii² 96 (Tod. 126; SEG 31.64; Harding no. 41); 99; 100; 1424.27; Add. 1424a.371; 1425.321; 1428.[152]; Add. 1428.[188]; 1429.[53]; 1445.5f.; 1446.1; 1622.491; 1635.3, 8, 27f., 30, 57f., [103], 118, 123 (Tod 125; *Insc. Délos* 98); Add. 1689.[1]; 2318.[246]; 3037.4; xiv 1098.6; SEG 26.72 (Harding no. 45). Panathenaic amphoras: Frel, *Amphoras* 21; Beazley, *Vase Painters* 413.

Strategos
TIMOTHEOS son of Konon of Anaphlystos (X) *PA* 13700; *APF* 507ff.
Xen. *Hell.* 6.2.2; Diod. 15.45.2ff. Hansen (*GRBS* 1983, 176) cites Xen. *Hell.* 5.4.66 for Timotheos' strategia in this year, which is quite uncertain, though some of his latter activities noticed under 376/5 could have extended into this year. The sources mentioned above refer to his being ordered home by two ambassadors after the conclusion of peace with Sparta, which peace he disturbed, however, by provocatively landing exiles from Zakynthos in their territory. There are problems of chronology

for this and the subsequent years which are discussed by Gray, *CQ* 1980, 306ff.; Tuplin, *Athenaeum* 1984, 537ff.; also and generally Cargill, *League* 64ff.

Hipparchoi

? --KLES of Erchia (II)
? [DEMOCH]ARES (? son of Demon) of Paiania (III) *PA* 3718; *APF* 144
IG ii² 102.19ff. (Tod 129; Harding no. 43). They were among the envoys to confirm the alliance with Amyntas of Makedon, the date of which is not certain. As Tod remarks, hipparchs are more likely in this role than phylarchs.

Tamias of Athene

EURYKLEID[ES]
IG ii² 1421.4 + Add. p. 799. The actual inventory of the year is ii² 1426 (Dinsmoor, *AJA* 1932, 167 n.1).

Tamiai of the other gods

PYTHOKLES son of Euthykles of Kedoi (I) *PA* 12443; *APF* 486
CHAIREPHILOS *PA* 15184
POLYDAMAS son of Euthyphron of Kerameis (V) *PA* 11915
ARCHEST[RATOS] *PA* 2404
[TEI]SAMENOS son of Aleximachos of Koile (VIII) *PA* 13444
MEGAKLEIDES son of My--
IG ii² 1445.6ff.; 1446.1ff. (SEG 21.551). The actual inventory of the year is 1446 +.

Epimeletes of dockyards

MNESIADES of Kothokidai (VI) *PA* 10259
IG ii² 1622.489f.

Epistatai

[LY]KOPADES of Euonymon (I)
-- of Paiania (III)
THERS-- of tribe IV
[? EXEKEST]IDES of Kothokidai (VI)
ANTIME--
Hesperia 1935, 167 (28) (Broneer). I am grateful to D. M. Lewis for elucidating this document, which may belong in 375/4 or 374/3. He suggests that the opening should be something like the following:

[τάδε παρέλαβον οἱ ᾑρημένοι ἐπὶ τὰ πομπε]ῖα τὰ χρυσᾶ ἐ[φ' Ἱππ]
[οδάμαντος ἄρχοντος καὶ τὰς Νίκας τὰς χρυσ]ᾶς καὶ τὰς οἴ[νοχ]
[όας καὶ τὸν ἄλλον κόσμον]

Then come the names of the relevant epistatai and the above from whom they received.

Amphiktyons to Delos

EPIGENES son of Metagenes of Koile (VIII) *PA* 4805

ANTIMACHOS son of Euthynomos of Marathon (IX) *PA* 1129
EPIKRATES son of Menestratos of Pallene (X) *PA* 4909; *APF* 182f.
-- son of --dos of Oe (VI)
NIKOMENES son of Hieron of Halai (VII) *PA* 10970

Grammateus

DIODOROS son of Olympiodoros of Skambonidai (IV) *PA* 3961
Insc. Délos 98.6ff., 59ff. (IG ii² 1635; Tod 125). See 377/6, 376/5. These
served into the next year, Idiotes having departed.

Envoy

?KALLIAS son of Hipponikos of Alopeke (X) *PA* 7826; *APF* 263ff.
Xen. *Hell.* 6.3.4. He was probably one of the envoys to Sparta to make
peace. See 387/6; Cawkwell, *CQ* 1976, 276 n.25.

COUNCIL AND ASSEMBLY

(i) IG ii² 96 (Tod 126; SEG 31.64; Harding no. 41) is a probouleumatic decree
for the admission of Corcyreans, Akarnanians and Kephallenians to the
Confederacy, about the scope and effect of which there is dispute (see
Tuplin, *Athenaeum* 1984, 545ff.). It gives us the names of two secretaries,
the second of pryt. Antiochis (second prytany) and restored from ii² 99:
Grammateis
PHILOKLES son of O-- *PA* 14530
[PHY]LAKOS of Oinoe (VIII or IX) *PA* 15037
Proposer
KR[ITI]OS *PA* 8798
For the first secretary, the omega seems to me to begin a patronymic, given
the space available; the only fourth-century name with this initial is
Ophelion (*PA* 15588) of Ikarion, where Philokles is an attested name (*PA*
14544, 14545). However, D.M. Lewis informs me he once read traces
which suggest The-- rather than omega.

(ii) IG ii² 97 (SEG 31.65; Harding no. 42) records a treaty involving Athens
and Corcyra, which Tod (127) also placed in this year. I am prepared to
accept the date and the interpretation of the document as a confederate
alliance; see above on ii² 96 and further Tuplin, *Athenaeum* 1984, 553ff.

(iii) IG ii² 98 (Tod p. 86; SEG 31.66), concerning arrangements with
Kephallenia, is dated here by association with ii² 96, but in re-editing the
inscription with a new fragment, Schweigert, *Hesperia* 1940, 321ff. (33),
attached the date 373/2.

(iv) IG ii² 99 is a proxeny decree of the second prytany, of Antiochis, for
Alkimos (for the secretary see above on ii² 96):
Bouleutes epistates
. . . ? . . . TES of Themakos (I)

(v) IG ii² 102 (Tod 129; Harding no. 43) records an alliance with Amyntas of Makedon, the date of which is not certain.

Sources for the common peace of this year are Xen. *Hell.* 6.2.1; Isok. 14.10, 15.109; Nepos *Tim.* 2.2; Diod. 15.38; cf. ?IG ii² 3774 (Tod 128); Philochoros *FGH* 328 F 151 (Harding no. 44). It was probably concluded on Hekatombaion 16; Tuplin, *Athenaeum* 1984, 564 n.77.

(vi) It seems from Aisch. 3.243 that as a result of his success at Corcyra Timotheos was granted a statue by the Athenians, a proposal which Hansen, *Sovereignty* no. 8, assumes was unsuccessfully challenged as unconstitutional on the analogy of honours to Chabrias and Iphikrates which were so challenged. I do not find this legitimate, nor does Aischines' appeal to the jurors (in 330!) have to mean that dikasts confirmed Timotheos' honour.

Nomothetai

(vii) SEG 26.72 (31.63; Harding no. 45) is a law of the nomothetai concerning silver coinage:
Proposer
NIKOPHON

374/3 (Ol. 101.3)

Archon
SOKRATIDES *PA* 13128
Dem. 49.6, 44, 59.33; Diod. 15.41.1; Suda *s.v.* Φιλόχορος; IG ii² Add. [1421]; 1424.21; Add. 1424a.50, 65; 1425.46, 65; Add. 1428.9; 1436.[9] (Schweigert, *Hesperia* 1938, 287); 1438.[2] (*Hesperia* 1938, 284 (16 A.3) (Schweigert)); 1622.538; 1635.58, [109], 118, 123 (Tod 125; *Insc. Délos* 98); SEG 16.[45]; 21.551 (IG ii² 1446+).

Strategoi
KTESIKLES *PA* 8861
Xen. *Hell.* 6.2.10f.; Diod. 15.46.3, 47.4ff. Diod. 15.46.3 says that the Athenians voted to help the Corcyreans and the Zakynthian exiles and sent Ktesikles to Zakynthos; later, after Timotheos failed to go to Corcyra and was deposed, Ktesikles was sent to Corcyra, where he dealt with internal problems and had some success against the besieging forces. As Timotheos' deposition and trial should be placed in 373/2, although Diodoros includes all this under 374/3, the sequence requires that Ktesikles' expedition to Corcyra, which also involves Iphikrates (along with Timotheos, erroneously) coming with a subsidiary force, must be in 373/2; this is clearly the basis upon which Hansen, *GRBS* 1983, 171, gives him generalships in both years. Xenophon, however, has no mention of

Zakynthos and has Ktesikles sent out to Corcyra *before* Timotheos is chosen to go there as well. I prefer to accept the version of Diodoros and believe that Xenophon's account resulted from confusion with the Zakynthian expedition. See Tuplin, *Athenaeum* 1984, 537ff. against Gray, *CQ* 1980, 322f.

TIMOTHEOS son of Konon of Anaphlystos (x) *PA* 13700; *APF* 507ff. Xen. *Hell.* 6.2.11ff.; Dem. 49.6ff., 13, 49; Diod. 15.47.3f., 7; ?Isaios 6.27. Chosen to go around the Peloponnese to Corcyra, he tried to find crews in the islands and/or Thrace (Diod.) and supposedly won allies for Athens (Diod.). He was about to depart in Mounychion (Dem. 49.6). See above on Ktesikles; also Cargill, *League* 69ff.

Tamiai of Athene
-- of Kephisia (I)
PROTO-- of tribe II
-- of Thria (VI)
PISTI[DES] of tribe VII
  Grammateus
  GLAUKE[TES]
IG ii² 1421.1ff. + Add. p. 799, with which as inventory go 1423, 1424 (SEG 21.549), 1689 (Woodward, *AE* 1937, 165) and, I am informed, *Hesperia* 1940, 320 (32), and *AM* 1941, 237 (7). For speculation on Glauketes' deme see Dinsmoor, *AJA* 1932, 165 n.4 (cf. 354/3).

Tamiai of the other gods
-- son of Dionysios of Kydathenaion (III)
-- of Anakaia (VIII)
LY--
SEG 21.551 (IG ii² 1446+).

Epimeletes of dockyards
ARIMNESTOS of Elaious (VIII) *PA* 1619
IG ii² 1622.536f.

Epistatai
NIKIAS (son of Nikeratos) of Kydantidai (II) *PA* 10809; *APF* 406
-- of Phrearrhioi (IV)
TELES[IAS ?of Probalinthos] (III)
DIOKLES (son of Diochares) of Pithos (VII) *PA* 4048; *NPA* 57; *APF* 158
[KALLISTRATOS] (son of Kallikrates) of Aphidna (IX) ?*PA* 8157 = 8130; *APF* 277ff.
THEOMN[ESTOS] of tribe IX
Hesperia 1935, 167 (28) (Broneer). See 375/4. For Nikias see Crosby, *Hesperia* 1941, 26. For Kallistratos (with reference to the statue of Nike) see also IG ii² 1424.33 + 1689 (Woodward, *AE* 1937, 165).

Amphiktyons to Delos
EPIGENES son of Metagenes of Koile (VIII)
ANTIMACHOS son of Euthynomos of Marathon (IX) *PA* 1129
EPIKRATES son of Menestratos of Pallene (X) *PA* 4909; *APF* 182f.
-- son of --dos of Oe (VI)
NIKOMENES son of Hieron of Halai (VII) *PA* 10970
  Grammateus
  DIODOROS son of Olympiodoros of Skambonidai (IV) *PA* 3961
See 375/4.

COUNCIL AND ASSEMBLY

The only decree assigned to this year, and that very dubiously, is SEG 16.45, from the tenth prytany, which is supposed to relate to a charge of theft against Glauketes (*PA* 2946; see Dem. 24.129).

373/2 (Ol. 101.4)

Archon
ASTEIOS *PA* 2641
Dem. 49.22,28,60,62,59.35,36; Arist. *Meteor.* 1.6 343b 20; *MP* A 71; Diod. 15.48.1; Paus. 7.25.4, 9.1.8; IG ii² 101; 1421.5; 1607.[1]; 1622.534; *Hesperia* 1934, 2 ([3]) (Meritt); 1939, 4 (2) (Schweigert); SEG 31.67.[14]. Panathenaic amphora: Beazley, *Vase Painters* 412.

Strategoi
TIMOTHEOS son of Konon of Anaphlystos (X) *PA* 13700; *APF* 507ff. See 374/3. He was deposed from office and tried for treason on the accusation of Iphikrates and Kallistratos, as was his treasurer Antimachos; Hansen, *Eisangelia* nos. 80 and 81, with Tuplin, *Athenaeum* 1984, 538ff., 566ff.

KTESIKLES *PA* 8861
See 374/3.

IPHIKRATES son of Timotheos of Rhamnous (IX) *PA* 7737; *APF* 248ff. Xen. *Hell.* 6.2.13f., 27ff.; Diod. 15.47.7, 16.57.2f.; Polyainos 3.9.39,48,55; Ael. Arist. 1.313 (Lenz); schol. Ael. Arist. *Pan.* 173.17 (III.282 Dindorf).
  For chronology see under Ktesikles 374/3. He is said to have replaced Timotheos and it is unclear whether he was one of the other regularly elected generals of the year; Tuplin, *Athenaeum* 1984, 539 n. 14. He went around the Peloponnese, making landings and overcoming cities in Kephallenia, whence he came to Corcyra; there he was successful in a naval engagement, later aiding friendly cities in Akarnania and making war against the Thyrians; he sailed to Kephallenia and exacted money, prepar-

ing for future action. Xenophon recounts all this together, but we could well be taken beyond this year and Iphikrates remained out until 371. On him, Chabrias and Kallistratos see Cawkwell, *Historia* 1973, 759ff.

KALLISTRATOS son of Kallikrates of Aphidna (IX) *PA* 8157; *APF* 277ff.
CHABRIAS son of Ktesippos of Aixone (VII) *PA* 15086; *APF* 560f.
Xen. *Hell.* 6.2.39. See above on Iphikrates, who is said to have asked for them as colleagues. For doubts on the date of their choice, which I do not share, see Dover, *JHS* 1960, 74 n.28.

THRASYBOULOS son of Thrason of Kollytos (II) *PA* 7305; *APF* 238ff.
Hesperia 1939, 4 ([2]) (Schweigert).

Taxiarchoi or Phylarchoi
. .⁴. . OKLES son of . . ⁵ . . tios of Kedoi (I)
THRASYMEDES son of Kallistratos of Acharnai (VI) ?*PA* 7365
KLEONYMOS son of Kleoxenos of Marathon (IX) cf. *PA* 8607
[AN]TIMACHOS son of . .⁴. . os of Pelekes (IV)
. .⁴. . AS son of . . ⁵ . . imos of Myrrhinous (III)
THEOPHILOS son of Eua[ngelos] of Hermos (V) ?*PA* 7138
CHAR[IDEM]O[S] son of [E]uni[k]-- of tribe VIII
PHILINOS son of . .⁴. . nes of Anaphlystos (X) cf. *PA* 14321
Hesperia 1939, 4 (2.5ff.) (Schweigert). They were officers under Thrasyboulos.

Epimeletai of dockyards
[OINOST]RATOS of Anagyrous (I) cf. *PA* 11361
PHANOSTRATOS of tribe II *PA* 14096
-- of Hagnous (V)
DEXANDRIDES of Acharnai (VI) *PA* 3210
ERGOBIOS of Halai (VII) *PA* 5050
PLATON of Anakaia (VIII) *PA* 11852
IG ii² 1607.1ff. and for Platon 1622.532f.

Amphiktyons to Delos
NIKOLEOS of Tho[rikos] (V) or Tho[rai] (X)
    Grammateus
    DIODOROS son of Olympiodoros of Skambonidai (IV) *PA* 3961
Insc. Délos 100.9, 11.

COUNCIL AND ASSEMBLY

(i) IG ii² 101 is an honorary decree of pryt. Akamantis for Alketas of Syracuse;
(ii) the secretary is also restored in what was probably also an honorary decree at *Hesperia* 1934, 2 (3) (Meritt), where we also have a proposer:
Grammateus
THOUDAITES of Diomeia (II) *PA* 7246

Proposer

ASTY[PHILOS] ?*PA* 2662

(iii) SEG 31.67 preserves the latter part of an Athenian decree to do with a proposal brought by envoys from a foreign state (that they join the Confederacy?), followed by the beginning of a decree of the allied synhedrion dated to the last day of Skirophorion.

On IG ii² 98 see 375/4.

372/1 (Ol. 102.1)

Archon

ALKISTHENES *PA* 639

Dem. 49.30, 59, 60, 62; 59.36; Diod. 15.50.1; Dion. *Lys.* 12; *Insc. Délos* 100.[2].

Strategoi

IPHIKRATES son of Timotheos of Rhamnous (IX) *PA* 7737; *APF* 248ff. Xen. *Hell.* 6.3.3, 4.1. Xenophon implies that he remained out; see 373/2.

CHABRIAS son of Ktesippos of Aixone (VII) *PA* 15086; *APF* 560ff.

KALLISTRATOS son of Kallikrates of Aphidna (IX) *PA* 8157; *APF* 277ff. Xen. *Hell.* 6.3.3 (Kallistratos). See 373/2. Kallistratos promised Iphikrates that if he could go home, he would secure money for the fleet or work for peace, which he did (see below envoys).

Amphiktyons to Delos

LYSIAS son of L--

--OS son of Archippos

-- of Oion (IV or VIII)

Insc. Délos 100.5ff. They evidently served into the archonship of Nausigenes (368/7).

Envoys

KALLIAS son of Hipponikos of Alopeke (X) *PA* 7826; *APF* 263ff.

AUTOKLES (? son of Strombichides of Euonymon (I)) *PA* 2727; *APF* 161f.

DEMOSTRATOS (? son of Aristophon of Azenia (VIII)) *PA* 3617, *APF* 65

ARISTOKLES *PA* 1851

KEPHISODOTOS (of Kerameis (V)) *PA* 8331

MELANOPOS (son of Laches of Aixone) (VII) *PA* 9788

LYKAITHOS *PA* 9189

?KALLISTRATOS son of Kallikrates of Aphidna (IX) *PA* 8157; *APF* 277ff. Xen. *Hell.* 6.3.2ff. They were envoys to Sparta in the matter of peace; Kallias is given a speech. It is by no means clear that Kallistratos was one of those chosen; Xenophon says he was also present. For the assumption that he was an envoy, however, see Mosley, *Envoys* 58ff. He would make up the number of ten if one accepted the argument of Tuplin (*LCM* 1977, 51ff.)

247

that the text should be read to include Strombichides and Aristophon as envoys, not patronymics; he also wonders if Aristophon would then be *the* Aristophon (*PA* 2108; *APF* 65f.). The problem is that Xenophon introduces the names as being 'of those chosen' (ἦν δὲ τῶν αἱρεθέντων), but while one can see why Kallias should be given a patronymic, no such reason seems to hold good for Autokles and Demostratos when the others are not so identified.

371/70 (Ol. 102.2)

Archon
PHRASIKLEIDES *PA* 14979
Dem. 59.37; *MP*A 72; Diod. 15.51.1; Dion. *Lys.* 12; Paus. 6.5.3, 8.27.8; IG ii² [143] (SEG 15.89); [190] (SEG 14.45); 1422.[12] (but see SEG 31.125); 1436.[19] (but see Schweigert, *Hesperia* 1938, 287); 1438.[2] (but see Schweigert, *Hesperia* 1938, 284 (16)); 1451.[5]; 1622.400f., 542; SEG 28.148.49, [51] (*Agora* xv.13a +). Panathenaic amphora: Beazley, *Vase Painters* 412.

Polemarchos
AIETES of Keiriadai (VIII) *PA* 294
Dem. 59.40. He dealt with the case mentioned by Demosthenes, dated at 59.37 after the peace made in Phrasikleides' archonship and the battle of Leuktra.

Strategoi
IPHIKRATES son of Timotheos of Rhamnous (IX) *PA* 7737; *APF* 248ff.
?CHABRIAS son of Ktesippos of Aixone (VII) *PA* 15086; *APF* 560ff.
Xen. *Hell.* 6.3.3, 4.1; Dion. *Lys.* 12. See 373/2, 372/1. Kallistratos had already returned; whether Chabrias was still out we cannot say. Iphikrates was brought back after the peace.

Tamias of Athene
CHARO[PIN]OS of Rh[a]m[nous](IX)
This is due to an unpublished reading by Woodward of IG ii² 1424a.2, which inscription is the inventory of this year; cf. Woodward, *AE* 1937, 165. On ii² 1422 see SEG 31.125.

Epimeletai of dockyards
AMYTHEON of Euonymon (I) *PA* 730
LACHARIDES of Eleusis (VIII) *PA* 9007
IG ii² 1622.398f., 540f.

Amphiktyons to Delos
LYSIAS son of L--
--OS son of Archippos
-- of Oion (IV or VIII)
See 372/1.

COUNCIL AND ASSEMBLY

(i) IG ii² 143 (SEG 15.89; 30.60) seems to be a decree in honour of the diaitetai.

(ii) IG ii² 190 (SEG 14.45) is a decree for a king of the Pelagonians, placed by restoration (SEG) in the prytany of Hippothontis in this year:
Grammateus
[ARCH]EP[TOLEMOS]
Proposer
[ARKE]TO[S]
Bouleutes epistates
[M]ENES

For the making of peace see Xen. *Hell.* 6.3f.; Aisch. 2.32; Diod. 15.50.4; for the date Dem. 59.37.

(iii) An honorary decree for Iphikrates seems to have been unsuccessfully challenged as unconstitutional by Harmodios: Lysias F XVIII; Dem. 23.130, 136; Aisch. 3.243; Dion. *Lys.*12; Hansen, *Sovereignty* no. 9.

SEG 28.148 now adds to *Agora* XV.13a and gives the names of bouleutai of tribe IV Leontis:
Phrearrhioi
-- son of --dikos
. . PO.D-- son of --emos
[A]POLLOD[. . OS] son of [Kephi]sokles
[M]ELESIA[S] son of --eles
[K]EDEIDE[S]
[S]OSIAS son of D--
[P]EISITHE[OS] son of [?Eu]xitheos
[X]ENOPHO[N] son of [?Tei]sis
[S]MI[K]R[IAS] son of [Eu]ripides
Sounion
PHILONEO[S] son of [A]meinonikos
TIMOTHEOS son of Hip[po]stratos
ALEXIPPOS son of Epigenes
POLYCHARMICHOS son of Pataikos
Deiradiotai
-- son of --os
[HE]RMODOROS son of [S]tra[t]on
Potamos Deiradiotes
. . . OROS son of Pan--
Skambonidai
LEOKRATES son of Hippokrates
HYPERANTHES son of Atarbion
DOSITHEOS son of Antigenes

Leukonoion
THEOROS son of Mnesistratos
KALLIKRATES son of Pamphilos
ARISTOMEDES son of Meton
Kettos
PHILOKRATES son of Amphitelides
MELANKOMAS son of Hierok[l]es
EUBOULOS son of Lysias
Potamos lower
DEMOKLES son of Anti[kl]es
PHILOXENOS son of Lysistratos
Potamos upper
THEAIOS son of Hippokles
Cholleidai
EPIKRATES son of Eukles
Halimous?
APOLE[X]IS son of Ap--
XENOPEITHES son of Xenokles
CHARISANDROS son of Exekestos
Pelekes
ALEXIMACHOS son of Cha[rinos]
CHARITHOS son of Amphio[n]
Hybadai
CHARIKLES son of Sosias
POLYKRATES son of Lysan--
Oion
PHANOSTRATOS son of Stra[tios]
Kolonai
PROTOMACHOS son of Pytho--
--OS son of Arxillas

370/69 (Ol. 102.3)

Archon
DYSNIKETOS of Phlya (VII) *PA* 4580
Dem. 46.13; *MP* A 73; Diod. 15.57.1; Paus. 4.27.9 (Dyskinetos); IG ii²
Add. 1424a.4; 1425.117, 122, 127; 1436.13 (Dynniketos); 1438.[2]
(Hesperia 1938, 284 (16 A.3) (Schweigert)); *Hesperia* 1938, 284 (16 A.[31]
(IG ii² 1438 +); Schweigert); SEG 19.133 (Dynniketos); 29.146 col. II.10
(Dynniketos).

Basileus
PHILON of Cholleidai (IV)
Polemarchos
MENANDROS of tribe II or IX

Thesmothetai

--ODOTOS of Lamptrai (I)
EUBOULOS (? son of Spintharos) of Probalinthos (III) ?*PA* 5369
...?... IDES of Eiresidai (V)
EUTHYKRATES of Phyle (VI)
...?... of Oion (VIII)
KTESIAS of Besa (X) ?*PA* 8841
SEG 19.133.3ff. Menandros' tribe is by elimination, so that there was an unknown grammateus of tribe II or IX. While the deme is correct and the chronology credible, we cannot be sure of the identity of Euboulos. I have assumed that the basileus is named after the archon, then the polemarch followed by the thesmothetai.

Strategos

IPHIKRATES son of Timotheos of Rhamnous (IX) *PA* 7737; *APF* 248ff. Xen. *Hell.* 6.5.49ff.; Nepos *Iph.* 2.5; Diod. 15.63.2 (369/8), cf. 65.6; Paus. 9.14.6f.; Polyainos 3.9.20,28,37. Chosen to go to the aid of the Spartans (see below on the Assembly), he went to Corinth, whence he conducted operations. Later he led the Athenians back from Arkadia to Corinth and, deciding to guard Oneion, failed to prevent the Thebans passing.

Tamias of Athene

KOROI[BOS]
IG ii² 1424a.4, Cf. 371/70.

Epimeletes of dockyards

CHARI[AS ? of Kydathenaion (III)] ?*PA* 15345
IG ii² 1609.20, which inscription I think belongs to this year; so Cawkwell, *Historia* 1973, 759ff., against Davies, *Historia* 1969, 309ff.

Amphiktyons to Delos

LYSIAS son of L--
--OS son of Archippos
-- of Oion (IV or VIII)
See 372/1.

Kleroucharchoi

EUKTE[MON] (son of Charias) [of Lousia] (VI) *PA* 5785 = 5800; *NPA* 79
EUTHIAS of Sounion (IV) *NPA* 76
IG ii² 1609.88f., for the date of which see above epimeletes of dockyards (Harding no. 47).

COUNCIL AND ASSEMBLY

(i) Xen. *Hell.* 6.5.33ff. reports a meeting of the assembly convened by a resolution of the council through concern at Theban activity in the Peloponnese; this was addressed by Spartans, Kleiteles of Corinth and

Prokles of Phleious and the decision was to help the Spartans. This may have been the occasion when Leptines spoke (Arist. *Rhet.* 3.10 1411a 4f.; cf. Plut. *Mor.* 803a).

(ii) Dem. 59.26f. records that Kallistratos persuaded the Athenians to help the Spartans and Xenokleides the poet opposed this.

Agora XV.13 can no longer be definitely ascribed to this or any other year; see SEG 29.148.

369/8 (Ol. 102.4)

Archon
LYSISTRATOS *PA* 9597
Diod. 15.61.1; Plut. *Mor.* 839d; IG ii² 103 (Tod 133; Osborne D 10); 107.35 (Tod 131; Harding no. 53); 1425.128, 129f., 131; 1436.[15]; 1438.[3] (*Hesperia* 1938, 286 (16 A.4) (Schweigert)); 1617.71; 1622.485; ?[5165] (SEG 14.140); *Insc. Délos* 88.

Strategos
CHABRIAS son of Ktesippos of Aixone (VII) *PA* 15086; *APF* 560ff.
Xen. *Hell.* 7.1.25; Diod. 15.68.1ff., 69; Plut. *Mor.* 193f; Paus. 9.15.4. He went to Corinth to oppose the Thebans; he joined in the fortification of approaches into the Peloponnese, drove the Boiotians out of Corinth and withstood another attack and also barred the way out of the territory of Epidauros for the Argives.

Epimeletai of dockyards
SONDRIDES of Euonymon (I) *PA* 13142
[E]RATON (son of Eration) of Ikarion (II) *PA* 5042
PHA[ENNOS?] of S[teiria?] (III) cf. *PA* 13920
PROKLES of Kolonai (IV) *PA* 12231 *bis*; *APF* 470
[KT]ESIPHANES of Thorikos (V) *NPA* 115
ANTHEMION of Perithoidai (VI) *PA* 941
PRAXITELES of Melite (VII) *PA* 12171
AR[IS]TO[K]L[ES] of Oinoe (VIII) *NPA* 29
[TI]MOTH[E]OS of Marathon (IX) *PA* 13709
IG ii² 1617.72ff.; 1622.483f. (Anthemion). For Phaennos, Ktesiphanes and Aristokles see Sundwall, *Epig. Beitr.* 36 nn.6,7, 37 n.1.

Amphiktyons to Delos
LYSIAS son of L--
--OS son of Archippos
-- of Oion (IV or VIII)
See 372/1.

COUNCIL AND ASSEMBLY

(i) IG ii² 103 (Tod 133; Osborne D 10) is a probouleumatic decree of the tenth prytany, of Erechtheis, in honour of Dionysios of Syracuse and his sons:
Grammateus
EXE[KESTOS] son of Pai[onid]es of Azenia (VIII) *PA* 4726
Bouleutes epistates
EUANGEL[OS] *PA* 5222
Proposer
[PA]NDIOS (? son of Sokles of Oion) (VIII) ?*PA* 11575
The possibility that the epistates was from Phrearrhioi (IV) arises from the presence of the name in *Agora* XV.13. For Pandios see below no. iv.

(ii) IG ii² 107.35ff. (Tod 131; Harding no. 53) is a reply to Mitylenian envoys:
Proposer
KALLISTRATOS (? son of Kallikrates of Aphidna) (IX) ?*PA* 8157; *APF* 277ff.

(iii) *Insc. Délos* 88 is a proxeny decree of the ninth prytany, of Leontis, proposed by the council for Pythodoros of Delos:
Grammateus
ARISTEIDES son of Strepheneos of Kydathenaion (III) *PA* 1707
Bouleutes epistates
SMIKRIAS of Athmonon (VII) *PA* 12741
Proposers
PHOXIAS *PA* 14942
EPIKRATES (son of Menestratos of Pallene) (X) *PA* 4909; *APF* 182f.

(iv) We may place here *AE* 1923, 36ff. (123) (Leonardos), which deals with repairs to the Amphiaraion at Oropos and also praises the priest of Amphiaraos Antikrates of Dekeleia:
Proposer
PANDIOS
The date has recently been discussed by Knoepfler (*Chiron* 1986, 71–98) and as this is a decree of the council, it is amenable to this year, in which a Pandios was on the council and is known as a proposer (restored in no. i above). Knoepfler (85f.) also notices men of the name other than the one whose identity is added above, especially a Pandios of Teithras (SEG 24.151.6, mid-century).

(v) Xen. *Hell.* 7.1.1ff. records discussion at Athens to decide the terms of alliance with the Spartans and their allies; the meeting is addressed by Timokrates of Sparta and Prokles of Phleious and the Athenians decide that each side should hold the leadership for five days after hearing Kephisodotos.

368/7 (Ol. 103.1)

Archon
NAUSIGENES *PA* 10544 + Add.
Philochoros *FGH* 328 F 223; *MP* A 74; Diod. 15.71.1; IG ii² 104.6 (Tod 134); [105 + 523](Tod 136; SEG 14.46; 31.68; Harding no. 52); 106 (Tod 135); 107 (Tod 131; Harding no. 53); 1174.8; 1425.222, 225, 228; Add. 1428.7, 56; 1436.[16]; 1438.[4] (*Hesperia* 1983, 284 (16 A.5) (Schweigert)); 1617.[92]; 1622.555; xiv 1098.10; *Insc. Délos* 100.[3]; ?*Hesperia* 1948, 34 (16.[35f.]) (Meritt) (but see SEG 15.120).

Strategoi
AUTOKLES (son of Strombichides of Euonymon) (I) *PA* 2727; *APF* 161f.
Diod. 15.71.3f. Sent to aid Alexandros of Pherai, he helped to cause the Boiotians to retreat.

IPHIKRATES son of Timotheos of Rhamnous (IX) *PA* 7737; *APF* 248ff.
Dem. 23.149, 151; Aisch. 2.27ff.; Nepos *Iph.* 3.2. He was sent to Amphipolis and drove Pausanias from Makedon at the request of Eurydike. He operated in this theatre until 365/4.

PHORM[ION] *PA* 14950
SPOUDIAS *PA* 12861
IG ii² 104.3f. (Tod 134). They took the oaths in the treaty with Leukas.

?CHABRIAS son of Ktesippos of Aixone (VII) *PA* 15086; *APF* 560ff.
Perhaps he remained in the Corinthiad; cf. Cawkwell, *Historia* 1973, 761.

Hipparchoi
NIKE--
--IKLES
IG ii² 104.1 (Tod 134). They took the oaths in the treaty with Leukas.

Epimeletai of dockyards
. . .⁷. . . os of Lamptrai (I)
[?THE]OBIOS of Kopros (VIII)
N . . .⁶. . . ELOS of Oa (III)
E--
?[P]RA[XIA]S of Xypete (VII) *NPA* 146
LYSIPHILOS of Rhamnous (IX) *PA* 9636
IG ii² 1617.93ff.; 1622.553f. (Lysiphilos).

Amphiktyons to Delos
LYSIAS son of L--
--OS son of Archippos
-- of Oion (IV or VIII)
See 372/1.

Envoys

TIMONOTHOS *PA* 13799
AUTOLYKOS (of Thorikos) (v) *PA* 2746
ARISTOPEITHES *PA* 2046
IG ii² 107.32ff. (Tod 131; Harding no. 53). Envoys to Lesbos in a mission which led to praise of the Mitylenians.

TIMAGORAS *PA* 13595
LEON *PA* 9101
Xen. *Hell.* 7.1.33ff.; Dem. 19.31, 137, 191; Plut. *Artax.* 22.5; *Pel.* 30.6; Athenaios 2.48d–e, 6.251b. They were sent to the King of Persia. Timagoras sided with Pelopidas and was condemned to death on his return home on the accusation of Leon (Hansen, *Eisangelia* no. 82). Dem. 19.191 seems to say they were co-envoys for four years, but this is doubted by Mosley, *GRBS* 1968, 157ff.

COUNCIL AND ASSEMBLY

(i) IG ii² 104 (Tod 134) records a treaty with Leukas from the first prytany, of Kekropis:
Grammateus
MNESIBOULO[S] *PA* 10264 = ?10265; *APF* 225
Bouleutes epistates
PHILIPPOS of Eiresidai (v) 14390

(ii) IG ii² 105 + 523 (Tod 136; SEG 14.46, 31.68; Harding no. 52) is an alliance with Dionysios of Syracuse restored in IG to the thirty-second day of the seventh prytany, of Aiantis, but other days are possible (Hansen, *GRBS* 1982,341 (*Ecclesia* 93); cf. SEG 32.58) and Lewis (SEG) doubts the restorations here recorded and now would like the prytany to be the second, as close as possible to 369/8:
Grammateus
MOSCHOS son of Thestios of Kydathenaion (III) *PA* 10461
Bouleutes epistates
. . .⁶. . . s son of Daippos [? of Marathon(IX)] *PA* 3101; *APF* 92
Proposer
[PAN]D[IOS] (? son of Sokles of Oion (VIII)) ?*PA* 11575
The secretary is restored from IG ii² 106 and 107; 105 has no patronymic.

(iii) IG ii² 106 (Tod 135) is a probouleumatic decree from the seventh prytany, of Aiantis, honouring Koroibos of Sparta (for the secretary see above):
Bouleutes epistates
PARAMYTHOS of Otryne (II) *PA* 11631
Proposer
DIOPHANTOS (son of Thrasymedes of Sphettos) (v) *PA* 4438

(iv) IG ii² 107 (Tod 131; Harding no. 53) is a probouleumatic decree of the same prytany praising the Mitylenians:

Bouleutes epistates
ARISTYLLOS of Erchia (II) *PA* 2131

Proposers
[DIO]PHA[NTOS] (son of Thrasymedes of Sphettos) (v) *PA* 4438
AUTOLYKOS (? of Thorikos (v)) *PA* 2746
There must be doubt that Autolykos is the same man as the envoy, unless we suppose that he is proposing to praise himself.

(v) For the alliance with Alexandros of Pherai and honours to him see IG ii² 116.39f.; Dem. 23.120; Diod. 15.71.3; Plut. *Pel.* 31.4, *Mor.* 193d–e.

367/6 (Ol. 103.2)

Archon
POLYZELOS *PA* 11960
Dem. 30.15; Diod. 15.75.1; Dion. *ad Amm.* 5 (Apollodoros *FGH* 244 F 38b); IG ii² 1428 + Add.; 1436.[17]; 1438.[5] (*Hesperia* 1938, 284 (16 A.6) (Schweigert)); 1450.[5]; 1451.7; 1617.[110]; 1622.500; *Hesperia* 1939, 5 (3.7) (Schweigert; Tod 137; Harding no. 54); SEG 12.100; *Agora* XV.14. Panathenaic amphora: Beazley, *Vase Painters* 413f.

Strategoi
IPHIKRATES son of Timotheos of Rhamnous (IX) *PA* 7737; *APF* 248ff. See 368/7.

TIMOMACHOS of Acharnai (VI) *PA* 13797; *APF* 280
Xen. *Hell.* 7.1.41f. He was in the Corinthiad, guarding Oneion, but failing to prevent the Thebans passing.

TIMOTHEOS son of Konon of Anaphlystos (X) *PA* 13700; *APF* 507ff.
Isok. 15.108, 111f.; Dem. 15.9f.; Deinarchos 1.14, 3.17; Arist. *Oik.* 2.2.3 1350b 5ff.; Nepos *Tim.* 1.2f.; Plut. *Mor.* 187c, 837c; Polyainos 3.10.10,?5; IG ii² 108.9f.

He was sent to aid Ariobarzanes. After his successful siege of Samos, he went on to win Sestos and Krithote. For the date see Schweigert, *AJPh* 1940, 197f.; Sealey, *Essays* 160 n.124. This continued into the next year, but I include the sources here.

CHARES son of Theochares of Angele (III) *PA* 15292; *APF* 568f.
Xen. *Hell.* 7.2.18ff.; Diod. 15.75.3. He was sent to help Phleious and was successful in two engagements against the Argives and also against the Sikyonians.

Tamiai of Athene
--KLEI[D]ES of Gargettos (II)
ALKIB[IO]S of Paiania (III) *PA* 605

--SIAS of Cholargos (V)
PHILOPHRON of Thria (VI) *PA* 14767
--[D]OROS of Marathon (IX)
HIEROMNEMON of Besa (X) *PA* 7504
IG ii² 1428.2ff., the inventory of the year.

Poletai
POLYEUKTOS of Lamptrai (I) *PA* 11948; *APF* 465
DEINIAS of Erchia (II) *PA* 3163; *APF* 96
THEAIOS of Paiania (III)
THEOTIMOS of Phrearrhioi (IV)
ARISTOGENES of Iphistiadai (V)
GLAUKON of Lakiadai (VI)
KEPHISOKLES of Peiraieus (VIII)
NIKOKLES of Anaphlystos (X)
  Grammateus
  EXEKESTOS (? son of Aristodemos) of Kothokidai (VI) *APF* 178
SEG 12.100; only the eight were listed.

The Eleven
PHAIAX of Aphidna (IX)
SEG 12.100.7.

Epimeletai of dockyards
. . . . R--
. . . . O . . . OIRO--
?[A]RIS[TAI]O[S] of Hermos (V)
?MEN[AICHM]O[S] of Pambotadai (I)
?TIMARETOS of Perithoidai (VI)
EUTHYDOMOS of Athmonon (VII) *PA* 5570
PH[I]LO[KL]ES of Phaleron (IX) *PA* 14564
IG ii² 1617.111ff.; 1622.498f. (Euthydomos). These are the readings of
IG, which differ somewhat from the earlier Sundwall, *Epig. Beitr.* 37.

COUNCIL AND ASSEMBLY

Prytanies of the year may be found at SEG 12.100: 1. Hippothontis; 2.
Antiochis; 3. Oineis; 4. Kekropis; 5. Aigeis; 7. Leontis; 9. Erechtheis.

Hesperia 1939, 5f. (3) (Schweigert; Tod 137; SEG 32.57; Harding no. 54) is
a decree of pryt. Oineis (third prytany) taking measures after the people of
Trichoneion, members of the Aitolian League, had detained those sent to
announce the sacred truce for the Eleusinian mysteries, Promachos (unpublished fragment) and Epigenes:
Grammateus
DEMOPHILOS son of Theoros of Kephale (V)

Bouleutes epistates
PHI[LI]PPOS of Semachidai (x)
Cf. Tod 146.4.
Proposer
KEPHISODOTOS (of Kerameis) (v) *PA* 8331

Agora XV.14 is a list of the victorious prytaneis of tribe I Erechtheis:
Euonymon
-- son of Nauphrades
-- son of --nomachos
-- son of Pytheides
[AUT]OKLES son of Androkles *APF* 162
[K]LEAICHMOS son of Menaichmos
ANAXIKRATES son of Anaximenes
EP[I]CHARINOS son of Philochares
[P]RA[X]IKLES son of Sophortos *APF* 469
ALEXIMACHOS son of Alexias *PA* 540
[N]AUSONIDES son of Eurrhemon
Anagyrous
[P]OLYKLES son of Polykrates *PA* 11988; *APF* 465f.
[EU]THYKLES son of Euthykrates
[B]ABYLAOS son of Xenokleides
[E]UKOLION son of Pyrrhakos cf. *APF* 196f.
[K]TESON son of Titon
[L]YSITHEOS
Kephisia
[E]URIPIDES son of Eurykleides
[D]IOPHANES son of Diophanes
--AS
TLETHYMOS son of Tlempolemos
LYSISTRATOS son of Nikoxenos
PYTHODOROS son of Aristion *PA* 12425; *APF* 564
Agryle lower
MNESITHEOS son of Proteas
PHILOKYDES son of Pantakles
Pergase lower
EPIKRATES son of Epiteles
PHILEUS son of Phelleus
Lamptrai coastal
ANDROMENES son of Theogenes
MENON son of Demophilos
PHILOKRATES son of Philinos
KLEINIAS son of Kannonos cf. *NPA* 158
DEMOTION son of Dem--
KALLIAS son of Epigenes *PA* 7873; *APF* 178f.

LYSANIAS son of Lysan[ias ?] ?*PA* 9316
EUTHYKRATES son of Euth[ykles] ?*PA* 5605; *APF* 193
PROKLEIDES
Themakos
NIKOPHON son of Timogen[es]
Agryle upper
THRASEAS son of Polyzelos
MENIPPOS son of Xenophantos
KALLIKLES son of Satyros
Kedoi
SOPHANES
THOUGEITON
Lamptrai lower
THOUKYDIDES son of Theokydes
HYGIAINON son of Chairedemos
DEMETRIOS son of Phileas
PYTHOKLES
[A]RISTOGENES
Phegous
--OS son of Lys--
Pergase upper?
--THEOS

366/5 (Ol. 103.3)

Archon
KEPHISODOROS *PA* 8342
Dem. 30.17; *MP* A 75; Diod. 15.76.1; Dion. *Isaios* 5, 7 (Isaios F 15.2;
Cawkwell, *C&M* 1962, 34f.); Athenaios 4.171d (or 323/2?); IG ii² 108;
1428.[5]; 1436.[18]; 1438.[5] (*Hesperia* 1938, 284 (16 A.6) (Schweigert));
1443.[213f.]; 1450.5f.; 1455.15; 1460.[29]; 1508.[14]; 1622.508; 2318.[247];
3025.2 (SEG 19.194: or 323/2?); xiv 1098.7.

Strategoi
TIMOTHEOS son of Konon of Anaphlystos (X) *PA* 13700; *APF* 507ff.
See 367/6; also Isaios F 15 and Dem. 23.130 with Cawkwell, *C&M* 1962,
35.

IPHIKRATES son of Timotheos of Rhamnous (IX) *PA* 7737; *APF* 248ff.
See 368/7.

?LYSISTRATOS *PA* 9598
Xen. *Poroi* 3.4.7. He was in command of aid sent to the Arkadians in this
year (Xen. *Hell*. 7.4.6) or 364/3 (Xen. *Hell*. 7.4.29).

CHABRIAS son of Ktesippos of Aixone (VII) *PA* 15086; *APF* 560ff.
Dem. 21.64 with schol.; Arist. *Rhet*. 1.7.13 1364a 19ff.; Diog. 3.23f.; schol.
Aisch. 3.85. He was tried for his life after the entrusting of Oropos to the

Thebans, Oropos having been seized by Themison of Eretria and Athenian forces sent (Xen. *Hell.* 7.4.1; Diod. 15.76.1); Hansen, *Eisangelia* nos. 83, 84.

CHARES son of Theochares of Angele (III) *PA* 15292; *APF* 568f.
Xen. *Hell.* 7.4.1, 5. He was called back from the Peloponnese when the Athenians sent their force to Oropos. He later came back to Kenchreiai with a fleet, but was sent away by the Corinthians.

Tamias of Athene
[M]OSCHOS son of Thestios of Kydathenaion (III) *PA* 10461
IG ii² 1428.6 + Add.

Epimeletes of dockyards
HEGESI[PPOS] of Melite (VII) *PA* 6349
IG ii² 1622.506f.

COUNCIL AND ASSEMBLY

(i) IG ii² 108 is evidently a probouleumatic decree of the fifth prytany, of Aiantis or Leontis, praising the Erythraians:
Grammateus
. . . ? . . . son of Demainetos [of Xypete (VII)?] *PA* 3266
Proposer
. . . . THEO[S]
On the deme and tribe of the secretary see Alessandri, *ASNP* 1982, 53ff.

(ii) Athenaios 4.171e records part of what seems to be a probouleumatic decree that councillors be allowed to share the holiday of the Apatouria; it belongs here or in 323/2:
Proposer
PHOKOS *PA* 15082

On the making of the alliance with the Arkadians see Xen. *Hell.* 7.4.2ff.
(iii) Demotion addressed the assembly and seems to have proposed that the generals should be instructed to see that Corinth was safe for the demos of the Athenians:
Proposer
DEMOTION *PA* 3646

365/4 (Ol. 103.4)

Archon
CHION *PA* 15552
Dem. 30.17; Diod. 15.77.1; IG ii² [216 + 261, 217] (SEG 14.47; see Harding, *Historia* 1976, 190ff.); 1436.[19]; 1438.[6] (*Hesperia* 1938, 284 (16 A.7) (Schweigert)); 3065.5; xiv 1098.1, 11.

Strategoi
IPHIKRATES son of Timotheos of Rhamnous (IX) *PA* 7737; *APF* 248ff.

See 368/7. He was removed from his command (Dem. 23.149); it is evident from Hansen, *GRBS* 1983, 169, 176, that he believes Timotheos' assumption of the command should be dated to 364/3.

TIMOTHEOS son of Konon of Anaphlystos (x) *PA* 13700; *APF* 507ff. Isok. 15.108, 113; Dem. 2.14, 23.149ff., 154; Deinarchos 1.14, 3.17; Arist. *Oik.* 2.2.23 1350a 23ff.; Nepos *Tim.* 1.2, 4; Polyainos 3.10.7,8,9,14,15.

See also 367/6, 366/5 and above on Iphikrates. He took over from the latter in the northern Aegean, attacked Amphipolis and then waged war with the Chalkidians with the aid of Perdikkas of Makedon, taking some cities.

Nauarchos
?KYDIAS *PA* 8924
Euboulos F 67 (Edmonds). Edmonds wants to date this fragment to *c.* 363. Kydias may have held this position, if this is what it was, when he opposed the klerouchy to Samos (see below). Hunter, *Eubulus* 153, dates the play *c.* 350–320 on very little.

COUNCIL AND ASSEMBLY

(i) IG ii² 216 + 261 = 217 is placed in this year by the restoration at SEG 14.47 and is not likely to be much wrong, if at all; see also Harding, *Historia* 1976, 190ff. The decree concerns the handing over of sacred objects from the old tamiai to the new:
Grammateus
KEPH[I]SIOS [? son of Epikrates of Ionidai (II)] ?*PA* 8290
Bouleutes epistates
AR[I]STO--

(ii) Also mentioned in this text is a decree which somehow regulated the procedure:
Proposer
ANDROTION (son of Andron of Gargettos) (II) *PA* 915 = 913; *APF* 33f. See also Dem. 22.69ff. This will have to be dated in this year or shortly before.

Kydias (cf. above nauarchos) spoke against the sending of klerouchs to Samos (Arist. *Rhet.* 2.6.24 1384b 32ff.).

364/3 (Ol. 104.1)

Archon
TIMOKRATES *PA* 13749
Dem. 30.15, 17; Diod. 15.78.1; Dion. *ad Amm.* 4 (Apollodoros *FGH* 244 F 347b); Plut. *Mor.* 844c, 845e; schol. Aisch. 2.31; IG ii² 1436.[20]; 1438.[7] (*Hesperia* 1938, 284 (16 A.8) (Schweigert)); ?[3038] (but see Amandry,

BCH 1976, 27f.); 3066.4; *Insc. Délos* 104; *Hesperia* 1971, 180 ([27]) (Stroud); 302 (8.6) (Camp). Panathenaic amphora: ?*Hesperia* Suppl. 10, 15 (15) (Talcott and Philippaki).

Strategoi
TIMOTHEOS son of Konon of Anaphlystos (X) *PA* 13700; *APF* 507ff.
Isok. 15.108, 113; Deinarchos 1.14; Nepos *Tim.* 1.2; Diod. 15.81.6; ?Justin 16.4.3f.; Polyainos 3.10.15. See also 365/4. Timotheos' operations, which continued into 363/2, when Poteidaia became his last gain, won several cities and relieved Kyzikos from seige. See Sealey, *Essays* 152, and on Justin Cawkwell, *CQ* 1972, 270, 272 n.1.

LACHES (? son of Laches of Aixone) (VII) *PA* 9018
Diod. 15.79.1. Unsuccessful with his fleet in an attempt to counter Theban ambitions to win over Rhodes, Chios and Byzantion.

ALKIMACHOS of Anagyrous (I) *PA* 616.
Schol. Aisch. 2.31. General in Thrace, he was unsuccessful against Amphipolis. See Sealey, *Essays* 152.

?LYSISTRATOS *PA* 9598
See 366/5.

Logistes
?TIMARCHOS son of Arizelos of Sphettos (V) *PA* 13636
Aisch. 1.107. Placed before 363/2 on the assumption that the list of offices in Aischines is in chronological order (see 363/2 archon in Andros). He is accused by Aischines of corruption.

Amphiktyons to Delos
ARISTON (son of Eukleon) of Aphidna (IX) *PA* 2152
  Grammateus
  PRAXITELES son of Praxiades of Kephale (V) *PA* 12170
Insc. Délos 104.4f.

COUNCIL AND ASSEMBLY

(i) Moysey, *AJAH* 1976, 182–9, has argued that IG ii² 119 and 141 (Tod 139) belong in this year. The former is in honour of King Tachos of Egypt:
Grammateus
PHANOKL[ES] *PA* 14044

(ii) Alessandri, *ASNP* 1982, 56ff., who argues that the annual secretary first appeared in 366/5 (see introduction), places IG ii² 145.11ff. in this year and Phanokles' name fits the available space for the secretary from Oinoe (VIII) at line 12 (but see 359/8); this is a probouleumatic decree of pryt. Leontis in honour of the heralds Eukles and Philokles:
Bouleutes epistates
EUPH--

Proposer
MELANOPOS (son of Laches of Aixone) (VII) *PA* 9788

(iii) IG ii² 141 (Tod 139; Harding no. 40) is an honorific decree for Straton, King of Sidon:
Proposers
KEPHISODOTOS (of Kerameis) (v) *PA* 8331
MENEXENOS *PA* 9972

363/2 (Ol. 104.2)

Archon
CHARIKLEIDES *PA* 15395
Dem. 21.178; Diod. 15.82.1; Plut. *Mor.* 845e; IG ii² 109a (Osborne D 11); 110 (Tod 143; Osborne T 56); 111 (Tod 142; SEG 31.71; Harding no. 55); ?1422.[12] (SEG 31.125); 1436.21, 23; 1438.[7] (*Hesperia* 1938, 284 (16 A.8) (Schweigert)); 1541.4; 1611.107; 1622.568; 2654.11; *Insc. Délos* 88.28; SEG 21.241; 527.2, 56, 67 (*LSS* no. 19); 27.12.6; 29.146 col. 11.14; *Hesperia* 1971, 302f. (8.16) (Camp). Panathenaic amphoras: Beazley, *Vase Painters* 414; Frel, *Amphoras* 23.

Strategoi
TIMOTHEOS son of Konon of Anaphlystos (x) *PA* 13700; *APF* 507ff.
IG ii² 110.6 (Tod 143). See also 364/3. He returned to Athens and commended the help of Menelaos the Pelagonian.

CHABRIAS son of Ktesippos of Aixone (VII) *PA* 15086; *APF* 560ff.
IG ii² 111.17ff. (Tod 142; SEG 31.71; Harding no. 55); ?Paus. 9.15.4. The inscription mentions arrangements with Keos. Pausanias talks of defeat by the Thebans at Lechaion in the Peloponnese.

ARISTOPHON son of Aristophanes of Azenia (VIII) *PA* 2108; *APF* 64ff.
Schol. Aisch. 1.64 (Hypereides F 40). General to Keos, apparently in this year (see below council and assembly).

HEGESILEOS (? of Probalinthos (III)) *PA* 6339
Xen. *Poroi* 3.4.7; Ephoros *FGH* 70 F 85; Diod. 15.84.2 (Hegelochos). He was general at Mantineia.

ERGOPHILOS *PA* 5062
Dem. 19.180; 23.104; Arist. *Rhet.* 2.3.13f. 1380b 10ff.; Harpokration and Suda *s.v.* Ἐργόφιλος; Photios *s.v.* Ἐργοκλῆς καὶ Ἐργόφιλος. General in the Hellespontine region, he was brought to trial and punished for betraying the Chersonese; Hansen, *Eisangelia* no. 86, and for date Sealey, *Essays* 152.

KALLISTHENES *PA* 8089
Aisch. 2.30f.; Arist. *Rhet.* 2.3.13f. 1380b 10ff. He defeated Perdikkas of

Makedon and made a truce with him which was adjudged premature and led to his execution; Hansen, *Eisangelia* no. 85; Sealey, *Essays* 152.

Hipparchos

KEPHISODOROS of Marathon (IX) *PA* 8376

Ephoros *FGH* 70 F 85; Paus. 8.9.10; Harpokration, Suda and Photios *s.v.* Κηφισόδωρος. He died at Mantineia.

Archon in Andros

?TIMARCHOS son of Arizelos of Sphettos (V) *PA* 13636

Aisch. 1.107f. The date is not specified, but if the offices described by Aischines are in chronological order (Cawkwell, *JHS* 1981, 51f. and n.47), then he held this position before his service as councillor in 361/60, for which position he will have been selected in 362/1. He is accused of misbehaviour by Aischines. Cf. Cargill, *League* 157f. and n.28.

Tamias of the other gods

CHAIRESTRATOS of Kollytos (II) *PA* 15165

IG ii² 1541.3.

Tamias of trireme funds

PHANOSTRATOS of Thorai (X) *PA* 14101

IG ii² 1622.546f.

Financial official?

LEPTINES of Koile (VIII) *PA* 9046; *APF* 340

IG ii² 1541.1. It seems he held a financial office of some (extraordinary?) sort; see *APF*.

Epistates of Eleusinion

AMPHIKTYON of Aphidna (IX) *PA* 776

IG ii² 1541.5. It looks as though he served until 357/6. That he was as described, and not epistates of Eleusis, seems to emerge from comparison with IG ii² 1666 (see 356/5); see also the Introduction, p. 13.

Amphiktyons to Delos

?THRASONIDES of Eupyridai (IV) *PA* 7398

Grammateus

?MENES son of Menekles of Pelekes (IV) *PA* 10028

Insc. Délos 104.6f. The query is whether they succeeded the previous board in this year, since there are doubts as to the length of service (see the Introduction, p. 18).

COUNCIL AND ASSEMBLY

This is the first year in which we have clear evidence that the secretary now served for the whole year; consequently he appears in all the inscriptions described below:

Grammateus
NIKOSTRATOS son of Philostratos of Pallene (X) *PA* 11043

(i) IG ii² 109a (Osborne D 11) is a probouleumatic decree dated to the thirtieth day of the second prytany, of Akamantis, dealing with Astykrates of Delphi and making him a citizen:
Bouleutes epistates
. . . ? . . . NES of Paiania (III)
Proposer
KRATINOS *PA* 8752

(ii) IG ii² 110 (Tod 143; Osborne T56) is a probouleumatic decree from the sixth prytany, of Oineis, honouring Menelaos the Pelagonian:
Bouleutes epistates
CHARIKLES of Leukonoion (IV) *PA* 15414
Proposer
SATYROS *PA* 12575

(iii) IG ii² 111 (Tod 142; SEG 31.71; Harding no. 55) is a decree of pryt. Aiantis establishing relations with Ioulis, evidently in similar terms to arrangements with other cities of Keos:
Bouleutes epistates
PHILITTIOS of Boutadai (VI) *PA* 14465
Proposer
ARISTOPHON son of Aristophanes of Azenia (VIII) *PA* 2108; *APF* 64ff.

(iv) Also at lines 5ff. reference is made to a sum of money due under a decree:
Proposer
MENEXENOS *PA* 9972 = ?9971; cf. *APF* 390

(v) Schol. Aisch. 1.64 also informs us of a successful challenge to a proposal concerning the Keans made by Aristophon and opposed by Hypereides (F VIII); Hansen, *Sovereignty* no. 10.

(vi) *Insc. Délos* 88.28ff. is a decree from the seventh prytany, of Hippothontis (but see the note at SIG I³ 158), extending proxeny to Pythodoros' nephew (see 369/8):
Bouleutes epistates
-- of Aphidna (IX)
Proposer
ANDROMENES *PA* 882 = ?883

(vii) SEG 21.241 is a decree concerning the listing of sacred gifts:
Bouleutes epistates
TI[M]--
Proposer
--NO[S]

362/1 (Ol. 104.3)

Archon

MOLON *PA* 10411

Dem. 50.4; Diod. 15.90.1; Dion. *Dein.* 13; IG ii² 112 (Tod 144; Harding no. 56); 113.[5]; 114 (Tod 146; Harding no. 58); 115; 120.[9]; 1436.24; 1438.[9] (*Hesperia* 1938, 284 (16 A.10) (Schweigert)); 1611.111; 1622.[433], 504; SEG 23.78.[25] (Reinmuth no. 1, but see Dow, *Essays Brendel* 81ff.); 27.13.6; 29.146 col. 11.3.

Strategoi

AUTOKLES son of Strombichides of Euonymon (I) *PA* 2727; *APF* 161f.
Dem. 23.104, 36.53, 50.12; Hypereides F XI. Sent to Thrace, he was recalled and deposed, evidently for contravening instructions, eight months later; he was impeached for treason and tried in the winter of 360; Hansen, *Eisangelia* no. 90.

MENON of Potamos (IV) *PA* 10085
Dem. 36.53; 50.12. Sent to replace Autokles, he saw out the year, but was himself impeached around the same time as Autokles; Hansen, *Eisangelia* no. 95.

Epimeletes of dockyards

THEO[D]OTOS of Aixone (VII) *PA* 6786
IG ii² 1622.502f.

Epistates of Eleusinion

AMPHIKTYON of Aphidna (IX) *PA* 776
See 363/2

COUNCIL AND ASSEMBLY

The secretary is found in IG ii² 112, 114 and 115:
Grammateus

AGATHARCHOS son of Agatharchos of Oe (VI) *PA* 33

(i) IG ii² 112 (Tod 144; Harding no. 56) is a decree of pryt. Oineis for alliance with Arkadians, Achaians, Eleians and Phleiasians:
Bouleutes epistates

XANTHIPPOS of Hermos (V) *PA* 11162
Proposer

PERIANDROS (son of Polyaratos of Cholargos) (V) *PA* 11800; *APF* 464

(ii) IG ii² 113 is restored to this year and the sixth prytany, of Pandionis, being a grant of isoteleia to Phanostratos and another and their descendants. Schwenk no. 60 follows Wilhelm in preferring 327/6, but there is not much left of the document.

(iii) IG ii² 114 (Tod 146; Harding no. 58) is a decree from the ninth prytany, of Erechtheis, concerning the sending of klerouchs to Poteidaia:
Bouleutes epistates
. . .⁶. . . s of Kerameis (v)
Proposer
PHIL[IPPO]S *PA* 14373

(iv) IG ii² 115 + Add. is also from the ninth prytany and is in honour of the Dieis of Thrace.

(v) The earliest measure of the year is to be found at Dem. 50.4ff. An assembly was held on Metageitnion 24, thus in the second prytany, which heard of troubles in the north; Miltokythes from Thrace had sent envoys asking for help and alliance and the Prokonnesians were asking for aid against the Kyzikenes. A vote was taken that the trierarchs should make ready their vessels, crews be selected and the fleet sent out:
Proposer
ARISTOPHON son of Aristophanes of Azenia (VIII) *PA* 2108; *APF* 64ff.

(vi) Then, at section 8, we hear of a vote that the bouleutai, on behalf of the demesmen, should bring forward the names of those who should pay the
(vii) advance eisphora. And at section 13 we find a decree in praise of Apollodoros for securing funds to crew his ship.

(viii) Dem. 23.104 records the decree passed when Autokles was about to sail concerning Miltokythes.

361/0 (Ol. 104.4)

Archon
NIKOPHEMOS *PA* 11067
Dem. 43.31, 46.13; Aisch. 1.109 with schol.; Diod. 15.95.1; Dion. *Dein.* 4, 9, 13; schol. Aisch. 1.53; IG ii² 116 (Tod 147; Harding no. 59); 1436.25; 1438.[9] (*Hesperia* 1938, 284 (16 A.10) (Schweigert)); 1611.[113]; 1617.125; 4894; SEG 23.78.1, 9f., [13] (Reinmuth no. 1, but see Lewis, *CR* 1973, 254; Dow, *Essays Brendel* 81ff.; Mitchel, *ZPE* 19 (1975), 234ff.); 27.14.5; 29.146 col. II.6.

Paredros
?[A]RISTOKRATES of Th[orikos] (v)
SEG 23.78.11. This is the suggestion of Dow, *Essays Brendel* 83, who also advises against the restoration of the demotic of the second paredros(?) named.

Strategoi
TIMOMACHOS of Acharnai (VI) *PA* 13797; *APF* 280
Dem. 19.180, 23.115, 36.53, 50.14,17f.,20f.,32,37,43ff.,48,51ff.; Aisch.

1.56 with schol.; Hypereides 4.1f. General in the north Aegean, he was impeached and condemned to death in his absence for betraying the Chersonese to Kotys, embezzlement and ordering the trierarch Kallippos to take the exiled Kallistratos from Methone to Thasos; Hansen, *Eisangelia* nos. 91, 92.

?PHILON (? son of Kallippos of Aixone (VII)) ?*PA* 14825; *APF* 274f.
Hypereides 4.1. His office is only an assumption from the context, as is the date; he fled before an impeachment for treason; Hansen, *Eisangelia* no. 89. The text describes him as ὁ ἐξ Ἀναίων, which in any case seems corrupt, as Davies points out, though he doubts the emendation to produce the demotic Αἰξωνεύς on the ground that it 'lacks palaeographical justification'; I doubt it because it would make him the only one in Hypereides' list to be given a demotic (even though an explanation could be found in the commonness of his name) and we seem to need some reference to his activity such as is provided for the following Theotimos.

?THEOTIMOS *PA* 7055
Hypereides 4.1. The office is again an assumption; he fled before an impeachment for treason for the loss of Sestos; Hansen, *Eisangelia* no. 94.

LEOSTHENES of Kephale (V) *PA* 9141; *APF* 342ff.
Aisch. 2.124; Hypereides 4.1; Diod. 15.95.2f.; Plut. *Phok.* 7.3; Polyainos 6.2.1f. Sent against Alexandros of Pherai at Peparethos and Panormos, he was defeated and condemned in absence for treason; Hansen, *Eisangelia* no. 88. I prefer to leave him in the year indicated by Diodoros.

CHARES son of Theochares of Angele (III) *PA* 15292; *APF* 568f.
Ain. Takt. 11.13ff.; Diod. 15.95.3. Though apparently sent to replace Leosthenes, he went to Corcyra, stirring up trouble. I do not follow Cargill, *League* 173ff., in referring this to the early 360s and, taking Aineias too literally, having Chares as garrison commander only.

?[CHARID]EMOS (son of Philoxenos of Acharnai (VI)) *PA* 15380; *APF* 570ff.
IG ii² 118.7, which concerns Poteidaia; the generalship is a deduction by Kirchner.

Ship commanders
LYKINOS of Pallene (X) *PA* 9207; *APF* 345
Dem. 50.53. Put onto a trireme as commander by Timomachos. *APF* says 'he was presumably an aide-de-camp of Timomachos'. Jordan, *TAPhA* 1970, 235 (= *Navy* 125), wants him as archon of the fleet.

KALLIPPOS son of Philon of Aixone (VII) *PA* 8065; *NPA* 106; *APF* 274ff.
Dem. 50.46ff. Sent in command of a ship to fetch Kallistratos and, when thwarted, took over a trierarchy to do so. Davies calls him 'an under-general of Timomachos'.

Tamias of Athene
HEGESANDROS son of Hegesias of Sounion (IV) *PA* 6307; *APF* 209
Aisch. 1.110f.; schol. Aisch. 1.109. This is a problem which does not seem
to have attracted attention, since he was also tamias to the general
Timomachos (Aisch. 1.55f., 95), who, it seems, must be in this year and not
earlier. But Aischines clearly separates the two positions in terms of
Hegesandros' relations with Timarchos. He is accused of lining his
pockets.

Epistates of Eleusinion
AMPHIKTYON of Aphidna (IX) *PA* 776
See 363/2.

Amphiktyon to Delos
? -- son of --ydikos of Kolonai (IV or X)
Insc. Délos 104–9.6 (IG ii² 1637 + Add.). The alternative date is 356/5,
which is preferred by *Insc. Délos*. The man could be secretary.

COUNCIL AND ASSEMBLY
The secretary comes from IG ii² 116, restored at 117a:
Grammateus
CHAIR[I]ON son of Charinau[t]es of Phaleron (IX) *PA* 15268

(i) IG ii² 116 (Tod 147; Harding no. 59) is a decree dated to the twelfth day of
pryt. Leontis for alliance between Athens and the Thessalians and their
respective allies:
Bouleutes epistates
ARCHIPPOS of Amphitrope (X) *PA* 2548
Proposer
E[X]EKESTIDES (? of Pallene (X)) or (? son of Charias of Thorikos (V)) *PA*
4710=?4721 or ?4718; *APF* 175f.
Lines 45ff. also commend Theaitetos of Erchia (II) (*PA* 6631) for his words
and deeds in carrying out his duty, which Hansen (*GRBS* 1983, 168) uses
to describe him as addressing the assembly; perhaps he was an envoy or
proxenos.

(ii) IG ii² 117 is a proxeny decree for Protomachos dated only by the restoration of the secretary; also restored is the dating to the fourteenth day of the
prytany, but there is doubt about this; Hansen, *GRBS* 1982, 342
(=*Ecclesia* 94).

(iii) IG ii² 118 is not internally dated; it involves praise of the Poteidaians and is
restored to the sixth day of the prytany, but Hansen (*GRBS* 1982, 342
(=*Ecclesia* 94)) suggests as an example of an alternative possibility that the
surviving letters could represent a secretary from Hermos (V); if that were
so, the inscription could not belong to this year. In any event, the following
emerge:

Bouleutes epistates
. . . .¹⁰. . . . . of Rhamnous (IX)
Proposer
[A]RI[STOPH]ON (son of Aristophanes of Azenia) (VIII) *PA* 2108; *APF* 64ff.

We know of another councillor of the year:
Bouleutes
TIMARCHOS son of Arizelos of Sphettos (V) *PA* 13636
Aisch. 1.109ff. relates his involvement with Hegesandros the tamias in embezzling public money; this was revealed at an assembly by Pamphilos; proceedings saw him voted out at first, but retained at the crucial vote of the council; Hansen, *Eisangelia* no. 143.

360/59 (Ol. 105.1)

Archon
KALLIMEDES *PA* 8035 + Add.
Diod. 16.2.1; Dion. *Dein.* 9; Diog. 2.6.56; schol. Aisch. 2.31; IG ii² 1436.27; 1438.11 (*Hesperia* 1938, 284 (16 A.12) (Schweigert)); 1611.114; 1622.415, 522, 560; [1637 + Add] (*Insc. Délos* 104–9: or 355/4); 1745.2 (*Agora* XV.17); SEG 27.15.6. Panathenaic amphoras: Frel, *Amphoras* 24.

Strategoi
KEPHISODOTOS (? of Acharnai (VI)) *PA* 8313
Dem. 19.180, 23.153,156,163f.,167ff.; Aisch. 3.51f. with schol. 3.51; Androtion *FGH* 324 F 19; Plut. *Mor.* 850f (Kephisodoros); schol. Dem. 4.46.
 General in the north without success, he made a pact with Charidemos which led to his removal from office and condemnation to a fine for thus betraying the Chersonese; Hansen, *Eisangelia* no. 96. For the demotic see Davies, *Wealth* 164.

MANTIAS (son of Mantitheos of Thorikos) (V) *PA* 9667; *APF* 365ff.
Diod. 16.2.6, 3.5. He aided the Makedonian pretender Argaios.

TIMOTHEOS son of Konon of Anaphlystos (X) *PA* 13700; *APF* 507ff.
Dem. 36.53; schol. Aisch. 2.31. He was accused after a lack of success at Amphipolis; Hansen, *Eisangelia* no. 93.

Epimeletai of dockyards
EXEKESTOS of Erchia (II) *PA* 4731
APEMON of Phlya (VII) *PA* 1351
LEOSTRATOS of Alopeke (X) *PA* 9152
IG ii² 1622.413f., 520f., 558f.

Epistates of Eleusinion
AMPHIKTYON of Aphidna (IX) *PA* 776
See 363/2.

Amphiktyons to Delos
?PYTHOGENES son of A--
? -- son of --es of Acharnai (VI)
? E--
  Grammateus
  ? -- of Lamptrai
Insc. Délos 104–9.2ff. (IG ii² 1637 +). The alternative date for this account
is 355/4, which is preferred by *Insc. Délos*.

COUNCIL AND ASSEMBLY

No decrees are firmly ascribed to this year; for IG ii² 119 see 364/3 (cf. ii²
200).

Agora XV.17 gives bouleutai of tribe VI Oineis:
Epikephisia
KLEOLEOS *PA* 8572
PHILON *PA* 14834
Phyle
THYON *PA* 7416
EUENIOS *PA* 5468
Ptelea
DIOKLES *PA* 4051
Hippotomadai
PHAIDRIADES *PA* 13932
Lakiadai
DEMONIKOS *PA* 3567; *APF* 112
ARISTONYMOS *PA* 2196
Boutadai
NAUTES *PA* 10612
Lousia
THEOTIMOS *PA* 7066
Perithoidai
ERGOKLES *PA* 5056; cf. *NPA* 71
ANTIPHON *PA* 1303
KALLIK[RA]TES *PA* 7978
Kothokidai
THRASYLEON *PA* 7330
TIMOSTRATOS *PA* 13820
Thria
NAUSIKRATES *PA* 10562
XENOKLEIDES *PA* 11199
NIKOMACHOS *PA* 10947
KLEOPOMPOS *PA* 8614
MEGAKLES *PA* 9701

ARCHILOCHOS *PA* 2513
NAUSIKRATES *PA* 10563
Oe
APOLEXIS *PA* 1358
K[T]ESIPHON *PA* 8898
POLYKR[A]TES *PA* 12023
P[O]LYIDOS *PA* 11967
CHARIADES *PA* 15317
OPSIOS *PA* 11510
Acharnai
SONDROS *PA* 13143
PHILONIDES *PA* 14894
AUTOKLES *PA* 2725
PYTHANDRIDES *PA* 12338
OPSIOS *PA* 11508
ATHENOKLES *PA* 283
ANTIDOROS *PA* 1028
DOROTHEOS *PA* 4607
EPISTRATOS *PA* 4949
ATARBION *PA* 2676
GLAUKON *PA* 3024
DEMOKRATES *PA* 3522; *APF* 391
DEMOSTHENES *PA* 3586
KALLITELES *PA* 8206
NIKON *PA* 11107; *APF* 358
PHANO[M]ACHOS *PA* 14072
PHILOKYDES *PA* 14646
DIOKLES *PA* 4019
PHILIPPIDES *PA* 14354
ARCHESTRATOS *PA* 2421
KEPHISOPHON *PA* 8411
KALLISTRATOS (? son of Kalliades) *PA* 8159

359/8 (Ol. 105.2)

Archon
EUCHARISTOS *PA* 6143
Diod. 16.4.1; Dion. *Dein.* 9; IG ii² 1436.28; 1438.[11] (*Hesperia* 1938, 284 (16 A.12) (Schweigert)); Add. 1593a.4; 1611.119; 1622.574f.; *Insc. Délos* 104–5.[17], 20; SEG 27.16.3.

Strategos
CHABRIAS son of Ktesippos of Aixone (VII) *PA* 15086; *APF* 56off. Dem. 23.171f., 176. He was general in Thrace, where he came to terms with Charidemos, terms which were rejected at Athens.

Tamias of trireme funds
NI[K]OMENES of Pallene (X) *PA* 10971
IG ii² 1622.573.

Epistates of Eleusinion
AMPHIKTYON of Aphidna (IX) *PA* 776
See 363/2.

Appendix: From this year begins a series of paired individuals from IG ii²
1696; they used to be taken as paredroi to the archons, but since Mitsos, *AE*
1950–51, 50 (34), we have evidence of their service continuing over more
than one year, so that the office is a mystery; see Dow, *Essays Brendel* 83. I
will merely record the names.
. . . . STHEN--
[ASO]POKLES (son of Theodoros)

COUNCIL AND ASSEMBLY

(i) IG ii² 145 has been recorded under 364/3, but Lewis (cf. *ABSA* 1954, 36f.)
has affirmed that he sees nothing against this year and would like as low a
date as possible.

(ii) SEG 21.246 is restored as in praise of envoys from the King of Makedon
and this year is suggested.

Insc. Délos 104–5.19ff. is dated to the second prytany and a date involving
the number eight for the day of Metageitnion; the following is restored as
ratifier from the prytaneis:
Bouleutes
[HIER]OMNEMON son of Te[i]simachos [? of Koile (VIII)] *PA* 7505

358/7 (Ol. 105.3)

Archon
KEPHISODOTOS *PA* 8314
MP A 75; Diod. 16.6.1; Dion. *ad Amm.* 8; *Isaios* 5, 7 (Isaios F 15; but see
366/5); *Dein.* 9; IG ii² Add. 248.[3]; 1436.29; 1438.[12] (*Hesperia* 1938, 284
(16 A.13) (Schweigert)); 1611.121; 1696.3.

Strategos
?CHARES son of Theochares of Angele (III) *PA* 15292; *APF* 568f.
Dem. 23.173; Nepos *Tim.* 3.1; Diod. 16.7.3; hyp. Isok. 8. That Chares
went to Euboia and thence to the Hellespont (as autokrator) in this year is
argued by Cawkwell, *JHS* 1981 52 and n.49, who also denies the truth of
the statement in hyp. Isok. 8 that his mission was originally to Amphipolis.

Archon at Arkesine
?ANDROTION son of Andron (of Gargettos) (II) *PA* 915 = 913; *APF* 33f.

IG xii 7, 5 (Tod 152; Harding no. 68). The inscription is hard to date exactly, but Androtion was a councillor in 356/5 and was at Arkesine for at least two years.

Tamias Paralou
MEIDIAS son of Kephisodoros of Anagyrous (I) *PA* 9719; *APF* 386f. Dem. 21.171ff.; cf. IG ii² 1612.291. He is accused of exploiting the Kyzikenes and shirking his duty with regard to Euboia.

Epistates of Eleusinion
AMPHIKTYON of Aphidna (IX) *PA* 776
See 363/2.

Envoys
ANTIPHON *PA* 1280
CHARIDEMOS *PA* 15370
Theopompos *FGH* 115 F 30a (Harding no. 61A). They went to Philip in the matter of possible friendship, I think probably in this year. Whatever actually happened, it does not seem any formal arrangement was made; de Ste Croix, *CQ* 1963, 110–18; Ellis, *Philip* 48ff.; Griffith, *Hist. Mac.* II.237ff.

Appendix
[AS]OPOKLES son of Theod[oros]
[AN]TIPHANES son of Charoiades
See 359/8 appendix.

COUNCIL AND ASSEMBLY

(i) IG ii² 120 begins with a decree of the council concerning the writing up of the objects in the Chalkotheke and is followed by a list of such objects. It may belong to this year, but see 353/2 (much more likely).

(ii) IG ii² 248 is a probouleumatic decree granting proxeny to Damoxenos of Taras which was dated before 354 by Johnson, *CPh* 1914, 424 (cf. Rhodes, *Boule* 249); Wilhelm (IG *ad loc.*) restored the archon of this year and the tribe of the secretary is amenable to this (he may also have appeared in ii² 203 = 155 (Schweigert, *Hesperia* 1941, 339)):
Grammateus
[HIE]RO[KLE]IDES of Lamptrai (I) *PA* 7468
Bouleutes epistates
. . . LIOS or . . . AIOS son of I--

(iii) There was a vote to assist Euboia (Arist. *Rhet.* 3.10.7 1411a 6ff.):
Proposer
KEPHISODOTOS of Kerameis (v) *PA* 8331

Dem. 23.172 (cf. 177) reports the assembly which considered the news of

(iv) Chabrias' arrangement with Charidemos and rejected it; a decree was passed to choose ten envoys, who were to renew the oaths with Kersebleptes or accept oaths from the other two Thracian kings and consider how to proceed with war:

Proposer

GLAUKON *PA* 3011

Nomothetai

(v) Dem. 47.21 apprises us of the law instituting naval symmories:

Proposer

PERIANDROS son of Polyaratos of Cholargos (v) *PA* 11800; *APF* 464

357/6 (Ol. 105.4)

Archon

AGATHOKLES *PA* 44

Dem. 47.44; *MP* A 78; Diod. 16.9.1; Dion. *Lys.* 12; *Dein.* 9; Paus. 10.2.3; IG ii² [121]; [122]; 123 (Tod 156; Harding no. 69) 124.19 (Tod 153; Harding no. 65); 1436.30f.; 1437.[4]; 1438.13 (*Hesperia* 1938, 284 (16 A.14) (Schweigert)); 1696.6; 1953.[2]; 2790A; 2839.[4]+2844.[5f.] (SEG 24.209.5); xiv 1098.12; ?*Hesperia* 1944, 229f. ([3]) (Meritt) (Osborne D 13, where caution is enjoined).

Strategoi

CHABRIAS son of Ktesippos of Aixone (VII) *PA* 15086; *APF* 56off.

CHARES son of Theochares of Angele (III) *PA* 15292; *APF* 568f.

[IPHIKRATES] (son of Timotheos) of Rhamnous (IX) *PA* 7737; *APF* 248ff.

MENON of Potamos (IV) *PA* 10085

PHILOCHARES of Rhamnous (IX) *PA* 14779

EXEKESTIDES (son of Charias) of Thorikos (v) *PA* 4718 = ?4712 = ?4710; *APF* 175

ALKI[MACHOS of Anagyrous (I)] *PA* 616

DIOKLES of Alopeke (X) *PA* 4015 = 3990; *APF* 157

IG ii² 124.10 (Menon), 20ff. (Tod 153; Harding no. 65). For Chabrias Dem. 20.80ff.; Nepos *Chab.* 4; Diod. 16.7.3f.; Plut. *Phok.* 6.1; for Chares Dem. 23.173; Nepos *Tim.* 3.1; Diod. 16.7.3, 21.1; hyp. Isok. 8; IG ii² 1953.3; for Diokles Dem. 21.174; Polyainos 5.29.

They all took the oath in the alliance with cities of Euboia, where Menon had evidently been. Diodoros says Chares and Chabrias were generals against the revolting allies; Chabrias died in the siege of Chios. Hansen, *Eisangelia* 62 n. 36, following Kahrstedt and Tod, has Chabrias deposed towards the end of 358/7 and thus erased from the treaty (on which see below). Thus he accepts that Chabrias was trierarch at Chios. The latter position is in fact only found in Nepos; Dem. 20.82 does *not* say he was trierarch, though it may be thought that the language used indicates he was not general. If ii² 124 belongs wholly in 357/6, Chabrias could have been erased from the document indeed because he was dead.

On Chares see 358/7. For the possibility that he does not belong in ii² 124 see Cawkwell, *C&M* 1962, 38f. n. 23. Diokles was in Euboia and made a truce with the Thebans. On Alkimachos cf. 354/3.

Archon at Arkesine
?ANDROTION son of Andron of Gargettos (II) *PA* 915 = 913; *APF* 33f. See 358/7.

Sitones
KALLISTHENES *PA* 8090
Dem. 20.33.

Epimeletes of dockyards
?SATYROS *PA* 12577
Dem. 22.63. The date cannot be exactly fixed; see Cawkwell, *C&M* 1962, 44.

Epistates of Eleusinion
AMPHIKTYON of Aphidna (IX) *PA* 776
See 363/2.

Epimeletai of tribe IV Leontis
CHAIRIMENES son of Lysanias of Deiradiotai
PHILONEOS son of Gnathios of Leukonoion
PHA-- son of [S]mi[k]-- of Aithalidai
IG ii² 2818. For the last name IG shows *ΦΛ*--, but no name beginning Phl-- is known. The only name from Aithalidai in *PA* which fits is no. 14031, Phanodemos.

Envoy
PEISIANAX (? of Sounion (IV)) ?*PA* 11776; *APF* 378
IG ii² 127.[15], 31 (Tod 157; Harding no. 70). As the decree comes in the first prytany of 356/5, he must have been envoy to Thrace and Illyria in this year.

Appendix
. . ⁵ . . OKLES son of Theodoros
. . ⁵ . . ES son of Krantos
See 359/8 appendix.

COUNCIL AND ASSEMBLY

The secretary is found or restored in IG ii² 121, 123, *Hesperia* 1939, 12(4) and 1944, 229ff.(3):

Grammateus
DIODOTOS son of Diokles of Angele (III) *PA* 3891; *APF* 156f.

(i) IG ii² 121 is a fragment from the sixth prytany:
Bouleutes epistates
[MELE]SIAS of Halai (II or VII) cf. *PA* 9811
Proposer
[ARIS]TOPHON (son of Aristophanes of Azenia) (VIII) *PA* 2108; *APF* 64ff.

(ii) IG ii² 122 is a fragment from the eighth prytany, of Hippothontis; the letters in line 5 may represent remains of a patronymic:
Bouleutes epistates
? -- son of --nes

(iii) IG ii² 123 (Tod 156; Harding no. 69) is a decree from the eighth day of the ninth prytany, of Aigeis, concerning the garrison on Andros:
Bouleutes epistates
[DIO]TI[M]OS of Oinoe (VIII or IX)
Proposer
[HEGE]SANDR[O]S (son of Hegesias of Sounion) (IV) *PA* 6307; *APF* 209

(iv) IG ii² 124 (Tod 153; Harding no. 65) is the alliance with the Euboian cities. Hansen, *Eisangelia* 62 n. 36, wants to believe that the treaty was actually concluded late in 358/7 and the oath not taken until early 357/6, thus accommodating the erasure of Chabrias' name due to an assumed deposition from office. I do not find this persuasive and note that it conflicts with Hansen's dating of Timotheos' speech (see below) to 357/6 (*GRBS* 1983, 176), as his words hardly seem appropriate when an alliance has already been concluded.

(v) IG ii² 125 (Tod 154; Harding no. 66) concerns aid to Eretria:
Proposer
HEGES[I]PP[OS] (son of Hegesias of Sounion) (IV) *PA* 6351; *APF* 209
The document concerns some who made an attack on Eretria, from which Hansen constructs *Eisangelia* no. 99.

(vi) IG ii² 126 (Tod 151; SEG 31.72; Harding no. 64) is part of an alliance with the Thracian kings (see Dem. 23.173).

(vii) IG ii² 147, fragments of an alliance with Chalkis, is tentatively assigned to this year.

On the suggested attribution of IG ii² 230 to this year see SEG 21.249.

(viii) *Hesperia* 1939, 12 (4) (Schweigert), concerns Elaious:
Bouleutes epistates
LYSIPP-- of Marathon (IX)

(ix) Osborne D 13 is cautious about following Meritt, *Hesperia* 1944, 229ff. (3), in ascribing to this year the granting of citizenship to Aristomenes (Meritt suggested he might be restored as an Andrian), but the secretary fits the demotic:

Bouleutes epistates
-- of Aphidna (IX)

(x) We learn from Dem. 47.20ff. of a proposal that the trierarchs should recover equipment from those of previous years:
Proposer
CHAIREDEMOS *PA* 15112

(xi) There was trouble with this and the council had to pass a decree that the recovery should take place by any means possible. See Hansen, *Eisangelia* no. 144.

(xii) From Dem. 7.42f. and hyp. 3f. we hear of a proposal concerning the Kardians and the holding of land in Kardian territory by Athenians:
Proposer
KALLIPPOS of Paiania (III) *PA* 8078
This was unsuccessfully challenged as unconstitutional; see Hansen, *Sovereignty* no. 11, who wants to place this soon after the treaty of IG ii² 126.

Dem. 8.74f. tells of an address to the people by Timotheos urging an expedition to Euboia, which may well belong to this year. Cawkwell, *Phoenix* 1978, 45, manages to extract from this a generalship for Timotheos, which the text does not justify.

356/5 (Ol. 106.1)

Archon
ELPINES *PA* 4673
Diod. 16.15.1; Dion. *Lys.* 12 (Elpinikes); *Dein.* 9; IG ii² 127 (Tod 157; Harding no. 70); 128 (Tod 159); 129; 1436.[33]; 1437.[7]; 1438.[14] (*Hesperia* 1938, 284 (16 A.15) (Schweigert)); 1541.7; 1614.[37]; 1622.404, 419, 481, 515f., 547; 1696.9; SEG 21.668.

Thesmothetes
?THRASYLLOS son of Apollodoros (born of Lakratides) of Leukonoion (IV) *PA* 7336; *APF* 44f.
Isaios 7.34. The office, which came before his adoption, seems to have been held recently as of the date of the speech, which is about 355/4: Parke, *JHS* 1939, 80ff.; Wevers, *Isaeus* 10, 16, 25, 67.

Strategoi
MENESTHEUS son of Iphikrates of Rhamnous (IX) *PA* 9988; *APF* 249ff.
TIMOTHEOS son of Konon of Anaphlystos (X) *PA* 13700; *APF* 507ff.
IPHIKRATES son of Timotheos of Rhamnous (IX) *PA* 7737; *APF* 248ff.
CHARES son of Theochares of Angele (III) *PA* 15292; *APF* 568f.
Lysias F LXV; Isok. 15.129; Philochoros *FGH* 328 F 152; Deinarchos 1.14, 3.17; Nepos *Iph.* 3.3; *Tim.* 3.2ff.; Diod. 16.21.1ff., 22.1f., 34.1; Dion. *Lys* 12; Plut. *Phok.* 7.3, *Mor.* 350f, 836d, cf. 187c, 788d; Polyainos 3.9.29;

schol. Dem. 4.19, ?3.31, cf. Dem. 2.28; Nepos *Chab.* 3.4; ?Plut. *Aratos* 16; IG ii² 127.17, 21 (Tod 157; Harding no. 70); Pap. fr. C. Wesseley, *Festschrift Hirschfeld* (1903) 100ff.

No source mentions them all together, but they commanded against the allies; they came into dispute as to whether or not to engage battle and after the defeat at Embata, Chares accused his colleagues of treason, Timotheos of having received bribes from the Chians and Rhodians and Menestheus in regard to his use of funds. The generals were suspended, Timotheos went into exile to avoid his fine, Iphikrates and Menestheus were acquitted; Hansen, *Eisangelia* nos. 100, 101, 102. Chares then joined Artabazos, in revolt from the Persian king, and may have taken Lampsakos and Sigeion.

?ANTIDOTOS
IG xii 5, 714. He is supposed as general on Andros in the Social War period, which must remain in doubt; see Cargill, *League* 158 n.28; cf. Accame, *La lega* 184 and n. 5.

Taxiarchoi
EUKRATES son of Strombichos of Euonymon (I) cf. *PA* 5768; *APF* 163
TIMOKRATES son of Timochares of Halai (II)
[T]IMOKEDES son of Gna[th]is of Eleusis (VIII) ?*PA* 13718; cf. 3049
SEG 21.668, where they are crowned by the demos and boule.

Epimeletai of dockyards
KTESIBIOS of Lamptrai (I) *PA* 8854
ANAXIPPOS (son of Thoudippos) of Araphen (II) *PA* 815; *APF* 229
MENIOS of Oe (VI) *PA* 10031
DEINIAS of Halai (VII) *PA* 3160
TIMOLAS of Rhamnous (IX) *PA* 13792
IG ii² 1622.402f., 417f., 479f., 513f., 545f.

Epistatai of Eleusinion
-- of Paionidai (IV)
DEMAINETOS *PA* 3267; cf. *APF* 103
NIKODEMOS son of Pistonides of Athmonon (VII) *PA* 10863; *NPA* 134
--NES son of Philippos of Hestiaia (II) *PA* 14393
MELANOPOS son of Hestiodoros of P-- *PA* 9793
IG ii² 1666.2ff.; 1541.6f. (Nikodemos). *PA* has Melanopos as secretary, which cannot be confirmed. A four-year tenure is assumed.

Amphiktyon to Delos
? -- son of --ydikos of Kolonai (IV or X)
Insc. Délos 104–9.6 (IG ii² 1637 + Add.). This is the date preferred by *Insc. Délos*; see 361/60.

Envoys
LYSIKRATES of Oinoe (VIII or IX) *PA* 9465

ANTIMACHOS *PA* 1108
[THRA]SON of Erchia (II) *PA* 7384; *APF* 239
IG ii² 127.36f. (Tod 157; Harding no. 70). They were sent to Ketriporis of
Thrace.

Appendix
.. 5 .. ACHOS son of Charidemos
[NEO]PTOLEMOS son of Archestratos
See 359/8 appendix.

The following may be called **eispraktores**. The first named was ap-
pointed to collect arrears of eisphora, but was ousted by Androtion, who
replaced him with a commission of ten. On date see Harding, *Historia*
1976, 192f.
EUKTEMON *PA* 5784
Dem. 22.48, 50; 24.159f.
ANDROTION son of Andron of Gargettos (II) *PA* 915 = 913; *APF* 33f.
TIMOKRATES son of Antiphon of Krioa (X) *PA* 13772; *APF* 513f.
Dem. 22.42, 47ff., passim; 24.8, 160ff., passim.

COUNCIL AND ASSEMBLY

The secretary is found in IG ii² 127, 128 and SEG 24.88:
Grammateus
LYSIAS son of Lys[imachos ?] of Pithos (VII) *PA* 9355
From this year secretaries are in forward order of tribes.

(i) IG ii² 127 (Tod 157; Harding no. 70) is a probouleumatic decree from the
eleventh day of the first prytany, of Hippothontis, recording an alliance
with Ketriporis of Thrace and his brothers, Lyppeios of Paionia and
Grabos of Illyria (cf. Diod. 16.22.3):
Bouleutes epistates
MNESARCH[OS] *PA* 10249
Proposer
KALLISTHE[NES] *PA* 8090

(ii) IG ii² 128 (Tod 159) is a probouleumatic decree from the ninth prytany, of
Antiochis, concerning dealings with Neapolis:
Bouleutes epistates
[?KALLISTOGE]ITON of Phegaia (II)
Proposer
POLYEUKTO[S] (son of Sostratos of Sphettos) (V) *PA* 11925 =
11934 = 11950

(iii) IG ii² 129 is a fragment of a proxeny decree for [Zop]yros.

(iv) IG ii² 148 bears no internal date, but is ascribed to this year; Hammond,
JHS 1937, 64 n. 80, placed it in 353. It is part of a treaty with Lokrians.

(v) SEG 24.88 now dates IG ii² 214 to this year and is restored as a proxeny decree:
Bouleutes epistates
A--
Proposer
...⁶... ON

(vi) There was an alliance with Phokis (Aisch. 3.118):
Proposer
HEGESIPPOS son of Hegesias of Sounion (IV) *PA* 6351; *APF* 209

Nomothetai
(vii) Dem. 20 concerns the law which sought to revoke all immunities from liturgies except for the descendants of the tyrannicides (cf. Libanius hyp. Dem. 20; Philostratos *Soph.* 1.23):
Proposer
LEPTINES of Koile (VIII) *PA* 9046; *APF* 340f.
For the syndikoi chosen to defend the law see 355/4.

For Dem. 22 and Androtion's proposal see 355/4. The speech provides certain details concerning this year. The council had failed to build ships as required and had themselves elected the tamias of the trireme builders (section 20). Androtion was a councillor and we learn of others from sections 38ff.:
Bouleutai
ANDROTION son of Andron of Gargettos (II) *PA* 915 = 913; *APF* 33f.
PHILIPPOS *PA* 14374
ANTIGENES *PA* 985
ARCHIAS of Cholargos (V) *PA* 2481
On Androtion's activities with regard to the collection of eisphora arrears see above appendix; the commission could have been drawn from the council. Cf. also Bultrighini, *QUCC* 1981, 87.

355/4 (Ol. 106.2)

Archon
KALLISTRATOS *PA* 8132
MP A 79; Diod. 16.23.1; Dion. *ad Amm.* 4; *Dein.* 9, 13 (Philochoros *FGH* 328 F 152); IG ii² 130 (SEG 19.49, 22.88, 24.85; Harding no. 73A); [131]; [133]; 1436.[34]; 1437.[8]; 1438.15 (*Hesperia* 1938, 284 (16 A.16) (Schweigert)); 1613.244f.; 1640.10; 1696.12; ? [5165] (cf. SEG 14.140); [1637 + Add.] (*Insc. Délos* 104–9: or 360/59); 1643 + Add. (*Insc. Délos* 104–12.93); *Insc. Délos* 104–21aB.[11]; SEG 27.17.6.

Strategoi
CHARES son of Theochares of Angele (III) *PA* 15292; *APF* 568f.

Diod. 16.22.2, 34.1; *FGH* 105.4 (Harding no. 72C); schol. Dem. 3.31, 4.19 (Harding no. 72A and B). As he was withdrawn in relation to the termination of the Social War, we may presume he remained general until then, though aiding Artabazos; see 356/5.

?MELANOPOS (son of Laches of Aixone) (VII) *PA* 9788
?Dem. 24.12f.; ? IG ii² 150.[5]. Demosthenes records him as envoy to Mausolos, which he could well have been as general; he is restored as general in the otherwise undated inscription, but D.M. Lewis advises that he cannot believe the text is as late as this.

Tamias
?GLAUKETES *PA* 2946
Dem. 24.129. Demosthenes seems to date this after the embassy of this year; he uses the words ταμιεύσας ἐν ἀκροπόλει and proclaims Glauketes' misdeeds. Given the date here adopted for Dem. 24 (354/3), I might suggest that Glauketes was tamias in this year and was envoy in the time he was off-duty or was allowed time off. Dinsmoor, *AJA* 1932, 165 n. 4, had him as the same man who was secretary to the treasurers in 374/3 (*q.v.*) and speculated on the deme, comparing IG ii² 130.6f. and wondering about Ankyle or Kolonai, but none of this seems legitimate.

Epistatai of Eleusinion
-- of Paionidai (IV)
DEMAINETOS *PA* 3267; cf. *APF* 103
NIKODEMOS son of Pistonides of Athmonon (VII) *PA* 10863; *NPA* 134
--NES son of Philippos of Hestiaia (III) *PA* 14393
MELANOPOS son of Hestiodoros of P-- *PA* 9793
See 356/5.

Amphiktyons to Delos
?PYTHOGENES son of A--
? -- son of --es of Acharnai (VI)
? E--

Grammateus
? -- of Lamptrai (I)
Insc. Délos 104–9.2ff. (IG ii² 1637 +). This is the preferred date of *Insc. Délos*; see 360/59.

Priest of Asklepios
EUTHYDEMOS of Eleusis (VIII) *PA* 5533
IG ii² 47.24 (*LSS* no. 11); 4962.11ff. (*LS* no. 21). See Schlaifer, *HSCPh* 1940, 243. Further on Euthydemos see Threpsiades, *Hesperia* 1939, 179f.; Ampolo, *RF* 1981, 187ff.

Envoys
MELANOPOS (son of Laches of Aixone) (VII) *PA* 9788
GLAUKETES *PA* 2946

ANDROTION (son of Andron of Gargettos) (II) *PA* 915 = 913; *APF* 33f.
Dem. 24.12, 127, 129; Libanius hyp. Dem. 24; hyp. ii Dem. 24. Envoys to
Mausolos of Karia and perhaps Egypt (Dem. 24.127 on Melanopos), their
vessel took a merchant ship off Naukratis and they retained the money
therein; see below. On Melanopos see above strategoi. On date see
Hornblower, *Mausolus* 215 and n. 271.

Appendix
[?HERA]KLEIDES son of Eukleios
[PAR]AMYTHOS son of Philinos
See 359/8 appendix.

COUNCIL AND ASSEMBLY

The secretary appears in IG ii² 130, 131, 132.19f. and 133; the restoration
in IG seems to me still to be the most probable (see Alessandri, *ASNP*
1982, 59), though I record also the variant suggested as an example by
Pečírka, *Enktesis* 37f.:
Grammateus
[PAN]DIOS or [RHAI]DIOS son of Sokles of Oion (VIII) *PA* 11575

(i) IG ii² 130 (SEG 19.49, 22.88, 24.85; Harding no. 73A) is a proxeny decree
for Sochares of Apollonia dated to the third day of the fifth prytany, of
Pandionis:
Bouleutes epistates
GLAUKETES *PA* 2950
On identity cf. above tamias.

Proposer
[A]RISTOPHO[N] (son of Aristophanes of Azenia) (VIII) *PA* 2108; *APF*
64ff.

(ii) IG ii² 131 is a fragment of an honorary decree from the sixth prytany (cf.
Hansen, *GRBS* 1984, 136):
Bouleutes epistates
. . . .¹⁰. . . . . of Paiania (III)

(iii) IG ii² 132 (with Pečírka, *Enktesis* 37f.) begins with a proxeny decree of the
council (cf. Hansen, *GRBS* 1984, 136):
Proposer
. . .⁶. . . ES

(iv) Then comes the beginning of a decree from the seventh prytany, of
Hippothontis (cf. Hansen, *GRBS* 1984, 136):
Bouleutes epistates
. . .⁷. . . ES
Proposer
. . . OI . . . or . . . OK . . .
Of the possible demes mentioned in IG for the epistates Anakaia is ruled

out as belonging to the tribe in prytany; the possibilities are in fact Aphidna, Aithalidai, Hagnous, Aigilia and Araphen. As for the proposer, in IG it is thought that the name may be Demokles or Philokles, but the association is made with the proposer of the earlier decree, which may be incorrect.

(v) IG ii² 133 is a proxeny decree for Philiskos of Sestos and his descendants, restored in IG to the ninth prytany, of Akamantis, but there are other possibilities for the number of the prytany (SEG 22.91):
Bouleutes epistates
. . . .^{10}. . . . . of Konthyle (III)
Proposer
. . .^{6}. . . IDES
Cf. Hansen, *GRBS* 1984, 137.

(vi) Given the dating of the priest of Asklepios (above), IG ii² 47 (*LSS* no. 11), an inventory followed by a decree regulating celebrations, must belong here:
Proposer
ATHENODO[ROS] *PA* 260
He is thus unlikely to be the same man as *PA* 259.

(vii) That IG ii² 150 somehow relates to this year is suggested by the restored presence therein of Lysitheides and Melanopos (but see above strategoi), both of whom appear at Dem. 24.1ff. concerning the investigation of the envoys.

(viii) Dem. 22 concerns the decree to honour the council of 356/5:
Proposer
ANDROTION son of Andron of Gargettos (II) *PA* 915 = 913; *APF* 33f.
This had been passed by the demos, but was challenged as unconstitutional; Hansen, *Sovereignty* no. 12. At the assembly meeting some made accusations against the council, among them Meidias (section 10).

Athens came to terms with the revolting allies, recognizing their loss to the alliance: Dem. 15.26; Diod. 16.22.2; schol. Dem. 3.28; cf. Isok. 16.

(ix) Dem. 24.11ff. tells us the following. There was a decree establishing a commission of enquiry into the matter of the envoys of this year:
Proposer
ARISTOPHON (son of Aristophanes of Azenia) (VIII) *PA* 2108; *APF* 64ff.
The subsequent assembly was addressed by the envoys, responding to one

(x) who then secured the passage of a measure regarding the recovery of the money:
Proposer
EUKTEMON *PA* 5784
This was unsuccessfully challenged by the envoys (cf. section 117; Hansen, *Sovereignty* no. 13), this in Skirophorion. The tale continues in 354/3 (which see for the dating).

Dem. 20.146ff. discourses on those chosen as advocates of Leptines' law and we may add Leptines himself; Hansen, *GRBS* 1983, 159ff., under the names:

Syndikoi

LEODAMAS (? son of Erasistratos) of Acharnai (VI) *PA* 9077; *APF* 523ff.
ARISTOPHON (son of Aristophanes) of Azenia (VIII) *PA* 2108; *APF* 64ff.
KEPHISODOTOS of Kerameis (V) *PA* 8331
DEINIAS of Erchia (II) *PA* 3163; *APF* 96
LEPTINES of Koile (VIII) *PA* 9046; *APF* 340

354/3 (Ol. 106.3)

Archon

DIOTIMOS *PA* 4372
Diod. 16.28.1; Dion. *ad Amm.* 4; *Dein.* 9, 13 (Philochoros *FGH* 328 F 152); IG ii^2 134; 135; 136.4, [9]; 137, 1436.[35]; 1437.[10], 24, 26; 1438.[15], [18], [20], 22, [23], [24], 25 (*Hesperia* 1938, 284 (16 A) (Schweigert)); 1613.203, 254; 1696.15; 2318.[259]; [2819]; SEG 26.220.7; *Hesperia* 1936, 399 (10.65) (Meritt); 1963, 173 (8.[18]) (IG ii^2 1517; Woodward, but see Linders, *Artemis* 38, 64f. – 353/2); 1971, 180 (?[27]) (Stroud); Agora I 7495 (unpublished).

Strategoi

CHARES son of Theochares of Angele (III) *PA* 15292; *APF* 568f.
Dem. 24.183; Theopompos *FGH* 115 F 249; Duris *FGH* 76 F 35; Herakleides F 2 (Edmonds); Antiphanes F 303 (Edmonds); Dion. *Dein.* 13; Plut. *Mor.* 187c, 788d; Polyainos 3.9.29, 13.2f., 4.2.22.

He was active in the Thraceward area; the actions at Diod. 16.34.3 are placed in this year by Hammond, *JHS* 1937, 64f., but I leave them in 353/2. Dionysios dates Chares' prosecution of Timotheos, Iphikrates and Menestheus to this year; see above 356/5. Aisch. 2.70ff. has been made to relate to 347/6; Hansen, *GRBS* 1977, 53 (= *Ecclesia* 45, 63f.).

?ALKIMACHOS of Anagyrous (I) *PA* 616
Dem. 47.50, 78; Harpokration and Suda *s.v.* Ἀλκίμαχος. He was general in 'the war with Philip', not later than 353 if the Demosthenic speech is correctly dated. But it seems the possibilities are more open; Hansen, *GRBS* 1983, 160, has 355/4(?). Cf. 357/6.

Theoric commissioners

?DIOPHANTOS son of Thrasymedes of Sphettos (V) *PA* 4438
?EUBOULOS son of Spintharos of Probalinthos (III) *PA* 5369
Aisch. 3.25; schol. Aisch. 3.24; schol. Dem. 1.1; Harpokration, Suda and Photios *s.v.* θεωρικά; cf. Dem. 20.137; translation of sources Harding no. 75.

For discussion see the introduction and Cawkwell, *JHS* 1963, 54ff. There is no certainty that the commission began this year or that the two men served concurrently. For Diophantos' patronymic see Hansen, *GRBS* 1983, 166.

Tamiai of Athene
[K]ALLISTRA[TOS] *PA* 8133
ST[REPHENEOS of Kydathenaion (III)?]
[?MEGAK]LEIDES of L[eukonoion (VI)?]
--[O]N of Acharnai (VI)
--ON of Aphidna (IX)
Grammateus
HAGN[ON ?of Prasiai (III) or Phegaia (II)]
IG ii² 1442. Only eight names seem to have been listed in this opening to an inventory. I owe the dating to D.M. Lewis, who restores it with a line of 32 letters; IG has 346/5, while the cards at the Institute for Advanced Study at Princeton say probably 350s; the identities of the tamiai of 345/4, as known from IG ii² 1443, rule out the involvement of that year, but no other two consecutive archons in the fourth century can be made to fit a line of 31 letters. For the secretary see Ferguson, *Treasurers* 144 and n.2.

Epistatai of Eleusinion
-- of Paionidai (IV)
DEMAINETOS *PA* 3267; cf. *APF* 103
NIKODEMOS son of Pistonides of Athmonon (VII) *PA* 10863; *NPA* 134
--NES son of Philippos of Hestiaia (III) *PA* 14393
MELANOPOS son of Hestiodoros of P-- *PA* 9793
See 356/5.

Amphiktyon to Delos
K . . . .⁸. . . . of Pallene (X)
Insc. Délos 104–12.4 (IG ii² 1643 + Add.).

Naopoios to Delphi
TELOKLES *PA* 13580
FD III.5, 19.34, 39.

Appendix
. .⁴. . IPPOS son of Agathokles
. . .⁶. . . MOS son of Lysippos
See 359/8 appendix.

COUNCIL AND ASSEMBLY
The secretary is found in IG ii² 134, 135, 136, 137 and the unpublished Agora I 7495, which confirms the demotic proposed by Ferguson, *Klio* 1915, 394; Alessandri, *ASNP* 1982, 7 n.1, 10, 59:
Grammateus
PROKLEIDES son of Anacharsis of Aphidna (IX) *PA* 12191

(i) IG ii² 134 is part of an honorary decree from the third prytany, of Pandionis or Akamantis, the latter if Dem. 24 is correctly dated (see below):
Proposer
KRATI[NOS] *PA* 8752

(ii) IG ii² 135 is the beginning of a decree from the sixth prytany, of Antiochis, in honour of Moschos of Nau[kratis].

(iii) IG ii² 136 is a probouleumatic proxeny decree of pryt. Kekropis for Apollonides of Halikarnassos:
Bouleutes epistates
M--
Proposer
PHILOTADES son of Phi[lostratos] of Pallene (x) *PA* 14927

(iv) IG ii² 137 is a decree of pryt. Oineis concerning religious matters:
Bouleutes epistates
THARREX of Lamptrai (I) *PA* 6584
Proposer
. . . . ? . . . . ES
Cf. Hansen, *GRBS* 1984, 137.

Dem. 14 unsuccessfully, I think (but see Jacoby, *FGH* III b Suppl. (i) 58), recommended changes to the naval symmories in the context of a debate during which some had evidently been advising aggression against the Persian king, a policy which did not win the day.

Nomothetai

(v) The unpublished Agora I 7495 is a law dated to the prytany of Antiochis (sixth prytany), seventh day of the prytany, and concerns the financing of a festival; the proposer is identified by association with the bouleutes of 335/4 (Hansen, *GRBS* 1983, 166):
Proposer
EPIKRATES (son of . .otetos of Pallene (x)) *PA* 4863; *APF* 182

(vi) The same man, one assumes, emerges from Dem. 24.27 as proposing on the eleventh day of the first prytany, of Pandionis (cf. section 26), a decree setting up nomothetai on the next day to deal with funds for the Panathenaia.

(vii) Dem. 24 belongs probably to this year (see Lewis, *ABSA* 1954, 32) and is an attack upon a law:
Proposer
TIMOKRATES son of Antiphon of Krioa (x) *PA* 13772; *APF* 513f.
This concerned state debtors and their sureties and we find at sections 39f. and 71 that it was proposed on the twelfth day of the first prytany, of Pandionis (on the genuineness of the documents cited see MacDowell, *JHS* 1975, 62). At section 71 we find who put Timokrates' law to the vote:

Epistates

ARISTOKLES of Myrrhinous (III) *PA* 1875
So the text, but Lewis, *ABSA* 1954, 32 wanted the deme to be
Myrrhinoutte (II), worried about the epistates of the nomothetai being
from the tribe in prytany.

353/2 (Ol. 106.4)

Archon

THOUDEMOS *PA* 7248
Diod. 16.32.1; Dion. *ad Amm.* 4; *Dein.* 9 (Eudemos), 13 (Philochoros *FGH*
328 F 153); IG ii² 138; 139; 140.14f. (*LSS* no. 13); 332 (Pritchett and
Neugebauer, *Calendars* 44); ?1145.[7]; 1437.[28] (*Hesperia* 1938, 287
(Schweigert)); 1438.21, [25], 27, [39] (*Hesperia* 1938, 284f. (16 A.22, 26, 28;
B.14) (Schweigert); SEG 19.129); 1517.[66] (Linders, *Artemis* 38);
1524.46; 1613.153, 257; 1696.18; xiv 1098.13; *Hesperia* 1950, 228 (13.[3],
[6]) (Crosby); 1963, 173 (8.[20f.]) (Woodward); *Insc. Délos* [104–12] (IG ii²
1643 + Add.: or 352/1).

Strategos

CHARES son of Theochares of Angele (III) *PA* 15292; *APF* 568f.
Diod. 16.34.3, 35.5. See 354/3. He took Sestos and was later in the Gulf of
Pagasai.

Officer

THRASYBOULOS (son of Thrason of Erchia) (II) *PA* 7304; *APF* 239
IG ii² 1613.270. While it seems he was serving with Chares, I see no
compulsion to believe that he was general.

Tamias of Athene

ARIS[T]--
IG ii² 1442.10. On this document see 354/3.

Epistatai of Eleusinion

-- of Paionidai (IV)
DEMAINETOS *PA* 3267; cf. *APF* 103
NIKODEMOS son of Pistonides of Athmonon (VII) *PA* 10863; *NPA* 134
--NES son of Philippos of Hestiaia (III) *PA* 14393
MELANOPOS son of Hestiodoros of P-- *PA* 9793
See 356/5.

Epistatai of Brauroneion

[S]TRATIPPOS *PA* 12921
KLEOTIMOS of Atene (X) *PA* 8626; *APF* 318
IG ii² 1524.40, 47 (Linders, *Artemis* 52 and n. 10).

Amphiktyons to Delos

. . . . N.S of Euonymon (I)

Hypogrammateus?
... PHILOS of Phrearrhioi (IV)
Insc. Délos 104–12.3f. (IG ii² 1643 + 1640), an inventory of this year or the next.

Naopoioi to Delphi
KYDIMOS *PA* 8934
THRASON (? of Erchia or Kollytos (II)) *PA* 7377 = ?7384 or ?7389; *APF* 239
FD III.5, 19.43.

NIKIADES (? of Halimous (IV)) cf. *PA* 10766, 10767
FD III.5, 19.53.

Appendix
...⁷... s son of Eumelos
...⁶... CHOS son of Thrasymedes
See 359/8 appendix.

COUNCIL AND ASSEMBLY

The secretary is found in IG ii² 138 and 139 (see Schweigert, *Hesperia* 1938, 286) and 1438 (SEG 19.129.14):
Grammateus
PHILOKEDES son of Dorotheos of Pallene (x) *PA* 4619

(i) IG ii² 138 + (*Hesperia* 1985, 309ff. (Walbank)) is a decree in honour of Xennias:
Proposer
EUTHYMA[CHOS] *PA* 5624

(ii) IG ii² 139 is a probouleumatic decree of unknown content:
Bouleutes epistates
... ESTRATOS of L[amptrai] (I)
Proposer
TIMONIDES *PA* 13855

(iii) IG ii² 332 (Schwenk no. 20–335/4) is dated to this year by Pritchett and Neugebauer, *Calendars* 44; the restoration of the prescript must remain in doubt, except perhaps for the prytany of Erechtheis:
Bouleutes epistates
[ARISTOK]RAT[ES]?

(iv) As IG ii² 1438 (SEG 19.129) concerns items in the Chalkotheke, Schweigert, *Hesperia* 1938, 281ff., correctly placed IG ii² 120 in this year (see 358/7).

(v) Dem. 23 is against the proposal of an honorary decree for Charidemos including special provisions for his safety:

Proposer
ARISTOKRATES *PA* 1897
This was still a probouleuma when it was challenged; Hansen, *Sovereignty* no. 14. We hear at sections 13f. and 110 of an assembly addressed by Aristomachos as envoy from Kersebleptes and Charidemos.

The Spartans and Megalopolitans sent envoys to Athens concerning their impending conflict and though Dem. 16 is in support of the latter, the Athenians decided not to intervene.

On the Athenian decision to send klerouchs to cities in the Chersonese see Diod. 16.34.4; cf. IG ii² 1613.297f.

Nomothetai
(vi) IG ii² 140 (SEG 30.62) is a law dated to the twenty-first day of the prytany of Pandionis (which is probably the tenth) concerning the aparche at Eleusis; the meeting was in the theatre of Dionysos:
Epistates
. . . . .[11]. . . . . s of Ikarion (II)
Proposer
MEID-- of Eleusis (VIII)

APPENDIX

Basileis
THEOGENES of Erchia (II) *PA* 6707
  Paredros
  STEPHANOS son of Antidorides of Eroiadai (VIII) *PA* 12887
Dem. 59.72, 81, 84, 121. At 59.72 Theogenes' deme is said to be Kothokidai (IV), but this may be a corruption; see *PA* and IG ii² 1903. The date may be the early 360s.

EUKTEMON son of Euboulides of Oion (IV) *PA* 5802; *APF* 80
Dem. 43.42ff. Sometime before 361/60.

Basileus or Polemarchos or Thesmothetes
AUTOLYKOS of Thorikos (V) *PA* 2746
That an Autolykos had been archon is known from Aisch. 1.81; Plut. *Mor.* 843d; Harpokration *s.v. Αὐτόλυκος*; cf. Lykourgos F III. He is assumed to be the man found in SEG 23.78, on whom see Dow, *Essays Brendel* 81ff.

Thesmothetai
[KALLI]AS son of Lykophron of Kydathenaion (III) *PA* 7872
IG ii² 1148.2f., 6.

ARISTOMACHOS of Kephale (V) *PA* 1974
Dem. 59.65. He evidently served before 371/70 and as he was of the same deme as Nausinikos, archon 378/7 (Dem. 59.71), that year is out.

Strategoi

It is likely enough, as always, that prominent men were generals in years other than those known to us, among them:

CHABRIAS son of Ktesippos of Aixone (VII) *PA* 15086; *APF* 560f.
Polyainos 2.22.3 tells of Ischolaos being besieged by Chabrias in Drys, which may belong about 374.

?NIKOTELES
SEG 30.114. He may have been general to Samos, though the token does not say he was general, perhaps in this period.

ANTISTHENES (? son of Antiphates of Kytherros (III)) *PA* 1184 = ?1194 = ?1196 = ?1197; *APF* 38f.
Xen. *Mem.* 3.4.1. See *APF* for discussion. The date may be around 370, despite the story being set in Sokrates' lifetime. If the identification is correct, we now know that he was choregic victor of 360/59 (SEG 27.15).

Osborne (*ABSA* 1971, 297–321, and *Naturalization* II.61ff.) has argued that IG ii² 207 belongs to the late 360s, but cf. Hansen, *GRBS* 1984, 134 n. 31; Moysey, *ZPE* 69 (1987), 93–100; Develin, *ZPE* 73 (1988), 75–81. In this there appear generals involved with Orontes, satrap of Mysia:
PHOKION son of Phokos *PA* 15076; *APF* 559
CHARIDEMOS son of Philoxenos of Acharnai (VI) *PA* 15380; *APF* 570ff.
CHARES son of Theochares of Angele (III) *PA* 15292; *APF* 568f.
PROXENOS son of Harmodios of Aphidna (IX) *PA* 12270; *APF* 478

Plut. *Phok.* 8.1 says that Phokion was general 45 times. Gehrke, *Phokion* 5ff., discusses these and on the basis of an age limit (which may or may not have been operative: Develin, *ZPE* 61 (1985), 153ff.) begins Phokion's career in the office around 371/70. We cannot know the years in which he was or was not in office, though his absences will have been few, beyond what specific evidence indicates and interpretative guesses. See also Tritle, *AJAH* 1981, 118–32, who wishes Phokion's deme to be Potamos (IV) on grounds which I do not find convincing.

Note: I see no necessary implication at Hypereides 4.28 that Aristophon was general, contrary to Beloch, *Att. Pol.* 318 (but cf. 363/2). Nor is it likely that Iphikrates was helping the Persians as Athenian general in the 370s (Diod. 15.29.4; see also schol. Ar. *Ploutos* 178).

Phylarchoi

THEOPHON *PA* 7180; *APF* 84
Isaios 11.41. Probably in the 370s.

DEMAINETOS son of Demeas of Paiania (III) *PA* 3276; *APF* 103f.
DEMEAS son of Demainetos of Paiania (III) *PA* 3323; *APF* 103f.
DEMOSTHENES son of Demainetos of Paiania (III) *PA* 3596; *APF* 103f.

IG ii² 3130. They will have held the position in different years, perhaps not all within this period.

Taxiarchoi?
-- son of --onides of tribe III
AUT-- son of Eur-- of tribe V
Hesperia 1963, 33 (30) (Meritt).

Lochagos
ASTYPHILOS son of Euthykrates of Araphen (II) *PA* 2665; *APF* 229f.
Isaios 9.14. He held the position on a number of occasions, perhaps as a mercenary on at least some, and died at Mitylene sometime after 371.

Tamias Paralou
ANTHIPPOS *PA* 955; *APF* 34
IG ii² 2966.3. He probably held this position, perhaps in this period.

Tamiai of Athene
Hesperia 1940, 324f. (34), is an inventory recording tamiai whom Schweigert thought might belong in 355/4 or 345/4; if the secretary cycle was in operation, they will belong to 354/3, with the secretary of the previous year mentioned, but this cannot be guaranteed and IG ii² 1442 has been placed in 354/3. D.M. Lewis informs me that his guess is 356/5, but the late 360s are possible.

A. **Grammateus**
   -- of Sounion (IV)

B. **Tamiai**
   --RATOS of Philaidai (II)
   --ENES of Phrearrhioi (IV)
   --of Acharnai (VI)

D. M. Lewis would place IG ii² 1439 in the late 360s; it has indications of the treasurers for three consecutive years:

A. ?[L]EON
   --ON of Athmonon (VII)

B. -- of Phyle (VI)

C. --ITES of Teithras (II)

Tamias of trireme funds
?[XAN]THIPPOS of G--, E-- or P-- *PA* 11160; *NPA* 167
IG ii² 1617.122. What is shown in IG would seem to allow any of the three letters shown to begin the demotic.

Epistatai of mint
The following come from SEG 21.667, dated before 356/5. Given the duplication of tribe IV, I do not guess at the tribes of men for whom the evidence is not specific:

-- of Anaphlystos (x)
-- DOROS son of . .⁴. . on
-- EMON son of Theo[ge]iton of Aphidna (IX) cf. *PA* 6681; *APF* 220
--S son of Phaidon of Phlya (VII)
--LOS son of Mnesi[th]eos of Lakiadai (VI)
--S son of Kallo[nid]es of Prospalta (V)
-- son of Smikri[on] of Leukonoion (IV)
-- of Leukonoion (IV)
-- of Paiania (III)
-- of Sybridai (I)
  Grammateus
  ?HIERO--

Epistatai of Brauroneion
SEG 21.256 seems to concern epistatai with some relation to Artemis of Brauron and there may be remains of the demotics of Iphistiadai (v) and Cholargos (v) or Cholleidai (IV).

Priests of Asklepios
The following are dated before the middle of the century:
NIKODEMOS *PA* 10855
IG ii² 4351.

ELPINES *PA* 4672
IG ii² 4352.

KTESIKLES of Hagnous (v) *PA* 8866
IG ii² 4400.

THEOPHILOS
AD 1963, B (i) 20.

Epimeletai of tribe III Pandionis
[MEIDOKR]ATES son of Meidokrates of Probalinthos
A . . . . ? . . . . son of [Anti]sthenes of Kytherros
-- of Paiania
SEG 21.515. The reading for the second name I owe to information from D.M. Lewis; for Antisthenes see above strategoi.

Demarchoi
? . . . KLES son of Kalli . . ⁵ . .
IG ii² 1173. The grounds are indeed slight for suggesting Acharnai: Whitehead, *Demes* 391.

NIKOSTRATOS of Halai (VII) ?*PA* 11019; *APF* 410
IG ii² 1175.22. See Whitehead, *ZPE* 47 (1982), 39f.

NIKON of Ikarion (II) *PA* 11110
IG ii² 1178.

Envoys
KALLISTRATOS son of Kallikrates of Aphidna (IX) *PA* 8157; *APF* 277ff.
Theopompos com. F 30 (Edmonds); Arist. *Rhet.* 3.17 1418b 13f.; Nepos
Epam. 6; Plut. *Mor.* 193c,d, 810f. He was sent to the Arkadians in the 360s;
362 (*PA*) seems unlikely.

-- of Euonymon (I)
--N son of Lykophron of Acharnai (VI) *PA* 9259
PH--
IG ii² 207d.27. Envoys to Orontes. For the date see above strategoi. The
letter ending the name of the son of Lykophron is as read by Osborne,
Naturalization II.63.

HAGNIAS son of Polemon of Oion (IV) *PA* 133; *APF* 82f.
Isaios 11.8. Humphreys, *CPh* 1983, 219ff., argues convincingly that his
embassy was in the 370s, possibly concerning Amyntas of Makedon in 371.

[EM]PEDOS of Oe (VI) *PA* 4696a
AISCHINES *PA* 333
--OROS of Acharnai (VI)
IG ii² 175.2ff. They were chosen with respect to oaths in arrangements
with Thessaly; Hansen, *GRBS* 1983, 159, has 361/60(?).

ANDRON of Kerameis (V) *PA* 924
LYSIA--
-- of Phlya (VII)
EUPHROSYNOS of Paiania (III) *PA* 6123
IG ii² 1128.39f. (Tod 162). In the matter of ruddle from Keos, probably in
the 350s.

HYPEREIDES son of Glaukippos of Kollytos (II) *PA* 13912; *APF* 517ff.
Hypereides F XXIV. His embassy to Thasos is dated 361/60 (?) by Hansen,
GRBS 1983, 177.

Unknown
A board of ten is found in IG ii² 2814, dated before the middle of the
century (*c.* 350 in SEG 32.241):
-- son of --res of Ankyle (II)
-- of Kydathenaion (III)
NIKIAS son of Nikides of Sphettos (V) *PA* 10825
EUKRATES son of Lysikrates of Epikephisia (VI) *PA* 5754
ARISTOBOULOS son of Boularchos of Phlya (VII) *PA* 1770
PHILOXENOS son of Antiphon of Eleusis (VIII) *PA* 14708
DIONYSIOS of tribe IX *PA* 4130
AISCHYLOS of tribe X *PA* 437
  Grammateus
  -- son of Elpines of E[uonymon] (I) *PA* 4675

Appendix

COUNCIL AND ASSEMBLY

(i) IG ii² 149 concerns the alliance with the Euboians and is dated before 355, but Cawkwell (*Phoenix* 1978, 45 n.14, 67 n.37) now wants it in 341/40 (contrast SEG 21.265).

(ii) IG ii² 152 is a proxeny decree of pryt. Akamantis for Timaphenides of Ainos, dated before 370 by Lewis, *ABSA* 1954, 38f.:
Grammateus
PHRYNON of Leukonoion (IV) *PA* 15030
Bouleutes epistates
KEDIKRA[TES] of Halai (II or VII) *PA* 8279
Proposer
DIO[G]E[IT]ON *PA* 3790

(iii) IG ii² 153 is of unknown content of pryt. Pandionis:
Grammateus
-- son of -- phon

(iv) IG ii² 154 is of unknown content and contains letters which may belong to names, but only the restoration of the demotic for Lamptrai (I) seems worth recording.

(v) IG ii² 156 is a bare fragment, but contains what are likely to be letters of a patronymic:
Grammateus
-- son of --isio--

(vi) IG ii² 157 is the beginning of a probouleumatic document of pryt. Aigeis which should be before 363/2:
Grammateus
. . .⁶. . . s son of Euphron of Phyle (VI)
Bouleutes epistates
[DE]XITHEOS of Hamaxanteia (VIII)
Proposer
? . . . .¹⁰. . . . of Poros (V)
D.M. Lewis informs me of difficulties with this text, particularly in that it seems too early for the proposer to have a demotic. If we do not restore a demotic to the proposer, the alternative would seem to be for lines 4 and 5: ἔδοξεν τῆι βο | [λῆι καὶ τῶι δήμωι . .]ριος εἶπ[ε]ν. The problem then is finding a name to complete what survives.

(vii) IG ii² 158 simply has the following:
Grammateus
. . .⁶. . . son of [Gl]aukippos of Atene (x) *PA* 2985
Lewis, *ABSA* 1954, 33, wondered whether this could be Nausias (cf. IG ii² 76; appendix to Section VI, no. xix).

(viii) IG ii² 159 is dated before 363/2 (Meritt, *Hesperia* 1940, 65):
Grammateus
[N]IKOXENOS son of Nikokles of Cholleidai (IV) *PA* 10987

(ix) IG ii² 165 simply has
DIIPPOS M--
who is not necessarily secretary, but IG ii² 4434, evidently the same document, has My--, which could be the demotic of Myrrhinous (III).

(x) Similarly, identification as secretary is unlikely for the following: IG ii² 166:
-- son of Leomedon

(xi) IG ii² 170:
[N]IKOTELES

(xii) IG ii² 171 is of pryt. Antiochis.

(xiii) IG ii² 172 is a probouleumatic renewal of the proxeny of Democharis son of Nymphaios (Walbank no. 81) dated to the third, fourth or fifth day of a prytany (Hansen, *GRBS* 1982, 342 no. 9 (=*Ecclesia* 94)):
Bouleutes epistates
[AR]ISTO[N] of Pergase (I) *PA* 2174
Proposer
[KRATI]NOS *PA* 8752

(xiv) IG ii² 179 concerns arrangements with Naxos which may belong in 376 or 364 (SEG 29.89).

(xv) IG ii² 182 is a probouleumatic proxeny decree for Apollodoros and an-
(xvi) other, with a rider from the man who had proposed a previous decree:
Proposer
PHILOKRAT[ES] (? son of Pythodoros of Hagnous (v)) *PA* 14576 = ?14599
The identification is not quite secure; for the patronymic see 347/6 envoys.

(xvii) IG ii² 188 is a probouleumatic proxeny decree with a rider:
Proposer
EPICHARES *PA* 4976

(xviii) IG ii² 189 has a rider:
Proposer
BLEPYROS son of Pei[thandros of Paionidai] (IV) *PA* 2881
The restoration of the man known as secretary in 343/2 (?) is all but certain;
(xix) he is a speculative candidate to be --OS of Paionidai in IG ii² 168 (apparently not grammateus therein).

(xx) For IG ii² 207 in the late 360s see above strategoi; it is a citizenship decree for Orontes (Osborne D 12) of pryt. Pandionis:
Bouleutes epistates
-- of Phlya (VII)

Appendix

Proposer
POLYKRATES son of Polykrates *not PA* 12027

(xxi) IG ii² 265 has been tentatively ascribed to this period by Pečírka, *Enktesis* 51ff., and I retain it here, even though Walbank, *ZPE* 63 (1986), 129–33, argues that it may have been originally a fifth-century decree:
Grammateus
PHEIDEL[EIDES]

(xxii) For IG ii² 404 in this period see SEG 19.50, 21.254. It is a renewal of the treaty with the cities of Keos; for the day and prytany see Hansen *GRBS* 1982, 346 no. 65 (= *Ecclesia* 98).

(xxiii) SEG 17.19 concerns arrangements with the Siphnians and is from the thirty-sixth day of the ninth prytany, dated *c.* 362–355.

(xxiv) For the recall of Xenophon from exile see the appendix to the last section no. xxxviii; the recall should fall in the 360s:
Proposer
EUBOULOS son of Spintharos of Probalinthos (III) *PA* 5369

Grammateis
AISCHINES son of Atrometos of Kothokidai (VI) *PA* 354; *APF* 543ff.
APHOBETOS son of Atrometos of Kothokidai (VI) *PA* 2775; *APF* 545
Dem. 19.70,98,200,237,249,314; Libanius hyp. Dem. 19; Plut. *Mor.* 840a,f. Dem. 19.249 says they rose from being hypogrammateis 'serving all the magistracies', including the demos and boule, to become grammateis.

The following spoke in the assembly: Meidias (Dem. 21.153,202); Melanopos (Plut. *Dem.* 13.3); Timarchos (hyp. Aisch. 1: he proposed more than a hundred decrees); Phokion (Plut. *Phok.* 7.3).

Nomothetai
(xxv) Dem. 24.61ff. informs us of a law amending the law on eisangelia passed before 353 (in general see Hansen, *Eisangelia* 12ff.):
Proposer
TIMOKRATES son of Antiphon of Krioa (x) *PA* 13772; *APF* 513f.

(xxvi) Dem. 24.138 tells of a proposed law of unknown content which almost resulted in the execution of its sponsor:
Proposer
PHILIPPOS son of Philippos

Agora xv.7 Provides us with victorious bouleutai of tribe VII Kekropis and, though given the date 390–360, probably belongs in this period:
Phlya
--SIS[T]RATOS son of Deinias *APF* 96
--LES son of --dotos

Halai
LEON son of Phila[gr]os *PA* 9110
ASTYPHILOS son of [Phil]agros *PA* 2664 = 2662 = 2663
--os son of --mos
-- son of --ares ?*PA* 1583
Melite
EXEK--
EUPHE--
PHILE--
HIER--
.Y--

Agora XV.11 has bouleutai of tribe VIII Hippothontis dated *c.* 400–350, but quite possibly around 375:
Thymaitadai?
POLYSTROPHOS son of Th--
AMEINIAS son of Lysa--
Eroiadai
CHARISANDROS son of Charikl[e]--
Keiriadai
PROTOMACHOS son of Herm--
HERMOKLES son of Hermo--

Agora XV.13 contains the victorious bouleutai of tribe IV Leontis dated 370/ 69 (?), which query must be reinforced and the date left open (SEG 29.148):
Kettos
AMPHITELES son of Amphitelides *PA* 792
TELESIPPOS son of Peisias *PA* 13539
ANTIKLEIDES son of Antikleides *PA* 10471; *APF* 36
Halimous
[P]RESBYCHARES son of Aristion *PA* 12186
NIKERATOS son of Leokrates *PA* 10735
THOUKRITOS son of Kephisodoros *PA* 7260
Potamos lower
CHARINOS son of Laches *PA* 15456
PHILIPPOS son of Philion *PA* 14414
Potamos upper
KLEONIKOS son of Stesarchos *PA* 8604
Skambonidai
ANTIKRATES son of Eukrates *PA* 1088
[PYTH]ODOROS son of Pythokles *PA* 12430
ARISTEIDES son of Himeraios *PA* 1715
Leukonoion
KALLIMACHOS son of Alkias *PA* 8020
CHARIADES son of [Ch]airokles *PA* 15315; cf. *NPA* 170

DIOGNETOS son of Diogenes *PA* 3864
Cholleidai
[AL]KISTHENES son of [Al]kibiades *PA* 643; *APF* 23
[NIK]ARCHOS son of [Ni]koxenos *PA* 10724
Phrearrhioi
ANTICHARES son of Philion *PA* 1315
PHILEAS son of Philion *PA* 14247
PEITHIADES son of Diodoros *PA* 11757
ARISTOKRATES son of Ariston *PA* 1927
EUANGELOS son of Cha[i]releides *PA* 5228
HEGEMON son of Labes *PA* 6301
PHANODEMOS *PA* 14035
THEMISTHOKLES (*sic*) *PA* 6665; *APF* 219
[ARCHES]TRATOS
Sounion
SP[EU]SI[K]LES son of Demet[r]ios *PA* 12843
[NI]KOMACHOS *PA* 10962
POLYXENOS son of Polykrates *PA* 12066
SMIKRON *PA* 12761
Deiradiotai
HAGNON son of Timokles *PA* 168
CHAIREPHON *PA* 15197
Potamos Deiradiotes
NIKON *PA* 11118
STRATONIKOS *PA* 12954
Pelekes
PHILEAS son of Philotheros *PA* 14245
HIEROKLEIDES son of Pheidon *PA* 7471
Hybadai
SIMON son of Simondes *PA* 12707
CHAIRION son of Pollis *PA* 15266
Oion
CLAUKOS son of Glauketes *PA* 3004; *APF* 83
Hekale
PHEIDESTRATOS son of Sosikles *PA* 14139
Kropidai
ENDEMOS son of Arrheneides *PA* 4699
Paionidai
MENESTRATOS son of Oinophilos *PA* 10013
THEOGENES son of Theodoros *PA* 6721
PHILOTHEROS son of Theophrastos *PA* 14504
Eupyridai
PHEIDESTRAT[OS] son of Chairestr[atos] *PA* 14141
ANTIRHETOS son of Aischeas *PA* 1182
Aithalidai

KTESIPPOS son of Ktesonides *PA* 8884
EUKLEIDES son of Eukles *PA* 5684
Kolonai
MENESTRATOS son of Menekrates *PA* 10010
HERMODOROS son of Hermolykos *PA* 5141

Agora XV.10 gives us bouleutai of tribe III Pandionis and a secretary, dated there *c.* 390–375, while Davies (*APF* 320) puts it in the 370s and Bourriot (*Historia* 1982, 418ff.) has *c.* 360 or later (cf. SEG 32.172):
Paiania
LY[S]-- son of --[k]les
-- son of --in--
-- son of --rhios
--OS son of Antikleides
-- son of Onetides
-- son of --phon
-- son of --os
--OS son of Leosthenes
--OROS son of Theodoros
[D]ORIKLEIDES
Konthyle
OPSIADES
Oa
DEMOKRATES son of Demodokos
ANDROKLES son of Lykinos
[EU]POLEMOS
[THRAS]YBOULOS son of Diodoros
Myrrhinous
--OS son of Polyeuktos
-- son of --es
-- son of --kles
--OS son of Lampon
Angele
MENEKLES son of Menestratos
MENANDROS son of Menes
ANTIMENES son of Antibios
Prasiai
TIMANDROS son of Timonides
EUDEKRATES son of Eukleides
Steiria
STRATOKLES son of Metalexis
KALLIMACHOS son of Lysimachos
KEPHISIOS son of Kephisodoros
Kytherros
HEGEMON son of Autophon

DEMONIKOS son of Admetos
Kydathenaion
ARCHIK[L]ES son of Ain--
MNESITHEOS son of Mnesige[nes]
KLEON son of Menexenos *APF* 320
EUAGORAS son of Dionysios
DEMOSTRATOS son of Lysanias
STRATON son of Stratios
PHILOSTRATOS son of Philinos
-- son of --dotos
L-- son of Diodotos
SOSIGE[NES] son of [L]ykinos
Probalinthos
ENDEMOS son of Endemos
PYTHODOROS son of Antiphilos
PITHON
Grammateus
CHAIRESTRATOS son of ? Thosko-- of Kollytos (II) ?*PA* 15165
It hardly seems that THOSKO can be correct.

Agora XV.15 contains bouleutai of tribe III Pandionis dated *c.* 360:
Kydathenaion
[SO]POLIS son of Kephisodoros *PA* 13155
[THE]OPHILOS son of Ariston *PA* 7146
[DE]MOPHILOS son of Aischron *PA* 3681
[D]AMOKRATES son of Gorgythos *PA* 3122
[PHI]LAIOS son of Kallaischros *PA* 7762
[DEM]E[T]RIOS son of Demostratos *PA* 3416
[KR]ATINOS son of Demostratos *PA* 8761
. . . . OS son of Philippos ?*PA* 14400 + Add.
Paiania upper?
-- son of --os
-- son of --tades
-- son of --nes
-- son of --on
Paiania lower
MNESIBOULOS son of Aristoteles *PA* 10267
Oa
DEMODOKOS son of Demokrates *PA* 3466
PAUSANIAS son of Paus[ani]as *PA* 11721
. EO . . s son of Ar--
Myrrhinous
SE--
EUDA--
Prasiai

ON--
I--
T--

Agora XV.16 retains names from tribe VII Kekropis before the middle of the century; that they are bouleutai is doubted (see also Rhodes, *ZPE* 38 (1980), 198), but I record the names:
MENON *PA* 10073
NIKANDRIDES *PA* 10676
ARIMNESTOS (? of Phlya) *PA* 1618a; cf. 1620
Sypalettos
TEISIMACHOS *PA* 13490
AUTOBOULOS (? son of Autosophos) *PA* 2705 + Add.
LYSIMACHOS *PA* 9528
DIODOTOS *PA* 3905a
Aixone
LEAIOS *PA* 9030
[CH]AIRIGENES *PA* 15225
[A]RCHEBIOS *PA* 2305a
[THR]ASIPPOS *PA* 7297a
--IKRATES
--[PH]ANES

Agora XV.492 is dated around 370. It is there stated that it may be a list of bouleutai and alternates, which I find attractive (see also SEG 31.132, where corrections are noted). There is restored in it Kleopompos of Thria, whose name appears among the bouleutai of 360/59, but in reference to him Rhodes, *ZPE* 38 (1980), 201, says of this list that the men are 'surely not bouleutae'.
Erechtheis (I)
Kephisia
[ANT]IK[LEIDES] or [CHAR]IK[LEIDES] ?*NPA* 116; *APF* 36
[AN]TIPHANES cf. *PA* 1236
[E]PAINETOS (? son of Antiphilos) *PA* 4753
Pergase upper
ARISTOMACH[OS] *PA* 1984
PHILIPPOS son of P-- *PA* 14412
PHILONIDES *PA* 14914; cf. *NPA* 167
Anagyrous
PLATON son of Ant-- *PA* 11851
HYPERBOLOS son of A-- *PA* 13908
PHILONOTHOS son of L-- *PA* 14687
PHILONIDES son of D-- *PA* 14890
PANTALEON son of P-- *PA* 11603
EUPHRONIAD[ES] *PA* 6102
SOKRATES *PA* 13103; *APF* 497

Appendix

EUTHYKRIT[OS] *PA* 5617
PANTOI[OS]
Sybridai
EUTHYKRAT[ES]
Agryle
. . . . S
. . . . YD--
. . . .T--
Phegous
EUKTEMONID[ES] *PA* 5778

Aigeis (II)
Otryne
PYRGION son of N--
ARISTOKL--
Araphen
CHARIMNE[STOS] *PA* 15428
HIEROKLE[IDES] *PA* 7464
THEOPEITH[ES] *PA* 7002
Ankyle
KIRRIA[S] or KIRRIA[DES] *PA* 8441
Phegaia
NIKOST[RATOS] *PA* 11055; *APF* 412
PHANIAS *PA* 14006 (Phania[des])
ANTIKR[ATES] *PA* 1089
SIMON son of Th-- *PA* 12708
XENOKL--
ANTIPHA[NES] *PA* 1248
Kydantidai
ARISTO--
PAMPHIL[OS] *PA* 11548
Erikeia
. . . . X--
. . .⁶. . . [E]NES son of Ch--
Kollytos
. . .⁷. . . son of Demophantos
-- son of --andros
. . .⁶. . . MOS son of Leokedes ?*PA* 9080
[NIKO]DEMOS son of Nikon
Halai
. . . OKLES son of Charias
[EU]KR[IT]OS son of Daitarchos
[A]NT[I]PATROS son of Komarchos
[N]AUKLES son of Nauarchos
NIKOKRATES son of Nikode[mos] *APF* 411

303

EUKLEIDES son of Euchares
NOMENIOS son of Kallias
NIKOSTRATOS son of Nikom-- *APF* 410f.
Ikarion
ARISTOGE--
NEOKLES son of Neodoros
ANTIDOTOS son of Euaine[tos]
PHRASIKLES son of Phrasik--
MNESIKLEIDES son of Go[rgiades]
TIMOGEN[ES] son of . . . o--

Leontis (IV)
-- son of --os or --as
-- son of --chos
-- son of --es
-- son of --telos
-- son of --[ch]ares
-- son of [S]tratonides *PA* 13005
-- son of [Th]rason

Akamantis (V)
--s son of Charis--

Oineis (VI)
Lousia
[O]NESIPHON son of Alki-- *PA* 11456
Phyle
[S]OPHANES son of Der[ketes]
[EU]ETHIDES son of So--
[PHI]LION son of Eua-- *PA* 14474
Thria
[EUPH]ANES son of S-- *PA* 6023
[KLEO]PHON son of O-- *PA* 8642
[KLEO]POMP[OS] ?*PA* 8614
[THEOG]ENE[S] *PA* 6710
Acharnai
DI--
HEPHA[IST]--
EUPHIL[ETOS] *PA* 6050
EUPHYL[IDES] *PA* 6127
NIKO--
PHANI[AS] ?*NPA* 161; *PA* 14011
EPINI[KOS] *PA* 4938
CHION son of L--
LYKIS[KOS] *PA* 9215
ARIST--

CHARIAD[ES] *PA* 15307
TELEPHON[OS] *PA* 13578
EUDRAST[OS] *PA* 5443
ONETORI[DES] *PA* 11460
PYTHODOR[OS] *PA* 12391; cf. *APF* 481
BATRACHO[S] *PA* 2844
EUKLEID[ES] *PA* 5676

Hippothontis (VIII)
Azenia
--s son of Antikles *PA* 1061
-- son of [A]ischron *PA* 397
[ARISTO]PHANES son of Aristomedes *PA* 2084
Keiriadai
.... [D]OROS son of Smikythos *PA* 12789
[NIKOS]TRATOS son of Nikostratos *PA* 11031
[EUKO]MOS son of Eukomion *PA* 5741
Kopros
[EUBOU]LIDES son of Euboulos *PA* 5329
[PHILI]PPIDES son of Kephalion *PA* 14357
[XEN]OTIMOS son of Xenokritos *PA* 11271 = ?11270
Anakaia
[THRA]SON son of Aristokles *PA* 7380
[KAL]LIDEMOS son of Xenotimos *PA* 7903
[ARI]STEIDES son of Exekestos *PA* 1697
[ARISTOK]LES son of Thr[a]so[n] *PA* 1859

Antiochis (X)
Anaphlystos
EI--
PHILT[ONIDES]
PHILO--
NAUKRATE[S] *PA* 10527
ERYMAIDE[S] *PA* 5182
PHILONIDES *PA* 14884
DIODOROS son of Th-- *PA* 3926
THEODOXOS *PA* 6747
KYDIPPOS *PA* 8937
LAIS[P]O[DIAS]
ATHEN--
Eroiadai
A--

Section VIII
352/1 to 337/6

352/1 (Ol. 107.1)

Archon
ARISTODEMOS *PA* 1798
Diod. 16.37.1; Dion. *ad Amm*. 1.4; *Dein*. 9, 13 (Philochoros *FGH* 328 F
154; Harding no. 77); *FGH* 255 (2); IG ii² 204.12 (*LS* no. 32; SEG 32.70;
Harding no. 78A); 1524.48f., 51f.; [1643 + Add.] (*Insc. Délos* 104–12: or
353/2); 1696.21; 3039.4; xii 8.63; SEG 15.120.[24]; 27.18.6; *Hesperia* 1950,
231 (13.130f.) (Crosby); 1963, 172 (8.[21f.], [28]) (Woodward).
Panathenaic amphora; Tarbell, *CR* 1900, 474.

Strategos
NAUSIKLES son of Klearchos of Oe (VI) *PA* 10552; *APF* 396f.
Diod. 16.37.3; cf. Dem. 18.115. He was sent with aid for the Phokians. On
his identity see Cawkwell. *CQ* 1962, 140 n.1 (but *APF* is not in doubt).
That he commanded the Athenians who confronted Philip at Thermopylai
is assumed, but not directly attested. I see no reason to reject Diodoros'
dating. The fake decree in Demosthenes mentions Imbros and has him as
hoplite general.

Epistates of Brauroneion
LYSIAS of Acharnai (VI) *PA* 9368
IG ii² 1524.49, 53f.; *Hesperia* 1963, 172 (8.22f.) (Woodward).

Priest of Asklepios
?THOUGENES *PA* 6689
IG ii² 1532.11, but the date is most uncertain.

The following names come from IG ii² 204.75ff. Five men from the boule
and ten from all Athenians were chosen to re-establish the boundaries of
the sacred land at Eleusis (A); one man from the boule and two from all
Athenians were chosen to consult the oracle at Delphi (B):

A. **From the boule:**
ARKEPHON of Lamptrai (I) *PA* 2226
--ES of Thria (VI)
-- of Hagnous (V)
From private citizens:
HIPPOKRATES of Kerameis (V) *PA* 7634
[CHAIR]E[PH]O[N] of Kedoi (I) *PA* 15200

EMMENIDES [of Koile] (VIII) *PA* 4689
-- of Sounion (IV)
[A]RISTEIDES of Oe (VI) *PA* 1713
GLAUKON of Perithoidai (VI) *PA* 3033
PHAIDROS *PA* 13953

B. **From private citizens:**
EUDIDAKTOS of Lamptrai (I) *PA* 5414
From the boule
--OS of Lamptrai (I)

Appendix
. . ⁵ . . KLES son of Astynomos
. . . OSTRATOS son of Archestratos
See 359/8 appendix.

COUNCIL AND ASSEMBLY

(i) IG ii² 204 (*LS* 32; SEG 32.70; Harding no. 78) concerns the sacred land at Eleusis (cf. above) and mentions at lines 54f. (see also Androtion *FGH* 324

(ii) F 30; Philochoros *FGH* 328 F 155) a previous decree on the matter:
Proposer
PHILOKRATES (son of Pythodoros of Hagnous) (V) *PA* 14576 = 14599

(iii) A vote of thanksgiving was passed for the defence of Thermopylai (Dem. 19.86 and schol.; Hansen (*GRBS* 1983, 166; 1984, 133) dates this 353/2):
Proposer
DIOPHANTOS son of Thrasymedes of Sphettos (V) *PA* 4438

Bouleutai
ARKEPHON of Lamptrai (I) *PA* 2226
--ES of Thria (VI)
-- of Hagnous (V)
--OS of Lamptrai (I)
See above on those chosen in IG ii² 204.

351/50 (Ol. 107.2)

Archon
THEELLOS *PA* 6641
Diod. 16.40.1 (Thessalos); Dion. *ad Amm.* 4; Dein. 9, 11 (Thellos); *FGH* 255 (2) (Thessalos); IG ii² [205]; 1436.[3]; 1440.22; 1517.[76]; 1524.55, 69; 1696.24; 2821.2 (*Agora* xv.19); ? *Insc. Délos* 104–21a B.[13], [14f.] (or 347/6 or 340/39).

Strategos
CHARIDEMOS son of Philoxenos of Acharnai (VI) *PA* 15380; *APF* 570ff. Dem. 3.5. He was sent to Thrace in late Boedromion to counter Philip, an expedition which was abandoned.

Tamiai of Athene
-- of Agryle (I)
ARISTAIOS son of Antikrates of Erchia (II) *PA* 1637; *APF* 362
MNESILOCHOS son of Mnesimachos of Konthyle (III) *PA* 10327
NI[K]-- of tribe IV
--ES son of Oinobios of Acharnai (VI) *PA* 11356
ANTITHEOS son of Archepolis of Phlya (VII) *PA* 1044
LAMPROKLES son of Aresias [? of Peiraieus] (VIII) *PA* 8992; *NPA* 116
  Grammateus
  AGATHYMOS son of Adeimantos of Thymaitadai (VIII) *PA* 79
IG ii² 1436.4ff.

Epistates of Brauroneion
[EX]EKESTOS of Aixone (VII) *PA* 4728
IG ii² 1524.70. This does not appear to be the name which was at line 55, but that is mutilated: . AR . . LADE. See Linders, *Artemis* 53, 55.

Priest of Asklepios
? --MOS
IG ii² 1532.33; the date is again uncertain.

Appendix
[AXIO]PISTOS son of The[odo]ros
. .⁴. . IGENES son of Polyeuktos
See 359/8 appendix.

COUNCIL AND ASSEMBLY

(i) IG ii² 205 (SEG 14.51) is a proxeny decree from the twenty-sixth day of pryt. Leontis for Demokrates of Lampsakos (on the proposer see Hansen, *GRBS* 1984, 137):
Grammateus
CHREMES son of Ph[iloitos of Ionidai] (II) *PA* 15566
Bouleutes epistates
[A]RISTAIO[S of Phaleron] (IX) *PA* 1634
Proposer
. . . .⁸. . . . S son of Aristy[l]los of Steiria (III) *PA* 2133

Although Dion. *ad Amm.* 4 places it in 352/1 (at least what he considers the first half), Ellis, *REG* 1966, 636-9, argues for this year for Dem. 4, in which the orator, as first speaker in a debate on the situation with regard to Philip,
(ii) unsuccessfully proposes the setting up of a force (see Hansen, *C&M* 1984, 58); thus I record
Proposer
DEMOSTHENES son of Demosthenes of Paiania (III) *PA* 3597; *APF* 113ff.
Dem. 15 is in response to an appeal for help from the Rhodian democrats, which Demosthenes supports, but help was not given.

Hansen, *GRBS* 1983, 160, suggests this year as that in which Androtion addressed the assembly concerning Karia (Arist. *Rhet.* 3.4.3 1406b 27).

350/49 (Ol. 107.3)

Archon
APOLLODOROS *PA* 1381 + Add.
Philochoros *FGH* 328 F 155 (Harding no. 78B); Diod. 16.46.1; Dion. *Dein.* 9, 11; *FGH* 255 (2); Suda *s.v.* Φιλόχορος; IG ii² 1436.1; 1440.26; 1517.[78f.]; 1524.71, 81; 1696.27; xiv 1098.8.

Strategoi
EPHIALTES = *PA* 6156
Philochoros *FGH* 328 F 155 (Harding no. 78B). General ἐπὶ τὴν χώραν, he went against the Megarians and marked out the sacred land.

?CHARIDEMOS son of Philoxenos of Acharnai (VI) *PA* 15380; *APF* 570ff. Philochoros *FGH* 328 F 50. Perhaps he continued in the Hellespont: see Cawkwell, *CQ* 1962, 131.

Tamiai of Athene
KTESIBIOS son of Tleson of Anagyrous (I) *PA* 8853
OINOPHIL[OS] of tribe II or III *PA* 11362
[PRAXITELES] son of [Pra]xiades of Kephale (V) = *PA* 12170
PHILEMON son of Lykourgos of Thria (VI) *PA* 14282
AUTOKLES son of Timeas of Aixone (VII) *PA* 2722
ANTIPHANES son of K-- of tribe VIII *PA* 1224
-- son of [Pa]mphilos of Besa (X) *PA* 11541
IG ii² 1436.1ff. Probably only 9 were listed in this inventory. The name of the secretary was never inscribed.

Epistatai of Brauroneion
[M]OIRAGENES of Kydathenaion (III) *PA* 10396
THRASON of Lamptrai (I) *PA* 7390
IG ii² 1524.72, 82.

Horistai
LAKRATEIDES *PA* 8969
HIEROKLEIDES *PA* 7460b
Androtion *FGH* 324 F 30; Philochoros *FGH* 328 F 155 (Harding no. 78B,C). Hierophant and daidouchos, they were chosen for the setting of the boundaries of the sacred land; see Clinton, *Sacred Officials* 17f.

Priest of Asklepios
?MENESTRATOS of Angele (III) *PA* 10001
IG ii² 4353; 4354. Note that Pritchett and Meritt, *Chronology* 79f., employed IG ii² 1753 as part of their argument for this date and this inscription has now been redated to *c.* 330 as *Agora* xv.47, partly on the assumption that this is the date of Menestratos' priesthood.

Appendix
-- son of Polemon[ikos]
-- son of ? . . . l.los
See 359/8 appendix.

COUNCIL AND ASSEMBLY

Grammateus
?-- of Paiania (III)
IG ii² 249.5 (cf. Johnson, *CPh* 1914, 424; Alessandri, *ASNP* 1982, 60f.).
If this is placed in the correct period and the demotic does belong to the
secretary, then the tribal cycle dictates this year. But the text is problematic
and the man concerned could be the proposer.

349/8 (Ol. 107.4)

Archon
KALLIMACHOS of Pergase (I) *PA* 8025
Diod. 16.52.1; Dion. *ad Amm.* 4, 9 (Philochoros *FGH* 328 F 49; Harding
no. 80), 10 (Philochoros *FGH* 328 F 156); *Dein.* 9; *FGH* 255 (2); Plut. *Mor.*
845d; Athenaios 5.217b; IG ii² 206; ?207 a.11 (but see the appendix to
Section VII; Osborne D 12); [208]; [209]; 1436.6; 1514.7; 1515.[1];
1524.[83]; 1582.62, 72 (cf. *Hesperia* 1941, 24; 1950, 302 (Crosby));
1620.44, 62; 1621.110; 2822.[1f.]; SEG 27.19.6.

Strategoi
PHOKION son of Phokos *PA* 15076; *APF* 559
Dem. 21.164 (cf. 162); Aisch. 2.169f.; Plut. *Phok.* 12ff.; ?Polyainos 5.21.
General to Euboia, he fought around Tamynai, subsequently expelling
Ploutarchos from Eretria and holding the strongpoint Zaretra; see Brunt,
CQ 1969, 248ff.; Carter, *Historia* 1971, 421. On IG ii² 207 as applying to
Phokion, Charidemos and Chares, see the appendix to Section VII.

CHARIDEMOS son of Philoxenos of Acharnai (VI) *PA* 15380; *APF* 570ff.
Philochoros *FGH* 328 F 50 (Harding no. 80); cf. Theopompos *FGH* 115 F
143. He was sent to aid the Olynthians, which he did against Pallene and
Bottiaia; Carter, *Historia* 1971, 424f.

CHARES son of Theochares of Angele (III) *PA* 15292; *APF* 568f.
Philochoros *FGH* 328 FF 49 (Harding no. 80), 51; schol. Ael. Arist. *Pan.*
179, 8, 9 (III.298f. Dindorf); Suda *s.v. Κάρανος*; cf. Lucian *Dem.* 37. He was
sent twice to aid the Olynthians; Cawkwell, *CQ* 1962, 130f.; Carter,
Historia 1971, 420f., 427f.

HEGESILEOS (? of Probalinthos (III)) *PA* 6339
Schol. Dem. 19.290 (Ulpian). He is said to have been general to Euboia,

tried for collusion with Ploutarchos to deceive the demos. His command and the year are problematic: see Carter, *Historia* 1971, 426; Gehrke, *Phokion* 11 n. 73. But the scholiast says he went when the Athenians sent help to Ploutarchos, which, if accurate, is suggestive, although Pausanias uses similar language with regard to Molottos (see 348/7 strategos).

Hipparchoi
MEIDIAS son of Kephisodoros of Anagyrous (I) *PA* 9719; *APF* 366f. Dem. 21.164ff., 174. Demosthenes accuses him of shirking his duty in Euboia; Carter, *Historia* 1971, 422ff.

KRATINOS (? of Erchia) (II) *PA* 8753 = ?8760, *APF* 321 Dem. 21.132 with schol. (Ulpian). He led the cavalry to Argoura and was assailed by Meidias. The identity was suggested to me by D.M. Lewis.

Phylarchos?
KLEOPHANES *PA* 8628 Plut. *Phok.* 13.3. He recalled the cavalry from flight and so is at least likely to be an officer with Phokion in Euboia; Davies, *Wealth* 153.

Taxiarchoi
MENITES son of Menon of Kydathenaion (III) = *PA* 10055 Aisch. 2.169f. He was sent with Aischines to report the victory in Euboia. For the name, rather than Temenides (*PA* 13555), see Lewis, *ABSA* 1955, 31; Davies, *Wealth* 152; this more nearly reflects the MS readings.

MANTITHEOS son of Mantias of Thorikos (v) *PA* 9676; *APF* 364ff. Dem. 39.17.

Officers?
THALLOS son of Kineas of Lamptrai (I) *PA* 6577; *APF* 492
GLAUKOS son of Polymedes *PA* 2994
Plut. *Phok.* 13.3. Their gallantry in Euboia may have been as officers.

Tamiai of Athene
[AMEINIAS] son of Philippos of Agryle (I) ?*PA* 677; *NPA* 163
[MNESAGO]RAS son of Mnesilochos of Halai (II) = *PA* 10238; *NPA* 130; *APF* 393
[TA]CHYKLES son of Phormion of Myrrhinous (III) *PA* 14957; *NPA* 158
HEGESIAS son of Hegias of Sounion (IV) *PA* 6331; *APF* 209
PLATON son of Isotimos of Iphistiadai (v) *PA* 11854
DEINON son of Deinias of Acharnai (VI) *PA* 3197; *NPA* 47
EXEKESTIDES son of Exekias of Xypete (VII) *NPA* 68
MORMIAS son of Eu[bou]los of Oinoe (VIII) = *PA* 10415; *NPA* 131
Grammateus
PISTIDES of Thorai (X) *PA* 11825
IG ii² 1436.6ff.; 2822.6ff. Only the eight were listed.

Epimeletai of dockyards
BLEPYROS son of Phyleides of Teithras (II) *PA* 2882
PHILOKALOS son of Exekias of Kerameis (V) *PA* 14506
ANTIPHON son of Archias of Kydathenaion (III) *PA* 1301
[KE]PHISOD[OROS or -OTOS] son of [E]uxitheos of Phrearrhioi (IV) *PA* 8305
--POS son of Aristo. . .os of Eleusis (VIII)
IG ii² 1620.45ff.

Epistates of Brauroneion
PHILOKEDES of Paionidai (IV) *PA* 14510
IG ii² 1524.84.

COUNCIL AND ASSEMBLY

The secretary is to be found in IG ii² 206, 208, 209;
Grammateus
DIEUCHES son of Demarchos of Phrearrhioi (IV) *PA* 3766

(i) IG ii² 206 is a probouleumatic proxeny decree of the ninth prytany, of Pandionis, for Theogenes of Naukratis; the proposer amends his own decree:
Bouleutes epistates
SOKERDES of Halai (II or VII) *PA* 13057
Proposer
HIEROKLEIDES son of Timostratos of Alopeke (X) *PA* 7463

(ii) IG ii² 208 is a probouleumatic decree, evidently in praise of Akarnanians:
Bouleutes epistates
EMM[EN]IDES of Koile (VIII) *PA* 4689
Proposer
ARCHEDEMOS son of Ar[chi]as of Paionidai (IV) *PA* 2325

(iii) IG ii² 209 has something to do with Eleusis (where it was found); given that the proposer is correctly identified, it is probouleumatic (cf. no. i above):
Bouleutes epistates
. . . .⁸. . . . DES of Gargettos (II)
Proposer
[HIEROKLEIDES son of Timos]tratos of Alopeke (X) *PA* 7463

(iv) IG ii² 210+259+EM 6874 (Schweigert, *Hesperia* 1937, 329ff.; Wilhelm, *Att. Urkunde* v.132ff.) is in praise of envoys from Akanthos and Dion.

(v) We come to Dem. 59.3ff.:
Bouleutes and Proposer
APOLLODOROS son of Pasion of Acharnai (VI) *PA* 1411; *APF* 428ff.
He brought before the council and then put as a probouleuma to the

assembly the proposal that the people should determine whether excess revenue should be for military purposes or go into the theoric fund. The vote was for military use, but an indictment for illegal motion was brought by Stephanos; Hansen, *Sovereignty* no. 18.

Nomothetai

(vi) Despite Cawkwell, *JHS* 1963, 59f., there is reason to accept the statement of schol. Dem. 1.1 that after Apollodoros' attempt a law was passed setting death as the penalty for trying to make theoric money available for military use:

Proposer

EUBOULOS son of Spintharos of Probalinthos (III) *PA* 5369

(vii) Dem. 21.173 indicates that laws were passed concerning the cavalry:

Proposer

MEIDIAS son of Kephisodoros of Anagyrous (I) *PA* 9719; *APF* 366f.

The autumn of this year provides the setting for Dem. 2, 1 and 3, the *Olynthiacs*, in that order (Ellis, *Historia* 1967, 108–12). I am not as sure as Hansen (*C&M* 1984, 58f.) that none of these speeches involved proposals as such, but they concern the need and the means by which to help the Olynthians. Hansen suggests that the third speech could have been in support of a proposal to appoint nomothetai to abrogate laws concerning the Theoric fund.

348/7 (Ol. 108.1)

Archon

THEOPHILOS *PA* 7106 + Add.

Dem. 37.6; Philochoros *FGH* 328 F 223; Diod. 16.53.1; Dion. *ad Amm.* 1.5 (Apollodoros *FGH* 244 F 38b), 10 (Philochoros *FGH* 328 F 156); *Dein.* 9 (Theomnestos); *FGH* 255 (3); Paus. 10.3.1; Athenaios 5.217b; Diog. 5.9; IG ii² 1441.5; 1514.10f.; 1515.5; 1582.76, 79, 83; 1622.551; 1748.11 (*Agora* XV.26.3); 2318.[271]; ?*Hesperia* 1950, 256 (17.[61], [66]) (Crosby). Panathenaic amphora: Frel, *Amphoras* 24.

Strategoi

CHARES son of Theochares of Angele (III) *PA* 15292; *APF* 568f.

Arist. *Rhet.* 3.10.7 1411a 6ff.; Philochoros *FGH* 328 F 51 (Harding no. 80). Sent to Olynthos (see 349/8), he will have been known to have been elected for this year and so have continued; see Carter, *Historia* 1971, 427f. He was questioned over his accounts.

?MOLOSSOS (MOLOTTOS) *PA* 10403 = ?10406

Plut. *Phok.* 14.1; Paus. 1.36.4. He succeeded Phokion in Euboia, probably as general for this year, and was captured by the enemy. See, however, Carter, *Historia* 1971, 426.

Exetastes
?TIMARCHOS son of Arizelos of Sphettos (v) *PA* 13636
Aisch. 1.113. He was accused of embezzlement when sent to inspect the
mercenaries at Eretria, perhaps in this year, as he was a councillor in 347/6.

Epimeletes of dockyards
PHILAGROS of Phaleron (IX) *PA* 14215
IG ii² 1622.549.

Priest of Asklepios
AMPHITEKTON of Prospalta (v) *NPA* 13
IG ii² 4427.

Envoys
KTESIPHON *PA* 8893
Aisch. 2.12f.; Dem. 19.12; hyp. Aisch. 2; hyp. ii Dem. 19. He was sent to
Philip in the matter of Phrynon's ransom money and also reported on
Philip's desire to end war. Hansen, *GRBS* 1983, 178, seems unjustified in
recording Phrynon himself as an envoy.

ARISTODEMOS (of Metapontum, the actor)
Aisch. 2.15ff.; Dem. 19.12; hyp. Aisch. 2; hyp. ii Dem. 19. He was sent to
Philip in the matter of Athenians caught in Olynthos; he was attacked for
delaying his report, which was that Philip wanted alliance. He received a
crown.

COUNCIL AND ASSEMBLY

(i) IG ii² 211 may belong to this year: it grants ateleia to Olynthians (? – see
Osborne x 12).

Aisch. 2.12ff. tells of envoys from Euboia addressing the assembly.
Phrynon of Rhamnous was captured by pirates and on his return persuaded the assembly to elect an envoy to see about recovering his ransom
money (see above Ktesiphon). Upon his report Ktesiphon was given a vote
(ii) of praise. Then came a motion that Philip be allowed to send envoys and a
herald concerning peace:
Proposer
PHILOKRATES son of Pythodoros of Hagnous (v) *PA* 14599 = 14576
This was unsuccessfully indicted as unconstitutional; Hansen, *Sovereignty*
no. 17.

Agora xv.26 provides bouleutai of tribe III Pandionis:
Paiania lower
[--D]OROS son of Sostratos *PA* 13364
Paiania upper
--RATOS son of Echedamas *PA* 6164

--THEOS son of Phanode[mos] *PA* 14034

[D]EMOPHILOS son of Dem[eas] or Dem[ophanes] *PA* 3686 or 3687; *APF* 104

XENOKLES *PA* 11230

Treasurer of tribe?

-- of Oa

347/6 (Ol. 108.2)

Archon

THEMISTOKLES *PA* 6650

Aisch. 3.62; *FGH* 255 (3); Diod. 16.56.1; Dion. *ad Amm.* 10,11 (Philochoros *FGH* 328 F 53); *Dein.* 9, 11; schol. Aisch. 1.109; IG ii² 212 (Tod 167; Harding no. 82); 213 (Tod 168; Harding no. 83); [214] (but see SEG 24.88; 356/5 *q.v.*); 215.[11]; ?[263]; 505.16; 1441.4; 1443.[92], 104, 216; 1455.17; 1514.12; 1515.6; 1519.10; 1521.[26f.] (but see Linders, *Artemis* 47); 1524.60f.; 1622.446f.; 2318.283; *Insc. Délos* 104–21 a B.[14f.] (or 351/50 or 340/39); Michel, *Recueil* 832.5; SEG 15.120.26; 19.51.5; 19.[52].

Strategoi

CHARES son of Theochares of Angele (III) *PA* 15292; *APF* 568f.
Aisch. 2.90,92; ?Polyainos 3.13.2f. General in the north, he wrote to Athens on the fate of Kersebleptes and the success of Philip.

PROXENOS son of Harmodios of Aphidna (IX) *PA* 12270; *APF* 478
Dem. 19.50, 52, 73f., 154f.; Aisch. 2.133f. Involved in Phokis, he later had to convey the envoys to Philip.

PHAIDROS son of Kallias of Sphettos (v) *PA* 13964; *APF* 525
IG ii² 213.8 (Tod 168; Harding no. 83). He was concerned with Mitylene.

Tamias of Athene

LEPTINES *PA* 9041; *APF* 341
IG ii² 1443.[216]; 1455.18. IG ii² 1441 is probably from the year's inventory.

Tamias of dockyards

EUTHYMACHOS of E-- *PA* 5634
IG ii² 1622.444. See Rhodes, *Boule* 119.

Epimeletes of springs

[KEPHISO]DOROS son of Kalli[as of Hagnous] (v)
IG ii² 215.9f. For the identity see IG *ad loc.*; cf. Develin, *ZPE* 57 (1984), 135.

Epistates of Brauroneion

CH--
IG ii² 1519.12.

Priest of Asklepios
ARISTARCHOS of Kothokidai (VI) *PA* 1664
IG ii² 4369; 4370.

Envoys
AISCHINES son of Atrometos of Kothokidai (VI) *PA* 354; *APF* 545ff.
Aisch. 2.79. 157; Dem. 19.11, 304ff. Sent to the Peloponnese, he spoke
before the Arkadians. For the date see Cawkwell, *CQ* 1978, 93ff.; Hansen,
GRBS 1983, 159 gives 348/7(?).

AISCHINES son of Atrometos of Kothokidai (VI) *PA* 354; *APF* 545ff.
DEMOSTHENES son of Demosthenes of Paiania (III) *PA* 3597; *APF* 113ff.
PHILOKRATES son of Pythodoros of Hagnous (V) *PA* 14599 =? 14576
PHRYNON of Rhamnous (IX) *PA* 15032
NAUSIKLES son of Klearchos of Oe (VI) *PA* 10552: *APF* 396f.
ARISTODEMOS
IATROKLES son of Pasiphon *PA* 7442
KIMON (? of Lakiadai) (VI) *PA* 8424; *APF* 309
KTESIPHON *PA* 8893
DERKYLOS son of Autokles of Hagnous (V) *PA* 3249 = 3248; *APF* 97f.
Aisch. 2 passim, 1.168,174,3.63f.,73,80f.; Dem. 5.9, 6.29, 19 passim,
18.17; *Epist.* 2.8; Plut. *Dem.* 16.1f., *Mor.* 841a; Lucian *Dem.* 16;
Philostratos *Soph.* 1.18, 2.1,32; hyp. Aisch. 1, 2; Libanius hyp. Dem. 19;
hyp. ii Dem. 19; Harpokration, Suda and Photios *s.v. Κτησιφῶν*;
Harpokration *s.v. Φρύνων*; Suda *s.v. Φρύνωνος*.

The same men were chosen to go to Philip to decide on terms for peace
and later to administer oaths for peace. On this business see Ellis, *Philip*
105ff.; Cawkwell, *Philip* 91ff.; Griffith, *Hist. Mac.* II.329ff. For
Philokrates' patronymic see *Hesperia* 1936, 393ff. (10.46, 111) (Meritt).

COUNCIL AND ASSEMBLY

The secretary is found in IG ii² 212 and 213:
Grammateus
LYSIMACHOS son of Sosidemos of Acharnai (VI) *PA* 9512; *APF* 358

(i) IG ii² 212 (Tod 167; Harding no. 82) is a decree of the eighth prytany, of
Aigeis, in honour of the 'Bosporan princes Spartakos, Pairisades and
Apollonios:
Bouleutes epistates
THEOPHILOS of Halimous (IV) *PA* 7125
Proposers
ANDROTION son of Andron of Gargettos (II) *PA* 915 = 913; *APF* 33f.
P[OLYEUKT]OS son of Timokrates of Krioa (X) *PA* 11946
This must have been passed at a meeting on Elaphebolion 8 or 16; see
Hansen, *GRBS* 1977, 50f. (= *Ecclesia* 42f.). At lines 53ff. it looks forward

to a meeting on the eighteenth, which we know to have taken place in connexion with the matters concerning the embassies (see below).

(ii) IG ii² 213 (Tod 168; Harding no. 83) is from the same day as no. i with the same epistates and concerns the renewal of the treaty with Mitylene:
Proposer
STEPHANOS son of Antidorides of Eroiadai (VIII or X) *PA* 12887

We may begin the considerable literary record of proceedings in this year with Dem. 19.10f., where we hear of Aischines addressing the council and assembly, supported by Ischandros, about Philip's designs and the need for envoys to Greek states to try to convene a meeting about war with Philip; subsequently Aischines reported on his embassy to Arkadia. We

(iii) learn more at 19.303ff., where we have the proposer of the decree for the embassies:
Proposer
EUBOULOS son of Spintharos of Probalinthos (III) *PA* 5369

The early stages of the business leading up to peace with Philip are to be read at Aisch. 2.16ff. Aristodemos (see 348/7 envoys) delayed his report, but he eventually spoke before council and assembly, after Demokrates persuaded the council to summon him, after they had heard from Iatrokles.

(iv) We learn of a bouleutes who proposed the crown for Aristodemos:
Bouleutes and proposer
DEMOSTHENES son of Demosthenes of Paiania (III) *PA* 3597; *APF* 113ff.

(v) Then came the proposal for the embassy to Philip concerning peace:
Proposer
PHILOKRATES son of Pythodoros of Hagnous (v) *PA* 14599 = ?14576

(vi) There was a proposal in the boule that envoys be chosen to go to the cities in which Aristodemos was bound to perform that he might be excused without penalty:
Proposer
DEMOSTHENES son of Demosthenes of Paiania (III) *PA* 3597; *APF* 113ff.
In what follows the major sources are Dem. 19 and Aisch. 2, with some additional information from other places, especially Dem. 18 and Aisch. 3. Members of the embassies (see above envoys) reported to and addressed the council and assembly, as also did Kephisophon (Dem. 18.21), Neoptolemos (Dem. 19.12, 315), Euboulos (Dem. 18.21) and Aristophon (Theopompos *FGH* 115 F 166). Out of the confusion Hansen, *Ecclesia* 69ff. (amending *GRBS* 1977, 54ff.), has created a scheme which I shall follow without indicating precise references for each detail (they are given by Hansen, whose views are criticized by Harris, *CQ* 1986, 366ff.).

The envoys returned and reported to the council late in Anthesterion or
(vii) in the first three days of Elaphebolion; probouleumata were passed giving
(viii) safe conduct to Philip's envoys and honouring the Athenian envoys:
Proposer
DEMOSTHENES son of Demosthenes of Paiania (III) *PA* 3597; *APF* 113ff.

Shortly after this, the envoys reported to the assembly and the bill for safe conduct for the Makedonian envoys was ratified, as eventually was De-
(ix) mosthenes' other proposal. He was also responsible for a decree ordering
(x) the prytaneis to conduct an assembly on Elaphebolion 8 and another, in the boule, granting proedria at the Dionysia to the envoys of Philip. On
(xi) Elaphebolion 8 he carried a decree which fixed assembly meetings to discuss and conclude peace and alliance on Elaphebolion 18 and 19. Before these there was the regular meeting of the assembly after the Dionysia in the precinct of Dionysos, perhaps on Elaphebolion 16.
(xii)　　On Elaphebolion 18 the proposal for peace and alliance was up for discussion:
Proposer
PHILOKRATES son of Pythodoros of Hagnous (v) *PA* 14599 = ?14576
There was conflict on the terms because of a proposal of the allied synhedrion, but on the next day, after the assembly had heard from the Makedonian Antipater, Philokrates' proposal was passed. At some stage, perhaps in the boule (though I am not confident in Hansen's argument), the envoys were chosen to administer the oaths for the peace. Then an assembly was held on Elaphebolion 25 with Demosthenes as proedros. A
(xiii) decree was carried that the allies should take the oath at once:
Proposer
PHILOKRATES son of Pythodoros of Hagnous (v) *PA* 14599 = ?14576
(xiv) Another decree was voted on, despite Demosthenes' objection, that Kritoboulos should take the oath on behalf of Kersebleptes:
Proposer
ALEXIMACHOS of Pelekes (IV) *PA* 545
(xv) A decree also gave instructions for the second embassy. On Mounichion 3
(xvi) it was voted in the boule that this embassy set out at once:
Proposer
DEMOSTHENES son of Demosthenes of Paiania (III) *PA* 3597; *APF* 113ff.
　　This is where Hansen's analysis ends. We continue with Dem. 19.58ff. The embassy returned on Skirophorion 13 and it will have been at the
(xvii) assembly on the sixteenth that there was passed the decree honouring Philip and appointing the envoys I include under 346/5, including a clause to the detriment of the Phokians (Dem. 19.47ff.):
Proposer
PHILOKRATES son of Pythodoros of Hagnous (v) *PA* 14599 = ?14576
On Skirophorion 27 an assembly was held in the Peiraieus concerning dockyard matters, which heard from Derkylos, newly arrived from Chalkis
(xviii) with a report of Philip's actions. In the wake of this (Dem. 19.125) measures were voted to bring in the women and children from the country and for fortifications and holding the Herakleia in the city; this is the decree mentioned at Dem. 18.37; 19.86 and schol.:
Proposer
KALLISTHENES *PA* 8090

(xix) At Aisch. 1.80ff. we learn of a councillor who, we find at Dem. 19.286f.,

proposed a measure that forbade the taking of arms to Philip:
Bouleutes and proposer
TIMARCHOS son of Arizelos of Sphettos (v) *PA* 13636

(xx) He had also proposed a decree concerning dwellings on the Pnyx which brought about the assembly of which Aischines informs us; there spoke the Areiopagite Autolykos and Pyrrhandros.

(xxi) Finally we have Aisch. 2.73, recording a decree that a message should be sent to Chares:
Proposer
KEPHISOPHON son of Kallibios of Paiania (III) *PA* 8417; *APF* 149
For the date see Hansen, *GRBS* 1977, 53f. (= *Ecclesia* 45f.).

346/5 (Ol. 108.3)

Archon
ARCHIAS *PA* 2449
Androtion *FGH* 324 F 52 = Philochoros *FGH* 328 F 52 (Harding no. 85A); *FGH* 255 (3); Diod. 16.59.1; Dion. *ad Amm.* 10; *Dein.* 9, 11; ?Plut. *Mor.* 850b (Xenias); IG ii^2 215, 218 (SEG 31.74); 1442.[3] (but see 354/3); 1443.[89], [91], [93], [95], [100], 102; 1461.11; 1514.24; 1515.[16f.]; 1516.4; 1622.390, 422; 1646.17 + Add. (*Insc. Délos* 104–22b); 2492.42f.; 3019.2; 3201.4f.; *Insc. Délos* 104–23.2, 104–24.13; Michel, *Recueil* 832.1; SEG 15.120.31, 16.125, 28.129.10; *Hesperia* 1935, 35 ([4]) (Oliver); 1936, 402 (10.166) (Meritt); 1950, 255 (18.[20]) (Crosby).

Tamias of trireme funds
EUTH[Y]NOS of Lamptrai (I) *PA* 5657
IG ii^2 1622.387.

Poletai
-- son of --rhos of Hermos (v)
[L]EOSTHENES
[THRA]SYMEDES son of L[y]simachos
SEG 16.125.2f.

Amphiktyons to Delos
　Grammateus
　. . . . .^{12}. . . . . son of --ilos of Aigilia (x)
Insc. Délos 104–23.10.

Naopoioi to Delos
L.CH-- son of [Ke]phisodoros of Sypalettos (VII) *PA* 8383
[AR]CHIPPOS son of Archestratos of Aphidna (IX) *PA* 2549; *APF* 474
　Grammateus
　ETEOCHARES son of Leochar[es] of Phrearrhioi (IV) *PA* 5219
Insc. Délos 104–23.1ff., 104–24.13ff.

346/5 (Ol. 108.3)

Naopoioi to Delphi
EUKTEMON son of Charias (? of Lousia) (VI) *PA* 5785 = ?5800
EPIKRATES *PA* 4861
FD III, 5, 19.74; cf. 91.23.

Demarchos
EUBOULIDES son of Antiphilos of Halimous (IV) *PA* 5323
Dem. 57.8 and passim. He was bouleutes in the same year.

Envoys
AISCHINES son of Atrometos of Kothokidai (VI) *PA* 354; *APF* 545ff.
APHOBETOS son of Atrometos of Kothokidai (VI) *PA* 2775; *APF* 545
DEMOSTHENES son of Demosthenes of Paiania (III) *PA* 3597; *APF* 113ff.
DERKYLOS son of Autokles of Hagnous (V) *PA* 3249 = 3248; *APF* 97f.
STEPHANOS (? son of Antidorides of Eroiadai) (VIII) *PA* 12887
Aisch. 2.94ff., 139ff., 162f., 178; Dem. 19.121ff.; hyp. ii Dem. 19. The matter has been obscured by rhetoric. An embassy of ten was chosen 'to the Amphiktyons', in fact to Philip in the matter of peace and actions against Phokis. Aischines cried off and Aphobetos was sent in his place; the envoys turned back when they heard that Philip had won Phokis. The same ten were then chosen, Aischines now being fit, to go to Philip and the Amphiktyonic Council.

COUNCIL AND ASSEMBLY

The secretary is to be found in IG ii² 215 and 218:
Grammateus
KEPHISODOROS son of Athenophanes of Phlya (VII) *PA* 8387

(i) IG ii² 215 is a probouleumatic decree from the eighth prytany, of Hippothontis, in honour of Kephisodoros son of Kallias of Hagnous:
Proposer
KALLI[KRA]TES son of Charopid[es] of Lamptrai (I) *PA* 7946 = 7973 = 8213

(ii) IG ii² 218 (SEG 31.74) is a probouleumatic decree from the ninth prytany, of Akamantis, in honour of Dioskourides of Abdera and his brothers:
Bouleutes epistates
PROTIAS of Acharnai (VI)
Proposers
EUBOULIDES son of An[t]iphilos of Halimous (IV) *PA* 5323
DIOPEITHES son of [Di]opeithes of Sphettos (V) *PA* 4328; *APF* 160

(iii) There was a revision of citizen lists in the demes; Aisch. 1.77, 86, 114; Androtion *FGH* 324 F 52 = Philochoros *FGH* 328 F 52 (Harding no. 85); schol. Aisch. 1.77:

Proposer
DEMOPHILOS *PA* 3664
For the controversy on this see Osborne, *ABSA* 1971, 329f. and n. 32.

For assemblies concerning the third embassy see above envoys.

It seems Aischines spoke at an assembly considering the request from
Thessalians and envoys from Philip that the latter be admitted to the
Amphiktyonic Council (Dem. 19.111ff.), which may have been the occasion for Dem. 5 in autumn 346, though Libanius thought that this speech
was written, but not delivered.

We know of a bouleutes from Dem. 57.8f.:
Bouleutes
EUBOULIDES son of Antiphilos of Halimous (IV) *PA* 5323
And we know of another who was chosen from the boule to oversee matters
concerning the dockyards:
MNESIKLES of Kollytos (II) *PA* 10314
IG ii² 1622.420ff.; see Rhodes, *Boule* 119, 239f.

345/4 (Ol. 108.4)

Archon
EUBOULOS *PA* 5343
FGH 255 (3); Diod. 16.66.1; Dion. *ad Amm.* 5 (Apollodoros *FGH* 244 F
38b), 10; *Dein.* 9, 11, 13; Diog. 5.9; IG ii² 219; 220.23; 1442.[10] (but see
354/3); 1443.3, 106, 111, 120; 1514.34; 1515.[26]; 1516.13; 1622.382;
2492.19, 20; 2655; *Insc. Délos* 104–24.3, 4; *Hesperia* 1950, 263f. (20. [7f.])
(Crosby).

Strategoi
PHILOCHARES son of Atrometos of Kothokidai (VI) *PA* 14775; *APF* 545
Dem. 19.237; Aisch. 2.149. He was general for the third consecutive year in
343/2. On the date of Dem. 19 and Aisch. 2 see Brunt, *CQ* 1969, 252 n.3.

?KEPHISOPHON (son of Kephalion) of Aphidna (IX) *PA* 8410; *APF* 292f.
IG ii² 1623.35ff.; 1629.483ff. Despite the lack of conclusion in *APF*, we
could date his expedition to Skiathos in this year. For at IG ii² 1443.106ff.
we have a dated reference to soldiers in Skiathos and at lines 111 and 120 we
are still in the same archon year; also at lines 112f. the restoration of
Kephisophon with demotic exactly fits for the man crowned by the
Samothrakians. Our knowledge of the workings of the theoric commission
is not such as to allow Kephisophon's position in that regard in 343/2 to
negate this conclusion.

Tamiai of Athene
CHAIRE[STRATOS?] son of [? Philemo]nides of Lamptrai (I) *NPA* 169
NIKOLAOS son of Nikoteles *PA* 10923

-- son of Sostratos of Prospalta (v)

POLYA[INOS?] son of [Euk]rates of Thria (VI) *NPA* 144

PHAIDRIAS son of Rhodon of Phlya (VII) *PA* 13945

. . . . .¹¹. . . . . son of [E]uthoinos of Dekeleia (VIII) *NPA* 76

DEXIADES son of D[exiades ?] of Phaleron (IX) *NPA* 47

THEOPHILOS son of Meni[sk]os of Atene (x) *PA* 7129

IG ii² 1443.3ff. Only eight were listed. The secretary's name was never inscribed.

Amphiktyons to Delos
THEOMENES of Oe (VI) *PA* 6957
  Grammateus
  ARISTHETAIROS of Anagyrous (I)
Insc. Délos 104–24.5f.

Naopoioi to Delos
  Grammateus
  PHILISTIDES son of Philippos of Kephale (v)
Insc. Délos 104–23.14f., 104–24.2.

Demarchos
DEMOSTHENES of Aixone (VII) *PA* 3583
IG ii² 2492.21f.

Priest of Asklepios
PATA[IKOS] (of Eleusis) (VIII) *PA* 11677; *APF* 442f.
IG ii² 1532.13f.; 4368.6.

Envoy
?EUKLEIDES *PA* 5678
Dem. 19.162 and schol. He was sent to Philip to complain about his activities in Thrace, perhaps in this year; cf. Hansen, *GRBS* 1983, 167.

COUNCIL AND ASSEMBLY

The secretary is found in IG ii² 219 and 220:
Grammateus
. . ⁵. . ENOS son of I . . . ? . . . of Oion (VIII)

(i) IG ii² 219, with the reading of Schweigert (*Hesperia* 1939, 172f. (3); see also Hansen, *GRBS* 1984, 137), is a fragment of the eighth prytany, day 16 or 21 (Hansen, *GRBS* 1982, 342 (= *Ecclesia* 94)):
Bouleutes epistates
DIO--
Proposer
? -- of Phrearrhioi (IV) or Eitea (v or x)

(ii) IG ii² 220.23ff. seems to be the decree ratified in the earlier parts honouring the Pellaneans; it is restored to the tenth day of the ninth prytany:

Bouleutes epistates
. . . . ? . . . . s of Eiresidai (V)
Proposer
[ARISTONYMOS] son of [Aris]to[n]ik[os]
For the latter see also lines 7f.

344/3 (Ol. 109.1)

Archon
LYKISKOS *PA* 9214
Dem. 58.28; Philochoros *FGH* 328 F 157 (Harding no. 86); *FGH* 255 (4);
Diod. 16.69.1; Dion. *ad Amm.* 1.10; Dein. 9, 11; IG ii² 221.9 (SEG 14.52);
1443.[1]; 1462.[16]; 1471.[62]; 1514.[59f.] (cf. Linders, *Artemis* 20f.);
1516.36 (cf. Linders, *Artemis* 26); 1518.[76] (Linders, *Artemis* 45);
1622.383; 2832; 3068.5; 3069.2; 3202.1f. (*Agora* XV.33); 4571.4.

Thesmothetes
-- of Hybadai (IV)
Dem. 58.27f. This was the brother of Theokrines, who used the latter as
adviser (?paredros) and was involved in the dismissal of the whole board of
archons (which was, however, reinstated).

Strategoi
PHILOCHARES son of Atrometos of Kothokidai (VI) *PA* 14775; *APF* 545
See 345/4.

?PHOKION son of Phokos *PA* 15076; *APF* 559
Plut. *Phok.* 15. It is extremely likely that he was general, but the specific
query is that the campaign to Megara mentioned by Plutarch may not
belong here. See Brunt, *CQ* 1969, 264f. and 252 n. 3, for Phokion in Cyprus
this year; Gehrke, *Phokion* 12ff., 225ff.

Tamias of Athene
-- son of --etos of Peiraieus (VIII)
IG ii² 1443.2. Only six or seven were listed in this inventory.

Tamias of stratiotic fund
NIKERAT[OS] (son of Nikias) of Kydantidai (II) *PA* 10742; *APF* 406f.
IG ii² 1443.13f. The inscription implies this year rather than 345/4.

Priest of Asklepios
LYSITHEOS of Trikorynthos (IX) *PA* 9407
IG ii² 1532.34; 4389.2ff.; 4390.2.

Syndikos
HYPEREIDES son of Glaukippos of Kollytos (II) *PA* 13912; *APF* 517ff.
Dem. 18.134; Plut. *Mor.* 840e, 850a. The people chose Aischines, but the
Areiopagos rejected him in favour of Hypereides to represent Athens in the
matter of who should have charge of the temple at Delos. Roux,

L'amphictionie 28, dates 345/4 or 344/3 and thinks the post was as pylagoras to Delphi.

Envoys
DEMOSTHENES son of Demosthenes of Paiania (III) *PA* 3597; *APF* 113ff. Dem. 6.19ff.; 18.79; Dion. *ad Amm.* 10. He went to the Peloponnese to agitate against Philip.

HEGESIPPOS son of Hegesias of Sounion (IV) *PA* 6351; *APF* 209f. Dem. 7.2; 19.331; Libanius hyp. Dem. 7. He went to Philip on the matter of Halonnesos; Hansen, *GRBS* 1983, 168, has this in 343/2.

?ARISTODEMOS (of Metapontum, the actor) Aisch. 3.83 (Harding no. 89A). He went on an embassy to Thessaly and Magnesia 'contrary to the terms of the peace' – perhaps in the context of Halonnesos? Hansen, *GRBS* 1983, 161, has 340/39 without a query.

Appendix: The agoranomoi of IG ii² 2823 are correctly dated to 129/8 at IG ii² Add. p. 348 and Pritchett, *Hesperia* 1942, 240 n. 39.

COUNCIL AND ASSEMBLY

(i) IG ii² 220 ratifies the honours to the Pellaneans (see 345/4) on day 16 or 21 of the prytany (Hansen, *GRBS* 1982, 342 (= *Ecclesia* 94)):
Bouleutes epistates
HIPPOCH--
Proposer
-- son of Oinobios of Rhamnous (IX) *PA* 11358

Plut. *Phok.* 15.1, if the year is correct (see above strategoi), tells of Phokion calling an assembly and revealing a message from the Megarians which resulted in a vote to send help.

There were a number of embassies to and from Athens this year. Androtion spoke in reply to one from Artaxerxes (Didymus *in Dem.* 8.14).
(ii) One from Philip, led by Python of Byzantion, elicited a reply proposed by the speaker of Dem. 7 (sections 23ff.):
Proposer
HEGESIPPOS son of Hegesias of Sounion (IV) *PA* 6351; *APF* 209f.
While some believe that it was at this assembly that Dem. 6, which contains no proposal, was delivered (Hansen, *C&M* 1984, 59), Markle, *Antichthon* 1981, 62–85, deals with the speech and accepts that it was produced at an assembly where envoys of Philip had complained about the words of Athenian orators and where envoys from Argos and Messene had objected
(iii) to Athenian support of Sparta. Then there is Demosthenes' embassy to the Peloponnese (Dem. 18.79):
Proposer
DEMOSTHENES son of Demosthenes of Paiania (III) *PA* 3597; *APF* 113ff.

343/2 (Ol. 109.2)

Archon

PYTHODOTOS *PA* 12386

Dem. 48.23ff.; *FGH* 255 (4); Diod. 16.70.1; Dion. *ad Amm*. 5 (Apollodoros *FGH* 244 F 38b), 10; Dein. 9, 13 (Philochoros *FGH* 328 F 158); Diog. 5.10; schol. Aisch. 3.83 (Harding no. 89A); IG ii² 223 a.1, 4, b.[7], 16, c.[15] (*Agora* xv.34); 224; [225] (Harding no. 89B); 1443.[6]; 1454.3; 1462.[7]; 1471.63; 1517.[55f.], [120] (see Linders, *Artemis* 37); 1524.134; 1525.8; 1526.19; 1532.1; 1590.2; 1622.383f.; 1699.[1] (*Agora* xv.493); 2318.[287]; *Insc. Délos* 104–27.[2], 17; *Hesperia* 1936, 401 (10.126) (Meritt); 1941, 40 ([7]) (Meritt) (*Agora* xv.35). Panathenaic amphora: Frel, *Amphoras* 19.

Strategoi

PHILOCHARES son of Atrometos of Kothokidai (VI) *PA* 14775; *APF* 545
See 345/4.

PHOKION son of Phokos *PA* 15076; *APF* 559
Aisch. 2.184.

CHARES son of Theochares of Angele (III) *PA* 15292; *APF* 568f.
Dem. 7.15 and schol., 58.38. He was stationed at Thasos. Dem. 7.15 complains about Philip using the generals to convey exiles from Makedon to Thasos and sending men to accompany the generals. Dem. 58.38 speaks of Chares appointing a rate of payment for the Ainians.

DIOPEITHES (? son of Diphilos of Sounion) (IV) *PA* 4327; *APF* 168
Dem. 8 passim, 9.15 (cf. 73), 12.3f., 16; Dion. *ad Amm*. 10; Dein. 13 (Philochoros *FGH* 328 F 158); Lucian *Dem*. 35, 37; Libanius hyp. Dem. 8; cf. schol. Aisch. 3.83 (Harding no. 89A).

He led out klerouchs to the Chersonese and grew ever more hostile to Makedon, aiding Kardia and operating in Thrace, among other things. Philip wrote to Athens complaining of his actions and his incitement of opposition to himself, matters which became the subject of debate at Athens. These actions would seem to extend into 341/40 and even in 340/39 Diopeithes may still have been in the Hellespontine area (see *APF*).

Tamiai of Athene

NIKANDROS son of [Eun]ikos of Lamptrai (I) *PA* 10688
-- of Gargettos (II)
CHARIAS son of Chairias of Sounion (IV) *NPA* 171
HIERON[YMOS] son of . . . .⁸. . . . of Kerameis (V)
EUMELIDES son of Arkeon of Acharnai (VI) *PA* 5830
-- son of --itheos of Melite (VII)
DEXIKRATES son of Dikaio[genes] of Eleusis (VIII) *NPA* 47
PHILINOS son of Pyrgion of Marathon (IX) *PA* 14330
  Grammateus

--IOS of Acharnai (VI)
IG ii² 1443.6ff. Only eight were listed. On Nikandros see SEG 14.84. The secretary depends upon an unpublished reading of Woodward.

Epistates of Brauroneion
KALLISTRATOS of Thorikos (V) *PA* 8168
IG ii² 1517.56f. (SEG 28.115 for the demotic).
    Grammateus
    OLYMPICHOS of Anaphlystos (X)
IG ii² 1517.2. See Linders, *Artemis* 34.

Amphiktyon to Delos
MNESI[S] son of Phil--
Insc. Délos 104–27.17.

Hieromnemon
MNESILOCHOS *PA* 10323
FD III, 5, 14.3, 27.

Pylagoras
DEMOSTHENES son of Demosthenes of Paiania (III) *PA* 3597; *APF* 113ff.
Aisch. 3.113f. Aischines charges him with corruption. Roux, *L'amphictionie* 28, gives the date as 341/40.

Naopoios to Delphi
EUKTEMON son of Charias (? of Lousia) (VI) *PA* 5785 = ?5800
FD III, 5, 19.96; cf. 91.23.

Envoys
DEMOSTHENES son of Demosthenes of Paiania (III) *PA* 3597; *APF* 113ff.
POLYEUKTOS son of Sostratos of Sphettos (V) *PA* 11950 = 11925 = 11934
HEGESIPPOS son of Hegesias of Sounion (IV) *PA* 6351; *APF* 209f.
LYKOURGOS son of Lykphron of Boutadai (VI) *PA* 9251; *APF* 350f.
?KLEITOMACHOS
Dem. 9.72; 18.244; Aisch. 3.97f., 256 (see 341/40); Plut. *Dem.* 17.3, *Mor.* 841e. They went on missions to counter Philip in the Peloponnese. Lykourgos should be included here to create a uniform tradition (*contra* Mosley, *TAPhA* 1965, 258). For Kleitomachos see Hansen, *GRBS* 1983, 171.

COUNCIL AND ASSEMBLY

The secretary is found in IG ii² 223c (*Agora* XV.34), 224 and 225:
Grammateus
KLEOSTRATOS son of Timosthenes of Aigilia (X) *PA* 8623

(i) IG ii² 224 is a decree from the fourth day of the tenth prytany, of Aigeis, honouring Kephallenians:

Bouleutes epistates
ARCHIKLEIDES of Paiania (III) *PA* 2492
Proposer
AR[ISTOPHO]N son of Aristophanes of Azenia (VIII) *PA* 2108; *APF* 64ff.

(ii) IG ii² 225 is a treaty with the Messenians and someone else from the same day and with the same epistates as 224.

(iii) IG ii² 223 (of which part c is *Agora* XV.34) is a dedication by the boule incorporating certain votes by the body and naming certain officers. The first proposal is in honour of Phanodemos:
Proposer
DEINOSTRATOS son of Deiniades of Ankyle (II) *PA* 3192 = 3191

(iv) The second concerns the honours to the boule:
Proposer
[PHA]NO[DEMOS] son of [Di]yllos of Thymaitadai (VIII) *PA* 14033

(v) Then there is further praise for the council:
Proposer
[KEPHI]SOPHON son of Kallibios of Paiania (III) *PA* 8417; *APF* 149

(vi) The next praises Eudoxos for the functions he has fulfilled:
Proposer
. . .⁶. . . ON son of Antikrates of Pambotadai (I) *PA* 1086

(vii) A similar measure follows:
Proposer
BRACHYLLOS son of Bathyllos of Erchia (II) *PA* 2928
The latter part also gives us the secretary and the following:
In charge of decrees
DEMOPHILOS son of Pantaleon of Agryle (I) *PA* 3669
In charge of the theoric fund
KEPHISOPHON son of Kephalion of Aphidna (IX) *PA* 8410; *APF* 292f.
I suspect he was not a commissioner as such, but an official of the council who was concerned with this area.
Tamiai of boule
ANTIKLES son of Aristokrates of Kydathenaion (III) *PA* 1067
DROMOKLEIDES son of Thrasymedes of Hagnous (v) *PA* 4567

(viii) Aisch. 3.224 indicates a proposal of the death penalty for Anaxinos of Oreus, who was acquiring things for Olympias, perhaps in this year (Hansen, *GRBS* 1983, 164):
Proposer
DEMOSTHENES son of Demosthenes of Paiania (III) *PA* 3597; *APF* 113ff.

(ix) Also in this year Demosthenes will have proposed an embassy to Euboia (Dem. 18.79).

(x) Dem. 7 is attributed to the man who ends by saying he will propose the answer to Philip's letter:

343/2 (Ol. 109.2)

Proposer

HEGESIPPOS son of Hegesias of Sounion (IV) *PA* 6351; *APF* 209f.

Agora xv.36 gives us bouleutai of tribe II Aigeis, dated to this year by the appearance of Deinostratos (see above); I assume, therefore, that *Agora* xv.493 is not a list of bouleutai and omit its names. Before the bouleutai I include the following, also found in *Agora* xv.37:

Grammateus of boule and demos

BLEPYROS son of Peithandros of Paionidai (IV) *PA* 2881

Philaidai

ANTIGENES son of Antidoros *PA* 1002

DIONYSIOS son of Hephaistion *PA* 4259

[L]YSIKLES son of Thrasymenes *PA* 9441

Ionidai

[CHR]EMES son of Philoitios *PA* 4802 = 15566

[E]PIGENES son of Androkles *PA* 4801

Halai

NIKERATOS son of Nikokrates *PA* 10734; *APF* 411

ANTIKRATES son of Phalanthos *PA* 1081

EUPOLIS son of Arrhileos *PA* 5939

EPIKRATES son of Nikomenes *PA* 4879; *APF* 410

[S]OKRATES son of Habron *PA* 13098

Phegaia

[A]KESTIDES son of Antiphanes *PA* 467; *APF* 191

SOTIMIDES son of Aischines *PA* 13400

[A]RISTI[O]N son of Philistides *PA* 1755

POLYKRATES son of Polyeuktos *PA* 12027

Ankyle

DEINOSTR[ATOS] son of De[ini]ades *PA* 3192 = 3191

PAUSIAS son of Sokrates *PA* 11730

Kydantidai

THEOMNESTOS son of Theomnestos *PA* 6969

Kolonos

ANTH[O]S son of Nikeratos *PA* 960

DEMETRIOS son of Speusikrates *PA* 3414

Bate

PYTHEAS son of Pythippos *PA* 12348

AMYNOMACHOS son of Philokrates *PA* 741

Araphen

MYRONIDES son of Kleon *PA* 10510; *APF* 229

MNESITHEOS son of Nikostratos *PA* 10288

Gargettos

MEGA[K]LES son of [E]uainetos *PA* 9700

EUNOMOS son of Euthynomos *PA* 5868

DEMOCHARES son of Charinos *PA* 3713

331

MENESTRATOS son of Straton *PA* 10004
Kollytos
AMEIN[I]AS son of Leokedes *PA* 681
NAUSISTRATOS son of Megakles *PA* 10594
POLYXENOS son of [S]mikythos *PA* 12063
Plotheia
POLYKRATES son of . . . .nes *PA* 12025

342/1 (Ol. 109.3)

Archon
SOSIGENES *PA* 13196
Philochoros *FGH* 328 FF 159 (Harding no. 91A), 161; *FGH* 255 (4); Diod.
16.72.1; Dion. *ad Amm.* 10; *Dein.* 9; Plut. *Mor.* 839d; Diog. 10.14; schol.
Aisch. 3.85; IG ii² [227]; 1455.[2]; 1517.[58], [61], 134 (Linders, *Artemis*
37); 1521.[65] (cf. Linders, *Artemis* 47); 1524.[150] (Linders, *Artemis* 59);
1622.384f.; 2318.[292]; 2320.[1]; 2331.1; 2932.2; xiv 1184; *Insc. Délos* 104–
27.3, 4, [17f.]; SEG 28.129.5, 14.

Strategoi
DIOPEITHES (? son of Diphilos of Sounion) (IV) *PA* 4327; *APF* 168
See 343/2.

KEPHISOPHON son of Kephalion of Aphidna (IX) *PA* 8410; *APF* 292f.
Philochoros *FGH* 328 F 159 (Harding no. 91A); schol. Aisch. 3.85. He led
the expedition to Oreos, which was successful, in Skirophorion.

Tamiai
--ON son of Aischines of Perithoidai (VI) *PA* 362
HIEROPHON son of Soi-- *PA* 7516
IG ii² 1455.3.

Epistates of Brauroneion
?PHILODEMO[S]
IG ii² 1517.61, 134f. (Linders, *Artemis* 40); 1524.[150] (Linders, *Artemis*
60). This reconstruction seems better than the proposal of Aristodemos of
Hamaxanteia (VIII) at *NPA* 29 = *PA* 1808.

Amphiktyons to Delos
-- son of Aristodemos of Leukonoion (IV)
-- of Paiania (III)
   Grammateus
     . . . . ? . . . . son of Diom . . o--
Insc. Délos 104–28a A.6ff.; 104–27.[4], 18.

Hieromnemon
?POLYKRITOS
FD III, 5, 14 II.11. He could be Athenian or Euboian.

Epimeletai of tribe ix Aiantis:
DION son of Noumenios of Phaleron
TIMOKRATES of Aphidna
POLYPHILOS son of Polymedes of Oinoe
Hesperia 1936, 402 (10.168ff.) (Meritt).

COUNCIL AND ASSEMBLY

(i) IG ii² 227 (not certainly of this year) is a fragment from the eighth prytany, of Aigeis:
Grammateus
KALLIADES of Euonymon (1) *PA* 7792
Bouleutes epistates?
TIM--

(ii) An alliance was made with Chalkis (Aisch. 2.92f.):
Proposer
DEMOSTHENES son of Demosthenes of Paiania (III) *PA* 3597; *APF* 113ff.

(iii) I assume also that it was in this year that Demosthenes proposed the expedition to Oreos, not 341/40 as at Hansen, *GRBS* 1983, 164; Dem. 18.79.

Dem. 8, 9 and 10 belong to this year, containing no proposals (Hansen, *C&M* 1984, 59f.; for the date of Dem. 10 see Markle, *Antichthon* 1981, 82f.). The first deals with Philip's complaint about Diopeithes, the second supports giving reinforcements to the latter, the third urges action and addresses the question of revenues.

The following are from *Hesperia* 1936, 397ff. (10.13, 117f.) (Meritt) and are bouleutai:
KEPHISODOROS son of Hag--
EUTHYKL[ES] son of Eukles of Kedoi (1) *APF* 486

341/40 (Ol. 109.4)

Archon
NIKOMACHOS *PA* 10936
Arist. *Met.* 1 345a 1; Philochoros *FGH* FF 55b (Harding no. 95c (2)), 160 (Harding no. 92), 161, 162 (Harding no. 95B); *FGH* 255 (4); Diod. 16.74.1; Dion. *ad Amm.* 10, 11 (Philochoros *FGH* 328 F 53); Dein. 9, 11, 13; schol. Aisch. 3.103; IG ii² ? 207a [11] (Osborne, *ABSA* 1971, 297ff.); 228 (Tod 174; Osborne D 15; Harding no. 94); [229]; 1455.[1]; 1456.28f.; 1517.[63]; ? 1518.[72f]; 1628.419; 1629.940; 1681.[24] (Davies, *Class. Stud. Capps* 86ff.); 1749.1 (*Agora* XV.38); 2318.[304]; 2320.16; *Insc. Délos* 104–27. [5]. Panathenaic amphoras: Beazley, *Black Figure* 414; Smets, *AC* 5 (1936), 87ff. no.116 (*Hesperia* Suppl. 10.15 no. 12).

Strategoi
DIOPEITHES (? son of Diphilos of Sounion) (IV) *PA* 4327; *APF* 168
See 343/2

PHOKION son of Phokos *PA* 15076; *APF* 559
Philochoros *FGH* 328 F 160 (Harding no. 92); Diod. 16.74; schol. Aisch.
3.103. He defeated and killed Kleitarchos, tyrant of Eretria, and installed
democracy.

CHARES son of Theochares of Angele (III) *PA* 15292; *APF* 568f.
Plut. *Phok.* 14.2f.; Hesychios *FGH* 390 F 1.28ff.; IG ii² 228.11ff. (Tod 174;
Osborne D 15; Harding no. 94); 1628.420; 1629.941. He was sent to help
the Byzantians and made exactions of the allies; Hesychios records some
success. The inscription IG ii² 228 concerns Elaious in the Chersonese.

?KALLIAS
Dem. 12.5. He is generally regarded as Kallias of Chalkis, but is accepted as
Athenian by Hansen, *GRBS* 1983, 169.

Tamiai
-- son of --ates of Phrearrhioi (IV)
DEMOPHILOS son of Demokl-- *PA* 3666
   Grammateus
   -- son of --imachos of Eleusis (VIII)
IG ii² 1455.1f., the inventory.

Amphiktyons to Delos
PHANOMACHOS son of Charmiades of Sounion (IV) *PA* 14077
PYTHODOROS son of Nikostratos of Acharnai (VI) *PA* 12413; *APF* 482
EUPOLEMOS son of Euthymenides of Myrrhinous (III) *PA* 5928
CHAIRIAS son of Euortios of Anaphlystos (X) *PA* 15218; *NPA* 169
ARCHENEOS son of Diphilos of Prospalta (V) *PA* 2368; *APF* 390
   Grammateus
   TEISIADES son of Teisippos of Sphettos (V) *PA* 13468
   Hypogrammateus
   EM-- or M--
Insc. Délos 42; 104–27.5; 104–28a A.3ff.; IG xii 5.113.2ff. The latter text,
from Paros, has Charmides for Charmiades and Chaire[mo]n for Chairias.

Naopoios to Delphi
EPIKRATES *PA* 4861
FD III, 5, 20.3.

Priest of Asklepios
EUNIKIDES of Halai (II) *PA* 5846
IG ii² 1533.7f.; Ferguson, *Priests* 145.

Envoys
DEMOSTHENES son of Demosthenes of Paiania (III) *PA* 3597; *APF* 113ff.

Dem. 18.244; Aisch. 3.96f., 256. He went to the Peloponnese for support. On the date see Brunt, *CQ* 1969, 255ff.

EPHIALTES *PA* 6156
Plut. *Mor*. 847f, 848e. He came back from Persia, reputedly, with money to incite politicians against Philip.

?HYPEREIDES son of Glaukippos of Kollytos (II) *PA* 13912; *APF* 517ff. Plut. *Mor*. 850a. To Rhodes. Berthold, *Historia* 1980, 45 n. 51, holds that this may as well belong to 323; Hansen, *GRBS* 1983, 177, has 342/1. Bartolini, *Iperide*, sends him to Chios on the strength of the *Chiakos* (which depends on emendation; F LXV).

?MENELAOS (? son of Menelochos of Myrrhinous) (III) *PA* 9963; *APF* 389 Lykourgos 1.24. He went to the Persian king. This is perhaps to be connected with Ephialtes' mission, but the source has no indication of date; it is at least before 330.

COUNCIL AND ASSEMBLY

The secretary is to be found in IG ii² 228.5f. and 229.3f.:
Grammateus
ONESIPPOS son of Smiky[thos] of Araphen (II) *PA* 11455

(i) IG ii² 228 (Tod 174; Osborne D 15; Harding no. 94) is a decree from the twenty-ninth day of the seventh prytany, of Pandionis, granting rights to the people of Elaious:
Bouleutes epistates
ARISTOMACHOS of Oion (IV or VIII) *PA* 1978
Proposer
HIPPOSTRATOS son of Etearchides of Pallene (X) *PA* 7669

(ii) IG ii² 229 is a decree restored to the thirty-seventh day of the tenth prytany, of Leontis, the last or penultimate day of the month (thus Skirophorion: for all this see Meritt, *Ath. Year* 10) honouring a Corinthian; on the proposer see Hansen, *GRBS* 1984, 137:
Proposer
-- son of --os of Phrearrhioi (IV)

(iii) IG ii² 230, the treaty with Eretria, is there reasonably dated to this year, though see SEG 21.249 for 357/6.

(iv) Aisch. 3.95ff. recounts Kallias' report to the assembly that he had secured support in the Peloponnese, which Demosthenes confirmed, as well as reporting on his own embassy to the Peloponnese and Akarnania. A motion ensued that envoys be sent to Eretria and Oreos:
Proposer
DEMOSTHENES son of Demosthenes of Paiania (III) *PA* 3597; *APF* 113ff.

(v) It seems he also proposed the expedition to Eretria (Dem. 18.79; Plut. *Dem.* 17.1).

(vi) At Dem. 18.83 we hear of a decree awarding a crown to Demosthenes:
Proposer
ARISTONIKOS son of Nikophanes of Anagyrous (1) *PA* 2025
Plut. *Mor.* 848d says this was opposed, but Demosthenes wants to give the opposite impression.

Agora XV.38 provides the bouleutai of tribe II Aigeis:
Erchia
THARRHIAS son of Tharrhiades *PA* 6590
KYDIAS son of Lysikrates *PA* 8928
CHAIREAS son of Paramythos *PA* 15100
[PH]YLARCHOS son of Paramythos *PA* 15042
XENOKLES son of Kalliades *PA* 11220
POLYKLEID[E]S son of Kallistratos *PA* 11970; *APF* 362
Gargettos
DIODOROS son of Philokles *PA* 3940
MEIXIAS son of Hegesias *PA* 9752
SMIKRIAS son of Philokedes *PA* 12743
AR[E]SIAS son of Pausias *PA* 1597
Philaidai
DIONYSIOS son of Hephaistion *PA* 4259
EUTHYKLES son of Ameinias *PA* 5586
EUTHYDIKOS son of Ameinias *PA* 5565
Kydantidai
PYTHION son of Aischronides *PA* 12370
DEMOSTRATOS son of Demostratos *PA* 3622
Ionidai
MELIEUS son of Il[i]oneus *PA* 10101
Ikarion
TIMOKRITOS son of Timokrates *PA* 13790; *APF* 513
ARISTOPHANES son of Eukleides *PA* 2088
ARCHENAUTES son of Archenautes *PA* 2357
ERATON son of Eration *PA* 5042
[A]RIGNOTOS son of Babyrias *PA* 1613
Hestiaia
POSEIDIPPOS son of Kallikrates *PA* 12126; *NPA* 145
Bate
LYSISTRATOS son of Polyeuktos *PA* 9615; *APF* 171
Kolonos
KALLIPHANES son of Kallikles *PA* 8222
THEAGES *PA* 6616
Kollytos

CHAIREPHON son of Thrason *PA* 15201; *APF* 239
ALEXIS son of Sosiades *PA* 552
PHEREKRATES son of Philokrates *PA* 14196
Plotheia
CHAIRIAS son of Chairias *PA* 15223
Otryne
PHILINOS son of Theodoros *PA* 14334
Erikeia
EPAMEINON son of Epainetos *PA* 4765
Halai
LYSIMACHIDES son of Lysipolis *PA* 9479
EUBIOS son of Autosthenes *PA* 5295
APOLLODOROS son of Archias *PA* 1404
EUNOSTIDES son of Theophantos *PA* 5878
KALLIMEDES son of Archemachos *PA* 8083
Teithras
DEMOSTHENES son of Demophon *PA* 3598
DEMOPHILOS son of Demokles *PA* 3689
KALLISTRATOS *PA* 8182; *APF* 111
PROKLEIDES son of Proxenides *PA* 12204
Phegaia
AKERATOS son of Archedemos *PA* 476
THEOMNESTOS *PA* 6978
THEODOROS son of Theognis *PA* 6908
Araphen
ELPINOS son of Sosigenes *PA* 4682
KALLIMACHOS son of Mnesitheos *PA* 8007
Myrrhinoutte
THEOPHILOS *PA* 7151
Ankyle
EUBIOS son of Eubiotos *PA* 5290
Diomeia
DOROTHEOS son of Theodoros *PA* 4609
Ankyle
MELESIPPOS son of Melesias *PA* 9820; *APF* 233
There follows a series of tribal decrees. Tharrhias of Erchia praises the
tamias of the tribe Poseidippos of Hestiaia. Aristophanes of Ikarion praises
the syllogeis, Diodoros of Gargettos, Timokritos of Ikarion, Tharrhias of
Erchia. Tharrhias praises the hieropoioi Poseidippos of Hestiaia,
Timokritos of Ikarion, Aristophanes of Ikarion, Chairias of Plotheia,
Kallistratos of Teithras, Pythion of Kydantidai, Eubios of Ankyle,
Theomnestos of Phegaia, Theophilos of Myrrhinoutte, Meliseus of
Ionidai. Diodoros praises Aristophanes of Ikarion.

340/39 (Ol. 110.1)

Archon
THEOPHRASTOS of Halai (II or VII) *PA* 7171
Aisch. 3.115; Philochoros *FGH* 328 FF 55b (Harding no. 95C (2)), 161, 162
(Harding no. 95B); *FGH* 255 (5); Diod. 16.77.1; Dion. *ad Amm.* 10, 11
(Philochoros *FGH* 328 FF 54a (Harding no. 95A), 56a (Harding no. 96A));
IG ii² [231]; 233 [a] (Harding no. 97), b.4, 7, 10 (Tod 175); 1455.4; 1457.21;
1462.[19]; 1533.9; 1628.[436]; 1629.957; 2318.316; 2320.30; 2394 (or 313/
12; Whitehead, *Demes* 384 no. 78); 2824 (or less likely 313/12); 3104 (or
313/12); *Insc. Délos* 104–21.[14f.] (or 351/50 or 347/6). Panathenaic
amphora: Beazley, *Black Figure* 415. IG ii² 1202 and *MDAI(A)* 1941,
218f. no. 1, probably belong in 313/12: Pickard-Cambridge, *Festivals²* 49
n.3 (Lewis); Whitehead, *Demes* 375f. nos. 12 and 13.

Paredros
?MNESARCHIDES (? son of Mnesarchos of Halai) (II) *PA* 10242 = 10245;
APF 392
Dem. 58.32. The identification is not secure, but a Mnesarchides was
paredros to an eponymous archon in the late 340s, being entrusted with a
case of maltreatment of an orphan. I place him here on the chance that his
deme might make him a suitable paredros to a possible associate.

Strategoi
CHARES son of Theochares of Angele (III) *PA* 15292; *APF* 568f.
Philochoros *FGH* 328 F 162 (Harding no. 95B); Plut. *Mor.* 188b; Steph.
Byz. *s.v.* Βόσπορος. Cf. 341/40. He was at Byzantion. He conferred with the
Persian generals and was unsuccessful in besieging Aristonymos in
Methymna.

PHOKION son of Phokos *PA* 15076; *APF* 559
Plut. *Phok.* 14.3ff., *Mor.* 188b–c, 851a; IG ii² 1628.437; 1629.958. He was
sent to Byzantion, where he was successful against Philip, following this up
with raids into Philip's territory. For a possible expedition to Megara see
344/3.

KEPHISOPHON son of Kephalion of Aphidna (IX) *PA* 8410; *APF* 292f.
IG ii² 1628.438; 1629.959; ?Plut. *Mor.* 850f. He was general to the
Hellespont with Phokion.

Tamiai
[NI]KOSTRATOS son of Nikiades of Halimous (IV) *PA* 11020; *APF* 95
MENAIO[S]

Grammateus
-- son of --rates of Trikorynthos (IX)
IG ii² 1455.5f. On the second name, a note on the card at the Institute for
Advanced Study at Princeton says that chi as last visible letter is indicated

on the squeeze, but D.M. Lewis tells me that on the Oxford squeeze he still reads *MENAIΩ*[*I*. . .] undotted.

PHILOKLES *PA* 14519
IG ii² 1457.21; 1462.20.

Epistates of navy
DEMOSTHENES son of Demosthenes of Paiania (III) *PA* 3597; *APF* 113ff.
Aisch. 3.222.

Epistatai of Eleusis
Grammateus
-- son of [K]leobo[ulos]
IG ii² 1543.2. The term was evidently four years.

Hieromnemon
DIOGNETOS of Anaphlystos (X) *PA* 3856
Aisch. 3.115ff.; *FD* III, 5, 22.19, 44. He fell sick and asked Aischines to speak for him.

Pylagorai
MEIDIAS son of Kephisodoros of Anagyrous (I) *PA* 9719; *APF* 386f.
THRASYKLES of Oion (IV or VIII) *PA* 7327
AISCHINES son of Atrometos of Kothokidai (VI) *PA* 354; *APF* 545ff.
Aisch. 3.115ff.; Dem. 18.149ff. Aischines was enlisted by the sick hieromnemon to speak for Athens on the matter of the Amphissans. See Roux, *L'amphictionie* 30ff.

Priest of Asklepios
DIOKLES of Myrrhinous (III) *PA* 3992; cf. 4041
IG ii² 1533.9; 4391.4.

Epimeletai of tribe II Aigeis?
[AN]DROKLES son of Andrios of Halai *PA* 857
PHILAGRO[S] (son of Diokles of Halai) *PA* 14208; *APF* 534f.
-- son of N[i]kokrates of Halai *PA* 10913; *APF* 411
IG ii² 2824.4f. IG doubts that they are epimeletai, *APF* accepts, after Pritchett, *AJPh* 1942, 429 n. 62. The date may be 313/12.

Tamias (? of tribe)?
GORGIADES son of Mnesikleides of Ikarion (II) *PA* 3062
IG ii² 2824.3f.; see the last entry.

COUNCIL AND ASSEMBLY

The secretary is found in IG ii² 231 and 233a:
Grammateus
ASPETOS son of [Dem]os[t]r[atos] of Kytherros (III) *PA* 2638

339

(i) IG ii² 231 is a decree from the eleventh day of the ninth prytany, of Hippothontis, granting proxeny to Phokinos, Nikandros and Dexippos, possibly Megarians:
Bouleutes epistates
ANDRO[K]L[ES] *PA* 852
Proposer
[DEMOSTHENES] son of De[m]o[sth]e[nes] of [Paiania] (III) *PA* 3597; *APF* 113ff.

(ii) IG ii² 232 is a probouleumatic decree (with a rider) honouring Aratos of Tenedos after praising the city itself:
Proposer
[PHILODEMOS] son of [Autokl]es of Eroiadai (X) *PA* 14488; *APF* 539

(iii) IG ii² 233 (Tod 175; Harding no. 97) is a decree from the eighth day of the prytany of Kekropis honouring Aratos and the Tenedians:
Bouleutes epistates
S--
Proposer
[KA]LLIKRATES son of Charopides of [Lamptrai] (I) *PA* 7946 = 7973 = 8213

(iv) IG ii² 234 is possibly in honour of the Chians.

(v) IG ii² 235 (Hansen, *GRBS* 1984, 138) is a probouleumatic proxeny decree for Apelles of Byzantion amended in the assembly:
Proposer
.... KR]ATES son of Athen--

A number of measures were passed this year:
Proposer
DEMOSTHENES son of Demosthenes of Paiania (III) *PA* 3597; *APF* 113ff.

(vi) There was his law reforming trierarchic arrangements: Dem. 18.102ff.;
(vii) Aisch. 3.55,222; Hypereides F 134; Lucian *Dem.* 36, 45. This survived a challenge; Hansen, *Sovereignty* no. 25. He was responsible for the war with Philip: Philochoros *FGH* 328 F 55 (Harding no. 95C). He brought about the
(viii) sending of forces to the north: Dem. 18.80; Plut. *Dem.* 17.2. He passed a
(ix) measure concerning the activities of the hieromnemon and pylagorai: Aisch. 3.125ff. This was after the pylagorai (see above) had reported to the assembly.

Plut. *Phok.* 14.3 tells of an angry assembly at which Phokion spoke, consequently being sent to the Hellespont.

339/8 (Ol. 110.2)

Archon
LYSIMACHIDES son of Lysimachos of Acharnai (VI) *PA* 9480; *APF* 357f.

FGH 255 (5); Diod. 16.82.1; Dion. *ad Amm.* 11 (Philochoros *FGH* 328 F 56a (Harding no. 96A)); *Dein.* 9; Diog. 4.2.14; IG ii² 1155a; 1457.22; 1462.[21]; 1533.18; 2493.12f.; 2833.[2] (*Agora* XV.41); [3133]; *Hesperia* 1934, 51 (38.5) (Meritt); 1937, 461 (9.2, 6) (Crosby: *Agora* XV.40); Suppl. 19.66ff. (Jameson); *AJPh* 1940, 358 (Schweigert).

Strategoi

PHOKION son of Phokos *PA* 15076; *APF* 559
Plut. *Phok.* 16.1ff. Probably in this year he was in the islands, whence he returned to engage in debate about terms with Philip.

?PROTOMACHOS
Hesychios *FGH* 390 F 1.31. He succeeded Chares and was successful against Thrakians, but the date may be doubted; see Jacoby's commentary.

CHARES son of Theochares of Angele (I:1) *PA* 15292; *APF* 568f.
PROXENOS son of Harmodios of Aphidna (IX) *PA* 12270; *APF* 478
Polyainos 4.2.8; *P.Ryl.* 490 II.24 (Chares); Deinarchos 1.74 (Proxenos). They were in command at Amphissa and deceived by Philip. See Wankel, *ZPE* 55 (1984), 47f. n. 18.

Taxiarchos

BOULAR[CHOS] son of Aristoboulos of Phlya (VII) *PA* 2912
IG ii² 1155a.2, b.2, 4, 7, 10.

Epistatai of Eleusis
Grammateus
-- son of Kleoboulos
See 340/39.

Hieromnemon
?PROTARCHOS
FD III, 5, 14 II.11; 21.8. He could well be Euboian.

Tamias at Delphi
THOUKYDIDES son of Kephisodotos
FD III, 5, 47.46f.

Priest of Asklepios
POLYXENOS (? of Sounion) (IV) cf. *PA* 12066
IG ii² 1533.19. See Ferguson, *Priests* 145.

Envoy
DEMOSTHENES son of Demosthenes of Paiania (III) *PA* 3597; *APF* 113ff.
Dem. 18.178ff., 211ff., 221, 237, 244; Aisch. 3.256; Deinarchos 1.16, 24; Diod. 16.85.1 (338/7). He was one of ten in negotiations with Thebes, perhaps on more than one visit (Deinarchos uses a plural).

COUNCIL AND ASSEMBLY

The secretary is found in SEG 16.52 and *AJPh* 1940, 358:
Grammateus
PHAIDROS son of [Me]idon of Cholleidai (IV)

(i) *AJPh* 1940, 358 (Schweigert) is a prytany decree from the second prytany, of Akamantis, restored to Boedromion 18:
Bouleutes epistates
. . . . .¹¹. . . . . son of [Ar]istippos

(ii) SEG 16.52 is a fragment of a probouleumatic decree from the thirty-second day of the tenth prytany, of Pandionis:
Bouleutes epistates
KALLIAS (? son of [Ka]lliklei[des]) of Phrearrhioi (IV) = ?*PA* 7896
Proposer
[TEL]EMACHOS son of Th[ea]ngelos of Acharnai (VI) = *PA* 13562

(iii) IG ii² 1155 contains decrees of the boule and the tribesmen honouring members of the tribe Kekropis for military achievements.

We hear of assembly meetings at which Demosthenes crossed swords with Ameiniades (Aisch. 3.130) and Phokion (Plut. *Phok.* 16) and, of course, he spoke at other assemblies (Dem. 18.191) and was the major voice against peace with Philip (Aisch. 3.149f.). An extended account is Dem. 18.169ff.

(iv) The news that Elatea had been taken came to the prytaneis; the next day the boule met and at an assembly there was a proposal for mobilization, an advance to Eleusis and the sending of envoys to Thebes:
Proposer
DEMOSTHENES son of Demosthenes of Paiania (III) *PA* 3597; *APF* 113ff.

(v) He also brought about the alliance with Thebes (also Aisch. 3.141ff. and in
(vi) general Diod. 16.84; Plut. *Dem.* 17f.) and with other states. He secured the
(vii) hiring of mercenaries to the Amphissans over Aischines' protests (Aisch.
(viii) 3.146). Philochoros *FGH* 328 F 56a (Harding no. 96A) records Demosthenes' decree that all monies be used for military purposes, i.e. that excess revenues go the stratiotic fund.

(ix) An honorary decree in praise of Demosthenes survived a challenge (Dem. 18.222ff., 249; Plut. *Mor.* 846a; Hansen, *Sovereignty* no. 26):
Proposers
DEMOMELES son of Demon of Paiania (III) *PA* 3554; *APF* 116
HYPEREIDES son of Glaukippos of Kollytos (II) *PA* 13912; *APF* 517ff.

338/7 (Ol. 110.3)

Archon
CHAIRONDAS son of Hegemon *PA* 15279
Dem. 18.54,84; Aisch. 3.27; Demetrios *FGH* 228 F 36; *FGH* 255 (5); Diod.

16.84.1; Dion. *Isok.* 1; *Dein.* 9; Plut. *Dem.* 24.2, *Mor.* 837e, 842f; IG ii²
[237] (Tod 178; Osborne D 16; SEG 31.76; Harding no. 100); 238a.[3];
1496.18; 1522.10; 1524.92, 96; 1533.29; 1627.428; 1628.396, 569; 1629.
915, 1045; 1631.[10]; 3023.5; *Hesperia* 1934, 51 (38.11); 65 (57) (Meritt:
but for other suggestions see Dow and Travis, *Hesperia* 1943, 163f.;
Finley, *Land and Credit* 161 no. 151 and p. 193; cf. Millett, *Opus* 1982,
221).

Strategoi
CHARES son of Theochares of Angele (III) *PA* 15292; *APF* 568f.
LYSIKLES *PA* 9422
Diod. 16.85.2, 88.1f. (Lysikles); Plut. *Mor.* 843d; Polyainos 4.2.8
(Chares); Stobaios *Flor.* 54.47 (Chares). They were generals in Boiotia and
at Chaironeia. Lysikles was condemned.

STRATOKLES (? of Lakiadai) (VI) *PA* 12931 = ?12941
Aisch. 3.143; Polyainos 4.2.2. He was general at Chaironeia; see Roberts,
Klio 1982, 367f. n. 5; Wankel, *ZPE* 55 (1984), 48. For identification see
Davies, *Wealth* 165. Hansen, *GRBS* 1983, 175, makes Aischines refer to
339/8.

. . .⁶. . . T-- of tribe VI
Bradeen, *Hesperia* 1964, 55ff. (*Agora* XVII.25). One would be tempted to
fill this out as Stratokles, whatever the space indicated, but Wankel (*ZPE*
55 (1984), 49) is hesitant and Stratokles is not reported to have died.

?NAUSIKLES son of Klearchos of Oe (VI) *PA* 10552; *APF* 396ff.
Wankel, *ZPE* 55 (1984), 46, thinks he was general because he is mentioned
as being crowned in the same passage (Dem. 18.114) as Charidemos and
Diotimos. He also believes one of these will have been at Chaironeia,
perhaps Nausikles.

CHARIDEMOS son of Philoxenos of Acharnai (VI) *PA* 15380; *APF* 569ff.
Dem. 18.114,116; Plut. *Phok.* 16.3; IG ii² 1496.[28ff.]. He was in charge
after Chaironeia, evidently in command of the hoplites, and joined in
success by Diotimos. See Gehrke, *Phokion* 61 and n. 52.

DIOTIMOS son of Diopeithes of Euonymon (I) *PA* 4384; *APF* 163f.
Dem. 18.114,116; IG ii² 1496.[22]; 1628.397; 1629.916; 1631.[11]. He was
general of the hippeis to Salamis. See above on Charidemos.

PHOKION son of Phokos *PA* 15076; *APF* 559
Plut. *Phok.* 16.3ff. We may accept that he was general when, Plutarch says,
he was entrusted with the city after Chaironeia. Gehrke, *Phokion* 61ff.,
thinks he replaced someone.

Tamias of stratiotic fund
KALLIAS son of Habron of Bate (II) *PA* 7856; *APF* 270
Plut. *Mor.* 842f. See Develin, *ZPE* 57 (1984), 135.

Sitones
DEMOSTHENES son of Demosthenes of Paiania (III) *PA* 3597; *APF* 113ff.
Dem. 18.248f.; Plut. *Mor.* 845f; cf. ?Aisch. 3.159; Deinarchos 1.80.
Chosen after Chaironeia, he came under attack for embezzlement.

Epistatai of Eleusis
  Grammateus
  -- son of Kleoboulos
See 340/39.

Hieromnemon
At *FD* III, 5, 47 1.34, 11.25 letters exist, but there is no restoration.

Priest of Asklepios
TEISIAS (? of Kephale) (V)
IG ii² 1533.29 (SEG 30.163). See Ferguson, *Priests* 145.

Envoys
DEMADES son of Demeas of Paiania (III) *PA* 3263; *APF* 99ff.
Dem. 18.285; Demades *Twelve Years* 9; Diod. 16.87; Suda *s.v.* Δημάδης.
His precise role in peace negotiations is unclear, but the Suda says he was
sent as envoy to Philip after Chaironeia on the matter of captives.

DEMOSTHENES son of Demosthenes of Paiania (III) *PA* 3597; *APF* 113ff.
Deinarchos 1.80. The circumstances are unclear, but he may have been
after help for Athens (but see *APF* 137).

AISCHINES son of Atrometos of Kothokidai (VI) *PA* 354; *APF* 545ff.
Dem. 18.282ff.; Aisch. 3.227. He went to negotiate with Philip.

?HYPEREIDES son of Glaukippos of Kollytos (II) *PA* 13912; *APF* 517ff.
Hypereides F 28. See Hansen, *GRBS* 1983, 177.

COUNCIL AND ASSEMBLY

The secretary is to be found in IG ii² 237 and 238; see Stamires, *Hesperia*
1957, 243 (SEG 17.24, 25); Alessandri, *ASNP* 1982, 62:
Grammateus
PHILIPPOS son of Antiph[emos] of [Eiresidai] (V) *PA* 14381

(i) IG ii² 236 (Tod 177; SEG 31.75; Harding no. 99) concerns the treaty with
Philip.

(ii) IG ii² 237 (Tod 178; Osborne D 16; SEG 31.76; Schwenk no. 1; Harding
no. 100) is a decree of the tenth prytany (Pečírka, *Enktesis* 49ff.), of
Pandionis, seemingly on the sixth day of the prytany, the penultimate day
of Thargelion (cf. Aisch. 3.27), honouring the Akarnanians and reaffirming as citizens Phormion and Karphinas:
Bouleutes epistates
. . . .⁸. . . . of Erchia (II)

Proposer

[HEGE]SIPPOS [son of Hegesias] of [Sounion] (IV) *PA* 6351; *APF* 209f.

(iii) IG ii² 238 (Schwenk no. 2) is a proxeny decree from the tenth prytany also for Drakontides and Hegesias of Andros.

A temporal connexion with the foregoing is found through Aisch. 3.27, where we learn that on the penultimate day of Thargelion there was a
(iv) motion that on Skirophorion 2 and 3 tribal assemblies should choose epimeletai and tamiai for work on the walls:

Proposer

DEMOSTHENES son of Demosthenes of Paiania (III) *PA* 3597; *APF* 113ff.
(v) Demosthenes was also responsible for other measures: for guard posts,
(vi) moats and fortifications (Dem. 18.248); for partial demobilisation and the
(vii) sending of embassies (Deinarchos 1.78ff.); probably on the powers of the
(viii) Areopagos (Deinarchos 1.62; Hansen, *GRBS* 1983, 164). Aischines also claims (3.159) that some decrees which stemmed from Demosthenes had another's name on them:

Proposer

NAUSIKLES son of Klearchos of Oe (VI) *PA* 10552; *APF* 396ff.

(ix) The same man proposed peace with and honours to Philip (Dem. 18.285;
(x) Demades *Twelve Years* 9; Diod. 16.87.3; Osborne T 68) and Athens' participation in common peace and the congress of Greek states, on which subject Phokion spoke (Plut. *Dem.* 16.4f.; Suda *s.v. Δημάδης*):

Proposer

DEMADES son of Demeas of Paiania (III) *PA* 3263; *APF* 99ff.

(xi) There was a decree, which was passed, survived a challenge, but never came into effect due to circumstances, to enfranchise *atimoi*, metics and slaves and send women, children and sacred objects to safety; Dem. 26.11; Lykourgos 1.16, 41; Hypereides FF 32, 33; Plut. *Mor.* 849a; Hansen, *Sovereignty* no. 27 (Osborne T 67):

Proposer and bouleutes

HYPEREIDES son of Glaukippos of Kollytos (II) *PA* 13912; *APF* 517ff. That he was councillor comes from Lucian *Parasit.* 42, where he is associated with
LYKOURGOS son of Lykophron of Boutadai (VI) *PA* 9251; *APF* 348ff.
(xii) The passage actually speaks of them putting together little motions and probouleumata.

Dem. 18.285 tells how he was appointed to speak over the dead despite the attacks of Aischines and Pythokles. Plut. *Mor* 803d records that Demokrates spoke at an assembly after the defeat.

Agora xv.39 is dated *c.* 340, but the gentleman now restored as secretary for this year appears at the bottom of this inscription and only restoration makes him the secretary of the council and demos, perhaps the position

more to be expected here, but economy suggests that we have here
bouleutai of tribe v Akamantis for this year:
Prospalta?
-- son of --nos
-- son of [Ch]airestrat[os]
-- son of [? Th]eophantos
--s son of Lysanias
. . . . P]EITHES son of Archinos
Thorikos
[SM]IKYTHOS son of Epiteles
[TH]OUKRITIDES son of Kallias = *PA* 7257; *APF* 272
DIONYSIOS son of Kalliades
[O]IAX son of Pedalion
[E]UKLEIDES son of Euthias
[AN]TIGENES son of Xenonides
Poros
[M]NESIKLES son of Pythokles
[TH]RASON son of Nikostratos
[ST]RATOS son of Melanopos

337/6 (Ol. 110.4)

Archon
PHRYNICHOS *PA* 15002
FGH 255 (5); Diod. 16.89.1; Dion. *Dein.* 9; IG ii² 239 (Tod 180); 240 (Tod
181; SEG 31.77); [241]; 242; 243; [276] (*Hesperia* 1940, 342 (Schweigert));
1255.3 (Schwenk no. 13); 1522.14, 16 (but see Linders, *Artemis* 26);
1524.93, 97f., 102; 1526.20; 1623.295; 2834; 4594; SEG 12.87 (Harding
no. 101); *Hesperia* 1934, 113 (178.[5]) (Meritt = 1943, 52ff. (12)); 1938, 292
([19]) (Schweigert); 1940, 325 (35) (Schweigert).

Strategos
DIOTIMOS son of Diopeithes of Euonymon (I) *PA* 4384; *APF* 163f.
It has been pointed out to me that IG ii² 1623.200ff. must give him a
generalship in this year, since Stesileides got Euphrainousa through a
decree of the boule proposed by Diophantos, who was on the council this
year (IG ii² 243).

Theoric commissioner
DEMOSTHENES son of Demosthenes of Paiania (III) *PA* 3597; *APF* 113ff.
Aisch. 3.24ff.; Dem. 18.113.

Teichopoios or epimeletes of walls
DEMOSTHENES son of Demosthenes of Paiania (III) *PA* 3597; *APF* 113ff.
Aisch. 3.14,17,23ff.; Dem. 18.113,118; Plut. *Mor.* 845f, 851a; schol. Aisch.

3.13, 17. See Cawkwell, *JHS* 1963, 56f., for him as theoric commissioner and teichopoios. He was selected in the latter role by his tribe (Aisch. 3.31).

Epistatai of Eleusis
  Grammateus
  -- son of Kleoboulos
See 340/39.

Priest of Asklepios
THEOPHA[NES] of Acharnai (VI) *PA* 7077
IG ii² 304 + 604.17ff. (SEG 18.11; Schwenk no. 14).

COUNCIL AND ASSEMBLY

The secretary is found or correctly restored in IG ii² 239, 240, 241, 242, 243, SEG 12.87, *Hesperia* 1938, 292 (19), 1940, 325 (35):
Grammateus
CHAIRESTRATOS son of Ameinias of Acharnai (VI) *PA* 15159

(i) IG ii² 239 (Tod 180) is a decree from the sixth prytany, of Akamantis, honouring Alkimachos (and Antipatros?) of Makedon (with proxeny?). This was dated to the fifth day of the prytany, Gamelion 7 (Schweigert, *Hesperia* 1940, 327; SEG 21.267), but the seventh of the month is the day of Apollo (Mikalson, *Calendar* 190) and Hansen, *GRBS* 1982, 342 (*Ecclesia* 94), tried Gamelion 5; Schwenk no. 4 has returned to Gamelion 10, also changing no.ix below, which Schweigert took to be from the same day as 239.

(ii) IG ii² 240 (Tod 181; SEG 31.77; Schwenk no. 7) is a proxeny decree from the tenth prytany, of Pandionis:
Bouleutes epistates
ANTIPHANES of Euonymon (I) *PA* 1232
Proposer
[D]E[MADES] son of [D]emeas of Paiania (III) *PA* 3263; *APF* 99ff.

(iii) IG ii² 241 (Schwenk no. 8) is the beginning of a decree from the same day and with the same personnel as the last one.

(iv) IG ii² 242 (Schwenk no. 10) is a probouleumatic decree from the last day of the same prytany:
Bouleutes epistates
[EU]THYKRATES (son of Drakontides) [of Aphidna] (IX) *PA* 5601
Proposer
[DIOPHANTOS] son of [Phrasikl]eides of Myrrhinous (III) *PA* 4435; *APF* 166

(v) IG ii² 243 (Schwenk no. 11) will be a probouleumatic decree of the same day, with the same personnel, honouring Kalliteles of Kydantidai.

(vi) The secretary of this year was restored in IG ii² 276 by Schweigert, *Hesperia* 1940, 342, though it could be around 342 (Hansen, *GRBS* 1983, 171; but see *GRBS* 1984, 138); it is Schwenk no. 12 and is a probouleumatic decree with a rider granting isoteleia to Asklepiodoros, restored to the same day as nos. iv and v above:

Bouleutes epistates
[EUTHY]KRATES (son of Drakontides) [of Aphidna] (IX) *PA* 5601
Proposers
-- of Potamos (IV)
KEPHISOPHON son of Kallibios of Paiania (III) *PA* 8417; *APF* 149

(vii) IG ii² 304 + 604 (SEG 18.11) comprise an honorific decree (for two doctors? – Schwenk no. 14).

(viii) *Hesperia* 1938, 292 (19) (Schweigert; Schwenk no. 9), honours the grammateus and is restored to the twenty-second day of the tenth prytany (of Pandionis), Skirophorion 16.

(ix) *Hesperia* 1940, 325 (35) (Schweigert), concerns Lemnos; on the dating see above no. i; Schwenk no. 5 offers the fifth day of the eighth prytany, Elaphebolion 18:

Bouleutes epistates
ERG--
Proposer
[D]EMAD[ES] son of [Demeas of Paiania] (III) *PA* 3263; *APF* 99ff.

(x) IG ii² 1623.210ff. mentions a decree of the council concerning trierarchy, which should be of this year:

Proposer
DIOPHANTOS (son of Phrasikleides) of Myrrhinous (III) *PA* 4435; *APF* 166

(xi) This is, I think, the likeliest year for the proposal that Euthykrates of Olynthos be given proxenia, which was challenged as unconstitutional, the result being unknown; Hypereides F 76; Suda *s.v.* Δημάδης; Hansen, *Sovereignty* no. 28:

Proposer
DEMADES son of Demeas of Paiania (III) *PA* 3264; *APF* 99ff.

(xii) An honorary decree was passed for Demosthenes, which was challenged, but the case was not tried until 330/29; Aisch. 3; Dem. 18; Plut. *Mor.* 846a; schol. Aisch. 2.1; hyp. Aisch. 3; Libanius hyp. Dem. 18; hyp. ii Dem.18; Harpokration *s.v.* Κτησιφῶν; Suda and Hesychios *s.v.* Αἰσχίνης; Hansen, *Sovereignty* no. 30:

Proposer
KTESIPHON *PA* 8894

Plut. *Phok.* 16.5 reports on Phokion's comments when the Athenians had to decide on sending triremes and cavalry to Philip.

Nomothetai

(xiii) IG ii² 244 is a law for the repair of walls, which Schwenk no. 3 puts in 338/7, which could be correct:

Proposer
[?KEPHISOPHON son of Kephalion] of Aphidna (IX) ?*PA* 8410; *APF* 292f.

(xiv) SEG 12.87 (Harding no. 101; Schwenk no. 6) is a law against tyranny from the ninth prytany, of Leontis:

Epistates
MENESTRATOS of Aixone (VII)
Proposer
EUKRATES son of Aristotimos of Peiraieus (VIII) *PA* 5762

APPENDIX

Paredroi of archon
ARISTOPHON son of Aristophanes of Azenia (VIII) *PA* 2108; *APF* 64ff.
Aisch. 1.158 – to the eponymous archon sometime before 343.

?[ATHE]NODOROS son of [Arist]oboulos of Phrearrhioi (IV)
?[SMIK]YTHOS son of Hippodamas of Kephisia (I)
Platon 1959, 221f. (3.4f.) (Oikonomides). The editor restored them as proedroi, but the suggestion that they were paredroi is on the cards at the Institute for Advanced Study at Princeton.

Strategoi
A[UTOKLES?]
IG ii² 264.17f. But this may not belong in this period; see below.

PHOKION son of Phokos *PA* 15076; *APF* 559
See the appendix to Section VII.

Hipparchos to Lemnos
PHEIDON of Thria (VI) *PA* 14178
SEG 30.114.

Phylarchoi
?ANACHARSIS son of Me-- (? of Kydathenaion) (III) *PA* 822
IG ii² 3135; 3136. For the deme see Davies, *Wealth* 153.

PHEIDON of Thria (VI) *PA* 14178
Mnesimachos F 4 (Edmonds). See Kroll and Mitchel, *Hesperia* 1980, 90f. This is dated to the 350s or 340s by Davies, *Wealth* 154.

Peripolarchos
?XENOKLES of Perithoidai (VI)
SEG 30.114.

Financial?
KEPHISOPHON son of Kallibios of Paiania (III) *PA* 8417; *APF* 149

At Dem. 19.293 we hear of an indictment in connexion with sacred money, this before 343. I do not share the confidence of *APF* that he was tamias, though he may have been in a position such as to receive money from the tamiai.

Theoric commission?

APHOBETOS son of Atrometos of Kothokidai (VI) *PA* 2775; *APF* 545
Aisch. 2.149 speaks of his brother as having been chosen ἐπὶ τὴν κοινὴν διοίκησιν; see Cawkwell, *JHS* 1963, 54. Hansen, *GRBS* 1983, 162, assumes the allusion is to election as treasurer (before 343).

Epimeletai of emporion
Grammateus

EUTHYPHEMOS *PA* 5660
Dem. 58.8 – in the 340s.

Religious officials

MEIDIAS son of Kephisodoros of Anagyrous (I) *PA* 9719; *APF* 386f.
Dem. 21.171 records that before 347 he was epimeletes of the mysteries, hieropoios, boönes and more. Dem. 21.15 indicates that he failed to be chosen epimeletes of the Dionysia in 349/8 (cf. *APF* 136 (G)).

DEMOSTHENES son of Demosthenes of Paiania (III) *PA* 3597; *APF* 113ff.
Dem. 21.114f. Before 347 he had been hieropoios, archetheoros to Nemean Zeus and hieropoios to the Eumenides.

Amphiktyons to Delos

-- of Phlya (VII)
?APELL--
Insc. Délos 104–15.2 (IG ii² 1650).

Naopoios to Delphi

KLEINOMACHOS son of Anthemokritos of Oion (IV or VIII) = *PA* 8516
FD III, 5, 91.2.

Priest of Asklepios

?TIMON *PA* 13837
IG ii² 4396. Dated ?335/4 at Pritchett and Meritt, *Chronology* 75, but on p. 80 it is noted that there is no clue but letter forms to the date.

Epimeletai on Lemnos

THEOPHILOS son of Meliton of Alopeke (X) *PA* 7126
IG xii 8.4.9f. (Myrine).

SA[URI]AS
IG xii 8.5.6 (Hephaistia).

Epimeletes of tribe IX Aiantis

NIKODEMOS son of Aristomenes of Oinoe
Hesperia 1936, 402 (10.159ff., 178) (Meritt) – before 346/5.

Demarchoi
GNATHIS (son of Timokedes) of Eleusis (VIII) *PA* 3048
IG ii² 1186.19.

A[RCHI]AS of Halai (II) = *PA* 2459
AE 1925–6, 168ff., 11f., 18. For identity see Whitehead, *Demes* no. 17.

ANTIPHILOS of Halimous (IV) *PA* 1266
Dem. 57.26, 60. Before 346/5.

EUXITHEOS son of Thoukritos of Halimous (IV) *PA* 5902; *APF* 93ff.
Dem. 57.63f. and passim. Before 346/5. From Dem. 57.25f. we hear that
his father Thoukritos had held sortitive deme offices.

. . . .¹⁰. . . . of Ikarion (II)
IG ii² 1179.3.

EUTHIPPOS of Teithras (II)
SEG 24.151.

Tamiai and synegoroi
So designated are those chosen by the boule and demos named in IG ii²
1251, dated after the middle of the century:
ANDROKYDES (son of Philagros) of Kydathenaion (III) *PA* 876
[N]IKERATOS *PA* 10731
[HE]GESIAS of L-- *PA* 6325
[PHI]LEAS son of Antiphon
ARISTEID[ES] *PA* 1682
[K]TESIAS
ARCHIPPOS
.KLE--
.O--
.T--S
. . . M--
--ILONIKES?
--IPPOS of Kephale (V)
--OSTRATOS of Poros (V)
--DOROS of Acharnai (VI)
--OKRATES of Halai (II or VII)
--ORT--
--OMA--
-- of Eleusis (VIII)
--s of Aphidna (IX)

Envoys
APHOBETOS son of Atrometos of Kothokidai (VI) *PA* 2775; *APF* 545
Aisch. 2.149. He went to Persia sometime before 343.

TIMARCHOS son of Arizelos of Sphettos (V) *PA* 13636
Aisch. 1.120. He served on a number of embassies before 346/5.

PHOKION son of Phokos *PA* 15076; *APF* 559
Nepos *Phoc.* 1.3. He went at some time as envoy to Philip. Gehrke, *Phokion* 64 and n. 64, puts this in 338/7, but I do not share his confidence.

Note: We have notices that seem unacceptable that in 339/8 Aristotle was on a embassy to Philip on behalf of Athens (Diog. 5.2) and that Xenokrates also went to Philip before 337 (Diog. 4.8f.).

Oath takers
In IG ii² 280.4ff. there is the following list in the matter of a treaty:
--LES son of Sopo[lis]
-- of Aigilia (x)
-- of Anaphlystos (x)
M--
-- son of --es of Kephisia (I)
--EON son of Per--
--S son of Dikaia-- or DIKAIA--
--TEL--
The last name is as read by D.M. Lewis.

Unknown
Hesperia 1968, 283f. (20) (Meritt: SEG 25.185), is a list of officials with only demotics surviving, showing five from Lamptrai (I), one from Prospalta (v), one from Halai (II or VII) and others unidentifiable.

IG ii² 1701 lists a college from after mid-century:
-- son of [--n]es of Lamptrai (I)
-- of Araphen (II)
-- son of --nides of Paiania (III)
-- son of --okles of Kettos (IV)
-- of Kerameis (v)
-- son of --tos of Acharnai (VI)
-- of Pithos (VII)
-- of Eleusis (VIII)
-- son of --es of Rhamnous (IX)
-- of Pallene (x)

IG ii² 2825 records a college from mid-century:
ARCHENEOS son of Archemachos of Anagyrous (I) *PA* 2366
MISGOLAS son of Naukrates of Kollytos (II) *PA* 10225
KALLIKRATIDES son of Kallikrates of Steiria (III) *PA* 7988
NIKESION son of Sosistratos of Sounion (IV) *PA* 10752
LYSANIAS son of Lysistratos of Thorikos (v) *PA* 9314
MNESISTRATOS son of Mnesimachos of Acharnai (VI) *PA* 10369
EUTHYDOMOS son of Demetrios of Melite (VII) *PA* 5573
EXEKESTOS son of Exekias of Anakaia (VIII) *PA* 4730
BOUTHEROS son of Dionysios of Marathon (IX) *PA* 2903

EUTHIPPOS son of Euthias of Pallene (x) *PA* 5499
Grammateus
CHAIRESTRATOS son of Phanostratos of Kephisia (I) *PA* 15164; *NPA* 169; *APF* 564
Hypogrammateus
IOPHON son of Sophokles of Kolonos (II) *PA* 7585

IG ii² 291 also records ten men, but not selected one per tribe and evidently without secretary – could they have been envoys? Davies, *APF* 219 n. 1, by pondering the restoration of the tenth man as Kallippos of Aixone (*PA* 8065), would create a date prior to 357, but I would prefer circumspection:
-- of Lamptrai (I)
--MOS of Hagnous (V)
--O]N of Lamptrai (I)
--ES of Lamptrai (I)
[THEMIST]OKLES of Phrearrhioi (IV) *PA* 6666; *APF* 219
--O]N of Trikorynthos (IX)
[TIMAS]ITHEOS (? son of Demainetos) of Kerameis (V) ?*PA* 13641 or 13640; *APF* 102f.
--LOS Marathon (IX)
--LES of Kephale (V)
--IP[P]OS of Aixone (VII)

IG ii² 1702 retains eight names in tribal order, dated after 350. As this comes from Eleusis, perhaps the board had something to do with matters there; D.M. Lewis suggests that in line 2 the restoration [ἱερο]ποιοί δ[is attractive:
SOTES of Lamptrai (I) *PA* 13399
SKAPHON of Philaidai (II) *PA* 12725 = ?12724
ELPINES (son of Elpinikos) of Probalinthos (III) *PA* 4676
HAGNOTHEOS of Kettos (IV) *PA* 153
PHILOTHEROS of Hagnous (V) *PA* 14501
LYSISTRATOS of Phyle (VI) *PA* 9629
LYSISTRATOS (? son of Kephisodoros) of Melite (VII) *PA* 9619; *APF* 425
[CHA]ROPINOS of Dekeleia (VIII) *PA* 15535

IG ii² 1703, tentatively dated to the fourth century, may be assigned to the present period if we compare Philistides with the son of Philistides who was involved in levying the metic tax about 342/1 (*Hesperia* 1936, 401 (10.125, 147) (Meritt)) and Lysias with the secretary of 356/5:
[?CHAIRESTR]ATOS son of Chai--
DEMANTHES son of Tima-- (? of Marathon) (IX) *PA* 3280 = ?3282; *APF* 106
PHILISTIDES son of Phi[l--] *PA* 14437
Grammateus
LYSIAS son of L-- *PA* 9356

Hypogrammateus
?L--

Note: Euboulos seems to have been active with others in the early years of this period (Dem. 3.29 and schol.), but in what capacity I hesitate to say. In general see Cawkwell, *JHS* 1963, 47ff.

COUNCIL AND ASSEMBLY

(i) IG ii² 185 and 251 are dated *c.* 350 by Osborne D 18 and 19 and I mention
(ii) them because they look forward respectively to the prytanies of Oineis and Pandionis.

(iii) IG ii² 226 (Osborne D 14) is a probouleumatic decree granting citizenship to Arybbas of Molossia, dated around 342.

(iv) IG ii² 253 is an honorific decree:
Proposer
-- son of --es of Sphettos (v)
On the latter see Hansen, *GRBS* 1984, 138

(v) IG ii² 263 could be of 347/6:
Bouleutes epistates
[KL]EAR[CHOS]
Proposer
-- of Kedoi (I), Kerameis (v) or Xypete (VII)

(vi) IG ii² 264 honours an Iatrokles, but D.M. Lewis informs me that he does not think it has anything to do with the Athenian Iatrokles and doubts that it belongs to this period.

(vii) IG ii² 289 (SEG 23.60; 32.93) is a probouleumatic proxeny decree with a rider:
Proposer
-- son of --os or --es of Azenia (VIII)
On the latter see Hansen, *GRBS* 1984, 138.

(viii) SEG 19.53 seems to be an honorary decree dated to the middle of the century and restored to produce the following:
Proposer
LEOS--
If this is correct, available known names are Leosthenes and Leostratos.

Dem. 18.70, 75 mentions a number of proposers of decrees concerning Philip and events in the north which must be dated 346–340:
Proposers
(ix) EUBOULOS son of Spintharos of Probalinthos (III) *PA* 5369
(x)(xi) ARISTOPHON son of Aristophanes of Azenia (VIII) *PA* 2108; *APF* 64ff.
(xii) DIOPEITHES son of Diopeithes of Sphettos (v) *PA* 4328; *APF* 160

(xiii) HEGESIPPOS son of Hegesias of Sounion (IV) *PA* 6351; *APF* 209f.
(xiv) PHILOKRATES son of Pythodoros of Hagnous (V) *PA* 14599 = 14576
(xv) KEPHISOPHON son of Kallibios of Paiania (III) *PA* 8417; *APF* 149

Two proposals of unknown content were successfully challenged as unconstitutional before 347 (Dem. 21.182; Hansen, *Sovereignty* nos. 19, 20):
Proposers
(xvi) SKITON
(xvii) SMIKROS

Two decrees concerning the Ainians before 342 were also challenged (Dem. 58.36ff.,43; Hansen, *Sovereignty* nos. 21, 22):
Proposers
(xviii) THOUKYDIDES *PA* 7265
(xix) DEMOSTHENES son of Demosthenes of Paiania (III) *PA* 3597; *APF* 113ff.

(xx) Likewise a decree concerning the Tenedians was challenged before 342 (Dem. 58.35; Hansen, *Sovereignty* no. 24):
Proposer
ANTIMEDON *PA* 1134

(xxi) The father of Epichares who proposed an honorary decree for Charidemos (Dem. 58.30ff.), correctly designated at Hansen, *Sovereignty* no. 23, appears as Epichares himself in Hansen, *GRBS* 1983, 166; *GRBS* 1984, 133.

(xxii) There was a decree protecting merchants passed before 342 (Dem. 58.53, 56):
Proposer
MOIROKLES (? son of Euthydemos of Eleusis (VIII)) *PA* 10400 = ?10401
For the patronymic and demotic cf. PA 5535; IG ii² 1191.

(xxiii) Two decrees of unknown content were successfully challenged as uncon-
(xxiv) stitutional before 336 (Hypereides 2.11):
Proposer
PHILIPPIDES *PA* 14351

(xxv) There is one said to have moved many decrees for others (Dem. 59.43):
Proposer
STEPHANOS son of Antidorides of Eroiadai (VIII or X) *PA* 12887

For Timarchos see the appendix to Section VII.

As for speakers in the assembly, Aisch. 1.64 tells of Hegesandros attacking Aristophon; we may include Meidias and Phokion from Section VII.

Nomothetai
(xxvi) A law restricting action in seizure of debtors' property on certain festive days was passed before 350 (Dem. 21.10):
Proposer
EUEGOROS (son of Philoinos of Paiania) (III) *PA* 5466; *APF* 360

As we come now to the boule, we may begin with the tamias who seems to be evidenced at Dem. 58.15 (τὰ κοινὰ διοικήσας):
Tamias of tribe
THEOKRINES of Hybadai (IV) *PA* 6946

Agora xv.18, augmented by SEG 28.150, gives bouleutai of tribe VII Kekropis from around the middle of the century:
Xypete
-- son of Antiphanes *PA* 1212
[?PHRY]NICHOS son of Aristokleides = *PA* 1156
PHILON son of Kleinias *PA* 14814
Sypalettos
AUTOBOULOS son of Aut[osophos] *PA* 2705 + Add.
DIOGE[N]E[S] son of Euthy[boulos ?]
Athmonon
-- son of --on
--AS son of Andron
[?MEID]ONIDES son of Meidon
[KAL]LIAS son of Kallias
. . . OPEITHES son of Demeas
Trinemeia
[CHAR]MYLOS son of Kallisth[e]nes ?*PA* 15524 + 8106 (IG ii² 1641 A.17, 23)

SEG 28,149 gives bouleutai of tribe VI Oineis around 350:
Perithoidai
XENOK[LES]
CHARM--
HABRON[--?]
Kothokidai
ARISTO--
THEOGEN[ES]

Agora xv.20 gives bouleutai dated *c.* 360–340, probably in this period:
Oineis (VI)
-- son of Andros[then]es *PA* 903

Kekropis (VII)
Melite
--ES son of Antikles *PA* 1062, *APF* 399
[ATHE]NODOROS son of De-- *PA* 264; *APF* 221
P[AN ?]TAINOS son of Euthy--
-- son of Demophilos *PA* 3667
[Xypete]? or [Pithos] (SEG 33.153)
AISCHRAI[OS] *PA* 372
THOUG[ENES?]
E--

Hippothontis (VIII)
Azenia
ARIST[O]MEDES son of Aristophon *PA* 2013 + Add.; *APF* 65f.
SPOUDIAS son of Philistides *PA* 12866
Anakaia
EX[E]K[IA]S son of Exe[kestos?] *PA* 4732
ANDROKLEID[ES] *PA* 848
[A]IS[CH]YLION son of Epichar-- *PA* 430
Dekeleia
[? ANTI]KLES son of Antiphan--
[K]ALLISTHENES son of Pro-- *PA* 8100
[M]EIDON son of Meidias *PA* 8269
[K]ALLAISCHRIDES *PA* 7750
Elaious
[KAL]LITELES son of Kal-- *PA* 8207
Hamaxanteia
[AIN]EAS son of Phyg--
[?DION]YSIO[S] *PA* 4146
But the latter is restored at SEG 28.145 as [Acherdo]usio[i]; it was not a
name.

Agora XV.21 gives bouleutai of tribe I Erechtheis around 350:
Lamptrai
KOMEAS
[BL]EPAIOS (son of Sokles) *PA* 2876
. . ⁵ . . IOS
. . . . OK--

Agora XV.22 gives bouleutai of tribe X Antiochis around the middle of the
century (on the first deme see Stanton, *ABSA* 1984, 306):
Kolonai
. . . . MEN[ES]
[EUPH]ANES son of Eu--
[IA]SIDEMOS son of Iasi[demos]
Thorai
PHORMION son of Chairephan[es]
KALLIKLES son of Gniphon
PROTOMACHOS son of Chion
ONETOR son of Mene--
Eroiadai
[PHI]LODEM[OS] son of [Autokles] *PA* 14488; *APF* 539

Agora XV.23 gives bouleutai from tribe IV Leontis from mid-century, along
with a secretary of the boule:
--K]RATES
--TIADES
--RRHIS?

Phrearrhioi
[LY]SANIAS son of Lysikrates *PA* 9328
[S]OSTRATOS son of Olympiodoros *PA* 13374 = 13373; *APF* 499
[D]IOGNIS *PA* 3880
KALLIADES *PA* 7803
DIAKRITOS son of Dieuches *PA* 3748
[?APOL]LONIDES
--ES
?
THEOGEN[ES] son of Stibon *PA* 6695
STIBON son of Kletos *PA* 12908
Grammateus of boule
A[N]TIMENES of Alopeke (x) *PA* 1139

The following, crowned about the middle of the century, was probably a bouleutes; *Agora* XV.24:
[CHA]RINOS son of Charon[ides] of [Euonymon] (1) *PA* 15440

Agora XV.29 gives bouleutai of tribe I Erechtheis:
. . . IOS son of T--
Euonymon
.ROUSELOS
[A]RESIAS son of Th--

Agora XV.31 gives bouleutai of tribe VII Kekropis after mid-century:
Xypete
--NOS son of Thrasyme[des]
--TOS son of Pausides
--LEOS son of Hippon
--IOS son of Androkl--
--ES son of Philistides
--ES son of Aristaios
-- son of [E]uxitheos
Halai
--S son of Nikodemos
-- son of --ysippos
-- son of --thykl--
-- son of [Ast]yphilos cf. *PA* 2662-2664
-- son of --sias
-- son of --on

Agora XV.32 gives us bouleutai of tribe III Pandionis from after mid-century (the prosopography is in fact ambiguous and it could well be in this period), as well as a secretary of boule and demos:
Paiania
?ANTH-- son of --s
--OS son of Demeas cf. *PA* 3323; *APF* 105

D[IPHIL]IDES son of [Di]philides *PA* 4660
NIKIAS son of Diophanes *PA* 10819
THOUKLES son of Theogenes *PA* 6943
CHAIRESTRATOS son of Chairestratos *PA* 15167; *APF* 574
EKPHANTOS son of Hagnotheos *PA* 4661
HERMOGENES son of Epizelos *PA* 5128
PHILOCHARES son of Philokydes *PA* 14778; *APF* 544
CHARES son of Charitaios *PA* 15301
AUTOKRATES son of Aischines *PA* 2744
Oa
ANTIPHANES son of Aristophanes *PA* 1250
EUPOLEMOS son of Makareus *PA* 5933
EUTHOINOS son of Philarchides *PA* 5510
KLEARISTOS son of Philarchides *PA* 8473
Konthyle
DEMOPHILOS son of Demonikos *PA* 3680
Myrrhinous
[EU]X[EN]OS son of Eu--n--
POLYKLES son of Thrasymachos *PA* 11997
CHARINOS son of Charias *PA* 15454
LYSIMACHOS son of Lysimenes *PA* 9524 (not 9424)
AISCHYLIDES son of Aristarchos *PA* 427
Angele
EUPHRANOR son of Euphraios *PA* 6091
PROKLEIDES son of Menekrates *PA* 12192
PA[USA]N[IA]S son of --es
Kytherros
MNESIGE[NE]S son of Kall[i]te[les]
DIODOTOS son of Diogenes *PA* 3901
Prasiai
EUDEMOS *PA* 5408
EUSTHENES son of Elpon *PA* 5991
HABRONICHOS son of Aristokles *PA* 22
Steiria
HEPHAISTODOROS son of Arizelos *PA* 6566
THEODOTOS son of Pausanias *PA* 6804
MELESIAS son of Aristoteles *PA* 9818
Kydathenaion
.E-- son of --ios
IOPHON son of Lysis *PA* 7586
ANTIPHON son of Pytheas *PA* 1302
TEISAMENOS son of Pythionikos *PA* 13445
SOPHILOS son of Stephanos *PA* 13417
ISOD[EM]OS son of Isodemos *PA* 7711
ARISTOKLES son of Hierokles *PA* 1872; *APF* 55

ARCH[I]AS son of Aresias *PA* 2221
ANDROKYDES son of Philagros *PA* 876
DIOKLES son of Dion *PA* 4037
Probalinthos
STEPHANOS son of Demylos *PA* 12892
KALLIKLES son of Phrynon *PA* 7935
ENDEMOS son of Eudemides *PA* 4700
TOLMAIOS son of Euthyneides *PA* 13878
THEOGENES son of Halios *PA* 6724
Grammateus of boule and demos
DOROS son of Smikythos of Melite (VII) *PA* 4624

SEG 28.151 gives a bouleutes from tribe VI Oineis around 340:
Thria
TEISIA[DES]

SEG 28.152 gives bouleutai of tribe VIII Hippothontis dated around 340–330:
Anakaia
EXEKEST[OS] son of Exekias ?*PA* 4730
Azenia
HAGNO[D]E[M]OS son of Pistodemos ?*PA* 138
AISCHRON son of Aischines cf. *PA* 397, 400
Hamaxanteia
TLEMPOLEMOS son of Agathymides
Auridai
LYSANIAS son of Philippos
-- son of G--?
Kopros
LE-- son of Le--
EUDI[KOS] son of Euthyd[ikos] cf. *PA* 5559; *APF* 191
Elaious
NIKOB[OULOS] son of Nikod[emos]

Section IX
336/5 to 322/1

336/5 (Ol. 111.1)

Archon

PYTHODELOS *PA* 12379

MP B 1; *FGH* 255 (6); Diod. 16.91.1; Dion. *Dein.* 4, 9 (Pythodemos); Arrian *Anab.* 1.1.1; IG ii² [328] (SEG 21.268); 330.7, [14], 29, 47; ?334 + (SEG 18.13; *LS* no. 33); 1522.[21f.]; 1524.98, 103, [115]; 1543.[2]; 1544.47; 1623.287; 1628.350, 369; 1629.870, 889; 1699.[1] (or 343/2?); SEG 17.[27]. Panathenaic amphoras: Beazley, *Black Figure* 415, 417; Frel, *Amphoras* 26ff.

Strategoi

DEINOKRATES (? son of Kleiombrotos of Acharnai) (VI) *PA* 3181 = ?3185; *APF* 353, 483

IG ii² 1628.351, 370; 1629.871, 890; see also Petrakos, *Praktika* 1984.

PHOKION son of Phokos *PA* 15076; *APF* 559

Plut. *Phok.* 17.1ff. He countered opposition to Alexander; see below Council and Assembly.

Financial administrator

LYKOURGOS son of Lykophron of Boutadai (VI) *PA* 9251; *APF* 348ff. Dem. *Epist.* 3.2; Hypereides F 118; Diod. 16.88.1; Dion. *Dein.* 11; Plut. *Mor.* 841b, 852b. On the date see *APF* and the Introduction, pp. 7f. In general see Mitchel, *Lykourgan Athens.* He was in office for four years: Develin, *ZPE* 57 (1984), 134.

Epistatai of Eleusis

ANTISTHENES son of Antikrates of Ikarion (II) *PA* 1191
AMPHIETIDES son of Theopompos of Paionidai (IV) *PA* 759
DEMOKLEIDES son of Philokles of Eitea (V) *PA* 3481
THEOPHILOS son of Kallimachos of Acharnai (VI) *PA* 7132
LAMPRIAS son of Lamprias of Sypalettos (VII) *PA* 8990
ALEXIMACHOS son of Teisamenos of Koile (VIII) *PA* 543
DIOXENOS son of Platon of Trikorynthos (IX) *PA* 4307

Grammateus

HAGNOTHEOS of Alopeke (X) *PA* 151

IG ii² 1543.[3ff.]; 1544.1ff. They served until 333/2.

363

Hieromnemon
ARCHIDEMOS *PA* 2488a
FD III, 5, 50 I.20.

COUNCIL AND ASSEMBLY

(i) IG ii² 328 (SEG 21.268; Schwenk no. 15) is a decree of the boule dated to the prytany of Akamantis day 28, Maimakterion 27, fourth prytany, or day 17, Metageitnion 27, second prytany (Hansen, *GRBS* 1982, 343 (= *Ecclesia* 95)):
Proposer
[LYKO]URGOS son of Ly[kophron] of [Boutadai] (VI) *PA* 9251; *APF* 348ff.

(ii) IG ii² 329 represents the renewal of the treaty with Alexander.

(iii) IG ii² 330.29ff. (Schwenk no. 18) has first a decree of the boule in honour of three hieropoioi, probably not syllogeis (Rhodes, *Boule* 130), but possibly bouleutai; it is dated to the fourteenth day of the month, the second of the ninth prytany (thus in Mounichion):
Proposer
AGASI[AS] [? son of Chairigenes of Ikarion (II)] *PA* 95 = ?97
I record the identification proposed in IG and repeated elsewhere, but it creates a problem, in that *Agora* XV.42 below includes the bouleutai of Ikarion and Agasias was not among them. Therefore either *Agora* XV.42 does not belong in this year or the identification in IG is wrong, which means that the name need not even be Agasias.

(iv) There follows the ratification by the demos, dated to the last day of the tenth prytany and Skirophorion:
Proposer
HIPPOCHARES of Alopeke (X) *A* 7670
See line 26.
Hieropoioi
PHYLEUS son of Pausanias of Oinoe (IX) *PA* 15045
[PAUS]ANIAS of Oinoe (IX) ?*PA* 11722
CHARIDEMOS of Oinoe (IX) *PA* 15390
The tribe is settled by *Agora* XV.72.204.

(v) SEG 17.27 (Schwenk no. 16) is a fragment dated to a day in the 20s of the prytany.

(vi) Honours were proposed for Philip (Demades, *Twelve Years* 9; Diod.
(vii) 16.92.1f.) and peace was proposed with Alexander (Demades, *Twelve Years* 14):
Proposer
DEMADES son of Demeas of Paiania (III) *PA* 3264; *APF* 99ff.

(viii) Honours for the proedroi presiding when honours for the King of

Makedon were voted were challenged as unconstitutional (Hypereides 2; Hansen, *Sovereignty* no. 32):
Proposer
PHILIPPIDES *PA* 14351

(ix) An honorary decree for Demades was voted and survived a challenge (Lex. Patm. *in* Dem. (ed. Sakkelion, *BCH* 1877, 1–16, 137–55) *s.v.* ἑκατόμπεδον; Hansen, *Sovereignty* no. 31):
Proposer
KEPHISODOTOS

(x) Plut. *Dem.* 22 (cf. Aisch. 3.160) tells how Demosthenes reported a dream to the council, having heard of Philip's death, and how, when the news was generally known, a decree of thanksgiving and a crown for the assassin were voted: Phokion spoke against this (Plut. *Phok.* 16.6).

Nomothetai
(xi) IG ii² 334 + (SEG 18.13; *LS* no. 33; Schwenk no. 17) is a law concerning the Panathenaia, which seems to belong to this year or the next:
Proposer
ARISTONIKOS son of Ari[stoteles of Marathon] (IX) *PA* 2028

(xii) It is followed by a probouleumatic decree of the demos.

(xiii) A law concerning the ephebes could be dated to this year (Lykourgos F 20):
Proposer
EPIKRATES (son of . . .otetos of Pallene) (x) *PA* 4863; *APF* 182f.

Dated to this year is *Agora* xv.42, a list of bouleutai (but see above no. iii):
Erechtheis (I)
Euonymon
ANYTOS *PA* 1325 = 1323; *APF* 41
[EPI]CHARES
ISONYMOS
PHILLES
ANTHEMION *APF* 41
ISEGOROS
HOMOPHRON
DEMOSTRATOS (? son of Lysi--) ?*PA* 3619
ANTIPHATES (son of Antiphanes)
MOSCHOS
Kedoi
PYTHIADES
HIERON
Agryle
LYSIPPOS
SOSIPPOS
EUTHIDIKOS

TIMOKRATES
HIPPON ?*PA* 7677
Pambotadai
LYKINOS
Anagyrous
DOKIMOS
ISOKRATES
TEISANDROS
D[EMA]INETOS
PHI[LIN]O[S]
ARCH[I]NOS
Kephisia
BLEPES
CHARIAS
STEPHANOS
LEONTIOS
ANTIPHATES
Pergase
ANTICHARMOS
NIKOMACHOS
ARISTOKRATES
EPITELES (son of Soinomos) *PA* 4963
Themakos
ANTIPHILOS
Phegous
MNESIPHON
Lamptrai
HEGEM[ACHOS]
XEN--
LAKRAT--
EUTHYMACHOS
AUTOKRATES
OPSIOS
ARISTOKLES
DIODOROS
ARCHIAS
POULYDAMAS
LYSITHEOS
ISONOMOS
ARCH[I]KR[ATES]
EUDE[M]OS (? son of . .o-- or of Epi--) ?*PA* 5402 or 5403

Aigeis (II)
Halai
. . .⁶. . . S

. .⁴. . MACHOS

[PHILOM]ELOS

[CHA]IR[ED]EMIDES

. . INIPPOS

Diomeia

[TIMAS]ITHEOS

Araphen

EUTHYKLES

KLEON *APF* 229

Phegaia

PYTHODOROS *PA* 12432; *APF* 484

[A]NTISTHENES

[P]OLYKRATES (son of Polyeuktos) *PA* 12027

Myrrhinoutte

[N]EOPTOLEMOS

Teithras

[PR]OKLEIDES (son of Proxenides) *PA* 12204

. . . SIS

. .⁴. . E[.]OS

EUPH[O]ROS

Ankyle

DION

SOST[RA]TOS

Ikarion

PEITH[ON] (son of Sosigenes) *PA* 11765

. . ON

[HAGN]OTHEOS

[POSEI]DIPPOS

. . .⁶. . . LOS

Kollytos

. . . OKLES

. . .⁷. . . ES

. . .⁷. . . S

Kolonos

PHILIPPOS

ANTHEMION

Hestiaia

SPINTHAROS

Bate

LEON

Erikeia

IASIMACHOS

Otryne

AGATHARCHOS

Plotheia

ARISTODEMOS
Erchia
NIKIAS
KALLIAS (? son of Egertios) ?*PA* 7863; *APF* 271f.
HEGETOR
BATHYLLOS
EUTHOINOS
DIOGNIS
Gargettos
KTEON (son of Mikon) *PA* 8830
PROKLES
DROMOKLES
KLEOKRITOS
Ionidai
[E]RXIMENES
Kydantidai
[K]ALLITELES (son of . . . .[8]. . . . es) *PA* 8211
[X]ENOKLES
Philaidai
PYTHOKLES
ANTIKLES
PHANOSTRATOS *PA* 14111

Pandionis (III)
Paiania
POLYARKES
PHANOKLES
SOSTHENES
DEMOKLES
SOTADES
BLEPSIAS
THRASYMEDES
PHILODEMOS (? son of Philokydes) *APF* 544
THEOPOMPOS
DEMADES (? son of Demeas) *PA* 3263; *APF* 99ff.
CHARINADES
THEODOROS
Kydathenaion
PYTHARATOS
THEODORIDES
ARISTODEMOS
DIODOROS
DEMETRIOS
PASIAS
HIPPEUS

THEOPHILOS
PHILODEMOS
PYTHEAS
LEOKRATES
ARISTOGENES
Probalinthos
LEPTIAS
CHARISANDROS
POLYKLES
MEIDOKRATES
THEOPHILOS
Oa
KI--
NIKO--
DION (son of Dion)
ANTIDOT[OS]
Konthyle
PROXENOS
Myrrhinous
MEIDON (? son of Epiteles)
DEINOKRATES
NIKANDROS
AISCHYLIDES (? son of Aristarchos) ?*PA* 427
KALLISTHENES ?*PA* 8103
THOUPHANES
Prasiai
TIMANDROS (? son of Timandros)
TIMOCHARES
CHARIAS
Steiria
CHARIDEMOS
MYRTILOS (? son of Chareleides)
THEOPOMPOS
Angele
EUTHYKRATES
HERMIPPOS
Kytherros
ARISTARCHOS
DIOKLES

Leontis (IV)
Sounion
. .⁴. . M]ACHOS
[KLEOPH]RADES
. .⁴. . LES

. . ⁴ . . INOS
Deiradiotai
. . MIAS
[A]GATHONIDES
Potamos
SOKLEIDES
PHOKION
DIOPEITHES
ARISTOKLES
ANTIPHANES
Phrearrhioi
ANTICHARES (? son of Philion) ?*PA* 1315
DEMARCHOS (? son of Dieuches)
NAUSISTRATOS
ARCHESTRATOS ?*PA* 2431
LYKON (son of Thersias) *PA* 9275
PHILOKLES ?*PA* 14565
ANDROMENES
KALLAISCHROS
Skambonidai
ARCHESTRATOS
KALLIADES
ARCHESTRATOS
Kettos
MELANOPIDES
SMIKYTHOS
DEMOPHILOS
Leukonoion
LYSANDRIDES
AKESTORIDES
DA[M]IAS
Halimous
EUBIODEMOS
ATHENODOROS
THEOGNETOS
Cholleidai
THEANGELOS
CHARIDEMOS
Aithalidai
NIKOSTRATOS
KALLIMACHOS
Paionidai
LYSISTRATOS
PHILEAS (son of Antigenes) *PA* 14242
ONOMAKLES

Kolonai
NIKOSTRATOS
ARISTOPHON
Hybadai
LACHES
LYSANIAS
Eupyridai
THEODOTOS
TIMOKLEIDES
Pelekes
PHEIDON
ONESION
Oion
CHIONIS
Kropidai
D[I]POLIS
Hekale
EMMENIDES

Akamantis (v)
Thorikos
DIONYSIOS (? son of Kalliades)
ARISTOPHANES
MNESIKRATES
HAGNODEMOS
KALLIPHANES (? son of Lysanias) ?*PA* 8221
Kephale
HIPPARCHIDES
PHILISTIDES
HIEROPHON ?*PA* 7517
EPAGROS
ERGOMELES
AGATHARCHOS
PROKLES
PHILONIDES
DEMOTELES
Poros
PHILOKRATES *PA* 14627; *APF* 547
ISCHYRIAS
STRATON
Kerameis
KALLIAS
THEOPOMPOS
EUKTEMON
MENESTRATOS

TIMOTHEOS
EUKLES
Eiresidai
KALLIAS
Hermos
EUANGELOS (? son of Theophilos) ?*PA* 5225
EUCHEIRIDES
Cholargos
TIMOKLES
PROXENOS
TELESARCHIDES
LYSIPHON (? son of Kephisophon) cf. ?*PA* 8419
Iphistiadai
MOLOTTOS
Eitea
KLEOBOULOS
DEMOKLEIDES (? son of Philokles) ?*PA* 3481
Sphettos
AUTOKLEIDES (? son of Euetion) *APF* 190
THRASON
TIMOKLES
PHILOKLES
EUTHYKRATES
Hagnous
SPEUSIAS
ISANDROS
KALLIPHEMOS
CHAIREDEMOS
LYSIMENES
Prospalta
HIEROPHON
EPI[KR]ATES (? son of Kallias) ?*PA* 4913
TIMONIDES
POLYEUKTOS
NIKOSTRATOS ?*PA* 11048 or 11049
Kikynna
EUPHILETOS
KALLIKRATES

335/4 (Ol. 111.2)

Archon
EUAINETOS *PA* 5242
MP B 2; Eratosthenes *FGH* 241 F 1d; *FGH* 255 (6); Diod. 17.2.1; Dion. *ad Amm.* 5 (Apollodoros *FGH* 244 F 38b); *Dein.* 9; IG ii² 330; [331] (SEG

21.270); [332] (but see 353/2); 333a.[13]; [363] (SEG 23.53); ?334 + (SEG 18.13; *LS* no. 33: see 336/5); 1524.117, 126f.; 1623.285; 1627.51; 1628.233; 1629.360; 1652.22 (*Insc. Délos* 104–30.23); 3042.3; SEG 21.[272]; *Hesperia* 1940, 328 ([36]) (Schweigert).

Strategos
DIOTIMOS son of Diopeithes of Euonymon (I) *PA* 4384; *APF* 163f.
Plut. *Mor.* 844a; IG ii² 414a.4 (*Hesperia* 1940, 340f. (Schweigert)). His expedition against the pirates resulted in success in 334/3 and the granting of honours.

Financial administrator
LYKOURGOS son of Lykophron of Boutadai (VI) *PA* 9251; *APF* 348ff.
See 336/5.

Epistatai of Eleusis
ANTISTHENES son of Antikrates of Ikarion (II) *PA* 1191
AMPHIETIDES son of Theopompos of Paionidai (IV) *PA* 759
DEMOKLEIDES son of Philokles of Eitea (V) *PA* 3481
THEOPHILOS son of Kallimachos of Acharnai (VI) *PA* 7132
LAMPRIAS son of Lamprias of Sypalettos (VII) *PA* 8990
ALEXIMACHOS son of Teisamenos of Koile (VIII) *PA* 543
DIOXENOS son of Platon of Trikorynthos (IX) *PA* 4307
Grammateus
HAGNOTHEOS of Alopeke (X) *PA* 151
See 336/5.

Epistates of Brauroneion
KALLIKRATIDES (? son of Kallikrates of Steiria) (III) *PA* 7985 = ? 7988
IG ii² 1524.127.

Envoys
PHOKION son of Phokos *PA* 15076; *APF* 559
Plut. *Phok.* 17.4f. He went to Alexander with an Athenian decree.

DEMOSTHENES son of Demosthenes of Paiania (III) *PA* 3597; *APF* 113ff.
Aisch. 3.161; Diod. 17.4.7; Plut. *Dem.* 23.3. Chosen to go to Alexander, he turned back.

DEMADES son of Demeas of Paiania (III) *PA* 3263; *APF* 99ff.
Diod. 17.15.4f.; Plut. *Dem.* 23.6. He persuaded Alexander against the exile of leading Athenians and in favour of Theban exiles.

COUNCIL AND ASSEMBLY
The secretary is found or restored in IG ii² 330, 331, 363, 1700.213 (*Agora* xv.43.227), SEG 21.272, *Hesperia* 1940, 328 (36):
Grammateus
PROXENOS son of Pylagoras of Acherdous (VIII) *PA* 12271

(i) IG ii² 330 (Schwenk no. 18) is a decree from the last day of the month, seventeenth of an unknown prytany (Meritt, *Ath. Year* 79), in honour of Phyleus (see 336/5 nos. iii and iv):

Proposer

THEODO[ROS son of Antiphanes of Alopeke] (x) *PA* 6854

(ii) IG ii² 331 (SEG 21.270; Schwenk no. 22) is from the last day of the month, Skirophorion because it is the thirty-fifth day of the tenth prytany, of Antiochis (or possibly the thirty-fourth or thirty-sixth: Hansen, *GRBS* 1982, 343 (=*Ecclesia* 95)):

Bouleutes epistates

--CHOS?

(iii) IG ii² 363, as dated to this year (SEG 23.53), is a decree in honour of Dionysios, restored by Meritt to the third day of the prytany, Anthesterion 11 (but see Hansen, *GRBS* 1982, 344 (=*Ecclesia* 96)), kyria ekklesia; Schwenk no. 67 dates it to 326/5 and it is problematic, but the secretary of this year can be fitted in and that of 326/5 is now known, though that does not rule out that date, as his patronymic and demotic remain unknown:

Proposer

[POLYEU]KTOS son of Sos[tratos] of Sphettos (v) *PA* 11925= 11934=11950

For the latter see SEG 12.89.

(iv) SEG 21.272 (Schwenk p. 128), still to be fully published, is a decree concerning Pythostratos from the twenty-third day of the tenth prytany, of Antiochis, Skirophorion 18; for the proposer see Hansen, *GRBS* 1983, 160:

Bouleutes epistates

. . .⁶. . . OS of Lamptrai (I)

Proposer

ALKIMACHOS son of . . .⁶. . . os or . . .⁶. . . es of Myrrhinoute (II) *PA* 622

(v) *Hesperia* 1940, 328 (36) (Schweigert; Schwenk no. 19), is a fragment from the fifth prytany, of Akamantis, Posideon 11 or 12:

Bouleutes epistates

[NI]KOKL[ES] of Rhamnous (IX)

Proposer

--N. .⁴. . or -- son of --n. .⁴. . of Paiania (III)

(vi) IG ii² 1623.28off. records a decree dealing with pirates:

Proposers

LYKOURGOS (son of Lykophron) of Boutadai (VI) *PA* 9251; *APF* 348ff.
ARISTONIKOS (son of Aristoteles) of Marathon (IX) *PA* 2023=2028

(vii) The Athenians voted assistance for the Thebans (Diod. 17.8.6; in general see Plut. *Dem.* 23):

Proposer

DEMOSTHENES son of Demosthenes of Paiania (III) *PA* 3597; *APF* 113ff. Phokion spoke against Demosthenes in this context (Plut. *Phok.* 17.1) and also in the debate when Alexander demanded the surrender of leading Athenians, when he was opposed by Lykourgos (Plut. *Phok.* 9.6, 17). Hypereides F LII may belong here. Diod. 17.15 reports the assembly also

(viii) and a decree in answer to Alexander:
Proposer
DEMADES son of Demeas of Paiania (III) *PA* 3263; *APF* 99ff.

(ix) Arrian *Anab.* 1.10.3 also has him responsible for the voting of the embassy.

Nomothetai
(x) IG ii² 333 (SEG 21.272; 31.78; Schwenk no. 21) is from the tenth prytany, of Antiochis, Skirophorion 6 (thus eleventh day of the prytany; see above no. iv) and concerns sacred matters:
Proposer
[LYKOUR]GOS son of Lykophr[on] of Boutadai (VI) *PA* 9251; *APF* 348ff.

(xi) I have postponed IG ii² 410 (SEG 22.94) as a transition to the boule. It includes the names of bouleutic hieropoioi, being in praise of them and certain priests, and though dated *c.* 330, it may as well be in this year, as Philostratos of Pallene was indeed a councillor (see the next entry); it is a decree of the council:
Proposer
-- son of --ktos of Skambonidai (IV)
Hieropoioi
EUNOMOS of Euonymon (I) *PA* 5869
SYBARITES of Gargettos (II) *PA* 13029
GNOSIAS son of Chairemon of Kydathenaion (III) *PA* 3061
PHILEAS son of Antigenes of Paionidai (IV) *PA* 14242
CHAIREPHANES of Sphettos (V) *PA* 15181
APOLLODOROS son of Euktemon of Ptelea (VI) *PA* 1443
[A]U[TOS]THENES son of Eu[k]l[eides?] of Xypete (VII) *PA* 2759; *APF* 75ff.
AMIANTOS of Auridai (VIII) *PA* 715
EPIKRATES son of Glaukon of Aphidna (IX) *PA* 4885
PHILOSTRATOS (son of Nikostratos) of Pallene (X) *PA* 14742

Agora xv.43 gives a list of bouleutai followed by officials:
Erechtheis (I)
-- son of --os or --es
KEPHISOKLES son of Kephisodotos
PYTHODELOS son of Pythodelos
ANDROKLES son of Androkles
ARI[S]TON son of Ariston
Pergase (lower)
KTESIPPOS son of Hagnodemos

SOSIKEDES son of Philonides
Pergase (upper)
ALKIMACHIDES son of Hegemachos ?*PA* 610
KLEONYMIDES son of Phokionides
Phegous
DEMYLOS son of Demakles
Themakos
EUTHIPPOS son of Pythippos

Aigeis (II)
-- son of --os or --es
--os son of --los or --les
[ANT]IPHON son of Antiphon
Hestiaia
POSEIDIPPOS son of Kal[l]ik[r]ates *PA* 12126; *NPA* 145
Otryne
ARCHESTRATOS son of Mnesarchides
Erikeia
CHAIREDEMOS son of Chairestratos
Bate
ANDROKLES son of Aristoleos
Kydantidai
SPINTHON son of Lamedon
PHEIDOLEOS son of Pheidostratos
Plotheia
THEODOROS *PA* 6896
Diomeia
ARIMNESTOS

Pandionis (III)
-- son of --os or --es
Probalinthos
DE-- son of . . .ios or . . .ias
ARCHENEOS son of Euklinos
ARCHESTRATOS son of Amynandros
POULYTION son of Polykles
NIKOSTRATOS son of Nikeas
Steiria
KEPHISOKLES son of Kephisodoros
ARISTOPHON son of Aristodemos
AISCHINES son of Kallimedes
Paiania lower
STRATON son of Kallistratos

Leontis (IV)
-- son of . . ^{5} . . osi[os]

ATHE[N]ODO[R]OS son of Noumenios
Halimous
TIMOKRATES son of Teleson
THORAX son of Lykophron
NIKOSTRATOS son of Nikiades *PA* 11020; *APF* 95
Eupyridai
LYSANIAS son of Lysiades
KTESINOS son of Kretheus
Kolonai
EUMELOS son of Aristophon
ANTIGENES son of Phaidromachos
Cholleidai
EUTHYDIKOS son of Thersippos
ARKEPHON son of Meidon
Potamos upper
ONOMAKLES son of Onomakritos
Oion
CHAIRESTRATOS son of Chariades

Akamantis (V)
-- son of --os or --es
THE-- son of . .⁴. . ylos
POLYDOROS son of Thougenes
PH[I]LON son of . . . 1 . .⁴. . es
Prospalta
NAUSIAS son of Nausikrates
EUMELOS son of Eumeliades
ANDROSTHENES son of Demokrates
DIKAIOS son of Dikaios
APOLLODOROS son of Archias
Hermos
CHARIAS *PA* 15342
KALLIKRATES
Eiresidai
THEOPHILOS son of Charisios

Oineis (VI)
--os son of --ros
HAGNON son of Hagnonides
THEOGENES son of Pleistos
MNESIKR[A]TES son of Lysikrates
EUNOMIDES son of Eunomion
GENNAIOS son of Pleistos
Perithoidai
DEMOKRATES son of Aristokrates

SOSTRATOS son of Smikythos
MNESIMACHOS son of Nouphrades

Kekropis (VII)
-- son of --los or --les
NEO[K]L[EID]ES son of Prox[e]nos
Sypalettos
AUTOBOULOS son of Autosophos ?*PA* 2705
SOSTRATOS son of Mikion
Pithos
CHAIRETIOS son of Chairimenes *PA* 15210
EUAINETOS son of Demainetos
CHAIRIPPOS son of Autokles *PA* 15249; *APF* 75
Daidalidai
PANTIADES son of Dexixenos

Hippothontis (VIII)
[Eleusis?]
--OS son of Ep[ik]ouros
SOSISTRATOS son of Menon
EUTHYSTRATOS son of Euthydemos
THRASYKLES son of Thrasyllos ?*PA* 7322; *APF* 241
PHOKIADES son of Polynikos
DIONYSODOTOS son of Pytharatos
Anakaia
PHILOMBROTOS son of Philokles
THRASON son of Thrasymedes
PHILON son of Philaios

Aiantis (IX)
PHILO-- son of Philo--
THEANGELOS son of Xenokles
KALLIXENOS son of Archeptolemos
ARISTODEMOS son of Aristophon

Antiochis (X)
--E[S] son of Diopeithes
Pallene
PHILOSTRA[T]OS son of Nikostratos *PA* 14742
. .[4]. . ANES son of . .[5]. . thos
EPIKRATES son of . . .otetos *APF* 182f.
THEMITEUS son of Euthyneus
THEODOROS son of Antidoros
LYSIDEMOS son of Lysitheos
Eitea
SOKRATES son of Kephisokles
AISCHYLOS son of Neokleides

378

Grammateus of demos
ANTIMENES son of Aristomenes of Teithras (II) *NPA* 17
Anagrapheus
ARISTOPHANES son of Hieronymos of Teithras (II) *NPA* 31
In charge of decrees
KRITON son of Erxidikos of Marathon (IX)
Antigrapheus
PISTOKLES son of Pistogenes of Anaphlystos (X) *NPA* 143
Tamias of boule
DIOGENES son of Diogenes of Melite (VII) *NPA* 53
Tamias of dedication
KONON son of Metrodoros of Kydathenaion (III) *NPA* 114; *APF* 401f.

334/3 (Ol. 111.3)

Archon
KTESIKLES *PA* 8863
MP B 3; *FGH* 255 (6); Diod. 17.17.1; Dion. *Dein.* 9; Plut. *Mor.* 844a; IG ii²
335 (SEG 21.274); [336a] (SEG 21.273; Osborne D 17); [405] (SEG
21.275; Osborne D 21); 414a (SEG 21.276); 1156.27, 50, 53 (Reinmuth no.
2); 1184.23f. (Schwenk no. 26); 1189.2 (Reinmuth no. 3); 1493.[2] (SEG
21.552); 1496.69, 91; 1524.125; 1544.[48f.]; 1623.[1]; 1652.[20] (*Insc.
Délos* 104–30); 1750 (*Agora* XV.44); [2970] (Reinmuth no. 4; see Mitchel,
Hesperia 1964, 349ff.); SEG 19.[196]; 23.78.[13] (Mitchel, *ZPE* 19 (1975),
234ff., and Dow, *Essays Brendel* 81ff., against Reinmuth no. 1).

Strategoi
DIOTIMOS son of Diopeithes of Euonymon (I) *PA* 4384; *APF* 163f.
See 335/4.

?PHAIDROS (son of Kallias of Sphettos) (V) *PA* 13964; *APF* 525
IG ii² 1623.239f. Probably in this year, possibly 335/4.

[KON]ON son of Timotheos [of Anaphlystos] (X) *PA* 8708; *APF* 511f.
[SOPHIL]OS son of A[risto]te[les of Phyle] (VI) *PA* 13422
IG ii² 2970.5f. (Reinmuth no. 4; Mitchel, *Hesperia* 1964, 349f.). Konon
was general in Peiraieus, Sophilos over the country, if the order reflects the
same as in 333/2.

Ephebic sophronistai
ADEISTOS son of Antimachos of Athmonon (VII) *PA* 205; *APF* 5
APHR-- of tribe I or X
IG ii² 1156.32, 41f., 47f., 59 (Reinmuth no. 2: Adeistos); 2970.3 (Reinmuth
no. 4: Aphr--).

Kosmetes
?AUTOLYKOS son of . . . . ? . . . . of Thorikos (V)

SEG 23.78.15, [18] (Mitchel, *ZPE* 19 (1975), 234ff., and Dow, *Essays Brendel* 81ff., against Reinmuth no. 1).

Financial administrator
LYKOURGOS son of Lykophron of Boutadai (VI) *PA* 9251; *APF* 348ff.
See 336/5.

Tamiai of Athene
-- of Kollytos (II)
NAUSISTRA[TOS] of tribe III (?)
-- of Acharnai (VI)
MELESIAS of Halai (VII) *PA* 9811
IG ii² 1493.2ff.

Tamias of stratiotic fund
DEMADES son of Demeas of Paiania (III) *PA* 3263; *APF* 99ff.
IG ii² 1493.[11ff.], [15ff.], [19ff.] (SEG 21.552; 22.133). At least by now the office was quadrennial; Develin, *ZPE* 57 (1984), 135.

Epimeletai of dockyards
ORSIMENES son of Eukti[menes of Paiania] (III) *PA* 11492
-- son of Philoktemon of Athmonon (VII) *PA* 14639
--MON son of Simonides of Alopeke (X) *PA* 12718
IG ii² 1623.1ff. (SEG 28.140).

Epimeletes of springs
PYTHEAS son of Sosidemos of Alopeke (X) *PA* 12346
IG ii² 338.9, 11ff. This was a four-year office; Develin, *ZPE* 57 (1984), 135f.

Epimeletes of Nikai, processional vessels and kosmos kanephorikos?
--AN]DROS of Gargettos (II)
IG ii² 1493.5f.

Epistatai of Eleusis
ANTISTHENES son of Antikrates of Ikarion (II) *PA* 1191
AMPHIETIDES son of Theopompos of Paionidai (IV) *PA* 759
DEMOKLEIDES son of Philokles of Eitea (V) *PA* 3481
THEOPHILOS son of Kallimachos of Acharnai (VI) *PA* 7132
LAMPRIAS son of Lamprias of Sypalettos (VII) *PA* 8990
ALEXIMACHOS son of Teisamenos of Koile (VIII) *PA* 543
DIOXENOS son of Platon of Trikorynthos (IX) *PA* 4307
  Grammateus
  HAGNOTHEOS of Alopeke (X) *PA* 151
See 336/5.

Naopoioi to Delphi
EUKTEMON son of Charias (? of Lousia) (VI) *PA* 5785 = ?5800
PYTHODOROS son of Python (? of Kedoi) (I) *APF* 486

EUTHYKRATES son of Euthy[krates ?] (of Amphitrope) (x) ?*PA* 5599; *APF* 70f.
FD III, 5, 48.13f.; cf. 91.23ff.

COUNCIL AND ASSEMBLY

The secretary is found or restored in IG ii² 335, 336a, 405, 414a:
Grammateus
MNESIPHILOS son of Mneson [of Phaleron] (IX) *PA* 10378

On the basis that IG ii² 1493 + 1494 + 1495 belonged to this year, Mitchel had two attempts at numbering prytanies of this year; in the second (*AJA* 1966, 66) this emerges as 4. Aigeis or Oineis; 5. Aiantis or Leontis; 8. Hippothontis; 9. Akamantis; 10. Kekropis. Osborne D 23 objects to this, wanting Hippothontis as fourth prytany in IG ii² 336, as in IG, but this is totally restored.

(i) IG ii² 335 (SEG 21.274; Schwenk no. 23) is a fragment dated to the ninth prytany, of Akamantis, Mounichion 24 or 25:
Bouleutes epistates
DEMO[KR . . . s of Paiania] (III)
Proposer
[DEMADES] son of [D]emeas [of Paiania] (III) *PA* 3263; *APF* 99ff.

(ii) IG ii² 336a (SEG 21.273; Osborne D 17; Schwenk no. 31) is a citizenship decree for Archippos of Thasos, referring to a probouleuma, dated to Maimakterion 11, twenty-first day of the prytany (the fourth – see above), kyria ekklesia:
Bouleutes epistates
. . . OTHEOS of Kyda(ntidai) (II) or Kyda(thenaion) (III)
Proposer
-- son of --ophron of Lakiadai (VI)

(iii) IG ii² 405 (SEG 21.275; Osborne D 21; Schwenk no. 24) is a citizenship decree for Amyntor son of Demetrios, restored to the same day and with the same personnel as IG ii² 335 +, the demotic of the epistates being certain.

(iv) IG ii² 414a (SEG 21.276; Schwenk no. 25) is dated to the same day as the last entry, the kappa of the name of the epistates now appearing, and is made to concern honours to Diotimos (cf. Plut. *Mor.* 844a):
Proposer
[LYKOURGOS] son of [L]ykphron [of Boutadai] (VI) *PA* 9251; *APF* 348ff.

(v) IG ii² 222 is plausibly placed in this year by Osborne D 22; it is a citizenship decree for Peisitheides of Delos.

(vi) IG ii² 1156.36ff. is a decree of the boule in praise of the epheboi of Kekropis and their sophronistes:

Proposer
HEGEMACHOS son of Chairemon of Perithoidai (VI) *PA* 6282

(vii) IG ii² 1623.313 records a decree concerning naval equipment:
Proposer
NAUSIKLES (son of Klearchos of Oe) (VI) *PA* 10552; *APF* 396ff.

Agora XV.44 gives bouleutai of tribe x Antiochis:
Anaphlystos
HIEROKLES son of Hieron *PA* 7486
ERATOSTRATOS son of Nausikydes *PA* 5036
KYKNOS son of Philochoros *PA* 8941
DEMETRIOS son of Pythippos *PA* 3388
[A]POLLODOROS son of Olympichos *PA* 1408; *APF* 516
EPIKRATES son of Alexiades *PA* 4884
THEAGENES son of Akesandros *PA* 6609
[PH]ILAIGIDES son of Leokedes *PA* 14216
PAUSANIAS son of Thrasyllos *PA* 11712
DEMETRIOS son of Kallippos *PA* 3386
Amphitrope
DIOKLES son of Philarchides *PA* 4017
AISCHYLOS son of Aischylos *PA* 440
Besa
KEPHISOSTRATOS son of Archias *PA* 8396
ARISTEUS son of Theogenes *PA* 1718
Atene
ARISTODAMAS son of Kallias *PA* 1793
GNATHIOS son of Euphiletos *PA* 3045
EUPHILETOS son of Gnathios *PA* 6060
Aigilia
KRATINOS son of Kratylos *PA* 8758
KRATIOS son of Kratylos *PA* 8765
ARISTODEMOS son of Epikrates *PA* 1805
PHAINIPPOS son of Sostratos *PA* 13981
EUXIPPOS son of Thersippos *PA* 5912
ARCHEDEM[O]S son of Pheidiades *PA* 2318
Thorai
KLEANDRIDES son of Kleandros *PA* 8463
CHARIKLES son of Athenodoros *PA* 15411
PHILOKLES son of Bison *PA* 14542
CHARIKLES *PA* 15410
Pallene
ARCHEBIOS son of Archenautes *PA* 2309
HEGESILEOS son of Deisitheos *PA* 6338
CHAIRESTRATOS son of Gniphon *PA* 15169
KLEOPEITHES son of Theopompos *PA* 8611

TIMOTHEOS son of Smikrias *PA* 13712
KEPHISIOS son of Kephisodemos *PA* 8295
THEODOTOS *PA* 6800
Alopeke
PHILOXENOS son of Xenophon *PA* 14704
DIOGENES son of Diogeiton *PA* 3813
AUTOPHONTIDES son of Deinias *PA* 2768
CHAIRESTRATOS son of Euxitheos *PA* 15156
ANTIMACHOS son of . .⁴. . n or . .⁵. . s
ANTIPHON son of Solon *PA* 1291
THEODOROS son of Antiphanes *PA* 6854
NIKON son of Archinos *PA* 11104
APHTHONETOS son of Pha[ne]s *PA* 2772
KLEON son of [? Di]agoras *PA* 8668
Krioa
THEOPHILOS son of Chaireas *PA* 7145
Kolonai
EPICHARINOS son of Euthykrates *PA* 5016
EUKRI[TO]S son of Eukritos *PA* 5770
Eitea
HIEROS son of Melanopos *PA* 7512
Eroiadai
ANTHIPPOS son of Anticha[r--] *PA* 956 (cf. Stanton, *ABSA* 1984, 289 n.2)
Semachidai
KOMAIOS son of Komon *PA* 8693; *APF* 320

333/2 (Ol. 111.4)

Archon

NIKOKRATES *PA* 10910

MP B 4; *FGH* 255 (6); Diod. 17.29.1; Dion. *Dein.* 9; Arrian *Anab.* 2.11.10; IG ii² 337.2, 26 (Tod 189; *LS* no. 34); 338 (vii 3499; SEG 25.484); 339a; [340]; [341]; [358] (Meritt, *Ath. Year* 84; but see SEG 21.326 – 307/6); 391.[9f.]; 1496.93, [124], [158]; 1544.[50]; 1623.[4]; 1652.[27] (*Insc. Délos* 104–30.28); 1653.1 (*Insc. Délos* 104–31); 2318.[320]; 2791 (SEG 32.238); 2976.[5] (Reinmuth no. 8.6); 3105 + (SEG 31.162); 4594a.3 (Reinmuth no. 11); SEG 21.680 (Reinmuth no. 6); 24.203.27f. (Schwenk no. 32); *Hesperia* 1940, 62 (8.[1], 11) (Meritt; Reinmuth no. 9). Panathenaic amphoras: Beazley, *Black Figure* 415; ?*Hesperia* Suppl. 10.15 (15).

Strategoi

?MENESTHEUS son of Iphikrates of Rhamnous (IX) *PA* 9988; *APF* 249ff. Dem. 17.20. The date is not secure for his command of a fleet in reaction to Makedonian retention of corn ships at Tenedos.

KONON son of Timotheos of Anaphlystos (x) *PA* 8708; *APF* 511f.
SOPHILOS son of Aristoteles of Phyle (VI) *PA* 13422
Reinmuth no.7.4ff. (SEG 21.681); no.8.9f. (IG ii² 2976); no.9.9ff.
(*Hesperia* 1940, 62); no. 5 (Travlos, *Praktika* 1954 (1957), 70f.). Konon
was again general in Peiraieus, Sophilos over the country.

Ephebic sophronistai
EPICHARES son of Epigenes of Oinoe (IX)
Reinmuth no. 6.3f. (SEG 21.680).

PHILOTHEOS son of Philokles of Sounion (IV)
Reinmuth no. 9 (*Hesperia* 1940, 62).

PERIK-- of [Anagyrous] (I)
SEG 31.162 (ii² 3105 +).

Kosmetes
. . . .⁸. . . . son of Ainesistratos of Acharnai (VI)
Reinmuth no. 8.11 (IG ii² 2976); no. 9.11.12f. (*Hesperia* 1940, 62 (8)).

Didaskaloi
?[MN]ESON son of Ariston
?-- of Paiania (III)
?[CH]A[RI]AS son of Arkeon
?-- son of --es of Myrrhinous (III)
Reinmuth no. 8.11ff. (IG ii² 2976).

[?LEOKRA]TES son of A. . .⁶. . . os of Pallene (x) *APF* 344
. . .⁷. . . s son of Ar. .aineas of Methone
Reinmuth no. 9. 1.33ff. (*Hesperia* 1940, 62).

I am informed that the two didaskaloi of Kekropis honoured in what is
Reinmuth no. 5 are:
CHAIRESTRATOS of Pallene (x) cf. *PA* 15169, 15170
AGATHANOR of Syracuse

Financial administrator
LYKOURGOS son of Lykophron of Boutadai (VI) *PA* 9251; *APF* 348ff.
See 336/5.

Tamias of stratiotic fund
DEMADES son of Demeas of Paiania (III) *PA* 3263; *APF* 99ff.
See 334/3 (there is no specific evidence for this year).

Epimeletai of dockyards
-- son of --emos of Paiania (III)
ARCHINOS son of Archinos of Deiradiotai (IV) *PA* 2524
[ARISTOD]EMOS son of Aristokles of Oinoe (VIII) *PA* 1878; cf. *NPA* 29
DEMOK-- of tribe IX
IG ii² 1623.4f.; for Aristodemos see *Hesperia* 1937, 455f. (Crosby).

Epimeletes of springs
PYTHEAS son of Sosidemos of Alopeke (X) *PA* 12346
See 334/3.

Antigrapheus
EUKLES
IG ii² 1673 + *AE* 1971, 83ff. (4) (Clinton), for the date of which see below.
He presumably operated only at Eleusis; cf. 329/8.

Epistatai of Eleusis
ANTISTHENES son of Antikrates of Ikarion (II) *PA* 1191
AMPHIETIDES son of Theopompos of Paionidai (IV) *PA* 759
DEMOKLEIDES son of Philokles of Eitea (V) *PA* 3481
THEOPHILOS son of Kallimachos of Acharnai (VI) *PA* 7132
LAMPRIAS son of Lamprias of Sypalettos (VII) *PA* 8990
ALEXIMACHOS son of Teisamenos of Koile (VIII) *PA* 543
DIOXENOS son of Platon of Trikorynthos (IX) *PA* 4307
Grammateus
HAGNOTHEOS of Alopeke (X) *PA* 151
See 336/5.

Amphiktyons to Delos
DIOKL[E]S of Kerameis (V) *PA* 4030; *APF* 157f.
ALK--
Grammateus
LYS--
Hypogrammateus
[L]YSIKLE[S] of Aigilia (X)
Insc. Délos 104–31 (IG ii² 1653).

Envoy
IPHIKRATES son of Iphikrates of Rhamnous (IX) *PA* 7736; *APF* 251
Arrian *Anab.* 2.15.2,4; Curtius 3.13.15. Sent to Dareios, he was captured
by Alexander. Curtius mentions him in error with Aristogeiton and
Dropides (see 330/29).

COUNCIL AND ASSEMBLY
The secretary is found or restored in IG ii² 336b (SEG 21.278), 338, 339a,
340:
Grammateus
ARCHELAS son of Chairias of Pallene (X) *PA* 2349

(i) IG ii² 336b (SEG 21.278; Osborne D 23; Schwenk no. 31) is a reaffirmation
of citizenship for Archippos of Thasos (see 334/3 no. ii), dated to the last
day of Elaphebolion, twenty-sixth of the prytany:
Symproedroi
THYMOCHARES of Te[ithras] (II) *PA* 7414

...?... of Kydathenaion (III)
EUXEN-- of tribe IV
--OS of Kephale (V)
E--
-- of Eleusis (VIII)
NIKI--
Proposer
--ES son of Aristarchos of Ph-- *PA* 1671
For the latter see Hansen, *GRBS* 1984, 138.

(ii) IG ii² 337 (Tod 189; *LS* no. 34; Schwenk no. 27) has two decrees giving the Kitians the right to build a shrine to Aphrodite. The first is of the boule in the first prytany, of Aigeis:
Bouleutes epistates
THEOPHILOS of Phegous (I) *PA* 7158
Proposer
ANTIDOTOS son of Apollodoros of Sypalettos (VII) *PA* 1019

(iii) The second is of the demos in the second prytany, of Pandionis:
Bouleutes epistates
PHANOSTRATOS of Philaidai (II) *PA* 14111
Proposer
LYKOURGOS son of Lykophron of Boutadai (VI) *PA* 9251; *APF* 348ff.

(iv) IG ii² 338 (vii 3499; SEG 25.484; Schwenk no. 28) is a decree from the first prytany, of Aigeis, Metageitnion 9, thirty-ninth day of the prytany, honouring Pytheas, the epimeletes of springs:
Bouleutes epistates
NIKIAS of Themakos (I) *PA* 10801
Proposer
CHAIRIONIDES son of Lysanias of Phlya (VII) *PA* 15269

(v) The ending is restored with the opening of the boule's decree of the previous day.

(vi) IG ii² 339a (SEG 16.54; 21.277; 26.75; Schwenk no. 29) is a proxeny decree for a Chian from the second prytany, of Pandionis, restored to Metageitnion 25, fifteenth day of the prytany, but this is not certain.

(vii) IG ii² 340 (Schwenk no. 30) is restored to the fourth prytany, Maimakterion 11, twelfth day of the prytany, kyria ekklesia:
Bouleutes epistates
[?NIKOKR]ATES of Phlya (VII)

IG ii² 341, I am informed, will be redated to 303/2.

(viii) IG ii² 1673 + *AE* 1971, 83ff. (4) (Clinton), may be of this year; line 9 mentions a decree which has something to do with Eleusis:

Proposer
CHARIKLEIDES *PA* 15396
(ix) This probably does not have a month date: SEG 32.167. Another deals with payments concerning the Eleusinion (line 65):
Proposer
LYKOURGOS (son of Lykophron of Boutadai) (VI) *PA* 9251; *APF* 348ff.

Aisch. 3.166f. tells of Demosthenes' words in the assembly in the context of the Spartan rising. This may be the year in which Phokion was called to speak in the boule about Alexander's request for triremes, which Demosthenes and Hypereides spoke against (Plut. *Phok.* 21.1; *Mor.* 847c, 848e; Gehrke, *Phokion* 75f.).

332/1 (Ol. 112.1)

Archon
NIKETES *PA* 10753
MP B 5; *FGH* 255 (7); Diod. 17.40.1 (Nikeratos); Dion. *Dein.* 9; Arrian *Anab.* 2.24.6 (Aniketos); IG ii² [344] (SEG 21.279; 32.92); 345; 346.[5]; 347; [368] (SEG 32.92); [420] (SEG 22.93); 1496.126; 1544.6; 1628.[3], [83f.]; 1653.[5] (*Insc. Délos* 104–31); 1672.[255]; 2318.[330]; 2792.2; 4594a.4 (Reinmuth no. 11); vii 4252; 4253; SEG 28.102.[17] (Schwenk no. 42); 103.25, 26f., 49, 52 (31.109A; Schwenk no. 43); *Hesperia* 1936, 414 ([11]) (Meritt; SEG 32.84); 1939, 26 ([6]) (Schweigert). Panathenaic amphoras: Beazley, *Black Figure* 415, 417.

Ephebic didaskaloi
[KAL]LAIS[CHR]OS son of Kallias of Paiania (III)
?PHILOKRA[T]E[S] son of [S]ostratos of Phrearrhioi (IV) *PA* 14629; *APF* 499
Reinmuth no. 10.7f. The date is not certain and Reinmuth's idea that Philokrates was one of the epimeletai of the shrine of Amphiaraos or the penteteric festival is problematic.

Financial administrator
?[XENOKLES] son of Xeinis of Sphettos (V) *PA* 11234; *APF* 414f.
Hesperia 1960, 2ff. (3.3, 8f.) (Meritt); cf. IG ii² 1191.22ff. He probably took over from Lykourgos for the next four years, but he could belong to the quadrennium beginning 328.

Tamias of stratiotic fund
DEMADES son of Demeas of Paiania (III) *PA* 3263; *APF* 99ff.
See 334/3 and Plut. *Mor.* 818e.

Tamias of trireme funds
DEMOKRATES of Eitea (V) *PA* 3525

IG ii² 1627.22f., 374f., 390ff.; 1628.5f., 85f., 533f., 547ff.; 1629.1010f., 1025f.; 1631.237f., 248ff.

Epistatai of Eleusis
KALLEAS son of Kallippos of Lamptrai (I) *PA* 7768
CHAIRIGENES son of Chairephon of Myrrhinous (III) *PA* 15228
POLYEUCHES son of Antagoras of Perithoidai (VI) *PA* 11956
POLYMEDES son of Dieitrephes of Phlya (VII) *PA* 12038
TEISIAS son of Dexitheos of Phlya (VII) *PA* 13482
PEISIAS son of Aristokrates of Marathon (IX) *PA* 11779
EUAINETOS son of Euthydikos of Anaphlystos (X) *PA* 5245
  Grammateus
  THOUKRITIDES son of Kallias of Thorikos (V) *PA* 7257; *APF* 272
IG ii² 1544.6ff. They served for four years.

Envoys
DIOPHANTOS (? son of Phrasikleides of Myrrhinous) (III) *PA* 4421 =
?4435; *APF* 166
ACHILLEUS *PA* 2796
Arrian *Anab.* 3.6.2. Sent to Alexander, they succeeded in their objectives, including the return of Athenian captives. Berve nos. 283 (with the alternative of *PA* 4419), 192.

HYPEREIDES son of Glaukippos of Kollytos (II) *PA* 13912; *APF* 517ff.
Hypereides F XXVII; Plut. *Mor.* 850b; Paus. 5.21.5; *P.Oxy.* 3360. He was sent to Elis to defend Kallippos.

COUNCIL AND ASSEMBLY

The secretary is found or restored in IG ii² 344, 345, 346, 347, 368, 420 (SEG 22,93), vii 4253, SEG 32.84, *Hesperia* 1939, 26 (6):
Grammateus
ARISTONOUS son of Aristonous of Anagyrous (I) *PA* 2038

(i) IG ii² 344 has been distinguished from 368 (SEG 32.92; but see the
(ii) discussion of Schwenk nos. 33, 82); the prescript of 344 being totally restored from 368, we have at least proxeny decrees from the same assembly, the second prytany, Boedromion 9, thirty-second day of the prytany:
Proposer
[POL]YEUKTOS son of Sostra[tos of Sphettos] (V) *PA* 11934 =
11925 = 11950

(iii) IG ii² 345 (Schwenk no. 36) is a decree honouring a Plataian from the eighth prytany, of Antiochis, Elaphebolion 19, seventh day of the prytany, assembly in the theatre of Dionysos:
Bouleutes epistates

N[IKOSTRATOS of Kopros] (VIII) *PA* 11037
Proposer
[LYKOURGOS son of Lykophron] of Boutadai (VI) *PA* 9251; *APF* 348ff.

The epistates in IG ii² 345 is restored from other decrees of the same day, 346 and 347, and is found also in *Hesperia* 1939, 26 (6) (Schweigert).

(iv) IG ii² 346 (Schwenk no. 37) is an honorific decree:
Proposer
DEMA[DES son of Demeas] of Paiania (III) *PA* 3263; *APF* 99ff.

(v) IG ii² 347 (Schwenk no. 38) honours the poet Amphis:
Proposer
[?ARISTOX]ENOS son of [Ke]phisodotos (? of Peiraieus (VIII)) *PA* 2044

(vi) *Hesperia* 1939, 26 (6) (Schwenk no. 39) is a proxeny decree for an Abderite:
Proposer
E[UBOIOS son of Kratistoleos of Anagyrous?] (I) *PA* 5313
On the latter see Hansen, *GRBS* 1984, 140.

(vii) IG ii² 420 (SEG 22.93) is restored to this year; the prytany dating cannot be relied upon (Hansen, *GRBS* 1982, 346 (= *Ecclesia* 98); Schwenk no. 35):
Proposer
[EU]RYKRAT[ES] or [EU]THYKRAT[ES]

IG vii 4252 and 4253 were passed at the same kyria ekklesia in the ninth prytany, of Erechtheis, Thargelion 11, twenty-third day of the prytany.

(viii) 4252 (Schwenk no. 40) honours the god Amphiaraos:
Bouleutes epistates
EPICHARES of Hagnous (V) *PA* 4982
Proposer
PHANODEMOS son of Diyllos of Thymaitadai (VIII) *PA* 14033

(ix) 4253 (SIG I³ 287; Schwenk no. 41) mentions a law on the shrine of
(x) Amphiaraos sponsored by Phanodemos and praises him; it is proboul-eumatic:
Proposer
DEMETRIOS son of Euktemon of Aphidna (IX) *PA* 3392

(xi) A decree concerning the Eleusinion is mentioned at IG ii² 1544.30; it may belong in this year or earlier, the date being uncertain; for the proposer cf. 352/1:
Proposer
EMMENIDES (? of Koile) (VIII) *PA* 4687 = ?4689

(xii) The decree which is now SEG 32.84 is from pryt. Kekropis; Hansen, *GRBS* 1982, 349 (= *Ecclesia* 101), has shown that this can be fifth, seventh or tenth prytany, the equations being (a) Poseideon 11 = pryt. 5.15 (Schwenk no. 34); (b) Anthesterion 20 = pryt. 7.13; (c) Skirophorion 11 = pryt. 10.16.

Dem. 17, which is surely not by Demosthenes (Hegesippos? – scholia p. 195 Dilts), may belong in this year, dealing with relations with Makedon and finally saying the speaker will move a proposal for war. For date see Cawkwell, *Phoenix* 1961, 74f.

(xiii)

331/30 (Ol. 112.2)

Archon
ARISTOPHANES *PA* 2078
FGH 255 (7); Diod. 17.49.1; Dion. *Dein.* 9; Arrian *Anab.* 3.7.1, 15.7; Philodemos *de Stoicis* (Usener, *Epicurea* 401); IG ii² [348]; 349 (Tod 193); ?[350] (SEG 32.85; but see Osborne D 39 – 318/17); ?[363] (but see 335/4); 1181 (Schwenk no. 46); 1496.137; [1575] (SEG 25.177); 1627.236; 1672.245, 256; 2318.333; ? [2835]; 4594a.5 (Reinmuth no. 11); ?*Hesperia* 1962, 401 (3.[4f.]) (Vanderpool: *Agora* xv.45 – or 330/29).

Financial administrator
?XENOKLES son of Xeinis of Sphettos (v) *PA* 11234; *APF* 414f. See 332/1.

Tamias of stratiotic fund
DEMADES son of Demeas of Paiania (III) *PA* 3263; *APF* 99ff. See 334/3 (there is no specific evidence for this year).

Epistatai of Eleusis
KALLEAS son of Kallippos of Lamptrai (I) *PA* 7768
CHAIRIGENES son of Chairephon of Myrrhinous (III) *PA* 15228
POLYEUCHES son of Antagoras of Perithoidai (VI) *PA* 11956
POLYMEDES son of Dieitrephes of Phlya (VII) *PA* 12038
TEISIAS son of Dexitheos of Phlya (VII) *PA* 13482
PEISIAS son of Aristokrates of Marathon (IX) *PA* 11779
EUAINETOS son of Euthydikos of Anaphlystos (X) *PA* 5245
  Grammateus
  THOUKRITIDES son of Kallias of Thorikos (v) *PA* 7257; *APF* 272
See 332/1.

Epimeletai of mysteries
EUTHYKRATES son of Drakontides of Aphidna (IX) *PA* 5601
K[A]LLIKRATES son of K[a]lli[kratides of Steiria?] (III) *PA* 7945 = ?7980
IG ii² 1672.244.

Hieromnemon
--EUS
FD III, 5, 54.6.

Priest of Asklepios
?PHANOSTRATOS of Erchia (II)
IG ii² 1944.3f. Other years are possible.

COUNCIL AND ASSEMBLY

With IG ii² 363 gone to 335/4 and 350 to 318/17 (Osborne D 39, despite SEG 32.85), 348 is the only evidence for the secretary:

Grammateus

NIKOSTRATOS

(i) IG ii² 348 (SEG 21.282; 23.54) honours an actor in the eighth prytany, of Akamantis, plausibly restored to (Elaphebolion) 19, sixth day of the prytany, assembly in the theatre of Dionysos, though other days are possible (Hansen, *GRBS* 1982, 343 (= *Ecclesia* 95); Schwenk no. 44):

Proposer

PHILEAS son of An[tigenes of Paionidai] (IV) *PA* 14232 = 14242

(ii) IG ii² 349 (Tod 193; Osborne T 66; Schwenk no. 45) honours Rheboulas of Thrace and dates to the tenth prytany, of Kekropis, Skirophorion 10, sixteenth day of the prytany:

Bouleutes epistates

[DO]ROTHE[OS] of Halai (II) *PA* 4603; *APF* 174

Proposer

NOTH[IPPOS son of Lysias] of Diomeia (II) *PA* 11131

Agora xv.45 (Schwenk no. 47) gives bouleutai of Teithras in tribe II Aigeis:

BLEPYR[OS son of Phyleides] *PA* 2882

MANTIK[LES]

--ANES son of An--

--I]NIADE[S] son of --es or --os

The date could be 330/29.

330/29 (Ol. 112.3)

Archon

ARISTOPHON *PA* 2107

Theophrastos *Char.* 7; *MP* B 6; *FGH* 255 (7); Diod. 17.62.1; Dion. *ad Amm.* 12; *Dein.* 9; Plut. *Dem.* 24.2; Arrian *Anab.* 3.22.2; IG ii² [351] (+624; Tod 198; SEG 21.283; 24.99); [352]; 360.31, 67; 1460.12; 1461.[19]; 1462.[22]; 1627.216; 1672.205f., 256; 1924 + 2409 (SEG 26.165)); 2318.[344]; ?[2835]; 3103; ?*Hesperia* 1962, 401 (3.[4f.]) (Vanderpool: *Agora* xv.45 – cf. 331/30).

Financial administrator

?XENOKLES son of Xeinis of Sphettos (V) *PA* 11234; *APF* 414f. See 332/1.

Epistatai of Eleusis

KALLEAS son of Kallippos of Lamptrai (I) *PA* 7768

CHAIRIGENES son of Chairephon of Myrrhinous (III) *PA* 15228

POLYEUCHES son of Antagoras of Perithoidai (VI) *PA* 11956
POLYMEDES son of Dieitrephes of Phlya (VII) *PA* 12038
TEISIAS son of Dexitheos of Phlya (VII) *PA* 13482
PEISIAS son of Aristokrates of Marathon (IX) *PA* 11779
EUAINETOS son of Euthydikos of Anaphlystos (X) *PA* 5245
  Grammateus
  THOUKRITIDES son of Kallias of Thorikos (V) *PA* 7257; *APF* 272
See 332/1.

Hieropoioi for the Pythais
PHANODEMOS son of Diyllos of Thymaitadai (VIII) *PA* 14033
BOETHOS son of Nausinikos of tribe V or X *PA* 2886
LYKOURGOS son of Lykophron of Boutadai (VI) *PA* 9251; *APF* 348ff.
DEMADES son of Demeas of Paiania (III) *PA* 3263; *APF* 99ff.
KLEARCHOS son of Nausikles of Aphidna (IX) *PA* 8480; *APF* 397
GLAUKETES son of Glaukos of Oion (IV) *PA* 2947; *APF* 83
NEOPTOLEMOS son of Antikles of Melite (VII) *PA* 10652; *APF* 399f.
KLEOCHARES son of Glauketes of Kephisia (I) *PA* 8647; *APF* 89
HIPPOKRATES son of Aristokrates of tribe V or X *PA* 7631
NIKERATOS son of Nikias of Kydantidai (II) *PA* 10742; *APF* 406f.
FD III, 1, 511. For the date see Charitonides, *Hesperia* 1961, 43f. against
Lewis, *ABSA* 1955, 34f.; Lewis is still for summer 326 in *Hesperia* 1968,
377 n.29. On available evidence it is likely that Boethos represented tribe X,
Hippokrates tribe V.

Priest of Asklepios
?DEMON son of Demomeles of Paiania (III) *PA* 3736; *APF* 116ff.
IG ii² 4969. Though a place in the cycle is not ruled out, *APF* has
arguments that the position might have been given out of the cycle; cf.
Schlaifer, *CPh* 1943, 39ff.

Envoys
ARISTOGEITON *PA* 1774
DROPIDES (of Aphidna) (IX) *PA* 4575 = 4576
Curtius 3.13.15; Arrian *Anab.* 3.24.4 (Dropides). They went to Dareios
and were captured by Alexander. For Dropides' demotic see *Hesperia*
1950, 261 (19.22) (Crosby). See Berve nos. 123 and 291 and 333/2.

KTESIPHON *PA* 8894
Aisch. 3.242. He went to Kleopatra after the death of Alexandros of
Epeiros. Berve no. 455, though patronymic and demotic come from the
spurious documents at Dem. 18.54 and 118.

COUNCIL AND ASSEMBLY
The secretary is found at IG ii² 351 and 352 (see SEG 29.88 on SEG 16.55):
Grammateus
ANTIDOROS son of Antinous of Paiania (III) *PA* 1031

(i) IG ii² 351+624 (Tod 198; SEG 21.283; 24.99) honours Eudemos of Plataia and is dated to the ninth prytany, of Leontis, Thargelion 11, nineteenth day of the prytany, though the equation is wrong and it perhaps should be the twenty-ninth day of the prytany (Hansen, *GRBS* 1982, 344 (= *Ecclesia* 96); more detail at Schwenk no. 48):

Bouleutes epistates
AN[TI]PHANE[S] of Euonymon (I) = *PA* 1232
Proposer
LYKOURGOS son of Lykophron [of Boutadai] (VI) *PA* 9251; *APF* 348ff. The name of the epistates is as at SEG 24.99.

(ii) IG ii² 352 (Schwenk no. 49) is a fragment from the same prytany, Thargelion 14, thirty-second day of the prytany, kyria ekklesia.

(iii) There were decrees for the condemnation of triremes (IG ii² 1627.247f.; 1628.464f.; 1629.728f.; 1631.104f.):

Proposer
DEMADES son of Demeas of Paiania (III) *PA* 3263; *APF* 99ff.

(iv) In this year or earlier there was a decree of the boule concerning naval equipment (IG ii² 1627.380, 386f., 394, 544; 1628.539, 544, 550f.; 1629.1016, 1021f., 1029; 1631.241f., 245f., 251):

Proposer
KALLISTRATOS of Thorikos (v) *PA* 8168

Oineis held tenth prytany: IG ii² 1672.7f.

329/8 (Ol. 112.4)

Archon
KEPHISOPHON *PA* 8404
Ath. Pol. 54.7; *FGH* 255 (7); Diod. 17.74.1; Dion. *Dein.* 9; IG ii² 353; 1256.4 (Schwenk no. 52); ?1461.[19]; 1462.23; 1497.[1f.]; 1627.229, 240; 1672.1, 257; 1925; 2318.361; 2836.2; 2837.2; ?3053.[2] (or 323/2); vii 4254.2.

Thesmothetai
ANTIKRATES son of Lysanias of Probalinthos (III) *PA* 1087
IG ii² 2836.

KLEONYMOS son of Kleemporos of Epieikidai (VII) *PA* 8683
IG ii² 2837.

Strategoi
The following are recorded in IG ii² 1672 as having sent grain from various places and I would not omit them on the ground that they are from klerouchies (cf. Davies, *Wealth* 166). Sopatros, Aischylos, Demetrios and Lysimachides are not specified as generals, being listed after an individual who is; if they were not generals, they would seem to have held some other

position of authority. The full list is at lines 271ff.; Philon also appears at lines 97, 102, 194, 208.

PHILON *PA* 14805 (Drymos)
MNESISTRATOS of Kytherros (III) *PA* 10372 (Skyros)
STHENYLLOS of Eiresidai (V) *PA* 12643 (Myrrhine)
?SOP[ATRO]S of Alopeke (X) (Myrrhine)
?AISCHYLOS of Erchia (II) (Myrrhine)
MNESIMACHOS of Hagnous (V) *PA* 10336 (Hephaistia)
?DEMETRIOS of Koile (VIII) (Hephaistia)
?LYSIMACHIDES of Hagnous (V) (Hephaistia)

Financial administrator
?XENOKLES son of Xeinis of Sphettos (V) *PA* 11234; *APF* 414f.
See 332/1.

Tamiai of the two goddesses
NIKOPHILOS of Alopeke (X) *PA* 11073
KERAMON of Phlya (VII) *PA* 8267
IG ii² 1672.2f., 35, 38, 113, 115, 135, 138, [212], [214], 249.

Antigrapheus
TELOPHILOS *PA* 13585
IG ii² 1672.12, 43, 118, 143. 'The one elected to keep a reckoning of expenditure', presumably only at Eleusis; cf. 333/2.

Epistatai of Eleusis
KALLEAS son of Kallippos of Lamptrai (I) *PA* 7768
CHAIRIGENES son of Chairephon of Myrrhinous (III) *PA* 15228
POLYEUCHES son of Antagoras of Perithoidai (VI) *PA* 11956
POLYMEDES son of Dieitrephes of Phlya (VII) *PA* 12038
TEISIAS son of Dexitheos of Phlya (VII) *PA* 13482
PEISIAS son of Aristokrates of Marathon (IX) *PA* 11779
EUAINETOS son of Euthydikos of Anaphlystos (X) *PA* 5245
  Grammateus
  THOUKRITIDES son of Kallias of Thorikos (V) *PA* 7257; *APF* 272
See 332/1.

Hieropoios at Eleusis
DEMOPHILOS (son of Demophilos) of Acharnai (VI) *PA* 3675; *APF* 498
IG ii² 1672.299.

Epimeletai of Amphiaraia at Oropos
PHANODEMOS son of Diyllos of Thymaitadai (VIII) *PA* 14033
LYKOURGOS son of Lykophron of Boutadai (VI) *PA* 9251; *APF* 348ff.
DEMADES son of Demeas of Paiania (III) *PA* 3263; *APF* 99ff.
SOPHILOS son of Aristoteles of Phyle (VI) *PA* 13422
THRASYLEON son of Theophon of Acharnai (VI) *PA* 7329
EPITELES son of Soinomos of Pergase (I) *PA* 4963 = ?4955

NIKERATOS son of Nikias of Kydantidai (II) *PA* 10742; *APF* 406f.
EPICHARES son of Agonochares of Paiania (III) *PA* 4999
THYMOCHARES son of Phaidros of Sphettos (V) *PA* 7412 = 7407 = 7409;
APF 525f.
KEPHISOPHON son of Lysiphon of Cholargos (V) *PA* 8419
IG vii 4254 (SIG I³.298; Schwenk no. 50).

Priest of Asklepios
?LEUKON son of [D]emeas of Phrearrhioi (IV) *PA* 9069
IG ii² 4393. The date could be 349/8.

Demarchos
PROKLES of Sounion (IV) *PA* 12237
IG ii² 1672.273. On his position see Whitehead, *ZPE* 47 (1982), 40ff.

Archon of Salamis?
TIMOTHEOS of Alopeke (X) *PA* 13698
IG ii² 1672.274. He sent grain from Salamis and there is every chance he
was archon.

Envoy
THEBAGENES of Eleusis (VIII) *PA* 7131
IG ii² 360.45. He was sent to Dionysios of Herakleia. On the date see below.

COUNCIL AND ASSEMBLY

The secretary is found or restored in IG ii² 353 and vii 4254:
Grammateus
SOSTRATIDES son of Echphantos of Eupyridai (IV) *PA* 13322

Prytanies may be found at IG ii² 1672: 1. Antiochis; 2. Antiochis (*sic*; this or
the previous prytany must be written by mistake); 5. Kekropis; 6.
Pandionis; 10. Akamantis. Add 3. Hippothontis (IG vii 4254); 4. Aigeis
(IG ii² 353).

(i) IG ii² 353 (Schwenk no. 51) honours a Larissan; it is from the fourth
prytany, of Aigeis, the last day of Pyanopsion, eleventh day of the prytany
(Hansen, *GRBS* 1982, 344 (= *Ecclesia* 96)):
Bouleutes epistates
. . . PPOS of Oa (III)
Proposer
DEMADES [son of Demeas of Paiania] (III) *PA* 3263; *APF* 99ff.

(ii) IG ii² 360.28ff. (Schwenk no. 68) has two decrees concerning praise for
(iii) Herakleides of Salamis which may belong in this year, as they mention his
actions in the previous archonship:
Proposer
TELEMACHOS son of Theangelos of Acharnai (VI) *PA* 13562

(iv) There follows a decree of the boule:
Proposer
KEPHISODOTOS son of Eucharides of Acharnai (VI) *PA* 8327

(v) IG vii 4254 (SIG I³.298; Schwenk no. 50) praises the epimeletai of the Amphiaraia; it is from the third prytany, of Hippothontis, Pyanopsion 16, thirty-third day of the prytany:
Bouleutes epistates
DEMOCHARES of Phlya (VII) *PA* 3723
Proposer
DEMOSTHENES son of Demokles of Lamptrai (I) *PA* 3593

(vi) IG ii² 1672.302f., which is of this year, mentions a decree of the council
(vii) concerning a sacrifice and one of the demos concerning pay to the hieropoioi, both proposed by the same man:
Proposer
LYKOURGOS son of Lykophron of Boutadai (VI) *PA* 9251; *APF* 348ff.

(viii) Walbank, *Hesperia* Suppl. 19.173ff., suggests that the document which is now SEG 32.86 might be part of the law regulating the Amphiaraia drawn up by Phanodemos (cf. IG vii 4253).

328/7 (Ol. 113.1)

Archon
EUTHYKRITOS *PA* 5611
MP B 7; *FGH* 255 (8); Diod. 17.82.1; Dion. *Dein* 9; IG ii² [354] (SEG 18.14; 21.285; 23.56); [355]; 360.70; [452] (SEG 21.284; 23.55; 25.68); 1497.[7f.]; 1628.11f.; 1629.275; 1630.13; 1672.249, 251; 3052.3; 4595.3; *Agora* xv.49.2; SEG 29.146 a 1.16; *Hesperia* 1968, 247.391 (Laing). Panathenaic amphora: Beazley, *Black Figure* 415.

Thesmothetes
TELESKOPOS son of Aristokritos of Rhamnous (IX)
Hesperia 1938, 95 (15.12ff.) (Meritt) – or 327/6 (Schwenk no. 61).

Note: While I have adopted on general grounds the idea that Lykourgos' twelve years of influence began in 336/5, I cannot believe that he held a second post as financial administrator beginning in this year. I do not think that Plut. *Mor.* 842e-f necessarily implies that he held any office when he died, but even if he did, I do not think we can say what it was (this against Davies, *APF* 351).

Tamias of trireme funds
POLYKRATES of Aphidna (IX) *PA* 12015
IG ii² 1628.13f.; 1629.275; 1632.14f.

Tamias of the two goddesses
KALLAISCHROS of Aphidna (IX) *PA* 7759
IG ii² 1672.250.

Hieropoioi at Eleusis
KRITOBOULOS of Kolonai (IV or X) *PA* 8805
NIKOMACHOS of Steiria (III) *PA* 10963
IG ii² 1672.252, 303.

Hieromnemon
APEMANTOS *PA* 1347a
FD III, 5, 16.43f.; 57 A.4.

Naopoios to Delphi
EPITELES son of Soinomos of Pergase (I) *PA* 4955 = 4963
FD III, 5, 57 B.11.

Priest of Asklepios
ANDROKLES son of [Kl]einias of Kerameis (v) *PA* 864; *NPA* 14
IG ii² 354.2f., 12f., 19f. (SEG 18.14).

COUNCIL AND ASSEMBLY

The secretary is found at IG ii² 354, 452 (SEG 21.284) and *Agora* xv.49.35:
Grammateus
PYTHODELOS son of Pythodelos of Hagnous (v) *PA* 12380

(i) IG ii² 354 (SEG 18.14; 21.285; 23.56; Hansen, *GRBS* 1982, 340
(*Ecclesia* 92); Schwenk no. 54) is a decree of the eighth prytany, of
Antiochis (the rest of the dating is disputed), in honour of the priest
Androkles:
Bouleutes epistates
EPIGENES of Eroiadai (VIII) *PA* 4795
Proposer
PROKLEIDES son of Panta[leon] of Kerameis (v) *PA* 12200
(ii) There follows a decree of the boule:
Proposer
EUETION son of Autokleides of Sphettos (v) *PA* 5463; *APF* 189f.

(iii) IG ii² 355 (Schwenk no. 55) seems to mention -- son of --os of Lamptrai (I)
in some capacity.

(iv) IG ii² 452 (SEG 21.284; 23.55; 25.68; Schwenk no. 53)) is restored to the
sixth prytany, of Akamantis, Gamelion 18, thirty-first day of the prytany at
SEG 21.284, but the calendar date is uncertain (Hansen, *GRBS* 1982, 347
(= *Ecclesia* 99)):
Bouleutes epistates
PAMPHILO[S] of Ph[egous] (I) *PA* 11559

Symproedroi
. . . .[8]. . . . of Halai (II)
O-- or TH-- of tribe III
-- of Cholleidai (IV)
A-- of tribe VI
-- of Melite (VII)
P-- of tribe VIII
-- of Oinoe (IX)
BOUL[IS of Thorai] (X) cf. *PA* 2916
Proposer
[LYKOURGOS son of Lykophro]n of Boutadai (VI) *PA* 9251; *APF* 348ff.

(v) *Agora* XV.49 (Schwenk no. 56) contains a decree of the boule:
Proposer
KALLISTHENES son of Charopides of Trinemeia (VII) *PA* 8106
This praises the epimeletai of the dedication who are the first three named
in the list of councillors, which is followed by named officials:
Bouleutai
PHILOSTRATOS son of Philinos of Acharnai (VI) *APF* 551
EUTHYKRATES son of Drakontides of Aphidna (IX) *PA* 5601
CHAIRESTRATOS son of Chairedemos of Rhamnous (IX)
OULIAS of Steiria (III)
[PH]ALANTHOS of Kerameis (V)
EUKRATES of Lamptrai (I) ?*PA* 5758; *APF* 197
LYKOURGOS of Melite (VII) *PA* 9254
KALLISTHENES son of Charopides of Trinemeia (VII) *PA* 8106
EUETION (son of Autokleides) of Sphettos (V) *PA* 5463; *APF* 189f.
EMPEDOS of Oe (VI)
THEOKRINES of Hybadai (IV) *PA* 6946
PHILOKRATES (? son of Philon) of Aixone (VII) ?*PA* 14600; *APF* 275f.
PROTOKLES of Kephisia (I)
BOULIS of Thorai (X) cf. *PA* 2916
DEMETRIOS (son of Euktemon) of Aphidna (IX) *PA* 3392
AMEINIAS of Agryle (I) *PA* 677
ANTIDOTOS (son of Apollodoros) of Sypalettos (VII) *PA* 1019
THEODOROS (? son of Antidoros) of Pallene (X)
EPIGETHES of Eroiadai (VIII or X)
NIKANDROS of Marathon (IX)
LYSITHEOS of Euonymon (I)
Tamias of council
SOTI[A]DES of Acharnai (VI)
Grammateus of council
SOKRATES (? son of Pyr--) of Paionidai (IV)

327/6 (Ol. 113.2)

Archon
HEGEMON *PA* 6291
FGH 255 (8); Dion. *Dein.* 9; Arrian *Anab.* 5.19.3; IG ii² [356] (Tod 199; SEG 21.286); [357] (SEG 21.287); [358] (but see SEG 21.326 – 307/6); 1497.10; 1527.42; 1628.[455], 630; 1629.1109f.; 1631.295; SEG 21.288 (25.69 – ? 307/6); 23.104; 24.159.506; *Hesperia* 1938, 95 (15.30) (Meritt) (Schwenk no. 61); 1947, 184 (90.2) (Pritchett: *Agora* xv.50).

Tamias Paralou
LYSANIAS son of Proxenos of Sounion (IV) *PA* 9323; *APF* 354
IG ii² 1628.8f.; 1629.689. He is best placed in this year, as we have a tamias for 326/5.

Hieromnemon
APEMANTOS *PA* 1347a
FD III, 5, 17.3; 58.59.

Naopoioi to Delphi
EPITELES son of Soinomos (of Pergase) (I) *PA* 4955 = 4963
PYTHODOROS son of Python (? of Kedoi) (I) *APF* 486
FD III, 5, 58.22, 29; cf. 91.24, 26.

COUNCIL AND ASSEMBLY

The secretary is found or restored at IG ii² 356, 357, SEG 21.288 (assuring the patronymic):

Grammateus
AUTOKLES son of Autias of Acharnai (VI) *NPA* 41

(i) IG ii² 356 (Tod 199; SEG 21.286; 23.57) honours Memnon of Rhodes; it is dated to the fourth prytany, of Hippothontis, though the seventh is an alternative (SEG; Schwenk no. 58), the penultimate day of the month, twenty-sixth of the prytany, kyria ekklesia.

(ii) IG ii² 357 (SEG 21.287) is a proxeny decree for an Eretrian, dated in IG and Schwenk no. 57 to the sixth prytany, of Aiantis, though the tenth has been suggested, the last day of the month, in the early days of the prytany (Hansen, *GRBS* 1982, 344 (= *Ecclesia* 96)).

(iii) SEG 21.288 seems to belong to this year (but cf. 25.69) and is honorific; it is from the ninth prytany, of Oineis, apparently Mounichion 21, but this is a problem (Schwenk no. 59; Hansen, *GRBS* 1982, 348 (= *Ecclesia* 100)):

Bouleutes epistates
PAMPHILOS (son of Chairephilos) of P[aiania] (III) *PA* 11555; *APF* 567
Proposer
-- of Thria (VI)

326/5 (Ol. 113.3)

Archon
CHREMES *PA* 15568
FGH 255 (8); Diod. 17.87.1; Dion. *Dein*. 9; IG ii² 359; [363] (but see 335/
4); [800] (SEG 21.289 and see below); 1157.[2], [13] (Schwenk no. 65);
1198.3 (Schwenk no. 66); 1472.[11f.]; 1628.298f., 341, 345, 357f., 381, 391,
406, 427, 444f., 487, 641; 1629.791, 861, 865, 878, 900, 910, 926, 948, 966f.,
1121; 1631.302f.; *Hesperia* 1985, 137–9 (Palagia and Clinton).

Strategoi
THRASYBOULOS son of Thrason of Erchia (II) *PA* 7304; *APF* 239
IG ii² 1628.40f.; 2969.4ff. He was concerned with the supply of corn.

DIOXANDROS *PA* 4526
IG ii² 1628.17f., 28. General to Samos.

. . .⁶. . . OS of Eroiadai (VIII) *APF* 540 n.1
IG ii² 1628.109f. General to Samos. I do not follow *APF* in the suggestion
of Philokles.

DIPHILOS of Aixone (VII) ?*PA* 4467 = ?4468; *APF* 168f.
IG ii² 1628.[119f.]; *Insc. Priene* 5.18. General to Samos.

Tamias Paralou
HEGEMON of Athmonon (VII) *PA* 6294; *APF* 208
IG ii² 1628.79f.

Tamias of rigging
ARISTOKLEIDES son of Thrasykles of Melite (VII)
SEG 24.159.341ff.

Hieromnemon
LYSISTRATOS *PA* 9601
FD III, 5, 20.44; 60 B.16.

Naopoioi to Delphi
PYTHODOROS son of Python (? of Kedoi) (I) *APF* 486
EPITELES son of Soinomos (of Pergase) (I) *PA* 4955 = 4963
THEOPHRON son of Euthyphron (? of Lamptrai) (I) *PA* 7178
FD III, 5, 20.33, 38; cf. 91.24, 27, 28; cf. p. 242.

Priest of Asklepios
PHILOKLES of Xypete (VII) *PA* 14553
IG ii² 4397.

Demarchos
DORO[THE]OS of Aixone (VII) *PA* 4601
IG ii² 1198.15f.; cf. 1196.4. See Whitehead, *ZPE* 47 (1982), 38f.

COUNCIL AND ASSEMBLY

The name of the secretary may now be asserted through *Hesperia* 1985, 137–9, taken with and helping to confirm the date of IG ii² 800:
Grammateus
KEPHISOKL[ES]

(i) IG ii² 359 is a prescript from the prytany of Erechtheis, restored as the seventh, Elaphebolion 8, thirtieth day of the prytany, kyria ekklesia, and this may stand (Hansen, *GRBS* 1982, 336f. (= *Ecclesia* 88f.); Schwenk no. 63, unconvincingly suggesting an Astypalaian honorand).

(ii) IG ii² 800 (SEG 21.289) is a fragment from the prytany of Leontis, restored with a query as the sixth:
Bouleutes epistates
[THE]OPOMPOS
Symproedroi
--MENES of Lamptrai (I)
-- of Paiania (III)
DEM--
-- ? of Oe (VI)
THEOKL[ES]
-- of Anaphlystos (X)
-- of Sphettos (V)
Proposer
-- son of --toros or --tores of Sy[bridai] (I)
For the latter, Schwenk no. 64 leaves Sy[palettios] as a possibility, but this seems too long.

(iii) IG ii² 1628.38f. records a decree concerning triremes:
Proposer
PO[LYEUKTOS] of Kydantidai (II) *PA* 11947 = ?11928 = ?11927

(iv) IG ii² 1629.520 mentions a decree concerning the collection of naval debts:
Proposer
DEMADES (son of Demeas) of Paiania (III) *PA* 3263; *APF* 99ff.

(v) He proposed another decree concerning epidoseis (IG ii² 1628.348f.; 1629.869; 1631.65).

(vi) *Hesperia* 1985, 137–9 (Palagia and Clinton), is a decree honouring the priest of Asklepios (who was probably Philokles in this year) from the prytany of Pandionis, which was probably the eighth prytany, possibly the ninth.

325/4 (Ol. 113.4)

Archon
ANTIKLES *PA* 1058
FGH 255 (8); Diod. 17.110.1; Dion. *ad Amm.* 12; *Dein.* 9; IG ii² 360; [361];
1203.3, 8 (Schwenk no. 70); 1472.[12]; 1628.458; 1629.351, 468, 560, 593,
609, 679, 794f., 816, 1132, 1162; 1631.[177f.], 198f., 310, 342, 355, 411;
1926; Add. 2833a.4 (*Hesperia* 1939, 39 (25) (Schweigert), 66 (60) (Meritt));
2838.1; SEG 24.159.448f.; *Hesperia* 1948, 39 (25.4) (Meritt: *Agora* xv.51).

Strategoi
PHILOKLES (? son of Phormion of Eroiadai) (VIII) *PA* 14541; *APF* 539ff.
Deinarchos 3.1, 12. General over Mounichia and the dockyards, he betrayed his promise not to admit Harpalos. For the date see *APF* 540. On
identity see, however, Reinmuth 67f., 73f.

?DEMETRIOS son of Phanostratos of Phaleron (IX) *PA* 3455; *APF* 107ff.
IG ii² 2971. The inscription records service as hipparch and three
generalships. Dow and Travis, *Hesperia* 1943, 145ff., put the latter in the
years 325/4 to 319/18, but see *APF* 108.

Naval officer
DIOPHANTOS son of Phrasikleides of Myrrhinous (III) *PA* 4435; *APF* 166
IG ii² 1629.618. The precise position is unknown.

Tamias of dockyards
KEPHISODOROS (son of Smikythos of Kydathenaion) (III) *PA* 8373
IG ii² 1631.357ff.

Tamias of rigging
ANTISTHENES of Phaleron (IX) *PA* 1202
IG ii² 1629.465.

Hieropoioi (κατ'ἐνιαυτόν)
[POLYE]UKTOS son of [? Harmo]dios of Themakos (I)
. .⁴. . L]YKOS son of Ka. . .it. .os of Ikarion (II)
. . . ? . . . IOS son of K[r]atio[s] of Kydathenaion (III)
-- of Leukonoion (IV)
-- son of --es of Kephale (V)
-- son of --os or --es of Perithoidai (VI)
[T]IMOKRATES son of Philinos of Eleusis (VIII)
IG ii² 2838 with fuller readings by Peek, *Kerameikos* III.13ff. no. 10.

Hieromnemon
HERMI[PPOS?]
BCH 1960, 459ff. line 6 (Daux). See Bousquet, *Mélanges Daux* 21ff.

Priest of Asklepios
ARCHIPPOS son of Arch-- of Koile (VIII)
IG ii² 4371 (=4428); *MDAI(A)* 1942, 55 (83) (Peek). Not *PA* 2406.

Demarchos
PO-- of Athmonon (VII)
IG ii² 1203.20 (Schwenk no. 70).

Oikistes
MILTIADES (? son of Kimon of Lakiadai) (VI) *PA* 10210; *APF* 309
IG ii² 1629.18f., 39, 60, 72f., 86f., 107f., 124f., 141f., 160f., 223f. (Tod 200).

COUNCIL AND ASSEMBLY

The secretary is found in IG ii² 360 and 361:
Grammateus
ANTIPHON son of Koroibos of Eleusis (VIII) *PA* 1294

(i) IG ii² 360 (Schwenk no. 68) is in honour of Herakleides of Salamis; it is from the fifth prytany, of Aigeis, eleventh day of the month (Posideon 11), thirty-fourth day of the prytany (see Meritt, *Ath. Year* 102f.):
Bouleutes epistates
PHILYLLOS of Eleusis (VIII) *PA* 14798
Proposer
DEMOSTHENES son of Demokles of Lamptrai (I) *PA* 3593

(ii) We may include here the decree of the boule at lines 66ff.
Proposer
PHYLEUS son of Pausanias of Oinoe (VIII or IX) *PA* 15045

(iii) IG ii² 361 (Schwenk no. 69) is a fragment from the tenth prytany, of Akamantis, Thargelion 22, fifth day of the prytany, from the boule:
Bouleutes epistates
ARCHEST[RAT]OS of Athmonon (VII) *PA* 2416
Proposer
-- of Alopeke (X)

(iv) There was a decree concerning naval equipment (IG ii² 1629.14f., 35f., 57, 103f., 120, 137f., 157):
Proposer
HAGNONIDES (son of Nikoxenos) of Pergase (I) *PA* 176

(v) Another concerned the squadron sent to the Adriatic (IG ii² 1629.21, 42, 63, 75, 89f., 110, 127, 144, 163, 170):
Proposer
KEPHISOPHON son of Lysiphon of Cholargos (V) *PA* 8419
Hypereides F LVI can be associated with this mission.

(vi) There was a decree of the boule concerning a quadrireme (IG ii² 1629.273):
Proposer
ALKIMACHOS son of . . .⁶. . . os or . . .⁶. . . es of Myrrhinoutte (II) *PA* 622

Dated to this year is the prosecution of Aristogeiton represented in Dem.

25 and 26 and Lykourgos FF 1–7 (Hansen, *Apagoge* no. 32); the prosecutors were appointed by the assembly:

Kategoroi

DEMOSTHENES son of Demosthenes of Paiania (III) *PA* 3597; *APF* 113ff.

LYKOURGOS son of Lykophron of Boutadai (VI) *PA* 9251; *APF* 348ff.

From Deinarchos 2.13 we evidently learn the following:

Bouleutes

ARISTOGEITON son of Kydimachos *PA* 1775

He also addressed the assembly.

324/3 (Ol. 114.1)

Archon

HEGESIAS son of Kephisodoros *PA* 6313

MP B 8; *FGH* 255 (9); Diod. 17.113.1 (Agesias); Arrian *Anab.* 7.28.1; IG ii² 362 (SEG 21.291); [363] (but see 335/4); [454] (SEG 21.293); [547] (SEG 21.292; 32.88); 1176. [9] (*CSCA* 1974, 293 (Stroud); Schwenk no. 76); 1257 (Schwenk no. 77); 1258.22 (Schwenk no. 78); 1631.[62], [89f.], [94f.], 143, [151], 318, 370, 386, 441; 2935.3f.; SEG 21.290; *Hesperia* 1941, 43 (11.[11]) (Meritt: *Agora* xv.53, with patronymic), 52 ([13]) (Meritt). Panathenaic amphoras: Beazley, *Black Figure* 415.

Strategoi

?DEMETRIOS son of Phanostratos of Phaleron (IX) *PA* 3455; *APF* 107ff. See 325/4.

PHEREKLEIDES son of Pherekles of Perithoidai (VI) *PA* 14187

Reinmuth no. 15 (*AE* 1918, 76, 99 (Leonardos)); cf. IG ii² 2968. He was general at Akte; on date see below ephebic officials.

DIKAIOGENES (son of Menexenos) of Kydathenaion (III) *PA* 3776; *APF* 147, 540

IG ii² 1631.380f.; Reinmuth no. 15 (*AE* 1918, 76, 99 (Leonardos)). He was general at Peiraieus.

LEOSTHENES son of Leosthenes of Kephale (V) *PA* 9142=9144; *APF* 342ff.

?Diod. 17.111.1ff.; 18.9.1ff.; Reinmuth no. 15 (*AE* 1918, 76, 99 (Leonardos)). He was general over the country. We are told, however, of his dealings with mercenaries who had come over from Asia, a tale which continues into 323/2. See Badian, *JHS* 1961, 27, 37ff. (on chronology).

Ephebic officials

The following come from Reinmuth no. 15, though the date cannot be regarded as secure:

Sophronistes

THYMOCHARES son of Demochares of Leukonoion (IV) *APF* 142

Kosmetes

PHILOKLES son of Phormion of Eroiadai (VIII) *PA* 14541; *APF* 539ff.
Didaskalos
PYTHA-- son of --okles of Dekeleia (VIII)
Epimeletes
NIKODOROS son of Philotheros of Acharnai (VI)

Financial administrator
MENESAICHMOS *PA* 9983
Dion. *Dein.* 11 (660 U.-R.). Presumably chosen for four years.

Poletai
ERGINOS son of Theoklitos of Kydathenaion (III)
ANTIGENES son of Aristomachos of Xypete (VII) ?*PA* 994
AE 1973, 175f.

Hieromnemon
EUTHYKLES
FD III, 5, 61 I.4, II A.16.

Naopoioi to Delphi
EPITELES son of Soinomos (of Pergase) (I) *PA* 4955 = 4963
THEOPHRON son of Euthyphron (? of Lamptrai) (I) *PA* 7178
FD III, 5, 61 II B.25f.; cf. 91.26f.; cf. p. 242.

Kategoroi
HYPEREIDES son of Glaukippos of Kollytos (II) *PA* 13912; *APF* 517ff.
PYTHEAS *PA* 12342
MENESAICHMOS *PA* 9983
HIMERAIOS son of Phanostratos of Phaleron (IX) *PA* 7578; *APF* 108
?PATROKLES or PROKLES *PA* 12208
STRATOKLES son of Euthydemos of Diomeia (II) *PA* 12938; *APF* 495
Deinarchos 1.20f. (Stratokles); Plut. *Mor.* 846c; Photios *Bibl.* p. 494 a.36ff.
Ten prosecutors were chosen against those charged with taking money
from Harpalos (Deinarchos 2.6) and these are the names which survive.
Patrokles/Prokles has been doubted; Badian, *JHS* 1961, 32 n. 113, 42ff.,
for chronology.

COUNCIL AND ASSEMBLY

The secretary is known from IG ii² 362 (SEG 21.291); 454 (SEG 21.293);
547 (SEG 21.292); *Agora* xv.53.17f. (especially); SEG 21.290; *Hesperia*
1941, 52 (13):
Grammateus
EUPHANES son of Phrynon of Rhamnous (IX)

(i) IG ii² 362 (Schwenk no. 73) is a prescript from the ninth prytany, of
Akamantis, Thargelion 18, twenty-ninth day of the prytany, kyria
ekklesia.

(ii) IG ii² 454 (SEG 21.293; Schwenk no. 75) is from the tenth prytany, of Erechtheis, Skirophorion 25:
Bouleutes epistates
CHARIDE[MOS] *PA* 15372
Symproedroi
--OS of Halai (II)
--S of Phrearrhioi (IV)
-- of Lakiadai (VI)
X-- of tribe VII
KALL-- of tribe X
Proposer
? -- son of --eri--
For the latter see Hansen, *GRBS* 1984, 139.

(iii) IG ii² 547 (SEG 21.292; Schwenk no. 74) has been restored to the tenth prytany, of Erechtheis, Thargelion 29, fifth day of the prytany, but this is not secure (Hansen, *GRBS* 1982, 348 (= *Ecclesia* 100)):
Symproedroi
[DION]YSIOS of K[ydathenaion] (III)
. . . .⁸. . . . of Hekale (IV)
[?AR]CHIN[OS]
EP--
--S of Alopeke (X)

(iv) IG ii² 1631.350f. mentions a decree of the council concerning a naval debt:
Proposer
POLYEUKTOS son of Kallikrates of Hestiaia (II) *PA* 11943

(v) At lines 655ff. is a decree of this year or earlier concerning naval equipment:
Proposer
DEMOPHILOS son of Demophilos of Acharnai (VI) *PA* 3675; *APF* 498

(vi) SEG 21.290 (Schwenk no. 71) is restored to the fifth prytany, of Aiantis, Posideon 28, thirty-first day of the prytany, but this is speculative.

(vii) *Hesperia* 1941, 52 (13) (Meritt; Schwenk no. 72), seems to be an honorific decree; it is from the sixth prytany, of Pandionis (the only restoration available).

(viii) I will not rehearse all the details of the Harpalos affair (see in general Plut. *Dem.* 25f.). There was a decree that the Areiopagos should investigate (Deinarchos 1.4, 61, 82f., 85f., 89; Hypereides 5.1):
Proposer
DEMOSTHENES son of Demosthenes of Paiania (III) *PA* 3597; *APF* 113ff.

(ix) He seems to have included a provision for death for himself if found guilty, as did another (Deinarchos 3.2, 5):
Proposer
PHILOKLES (son of Phormion of Eroiadai) (VIII) *PA* 14541; *APF* 539ff.

(x) A number of other measures are attributed to Demosthenes: that Harpalos

be arrested and his money confiscated (Hypereides 5.8f.; Deinarchos
(xi) 1.68f., 89); honouring Diphilos (Deinarchos 1.43; F 41); that no one should
(xii) believe in any but the traditional gods (Deinarchos 1.94). The latter was
over the request for divine honours from Alexander, in which debate there
spoke Diphilos (Deinarchos F 41), Lykourgos (Plut. *Mor.* 842d) and
(xiii) Pytheas (Plut. *Mor.* 804b), while a decree that Alexander's claims be
recognized was successfully challenged as unconstitutional (Athenaios
5.251b; Aelian *VH* 5.12; Hansen, *Sovereignty* no. 38):
Proposer
DEMADES son of Demeas of Paiania (III) *PA* 3263; *APF* 99ff.
(xiv) Nevertheless such a decree was in fact passed, as it is claimed Demosthenes
eventually supported it (Hypereides 5.31; Deinarchos 1.94).

We may note Leosthenes' secret consultation with the boule (Diod.
17.111.3).

Agora XV.53 records officers of the council. Alessandri, *ASNP* 1982, 66f.,
challenges Meritt's identification of the document as a dedicatory base and
prefers it to be in honour of the prytaneis of a tribe, for him Erechtheis, as in
line 9 he would restore the demotic [ἐκ Κηδ]ῶν instead of an indication of
the archon (cf. SEG 32.175, where the line references are confusing as
between the first publication and that in *Agora* XV). This would help with
the mystery of the name at line eight and would produce:
Bouleutai
--NIAS son of Theopompos
Kedoi
H--IAS son of Kephisodoros
Thus the first official here mentioned might be doubtful:
Tamias of council
-- son of --ates
Grammateus of demos
[CH]ARIPPOS son of Ph[il]on of Rhamnous (IX)
Anagrapheus
--IDES son of Kichonides of Paiania (III)
In charge of laws
EIRENOKLE[S] of Athmonon (VII)

Officials of the boule are the following:
Syllogeis (hieropoioi)
EUTHYKRITOS *PA* 5612
LYSIKLES son of Eirenipp[os] *PA* 9426
IG ii² 1257 A.3, B.4 (Schwenk no. 77).

323/2 (Ol. 114.2)

Archon
KEPHISODOROS *PA* 8347

MP B 9; *FGH* 255 (9); Diod. 18.2.1; Dion. *ad Amm.* 5 (Apollodoros *FGH* 244 F 38b); *Dein.* 9; Arrian *Ind.* 21.1; Athenaios 4.171d (or 366/5); IG ii² [343] (SEG 24.103); 365 (SEG 21.294); 366; [367] (SEG 21.295; 26.81); 368.[19] (SEG 21.296); 369 (SEG 21.298; Osborne D 25); 448 (SEG 21.297; 23.59; 26.82; Osborne D 24); 505.16f.; 1631.325, 347, 443, 507; 1632.24; [3025] (or 366/5); [3053] (or 329/8); 3054.4. Panathenaic amphora: Beazley, *Black Figure* 415.

Strategoi
?DEMETRIOS son of Phanostratos of Phaleron (IX) *PA* 3455; *APF* 107ff.
See 325/4.

[DIK]AIOGENES (son of Menexenos) of Kydathenaion (III) *PA* 3776; *APF* 147, 540
IG ii² 1631.214f. General at Peiraieus. Reinmuth (67, 70) wrongly dates this to 325/4.

PHAIDROS son of Kallias of Sphettos (V) *PA* 13964; *APF* 525
Strabo 10.1.6; ?IG ii² 682.2f. He destroyed Styra in Euboia.

PHOKION son of Phokos *PA* 15076; *APF* 559
Plut. *Phok.* 24.1ff.; Polyainos 3.12. He was chosen general against the Boiotians.

LEOSTHENES son of Leosthenes of Kephale (V) *PA* 9142 = 9144; *APF* 342ff.
Hypereides 6 passim; Diod. 18.9, 11.3ff.; Strabo 9.5.10; Plut. *Dem.* 27.1; *Timol.* 6.5; *Phok.* 23.1ff.; *Pyrrhos* 1.4; *Mor.* 486d, 546a, 803a, 849f; Justin 13.5.12; Arrian *FGH* 156 F 1.9; Paus. 1.1.3, 25.5, 29.13, 3.6.1.
  See also 324/3. General in the Lamian War, he lost his life.

ANTIPHILOS *PA* 1264
Diod. 18.13.6, 15.7; Plut. *Phok.* 24.1f., 25.3. Chosen to replace Leosthenes, he commanded the Greeks in success against the Makedonians in Thessaly.

Nauarchos
EUETION (? son of Pythangelos of Kephisia) (I) *PA* 5461 = ?5462; *APF* 190
Diod. 18.15.9; IG ii² 505.18, 25; cf. 506.10f. He was twice defeated by the Makedonian fleet.

Financial administrator
MENESAICHMOS *PA* 9983
See 324/3.

Tamias of trireme funds
--OS of Pambotadai (I)
IG ii² 1631.504f.

Envoys

POLYEUKTOS son of Sostratos of Sphettos (v) *PA* 11925 = 11934 = 11950
Plut. *Mor.* 846c-d. He went to Arkadia.

HYPEREIDES son of Glaukippos of Kollytos (II) *PA* 13912; *APF* 517ff.
Justin 13.5.10. He went to seek support in the Peloponnese. For another
possible mission see 341/40.

COUNCIL AND ASSEMBLY

The secretary is found or restored in IG ii² 343 (SEG 24.103), 365 (SEG
21.294), 367 (SEG 21.295), 368 (SEG 21.296), 369+ (SEG 21.298;
Osborne D 25), 448 (SEG 21.297; 26.81; Osborne D 24):
Grammateus
ARCHIAS son of Pythodoros of Alopeke (x)

(i) IG ii² 343 (SEG 24.103) honours Apollonides of Sidon:
Bouleutes epistates
EPAMEI[NON ? of Erchia] (II) *PA* 4759 = 4760 = ?4766
Proposer
-- of Anagyrous (I)
I do not wish to say that dotted letters in the texts are part of the latter's
name. The document is totally restored to this year and to the fifth prytany,
of Pandionis, Posideon 25, twenty-first day of the prytany, kyria ekklesia.
Osborne, *Naturalization* II.104, and Schwenk no. 84 retain the same day as
ii² 448, Posideon 16, twenty-second day of the prytany, but see also
Hansen, *GRBS* 1982, 346f. (= *Ecclesia* 98f.). The demotic of the epistates
fits the space in 448, where Osborne reads EPAME[, Schwenk EPAMEIN[.

(ii) IG ii² 448 (SEG 21.297; 26.81; Osborne D 24 (text D 38); Schwenk no. 83)
is a citizenship decree for Euphron of Sikyon:
Proposers
EUPHILETOS son of Euphile[tos ? of Kephisia] (I) *PA* 6054; *APF* 206
PAMPHILOS son of Euphiletos (? of Kephisia) (I) *PA* 11531; *APF* 206
Schwenk prefers Kikynna (v) for the deme, following Charitonides (see
Agora xv.42.326).

(iii) IG ii² 365 (SEG 21.294; 30.66; Schwenk no. 79) praises Lapyris of Kleonai
and is thought by Walbank to deal with reports on the Nemean festival; it is
dated to the first prytany, of Hippothontis, Hekatombaion 11, eleventh
day of the prytany:
Bouleutes epistates
TIMOSTRA[T]O[S] *PA* 13816
Proposer
EPITEL[ES] son of S[o]in[omos] of Pergase (I) *PA* 4963

(iv) IG ii² 366 (Schwenk no. 80) is an honorific decree from the second prytany,
of Aigeis, sixteenth day of the prytany:

Bouleutes epistates
HEGESIAS of Marathon (IX) *PA* 6326
Proposer
ARI . . .⁶. . .
On the latter see Hansen, *GRBS* 1984, 139.

(v) IG ii² 367 (SEG 21.295; 26.81: 32.91; Schwenk no. 81) concerns the Phokians; it is from the third prytany, thirty-sixth day, ekklesia kyria, but the date in Pyanopsion is uncertain (IG has 18, Meritt and Schwenk 19, Pritchett and Neugebauer, *Calendars* 25):
Proposer
-- son of --doros of Melite (VII)
On the latter see Hansen, *GRBS* 1984, 139.

(vi) IG ii² 368.19ff. (SEG 21.296; Schwenk no. 82) concerns the proxeny of Theophantos; the prytany is the fifth, of Pandionis, the month Posideon, the rest uncertain (Hansen, *GRBS* 1982, 345 (= *Ecclesia* 97)).

(vii) IG ii² 369 + (SEG 21.298; Osborne D 25; Schwenk no. 85) is a citizenship decree for a Bosporan from the eighth prytany, of Oineis.

(viii) IG ii² 370 (SEG 21.299) is the heading of an alliance with the Aitolians dated to this year (cf. Diod. 17.111.3, 18.9.5, 11.1).

(ix) There is a chance that the honorific decree SEG 21.340 may belong here.

(x) A law concerning the navy belongs in this year or earlier (IG ii² 1631.511; 1632.19):
Proposer
DIPHILOS (son of Diopeithes of Sounion) (IV) *PA* 4467 = 4487; *APF* 168f.

(xi) For the decree concerning the Apatouria mentioned at Athenaios 4.171e see 366/5 (ii).

(xii) Diod. 18.10 reports the assembly at which a decree was passed for
(xiii) mobilisation and the sending of envoys. Late in the year, it seems, a decree was passed for the return of Demosthenes from exile (Plut. *Dem.* 27.6; *Mor.* 846d):
Proposer
DEMON son of Demomeles of Paiania (III) *PA* 3736; *APF* 116ff.

Plut. *Phok.* 22.3f. has an assembly on the news of Alexander's death which pits Phokion against Demades and in c. 23 he is at odds with Leosthenes and Hypereides; c. 24 again has him speaking.

322/1 (Ol. 114.3)

Archon
PHILOKLES *PA* 14524
MP B 10; *FGH* 255 (9); Diod. 18.26.1; Dion. *Dein.* 9; Diog. 5.10

(Apollodoros *FGH* 244 F 38); anon. *de com.* 3.59 (Koster); IG ii² [371]; [372] (SEG 21.300; 23.60); 373.16 (SEG 21.301); [375] (SEG 21.302); 377.7; 1468.13f.; 1469.167; 1472.16; 2839.[4].

Strategoi

ANTIPHILOS *PA* 1264
Diod. 18.17.6 and see 323/2. He was in command at Krannon, which defeat occurred in Metageitnion (Plut. *Dem.* 28.1).

?CHARIAS son of Euthykrates of Kydathenaion (III) *PA* 15346; *APF* 193
Davies, *Wealth* 166, puts this here without a query, but it seems to have no justification from IG ii² 2847 nor is it so dated in *APF*.

?THYMOCHARES son of Phaidros of Sphettos (V) *PA* 7412; *APF* 525f.
This is equally shaky, for it depends on the invention of a campaign to Cyprus to accommodate the generalship mentioned at IG ii² 682.4ff.

Financial administrator

MENESAICHMOS *PA* 9983
See 324/3.

Envoys

PHOKION son of Phokos *PA* 15076; *APF* 559
DEMADES son of Demeas of Paiania (III) *PA* 3263; *APF* 99ff.
XENOKRATES son of Agathenor of Chalkedon
Diod. 18.18.2f.; Plut. *Phok.* 26.3f., 27; Diog. 4.9 (Xenokrates). They were involved in negotiations with Antipatros, Xenokrates, the head of the Akademy, being added to the second embassy.

DEMETRIOS son of Phanostratos of Phaleron (IX) *PA* 3455; *APF* 107ff.
Demetrios *On Style* 5.289. Possibly he was on the last mentioned embassy.

COUNCIL AND ASSEMBLY

The secretary is found or restored in IG ii² 371, 372, 373, 375, 376:
Grammateus

EUTHYGENES son of Hephaistodemos of Kephisia (I) *PA* 5512

(i) IG ii² 371 is a fragment from the seventh prytany, in Anthesterion, a proxeny decree if correctly associated with 308 (see Schwenk no. 86).

(ii) IG ii² 372 (SEG 21.300; 23.60; Schwenk no. 87) is a fragment from the eighth prytany, possibly Elaphebolion 18 or 19 at the assembly in the precinct of Dionysos, sixth, eighth or ninth day of the prytany (Hansen, *GRBS* 1982, 345 (=*Ecclesia* 97)):
Proposer

[DEMADE]S son of Deme[as of Paiania] (III) *PA* 3263; *APF* 99ff.

(iii) IG ii² 373.16ff. (SEG 21.301; Schwenk no. 88) is evidently a probouleumatic decree (though the procedure is problematic: see

411

Schwenk) honouring Euenor of Akarnania; it is from the ninth prytany, of Oineis, Thargelion 2, twenty-third day of the prytany, but there seems to be a mason's error here (Hansen, *GRBS* 1982, 345 (= *Ecclesia* 97)):

Bouleutes epistates
EUALKOS of Phaleron (IX) *PA* 5264
Proposer
DIOPHANTOS son of Phrasikleides of Myrrhinous (III) *PA* 4435; *APF* 166

(iv) IG ii² 375 (SEG 21.302; Schwenk no. 89) is from the tenth prytany, of Pandionis, the last day of Thargelion (though this seems to be in error for Skirophorion), thirty-fifth or thirty-seventh day of the prytany (Hansen, *GRBS* 1982, 345 (= *Ecclesia* 97)):

Bouleutes epistates
?[A]N[T]ID[O]TO[S] of [Th]ri[a] (VI)
Proposer
HEGEM[ON ?]

(v) IG ii² 376 (Schwenk no. 90) is a fragment restored to the last day of Posideon or Gamelion.

(vi) IG ii² 377 (Schwenk no. 91) is little more than letters.

(vii) After the Greek defeat, a bill was passed establishing the death sentence for anti-Makedonian orators:

Proposer
DEMADES son of Demeas of Paiania (III) *PA* 3263; *APF* 99ff.

(viii) He was also responsible for the decree for envoys to Antipatros: Plut. *Phok.* 26.2f., which has Phokion speaking to the people. Demochares also spoke (Plut. *Mor.* 847d).

APPENDIX

Basileus
[E]XEKESTIDES son of [Nikokr]ates of Alopeke (X)
  Paredroi
  NIKOKRATES son of Exekes[tides of Alopeke] (X)
  KLEAINETOS son of Meno[n]
SEG 32.240. They could come within our period, but could be later. Note that SEG misreports the date in the original publication.

Paredros of basileus
EUTHYDEMOS *PA* 5518
IG ii² 1230.3. Perhaps within our period.

Polemarchos
DEMOTELES son of Ant[i]machos of Halai (II or VII) *PA* 3636; *APF* 26
IG ii² 1578.1 – *c.* 330 (cf. Lewis, *Hesperia* 1959, 236).

Thesmothetes
TIMOK[RATES] son of T-- of tribe IV or IX
Hesperia 1934, 44 (32.2, 8f.) = 1946, 189 (35) (Meritt) – possibly 320s.

Basileus or polemarchos or thesmothetes
PISTIAS *PA* 11823
Deinarchos 1.53. See Hansen, *Eisangelia* no. 117.

Note: Plut. *Mor.* 817c cites Demosthenes as speaking of himself as thesmothetes, but this is a misunderstanding of Dem. 21.30ff. at 33.

Strategoi
NAUSIKLES son of Klearchos of Oe (VI) *PA* 10552; *APF* 396f.
IG ii² 1623.329f. Before 334/3; cf. Dem. 18.114.

PHEREKLEIDES son of Pherekles of Perithoidai (VI) *PA* 14187
IG ii² 2968.5ff. He was general over the country about, but not in, 333/2; see Reinmuth 67.

PHILEMONIDES
Hesperia Suppl. 8.274.3 (Pritchett: Reinmuth no. 12). General in the 330s; cf. Davies, *Wealth* 165.

POLYEUKTOS (? of Kydantidai) (II) ?*PA* 11947
Hypereides FF 155–7. General between 360 and 322, probably late in that period. See Hansen, *GRBS* 1983, 175.

?CHARES son of Theochares of Angele (III) *PA* 15292; *APF* 568f.
Plut. *Mor.* 848e speaks of him commanding a mercenary force at Tainaron, perhaps after the death of Agis and not as Athenian strategos; see Badian, *JHS* 1961, 26 and nn. 69 and 70.

DIOTI[MOS] (son of Diopeithes of Euonymon) (I) *PA* 4384; *APF* 163f.
IG ii² 408.8f., possibly to be dated at the period of corn shortage, 330–326.

PHILOKLES (? son of Phormion of Eroiadai) (VIII) *PA* 14541; *APF* 539ff.
Deinarchos 3.12. He was general more than ten times before 324/3, one of which occasions is placed in 325/4.

Note: On Phokion see the appendix to Section VII. The generalship of Derkylos at IG ii² 1187.1f. is now dated to 319/18 (Mitchel, *Hesperia* 1964, 337ff.).

Officer
[?OLYMPI]ODOROS (son of Diotimos of Euonymon) (I) *PA* 11401; *APF* 164f.
IG ii² 408.8f. He was to see to the escort of corn. On the identity see *APF*. On date see above on the general Diotimos.

Taxiarchoi
PROKLEIDES (? of Thorai) (X)
SEG 3.116 – *c.* 330. For the demotic see Davies, *Wealth* 152.

DIAITOS of Pambotadai (I)
DEMOPHON of Erchia (II)
--RES of tribe VII
L-- of Marathon (IX)
G-- of Aigilia (X)
SEG 17.85 – second half of the century.

Peripolarchos
ARISTOMENES son of Kannonos of Philaidai (II) *PA* 2006
IG ii² 2968.5ff. He was honoured along with the general Pherekleides (see above).

Hipparchoi
LYKOPHRON *PA* 9255
Hypereides 1.17f. For three years on Lemnos before 333.

PHILOKLES (? son of Phormion of Eroiadai) (VIII) *PA* 14541; *APF* 539ff.
Deinarchos 3.12. Three or four times before 324/3.

?DEMETRIOS son of Phanostratos of Phaleron (IX) *PA* 3455; *APF* 107ff.
IG ii² 2971.18, 33. See under 325/4 strategoi.

[?EUE]TION son of Pythangelos of Kephisia (I) *PA* 5462; *APF* 190
EPILYKOS son of Nikostra[tos of Gargettos] (II) *APF* 312
Hesperia 1937, 462 (10) (Crosby) – before 325.

ANTIKRATES son of Sokrates of Hermos (V)
PATROKLES son of Hierokles of Philaidai (II)
Hesperia 1953, 51 (Thompson).

ANTID[O]ROS of Thria (VII)
SEG 30.114.

Phylarchoi
LYKOPHRON *PA* 9255
Hypereides 1.17. Before being hipparch (see above).

DEMETRIOS son of [Anti]phanes of Alopeke (X)
SEG 3.115.5 – possibly in this period.

EUTHYKRATES of Pergase (I)
MOIRAGENES of Ikarion (II)
[HA]GNODEMOS of Paiania (III)
Hesperia 1940, 58 (6) (Meritt). A date around 380 is not necessary.

--ON of Oe (VI)
Hesperia 1946, 176f. (24) (Meritt) – *c.* 325.

Ephebic officers
The following come from Reinmuth no. 12 (*Hesperia* Suppl. 8.273ff. (Pritchett)):

Appendix

Sophronistes
CHEIMEUS (? son of Kikon of Lakiadai) (VI) ?*PA* 15545; *APF* 574

Didaskalos?
PHILIPPOS

Akontistes
KEPHISIPPOS

Paidotribes
?S--ON
SEG 32.206.

Tamiai Paralou
?MEIXIGENES son of [M]ikon of Cholleidai (IV) *PA* 9754; *APF* 58
DIOPHANTOS *APF* 166
IG ii² 1254.2, 6ff., 17f. – second half of the century.

ONESANDROS son of Ithaimenes of Eleusis (VIII) *APF* 420
Hesperia 1961, 268 (93.5) (Meritt) – second half of the century.

?KONON son of Kleisthenes of Athmonon (VII) *APF* 321
REG 1931, 296 (2.3, 6f.) = Dain, *Insc. Bardo* 27 – possibly in our period.

Tamias
?[TH]ALLOS son of [Ph]anotheos of Paiania (III) *PA* 6581
IG ii² 3208 – possibly in our period, but it is not clear what sort of tamias he was.

Note: D. M. Lewis informs me of his opinion that *MDAI(A)* 1941, 235ff. (7), goes with IG ii² 1469, so that the tamias there found was active after 321.

Tamiai of trireme funds
?APHRO--
?ARCHI-- of Anaphlystos (X)
IG ii² 1624.26, 29, where the restoration is not certain.

ANTIPHON of Erchia (II) *PA* 1296
EUPOLE[MO]S (son of Euthymenides) of Myrrhinous (III) *PA* 5928
LEOTROPHIDES of Kropidai (IV) *PA* 9158
IG ii² 1627.33f., 73f., 76f., 155f.; 1629.343f. They must antedate 330/29 and if tribal rotation applied to the position, Antiphon could belong to 335/4, Eupolemos to 334/3, Leotrophides to 333/2, and if Archi-- above was tamias, his year could be 337/6.

Tamiai?
The following come from *Hesperia* 1946, 178 (25), with SEG 14.112; Meritt believes this may be a list of tamiai, whereby the demotic of the secretary would fit 325/4 in the cycle:
--O-- of tribe I

PH[ILOI]TIOS of Ionidai (II)
SO[SI]MACHOS of Myrrhinous (III)
KALLIMEDON of Cholleidai (IV) *PA* 8033
P . . . IOS of tribe V
--ES of Acharnai (VI)
--S of Phlya (VII)
-- of Oinoe (VIII)
[DE]MOKLEIDES or [TI]MOKLEIDES of Aphidna (IX)
. .⁴. .ODOROS of Alopeke (X)
Grammateus
ARISTOKLEIDES son of Aristokles of Sounion (IV)

Financial
DIONYSIOS *PA* 4095
Deinarchos F 13 – ἐπὶ τῆς διοικήσεως.

Poletai?
-- ? son of Stry--
EUPOLIS ? son of Eu[themon of Halai] (VII) ?*PA* 5940; *APF* 198
EUKRATES son of Ma--
Grammateus
TIMO--
Hesperia 1957, 19 (58) (Crosby) – last third of the century.

Note: Davies, *APF* 137, takes Plut. *Mor.* 851b to ascribe, erroneously (?), a second position as sitones to Demosthenes in the early 320s, but the reference is general and not, I think, to an arche (perhaps it was in the subscription of 328/7: Dem. 34.38f.; IG ii² 360).

Epimeletes of pompeia
KEPHISO--
IG ii² 1494.4. Dated *c.* 334/3, but there are problems with the text which, I am informed, combines 1493, 1494, 1495, 1497 and *Hesperia* 1937, 456f. (6) (Crosby).

Epistates
NEOPTOLEMOS son of Antikles of Melite (VII) *PA* 10652; *APF* 399f.
Dem. 18.114. He was epistates of many works and if he could be restored at IG ii² 1231 instead of Tlepolemos (Raubitschek unpublished; this in spite of Threatte, *Grammar* 1.490), he was epimeletes of certain rites and adorned the shrine of Plouton (I owe this to D.M. Lewis).

Epistatai of the temple of Zeus Soter
-- son of Plei[stias] of Ana-- *PA* 11866
-- son of Ep[i]phanes of Azenia (VIII) *PA* 4970
LE[OCH]ARES son of Le[ok]rat[es] of Pallene (X) *PA* 9175; *APF* 344
[KL]EO--
ARIS[T]EIDES son of Arist[on] of Pergase (I) *PA* 1714

Grammateus
[EPI]KRA[TES]
IG ii² 1669.2ff. – after the middle of the century.

Epistates of the Akademy
ARISTOMACHOS *PA* 1961
Hypereides 5.26. This mysterious post dates before 324/3.

Note: This may be the place to list the functions fulfilled by
LYKOURGOS son of Lykophron of Boutadai (VI) *PA* 9251; *APF* 348ff.
The evidence is set out in the testimonia in the Teubner edition of
Lykourgos; cf. Paus. 1.29.16 and Hypereides F 118 and below IG ii² 3207:
a. Elected over preparation for war (cf. b–f).
b. Provided 400 triremes.
c. Built dockyards (Hypereides).
d. Finished shipsheds.
e. Finished skeuotheke.
f. Built harbours (Hypereides).
g. Built gymnasion in Lykeion.
h. Built palaistra.
i. Finished the theatre of Dionysos as epistates.
j. Completed other buildings.
k. Put foundation walls around the Panathenaic stadion.
l. Reorganized and saw to making of cult equipment for Athene.
m. Saw to the Odeion (Hypereides).

Hieropoios to Delphi?
TIMOKRATES son of Nikomachos of Acharnai (VI)
SEG 25.568.

Note: It may be doubted that --teles son of Medeios at IG ii² 4648 was a
state hieropoios.

Plouton and the Furies
IG ii² 1933 gives us names associated with this cult about our period; D.M.
Lewis informs me that 1934 cannot belong to this period (cf. Clinton,
Sacred Officials 22):
KRITODEMOS son of [E]ndios of Lamptrai (I) *PA* 8812; *APF* 179
EPIKRATES son of [Pe]isianax [of Sounion] (IV) *APF* 378
THRASYLLOS son of [Th]rasyllos [of Dekeleia] (VIII) *PA* 7341; *APF* 241
ANTIGENES son of Xenokles of Oe (VI) *PA* 995
PYRRHOS son of Pythodoros of Acherdous (VIII) *PA* 12514
BOULARCHOS son of [B]oular[ch]os of Phlya (VII) *PA* 2913
APOLLODOROS son of Apollodo[ros] *PA* 1392
ETEOKLES son of Chremonides [of Aithalidai] (IV)
PHILOTIMOS son of Akestothemi[s] *PA* 14747
[A]RIST[ODE]M[OS] son of Aristodemos *PA* 1802

Epimeletai of tribe?
[KLEOPEITHE]S son of Theopompos of Pallene (X) *PA* 8611
--O]N son of Theophilos of Anaphlystos (X) *PA* 7128
IG ii² 1596.21ff. For the suggestion of the 320s see Lewis in *Problèmes de la terre* 191.

Epimeletai of tribe III Pandionis
[PHEIDIPPOS] son of [Ph]eidon of Paiania *PA* 14162; *APF* 567
. . . ? . . . AS son of Kallisthen[es of ?Myrrhinous] *PA* 8103
NIKOMACHOS son of Thra[s. . ⁵ . .] of Kydathenaion *PA* 10951; *APF* 253
IG ii² 1152.3ff. (= 596) – perhaps after our period. The restoration of Myrrhinous depends on trittys distribution, not a safe assumption.

Demarchoi
PHILOTHEROS of Aixone (VII) *PA* 14502
IG ii² 1197.20 – *c.* 330

PHI[LERIPHOS] son of [A]ischeas of Halai (VII) *APF* 535, 537f.
IG ii² 1598.37f. – 320s ? For the restoration, rather than Philippos, see SEG 21.573 and Whitehead, *Demes* no. 16.

ISCHYRIAS of Halai (II)
SEG 2.7.6 – between 330 and 325 and before the next man.

KYBERNIS of Halai (II)
SEG 2.7.20. See the last entry.

--AIOS son of [Sos]igenes of Ikarion (II)
SEG 22.117.1, 7 – about 330 and before the next man.

THOUKYDIDES of Ikarion (II) *PA* 7273
SEG 22.117.6f. See the last entry.

MNESARCHIDE[S] of Oinoe (VIII)
IG ii² 1594.51 – 320s?

A[N]TIPA[TROS] of Sphettos (V)
IG ii² 1601.17 – 320s? See Whitehead, *Demes* no. 47.

Paredros of demarchos?
CHARISANDROS son of Charisiades of Halimous (IV)
SEG 2.7.3, 11ff. He was honoured for duties as substitute for the demarch about 330–325.

COUNCIL AND ASSEMBLY

(i) Potter, *ABSA* 1984, 229–35, has argued that IG ii² 399 may belong at this time; the argument is very speculative, but the document may belong in this period; it honours Eurylochos of Kydonia and is dated to the tenth day of the prytany or shortly thereafter:

Bouleutes epistates
PAMPHILOS of Phi[laidai] (II)
Proposer
DEMADES son of De[meas of Paiania] (III) *PA* 3263; *APF* 99ff.
For the epistates, Philaidai is the only demotic available, though Potter's text leaves too much room for it.

(ii) IG ii² 403 (*LS* no. 35) is a probouleumatic decree concerning repair to the statue of Athene:
Bouleutes epistates
. . . .⁸. . . . s of Kerameis (v)
Proposer
-- of Lakiadai (VI)
On the latter see Hansen, *GRBS* 1984, 139.

(iii) IG ii² 413 may have the following:
Proposer?
LYKOU[RGOS] (son of Lykophron of Boutadai) (VI) *PA* 9251; *APF* 348ff.

(iv) IG ii² 415 is a probouleumatic decree of about 330/29 in honour of the anagrapheus; it is dated to the last day of Skirophorion, thirty-fourth of the prytany; cf. Walbank, *Hesperia* 1982, 44:
Bouleutes epistates
DEMETRIOS of Erchia (II) *PA* 3400
Proposer
[HI]ERONYMOS son of Oikopheles of Rhamnous (IX) *PA* 7570
Anagrapheus
KALLIKRA[T]IDES son of Kallikrates of Steiria (III) *PA* 7988

(v) IG ii² 421 honours an Amphipolitan; it is dated before 318/17:
Bouleutes epistates
MNESIKLES of A-- *PA* 10309
Proposer
[DEMOPHILOS] son of [De]mophilos of Acharnai (VI) *PA* 3675; *APF* 498
The alpha of Mnesikles' demotic is an unpublished reading communicated by D.M. Lewis.

(vi) IG ii² 422 honours a Histiaian before 318/17:
Proposer
-- son of --os or --es or --as of Oion (IV or VIII)

(vii) IG ii² 436 has the following:
Proposer
-- son of --os or --es or --as of An--
Hansen, *GRBS* 1984, 139, suggests the possible restoration of Meidias son

of Meidias of Anagyrous (I) (*PA* 9720; *APF* 387), but this is obviously speculative.

(viii) IG ii² 1628.300 records a decree concerning naval equipment before 326:
Proposer
HEGEMON *PA* 6290

IG ii² 3207, taken as the bottom part of 457, refers to honours for Lykourgos, first in the boule:
Proposers
(ix) DEMEAS of Sphettos (V) *PA* 3325
(x) DIOPHANES of Kephisia (I) *PA* 4409
(xi) KTESIKLES of Bate (II) *PA* 8868
(xii) In boule and demos:
(xiii) **Proposer**
THEOMENES of Oe (VI) *PA* 6957
(xiv) Unspecified:
-- of Myrrhinous (III)

(xv) *Hesperia* 1940, 332f. (39) (Schweigert), is dated *c.* 330:
Proposer
-- son of --mo--
Hansen (*GRBS* 1984, 140) suggests, with no confidence, the possibility of Moirokles son of Euthydemos of Eleusis (VIII) (*PA* 10400 = 10401).

(xvi) *Hesperia* 1944, 231ff. (5) (Meritt: Osborne D 26), is a citizenship decree for a Plataian dated just before 321/20:
Bouleutes epistates
--IKOS of Thorai (X)
Proposer
DEMEAS son of Dem[ades of Paiania] (III) *PA* 3322; *APF* 101f.

(xvii) *Hesperia* 1974, 322 (3) (Camp), is a probouleumatic proxeny decree for Sopatros of Akragas before 324:
Proposer
[LYKOURGO]S son of Lyko[phron of Boutadai] (VI) *PA* 9251; *APF* 348ff.

(xviii) *MDAI(A)* 1957, 156ff. (1), is a decree concerning Samos:
Proposer
ARISTOPHON

A number of decrees are attributed to
Proposer
DEMOSTHENES son of Demosthenes of Paiania (III) *PA* 3597; *APF* 113ff.
(xix) Deinarchos 1.43 records citizenship decrees for Chairephilos and his sons,
(xx)(xxi) Epigenes and Konon (Osborne TT 75–78, 80, 81), also honours for
(xxii) Bosporan princes, possibly all around 330; Aisch. 3.85 and Hypereides
(xxiii) 5.20 record citizenship decrees for Kallias and Taurosthenes of Chalkis

(Osborne TT 73, 74); anon *de com.* 3.46ff. (Koster) records a citizenship
(xxiv) decree for Antiphanes, but this is problematic (Osborne T 79); Deinarchos
(xxv) F 42 refers to a decree of unspecified content which was indicted as unconstitutional (Hansen, *Sovereignty* no. 37).

(xxvi) A decree honouring Neoptolemos was passed in the period 338–330 (Dem.
18.114; Plut. *Mor.* 843f):
Proposer
LYKOURGOS son of Lykophron of Boutadai (VI) *PA* 9251; *APF* 348ff.

(xxvii) Dem. 26.17 (cf. 25.94) and Deinarchos 2.12 suggest a number of decrees from:
Proposer
ARISTOGEITON son of Kydimachos *PA* 1775
(xxviii) That concerning the trial and execution of Hierokles was successfully challenged as unconstitutional (Dem. 25.40, 68, 87; hyp. i, ii, iii Dem. 25; Hansen, *Sovereignty* no. 29).

(xxix) A decree that the tribes Akamantis and Hippothontis should relinquish their share of Oropos to Amphiaraos was successfully challenged as unconstitutional (Hypereides 4.15ff.; Hansen, *Sovereignty* no. 35):
Proposer
POLYEUKTOS of Kydantidai (II) *PA* 11947 = 11928 = ?11927

(xxx) A decree concerning public water supply was also attacked after 335 (Deinarchos F 18; Hansen, *Sovereignty* no. 33):
Proposer
STEPHANOS *PA* 12879

(xxxi) Plut. *Mor.* 850b records an honorary decree for Phokion which must be before 322; the archon mentioned is the fictitious Xenias and if this is a corruption, 346/5 (Archias) or 324/3 (Hegesias) are possible years; it was indicted as unconstitutional (Hansen, *Sovereignty* no. 39):
Proposer
MEIDIAS son of Meidias of Anagyrous (I) *PA* 9720; *APF* 387

Speakers in the assembly are Aristogeiton (Dem. 25.41f., 64; *Ep.* 3.16; Deinarchos 2.12); Aphareus (Plut. *Mor.* 839c); Demeas of Paiania (Athenaios 13.591f); Euxenippos (Hypereides 4.14); Kephisodoros (Timokles F 17 Edmonds); Moirokles, Pataikos and Taureas (Dem. *Ep.* 3.16); Polycharmos (Plut. *Mor.* 726b – date uncertain); Hypereides (Athenaios 13.591f).

Nomothetai
(xxxii) Before 330 a law was passed affecting the duties of the theoric commission (Aisch. 3.25):
Proposer
HEGEMON *PA* 6290

(xxxiii) Nomoi were proposed before 322 (Athenaios 6.226a (Alexis F 126 Edmonds)):
Proposer
ARISTONIKOS son of Aristoteles of Marathon (IX) *PA* 2023 = 2028

Proposer
LYKOURGOS son of Lykophron of Boutadai (VI) *PA* 9251; *APF* 348ff.
(xxxiv) Plut. *Mor.* 841f–842a records laws concerning comic actors; concerning
(xxxv) the statues and texts of dramatists; against buying freeborn captives for
(xxxvi) slaves; concerning the festival of Poseidon; concerning women going to
(xxxvii) Eleusis by carriage.
(xxxviii)

SEG 28.52 has a decree of the boule praising the tamias (of the boule) and a list of bouleutai of tribe IV Leontis, dated *c.* 333:
Tamias of boule
P . . . ON of Paionidai or Cholleidai (IV)
Bouleutai
[Skambonidai?]
-- son of Aito[l]ides?
LYKOPH[RON] son of [L]ykophron
PANT[EN]OR son of Euenor
Potamos lower
EPITELES son of Epimedes
Kropidai
NAUS[I]STRATOS son of Dipolis
Oion
KLEARCHOS son of Damasias
Eupyridai˙
EPAINETOS son of Smikythos
NIKODEMOS son of Nikeratos
Potamos Deiradiotes
THEOXENOS son of Theogenes cf. *PA* 6985
NIKOSTRATOS son of Stratonikos cf. *PA* 12954
Aithalidai
THERIKLES son of Therimachos
HAGNON son of Hagnias cf. *PA* 128
Hybadai
HYPSIMOS son of Diognetos *PA* 13915; *APF* 520f.
MOSCHOS son of Keph[i]sodoros
Phrearrhioi
KALLISTRATOS son of Eukles cf. *PA* 8151
XEN--
MNESIS[TRATOS?]
SIMON
DIOPE[ITHES son of Diokleides] *PA* 4329; *APF* 161
ARISTO--

MNESONI[DES]
ANTIPHANES
XENOKLE[IDES]
Potamos upper
LACHES son of Ch[arinos] cf. *PA* 9025
HEPHAISTODO[ROS]
Sounion
AUTOKLES
KTESAR[CH]O[S]
CHARIAS son of Pos--
EPICHARES son of Pat[aikos]
Hekale
TELOKLES son of Kle--
Kettos
CHAIRESTRATOS
SOPHILOS son of S-- cf. *PA* 13415
AMEINO[KLES] cf. *PA* 696
Pelekes
DIO--

Agora xv.46 provides bouleutai from around 330:
Leontis (IV)
--ES

Akamantis (V)
--POS
Iphistiadai
[D]IOTIMOS *PA* 4388
Kikynna
NIKIAS *PA* 10805
DIAKRITOS *PA* 3747

Kekropis (VII)
Phlya
MENEST[RATOS] ?*PA* 10019
ANDROKLE[S]
TIMOKLES
ARISTOMENES
[E]UANGELIDE[S]

Hippothontis (VIII)
--S
--KLES
--KLES
--KLES
--TOS
--EOS

Aiantis (IX)
--S
--R.OS
[?PHIL]ONIDES
[PH]ILANTHES *PA* 12221
[?KOROI]BOS
--KIAS
E--SIDES
Phaleron
AUTOBIOS *PA* 2703
BOETHOS *PA* 2895
EUKRATES *PA* 5766
KALLIKRATES son of Hippo-- *PA* 7982
KALLIKRATES son of Kal-- *PA* 7983
PHOKOS *PA* 15085
PHILON *PA* 14877
DIONYSIOS *PA* 4254
D[EME]TRIOS?

Antiochis (X)
[Alopeke]
--E[S] son of Glaukon *PA* 3015
ANDROKLEIDES *PA* 847
PHYSON (? son of Pytharchos) *PA* 15061
PYTHEAS *PA* 12344
KTESIKLEIDES (son of Kteson) *PA* 8859
LOKRION *PA* 9185
THEOPOMPOS *PA* 7021
ERATOKLES *PA* 5032
PHILEMONIDES *PA* 14265
Anaphlystos
ARKESILAS *PA* 2213
KLEOMEDON *PA* 8583
EUKRATES *PA* 5751
RHIKON *PA* 12530
KINEAS *PA* 8435
PHILTONIDES *PA* 14793
AUTOKLEIDES *PA* 2710
AGATHON *PA* 85
DRAKALION *PA* 4540
CHAIRESTRATOS *PA* 15158

Agora XV.47 has bouleutai of tribe III Pandionis from around 330:
Paiania
STRATONIDES son of Sosigenes *PA* 13010
PRAXIAS son of Anthemion *PA* 12160
THEOMNESTOS son of Dion *PA* 6972

ARCHIDAMOS son of Archikleides *PA* 2487
THEODOTOS son of Antiphates *PA* 6799
ALKIMACHOS son of Andron *PA* 624; *APF* 22
LYSIPPOS son of Philinos *PA* 9564
ANTIGENES son of Timostratos *PA* 996
CHIONIS son of Demostratos *PA* 15550=?3627; *APF* 105
ETEANDROS son of [Ch]armantides *PA* 5211; *APF* 574
Konthyle
CHAIREAS son of Melesippos *PA* 15102
Oa
--ODEMOS son of Deikiros (?)
Prasiai
ARISTOKLES son of Aristokleides
Angele
THEOGENES son of Ergophilos *PA* 6697
MELETOS son of Menestratos *PA* 9827
NIKIAS son of Chaireleides *PA* 10790
Myrrhinous
POLYDAMAS son of Aristodamas *PA* 11917
SOSIGENES son of Sosigenes *PA* 13213
NIKESIAS son of Telokles
[AN]TIPHANES son of Antimenes *PA* 1241
EUTHYKRATES son of Euthykrates *PA* 5607
--CHIAS son of Eukleides *PA* 5691
Steiria
[DE]INIAS son of Deinokrates *PA* 3171
ZOP[Y]ROS son of Kratynon *PA* 6271
CHARIAS son of Aristokles *PA* 15360
Probalinthos
LYSANIAS son of Aristokleides *PA* 9322
KLEOMEDES son of Aristokleides *PA* 8597
MNESARCHOS son of Timostratos *PA* 10255
EUTHYDEMOS son Euk[r]ates *PA* 5543

Agora xv.48 has bouleutai of tribe VI Oineis around 330:
-- son of --ades
-- son of --oklitos
-- son of --omach[os]?
-- son of --dos or --des
-- son of --kios
-- son of --os or --es or --as
-- son of --oulos
-- son of --nides
-- son of --esippos
-- son of --ophon
Oe

OIN[O--]

. . LON--

[EU]PHRO[N]I[OS] (? son of Polykrates) ?*PA* 6111

E--

EUD--

.O.I--

--OGEN[ES]

Kothokidai

EUA[G]I[ON?]

Epikephisia

KALLIMACH[OS]

Agora XV.52 has bouleutai of tribe IV Leontis around 325; the first two queries in square brackets are suggestions of D.M. Lewis:

[Paionidai?]

-- son of --chos

[?OINOPHILOS] son of [Me]nestratos *PA* 9999; cf. 10013

Eupyridai

-- son of [P]olykles *PA* 11984

[?SOSTRATIDE]S son of Ekphantos *PA* 4657 = ?13322

?

-- son of [A]mynandros *PA* 735

-- son of Athenotimos *PA* 284

?

-- son of [Ka]llistratos *PA* 8151

-- son of --okles

?

-- son of --[d]oros

-- son of --os or --es or --as

[Phrearrhioi]

K--

DIO--

LYKINOS *PA* 9210

PHANIAS son of Agan[or] *PA* 14028

LEUKON son of Demeas *PA* 9069

EUBOULOS son of Diodoros *PA* 5373

ARISTOKRITOS son of Autophanes *PA* 1936

Sounion

ANDROMENES son of Chalkideus *PA* 888

DIOPHANES son of Diopeithes *PA* 4413; *APF* 167f.

THOUTIMIDES son of Phanias *PA* 7280

DIONYSIPHILOS son of Thougeiton *PA* 4270

Potamos Deiradiotes

PYRRHOS son of [Euth]ymachos *PA* 12523 = ?12522

POLYK[LE]S son of Heortios *PA* 12000

Agora XV.54, dated *c.* 321, has bouleutai of tribe VI Oineis:

Appendix

[Acharnai]
[TH]RASYLL[OS] son of [L]eonteus
TIMODEMO[S] son of Kephisodot[os] ?*PA* 13680
Phyle
[THO]UDOSIO[S]

Agora xv.55 is also dated *c.* 321 and has bouleutai of tribe x Antiochis:
[Anaphlystos]
--s son of Leo[k]ra[tes] cf. *PA* 9087
--s son of ?Chai[r]e[philo]s *PA* 15185
-- son of ?--m]a[ch]os
-- son of [Ar]istaios *PA* 1635
--s son of Poithikos *PA* 11877
-- son of Euangelos *PA* 5223
--os son of Philinos *PA* 14312
--os son of Lysimachos *PA* 9494
--OKL[E]S son of Nikokles *PA* 10894
?
-- son of --on
-- son of --sinikos
[Semachidai?]
-- son of --ikos
[Eitea?]
[OL]YM[P]IO[D]O[R]OS son of Olympiodoros *PA* 11392; *APF* 516
--AS son of Antiphanes *PA* 1220
[Eroiadai?]
--MENES son of Nausichares *PA* 10602
[Atene?]
--OS son of Menippos *PA* 10036
-- son of Lysiades *PA* 9338
--OS son of Lysiades *PA* 9339
Alopeke
. .⁴. . KLES
. .⁴. . ST]RATOS son of Nikostratos *PA* 11018
. .⁴ . . MON son of Lyson *PA* 9644
. .⁵ . . DES son of Nikodromos *PA* 10875
[K]T[ESI]KLEIDES son of Kteson *PA* 8859
[M]ELESIAS son of Melesippos *PA* 9810; *APF* 233
[DEM]OPHILOS son of Leostratos *PA* 9151 = 3672
. . . YKLES son of Oinobios *PA* 11354
[TH]OUDES son of Thoudiades *PA* 7249
[CH]AIREDEMOS son of Archelas *PA* 15118
[D]IOPHANES son of Euteles *PA* 4403
[HIPP]ONIKOS son of Kallias *PA* 7660; *APF* 269
Kolonai
[ANTI]OCHIDES son of Demokrates *PA* 1151

Addenda

Professor Lewis has communicated to me the details of an unpublished inscription of 422/1, which is in fact a republication of around 403, being preceded by lines from that time. It is an honorary decree for Polypeithes of Siphnos from the nineteenth day of pryt. Akamantis and provides the following:

Grammateus
ARCHIKLES of Halai (II or VII) *PA* 2495
Bouleutes epistates
DIDYMIAS
Proposer
ALKIBIADES (son of Kleinias of Skambonidai) (IV) *PA* 600; *APF* 9ff.
The secretary's identity means that IG i³ 91 and 92 (App. V xi and xii) must now also be placed in 422/1.

Indexes

Index I: Persons

In this index will be found all who appear in the annalistic text, each assigned a number for future reference. Alternative names are included in brackets and then appear separately in their place as the number of the first entry plus 'a', 'b' as necessary. Thus we try to preserve the number of individuals who appear, but this is complicated by choices in prosopographical identification and subjective criteria which may leave probable identifications unmade. All suggested *PA* equivalences are included, so we have, e.g., no. 1278 as *PA* 4721 = 4710 and as Prop. 361 i, and no. 1279 as *PA* 4718 = 4710 and Prop. 361 i. On the other hand, as with nos. 2932 and 2933, two separate individuals may be listed, although they are identified in *PA*. Another problem arises with no. 503, who, because of identity suggested, has three entries as bouleutes, when an individual can only be allowed two.

All question marks and square brackets attached to entries in the main text have been removed, so that a question mark in the index indicates that the *office* is unknown. The index is effectively a guide to where people will be found. Users should in any case refer for any individual from the index to the text. Dates, too, have been simplified to the first year in the archon-year formula, except that 411 and 411/10 remain distinguished. Offices are listed according to the order used in the text.

The index proceeds first by alphabetization according to the spellings adopted (note again my retention of 'Thucydides' for the historian, 'Thoukydides' for others). With each letter we have: (i) those for whom only initial letter(s) of the name survive; (ii) those who show in addition a patronymic; (iii) those who show (patronymic or not) an indication of tribe (for those with demes see below); (iv) the list of those with full name, homonyms being organized in order as those with simple name, then those with patronymic only, those with tribe (patronymic or not), those with demotic, alphabetically by demotic, homonyms with full nomenclature being further ordered alphabetically by patronymic and/or chronologically.

The second part of this index is of incomplete names without initial letter(s). First come those whose name does not survive at all: (i) with

433

patronymic, whole or part, alphabetically; (ii) with tribe, in tribal order and within that alphabetically by patronymic; (iii) two with the initial remains of demotics. Then we list the letters of those names which have survived, arranged alphabetically by letter and chronologically, regardless of whatever other elements occur.

The third part consists of all incomplete names with demotics attached, arranged alphabetically by demes: (i) those whose name is completely lost; (ii) those without initial letter(s); (iii) those with initial letter(s); (iv) those with incomplete patronymic, then those with at least initial letter(s) of patronymic, alphabetically by patronymic, whatever else survives.

The following abbreviations are used:

A(rchon): usually eponymous
Amph(iktyon)
App(endix)
Arch(on): other than the nine archons
Askl.: Priest of Asklepios
Ass.: speaker in the Assembly
Athl(othetes)
Bas(ileus)
Boul(eutes)
Braur(oneion)
Decrees: Secretary in charge of decrees
Dem(archos)
Didask(alos)
dock(yards)
Env(oy)
Ep(istates)
Epim(eletes)
Fin(ancial)
Gr(ammateus): the official of the council unless otherwise specified
Hell(enotamias)
Hier(opoios)
Hieromn(emon)
Hipp(archos)
Hypogr(ammateus)
Laws: Secretary in charge of laws
Misc(ellaneous)
Naop(oios)
Par(edros)
Phyl(archos)
Pol(emarchos)
Prop(oser)
Pylag(oras)
S(trategos)
Sophr(onistes)

strat(iotic fund)
Syngr(ammateus)
Tam(ias): alone of Athene or the mixed board, otherwise
Tam. o.g.: of the other gods
Tax(iarchos)
Thesm(othetes)
trir(eme)

1. A--: Env. 424.
2. A . . ⁶ . . . /AR . . ⁶ . . . : Prop. App. V xxi.
3. A--: Boul. 356 v.
4. AI . . .⁷. . . . : Gr. 455.
5. AIN--: Gr. App. v xviii.
6. AL . . ⁵ . . . /AN . . ⁵ . . . : Prop. App. V xxix.
7. ALK--: Amph. Delos 333.
(6a.) AN . . ⁵ . . . /AL . . ⁵ . . . : Prop. App. V xxix.
8. ANDR--: Gr. Tam. 443.
9. ANT--: Gr. Hell. 418.
10. ANT--: Gr. Amph. Delos 393–389.
11. ANTI--: Ep. App. V.
12. ANTIME--: Ep. 375.
13. APELL-: Amph. Delos App. VIII.
14. APHRO--: Tam. trir. funds App. IX.
15. AR--: Boul. App. IV iv.
16. AR . . ⁶ . . . : Gr. 416.
17. AR--: Eleusis App. V.
(2a.) AR . . ⁶ . . . /A . . ⁶ . . . : Prop. App. V xxi.
18. ARCHE . ⁴ . . : Prop. 405 i.
19. ARI . . ⁶ . . . : Prop. 323 iv.
20. ARIST--: Tam. 353/2.
21. ARISTO--: Boul. 365 i.

22. A-- of tribe II: Tam. 389.
23. A-- of tribe VI: Symproedros 328 iv.
24. AGA-- of tribe V: Boul. 424 vi.
25. ANT-- of tribe I: Boul. 381.
26. APHR-- of tribe I/X: Sophr. 334.
27. ARIS-- of tribe I: Boul. 381.
28. AUT-- s. of Eur-- of tribe V: Tax. App. VII.

29. ACHILLEUS (*PA* 2796): Env. 332.
30. ADEIMANTOS (*PA* 189): A. 477.
31. ADEIMANTOS s. of Leukolophides of Skambonidai IV (*PA* 202): S. 407, 406, 405; Ass. 405.
32. ADEISTOS s. of Antimachos of Athmonon VII (*PA* 205; *APF* 5): Sophr. 334.
33. ADOUSIOS (*PA* 207): Boul.-Prop. 418 i.
34. AGAKLES: Env. 424.
35. AGASIAS s. of Chairigenes of Ikarion II (*PA* 95 = 97): Boul.-Prop. 336 iii.

36. AGATHANOR of Syracuse: Didask. 333.
37. AGATHARCHOS of Kephale V: Boul. 336.
38. AGATHARCHOS s. of Agatharchos of Oe VI (*PA* 33): Gr. 362.
39. AGATHARCHOS of Otryne II: Boul. 336.
40. AGATHOKLES (*PA* 44): A. 357.
41. AGATHON of Anaphlystos X (*PA* 85): Boul. App. IX.
42. AGATHONIDES of Deiradiotai IV: Boul. 336.
43. AGATHYMOS s. of Adeimantos of Thymaitadai VIII (*PA* 79): Gr. Tam. 351.
44. AGYRRHIOS of Kollytos II (*PA* 179; *APF* 278f.): S. 389; Gr. 403 i, iii; Prop. App. V xliii, App. VI xxx, xxxii, xxxiii.
45. AIETES of Keiriadai VIII (*PA* 294): Pol. 371.
46. AINEAS (*PA* 296): Boul. App. IV xxv.
47. AINEAS s. of Phyg-- of Hamaxanteia VIII: Boul. App. VIII.
48. AISCHINES (*PA* 328): Fin. 446.
49. AISCHINES (*PA* 341): Thirty 404.
50. AISCHINES (*PA* 333): Env. App. VII.
51. AISCHINES s. of Atrometos of Kothokidai VI (*PA* 354; *APF* 543ff.): Pylag. 340; Env. 347, 346, 338; Hypogr.-Gr. App. VII; Ass. 347, 346, 339, 338.
52. AISCHINES of Perithoidai VI: Hell. 418.
53. AISCHINES s. of Kallimedes of Steiria III: Boul. 335.
54. AISCHRAIOS of Xypete VII (*PA* 372): Boul. App. VIII.
55. AISCHRON s. of Aischines of Azenia VIII: Boul. App. VIII.
56. AISCHRON of Marathon IX (*PA* 408): Hell. 430.
57. AISCHYLIDES: Eleusis App. V.
58. AISCHYLIDES s. of Aristarchos of Myrrhinous III (*PA* 427): Boul. App. VIII, 336.
59. AISCHYLION s. of Epichar-- of Anakaia VIII (*PA* 430): Boul. App. VIII.
60. AISCHYLOS (*PA* 434): Gr. App. IV xxviii.
61. AISCHYLOS: Hell. 429.
62. AISCHYLOS (*PA* 435): Gr. 412 ii.
63. AISCHYLOS of tribe X (*PA* 437): ? App. VII.
64. AISCHYLOS s. of Aischylos of Amphitrope X (*PA* 440): Boul. 334.
65. AISCHYLOS of Ankyle II: Hell. 409.
66. AISCHYLOS s. of Neokleides of Eitea X: Boul. 335.
67. AISCHYLOS of Erchia II: S. 329.
68. AISIMOS (*PA* 311; *NPA* 8): Env. 384, 378; Ass. 396.
69. AKERATOS s. of Archedemos of Phegaia II (*PA* 476): Boul. 341.
70. AKESTIDES s. of Antiphanes of Phegaia II (*PA* 467; *APF* 191): Boul. 343.
71. AKESTORIDES (*PA* 470; *APF* 296): A. 504.
72. AKESTORIDES (*PA* 471 = 472; *APF* 296): A. 474.
73. AKESTORIDES of Leukonoion IV: Boul. 336.
74. ALEXIAS (*PA* 528): A. 405.
75. ALEXIKLES (*PA* 535): S. 411.
76. ALEXIMACHOS s. of Alexias of Euonymon I (*APF* 540): Boul. 367.
77. ALEXIMACHOS s. of Teisamenos of Koile VIII (*PA* 543): Ep. Eleusis 336–333.

78. ALEXIMACHOS of Pelekes IV (*PA* 545): Prop. 347 xiv.
79. ALEXIMACHOS s. of Charinos of Pelekes IV: Boul. 371.
80. ALEXIPPOS s. of Epigenes of Sounion IV: Boul. 371.
81. ALEXIS s. of Sosiades of Kollytos II (*PA* 552): Boul. 341.
82. ALKAIOS (*PA* 572): A. 422.
83. ALKIBIADES s. of Kleinias of Skambonidai IV (*PA* 597; *APF* 15f.): Prop. App. IV xxxix.
84. ALKIBIADES s. of Kleinias of Skambonidai IV (*PA* 600; *APF* 9ff.): S. 420, 419, 418, 417, 416, 415, 411/10, 410, 409, 408, 407; Taktes 425; Env. 418; Prop. 419, 407 iv–vii, App. V xli, Addenda; Ass. 420, 416, 408.
85. ALKIBIOS of Paiania III (*PA* 605): Tam. 367.
86. ALKIDEMOS of Myrrhinous III (*PA* 607): Tam. 400.
87. ALKIMACHIDES s. of Hegemachos of Pergase (upper) I (*PA* 610): Boul. 335.
88. ALKIMACHOS of Anagyrous I (*PA* 616): S. 364, 357, 354.
89. ALKIMACHOS s. of Kephisios of Angele III (*PA* 615): Env. 378.
90. ALKIMACHOS s. of . . ?. . . os/es of Myrrhinoutte II (*PA* 622): Prop. 335 iv, 325 vi.
91. ALKIMACHOS of Paiania (upper) III (*PA* 624): Boul. App. VI.
92. ALKIMACHOS s. of Andron of Paiania III (*PA* 624; *APF* 22): Boul. App. IX.
93. ALKIPHRON of Anaphlystos x (*PA* 644): Tam. o.g. 429.
94. ALKISTHENES (*PA* 639): A. 372.
95. ALKISTHENES s. of Alkibiades of Cholleidai IV (*PA* 643; *APF* 23): Boul. App. VII.
96. ALKMAION (*PA* 647 = 652; *APF* 382): A. 505.
97. ALKMAION s. of Megakles (*PA* 651; *APF* 371): S. 591.
98. ALKMEON: Hier. 558.
99. AMEINIADES (*PA* 662): Tam. 411/10.
100. AMEINIADES (*PA* 664): Ass. 339.
101. AMEINIADES s. of Philemon (*PA* 666): Env. 430.
102. AMEINIAS (*PA* 670): A. 423.
103. AMEINIAS of Agryle I (*PA* 677): Boul. 328.
104. AMEINIAS s. of Philippos of Agryle I (*PA* 677; *NPA* 163): Tam. 349.
105. AMEINIAS s. Leokedes of Kollytos II (*PA* 681): Boul. 343.
106. AMEINIAS of Sphettos v (*PA* 685): Gr. App. VI xiii, xiv.
107. AMEINIAS s. of Lysa-- of Thymaitadai VIII: Boul. App. VII.
108. AMEINOKLES (DEINOKRATES): Gr. App. V xxxvii.
109. AMEINOKLES of Kettos IV: Boul. App. IX.
110. AMEIPSIAS (*PA* 709): Boul. 394 ii.
111. AMEIPSIAS s. of Lykomedes of Thorikos v (*PA* 710): Tam. 376.
112. AMEMPTOS (*PA* 713): Athl. 415.
113. AMIANTOS of Auridai VIII (*PA* 715): Boul.-Hier. 335.
114. AMOIBICHOS of Lamptrai I (*PA* 727): Ep. App. IV.
115. AMPHIAS of tribe IX: Epim. tribe 407.
116. AMPHIETIDES s. of Theopompos of Paionidai IV (*PA* 759): Ep. Eleusis 336–333.
117. AMPHIKEDES of tribe IX: Epim. tribe 407.
118. AMPHIKRATES (*PA* 768): Gr. App. V xxxii.

119. AMPHIKTYON of Aphidna IX (*PA* 776): Ep. 363–357.
120. AMPHILOCHOS: Tax. 410.
121. AMPHISTHENES of Oa III (*PA* 788): Boul. App. VI.
122. AMPHISTHENES of Potamos IV (*PA* 786): Gr. Ep. Eleusis 408.
123. AMPHITEKTON of Prospalta V (*NPA* 13): Askl. 348.
124. AMPHITELES s. of Amphitelides of Kettos IV (*PA* 792): Boul. App. VII.
125. AMYNIAS s. of Pronapes of Prasiai III (*PA* 737; *APF* 471): Env. 423.
126. AMYNOMACHOS s. of Philokrates of Bate II (*PA* 741): Boul. 343.
127. AMYTHEON (EUETHION) (*APF* 93): Gr. 410 vi.
128. AMYTHEON of Euonymon I (*PA* 730): Epim. dock. 371.
129. ANACHARSIS s. of Me-- of Kydathenaion III (*PA* 822): Phyl. App. VIII.
130. ANAITIOS of Sphettos V (*PA* 800): Hell. 410; Thirty 404.
131. ANAXIKRATES (*PA* 805): S. 451.
132. ANAXIKRATES s. of Anaximenes of Euonymon I: Boul. 367.
133. ANAXIKRATES of Lamptrai I (*PA* 811): Tam. 417.
134. ANAXION (*PA* 817; *APF* 26): Tam. 550.
135. ANAXIPPOS s. of Thoudippos of Araphen II (*PA* 815; *APF* 229): Epim. dock. 356.
136. ANCHISES (*PA* 182): A. 488.
137. ANDOKIDES (*PA* 826; *APF* 27): Tam. 550.
138. ANDOKIDES s. of Leogoras of Kydathenaion III (*PA* 827; *APF* 29f.): S. 447, 446, 441; Env. 446.
139. ANDOKIDES s. of Leogoras of Kydathenaion III (*PA* 828; *APF* 29ff.): Tam. 401; Env. 392; Ass. 392.
140. ANDROKLEIDES of Alopeke X (*PA* 847): Boul. App. IX.
141. ANDROKLEIDES of Anakaia VIII (*PA* 848): Boul. App. VIII.
142. ANDROKLES (*PA* 852): Boul. 340 i.
143. ANDROKLES s. of Androkles of tribe I: Boul. 335.
144. ANDROKLES s. of Aristoleos of Bate II: Boul. 335.
145. ANDROKLES s. of Andrios of Halai II (*PA* 857): Epim. tribe 340.
146. ANDROKLES s. of Kleinias of Kerameis V (*PA* 864; *NPA* 14): Askl. 328.
147. ANDROKLES s. of Lykinos of Oa III: Boul. App. VII.
148. ANDROKLES of Phlya VII (*PA* 873): Tam. 426.
149. ANDROKLES of Phlya VII: Boul. App. IX.
150. ANDROKLES of Pithos VII (*PA* 870): Theoros 423.
151. ANDROKYDES s. of Philagros of Kydathenaion III (*PA* 876): Tam.-Synegoros App. VIII; Boul. App. VIII.
152. ANDROMENES (*PA* 882 = 883): Prop. 363 vi.
153. ANDROMENES s. of Theogenes of Lamptrai (coast) I: Boul. 367.
154. ANDROMENES of Phrearrhioi IV: Boul. 336.
155. ANDROMENES s. of Chalkideus of Sounion IV (*PA* 888): Boul. App. IX.
156. ANDRON s. of Androtion of Gargettos II (*PA* 921; *APF* 34): Prop. 411/10 ii.
157. ANDRON of Kerameis V (*PA* 924): Env. App. VII.
158. ANDROSTHENES s. of Demokrates of Prospalta V: Boul. 335.
159. ANDROTION s. of Andron of Gargettos II (*PA* 913 = 915; *APF* 33f.): Arch. Arkesine 358–357; Eispraktor 356; Env. 355; Boul. App. VI xiii, 356; Prop. 365 ii, 355 viii, 347 i; Ass. 351, 344.
160. ANTENOR (ANTENORIDES): Hier. 566.

(160a.) ANTENORIDES (ANTENOR): Hier. 566.
161. ANTHEMION of Anaphlystos x (*PA* 939): Tam. 398.
162. ANTHEMION of Euonymon I (*APF* 41): Boul. 336.
163. ANTHEMION of Kolonos II: Boul. 336.
164. ANTHEMION of Perithoidai VI (*PA* 941): Epim. dock. 369.
165. ANTHIPPOS (*PA* 955; *APF* 34): Tam. Paralou App. VII.
166. ANTHIPPOS s. of Antichar-- of Eroiadai x (*PA* 956): Boul. 334.
167. ANTHOS s. of Nikeratos of Kolonos II (*PA* 960): Boul. 343.
168. ANTIBIOS: Prop. App. IV ii.
169. ANTICHARES (*PA* 1309): Prop. 408 i.
170. ANTICHARES s. of Philion of Phrearrhioi IV (*PA* 1315): Boul. App. VII,
336.
171. ANTICHARMOS of Pergase I: Boul. 336.
172. ANTIDOROS (ANTIDOTOS): Gr. 446.
173. ANTIDOROS of Acharnai VI (*PA* 1028): Boul. 360.
174. ANTIDOROS s. of Antinous of Paiania III (*PA* 1031): Gr. 330.
175. ANTIDOROS of Thria VI: Hipp. App. IX.
176. ANTIDOTOS (*PA* 1016): A. 451.
(172a.) ANTIDOTOS (ANTIDOROS): Gr. 446.
177. ANTIDOTOS: S. 356.
178. ANTIDOTOS s. of Euainetos of Ikarion II: Boul. App. VII.
179. ANTIDOTOS of Oa III: Boul. 336.
180. ANTIDOTOS s. of Apollodoros of Sypalettos VII (*PA* 1019): Boul.-Prop.
333 ii; Boul. 328.
181. ANTIDOTOS of Thria VI: Boul. 322 iv.
182. ANTIGENES (*PA* 983): A. 407.
183. ANTIGENES (*PA* 985): Boul. 356.
184. ANTIGENES s. of Phaidromachos of Kolonai IV: Boul. 335.
185. ANTIGENES s. of Xenokles of Oe VI (*PA* 995): Plouton App. IX.
186. ANTIGENES s. of Timostratos of Paiania III (*PA* 996): Boul. App. IX.
187. ANTIGENES s. of Antidoros of Philaidai II (*PA* 1002): Boul. 343.
188. ANTIGENES s. of Xenonides of Thorikos V: Boul. 338.
189. ANTIGENES s. of Aristomachos of Xypete VII (*PA* 994): Poletes 324.
190. ANTIKLEIDES (CHARIKLEIDES) of Kephisia I (*NPA* 116; *APF* 36):
Boul. App. VII.
191. ANTIKLEIDES s. of Antikleides of Kettos IV (*PA* 1047; *APF* 36): Boul.
App. VII.
192. ANTIKLES (*PA* 1052): Syngr. Ep. 446, 443, 441, 439, 438, 437; Gr. Ep.
436, 435, 434, 433.
193. ANTIKLES (*PA* 1058): A. 325.
194. ANTIKLES s. of Antiphon-- of Dekeleia VIII: Boul. App. VIII.
195. ANTIKLES s. of Aristokrates of Kydathenaion III (*PA* 1067): Tam. boule
343.
196. ANTIKLES of Melite VII (*PA* 1051; *APF* 399): S. 440, Prop. 446 ii, App.
V iv.
197. ANTIKLES of Philaidai II: Boul. 336.
198. ANTIKRATES of tribe V (*PA* 1076): Boul. App. V xi, xii.
199. ANTIKRATES s. of Phalanthos of Halai II (*PA* 1081): Boul. 343.
200. ANTIKRATES s. of Sokrates of Hermos V: Hipp. App. IX.

201. ANTIKRATES of Phegaia II (*PA* 1089): Boul. App. VII.
202. ANTIKRATES s. of Lysanias of Probalinthos III (*PA* 1087): Thesm. 329.
203. ANTIKRATES s. of Eukrates of Skambonidai IV (*PA* 1088): Boul. App. VII.
204. ANTIKRATIDES: Gr. App. V xix.
205. ANTIMACHOS (*PA* 1108): Env. 356.
206. ANTIMACHOS s. of . ⁴. . n/. .⁵ . . . s of Alopeke x: Boul. 334.
207. ANTIMACHOS of Hermos v (*PA* 1123; *APF* 37): Par. S. 416.
208. ANTIMACHOS s. of Euthynomos of Marathon IX (*PA* 1129): Amph. Delos 377–374.
209. ANTIMACHOS of Oa III (*PA* 1131): Tam. o.g. 421.
210. ANTIMACHOS s. of . ⁴. . os of Pelekes IV: Tax./Phyl. 373.
211. ANTIMEDES of Kydathenaion III: Tam. 431.
212. ANTIMEDON (*PA* 1134): Prop. App. VIII xx.
213. ANTIMENES of Alopeke x (*PA* 1139): Gr. boule App. VIII.
214. ANTIMENES s. of Antibios of Angele III: Boul. App. VII.
215. ANTIMENES s. of Aristomenes of Teithras II (*NPA* 17): Gr. demos 335.
216. ANTIOCHIDES (*PA* 1149): A. 435.
217. ANTIOCHIDES of tribe III (*PA* 1150): Boul. 418 i.
218. ANTIOCHIDES of Alopeke x: Logistes 407.
219. ANTIOCHIDES s. of Demokrates of Kolonai x (*PA* 1151): Boul. App. IX.
220. ANTIOCHOS (*PA* 1153): Kybernetes 407.
221. ANTIPATROS (*PA* 1162): A. 389.
222. ANTIPATROS s. of Komarchos of Halai II: Boul. App. VII.
223. ANTIPATROS of Sphettos v: Dem. App. IX.
224. ANTIPHANES (*PA* 1209): Tam. 403.
225. ANTIPHANES s. of Charoiades: App. 358.
226. ANTIPHANES of tribe v (*PA* 1221): Phyl. 394.
227. ANTIPHANES s. of K-- of tribe VIII (*PA* 1224): Tam. 350.
228. ANTIPHANES of Euonymon I (*PA* 1232): Boul. 337 ii, iii, 330 i.
229. ANTIPHANES of Kephisia I: Boul. App. VII.
230. ANTIPHANES s. of Antimenes of Myrrhinous III (*PA* 1241): Boul. App. IX.
231. ANTIPHANES s. of Aristophanes of Oa III (*PA* 1250): Boul. App. VIII.
232. ANTIPHANES of Phegaia II (*PA* 1248): Boul. App. VII.
233. ANTIPHANES of Phrearrhioi IV: Boul. App. IX.
234. ANTIPHANES of Potamos IV: Boul. 336.
235. ANTIPHANIDES of Euonymon I (*PA* 1251): Tam. o.g. 418.
236. ANTIPHATES (*PA* 1254): Tam. 440.
237. ANTIPHATES s. of Antiphanes of Euonymon I: Boul. 336.
238. ANTIPHATES of Kephisia I: Boul. 336.
239. ANTIPHATES of Kytherros III (*PA* 1260 = 1261; *APF* 38): Pentekontarchos 405.
240. ANTIPHILOS (*PA* 1264): S. 323, 322.
241. ANTIPHILOS of Anaphlystos x: Tam. 442.
242. ANTIPHILOS of Halimous IV (*PA* 1266): Dem. App. VIII.
243. ANTIPHILOS of Themakos I: Boul. 336.
244. ANTIPHON (*PA* 1280): Env. 358.
245. ANTIPHON s. of Lysonides (*PA* 1283; *APF* 327f.): S. 411, App. V; Env. 411.

246. ANTIPHON s. of Antiphon of tribe II: Boul. 335.
247. ANTIPHON s. of Solon of Alopeke x (*PA* 1291): Boul. 334.
248. ANTIPHON s. of Koroibos of Eleusis VIII (*PA* 1294): Gr. 325.
249. ANTIPHON of Erchia II (*PA* 1296): Tam. trir. funds App. IX.
250. ANTIPHON s. of Antiphon of Krioa x (*PA* 1285): Tam. 407.
251. ANTIPHON s. of Archias of Kydathenaion III (*PA* 1301): Epim. dock. 349.
252. ANTIPHON s. of Pytheas of Kydathenaion III (*PA* 1302): Boul. App. VIII.
253. ANTIPHON of Perithoidai VI (*PA* 1303): Boul. 360.
254. ANTIPHON of Rhamnous IX: Tam. o.g. 429.
255. ANTIPHON of Skambonidai IV (*PA* 1277): A. 418.
256. ANTIRHETOS s. of Aischeas of Eupyridai IV (*PA* 1182): Boul. App. VII.
257. ANTISTHENES of Hermos V (*PA* 1190): Hell. 411.
258. ANTISTHENES s. of Antikrates of Ikarion II (*PA* 1191): Ep. Eleusis 336–333.
259. ANTISTHENES s. of Antiphates of Kytherros III (*PA* 1184 = 1194 = 1196 = 1197; *APF* 38f.): S. App. VII.
260. ANTISTHENES of Phaleron IX (*PA* 1202): Tam. rigging 325.
261. ANTISTHENES of Phegaia II: Boul. 336.
262. ANTITHEOS s. of Archepolis of Phlya VII (*PA* 1044): Tam. 351.
263. ANYTOS (*PA* 1322; *APF* 41): Sitophylax 388.
264. ANYTOS of Euonymon I (*PA* 1323 = 1325; *APF* 41): Boul. 336.
265. ANYTOS s. of Anthemion of Euonymon I (*PA* 1324; *APF* 40f.): S. 409, App. VI; Ass. 396.
266. APEMANTOKLES of Trikorynthos IX (*PA* 1344): Boul. App. VI ii.
267. APEMANTOS (*PA* 1347a): Hieromn. 328, 327.
268. APEMON of Phlya VII (*PA* 1351): Epim. dock. 360.
269. APHAREUS s. of Isokrates of Erchia II (*PA* 2769; *APF* 246f.): Ass. App. IX.
270. APHAREUS of Pithos VII (*PA* 2770): Tam. 384.
271. APHOBETOS s. of Atrometos of Kothokidai VI (*PA* 2775; *APF* 545): Theorikon App. VIII; Hypogr.-Gr. App. VII; Env. 346, App. VIII.
272. APHTHONETOS s. of Phanes of Alopeke x (*PA* 2772): Boul. 334.
273. APOLEXIS s. of Ap-- of Halimous IV: Boul. 371.
274. APOLEXIS s. of Smikythos of Iphistiadai V: Ep. 421.
275. APOLEXIS of Oe VI (*PA* 1358): Boul. 360.
276. APOLLODOROS (*PA* 1375): A. 430.
277. APOLLODOROS (*PA* 1381 + Add.): A. 350.
278. APOLLODOROS s. of Apollodoros (*PA* 1392): Plouton App. IX.
279. APOLLODOROS s. of Pasion of Acharnai VI (*PA* 1411; *APF* 428ff.): Boul.-Prop. 349 v.
280. APOLLODOROS s. of Olympichos of Anaphlystos x (*PA* 1408; *APF* 516): Boul. 334.
281. APOLLODOROS s. of Kritias of Aphidna IX (*PA* 1410): Gr. Tam. 432.
282. APOLLODOROS s. of Archias of Halai II (*PA* 1404): Boul. 341.
283. APOLLODOROS of Kyzikos (*PA* 1458): S. App. VI.
284. APOLLODOROS s. of Archias of Prospalta V: Boul. 335.
285. APOLLODOROS s. of Euktemon of Ptelea VI (*PA* 1443): Boul.-Hier. 335.
286. APOLLONIDES of Phrearrhioi IV: Boul. App. VIII.

287. APSEPHION (*PA* 2805): A. 469.

288. APSEPHION (*PA* 2806): Boul. 415.

289. APSEPHION s. of Apsithyllos: Amph. Delos 410.

290. APSEUDES (*PA* 2801; *APF* 112): A. 433.

291. ARCHANDROS of Paiania (upper) III (*PA* 2297): Boul. App. VI.

292. ARCHEBIOS of Aixone VII (*PA* 2305a): Boul. App. VII.

293. ARCHEBIOS s. of Archenautes of Pallene x (*PA* 2309): Boul. 334.

294. ARCHEDEMIDES (*PA* 2314): A. 464.

295. ARCHEDEMOS: Prop. App. IV vii.

296. ARCHEDEMOS s. of Pheidiades of Aigilia x (*PA* 2318): Boul. 334.

297. ARCHEDEMOS of Marathon IX: Logistes 407.

298. ARCHEDEMOS of Paionidai IV: Logistes 407.

299. ARCHEDEMOS s. of Archias of Paionidai IV (*PA* 2325): Boul.-Prop. 349 ii.

300. ARCHEDEMOS of Pelekes IV (*PA* 2326): Logistes 406; Env. App. VI.

301. ARCHEDEMOS of Skambonidai IV: Dem. 402.

302. ARCHELAS s. of Chairias of Pallene x (*PA* 2349): Gr. 333.

303. ARCHENAUTES of Ikarion II: S. 433.

304. ARCHENAUTES s. of Archenautes of Ikarion II (*PA* 2357): Boul. 341.

305. ARCHENEOS s. of Archemachos of Anagyrous I (*PA* 2366): ? App. VIII.

306. ARCHENEOS s. of Euklinos of Probalinthos III: Boul. 335.

307. ARCHENEOS s. of Diphilos of Prospalta v (*PA* 2368; *APF* 390): Amph. Delos 341.

308. ARCHEPTOLEMOS: Gr. 371 ii.

309. ARCHEPTOLEMOS s. of Hippodamos of Agryle I (*PA* 2384): Env. 411.

310. ARCHESTRATIDES (*PA* 2394): A. 577.

311. ARCHESTRATOS: Prop. 462 ii.

312. ARCHESTRATOS (*PA* 2397): Gr. 442.

313. ARCHESTRATOS (*PA* 2411): Prop. 424 v, vi.

314. ARCHESTRATOS (*PA* 2402): Boul.-Prop. 405 vii.

315. ARCHESTRATOS (*PA* 2404): Tam. o.g. 375.

316. ARCHESTRATOS of Acharnai VI (*PA* 2421): Boul. 360.

317. ARCHESTRATOS of Athmonon VII (*PA* 2416): Boul. 325 iii.

318. ARCHESTRATOS s. of Mnesarchides of Otryne II: Boul. 335.

319. ARCHESTRATOS of Phlya VII (*PA* 2398): Tam. 429.

320. ARCHESTRATOS s. of Lykomedes of Phlya VII (*PA* 2411; *APF* 346): S. 433; Prop. 446 ii.

321. ARCHESTRATOS of Phrearrhioi IV (*PA* 2430): S. 406.

322. ARCHESTRATOS of Phrearrhioi IV: Boul. App. VII.

323. ARCHESTRATOS of Phrearrhioi IV (*PA* 2431): Boul. 336.

324. ARCHESTRATOS s. of Amynandros of Probalinthos III: Boul. 335.

325. ARCHESTRATOS of Skambonidai IV: Boul. 336.

326. ARCHESTRATOS of Skambonidai IV: Boul. 336.

327. ARCHIAS: A. 497.

328. ARCHIAS: Boul.-Prop. 458.

329. ARCHIAS: (*PA* 2447): A. 419.

330. ARCHIAS: (*PA* 2449): A. 346.

331. ARCHIAS s. of Pythodoros of Alopeke x: Gr. 323.

332. ARCHIAS of Cholargos v (*PA* 2481): Boul. 356.

333. ARCHIAS of Halai II (*PA* 2459): Dem. App. VIII.
334. ARCHIAS s. of Aresias of Kydathenaion III (*PA* 2221): Boul. App. VIII.
335. ARCHIAS of Lamptrai I: Boul. 336.
336. ARCHIDAMOS s. of Archikleides of Paiania III (*PA* 2487): Boul. App. IX.
337. ARCHIDEMOS (*PA* 2488a): Hieromn. 336.
338. ARCHIKLEIDES of Paiania III (*PA* 2492): Boul. 343 i, ii.
339. ARCHIKLES of Halai II/VII (*PA* 2495): Gr. App. V xi, xii; Addenda.
340. ARCHIKLES s. of Ain-- of Kydathenaion III: Boul. App. VII.
341. ARCHIKRATES of Lamptrai I: Boul. 336.
342. ARCHILLOS of K-- (*PA* 2509): Ep. App. IV.
343. ARCHILOCHOS of Thria VI (*PA* 2513): Boul. 360.
344. ARCHINOS: Symproedros 324 iii.
345. ARCHINOS of Anagyrous I: Boul. 336.
346. ARCHINOS s. of Archinos of Deiradiotai IV (*PA* 2524): Epim. dock. 333.
347. ARCHINOS of Koile VIII (*PA* 2526): S. App. VI; Prop. App. V xliii, 403 iii, v, vi; Ass. 403.
348. ARCHIPPOS: Tam.-Synegoros App. VIII.
349. ARCHIPPOS of Amphitrope x (*PA* 2548): Boul. 361 i.
350. ARCHIPPOS s. of Archestratos of Aphidna IX (*PA* 2549; *APF* 474): Naop. Delos 346.
351. ARCHIPPOS s. of Arch-- of Koile VIII: Askl. 325.
352. ARESAICHMOS of Agryle I (*PA* 1592): Tam. 408.
353. ARESIAS (*PA* 1596): Thirty 404.
354. ARESIAS s. of Ph-- of Euonymon I: Boul. App. VIII.
355. ARESIAS s. of Pausias of Gargettos II (*PA* 1597): Boul. 341.
356. ARIGNOTOS s. of Babyrias of Ikarion II (*PA* 1613): Boul. 341.
357. ARIMNESTOS (*PA* 1618): A. 416.
358. ARIMNESTOS of Diomeia II: Boul. 335.
359. ARIMNESTOS of Elaious VIII (*PA* 1619): Epim. dock. 374.
360. ARIMNESTOS of Phlya VII (*PA* 1618a): Boul. App. VII.
361. ARISTAICHMOS (*PA* 1638): A. 621.
362. ARISTAINETOS (.. LE.AINETOS): Boul. App. V xxx.
363. ARISTAIOS s. of Antikrates of Erchia II (*PA* 1637; *APF* 362): Tam. 351.
364. ARISTAIOS of Hermos v: Epim. dock. 367.
365. ARISTAIOS of Phaleron IX (*PA* 1634): Boul. 351 i.
366. ARISTARCHOS of Dekeleia VIII (*PA* 1663; *APF* 48): S. 411.
367. ARISTARCHOS of Kothokidai VI (*PA* 1664): Askl. 347.
368. ARISTARCHOS of Kytherros III: Boul. 336.
369. ARISTEIDES (*PA* 1682): Tam.-Synegoros App. VIII.
370. ARISTEIDES s. of Archippos (*PA* 1685): S. 425.
371. ARISTEIDES s. of Lysimachos of Alopeke x (*PA* 1695; *APF* 48ff.): A. 489; S. 490, 479, 478; Epim. revenues App. III; Env. 479; Prop. 480 iii-v, 479 i, App. IV xxxviii.
372. ARISTEIDES s. of Exekestos of Anakaia VIII (*PA* 1697): Boul. App. VII.
373. ARISTEIDES s. of Strepheneos of Kydathenaion III (*PA* 1707): Gr. 369 iii.
374. ARISTEIDES of Oe VI (*PA* 1713): Horistes 352.
375. ARISTEIDES s. of Ariston of Pergase I (*PA* 1714): Ep. App. IX.

376. ARISTEIDES s. of Himeraios of Skambonidai IV (*PA* 1715): Boul. App. VII.

377. ARISTEUS s. of Theogenes of Besa X (*PA* 1718): Boul. 334.

378. ARISTHETAIROS of Anagyrous I: Gr. Amph. Delos 345.

379. ARISTION (*PA* 1732): A. 421.

380. ARISTION (*PA* 1734): Prop. App. VI xviii.

381. ARISTION s. of Ari-- of Hagnous V (*PA* 1738): Boul. 378.

382. ARISTION s. of Aristonymos of Pallene X (*PA* 2198): Antigrapheus App. VI.

383. ARISTION s. of Philistides of Phegaia II (*PA* 1755): Boul. 343.

384. ARISTOBOULOS s. of Boularchos of Phyla VII (*PA* 1770): ? App. VII.

385. ARISTODAMAS s. of Kallias of Atene X (*PA* 1793): Boul. 334.

386. ARISTODEMOS (*PA* 1798): A. 352.

387. ARISTODEMOS s. of Aristodemos (*PA* 1802): Plouton App. IX.

388. ARISTODEMOS s. of Aristophon of tribe IX: Boul. 335.

389. ARISTODEMOS s. of Epikrates of Aigilia X (*PA* 1805): Boul. 334.

390. ARISTODEMOS of Bate II (*PA* 1812): Hell. App. V.

391. ARISTODEMOS of Kydathenaion III: Boul. 336.

392. ARISTODEMOS of Metapontum: Env. 348, 347, 344; Ass. 347.

393. ARISTODEMOS s. of Aristokles of Oinoe VIII (*PA* 1878): Epim. dock. 333.

394. ARISTODEMOS of Plotheia II: Boul. 336.

395. ARISTODIKOS (*PA* 1829): Hier. 566.

396. ARISTOGEITON (*PA* 1774): Env. 330.

397. ARISTOGEITON s. of Kydimachos (*PA* 1775): Boul. 325; Prop. App. IX xxvii, xxviii; Ass. 325, App. IX.

398. ARISTOGENES (*PA* 1781): S. 406.

399. ARISTOGENES of Iphistiadai V: Poletes 367.

400. ARISTOGENES of Kydathenaion III: Boul. 336.

401. ARISTOGENES of Lamptrai (lower) I: Boul. 367.

402. ARISTOKLEIDES s. of Thrasykles of Melite VII: Tam. rigging 326.

403. ARISTOKLEIDES s. of Aristokles of Sounion IV: Gr. Tam. App. IX.

404. ARISTOKLES (*PA* 1847; *APF* 331f.): A. 605.

405. ARISTOKLES (*PA* 1851): Env. 372.

406. ARISTOKLES s. of Thrason of Anakaia VIII (*PA* 1859): Boul. App. VII.

407. ARISTOKLES of Hamaxanteia VIII (*PA* 1858; *APF* 55): Tam. 398.

408. ARISTOKLES of Kerameis V (*PA* 1866): Ep. 420.

409. ARISTOKLES s. of Hierokles of Kydathenaion III (*PA* 1872; *APF* 55): Boul. App. VIII.

410. ARISTOKLES of Lamptrai I: Boul. 336.

411. ARISTOKLES of Myrrhinous III (*PA* 1850/1851): Gr. 394 V.

412. ARISTOKLES of Myrrhinous III/Myrrhinoutte II (*PA* 1875): Ep. Nomothetai 354 vii.

413. ARISTOKLES of Oinoe VIII (*NPA* 29): Epim. dock. 369.

414. ARISTOKLES of Potamos IV: Boul. 336.

415. ARISTOKLES s. of Aristokleides of Prasiai III: Boul. App. IX.

416. ARISTOKRATES: Gr. App. IV x.

417. ARISTOKRATES (*PA* 1894): A. 399.

418. ARISTOKRATES: Boul. 353 iii.

419. ARISTOKRATES (*PA* 1897): Boul.-Prop. 353 v.

420. ARISTOKRATES of Euonymon I (*PA* 1911): Hell. 415.
421. ARISTOKRATES s. of Aischines of Kephale V (*PA* 1913 = 1895): Gr. 394 ii.
422. ARISTOKRATES of Pergase I: Boul. 336.
423. ARISTOKRATES of Phaleron IX (*PA* 1925; *APF* 60): Hell. 421.
424. ARISTOKRATES s. of Ariston of Phrearrhioi IV (*PA* 1927): Boul. App. VII.
425. ARISTOKRATES of Thorikos V: Par. A. 361.
426. ARISTOKRATES s. of Skellias of Trinemeia VII (*PA* 1904; *APF* 56f.): S. 413, 410, 407, 406; Tax. 411; Oath 422.
427. ARISTOKRITOS s. of Autophanes of Phrearrhioi IV (*PA* 1936): Boul. App. IX.
428. ARISTOMACHOS (*PA* 1956): Boul. 412 vii.
429. ARISTOMACHOS (*PA* 1961): Ep. Akademy App. IX.
430. ARISTOMACHOS of Kephale V (*PA* 1974): Thesm. App. VII.
431. ARISTOMACHOS of Oion IV/VIII (*PA* 1978): Boul. 341 i.
432. ARISTOMACHOS of Pergase (upper) I (*PA* 1984): Boul. App. VII.
433. ARISTOMEDES s. of Aristophanes of Azenia VIII (*PA* 2011; *APF* 65): Tam. 400.
434. ARISTOMEDES s. of Aristophon of Azenia VIII (*PA* 2013 + Add.; *APF* 65f.): Boul. App. VIII.
435. ARISTOMEDES s. of Meton of Leukonoion IV: Boul. 371.
436. ARISTOMENES (*PA* 1990): A. 570.
437. ARISTOMENES s. of Kannonos of Philaidai II (*PA* 2006): Peripolarchos App. IX.
438. ARISTOMENES of Phlya VII: Boul. App. IX.
439. ARISTON (*PA* 2136): A. 454.
440. ARISTON s. of Ariston of tribe I: Boul. 335.
441. ARISTON s. of Eukleon of Aphidna IX (*PA* 2152): Amph. Delos 364.
442. ARISTON of Pergase I (*PA* 2174): Boul. App. VII xiii.
443. ARISTONIKOS s. of Nikophanes of Anagyrous I (*PA* 2025): Prop. 341 vi.
444. ARISTONIKOS s. of Aristoteles of Marathon IX (*PA* 2028): Prop. 336 xi, 335 vi, App. IX xxxiii.
445. ARISTONOUS s. of Aristonous of Anagyrous I (*PA* 2038): Gr. 332.
446. ARISTONYMOS: Env. 424.
447. ARISTONYMOS s. of Aristonikos: Prop. 345 ii.
448. ARISTONYMOS of Lakiadai VI (*PA* 2196): Boul. 360.
449. ARISTOPEITHES (*PA* 2046): Env. 368.
450. ARISTOPHANES (*PA* 2078): A. 331.
451. ARISTOPHANES s. of Nikophemos (*PA* 2082; *APF* 201f.): Env. 394, 390.
452. ARISTOPHANES s. of Aristomedes of Azenia VIII (*PA* 2084): Boul. App. VII.
453. ARISTOPHANES s. of Eukleides of Ikarion II (*PA* 2088): Boul.-Hier. 341.
454. ARISTOPHANES s. of Philippos of Kydathenaion III (*PA* 2090): Boul. App. VI.
455. ARISTOPHANES s. of Hieronymos of Teithras II (*NPA* 31): Anagrapheus 335.
456. ARISTOPHANES of Thorikos V: Boul. 336.

457. ARISTOPHON (*PA* 2102): Env. 411.

458. ARISTOPHON (*PA* 2107): A. 330.

459. ARISTOPHON: Prop. App. IX xviii.

460. ARISTOPHON of Aithalidai IV (*PA* 2109): Hell. 405.

461. ARISTOPHON of Athmonon VII: Tam. o.g. 421.

462. ARISTOPHON s. of Aristophanes of Azenia VIII (*PA* 2108; *APF* 64ff.):
Par. A. App. VIII; S. 363, App. VII note; Env. App. VI, 372; Syndikos
355; Prop. 403 viii, x, xi, 363 iii, v, 362 v, 361 iii, 357 i, 355 i, ix, 343 i,
App. VIII x, xi; Ass. 347.

463. ARISTOPHON of Kolonai IV: Boul. 336.

464. ARISTOPHON s. of Naukles of Lakiadai VI (*PA* 2115; *APF* 66): Tam.
377.

465. ARISTOPHON s. of Aristodemos of Steiria III: Boul. 335.

466. ARISTOTELES s. of Euphiletos of Acharnai VI (*PA* 2061): Gr. 378 v.

467. ARISTOTELES of Marathon IX (*PA* 2065): Env. 378; Prop. 378 iv.

468. ARISTOTELES of Thorai X: Hell. 421.

469. ARISTOTELES s. of Timokrates of Thorai X (*PA* 2055 = 2057): S. 431,
411; Nauarchos 426; Thirty 404.

470. ARISTOXENOS (*PA* 2042): Gr. 418 i.

471. ARISTOXENOS s. of Kephisodotos of Peiraieus VIII (*PA* 2044): Prop. 332
v.

472. ARISTYLLOS of Erchia II (*PA* 2131): Boul. 368 iv.

473. ARISTYLLOS s. of Hellespontios of Erchia II (*PA* 2132): Tam. 444.

474. ARISTYLLOS of Melite VII: Ep. 434.

475. ARKEPHON s. of Meidon of Cholleidai IV: Boul. 335.

476. ARKEPHON of Lamptrai I (*PA* 2226): Horistes-Boul. 352.

477. ARKESILAS of Anaphlystos X (*PA* 2213): Boul. App. IX.

478. ARKETOS: Prop. 371 ii.

479. ARRHENEIDES: Gr. Ep. 442.

480. ASOPIOS s. of Phormion of Paiania III (*PA* 2669): S. 428.

481. ASOPODOROS of Kydathenaion III (*PA* 2672): Tam. 411.

482. ASOPOKLES s. of Theodoros: App. 359, 358.

483. ASPETOS s. of Demostratos of Kytherros III (*PA* 2638): Gr. 340.

484. ASTEIOS (*PA* 2641): A. 373.

485. ASTYPHILOS: Gr. Ep. App. IV.

486. ASTYPHILOS (*PA* 2662): Prop. 378 iii, 373 ii.

487. ASTYPHILOS s. of Euthykrates of Araphen II (*PA* 2665; *APF* 229f.):
Lochagos App. VII.

488. ASTYPHILOS s. of Philagros of Halai VII (*PA* 2662 = 2663 = 2664): Boul.
App. VII.

489. ASTYPHILOS of Kydantidai II (*PA* 2661): A. 420.

490. ATARBION of Acharnai VI (*PA* 2676): Boul. 360.

491. ATHEMION of Rhamnous IX: Hell. 404.

492. ATHENION of Araphen II (*PA* 240): Env. 384.

493. ATHENODOROS: Boul. 381.

494. ATHENODOROS (*PA* 260): Prop. 355 vi.

495. ATHENODOROS of tribe II/VI (*PA* 259): Boul. App. IV xxxvi; Prop. App.
VI vii.

496. ATHENODOROS s. of Noumenios of tribe IV: Boul. 335.
497. ATHENODOROS of Halimous IV: Boul. 336.
498. ATHENODOROS of Melite VII (*PA* 274; *APF* 221): Hell. 407.
499. ATHENODOROS s. of De-- of Melite VII (*PA* 264; *APF* 221): Boul. App. VIII.
500. ATHENODOROS s. of Aristoboulos of Phrearrhioi IV: Par. A. App. VIII.
501. ATHENOKLES of Acharnai VI (*PA* 283): Boul. 360.
502. AUTOBIOS of Phaleron IX (*PA* 2703): Boul. App. IX.
503. AUTOBOULOS s. of Autosophos of Sypalettos VII (*PA* 2705 + Add.): Boul. App. VII, App. VIII, 335.
504. AUTOKLEIDES of Anaphlystos X (*PA* 2710): Boul. App. IX.
505. AUTOKLEIDES s. of Sostratos of Phrearrhioi IV (*PA* 2713): Gr. Tam. 412.
506. AUTOKLEIDES of Rhamnous IX: Dem. App. IV.
507. AUTOKLEIDES s. of Euetion of Sphettos V (*APF* 190): Boul. 336.
508. AUTOKLES: S. App. VIII.
509. AUTOKLES of Acharnai VI (*PA* 2725): Boul. 360.
510. AUTOKLES s. of Autias of Acharnai VI (*NPA* 41): Gr. 327.
511. AUTOKLES s. of Timeas of Aixone VII (*PA* 2722): Tam. 350.
512. AUTOKLES of Alopeke X (*PA* 2723): Tam. o.g. 420.
513. AUTOKLES s. of Tolmaios of Anaphlystos X (*PA* 2724 = 2717; *APF* 74): S. 425, 424, 418.
514. AUTOKLES s. of Androkles of Euonymon I (*APF* 162): Boul. 367.
515. AUTOKLES s. of Strombichides of Euonymon I (*PA* 2727; *APF* 161f.): S. 368, 362; Env. 372; Prop. 368 iv.
516. AUTOKLES of Peiraieus VIII: Ep. App. IV.
517. AUTOKLES of Sounion IV: Boul. App. IX.
518. AUTOKRATES of Lamptrai I: Boul. 336.
519. AUTOKRATES s. of Aischines of Paiania III (*PA* 2744): Boul. App. VIII.
520. AUTOLYKOS of Thorikos V (*PA* 2746): Bas./Pol./Thesm. App. VII; Env. 368; Ass. 347.
521. AUTOLYKOS s. of ....⁹..... of Thorikos V: Kosmetes 334.
522. AUTOPHONTIDES s. of Deinias of Alopeke X (*PA* 2768): Boul. 334.
523. AUTOSTHENES (*PA* 2756a): A. 668.
524. AUTOSTHENES s. of Eukleides of Xypete VII (*PA* 2759; *APF* 75ff.): Boul.-Hier. 335.
525. AXIOCHOS s. of Alkibiades of Skambonidai IV (*PA* 1329 = 1330; *APF* 16f.): Boul.-Prop. 407 i.
526. AXIOPISTOS s. of Theodoros: App. 351.

527. B--: Bas./Pol./Thesm. 402.

528. BABYLAOS s. of Xenokleides of Anagyrous I: Boul. 367.
529. BATHYLLOS of Erchia II: Boul. 336.
530. BATRACHOS of Acharnai VI (*PA* 2844): Boul. App. VII.
531. BLEPAIOS s. of Sokles (*PA* 2876): Boul. App. VIII.
532. BLEPES of Kephisia I: Boul. 336.
533. BLEPSIAS of Paiania III: Boul. 336.

534. BLEPYROS: Ep. 436.
535. BLEPYROS s. of Peithandros of Paionidai IV (*PA* 2881): Gr. boule and demos 343; Prop. App. VII xviii.
536. BLEPYROS s. of Phyleides of Teithras II (*PA* 2882): Epim. dock. 349; Boul. 331.
537. BOETHOS of tribe IX (*PA* 2883): Boul. 410 i.
538. BOETHOS s. of Nausinikos of tribe X/V (*PA* 2886): Hier. 330.
539. BOETHOS of Phaleron IX (*PA* 2895): Boul. App. IX.
540. BOIOTOS: Fin. App. VI.
541. BOULARCHOS s. of Aristoboulos of Phlya VII (*PA* 2912): Tax. 339.
542. BOULARCHOS s. of Boularchos of Phlya VII (*PA* 2913): Plouton App. IX.
543. BOULIS of Thorai X: Symproedros 328 iv.
544. BOUTALION of Marathon IX: Tam. o.g. 420.
545. BOUTHEROS s. of Dionysios of Marathon IX (*PA* 2903): ? App. VIII.
546. BRACHYLLOS s. of Bathyllos of Erchia II (*PA* 2928): Boul.-Prop. 343 vii.
547. BROSYNIDES of Kephisia I (*PA* 2929): Ep. 409.
548. BRYSON: Hier. 566.

549. CH--: Ep. Braur. 347.
550. CHA--: Ep. 441.
551. CHA--: Ep. Eleusis 407.
552. CHAIRE--: Tam. 408.
553. CHAIRE--: Hell. 404.
554. CHARI--: Tam. o.g. 429.

555. CH . . . .[10] . . . . . of tribe IV: S. 439.

556. CHABRIAS s. of Ktesippos of Aixone VII (*PA* 15086; *APF* 560f.): S. 390, 388, 379, 378, 377, 376, 373, 372, 371, 369, 368, 366, 363, 359, 357, App. VII.
557. CHAIREAS s. of Paramythos of Erchia II (*PA* 15100): Boul. 341.
558. CHAIREAS s. of Epigonos of Hagnous V (*PA* 15099): Ep. 421.
559. CHAIREAS s. of Melesippos of Konthyle III (*PA* 15102): Boul. App. IX.
560. CHAIREAS s. of Archestratos of Phlya VII (*PA* 15093; *APF* 346): S. 411/10.
561. CHAIREDEMIDES of Halai II: Boul. 336.
562. CHAIREDEMOS (*PA* 15112): Prop. 357 x.
563. CHAIREDEMOS (*PA* 15117): Boul. App. VI xv.
564. CHAIREDEMOS s. of Archelas of Alopeke X (*PA* 15118): Boul. App. IX.
565. CHAIREDEMOS s. of Chairestratos of Erikeia II: Boul. 335.
566. CHAIREDEMOS of Hagnous V: Boul. 336.
567. CHAIRELEIDES s. of Charixenos of Aphidna IX (*PA* 15135; *APF* 476): Tam. 444.
568. CHAIRELEOS (*PA* 15137; *APF* 85): Thirty 404.
569. CHAIREMON (CHAIRIAS) s. of Euortios of Anaphlystos X (*PA* 15218; *NPA* 169): Amph. Delos 341.
570. CHAIREMONIDES: Prop. App. VI xxxviii.

571. CHAIRENEOS of Lamptrai I: Gr.? 378.
572. CHAIREPHANES (PA 15175): A. 452.
573. CHAIREPHANES of Sphettos V (PA 15181): Boul.-Hier. 335.
574. CHAIREPHILOS (PA 15184): Tam. o.g. 375.
575. CHAIREPHON of Deiradiotai IV (PA 15197): Boul. App. VII.
576. CHAIREPHON of Kedoi I (PA 15200): Horistes 352.
577. CHAIREPHON s. of Thrason of Kollytos II (PA 15201; APF 239): Boul. 341.
578. CHAIRESTRATOS (PA 15147): Prop. App. IV xxxi.
579. CHAIRESTRATOS s. of Chai--: ? App. VIII.
580. CHAIRESTRATOS s. of Ameinias of Acharnai VI (PA 15159): Gr. 337.
581. CHAIRESTRATOS s. of Euxitheos of Alopeke X (PA 15156): Boul. 334.
582. CHAIRESTRATOS of Anaphlystos X (PA 15158): Boul. App. IX.
583. CHAIRESTRATOS s. of Phanostratos of Kephisia I (PA 15164; NPA 169; APF 564): Gr.? App. VIII.
584. CHAIRESTRATOS of Kettos IV: Boul. App. IX.
585. CHAIRESTRATOS of Kollytos II (PA 15165): Tam. o.g. 363.
586. CHAIRESTRATOS s. of Thosko-- of Kollytos II: Gr. App. VII.
587. CHAIRESTRATOS s. of Philemonides of Lamptrai I (NPA 169): Tam. 345.
588. CHAIRESTRATOS s. of Chariades of Oion IV: Boul. 335.
589. CHAIRESTRATOS s. of Chairestratos of Paiania III (PA 15167; APF 574): Boul. App. VIII.
590. CHAIRESTRATOS of Pallene X: Didask. 333.
591. CHAIRESTRATOS s. of Gniphon of Pallene X (PA 15169): Boul. 334.
592. CHAIRESTRATOS s. of Chairedemos of Rhamnous IX: Epim.-Boul. 328.
593. CHAIRETIOS s. of Chairimenes of Pithos VII (PA 15210): Boul. 335.
(569a.) CHAIRIAS (CHAIREMON) s. of Euortios of Anaphlystos X (PA 15218; NPA 169): Amph. Delos 341.
594. CHAIRIAS s. of Chairias of Plotheia II (PA 15223): Boul.-Hier. 341.
595. CHAIRIGENES of Aixone VII (PA 15225): Boul. App. VII.
596. CHAIRIGENES s. of Chairephon of Myrrhinous III (PA 15228): Ep. Eleusis 332–329.
597. CHAIRIKLES of Pallene X: Tam. o.g. 418.
598. CHAIRIMENES of tribe IV (PA 15232): Boul. 410 iv.
599. CHAIRIMENES s. of Lysanias of Deiradiotai IV: Epim. tribe 357.
600. CHAIRION s. of Kleidikos/Kleidemos (PA 15258 = 15254 = 15257; APF 13): Tam. 550.
601. CHAIRION of Eleusis VIII (PA 15263): Gr. Tam. 399.
602. CHAIRION s. of Pollis of Hybadai IV (PA 15266): Boul. App. VII.
603. CHAIRION s. of Charinautes of Phaleron IX (PA 15268): Gr. 361.
604. CHAIRIONIDES s. of Lysanias of Phlya VII (PA 15269): Prop. 333 iv.
605. CHAIRIPPOS s. of Autokles of Pithos VII (PA 15249; APF 75): Boul. 335.
606. CHAIRONDAS s. of Hegemon (PA 15279): A. 338.
607. CHALKIDEUS of Melite VII (PA 15282; APF 568): Gr. Hell. 442.
608. CHARES (PA 15285): A. 472.
609. CHARES (PA 15286): Env. 446.

I: Persons

610. CHARES s. of Theochares of Angele III (*PA* 15292; *APF* 568f.): S. 367, 366, 361, 358, 357, 356, 355, 354, 353, App. VII, 349, 348, 347, 343, 341, 340, 339, 338, App. IX.

611. CHARES s. of Charitaios of Paiania III (*PA* 15301): Boul. App. VIII.

612. CHARIADES of Acharnai VI (*PA* 15307): Boul. App. VII.

613. CHARIADES s. of Charias of Agryle I (*PA* 15310; *APF* 569): Tam. 404; Hell. 407; Ep. 409.

614. CHARIADES s. of Chairokles of Leukonoion IV (*PA* 15315): Boul. App. VII.

615. CHARIADES of Oe VI (*PA* 15317): Boul. 360.

616. CHARIADES of Paiania (upper) III (*PA* 15318): Boul. App. VI.

617. CHARIAS (*PA* 15322; *APF* 27f.): see App. II.

618. CHARIAS (*PA* 15323): Gr. 433 i, ii.

619. CHARIAS (*PA* 15324): A. 415.

620. CHARIAS s. of Arkeon: Didask. 333.

621. CHARIAS of tribe VI (*PA* 15331): Boul. 410 ii.

622. CHARIAS of Araphen II (*PA* 15338): Tam. 397.

623. CHARIAS of Daidalidai VII (*PA* 15340): Hell. 432.

624. CHARIAS of Hermos V (*PA* 15342): Boul. 335.

625. CHARIAS of Kephisia I: Boul. 336.

626. CHARIAS of Kydathenaion III (*PA* 15345): Epim. dock. 370.

627. CHARIAS s. of Euthykrates of Kydathenaion III (*PA* 15346; *APF* 193): S. 322.

628. CHARIAS of Pelekes IV (*PA* 15358): Tam. 398.

629. CHARIAS of Prasiai III: Boul. 336.

630. CHARIAS s. of Chairias of Sounion IV (*NPA* 171): Tam. 343.

631. CHARIAS s. of Pos-- of Sounion IV: Boul. App. IX.

632. CHARIAS of Aristokles of Steiria III (*PA* 15360): Boul. App. IX.

633. CHARIAS s. of Chariades of Sybridai I (*PA* 15361): Tam. 377.

634. CHARIDEMOS (*PA* 15370): Env. 358.

635. CHARIDEMOS (*PA* 15372): Boul. 324 ii.

636. CHARIDEMOS s. of Eunik-- of tribe VIII: Tax./Phyl. 373.

637. CHARIDEMOS s. of Philoxenos of Acharnai VI (*PA* 15380; *APF* 570ff.): S. 361, App. VII, 351, 350, 349, 338.

638. CHARIDEMOS of Cholleidai IV: Boul. 336.

639. CHARIDEMOS s. of Theoteles of Lamptrai I (*PA* 15386): Gr. App. VI vii.

640. CHARIDEMOS of Oinoe IX (*PA* 15390): Hier.-Boul. 336 iv.

641. CHARIDEMOS of Steiria III: Boul. 336.

642. CHARIKLEIDES (*PA* 15395): A. 363.

643. CHARIKLEIDES (*PA* 15396): Prop. 333 viii.

(190a.) CHARIKLEIDES (ANTIKLEIDES) of Kephisia I: Boul. App. VII.

644. CHARIKLES s. of Apollodoros of tribe VI (*PA* 15407; *APF* 502f.): S. 414; Zetetes 415; Thirty 404.

645. CHARIKLES s. of Sosias of Hybadai IV: Boul. 371.

646. CHARIKLES of Leukonoion IV (*PA* 15414): Boul. 363 ii.

647. CHARIKLES of Thorai X (*PA* 15410): Boul. 334.

648. CHARIKLES s. of Athenodoros of Thorai X (*PA* 15411): Boul. 334.

649. CHARIMNESTOS of Araphen II (*PA* 15428): Boul. App. VII.

650. CHARINADES of Paiania III: Boul. 336.
651. CHARINOS (*PA* 15434): Prop. 433 v.
652. CHARINOS of Athmonon VII (*PA* 15443): Boul. 378 iv.
653. CHARINOS s. of Charonides of Euonymon I (*PA* 15440): Boul. App. VIII.
654. CHARINOS s. of Charias of Myrrhinous III (*PA* 15454): Boul. App. VIII.
655. CHARINOS s. of Aleximachos of Pelekes IV (*PA* 15435 = 15455): Tam. 418.
656. CHARINOS s. of Laches of Potamos (lower) IV (*PA* 15456): Boul. App. VII.
657. CHARIPPOS s. of Philon of Rhamnous IX: Gr. demos 324.
658. CHARISANDROS (*PA* 15471): A. 376.
659. CHARISANDROS s. of Charikle-- of Eroiadai VIII: Boul. App. VII.
660. CHARISANDROS s. of Exekestos of Halimous IV: Boul. 371.
661. CHARISANDROS s. of Charisiades of Halimous IV: Par. Dem. App. IX.
662. CHARISANDROS of Paiania (upper) III (*PA* 15482): Boul. App. VI.
663. CHARISANDROS of Probalinthos III: Boul. 336.
664. CHARISIOS: Bas./Pol./Thesm. 402.
665. CHARISOS s. of Melanthios of Acharnai VI (*PA* 15492): Tam. 444.
666. CHARITHOS s. of Amphion of Pelekes IV: Boul. 371.
667. CHARITIMIDES (*PA* 15497): Nauarchos 460.
668. CHARMANTIDES of Paiania III (*PA* 15501; *APF* 573): Tam. 427.
669. CHARMIDES s. of Glaukon (*PA* 15512; *APF* 330f.): Arch. Peiraieus 404.
670. CHARMIDES of Lamptrai I (*PA* 15514): Tam. o.g. 420.
671. CHARMIDES of Lamptrai I: Boul. App. VI xvii.
672. CHARMINOS (*PA* 15517): S. 412.
673. CHARMOS (*PA* 15520; *APF* 451): Pol. 557.
674. CHARMYLOS s. of Kallisthenes of Trinemeia VII (*PA* 15524 + 8106): Boul. App. VIII.
675. CHAROIADES s. of Euphiletos (*PA* 15528 = 15529): Gr. App. IV xxxi; S. 427.
676. CHAROPIDES of Skambonidai IV (*PA* 15534): Hell. 424.
677. CHAROPINOS of Dekeleia VIII (*PA* 15535): ? App. VIII.
678. CHAROPINOS of Rhamnous IX: Tam. 371.
679. CHARTADES of Sounion IV (*PA* 15538): Amph. Delos 413.
680. CHEILON of Kephisia I: Boul. 386.
681. CHEIMEUS s. of Kikon of Lakiadai VI (*PA* 15545; *APF* 574): Sophr. App. IX.
682. CHELONION s. of Theog-- (*PA* 15546): Gr. 394.
683. CHION (*PA* 15552): A. 365.
684. CHION s. of L-- of Acharnai VI: Boul. App. VII.
685. CHIONIS of Oion IV: Boul. 336.
686. CHIONIS s. of Demostratos of Paiania III (*PA* 15550 = 3627; *APF* 105): Boul. App. IX.
687. CHIONIS of Prospalta V: Tam. o.g. 420.
688. CHREMES (*PA* 15568): A. 326.
689. CHREMES s. of Philoitios of Ionidai II (*PA* 15566 = 4802): Gr. 351; Boul. 343.

690. CHREMON (*PA* 15570): Boul. 405; Thirty 404.
691. CHROMON: Prop. App. IV xxvii.

692. D--: Ep. 437.
693. D--: Hell. 425.
694. D--: Hier. Eleusis App. V.
695. DEM--: Symproedros 326 ii.
696. DEME--: Ep. App. IV.
697. DI--: Ep. 435.
698. DIO--: Boul. 345 i.
699. DOR--: Gr. App. VI xxvi.

700. DEMOK-- of tribe IX: Epim. dock. 333.
701. DI-- of tribe III: Tam. 397.
702. DI. .AL-- (LI. .AL--) of tribe VII: Tam. 385.

703. DAIPHRON (*PA* 3105): Boul. 387 i.
704. DAMASIAS (*PA* 3109): A. 639.
705. DAMASIAS (*PA* 3110): A. 582, 581, 580.
706. DAMIAS of Leukonoion IV: Boul. 336.
707. DAMIPPOS of Phyle VI: Gr. Hell. 429.
708. DAMOKRATES s. of Gorgythos of Kydathenaion III (*PA* 3122): Boul. App. VII.
709. DEINIAS of Erchia II (*PA* 3163; *APF* 96): Poletes 367; Syndikos 355.
710. DEINIAS of Halai VII (*PA* 3160): Epim. dock. 356.
711. DEINIAS s. of Euages of Philaidai II (*PA* 3173; *APF* 186): Gr. Tam. 444.
712. DEINIAS s. of Deinokrates of Steiria III (*PA* 3171): Boul. App. IX.
(108a.) DEINOKRATES (AMEINOKLES): Gr. App. V xxxvii.
713. DEINOKRATES s. of Kleiombrotos of Acharnai VI (*PA* 3181 = 3185; *APF* 353, 483): S. 336.
714. DEINOKRATES of Myrrhinous III: Boul. 336.
715. DEINON s. of Deinias of Acharnai VI (*PA* 3197; *NPA* 47): Tam. 349.
716. DEINOSTRATOS s. of Deiniades of Ankyle II (*PA* 3192 = 3191): Boul.-Prop. 343 iii.
717. DEMADES s. of Demeas of Paiania III (*PA* 3263; *APF* 99ff.): Tam. strat. 334–331; Hier. 330; Epim. Amphiaraia 329; Env. 338, 335, 322; Boul. 336; Prop. 338 ix, x, 337 ii, iii, ix, xi, 336 vi, vii, 335 viii, ix, 334 i, iii, 332 iv, 330 iii, 329 i, 326 iv, v, 324 xiii, 322 ii, vii, viii, App. IX i; Ass. 323.
718. DEMAINETOS (*PA* 3267): Ep. 356–353.
719. DEMAINETOS of Anagyrous I: Boul. 336.
720. DEMAINETOS s. of Demeas of Paiania III (*PA* 3276 = 3265; *APF* 104f.): S. 396, 388, 387; Phyl. App. VII.
721. DEMANTHES s. of Tima-- of Marathon IX (*PA* 3280 = 3282; *APF* 106): ? App. VIII.
722. DEMARATOS (*PA* 3283): S. 414.
723. DEMARCHOS s. of Dieuches of Phrearrhioi IV: Boul. 336.
724. DEMEAS s. of Demades of Paiania III (*PA* 3322; *APF* 101f.): Prop. App. IX xvi; Ass. App. IX.
725. DEMEAS s. of Demainetos of Paiania III (*PA* 3323; *APF* 103f.): Phyl. App. VII.

726. DEMEAS of Sphettos V (*PA* 3325): Boul.-Prop. App. IX ix.
727. DEMETRIOS s. of Antiphanes of Alopeke X: Phyl. App. IX.
728. DEMETRIOS s. of Kallippos of Anaphlystos X (*PA* 3386): Boul. 334.
729. DEMETRIOS s. of Pythippos of Anaphlystos X (*PA* 3388): Boul. 334.
730. DEMETRIOS s. of Euktemon of Aphidna IX (*PA* 3392): Boul.-Prop. 332 X; Boul. 328.
731. DEMETRIOS of Erchia II (*PA* 3400): Boul. App. IX iv.
732. DEMETRIOS (MELANTHIOS) of Hamaxanteia VIII: Logistes 407.
733. DEMETRIOS of Koile VIII: S. 329.
734. DEMETRIOS of Kollytos II (*PA* 3413): Gr. 423.
735. DEMETRIOS s. of Speusikrates of Kolonos II (*PA* 3414): Boul. 343.
736. DEMETRIOS of Kydathenaion III: Boul. 336.
737. DEMETRIOS s. of Demostratos of Kydathenaion III (*PA* 3416): Boul. App. VII.
738. DEMETRIOS s. of Phileas of Lamptrai (lower) I: Boul. 367.
739. DEMETRIOS of Phaleron IX: Boul. App. IX.
740. DEMETRIOS s. of Phanostratos of Phaleron IX (*PA* 3455; *APF* 107ff.): S. 325, 324, 323; Hipp. App. IX; Env. 322.
741. DEMOCHARES: Hell. 435.
742. DEMOCHARES s. of Charinos of Gargettos II (*PA* 3713): Boul. 343.
743. DEMOCHARES s. of Laches of Leukonoion IV (*PA* 3716; *APF* 142); Ass. 322.
744. DEMOCHARES s. of Demon of Paiania III (*PA* 3718; *APF* 144): Hipp. 375.
745. DEMOCHARES of Phlya VII (*PA* 3723): Boul. 329 v.
746. DEMOCHARES s.of Simylos of Potamos IV (*PA* 3721; *APF* 142): Tam. 444.
747. DEMODOKOS of Anagyrous I (*PA* 3464): S. 425; Hell. App. V; Misc. App. V.
748. DEMODOKOS s. of Demokrates of Oa III (*PA* 3466): Boul. App. VII.
749. DEMOKEDES s. of Archekomos of Paiania (upper) III (*PA* 3471): Boul. App. VI.
750. DEMOKLEIDES (*PA* 3475): Prop. App. V xxiii.
751. DEMOKLEIDES (*PA* 3476): Env. 384.
752. DEMOKLEIDES of tribe II (*PA* 3474): S. 446, 439; Prop. 446 iv.
753. DEMOKLEIDES (TIMOKLEIDES) of Aphidna IX: Tam. App. IX.
754. DEMOKLEIDES s. of Philokles of Eitea V (*PA* 3481): Ep. Eleusis 336–333; Boul. 336.
755. DEMOKLES (*PA* 3484): Boul. App. VI iv.
756. DEMOKLES of Kephale V (*PA* 3499): Tam. 398.
757. DEMOKLES of Paiania III: Boul. 336.
758. DEMOKLES s. of Antikles of Potamos (lower) IV: Boul. 371.
759. DEMOKRATES of Acharnai VI (*PA* 3522; *APF* 391): Boul. 360.
760. DEMOKRATES s. of Demokles of Aphidna IX (*PA* 3521; *APF* 475): Ass. 338.
761. DEMOKRATES of Eitea V (*PA* 3525): Tam. trir. funds 332.
762. DEMOKRATES s. of Demodokos of Oa III: Boul. App. VII.
763. DEMOKRATES s. of Aristokrates of Perithoidai VI: Boul. 335.
764. DEMOKRATES of Rhamnous IX (*PA* 3537): Tam. 399.

765. DEMOKRITOS s. of Phanias: Amph. Delos 410.
766. DEMOKRITOS of Alopeke x (*PA* 3548): Hier. Eleusis 420.
767. DEMOMELES s. of Demon of Paiania III (*PA* 3554; *APF* 116): Prop. 339 ix.
768. DEMON s. of Demomeles of Paiania III (*PA* 3736; *APF* 116ff.): Askl. 330; Prop. 323 xiii.
769. DEMONIKOS of Alopeke x (*PA* 3562): Gr. 411/10 ii.
770. DEMONIKOS s. of Admetos of Kytherros III: Boul. App. VII.
771. DEMONIKOS of Lakiadai VI (*PA* 3567; *APF* 112): Boul. 360.
772. DEMOPHANES of Rhamnous IX (*APF* 140): Dem. App. IV.
773. DEMOPHILOS (*PA* 3661): Boul. 401.
774. DEMOPHILOS (*PA* 3662): A. 381.
775. DEMOPHILOS (*PA* 3664): Prop. 346 iii.
776. DEMOPHILOS s. of Demokl-- (*PA* 3666): Tam. 341.
777. DEMOPHILOS s. of Demophilos of Acharnai VI (*PA* 3675; *APF* 498): Hier. Eleusis 329; Prop. 324 v, App. IX v.
778. DEMOPHILOS s. of Pantaleon of Agryle I (*PA* 3669): Decrees 343.
779. DEMOPHILOS s. of Leostratos of Alopeke x (*PA* 9151 = 3672): Boul. App. IX.
780. DEMOPHILOS s. of Theoros of Kephale v: Gr. 367.
781. DEMOPHILOS of Kettos IV: Boul. 336.
782. DEMOPHILOS s. of Demonikos of Konthyle III (*PA* 3680): Boul. App. VIII.
783. DEMOPHILOS s. of Aischron of Kydathenaion III (*PA* 3681): Boul. App. VII.
784. DEMOPHILOS s. of Demeas/Demophanes of Paiania (upper) III (*PA* 3686/3687; *APF* 104): Boul. 348.
785. DEMOPHILOS s. of Demokles of Teithras II (*PA* 3689): Boul. 341.
786. DEMOPHON (*PA* 3693): S. 379.
787. DEMOPHON of Anagyrous I: Boul. 381.
788. DEMOPHON of Erchia II: Tax. App. IX.
789. DEMOS s. of Pyrilampes (*PA* 3573; *APF* 330): Env. App. VI.
790. DEMOSTHENES of Acharnai VI (*PA* 3586): Boul. 360.
791. DEMOSTHENES of Aixone VII (*PA* 3583): Dem. 345.
792. DEMOSTHENES s. of Alkisthenes of Aphidna IX (*PA* 3585; *APF* 112f.): S. 427, 425, 424, 418, 414, 413; Oath 422.
793. DEMOSTHENES s. of Demokles of Lamptrai I (*PA* 3593): Prop. 329 v, 325 i.
794. DEMOSTHENES s. of Demainetos of Paiania III (*PA* 3596; *APF* 103f.): Phyl. App. VII.
795. DEMOSTHENES s. of Demosthenes of Paiania III (*PA* 3597; *APF* 113ff.): Theorikon 337; Ep. navy 340; Sitones 338; Teichopoios 337; Hier. App. VIII; Pylag. 343; Kategoros 325; Env. 347, 346, 344, 343, 341, 339, 338, 335; Boul.-Prop. 347 iv, vi–xi, xvi; Prop. 351 ii, 344 iii, 343 viii, ix, 342 ii, iii, 341 iv, v, 340 i, vi–ix, 339 iv–viii, 338 iv–vii, App. VIII xix, 335 vii, 324 viii, x–xii, App. IX xix–xxv; Ass. 354, 353, 351, 349, 346, 344, 342, 341, 339, 336, 333, 324.
796. DEMOSTHENES s. of Demophon of Teithras II (*PA* 3598): Boul. 341.
797. DEMOSTRATOS (*PA* 3611; *APF* 105f.): Prop. 416 iii.

798. DEMOSTRATOS: Prop. App. V xi.

799. DEMOSTRATOS (*PA* 3620): A. 390.

800. DEMOSTRATOS s. of Aristophon of Azenia VIII (*PA* 3617; *APF* 65): Env. 372.

801. DEMOSTRATOS s. of Lysi-- of Euonymon I (*PA* 3619): Boul. 336.

802. DEMOSTRATOS of Kerameis V (*PA* 3612): A. 393.

803. DEMOSTRATOS s. of Demostratos of Kydantidai II (*PA* 3622): Boul. 341.

804. DEMOSTRATOS s. of Lysanias of Kydathenaion III: Boul. App. VII.

805. DEMOSTRATOS of Xypete VII (*PA* 3625): Gr. Tam. 440.

806. DEMOTELES s. of Antimachos of Halai II/VII (*PA* 3636; *APF* 26): Pol. App. IX.

807. DEMOTELES of Kephale V: Boul. 336.

808. DEMOTION (*PA* 3645): A. 470.

809. DEMOTION (*PA* 3646): Prop. 366 iii.

810. DEMOTION s. of Dem-- of Lamptrai (coast) I: Boul. 367.

811. DEMYLOS s. of Demakles of Phegous I: Boul. 335.

812. DERKYLOS (*PA* 3247): 423 note.

813. DERKYLOS s. of Autokles of Hagnous V (*PA* 3248 = 3249; *APF* 97f.): Env. 347, 346; Ass. 347.

814. DERKYLOS of Poros V (*PA* 3250; *APF* 98): Tam. 400.

815. DEXANDRIDES of Acharnai VI (*PA* 3210): Epim. dock. 373.

816. DEXIADES s. of Dexiades of Phaleron IX (*NPA* 47): Tam. 345.

817. DEXIKRATES of Aigilia X (*PA* 3226): S. 410.

818. DEXIKRATES s. of Dikaiogenes of Eleusis VIII (*NPA* 47): Tam. 343.

819. DEXILEOS: Hier. 558.

820. DEXITHEOS (MNESITHEOS): Hier. 558.

821. DEXITHEOS (*PA* 3215): A. 385.

822. DEXITHEOS (*PA* 3214): Gr. App. VI iv, v.

823. DEXITHEOS of tribe VIII (*PA* 3217): Tam. 384.

824. DEXITHEOS of Hamaxanteia VIII: Boul. App. VII vi.

825. DEXITHEOS of Phlya VII/Thria VI (*PA* 3221): Tam. 416.

826. DIAITOS of Pambotadai I: Tax. App. IX.

827. DIAKRITOS of Kikynna V (*PA* 3747): Boul. App. IX.

828. DIAKRITOS s. of Dieuches of Phrearrhioi IV (*PA* 3748): Boul. App. VIII.

829. DIEITREPHES (*PA* 3756): A. 384.

830. DIEITREPHES s. of Nikostratos of Skambonidai IV (*PA* 3755): S. 414, 411; Hipp. App. V: Phyl. App. V; Boul.-Prop. 408 i.

831. DIERXIS of Marathon IX (*PA* 3761): Tam. 442.

832. DIEUCHES s. of Demarchos of Phrearrhioi IV (*PA* 3766): Gr. 349.

833. DIIPPOS of Myrrhinous III: Gr. App. VII ix.

834. DIKAIOGENES s. of Menexenos of Kydathenaion III (*PA* 3773; *APF* 145): S. 459.

835. DIKAIOGENES s. of Menexenos of Kydathenaion III (*PA* 3776; *APF* 147, 540): S. 324, 323.

836. DIKAIOS s. of Dikaios of Prospalta V: Boul. 335.

837. DIKTYS s. of Epikleides of Eleusis VIII: Par. A. 394.

838. DIKTYS of Koile VIII: Ep. 434.

839. DIODES of Kephisia I (*PA* 3882a): Ep. 409.
840. DIODES of Paionidai IV: Gr. Hell. 447.
841. DIODOROS (*PA* 3916): Officer 408.
842. DIODOROS s. of Th-- of Anaphlystos X (*PA* 3926): Boul. App. VII.
843. DIODOROS s. of Philokles of Gargettos II (*PA* 3940): Boul.-Syllogeus 341.
844. DIODOROS of Kydathenaion III: Boul. 336.
845. DIODOROS of Lamptrai I: Boul. 336.
846. DIODOROS of Paiania (lower) III: Boul. App. VI.
847. DIODOROS s. of Olympiodoros of Skambonidai IV (*PA* 3961): Gr. Amph. Delos 377–373.
848. DIODOTOS s. of Eukrates (*PA* 3889): Prop. 428 iii.
849. DIODOTOS of tribe VII/VIII (*NPA* 54): Tam. 401.
850. DIODOTOS s. of Diokles of Angele III (*PA* 3891; *APF* 156ff.): Gr. 357.
851. DIODOTOS s. of Diogenes of Kytherros III (*PA* 3901): Boul. App. VIII.
852. DIODOTOS of Paiania (upper) III: Boul. App. VI.
853. DIODOTOS of Sypalettos VII (*PA* 3905a): Boul. App. VII.
854. DIOGEITON (*PA* 3790): Prop. App. VII ii.
855. DIOGEITON of Acharnai VI (*PA* 3794): Tam. 398; Epim. dock. 377.
856. DIOGENES (*PA* 3802): Gr. Ep. 434.
857. DIOGENES s. of Diogeiton of Alopeke X (*PA* 3813): Boul. 334.
858. DIOGENES s. of Diogenes of Melite VII (*NPA* 53): Tam. boule 335.
859. DIOGENES s. of Euthyboulos of Sypalettos VII: Boul. App. VIII.
860. DIOGNETOS (*PA* 3847): A. 492.
861. DIOGNETOS (*PA* 3848): Prop. 446 ii.
862. DIOGNETOS of Anaphlystos X (*PA* 3856): Hieromn. 340.
863. DIOGNETOS s. of Nikeratos of Kydantidai II (*PA* 3863 = 3850: *APF* 405): Zetetes 415; Eleven App. V.
864. DIOGNETOS s. of Diogenes of Leukonoion IV (*PA* 3864): Boul. App. VII.
865. DIOGNETOS of Phrearrhioi IV (*PA* 3875): Gr. 409.
866. DIOGNIS of Erchia II: Boul. 336.
867. DIOGNIS s. of Isandros of Peiraieus VIII (*PA* 3879): Gr. Tam. 431.
868. DIOGNIS of Phrearrhioi IV (*PA* 3880): Boul. App. VIII.
869. DIOKLES (*PA* 3983): Prop. 410 v.
870. DIOKLES (*PA* 3984): A. 409.
871. DIOKLES (*PA* 4006): Thirty 404.
872. DIOKLES (*PA* 3989): Prop. App. VI xxxix.
873. DIOKLES of Acharnai VI (*PA* 4019): Boul. 360.
874. DIOKLES of Alopeke X (*PA* 4015 = 3990; *APF* 157): S. 357.
875. DIOKLES s. of Philarchides of Amphitrope X (*PA* 4017): Boul. 334.
876. DIOKLES of Kerameis V (*PA* 4030; *APF* 157f.): Amph. Delos 333.
877. DIOKLES s. of Dion of Kydathenaion III (*PA* 4037): Boul. App. VIII.
878. DIOKLES of Kytherros III: Boul. 336.
879. DIOKLES of Myrrhinous III (*PA* 3992): Askl. 340.
880. DIOKLES of Pambotadai I: Epim. dock. 378.
881. DIOKLES s. of Diochares of Pithos VII (*PA* 4048; *NPA* 57; *APF* 158): Ep. 374.
882. DIOKLES of Ptelea VI (*PA* 4051): Boul. 360.

883. DIOMEDES s. of Lykomedes of Phlya VII (*PA* 4072; *APF* 347): Tam. 398.
884. DIOMEDON (*PA* 4065): S. 412, 406; Ass. 406.
885. DION (DIOTIMOS): Gr. App. IV vii.
886. DION of tribe V/VI: Tam. 399.
887. DION of Ankyle II: Boul. 336.
888. DION of Lamptrai I (*PA* 4491 = 4508): Env. 393.
889. DION s. of Dion of Oa III: Boul. 336.
890. DION s. of Noumenios of Phaleron IX: Epim. tribe 342.
891. DIONCHIS s. of Xenokles of Phlya VII (*PA* 3881): Tam. 444.
892. DIONYSIOS (*PA* 4085): Hell. 433.
893. DIONYSIOS (*PA* 4092): S. 387.
894. DIONYSIOS (*PA* 4095): Fin. App. IX.
895. DIONYSIOS of tribe IX (*PA* 4130): ? App. VII.
896. DIONYSIOS of Acharnai VI (*PA* 4158; *APF* 159): Hell. 430.
897. DIONYSIOS of Kydathenaion III (*PA* 4198): Hell. 410.
898. DIONYSIOS of Kydathenaion III: Symproedros 324 iii.
899. DIONYSIOS s. of Eukleides of Peiraieus VIII (*PA* 4241): Tam. 444.
900. DIONYSIOS of Phaleron IX (*PA* 4254): Boul. App. IX.
901. DIONYSIOS s. of Hephaistion of Philaidai II (*PA* 4259): Boul. 343, 341.
902. DIONYSIOS s. of Kalliades of Thorikos V: Boul. 338, 336.
903. DIONYSIPHILOS s. of Thougeiton of Sounion IV (*PA* 4270): Boul. App. IX.
904. DIONYSODOROS (*PA* 4278): Tax. 405.
905. DIONYSODOTOS s. of Pytharatos of Eleusis VIII: Boul. 335.
906. DIOPEITHES (*PA* 4309): Prop. 438 iii.
907. DIOPEITHES (*PA* 4308): Prop. 430 i.
908. DIOPEITHES s. of Diokleides of Phrearrhioi IV (*PA* 4329; *APF* 161): Boul. App. IX.
909. DIOPEITHES of Potamos IV: Boul. 336.
910. DIOPEITHES s. of Diphilos of Sounion IV (*PA* 4327; *APF* 168): S. 343, 342, 341.
911. DIOPEITHES s. of Diopeithes of Sphettos V (*PA* 4328; *APF* 160): Prop. 346 ii, App. VIII xii.
912. DIOPHANES s. of Euteles of Alopeke X (*PA* 4403): Boul. App. IX.
913. DIOPHANES s. of Diophanes of Kephisia I: Boul. 367.
914. DIOPHANES of Kephisia I (*PA* 4409): Boul.-Prop. App. IX x.
915. DIOPHANES s. of Diopeithes of Sounion IV (*PA* 4413; *APF* 167f.): Boul. App. IX.
916. DIOPHANTOS: Syngrapheus 410.
917. DIOPHANTOS (*PA* 4417): A. 395.
918. DIOPHANTOS (*APF* 166): Tam. Paralou App. IX.
919. DIOPHANTOS of Aphidna IX: Tam. o.g. 418.
920. DIOPHANTOS s. of Phrasikleides of Myrrhinous III (*PA* 4435 = 4421; *APF* 166): Officer 325; Env. 332; Boul.-Prop. 337 iv, v, x; Prop. 322 iii.
921. DIOPHANTOS s. of Thrasymedes of Sphettos V (*PA* 4438): Theorikon 354; Boul.-Prop. 368 iii, iv; Prop. 352 iii.
922. DIOTIMOS (*PA* 4364): Gr. Hell. 452.
(885a.) DIOTIMOS (DION): Gr. App. IV vii.

923. DIOTIMOS (*PA* 4366): A. 428.
924. DIOTIMOS (*PA* 4370; *APF* 162f.): S. 390, 389, 388, 387; Nauarchos App. VI; Phrourarchos 376.
925. DIOTIMOS (*PA* 4372): A. 354.
926. DIOTIMOS s. of Diopeithes of Euonymon I (*PA* 4384; *APF* 163f.): S. 338, 337, 335, 334, App. IX.
927. DIOTIMOS s. of Strombichos of Euonymon I (*PA* 4386; *APF* 161): S. 433; S./Nauarchos App. IV; Env. App. IV.
928. DIOTIMOS of Iphistiadai V (*PA* 4388): Boul. App. IX.
929. DIOTIMOS of Oinoe VIII/IX: Boul. 357 iii.
930. DIOXANDROS (*PA* 4526): S. 326.
931. DIOXENOS s. of Platon of Trikorynthos IX (*PA* 4307): Ep. Eleusis 336–333.
932. DIOXIS of Kephisia I (*PA* 4531): Amph. Delos 413.
933. DIPHILIDES s. of Diphilides of Paiania III (*PA* 4660): Boul. App. VIII.
934. DIPHILOS (*PA* 4462): A. 442.
935. DIPHILOS (*PA* 4464): S./Nauarchos 413.
936. DIPHILOS of Aixone VII (*PA* 4467 = 4468; *APF* 168f.): S. 326; Ass. 324.
937. DIPHILOS s. of Diopeithes of Sounion IV (*PA* 4487 = 4467; *APF* 168f.): Prop. 323 x.
938. DIPOLIS of Kropidai IV: Boul. 336.
939. DIYLLOS of Erchia II (*PA* 4450): Hier. 410.
940. DOKIMOS of Anagyrous I: Boul. 336.
941. DORIKLEIDES of Paiania III: Boul. App. VII.
942. DOROS s. of Smikythos of Melite VII (*PA* 4624): Gr. boule and demos App. VIII.
943. DOROTHEOS (*PA* 4589): Env. 409.
944. DOROTHEOS (*PA* 4590): Gr. Tam. 408.
945. DOROTHEOS: Gr. 408 ii.
946. DOROTHEOS of Acharnai VI (*PA* 4607): Boul. 360.
947. DOROTHEOS of Aixone VII (*PA* 4601): Dem. 326.
948. DOROTHEOS of Anagyrous I (*PA* 4605; *APF* 174): Tam. 389.
949. DOROTHEOS s. of Theodoros of Diomeia II (*PA* 4609): Boul. 341.
950. DOROTHEOS of Halai II (*PA* 4603; *APF* 174): Boul. 331 ii.
951. DORYPHILOS of Ikarion II (*PA* 4537): Hell. 442.
952. DOSITHEOS s. of Antigenes of Skambonidai IV: Boul. 371.
953. DRAKALION of Anaphlystos X (*PA* 4540): Boul. App. IX.
954. DRAKON (*PA* 4553): Thesmothetes 621.
955. DRAKONTIDES of Aphidna IX (*PA* 4546): Thirty 404; Prop. 404 i.
956. DRAKONTIDES s. of Leogoras of Thorai X (*PA* 4551; *APF* 173): S. 433; Boul. 446 ii; Prop. 438 iv.
957. DROMOKLEIDES (*PA* 4564): A. 475.
958. DROMOKLEIDES: Gr. Tam. 404.
959. DROMOKLEIDES s. of Thrasymedes of Hagnous V (*PA* 4567): Tam. boule 343.
960. DROMOKLES of Gargettos II: Boul. 336.
961. DROPIDES (*PA* 4572; *APF* 322): A. 645.
962. DROPIDES s. of Dropides (*PA* 4573; *APF* 322ff.): A. 593.

963. DROPIDES of Aphidna IX (*PA* 4575 = 4576): Env. 330.
964. DYSNIKETOS of Phlya VII (*PA* 4580): A. 370.

965. E--: Ep. Eleusis App. V.
966. E--(ECH . . .⁷. . . .): Prop. App. V xxviii.
967. E--: Tam. o.g. 376.
968. E--: Epim. dock. 368.
969. E--: Amph. Delos 360/355.
970. E--: Symproedros 333 i.
(966a.) ECH . . .⁷. . . . (E--): Prop. App. V xxviii.
971. EM-- (M--): Hypogr. Amph. Delos 341.
972. EP--: Ep. App. IV.
973. EP--: Symproedros 324 iii.
974. ERG--: Boul. 337 ix.
975. EU--: Boul. Prop. 403 ii.
976. EUA--: Prop. App. IV xvii.
977. EUK--: Gr. Hell. 445.
978. EUPH--: Boul. 364 ii.
979. EUTH--: Hier. 429.

980. E . . . EDES (N . . . . DES) of tribe V: Boul. App. IV iii.
981. E--SIDES of tribe IX: Boul. App. IX.
982. EP-- of tribe VIII: Hell. 432.
983. EUTH-- of tribe I: Boul. 381.
984. EUXEN-- of tribe IV: Symproedros 333 i.

985. ECHOS of Thymaitadai VIII: Boul. App. VI.
986. EIRENOKLES of Athmonon VII: Laws 324.
987. EKPHANTOS s. of Hagnotheos of Paiania III (*PA* 4661): Boul. App. VIII.
988. ELPIAS: Prop. App. IV xxv.
989. ELPINES (*PA* 4673): A. 356.
990. ELPINES (PA 4672): Askl. App. VII.
991. ELPINES of Euonymon I: Boul. 408.
992. ELPINES s. of Elpinikos of Probalinthos III (*PA* 4676): ? App. VIII.
993. ELPINOS s. of Sosigenes of Araphen II (*PA* 4682): Boul. 341.
994. EMMENIDES of Hekale IV: Boul. 336.
995. EMMENIDES of Koile VIII (*PA* 4687 = 4689): Horistes 352; Boul. 349 ii; Prop. 332 xi.
996. EMPEDOS of Oe VI (*PA* 4696a): Env. App. VII.
997. EMPEDOS of Oe VI: Boul. 328.
998. ENDEMOS s. of Arrheneides of Kropidai IV (*PA* 4699): Boul. App. VII.
999. ENDEMOS s. of Eudemides of Probalinthos III (*PA* 4700): Boul. App. VIII.
1000. ENDEMOS s. of Endemos of Probalinthos III: Boul. App. VII.
1001. ENDIOS of Agryle (upper) I: Boul. 408.
1002. ENLOGIMOS: Ep. App. IV.
1003. EPAGROS of Kephale V: Boul. 336.
1004. EPAINETOS (*PA* 4746): Bas. 636.

1005. EPAINETOS s. of Smikythos of Eupyridai IV: Boul. App. IX.
1006. EPAINETOS s. of Antiphilos of Kephisia I (*PA* 4753): Boul. App. VII.
1007. EPAMEINON (*PA* 4758): A. 429.
1008. EPAMEINON of Erchia II (*PA* 4759 = 4760 = 4766): Boul. 323 i, ii.
1009. EPAMEINON s. of Epainetos of Erikeia II (*PA* 4765): Boul. 341.
1010. EPHIALTES (*PA* 6156): S. 350: Env. 341.
1011. EPHIALTES s. of Sophonides (*PA* 6157): S. 465; Prop. 462 ii.
1012. EPICHARES (*PA* 4991): Boul. 404.
1013. EPICHARES (*PA* 4976): Prop. App. VII xvii.
1014. EPICHARES of Euonymon I (*PA* 4986): Tam. 398.
1015. EPICHARES of Euonymon I: Boul. 336.
1016. EPICHARES of Hagnous V (*PA* 4982): Boul. 332 viii, x.
1017. EPICHARES of Lamptrai I (*PA* 4991): Ten 404.
1018. EPICHARES s. of Epigenes of Oinoe IX: Sophr. 333.
1019. EPICHARES s. of Agonochares of Paiania III (*PA* 4999): Epim.
    Amphiaraia 329.
1020. EPICHARES s. of Pataikos of Sounion IV: Boul. App. IX.
1021. EPICHARINOS s. of Epichares/Epicharinos of tribe X: Tam. 444.
1022. EPICHARINOS of Amphitrope X (*PA* 5004): Ep. 437.
1023. EPICHARINOS s. of Philochares of Euonymon I: Boul. 367.
1024. EPICHARINOS s. of Euthykrates of Kolonai X (*PA* 5016): Boul. 334.
1025. EPICHARINOS of Peiraieus VIII: Gr. 440.
1026. EPIGENES (*PA* 4779): Boul. 407 vi.
1027. EPIGENES s. of Lysandros of Aigilia X (*PA* 4788): Gr. Tam. 420.
1028. EPIGENES of Eroiadai VIII (*PA* 4795): Boul. 328 i.
1029. EPIGENES s. of Androkles of Ionidai II (*PA* 4801): Boul. 343.
1030. EPIGENES s. of Metagenes of Koile VIII (*PA* 4805): Amph. Delos
    377–374.
1031. EPIGETHES of Eroiadai VIII/X: Boul. 328.
1032. EPIKLES of Thorikos V: Gr. Ep. 435.
1033. EPIKOUROS of Kopros VIII: Hell. 409.
1034. EPIKRATES (*PA* 4863): Hell. 429.
1035. EPIKRATES (*PA* 4861): Naop. Delphi 346, 341.
1036. EPIKRATES: Gr. Ep. App. IX.
1037. EPIKRATES of tribe VIII: Tam. 399.
1038. EPIKRATES s. of Alexiades of Anaphlystos X (*PA* 4884): Boul. 334.
1039. EPIKRATES s. of Glaukon of Aphidna IX (*PA* 4885): Boul.-Hier. 335.
1040. EPIKRATES s. of Eukles of Cholleidai IV: Boul. 371.
1041. EPIKRATES s. of Nikomenes of Halai II (*PA* 4879; *APF* 410): Boul. 343.
1042. EPIKRATES of Kephisia I (*PA* 4859; *APF* 181): Env. 394, 392.
1043. EPIKRATES s. of . .otetos of Pallene X (*PA* 4863; *APF* 182): Boul. 335;
    Prop. 354 v, vi, 336 xiii.
1044. EPIKRATES s. of Menestratos of Pallene X (*PA* 4909; *APF* 182f.): Amph.
    Delos 377–374; Boul.-Prop. 369 iii.
1045. EPIKRATES s. of Epiteles of Pergase (lower) I: Boul. 367.
1046. EPIKRATES s. of Kallias of Prospalta V (*PA* 4913): Boul. 336.
1047. EPIKRATES s. of Peisianax of Sounion IV (*APF* 378): Plouton App. IX.
1048. EPILYKOS (*PA* 4922; *APF* 296): Pol. App. I.
1049. EPILYKOS s. of Teisandros (*PA* 4925; *APF* 297): Env. 424; Gr. 424.

1050. EPILYKOS s. of Nikostratos of Gargettos II (*APF* 312): Hipp. App. IX.

1051. EPIMEDES s. of An-- of Hagnous V (*PA* 4936): Boul. 378.

1052. EPINIKOS of Acharnai VI (*PA* 4938): Boul. App. VII.

1053. EPISTRATOS of Acharnai VI (*PA* 4949): Boul. 360.

1054. EPITELES s. of Soinautes of Pergase I (*PA* 4953 = 4962): S. 448.

1055. EPITELES s. of Soinomos of Pergase I (*PA* 4963 = 4955): Epim.
Amphiaraia 329; Naop. Delphi 328, 327, 326, 324; Boul. 336; Prop. 323
iii.

1056. EPITELES s. of Epimedes of Potamos (lower) IV: Boul. App. IX.

1057. ERASINIDES (*PA* 5021): S. 406; Boul.-Prop. 410 V.

1058. ERASISTRATOS: Hell. 407.

1059. ERASISTRATOS (*PA* 5028): Thirty 404.

1060. ERASISTRATOS of Acharnai VI (*PA* 5024; *APF* 322): S. App. IV.

1061. ERATOKLES of Alopeke X (*PA* 5032): Boul. App. IX.

1062. ERATON s. of Eration of Ikarion II (*PA* 5042): Epim. dock. 369; Boul.
341.

1063. ERATOSTHENES (*PA* 5035; *APF* 184f.): Thirty 404.

1064. ERATOSTRATOS s. of Nausikydes of Anaphlystos X (*PA* 5036): Boul.
334.

1065. ERGAMENES of Acharnai VI (*PA* 5046): Hell. 421.

1066. ERGINOS s. of Theoklitos of Kydathenaion III: Poletes 324.

1067. ERGOBIOS of Halai VII (*PA* 5050): Epim. dock. 373.

1068. ERGOKLES (*PA* 5052; *APF* 542): S. 390.

1069. ERGOKLES s. of Aristeides of Besa X (*PA* 5055): Hell. 418.

1070. ERGOKLES of Perithoidai VI (*PA* 5056): Boul. 360.

1071. ERGOMELES of Kephale V: Boul. 336.

1072. ERGOPHILOS (*PA* 5062): S. 363.

1073. ERGOPHILOS of Anaphlystos X: Gr. Hell. 439.

1074. EROTION of Eleusis VIII (*PA* 13402): Gr. 406 i.

1075. ERXIKLEIDES (*PA* 5180): A. 548.

1076. ERXIMENES of Ionidai II: Boul. 336.

1077. ERYMAIDES of Anaphlystos X (*PA* 5182): Boul. App. VII.

1078. ERYXIS of Kephisia I: Boul. 408.

1079. ETEANDROS s. of Charmantides of Paiania III (*PA* 5211; *APF* 574):
Boul. App. IX.

1080. ETEARCHOS of Kydathenaion III (*PA* 5215): Gr. Ep. 409.

1081. ETEOCHARES s. of Leochares of Phrearrhioi IV (*PA* 5219): Gr. Naop.
Delos 346.

1082. ETEOKLES s. of Chremonides of Aithalidai IV: Plouton App. IX.

1083. EUAGION of Kothokidai VI: Boul. App. IX.

1084. EUAGORAS s. of Dionysios of Kydathenaion III: Boul. App. VII.

1085. EUAINETOS (*PA* 5242): A. 335.

1086. EUAINETOS s. of Euthydikos of Anaphlystos X (*PA* 5245): Ep. Eleusis
332–329.

1087. EUAINETOS s. of Demainetos of Pithos VII: Boul. 335.

1088. EUAINETOS of Rhamnous IX: Dem. App. IV.

1089. EUAITELOS (EUANGELOS) of tribe IX: Epim. tribe 407.

1090. EUALKOS of Phaleron IX (*PA* 5264): Boul. 322 iii.

1091. EUANDROS: Prop. 386.

1092. EUANDROS s. of Erithalion of Euonymon I (*PA* 5271 = 5267; *APF* 187f.): A. 382; Gr. Tam. 411; Boul. 404.
1093. EUANGELIDES of Phlya VII: Boul. App. IX.
(1089a.) EUANGELOS (EUAITELOS) of tribe IX: Epim. tribe 407.
1094. EUANGELOS s. of Theophilos of Hermos V (*PA* 5225): Boul. 336.
1095. EUANGELOS of Phrearrhioi IV (*PA* 5222): Boul. 369 i.
1096. EUANGELOS s. of Chaireleides of Phrearrhioi IV (*PA* 5228): Boul. App. VII.
1097. EUATHLOS (*PA* 5238): Synegoros 427.
1098. EUATHLOS of Kerameis V (*PA* 5239): Tam. 397.
1099. EUBIODEMOS of Halimous IV: Boul. 336.
1100. EUBIOS of Aithalidai IV (*PA* 5293): Tam. 397; Ep. Eleusis 407.
1101. EUBIOS s. of Eubiotos of Ankyle II (*PA* 5290): Boul.-Hier. 341.
1102. EUBIOS s. of Autosthenes of Halai II (*PA* 5295): Boul. 341.
1103. EUBOIOS s. of Kratistoleos of Anagyrous I (*PA* 5313): Prop. 332 vi.
1104. EUBOLIDES of Oion IV/VIII: Tam. 441.
1105. EUBOULIDES s. of Epikleides of Eleusis VIII (*PA* 5325 + Add. = 5317): A. 394, Env. 392.
1106. EUBOULIDES s. of Antiphilos of Halimous IV (*PA* 5323): Dem. 346; Boul.-Prop. 346 ii.
1107. EUBOULIDES s. of Euboulos of Kopros VIII (*PA* 5329): Boul. App. VII.
1108. EUBOULOS (*PA* 5343): A. 345.
1109. EUBOULOS s. of Philogeiton of Acharnai VI (*PA* 5354): Gr. Tam. 427.
1110. EUBOULOS of Erchia II (*PA* 5357): Gr. Tam. o.g. 418.
1111. EUBOULOS s. of Lysias of Kettos IV: Boul. 371.
1112. EUBOULOS s. of Diodoros of Phrearrhioi IV (*PA* 5373): Boul. App. IX.
1113. EUBOULOS s. of Spintharos of Probalinthos III (*PA* 5369): Thesm. 370; Theorikon 354; Prop. App. VI xxxvi, App. VII xxiv, 349 vi, 347 iii, App. VIII ix; Ass. 347.
1114. EUCHARES: Gr. 377.
1115. EUCHARIDES s. of Euchares of Aphidna IX (*PA* 6144): Thesm. 444; Gr. Ep. App. IV.
1116. EUCHARISTOS (*PA* 6143): A. 359.
1117. EUCHEIRIDES of Hermos V: Boul. 336.
1118. EUDEKRATES s. of Eukleides of Prasiai III: Boul. App. VII.
1119. EUDEMOS of Kydathenaion III (*PA* 5401): Prop. 382.
1120. EUDEMOS s. of . . .o--/Epi-- of Lamptrai I (*PA* 5402/5403): Boul. 336.
1121. EUDEMOS of Prasiai III (*PA* 5408): Boul. App. VIII.
1122. EUDIDAKTOS of Lamptrai I (*PA* 5414): Horistes 352.
1123. EUDIKOS (*PA* 5417; *APF* 189): Tam. 550.
1124. EUDIKOS (*PA* 5419): Prop. 410 v.
1125. EUDIKOS s. of Euthydikos of Kopros VIII: Boul. App. VIII.
1126. EUDRAMON of Acherdous VIII (*PA* 5442): Gr. App. VI xi.
1127. EUDRASTOS of Acharnai VI (*PA* 5443): Boul. App. VII.
1128. EUEGOROS s. of Philoinos of Paiania III (*PA* 5466; *APF* 360): Prop. App. VIII xxvi.
1129. EUENIOS of Phyle VI (*PA* 5468): Boul. 360.
1130. EUETHIDES s. of So-- of Phyle VI: Boul. App. VII.
(127a.) EUETHION (AMYTHEON *APF* 93): Gr. 410 vi.

1131. EUETION of Kephisia I/Sphettos V (*PA* 5460; *APF* 190): S. 414.
1132. EUETION s. of Pythangelos of Kephisia I (*PA* 5461 = 5462; *APF* 190): Hipp. App. IX; Nauarchos 323.
1133. EUETION s. of Autokleides of Sphettos V (*PA* 5463; *APF* 189f.): Boul.-Prop. 328 ii.
1134. EUKLEIDES (*PA* 5672 = 5680 = 5689): S. 410; Thirty 404.
1135. EUKLEIDES (*PA* 5673): Gr. 408 i.
1136. EUKLEIDES (*PA* 5674): A. 403.
1137. EUKLEIDES (*PA* 5678): Env. 345.
1138. EUKLEIDES of tribe IX: Tax. 413.
1139. EUKLEIDES of Acharnai VI (*PA* 5676): Boul. App. VII.
1140. EUKLEIDES s. of Eukles of Aithalidai IV (*PA* 5684): Boul. App. VII.
1141. EUKLEIDES of Ankyle II (*PA* 5683): Ep. 420.
1142. EUKLEIDES s. of Euchares of Halai II: Boul. App. VII.
1143. EUKLEIDES s. of Euthias of Thorikos V: Boul. 338.
1144. EUKLES: Gr. App. IV xi.
1145. EUKLES (*PA* 5704): S. 424.
1146. EUKLES: Antigrapheus Eleusis 333.
1147. EUKLES s. of Molon (*PA* 5709): A. 427.
1148. EUKLES of Kerameis V: Boul. 336.
1149. EUKOLION s. of Pyrrhakos of Anagyrous I: Boul. 367.
1150. EUKOMOS s. of Eukomion of Keiriadai VIII (*PA* 5741): Boul. App. VII.
1151. EUKRATES (*PA* 5742): A. 592.
1152. EUKRATES: Prop. 422 ii.
1153. EUKRATES s. of Ma--: Poletes App. IX.
1154. EUKRATES of Anaphlystos X (*PA* 5751): Boul. App. IX.
1155. EUKRATES s. of Lysikrates of Epikephisia VI (*PA* 5754): ? App. VII.
1156. EUKRATES s. of Strombichos of Euonymon I: Tax. 356.
1157. EUKRATES s. of Nikeratos of Kydantidai II (*PA* 5757; *APF* 404f.): S. 412, 405.
1158. EUKRATES of Lamptrai I (*PA* 5758; *APF* 197): Boul. 328.
1159. EUKRATES of Melite VII (*PA* 5759): S. 432.
1160. EUKRATES s. of Aristotimos of Peiraieus VIII (*PA* 5762): Prop. 337 xiv.
1161. EUKRATES of Phaleron IX (*PA* 5766): Boul. App. IX.
1162. EUKRITOS s. of Daitarchos of Halai II: Boul. App. VII.
1163. EUKRITOS s. of Eukritos of Kolonai X (*PA* 5770): Boul. 334.
1164. EUKTEMON: Boul. 407 ii.
1165. EUKTEMON (*PA* 5784): Eispraktor 356; Prop. 355 x.
1166. EUKTEMON of Kephisia I (*PA* 5782): S. 412.
1167. EUKTEMON of Kerameis V: Boul. 336.
1168. EUKTEMON of Kydathenaion III/Kytherros III (*PA* 5799 + Add.): A. 408.
1169. EUKTEMON s. of Charias of Lousia VI (*PA* 5785 = 5800; *NPA* 79): Kleroucharchos 370; Naop. Delphi 346, 343, 334.
1170. EUKTEMON s. of Euboulides of Oion IV (*PA* 5802; *APF* 80): Bas. App. VII.
1171. EUKTEMONIDES of Phegous I (*PA* 5778): Boul. App. VII.
1172. EUMACHOS of Euonymon I (*PA* 5342): S. 411/10, 410.
1173. EUMATHES of Phaleron IX (*PA* 5807): Thirty 404.

1174. EUMELIDES s. of Arkeon of Acharnai VI (*PA* 5830): Tam. 343.

1175. EUMELOS s. of Aristophon of Kolonai IV: Boul. 335.

1176. EUMELOS s. of Eumeliades of Prospalta V: Boul. 335.

1177. EUNIKIDES of Halai II (*PA* 5846): Askl. 341.

1178. EUNOMIDES s. of Eunomion of tribe VI: Boul. 335.

1179. EUNOMOS (*PA* 5861): Nauarchos 389; Env. 394.

1180. EUNOMOS of Euonymon I (*PA* 5869): Boul.-Hier. 335.

1181. EUNOMOS s. of Euthynomos of Gargettos II (*PA* 5868): Boul. 343.

1182. EUNOSTIDES s. of Theophantos of Halai II (*PA* 5878): Boul. 341.

1183. EUPEITHES of tribe VII (*PA* 5918): Boul. 434 i, ii.

1184. EUPHANES s. of Eu-- of Kolonai X: Boul. App. VIII.

1185. EUPHANES s. of Phrynon of Rhamnous IX: Gr. 324.

1186. EUPHANES s. of S-- of Thria VI (*PA* 6023): Boul. App. VII.

1187. EUPHEMOS: Prop. 458.

1188. EUPHEMOS (*PA* 6034): A. 417.

1189. EUPHEMOS (*PA* 6035): Env. 415.

1190. EUPHEMOS of Kollytos II (*PA* 6042; *APF* 206): Tam. 421.

1191. EUPHILETOS of Acharnai VI (*PA* 6050): Boul. App. VII.

1192. EUPHILETOS s. of Gnathios of Atene X (*PA* 6060): Boul. 334.

1193. EUPHILETOS of Kephisia I (*PA* 6067; *APF* 206): Tam. 420; Ep. Eleusis 409.

1194. EUPHILETOS s. of Euphiletos of Kephisia I/Kikynna V (*PA* 6054; *APF* 206): Prop. 323 ii.

1195. EUPHILETOS of Kikynna V: Boul. 336.

1196. EUPHOROS of Teithras II: Boul. 336.

1197. EUPHRANOR s. of Euphraios of Angele III (*PA* 6091): Boul. App. VIII.

1198. EUPHRONIADES of Anagyrous I (*PA* 6102): Boul. App. VII.

1199. EUPHRONIOS s. of Polykrates of Oe VI (*PA* 6111): Boul. App. IX.

1200. EUPHROSYNOS of Paiania III (*PA* 6123): Env. App. VII.

1201. EUPHYLIDES of Acharnai VI (*PA* 6127): Boul. App. VII.

1202. EUPOLEMOS s. of Euthymenides of Myrrhinous III (*PA* 5928): Tam. trir. funds App. IX; Amph. Delos 341.

1203. EUPOLEMOS of Oa III: Boul. App. VII.

1204. EUPOLEMOS s. of Makareus of Oa III (*PA* 5933): Boul. App. VIII.

1205. EUPOLIS of Aphidna IX: Hell. 410.

1206. EUPOLIS s. of Arrhileos of Halai II (*PA* 5939): Boul. 343.

1207. EUPOLIS s. of Euthemon of Halai VII (*PA* 5940; *APF* 198): Poletes App. IX.

1208. EUREKTES of Atene X (*PA* 5759): Tam. 432.

1209. EURIPIDES s. of Eurykleides of Kephisia I: Boul. 367.

1210. EURIPPIDES s. of Adeimantos of Myrrhinous III (*PA* 5955 = 5949 = 5956; *APF* 202ff.): Env. 394; Boul.-Prop. App. VI xxvii; Prop. App. VI xxxiv.

1211. EURYKLEIDES: Tam. 375.

1212. EURYKRATES (EUTHYKRATES): Prop. 332 vii.

1213. EURYMEDON s. of Thoukles of Myrrhinous III (*PA* 5973; *APF* 334): S. 427, 426, 425, 423, 414, 413.

1214. EURYPTOLEMOS s. of Peisianax of Sounion IV (*PA* 5981 = 5985; *APF* 377ff.): Env. 409; Ass. 406.

1215. EUSTHENES s. of Elpon of Prasiai III (*PA* 5991): Boul. App. VIII.

1216. EUTHEMON (*PA* 5473): Gr. Ep. App. IV.

1217. EUTHIAS s. of Aischron of Anaphlystos X (*PA* 5484): Gr. Tam. 433.

1218. EUTHIAS s. of Peisias of Kettos IV (*PA* 5486): Gr. Tam. 376.

1219. EUTHIAS of Sounion IV (*NPA* 76): Kleroucharchos 370.

1220. EUTHIDIKOS of Agryle I: Boul. 336.

1221. EUTHIPPOS (*PA* 5494): A. 461.

1222. EUTHIPPOS: Gr. App. V xl.

1223. EUTHIPPOS s. of Euthias of Pallene X (*PA* 5499): ? App. VIII.

1224. EUTHIPPOS of Teithras II: Dem. App. VIII.

1225. EUTHIPPOS s. of Pythippos of Themakos I: Boul. 335.

1226. EUTHOINOS of Erchia II: Boul. 336.

1227. EUTHOINOS s. of Philarchides of Oa III (*PA* 5510): Boul. App. VIII.

1228. EUTHYDEMOS (*PA* 5514): A. 555.

1229. EUTHYDEMOS (*PA* 5515): A. 431.

1230. EUTHYDEMOS (*PA* 5518): Par. Bas. App. IX.

1231. EUTHYDEMOS s. of Eudemos (*PA* 5521): S. 422, 418, 414, 413; Officer 414; Oath 422.

1232. EUTHYDEMOS of Eleusis VIII (*PA* 5533): Askl. 355.

1233. EUTHYDEMOS s. of Eukrates of Probalinthos III (*PA* 5543): Boul. App. IX.

1234. EUTHYDIKOS of tribe V (*PA* 5555): Boul. 409.

1235. EUTHYDIKOS s. of Thersippos of Cholleidai IV: Boul. 335.

1236. EUTHYDIKOS s. of Ameinias of Philaidai II (*PA* 5565): Boul. 341.

1237. EUTHYDOMOS of Athmonon VII (*PA* 5570): Epim. dock. 367.

1238. EUTHYDOMOS s. of Demetrios of Melite VII (*PA* 5573): ? App. VIII.

1239. EUTHYGENES s. of Hephaistodemos of Kephisia I (*PA* 5512): Gr. 322.

1240. EUTHYKLES (*PA* 5575): A. 398.

1241. EUTHYKLES: Hieromn. 324.

1242. EUTHYKLES s. of Euthykrates of Anagyrous I: Boul. 367.

1243. EUTHYKLES of Araphen II: Boul. 336.

1244. EUTHYKLES s. of Eukles of Kedoi I (*APF* 486): Boul. 342.

1245. EUTHYKLES s. of Ameinias of Philaidai II (*PA* 5586): Boul. 341.

(1212a.) EUTHYKRATES (EURYKRATES): Prop. 332 vii.

1246. EUTHYKRATES s. of Euthykrates of Amphitrope X (*PA* 5599; *APF* 70f.): Naop. Delphi 334.

1247. EUTHYKRATES of Angele III: Boul. 336.

1248. EUTHYKRATES s. of Drakontides of Aphidna IX (*PA* 5601): Epim. mysteries 331; Boul. 337 iv–vi; Boul.-Epim. 328.

1249. EUTHYKRATES of Kydathenaion III: Tam. o.g. 418.

1250. EUTHYKRATES s. of Euthykles of Lamptrai (coast) I (*PA* 5605; *APF* 193): Boul. 367.

1251. EUTHYKRATES s. of Euthykrates of Myrrhinous III (*PA* 5607): Boul. App. IX.

1252. EUTHYKRATES of Pergase I: Phyl. App. IX.

1253. EUTHYKRATES of Phyle VI: Thesm. 370.

1254. EUTHYKRATES of Sphettos V: Boul. 336.

1255. EUTHYKRATES of Sybridai I: Boul. App. VII.

1256. EUTHYKRITOS (*PA* 5611): A. 328.

1257. EUTHYKRITOS (*PA* 5612): Boul.-Hier.-Syllogeus 324.
1258. EUTHYKRITOS of Anagyrous I (*PA* 5617): Boul. App. VII.
1259. EUTHYMACHOS (*PA* 5624): Prop. 353 i.
1260. EUTHYMACHOS s. of Alkimachos of Agryle I: Gr. 402.
1261. EUTHYMACHOS of E-- (*PA* 5634): Tam. dock. 347.
1262. EUTHYMACHOS of Lamptrai I: Boul. 336.
1263. EUTHYMENES (*PA* 5640): A. 437.
1264. EUTHYNOS (*PA* 5654): A. 450.
1265. EUTHYNOS (*PA* 5655): A. 426.
1266. EUTHYNOS of Lamptrai I (*PA* 5657): Tam. trir. funds 346.
1267. EUTHYPHEMOS (*PA* 5660): Gr. Epim. emporion App. VIII.
1268. EUTHYSTRATOS s. of Euthydemos of Eleusis VIII: Boul. 335.
1269. EUXENIPPOS s. of Ethelokrates of Lamptrai I (*PA* 5886 = 5888): Ass. App. IX.
1270. EUXENOS s. of Eu--n-- of Myrrhinous III: Boul. App. VIII.
1271. EUXENOS s. of Euphanes of Prospalta V (*PA* 5899): Gr. Tam. 417.
1272. EUXIPPOS s. of Thersippos of Aigilia X (*PA* 5912): Boul. 334.
1273. EUXITHEOS (*PA* 5901): Prop. App. V xxxii.
1274. EUXITHEOS (*PA* 5901): Boul. App. VI xi.
1275. EUXITHEOS s. of Thoukritos of Halimous IV (*PA* 5902; *APF* 93ff.): Dem. App. VIII.
1276. EXEKESTIDES s. of Nikokrates of Alopeke X: Bas. App. IX.
1277. EXEKESTIDES of Kothokidai VI: Ep. 375.
1278. EXEKESTIDES of Pallene X (*PA* 4721 = 4710; *APF* 175f.): Env. 378; Prop. 361 i.
1279. EXEKESTIDES s. of Charias of Thorikos V (*PA* 4718 = 4710 = 4712; *APF* 175f.): S. 357; Prop. 361 i.
1280. EXEKESTIDES s. of Exekias of Xypete VII (*NPA* 68): Tam. 349.
1281. EXEKESTOS of Aixone VII (*PA* 4728): Ep. Braur. 351.
1282. EXEKESTOS s. of Exekias of Anakaia VIII (*PA* 4730): ? App. VIII; Boul. App. VIII.
1283. EXEKESTOS of Athmonon VII: Gr. Tam. 446.
1284. EXEKESTOS s. of Paionides of Azenia VIII (*PA* 4726): Gr. 369 i.
1285. EXEKESTOS of Erchia II (*PA* 4731): Epim. dock. 360.
1286. EXEKESTOS s. of Aristodemos of Kothokidai VI (*APF* 178): Gr. Poletai 367.
1287. EXEKIAS s. of Exekestos of Anakaia VIII (*PA* 4732): Boul. App. VIII.

1288. GENNAIOS s. of Pleistos of tribe VI: Boul. 335.
1289. GLAUKETES: Gr. Tam. 374.
1290. GLAUKETES (*PA* 2946): Tam. 355; Env. 355.
1291. GLAUKETES (*PA* 2950): Boul. 355 i.
1292. GLAUKETES Athenaios (*PA* 2951): see S. 441.
1293. GLAUKETES s. of Glaukos of Oion IV (*PA* 2947; *APF* 83): Hier. 330.
1294. GLAUKIAS s. of Aischines of Kydathenaion III (*PA* 2968): Tam. 444.
1295. GLAUKINOS (*PA* 2975): A. 439.
1296. GLAUKIPPOS (*PA* 2979): A. 410.
1297. GLAUKON: Gr. Ep. App. IV.
1298. GLAUKON (*PA* 3011): Prop. 358 iv.

1299. GLAUKON of Acharnai VI (*PA* 3024): Boul. 360.
1300. GLAUKON s. of Leagros of Kerameis V (*PA* 3027; *APF* 91): S. 441, 439, 435, 433.
1301. GLAUKON of Lakiadai VI: Poletes 367.
1302. GLAUKON of Perithoidai VI (*PA* 3033): Horistes 352.
1303. GLAUKOS s. of Polymedes (*PA* 2994): Officer 349.
1304. GLAUKOS of tribe IV: Boul.-Prop. App. IV xiv.
1305. GLAUKOS s. of Glauketes of Oion IV (*PA* 3004; *APF* 83): Boul. App. VII.
1306. GLYKON (*PA* 3042): Prop. 438 ii.
1307. GNATHIOS (*PA* 3043): Boul.-Prop. 394 i.
1308. GNATHIOS s. of Euphiletos of Atene X (*PA* 3045): Boul. 334.
1309. GNATHIS s. of Timokedes of Eleusis VIII (*PA* 3048): Dem. App. VIII.
1310. GNATHON of Lakiadai VI: Prop. App. VI xxviii.
1311. GNOSIAS s. of Chairemon of Kydathenaion III (*PA* 3061): Boul.-Hier. 335.
1312. GORGIADES s. of Mnesikleides of Ikarion II (*PA* 3062): Tam. tribe 340.
1313. GORGOINOS s. of Oineides of Ikarion II (*PA* 3082): Tam. o.g. 423.
1314. GYLON of Kerameis V (*PA* 3098): Phrourarchos App. V.

1315. HIERO--: Gr. Ep. mint App. VII.
1316. HIPPOCH--: Boul. 344 i.
1317. HIPPOK--: Hell. 405.

1318. HABRON (*PA* 3; *APF* 270): A. 518.
1319. HABRON (*PA* 3): A. 458.
1320. HABRON of Perithoidai VI: Boul. App. VIII.
1321. HABRONICHOS s. of Lysikles of Lamptrai I (*PA* 20; *APF* 1): Env. 479.
1322. HABRONICHOS s. of Aristokles of Prasiai III (*PA* 22): Boul. App. VIII.
1323. HAGNIAS s. of Polemon of Oion IV (*PA* 133; *APF* 82f.): Env. 397, App. VII.
1324. HAGNODEMOS of tribe II (*PA* 136): Boul. 424 i.
1325. HAGNODEMOS s. of Pistodemos of Azenia VIII (*PA* 138): Boul. App. VIII.
1326. HAGNODEMOS of Dekeleia VIII (*PA* 140): Tam. 390.
1327. HAGNODEMOS of Paiania III: Phyl. App. IX.
1328. HAGNODEMOS of Thorikos V: Boul. 336.
1329. HAGNON s. of Hagnonides of tribe VI: Boul. 335.
1330. HAGNON s. of Hagnias of Aithalidai IV: Boul. App. IX.
1331. HAGNON s. of Timokles of Deiradiotai IV (*PA* 168): Boul. App. VII.
1332. HAGNON of Prasiai III/Phegaia II: Gr. Tam. 354.
1333. HAGNON s. of Nikias of Steiria III (*PA* 171; *APF* 227f.): S. 440, 437, 431, 430, 429; Proboulos 412; Oath 422; Prop. 438 iv.
1334. HAGNONIDES s. of Nikoxenos of Pergase I (*PA* 176): Prop. 325 iv.
1335. HAGNOTHEOS of Alopeke X (*PA* 151): Gr. Ep. Eleusis 336–333.
1336. HAGNOTHEOS of Ikarion II: Boul. 336.
1337. HAGNOTHEOS of Kettos IV (*PA* 153): ? App. VIII.
1338. HARPAKTIDES (*PA* 2249): A. 511.
1339. HEDYLOS of Philaidai II: Hell. 421.

1340. HEGELEOS of Alopeke x (*PA* 6277): Tam. 400.

1341. HEGEMACHOS of Lamptrai I: Boul. 336.

1342. HEGEMACHOS s. of Chairemon of Perithoidai VI (*PA* 6282): Boul. -Prop. 334 vi.

1343. HEGEMON (*PA* 6291): A. 327.

1344. HEGEMON: Prop. 322 iv.

1345. HEGEMON (*PA* 6290): Prop. App. IX viii, xxxii.

1346. HEGEMON of Athmonon VII (*PA* 6294; *APF* 208): Tam. Paralou 326.

1347. HEGEMON s. of Autophon of Kytherros III: Boul. App. VII.

1348. HEGEMON s. of Labes of Phrearrhioi IV (*PA* 6301): Boul. App. VII.

1349. HEGESANDROS of tribe x (*PA* 6305): Boul. App. IV xxxi.

1350. HEGESANDROS s. of Hegesias of Sounion IV (*PA* 6307; *APF* 209): Tam. 361; Prop. 357 iii; Ass. App. VIII.

1351. HEGESIAS (*PA* 6309): A. 556.

1352. HEGESIAS s. of Kephisodoros (*PA* 6313): A. 324.

1353. HEGESIAS of L-- (*PA* 6325): Tam.-Synegoros App. VIII.

1354. HEGESIAS of Marathon IX (*PA* 6326): Boul. 323 iv.

1355. HEGESIAS s. of Hegias of Sounion IV (*PA* 6331; *APF* 209): Tam. 349.

1356. HEGESIAS of Teithras II/Tyrmeidai VI/Trikorynthos IX (*PA* 6332): Ep. 438.

1357. HEGESILEOS s. of Deisitheos of Pallene x (*PA* 6338): Boul. 334.

1358. HEGESILEOS of Probalinthos III (*PA* 6339): S. 363, 349.

1359. HEGESIPPOS of Melite VII (*PA* 6349): Epim. dock. 366.

1360. HEGESIPPOS s. of Hegesias of Sounion IV (*PA* 6351; *APF* 209): Env. 344, 343; Prop. 357 v, 356 vi, 344 ii, 343 x, 338 ii, App. VIII xiii; Ass.-Prop. 332 xiii.

1361. HEGESTRATOS (*PA* 6309): A. 560.

1362. HEGETOR of Erchia II: Boul. 336.

1363. HELIODOROS of Konthyle III (*PA* 6416): Boul. App. VI.

1364. HENIOCHIDES (*PA* 6427): A. 615.

1365. HEPHAISTODOROS of Potamos (upper) IV: Boul. App. IX.

1366. HEPHAISTODOROS s. of Arizelos of Steiria III (*PA* 6566): Boul. App. VIII.

1367. HERAKLEIDES s. of Eukleios: App. 355.

1368. HERAKLEIDES of Klazomenai (*PA* 6489): S. App. VI; Prop. App. VI xxxi.

1369. HERMIPPOS: Hieromn. 325.

1370. HERMIPPOS of Angele III: Boul. 336.

1371. HERMIPPOS of Poros v (*PA* 5116): Env. 384.

1372. HERMODOROS: Prop. 424 vi.

1373. HERMODOROS s. of Straton of Deiradiotai IV: Boul. 371.

1374. HERMODOROS s. of Hermolykos of Kolonai IV (*PA* 5141): Boul. App. VII.

1375. HERMOGENES (*PA* 5119; *APF* 269f.): Env. 393.

1376. HERMOGENES s. of Epizelos of Paiania III (*PA* 5128): Boul. App. VIII.

1377. HERMOKLES s. of Hermo-- of Keiriadai VIII: Boul. App. VII.

1378. HERMOKREON (*PA* 5160): A. 501

1379. HERMON (*PA* 5170): Peripolarchos 411; Arch. Pylos 410.

1380. HESTIAIOS (*PA* 5194): Prop. App. IV xiv.

1381. HESTIODOROS s. of Aristokleides (*PA* 5207): S. 430.

1382. HEURETES of Alopeke x (*PA* 5943): Tam. 396.

1383. HIEROKLEIDES (*PA* 7460b): Horistes 350.

1384. HIEROKLEIDES of tribe VII (*PA* 7462): Boul. 425 iii.

1385. HIEROKLEIDES s. of Timostratos of Alopeke x (*PA* 7463): Boul.-Prop. 349 i, iii.

1386. HIEROKLEIDES of Araphen II (*PA* 7464): Boul. App. VII.

1387. HIEROKLEIDES of Lamptrai I (*PA* 7468): Gr. 358.

1388. HIEROKLEIDES s. of Pheidon of Pelekes IV (*PA* 7471): Boul. App. VII.

1389. HIEROKLES of tribe x (*PA* 7482): Boul. 408 i.

1390. HIEROKLES s. of Hieron of Anaphlystos x (*PA* 7486): Boul. 334.

1391. HIEROKLES s. of Archestratos of Athmonon VII (*PA* 7485): Par. Hell. 418.

1392. HIEROMNEMON of Besa x (*PA* 7504): Tam. 367.

1393. HIEROMNEMON s. of Teisimachos of Koile VIII (*PA* 7505): Boul. 359.

1394. HIERON (*PA* 7525): Thirty 404.

1395. HIERON of Kedoi I: Boul. 336.

1396. HIERON of Paiania (upper) III (*PA* 7542): Boul. App. VI.

1397. HIERONYMOS (*PA* 7552): S. 395.

1398. HIERONYMOS of tribe IV (*PA* 7560): Hell. 432.

1399. HIERONYMOS s. of . . . ⁸ . . . . of Kerameis v: Tam. 343.

1400. HIERONYMOS s. of Oikopheles of Rhamnous IX (*PA* 7570): Boul.-Prop. App. IX iv.

1401. HIEROPHON s. of Antimnestos (*PA* 7515): Nauarchos 426.

1402. HIEROPHON s. of Soi-- (*PA* 7516): Tam. 342.

1403. HIEROPHON of Kephale v (*PA* 7517): Boul. 336.

1404. HIEROPHON of Prospalta v: Boul. 336.

1405. HIEROS s. of Melanopos of Eitea x (*PA* 7512): Boul. 334.

1406. HIMERAIOS s. of Phanostratos of Phaleron IX (*PA* 7578; *APF* 108): Kategoros 324.

1407. HIPPARCHIDES of Kephale v: Boul. 336.

1408. HIPPARCHOS s. of Charmos of Kollytos II/Cholargos v (*PA* 7600; *APF* 451): A. 496.

1409. HIPPEUS of Kydathenaion III: Boul. 336.

1410. HIPPIAS s. of Peisistratos (*PA* 7605; *APF* 446ff.): Tyrant 528; A. 526.

1411. HIPPOCHARES of Alopeke x (*PA* 7670): Boul.-Prop. 336 iv.

1412. HIPPODAMAS (*PA* 7610): A. 375.

1413. HIPPODAMAS of tribe I (*PA* 7611): S. 459.

1414. HIPPOKLEIDES s. of Teisandros (*PA* 7617; *APF* 295f.): A. 566.

1415. HIPPOKLES (*PA* 7619): Ten 404.

1416. HIPPOKLES s. of Menippos (*PA* 7620): S./Nauarchos 413.

1417. HIPPOKRATES: Prop. App. IV xxi.

1418. HIPPOKRATES s. of Aristokrates of tribe v/x (*PA* 7631): Hier. 330.

1419. HIPPOKRATES s. of Ariphron of Cholargos v (*PA* 7640 = 7628; *APF* 456): S. 426, 424; Prop. 427 iii.

1420. HIPPOKRATES of Kerameis v (*PA* 7634): Horistes 352.

1421. HIPPOLOCHOS (*PA* 7646): Thirty 404.

1422. HIPPOMACHOS (*PA* 7650): Thirty 404.

1423. HIPPOMENES (*PA* 7554): Prop. App. V xiii.

1424. HIPPON of Agryle I (*PA* 7677): Boul. 336.
1425. HIPPONIKOS: Prop. App. IV xix.
1426. HIPPONIKOS s. of Kallias of Alopeke x (*PA* 7658; *APF* 262f.): S. 426; Officer 424; Gr. 444.
1427. HIPPONIKOS s. of Kallias of Alopeke x (*PA* 7660; *APF* 269): Boul. App. IX.
1428. HIPPOSTRATOS s. of Etearchides of Pallene x (*PA* 7669): Prop. 341 i.
1429. HOMOPHRON of Euonymon I: Boul. 336.
1430. HYBRILIDES (*PA* 13896): A. 491.
1431. HYGIAINON of tribe VII: Boul. 426 iii, iv.
1432. HYGIAINON s. of Chairedemos of Lamptrai (lower) I: Boul. 367.
1433. HYPERANTHES s. of Atarbion of Skambonidai IV: Boul. 371.
1434. HYPERBOLOS (*PA* 13907): Gr. App. VI x.
1435. HYPERBOLOS s. of A-- of Anagyrous I (*PA* 13908): Boul. App. VII.
1436. HYPERBOLOS s. of Antiphanes of Perithoidai VI (*PA* 13910; *APF* 517): S. 425; Hieromn. 424; Boul.-Prop. 421 ii; Prop. 418.
1437. HYPEREIDES s. of Glaukippos of Kollytos II (*PA* 13912; *APF* 517ff.): Env. App. VII, 341, 338, 332, 323; Syndikos 344; Kategoros 324; Boul.-Prop. 338 xi, xii; Prop. 339 ix; Ass. 333, 325, 323, App. IX.
1438. HYPSICHIDES (*PA* 13916): A. 481.
1439. HYPSIMOS s. of Diognetos of Hybadai IV (*PA* 13915; *APF* 520f.): Boul. App. IX.

1440. IASIDEMOS s. of Iasidemos of Kolonai x: Boul. App. VIII.
1441. IASIMACHOS of Erikeia II: Boul. 336.
1442. IASON: Gr. App. IV xxi.
1443. IATROKLES s. of Pasiphon (*PA* 7442): Env. 347; Ass. 347.
1444. IDIOTES s. of Theogenes of Acharnai VI (*PA* 7445): Amph. Delos 376.
1445. IOLKOS of tribe VIII (*PA* 7739): Oath 422.
1446. IOPHON s. of Sophokles of Kolonos II (*PA* 7585): Hypogr. ? App. VIII.
1447. IOPHON s. of Lysis of Kydathenaion III (*PA* 7586): Boul. App. VIII.
1448. IPHIKRATES s. of Iphikrates of Rhamnous IX (*PA* 7736; *APF* 251): Env. 333.
1449. IPHIKRATES s. of Timotheos of Rhamnous IX (*PA* 7737; *APF* 248ff.): S. 393, 392, 391, 390, 389, 388, 387, 373, 372, 371, 370, 368, 367, 366, 365, 357, 356, App. VII S. note.
1450. ISAGORAS s. of Teisandros (*PA* 7680): A. 508.
1451. ISANDROS of Hagnous v: Boul. 336.
1452. ISARCHOS (*PA* 7685): A. 424.
1453. ISCHYRIAS of Halai II: Dem. App. IX.
1454. ISCHYRIAS of Poros v: Boul. 336.
1455. ISEGOROS of Euonymon I: Boul. 336.
1456. ISODEMOS s. of Isodemos of Kydathenaion III (*PA* 7711): Boul. App. VIII.
1457. ISODIKOS of tribe IX: Toxarchos 413.
1458. ISOKRATES of Anagyrous I: Boul. 336.
1459. ISONOMOS of Lamptrai I: Boul. 336.
1460. ISONYMOS of Euonymon I: Boul. 336.

1461. ISOTIMIDES (*PA* 7721): Prop. 415 x.
1462. ISTHMIONIKOS (*PA* 7689 = 7690; *APF* 403f.): Oath 422.

1463. K--: A. 551.
1464. K--: Tam. o.g. 429.
1465. KA--: Ep. 446.
1466. KA--: Gr. Eisagogeis 425.
1467. KALLI--: Tam. 407.
1468. KALLIK--: Gr. App. V xxxiii.
1469. KEPHISO--: Epim. pompeia App. IX.
1470. KIN--: Prop. App. IV xxxiii.
1471. KLEO--: Prop. App. V xvii.
1472. KLEO--: Ep. App. IX.
1473. KR . . . S: Gr. Taktai 434.

1474. KAL-- of tribe IX/X: Tam. 390.
1475. KALL-- of tribe X: Symproedros 324 ii.

1476. KALESIAS of Kydathenaion III (*PA* 7748): Boul. App. VI.
1477. KALLAISCHRIDES of Dekeleia VIII (*PA* 7750): Boul. App. VIII.
1478. KALLAISCHROS of Aphidna IX (*PA* 7759): Tam. two goddesses 328.
1479. KALLAISCHROS of Eupyridai IV (*PA* 7760; *APF* 327f.): Tam. 412.
1480. KALLAISCHROS s. of Kallias of Paiania III: Didask. 332.
1481. KALLAISCHROS of Phrearrhioi IV: Boul. 336.
1482. KALLEAS (*PA* 7766): A. 377.
1483. KALLEAS s. of Kallippos of Lamptrai I (*PA* 7768): Ep. Eleusis 332–329.
1484. KALLIADES: A. 523.
1485. KALLIADES (*PA* 7773): A. 480.
1486. KALLIADES: S. 430.
1487. KALLIADES (*PA* 7776): Tax. 405.
1488. KALLIADES (*PA* 7777): Gr. 384 ii.
1489. KALLIADES of Anakaia VIII: Tam. 426.
1490. KALLIADES of Euonymon I (*PA* 7792): Gr. 342.
1491. KALLIADES of Phrearrhioi IV (*PA* 7803): Boul. App. VIII.
1492. KALLIADES of Skambonidai IV: Boul. 336.
1493. KALLIAS: Gr. Hier. 558.
1494. KALLIAS (*PA* 7807): A. 456.
1495. KALLIAS (*PA* 7827): Prop. 434 i, ii, 433 i, ii.
1496. KALLIAS: Boul.-Prop. App. IV xx.
1497. KALLIAS (*PA* 7810): Prop. 424 i.
1498. KALLIAS: S. 341; Ass. 341.
1499. KALLIAS s. of Kalliades (*PA* 7827): S. 432.
1500. KALLIAS s. of Kratios: see Env. 508.
1501. KALLIAS s. of Hipponikos of Alopeke X (*PA* 7825; *APF* 258ff.): Env. 465, 450, 446.
1502. KALLIAS s. of Hipponikos of Alopeke X (*PA* 7826; *APF* 259ff.): S. 391; Env. 387, 375, 372.
1503. KALLIAS of Angele III (*PA* 7841): A. 406.
1504. KALLIAS s. of Kallias of Athmonon VII: Boul. App. VIII.

1505. KALLIAS s. of Habron of Bate II (*PA* 7856; *APF* 270): Tam. strat. 338.

1506. KALLIAS of Eiresidai V: Boul. 336.

1507. KALLIAS s. of Egertios of Erchia II (*PA* 7863; *APF* 271f.): Boul. 336.

1508. KALLIAS of Euonymon I: Hell. 410.

1509. KALLIAS of Kerameis V: Boul. 336.

1510. KALLIAS s. of Lykophron of Kydathenaion III (*PA* 7872): Thesm. App. VII.

1511. KALLIAS s. of Epigenes of Lamptrai (coast) I (*PA* 7873; *APF* 178f.): Boul. 367.

1512. KALLIAS of Oa III: Boul. 403 i.

1513. KALLIAS of Oa III: Epim. dock. 377.

1514. KALLIAS s. of Kallikleides of Phrearrhioi IV (*PA* 7896): Boul. 339 ii.

1515. KALLIAS of Skambonidai IV (*PA* 7887): A. 412.

1516. KALLIBIOS s. of Kephisophon of Paiania III (*PA* 7900; *APF* 148f.): Gr. 378 iv.

1517. KALLIDEMOS s. of Xenotimos of Anakaia VIII (*PA* 7903): Boul. App. VII.

1518. KALLIKLES s. of Satyros of Agryle (upper) I: Boul. 367.

1519. KALLIKLES s. of Phrynon of Probalinthos III (*PA* 7935): Boul. App. VIII.

1520. KALLIKLES s. of Gniphon of Thorai X: Boul. App. VIII.

1521. KALLIKRATES: Prop. 439.

1522. KALLIKRATES of Hermos V: Boul. 335.

1523. KALLIKRATES of Kikynna V: Boul. 336.

1524. KALLIKRATES s. of Charopides of Lamptrai I (*PA* 7946 = 7973 = 8213): Boul.-Prop. 346 i; Prop. 340 iii.

1525. KALLIKRATES s. of Pamphilos of Leukonoion IV: Boul. 371.

1526. KALLIKRATES of Perithoidai VI (*PA* 7978): Boul. 360.

1527. KALLIKRATES s. of Hippo-- of Phaleron IX (*PA* 7982): Boul. App. IX.

1528. KALLIKRATES s. of Kal-- of Phaleron IX (*PA* 7983): Boul. App. IX.

1529. KALLIKRATES s. of Kallikratides of Steiria III (*PA* 7945 = 7980): Epim. mysteries 331.

1530. KALLIKRATIDES s. of Kallikrates of Steiria III (*PA* 7988 = 7985): Ep. Braur. 335; Anagrapheus App. IX iv; ? App. VIII.

1531. KALLIMACHOS (*PA* 7992): A. 446.

1532. KALLIMACHOS: Prop. App. IV ii.

1533. KALLIMACHOS Aithalidai IV: Boul. 336.

1534. KALLIMACHOS of Aphidna IX (*PA* 8008): Pol. 490.

1535. KALLIMACHOS s. of Mnesitheos of Araphen II (*PA* 8007): Boul. 341.

1536. KALLIMACHOS of Epikephisia VI: Boul. App. IX.

1537. KALLIMACHOS of Hagnous V (*PA* 8002): Hell. 411/10.

1538. KALLIMACHOS s. of Alkias of Leukonoion IV (*PA* 8020): Boul. App. VII.

1539. KALLIMACHOS of Pergase I (*PA* 8025): A. 349.

1540. KALLIMACHOS s. of Lysimachos of Steiria III: Boul. App. VII.

1541. KALLIMEDES (*PA* 8035 + Add.): A. 360.

1542. KALLIMACHOS s. of Archemachos of Halai II (*PA* 8083): Boul. 341.

1543. KALLIMACHOS (*PA* 8030; *APF* 279): Env. 393.

1544. KALLIMEDON of Cholleidai IV (*PA* 8033): Tam. App. IX.

1545. KALLIPHANES s. of Kallikles of Kolonos II (*PA* 8222): Boul. 341.

1546. KALLIPHANES s. of Lysanias of Thorikos V (*PA* 8221): Boul. 336.

1547. KALLIPHEMOS of Hagnous V: Boul. 336.

1548. KALLIPPIDES of Euonymon I: Gr. Tam. o.g. 420.

1549. KALLIPPOS s. of Philon of Aixone VII (*PA* 8065; *NPA* 106; *APF* 274ff.): Ship commander 361.

1550. KALLIPPOS of Paiania III (*PA* 8078): Prop. 357 xii.

1551. KALLISTHENES (*PA* 8088): Prop. 415 i.

1552. KALLISTHENES (*PA* 8088): Env. 393.

1553. KALLISTHENES (*PA* 8089): S. 363.

1554. KALLISTHENES (*PA* 8090): Sitones 357; Boul.-Prop. 356 i; Prop. 347 xviii.

1555. KALLISTHENES of tribe X: Boul. 403 iv.

1556. KALLISTHENES s. of Pro-- of Dekeleia VIII (*PA* 8100): Boul. App. VIII.

1557. KALLISTHENES of Myrrhinous III (*PA* 8103): Boul. 336.

1558. KALLISTHENES s. of Charopides of Trinemeia VII (*PA* 8106): Boul.-Prop. 328 v.

1559. KALLISTOGEITON of Phegaia II: Boul. 356 ii.

1560. KALLISTRATOS (*PA* 8132): A. 355.

1561. KALLISTRATOS (*PA* 8133): Tam. 354.

1562. KALLISTRATOS of Acharnai VI (*PA* 8148 [8158]): S. 441, 439; Gr. Ep. App. IV.

1563. KALLISTRATOS s. of Kalliades of Acharnai VI (*PA* 8159): Boul. 360.

1564. KALLISTRATOS s. of Kallikrates of Aphidna IX (*PA* 8157 = 8130; *APF* 277ff.): S. 378, 373, 372; Ep. 374; Env. 372, App. VII; Prop. App. VI xxiv, 369 ii; Ass. 370.

1565. KALLISTRATOS of Marathon IX (*PA* 8174): Tam. 410.

1566. KALLISTRATOS s. of Empedos of Oe VI (*PA* 8142 = 8125): S. 418; Hipp. 413; Gr. 429.

1567. KALLISTRATOS s. of Eukles of Phrearrhioi IV: Boul. App. IX.

1568. KALLISTRATOS of Teithras II (*PA* 8182; *APF* 111): Boul.-Hier. 341.

1569. KALLISTRATOS of Thorikos V (*PA* 8168): Ep. Braur. 343; Boul.-Prop. 330 iv.

1570. KALLITELES of Acharnai VI (*PA* 8206): Boul. 360.

1571. KALLITELES s. of Kal-- of Elaious VIII (*PA* 8207): Boul. App. VIII.

1572. KALLITELES s. of . . . ⁸ . . . . es of Kydantidai II (*PA* 8211): Boul. 336.

1573. KALLIXE(I)NOS (*PA* 8042): Boul.-Prop. 406 iii.

1574. KALLIXENOS s. of Archeptolemos of tribe IX: Boul. 335.

1575. KANNONOS (*PA* 8249): Prop. App. IV xlvi.

1576. KARKINOS s. of Xenotimos of Thorikos V (*PA* 8254; *APF* 283): S. 432, 431.

1577. KEBRIS (*PA* 8263): A. App. III.

1578. KEDEIDES of Phrearrhioi IV: Boul. 371.

1579. KEDIKRATES of Halai II/VII (*PA* 8279): Boul. App. VII ii.

1580. KEDON (*PA* 8280): Officer 376.

1581. KEPHALOS of Kollytos II (*PA* 8277): Env. 384; Prop. 387 ii, 379 iii, App. VI xxxvii.

1582. KEPHISES of Kephisia I: Boul. 408.

1583. KEPHISIOS s. of Epikrates of Ionidai II (*PA* 8290): Gr. 365 i.

1584. KEPHISIOS s. of Kephisodemos of Pallene x (*PA* 8295): Boul. 334.
1585. KEPHISIOS s. of Kephisodoros of Steiria III: Boul. App. VII.
1586. KEPHISIPPOS: Akontistes App. IX.
1587. KEPHISODOROS (*PA* 8342): A. 366.
1588. KEPHISODOROS (*PA* 8347): A. 323.
1589. KEPHISODOROS (*PA* 8351): Ass. App. IX.
1590. KEPHISODOROS s. of Hag--: Boul. 342.
1591. KEPHISODOROS of tribe VIII (*PA* 8356): Boul. 412 ii.
1592. KEPHISODOROS s. of Kallias of Hagnous V: Epim. springs 347.
1593. KEPHISODOROS s. of Smikythos of Kydathenaion III (*PA* 8373): Tam. dock. 325.
1594. KEPHISODOROS of Marathon IX (*PA* 8376): Hipp. 363.
1595. KEPHISODOROS s. of Athenophanes of Phlya VII (*PA* 8387): Gr. 346.
1596. KEPHISODOROS (KEPHISODOTOS) s. of Euxitheos of Phrearrhioi IV (*PA* 8305): Epim. dock. 349.
1597. KEPHISODOTOS: Hell. 409.
1598. KEPHISODOTOS (*PA* 8312): S. 405.
1599. KEPHISODOTOS (*PA* 8314): A. 358.
1600. KEPHISODOTOS: Prop. 336 ix.
1601. KEPHISODOTOS of Acharnai VI (*PA* 8313): S. 360.
1602. KEPHISODOTOS s. of Eucharides of Acharnai VI (*PA* 8327): Boul.-Prop. 329 iv.
1603. KEPHISODOTOS of Kerameis V (*PA* 8331): Env. 372; Syndikos 355; Prop. 367, 364 iii, 358 iii; Ass. 369.
(1596a.) KEPHISODOTOS (KEPHISODOROS) s. of Euxitheos of Phrearrhioi IV (*PA* 8305): Epim. dock. 349.
1604. KEPHISOKLES: Gr. 326.
1605. KEPHISOKLES s. of Kephisodotos of tribe I: Boul. 335.
1606. KEPHISOKLES of Peiraieus VIII: Poletes 367.
1607. KEPHISOKLES s. of Kephisodoros of Steiria III: Boul. 335.
1608. KEPHISOPHON (*PA* 8404): A. 329.
1609. KEPHISOPHON of Acharnai VI (*PA* 8411): Boul. 360.
1610. KEPHISOPHON s. of Kephalion of Aphidna IX (*PA* 8410; *APF* 292f.): S. 345, 342, 340; Theorikon 343; Prop. 337 xiii.
1611. KEPHISOPHON s. of Lysiphon of Cholargos V (*PA* 8419): Epim. Amphiaraia 329; Prop. 325 v.
1612. KEPHISOPHON s. of Kephisodoros of Hermos V (*PA* 8413): Gr. Tam. 426.
1613. KEPHISOPHON of Paiania III (*PA* 8416 = 8400 = 8401 = 8415; *APF* 148): Tam. 398; Env. 404; Gr. 403 ii; Boul. 403 iii; Boul.-Prop. 403 i.
1614. KEPHISOPHON s. of Kallibios of Paiania III (*PA* 8417; *APF* 149): Fin. App. VIII; Boul.-Prop. 343 v; Prop. 347 xxi, 337 vi, App. VIII xv; Ass. 347.
1615. KEPHISOSTRATOS s. of Archias of Besa X (*PA* 8396): Boul. 334.
1616. KERAMON of Phlya VII (*PA* 8267): Tam. two goddesses 329.
1617. KICHESIPPOS of Myrrhinous III (*PA* 8449): Gr. Ep. 440.
1618. KIMON of Lakiadai VI (*PA* 8424; *APF* 309): Env. 347.
1619. KIMON s. of Miltiades of Lakiadai VI (*PA* 8429; *APF* 302ff.): S. 478,

477, 476, 469, 466, 465, 464, 463, 462, 451; Env. 480, 452; Prop. 462 i,
App. IV xxxvii.

1620. KINEAS of Anaphlystos X (*PA* 8435): Boul. App. IX.

1621. KINESIAS (*PA* 8437): Gr. Hier. 566.

1622. KINESIAS s. of Meles (*PA* 8438): Boul.-Prop. 394 iii.

1623. KIRRIADES (KIRRIAS) of Ankyle II (*PA* 8441): Boul. App. VII.

(1623a.) KIRRIAS (KIRRIADES) of Ankyle II (*PA* 8441): Boul. App. VII.

1624. KLEAICHMOS s. of Menaichmos of Euonymon I: Boul. 367.

1625. KLEAINETOS s. of Menon: Par. Bas. App. IX.

1626. KLEANDRIDES s. of Kleandros of Thorai X (*PA* 8463): Boul. 334.

1627. KLEARCHOS: Prop. 449 ii.

1628. KLEARCHOS: Boul. App. VIII v.

1629. KLEARCHOS of Agryle (lower) I: Gr. 408 iii; Boul. 408.

1630. KLEARCHOS s. of Nausikles of Aphidna IX (*PA* 8480; *APF* 397): Hier.
330.

1631. KLEARCHOS s. of Damasias of Oion IV: Boul. App. IX.

1632. KLEARISTOS s. of Philarchides of Oa III (*PA* 8473): Boul. App. VIII.

1633. KLEIDEMOS s. of Aines-- (*PA* 8495): Gr. 383.

1634. KLEIGENES of Halai II/VII (*PA* 8488): Gr. 410 i.

1635. KLEINIAS s. of Kannonos of Lamptrai (coast) I: Boul. 367.

1636. KLEINIAS s. of Alkibiades of Skambonidai IV (*PA* 8510; *APF* 16): Prop.
448.

1637. KLEINOMACHOS s. of Anthemokritos of Oion IV/VIII (*PA* 8516): Naop.
Delphi App. VIII.

1638. KLEIPPIDES s. of Deinias of Acharnai VI (*PA* 8521): S. 429.

1639. KLEISOPHOS of Euonymon I (*PA* 8529): Gr. Tam. 402.

1640. KLEISTHENES s. of Megakles (*PA* 8526; *APF* 375): A. 525; Nomothetes
508; see Env. 508.

1641. KLEISTHENES s. of Sibyrtios (*PA* 8525): Theoros 423.

1642. KLEITOMACHOS: Env. 343.

1643. KLEITOPHON s. of Aristonymos (*PA* 8546): Prop. 412 vi.

1644. KLEITOPHON of Thorai X (*PA* 8548): S. 441.

1645. KLEOBOULOS s. of Glaukos of Acharnai VI (*PA* 8558; *APF* 544): S. 396/
388.

1646. KLEOBOULOS of Eitea V: Boul. 336.

1647. KLEOCHARES s. of Glauketes of Kephisia I (*PA* 8647; *APF* 89): Hier.
330.

1648. KLEOKRITOS (*PA* 8569): A. 413.

1649. KLEOKRITOS of Gargettos II: Boul. 336.

1650. KLEOLEOS of Epikephisia VI (*PA* 8572): Boul. 360.

1651. KLEOMEDES (*PA* 8596): Thirty 404.

1652. KLEOMEDES s. of Lykomedes of Phlya VII (*PA* 8598; *APF* 347): S. 418,
417, 416.

1653. KLEOMEDES s. of Aristokleides of Probalinthos III (*PA* 8597): Boul.
App. IX.

1654. KLEOMEDON of Anaphlystos X (*PA* 8583): Boul. App. IX.

1655. KLEON (*PA* 8663): Boul. 399 ii.

1656. KLEON s. of Diagoras of Alopeke X (*PA* 8668): Boul. 334.

1657. KLEON of Araphen II (*APF* 229): Boul. 336.

1658. KLEON s. of Thoudippos of Araphen II (*PA* 8669; *APF* 229): Tam. 377.

1659. KLEON s. of Kleainetos of Kydathenaion III (*PA* 8674; *APF* 318ff.): S. 425, 424, 423, 422; Kataskopos 425; Boul. App. V; Prop. 428 ii, iv, 426 v, 424 ix, App. V xlii; Ass. 425.

1660. KLEON s. of Menexenos of Kydathenaion III (*APF* 320): Boul. App. VII.

1661. KLEONIKOS s. of Stesarchos of Potamos (upper) IV (*PA* 8604): Boul. App. VII.

1662. KLEONYMIDES s. of Phokionides of Pergase (upper) I: Boul. 335.

1663. KLEONYMOS (*PA* 8880): Synegoros 427.

1664. KLEONYMOS: Boul.-Prop. 426 i; Prop. 426 ii–iv.

1665. KLEONYMOS: Prop. 415 iv.

1666. KLEONYMOS: Prop. App. V v.

1667. KLEONYMOS: Prop. App. V xl.

1668. KLEONYMOS s. of Kleemporos of Epieikidai VII (*PA* 8683): Thesm. 329.

1669. KLEONYMOS s. of Kleoxenos of Marathon IX: Tax./Phyl. 373.

1670. KLEOPEITHES s. of Theopompos of Pallene X (*PA* 8611): Boul. 334; Epim. tribe App. IX.

1671. KLEOPHANES (*PA* 8628): Phyl. 349.

1672. KLEOPHON s. of Kleippides of Acharnai VI (*PA* 8638): S. App. V; Prop. 410 vii; Ass. 411/10, 405.

1673. KLEOPHON s. of O-- of Thria VI (*PA* 8642): Boul. App. VII.

1674. KLEOPHRADES: Gr. 415 i.

1675. KLEOPHRADES of Sounion IV: Boul. 336.

1676. KLEOPOMPOS s. of Kleinias of Skambonidai IV/Thria VI (*PA* 8613; *APF* 16): S. 431, 430.

1677. KLEOPOMPOS of Thria VI (*PA* 8614): Boul. 360, App. VII.

1678. KLEOSTRATOS s. of Timosthenes of Aigilia X (*PA* 8623): Gr. 343.

1679. KLEOTIMOS of Atene X (*PA* 8626; *APF* 318): Ep. Braur. 353.

1680. KLESOPHOS: Boul. 405 iii.

1681. KLYTIAS of Pergase I (*PA* 8795): Tam. 442.

1682. KOMAIOS s. of Komon of Semachidai X (*PA* 8693; *APF* 320): Boul. 334.

1683. KOMEAS (*PA* 8955): A. 561.

1684. KOMEAS of Lamptrai I: Boul. App. VIII.

1685. KONON (*PA* 8699; *APF* 507): A. 462.

1686. KONON s. of Timotheos of Anaphlystos X (*PA* 8707; *APF* 506ff.): S. 411/10, 407, 406, 405; S./Nauarchos 414; Env. 393.

1687. KONON s. of Timotheos of Anaphlystos X (*PA* 8708; *APF* 511f.): S. 334, 333.

1688. KONON s. of Kleisthenes of Athmonon VII (*APF* 321): Tam. Paralou App. IX.

1689. KONON s. of Metrodoros of Kydathenaion III (*NPA* 114; *APF* 401f.): Tam. dedication 335.

1690. KOROIBOS: Tam. 370.

1691. KOROIBOS of tribe IX: Boul. App. IX.

1692. KRATES: Hier. 566.

1693. KRATES (*PA* 8740): A. 434.

1694. KRATES (*PA* 8741): Gr. 407 vi.

1695. KRATES s. of Naupon of Lamptrai I (*PA* 8746): Gr. Tam. 434.
1696. KRATINOS (*PA* 8750): S. 476.
1697. KRATINOS (*PA* 8752): Boul.-Prop. 363 i, App. VII xiii; Prop. 354 i.
1698. KRATINOS s. of Kallimedes of tribe VI (*PA* 8755): Tax. App. IV.
1699. KRATINOS s. of Kratylos of Aigilia X (*PA* 8758): Boul. 334.
1700. KRATINOS of Erchia II (*PA* 8753 = 8760; *APF* 321): Hipp. 349.
1701. KRATINOS s. of Demostratos of Kydathenaion III (*PA* 8761): Boul. App. VII.
1702. KRATINOS of Sphettos V (*PA* 8757a): Env. 392.
1703. KRATIOS s. of Kratylos of Aigilia X (*PA* 8765): Boul. 334.
1704. KREON (*PA* 8781): A. 684.
1705. KREON of Skambonidai IV (*PA* 8785): S. 441.
1706. KRITIADES s. of Phaeinos of Teithras II (*PA* 8788): Gr. 433.
1707. KRITIAS: A. App. II.
1708. KRITIAS s. of Dropides (*PA* 8789; *APF* 322, 326): A. 600.
1709. KRITIAS s. of Kallaischros (*PA* 8792; *APF* 326f.): Thirty 404; Prop. 411/10 i, iii.
1710. KRITIOS (*PA* 8798): Boul.-Prop. 375 i.
1711. KRITOBOULOS of Kolonai IV/X (*PA* 8805): Hier. Eleusis 328.
1712. KRITODEMOS s. of Endios of Lamptrai I (*PA* 8812; *APF* 179): Plouton App. IX.
1713. KRITON s. of Erxidikos of Marathon IX: Decrees 335.
1714. KTEON s. of Mikon of Gargettos II (*PA* 8830): Boul. 336.
1715. KTESARCHOS of Sounion IV: Boul. App. IX.
1716. KTESIAS: Tam. App. IV.
1717. KTESIAS (*PA* 8838): Prop. App. IV xxxvi.
1718. KTESIAS: Tam.-Synegoros App. VIII.
1719. KTESIAS of Besa X (*PA* 8841): Thesm. 370.
1720. KTESIBIOS s. of Tleson of Anagyrous I (*PA* 8853): Tam. 350.
1721. KTESIBIOS of Lamptrai I (*PA* 8854): Epim. dock. 356.
1722. KTESIKLEIDES s. of Kteson of Alopeke X (*PA* 8859): Boul. App. IX (twice).
1723. KTESIKLES (*PA* 8861): S. 395, 374, 373.
1724. KTESIKLES (*PA* 8863): A. 334.
1725. KTESIKLES of Bate II (*PA* 8868): Boul.-Prop. App. IX xi.
1726. KTESIKLES of Hagnous V (*PA* 8866): Askl. App. VII.
1727. KTESINOS s. of Kretheus of Eupyridai IV: Boul. 335.
1728. KTESION (*PA* 8903): Tam. 440.
1729. KTESIPHANES of Thorikos V (*NPA* 115): Epim. dock. 369.
1730. KTESIPHON (*PA* 8893): Env. 348, 347; Ass. 348.
1731. KTESIPHON (*PA* 8894): Env. 330; Prop. 337 xii.
1732. KTESIPHON of Oe VI (*PA* 8898): Boul. 360.
1733. KTESIPPOS s. of Ktesonides of Aithalidai IV (*PA* 8884): Boul. App. VII.
1734. KTESIPPOS s. of Hagnodemos of Pergase (lower) I: Boul. 335.
1735. KTESON s. of Titon of Anagyrous I: Boul. 367.
1736. KTESONIDES of Prasiai III (*PA* 8917): Tam. o.g. 420.
1737. KTESOS of Sypalettos VII (*PA* 8904): Gr. Ep. Eleusis 409.
1738. KYBERNIS of Halai II: Dem. App. IX.
1739. KYDENOR s. of Kydenor of Alopeke X (*PA* 8921): Gr. App. VI viii.

1740. KYDIAS (*PA* 8924): Nauarchos 365; Ass. 365.
1741. KYDIAS s. of Lysikrates of Erchia II (*PA* 8928): Boul. 341.
1742. KYDIMOS (*PA* 8934): Naop. Delphi 353.
1743. KYDIPPOS of Anaphlystos X (*PA* 8937): Boul. App. VII.
1744. KYKNEAS of tribe VII (*PA* 8940): Boul. App. V viii.
1745. KYKNOS s. of Philochoros of Anaphlystos X (*PA* 8941): Boul. 334.
1746. KYNEGEIROS s. of Euphorion of Eleusis VIII (*PA* 8944): S. 490.
1747. KYPSELOS s. of Agamestor (*PA* 8951; *APF* 295ff.): A. 597.

1748. L--: Prop. App. IV v.
1749. L--: Hypogr.? App. VIII.
1750. LEOS--: Prop. App. VIII viii.
1751. LY--: Tam. o.g. 374.
1752. LYS--: Hell. 429.
1753. LYS--: Gr. Amph. Delos 333.
1754. LYSIA--: Env. App. VII.
1755. LYSIK--: Tam. 403.

(702a.) LI . . AL-- (DI . . AL--) of tribe VII: Tam. 385.
1756. LY-- of tribe VI: Boul. App. V xx.

1757. LACHARIDES of Eleusis VIII (*PA* 9007): Epim. dock. 371.
1758. LACHES (*PA* 9011): A. 400.
1759. LACHES of Aixone VII (*PA* 9012): Tax. 394.
1760. LACHES s. of Laches of Aixone VII (*PA* 9018): S. 364.
1761. LACHES s. of Melanopos of Aixone VII (*PA* 9019): S. 427, 426, 422, 418;
    Officer 424; Oath 422; Prop. 424 iii, viii.
1762. LACHES of Hybadai IV: Boul. 336.
1763. LACHES s. of Charinos of Potamos (upper) IV: Boul. App. IX.
1764. LAISPODIAS of Anaphlystos X: Boul. App. VII.
1765. LAISPODIAS s. of Andronymis of Koile VIII (*PA* 8963): S. 414; Env. 411.
1766. LAKEDAIMONIOS s. of Kimon of Lakiadai VI (*PA* 8965; *APF* 305f.): S.
    433; Hipp. App. IV.
1767. LAKONIDES of Hagnous V (*PA* 8976): Boul. 378.
1768. LAKRATEIDES (*PA* 8967): A. App. II.
1769. LAKRATEIDES (*PA* 8969): Horistes 350.
1770. LAMACHOS s. of Xenophanes of Oe VI (*PA* 8981): S. 436, 425, 424, 416,
    415, 414, App. V; Env. 426; Oath 422.
1771. LAMPIDES of Peiraieus VIII: S. 441.
1772. LAMPON (*PA* 8996): Oath 422; Prop. App. V viii.
1773. LAMPRIAS s. of Lamprias of Sypalettos VII (*PA* 8990): Ep. Eleusis 336–
    333.
1774. LAMPROKLES s. of Aresias of Peiraieus VIII (*PA* 8992; *NPA* 116): Tam.
    351.
1775. LAMPROKLES of Phlya VII (*PA* 8994): Tam. 399.
1776. LEAGROS s. of Glaukon of Kerameis V (*PA* 9028; *APF* 90f.): S. 465.
1777. LEAIOS of Aixone VII (*PA* 9030): Boul. App. VII.
1778. LEARCHOS s. of Kallimachos (*PA* 9031): Env. 430.
1779. LEOCHARES of Alopeke X (*PA* 9166): Tam. 415.

1780. LEOCHARES s. of Leokrates of Pallene x (*PA* 9175; *APF* 344): Ep. App. IX.

1781. LEODAMAS s. of Erasistratos of Acharnai VI (*PA* 9077; *APF* 523): Env. App. VI; Syndikos 355.

1782. LEOGORAS (*PA* 9074; *APF* 27f.): see App. II.

1783. LEOGORAS (*APF* 30): S. 453.

1784. LEOGORAS (*PA* 9072): Env. 426.

1785. LEOKRATES s. of Stroibos (*PA* 9084): S. 479, 459, 458, 457.

1786. LEOKRATES of Kydathenaion III: Boul. 336.

1787. LEOKRATES s. of A . . ᵌ . . . os of Pallene x (*APF* 344): Didask. 333.

1788. LEOKRATES s. of Hippokrates of Skambonidai IV: Boul. 371.

1789. LEON: Gr. Hell. 453.

1790. LEON (*PA* 9099): Prop. App. IV iii.

1791. LEON: Prop. App. IV xii.

1792. LEON (*PA* 9100): S. 412.

1793. LEON (*PA* 9101): Env. 368.

1794. LEON: Tam. App. VII.

1795. LEON of tribe x (*PA* 9100): Oath 422.

1796. LEON of Bate II: Boul. 336.

1797. LEON s. of Philagros of Halai VII (*PA* 9110): Boul. App. VII.

1798. LEONTICHOS (*PA* 9036): S. 387.

1799. LEONTIOS of Kephisia I: Boul. 336.

1800. LEOSTHENES: Poletes 346.

1801. LEOSTHENES of Kephale V (*PA* 9141; *APF* 342ff.): S. 361.

1802. LEOSTHENES s. of Leosthenes of Kephale V (*PA* 9142 = 9144; *APF* 342ff.): S. 324, 323; Ass. 323.

1803. LEOSTRATOS (*PA* 9147): A. 671.

1804. LEOSTRATOS (*PA* 9148): A. 484.

1805. LEOSTRATOS of Alopeke x (*PA* 9152): Epim. dock. 360.

1806. LEOTROPHIDES (*PA* 9159): S. 409.

1807. LEOTROPHIDES of Kropidai IV (*PA* 9158): Tam. trir. funds App. IX.

1808. LEPTIAS of Probalinthos III: Boul. 336.

1809. LEPTINES (*PA* 9041; *APF* 341): Tam. 347.

1810. LEPTINES of Koile VIII (*PA* 9046; *APF* 340): Fin. 363; Syndikos 355; Prop. 356 vii; Ass. 370.

1811. LEUKAIOS s. of Komarchos of Aphidna IX (*PA* 9051): Gr. Tam. 413.

1812. LEUKOLOPHOS: Arch. Salamis 402.

1813. LEUKON s. of Demeas of Phrearrhioi IV (*PA* 9069): Askl. 329; Boul. App. IX.

1814. LOBON of Kedoi I (*PA* 9184): Gr. 410 v.

1815. LOKRION of Alopeke x (*PA* 9185): Boul. App. IX.

1816. LYKAITHOS (*PA* 9189): Env. 372.

1817. LYKIDES (*PA* 9194): Boul.-Prop. 480 i.

1818. LYKINOS of Pallene x (*PA* 9207; *APF* 345): Ship commander 361.

1819. LYKINOS of Pambotadai I: Boul. 336.

1820. LYKINOS of Phrearrhioi IV (*PA* 9210): Boul. App. IX.

1821. LYKISKOS (*PA* 9213): Prop. 406 iv.

1822. LYKISKOS (*PA* 9214): A. 344.

1823. LYKISKOS of Acharnai VI (*PA* 9215): Boul. App. VII.

1824. LYKON of Kephisia I (*PA* 9272): Epim. dock. 378.

1825. LYKON s. of Thersias of Phrearrhioi IV (*PA* 9275): Boul. 336.

1826. LYKON of Prasiai III (*PA* 9274): Tam. 419.

1827. LYKOPADES of Euonymon I: Ep. 375.

1828. LYKOPHRON (*PA* 9255): Hipp. App. IX; Phyl. App. IX.

1829. LYKOPHRON s. of Lykophron of Skambonidai IV: Boul. App. IX.

1830. LYKOS of Koile VIII (*PA* 9022): Tam. 442.

1831. LYKOURGOS of Boutadai VI (*PA* 9246; *APF* 349): S. 476.

1832. LYKOURGOS s. of Lykophron of Boutadai VI (*PA* 9251; *APF* 350f.): Fin.
      administrator 336–333; Epim. Amphiaraia 329; Hier. 330; Kategoros
      325; Env. 343; Various App. IX; Boul.-Prop. 338 xii, 336 i; Prop. 335 vi,
      x, 334 iv, 333 iii, ix, 332 iii, 330 i, 329 vi, vii, 328 iv, App. IX iii, xvii,
      xxvi, xxxiv–xxxviii; Ass. 335, 324.

1833. LYKOURGOS of Melite VII (*PA* 9254): Boul. 328.

1834. LYSAGORAS (*PA* 9275a): A. 509.

1835. LYSANDRIDES of Leukonoion IV: Boul. 336.

1836. LYSANIAS (*PA* 9299): A. 466.

1837. LYSANIAS (*PA* 9300): A. 443.

1838. LYSANIAS: Prop. App. IV xiii.

1839. LYSANIAS s. of Philippos of Auridai VIII: Boul. App. VIII.

1840. LYSANIAS s. of Lysiades of Eupyridai IV: Boul. 335.

1841. LYSANIAS of Hybadai IV: Boul. 336.

1842. LYSANIAS s. of Lysanias of Lamptrai (coast) I (*PA* 9316): Boul. 367.

1843. LYSANIAS s. of Lysikrates of Phrearrhioi IV (*PA* 9328): Boul. App.
      VIII.

1844. LYSANIAS s. of Aristokleides of Probalinthos III (*PA* 9322): Boul. App.
      IX.

1845. LYSANIAS s. of Proxenos of Sounion IV (*PA* 9323; *APF* 354): Tam.
      Paralou 327.

1846. LYSANIAS s. of Lysistratos of Thorikos V (*PA* 9314): ? App. VIII.

1847. LYSIADES (*PA* 9332a): A. 682.

1848. LYSIADES (*PA* 9333): Gr. 401.

1849. LYSIAS (*PA* 9351): S. 406.

1850. LYSIAS s. of L--: Amph. Delos 372–368.

1851. LYSIAS s. of L-- (*PA* 9356): Gr.? App. VIII.

1852. LYSIAS of Acharnai VI (*PA* 9368): Ep. Braur. 352.

1853. LYSIAS s. of Lysimachos of Pithos VII (*PA* 9355): Gr. 356.

1854. LYSIDEMOS s. of Lysitheos of Pallene X: Boul. 335.

1855. LYSIDIKOS of Gargettos II (*PA* 9388): Gr. Tam. 419.

1856. LYSIKLES (*PA* 9417): S. 428; Prop. App. IV xxii.

1857. LYSIKLES (*PA* 9422): S. 338.

1858. LYSIKLES s. of E-- (*PA* 9418): Gr. 407 iii.

1859. LYSIKLES s. of Eirenippos (*PA* 9426): Boul.-Hier.-Syllogeus 324.

1860. LYSIKLES of Aigilia X: Hypogr. Amph. Delos 333.

1861. LYSIKLES s. of Drakontides of Bate II (*PA* 9432; *APF* 170): Gr. Tam.
      416.

1862. LYSIKLES s. of Thrasymenes of Philaidai II (*PA* 9441): Boul. 343.

1863. LYSIKRATES (*PA* 9442): A. 453.

1864. LYSIKRATES (*PA* 9443): S. App. V.

1865. LYSIKRATES of Oinoe VIII/IX (*PA* 9465): Env. 356.
1866. LYSIMACHIDES (LYSIMACHOS) (*PA* 9475): A. 445.
1867. LYSIMACHIDES s. of Lysimachos of Acharnai VI (*PA* 9480; *APF* 357f.): A. 339.
1868. LYSIMACHIDES of Hagnous V: S. 329.
1869. LYSIMACHIDES s. of Lysipolis of Halai II (*PA* 9479): Boul. 341.
1870. LYSIMACHOS (*APF* 48): Tam. 550.
(1866a.) LYSIMACHOS (LYSIMACHIDES) (*PA* 9475): A. 445.
1871. LYSIMACHOS (*PA* 9486): Hipp. 404.
1872. LYSIMACHOS s. of Sosidemos of Acharnai VI (*PA* 9512; *APF* 358): Gr. 347.
1873. LYSIMACHOS of Kedoi I: Tam. o.g. 421.
1874. LYSIMACHOS of Kolonai IV/X (*PA* 9518): Gr. 399 ii.
1875. LYSIMACHOS of Myrrhinous III (*PA* 9523): A. 436.
1876. LYSIMACHOS s. of Lysimenes of Myrrhinous III (*PA* 9524): Boul. App. VIII.
1877. LYSIMACHOS of Sypalettos VII (*PA* 9528): Boul. App. VII.
1878. LYSIMENES of Hagnous V: Boul. 336.
1879. LYSIPHILOS of Rhamnous IX (*PA* 9636): Epim. dock. 368.
1880. LYSIPHON s. of Kephisophon of Cholargos V: Boul. 336.
1881. LYSIPPIDES of Thorikos V: Dem. App. VI.
1882. LYSIPPOS of Agryle I: Boul. 336.
1883. LYSIPPOS s. of Philinos of Paiania III (*PA* 9564): Boul. App. IX.
1884. LYSISTRATOS (*PA* 9591): S. 476.
1885. LYSISTRATOS (*PA* 9592): A. 467.
1886. LYSISTRATOS (*PA* 9597): A. 369.
1887. LYSISTRATOS (*PA* 9598): S. 366/364.
1888. LYSISTRATOS (*PA* 9601): Hieromn. 326.
1889. LYSISTRATOS (SOSISTRATOS *PA* 13290) of Aigilia X: Tam. o.g. 421.
1890. LYSISTRATOS s. of Polyeuktos of Bate II (*PA* 9615; *APF* 171): Boul. 341.
1891. LYSISTRATOS s. of Nikoxenos of Kephisia I: Boul. 367.
1892. LYSISTRATOS of Kothokidai VI: Tam. o.g. 420.
1893. LYSISTRATOS s. of Kephisodoros of Melite VII (*PA* 9619; *APF* 425): ? App. VIII.
1894. LYSISTRATOS of Paionidai IV: Boul. 336.
1895. LYSISTRATOS s. of Morychides of Pallene X (*PA* 9624): Gr. Tam. 425.
1896. LYSISTRATOS of Phyle VI (*PA* 9629): ? App. VIII.
1897. LYSITHEOS (*PA* 9398): A. 465.
1898. LYSITHEOS of Anagyrous I: Boul. 367.
1899. LYSITHEOS of Euonymon I: Boul. 328.
1900. LYSITHEOS of Lamptrai I: Boul. 336.
1901. LYSITHEOS of Thymaitadai VIII (*PA* 9405; *APF* 355): Hell. 407.
1902. LYSITHEOS of Trikorynthos IX (*PA* 9407): Askl. 344.

1903. M--: Ep. 434.
1904. M--: Boul. 354 iii.
(971a.) M--: (EM--): Hypogr. Amph. Delos 341.

1905. M--: Oath App. VIII.
1906. MY--: Boul. App. VI xxvi.

1907. MANTIAS s. of Mantitheos of Thorikos v (*PA* 9667; *APF* 364ff.): S. 360; Tam. dock. 377.
1908. MANTIKLES of Teithras II: Boul. 331.
1909. MANTITHEOS (*PA* 9670): Officer 408; Env. 409; Boul. 415.
1910. MANTITHEOS of Thorikos v (*PA* 9674; *APF* 364f.): Ass. App. VI.
1911. MANTITHEOS s. of Mantias of Thorikos v (*PA* 9676; *APF* 364ff.): Tax. 349.
1912. MECHANION (*PA* 10162): Gr. App. IV.
1913. MEGAKLEIDES s. of My--: Tam. o.g. 375.
1914. MEGAKLEIDES of Leukonoion IV (*PA* 9687): Gr. 426 i.
1915. MEGAKLEIDES of Leukonoion IV: Tam. 354.
1916. MEGAKLES (*PA* 9688; *APF* 370f.): A. 632.
1917. MEGAKLES s. of Hippokrates of Alopeke x (*PA* 9695; *APF* 379): see Env. 508.
1918. MEGAKLES s. of Megakles of Alopeke x (*PA* 9697; *APF* 381): Gr. Tam. 428; Env. 426.
1919. MEGAKLES s. of Euainetos of Gargettos II (*PA* 9700): Boul. 343.
1920. MEGAKLES of Thria VI (*PA* 9701): Boul. 360.
1921. MEIDIAS s. of Kephisodoros of Anagyrous I (*PA* 9719; *APF* 386f.): Hipp. 349; Tam. Paralou 358; Epim. mysteries App. VIII; Hier. App. VIII; Boones App. VIII; Pylag. 340; Prop. 349 vii; Ass. 355, App. VII, App. VIII.
1922. MEIDIAS s. of Meidias of Anagyrous I (*PA* 9720; *APF* 387): Prop. App. IX xxxi.
1923. MEIDOKRATES of Probalinthos III: Boul. 336.
1924. MEIDOKRATES s. of Meidokrates of Probalinthos III: Epim. tribe App. VII.
1925. MEIDON s. of Meidias of Dekeleia VIII (*PA* 8269): Boul. App. VIII.
1926. MEIDON of Euonymon I (*PA* 9739): Tam. 400.
1927. MEIDON s. of Epiteles of Myrrhinous III: Boul. 336.
1928. MEIDONIDES s. of Meidon of Athmonon VII: Boul. App. VIII.
1929. MEIXIAS s. of Hegesias of Gargettos II (*PA* 9752): Boul. 341.
1930. MEIXIGENES s. of Mikon of Cholleidai IV (*PA* 9754; *APF* 58): Tam. Paralou App. IX.
1931. MELANKOMAS s. of Hierokles of Kettos IV: Boul. 371.
1932. MELANOPIDES of Kettos IV: Boul. 336.
1933. MELANOPOS s. of Laches of Aixone VII (*PA* 9788): S. 355; Env. 372, 355; Boul.-Prop. 364 ii; Ass. App. VII.
1934. MELANOPOS s. of Hestiodoros of P-- (*PA* 9793): Ep. 356–353.
1935. MELANTHIOS (*PA* 9768): S. 411.
(732a.) MELANTHIOS (DEMETRIOS of Hamaxanteia VIII): Logistes 407.
1936. MELANTHIOS s. of Phalanthos (*PA* 9764): S. 499.
1937. MELESANDROS (*PA* 9803): S. 430.
1938. MELESANDROS: S. 414.
1939. MELESIAS: Hier. 558.

1940. MELESIAS s. of Melesippos of Alopeke x (*PA* 9810; *APF* 233): Boul. App. IX.

1941. MELESIAS s. of Thoukydides of Alopeke x (*PA* 9813; *APF* 232f.): Env. 411.

1942. MELESIAS of Halai II/VII: Boul. 357 i.

1943. MELESIAS of Halai VII (*PA* 9811): Tam. 334.

1944. MELESIAS s. of Polykles of Oa III: Gr. Tam. 429.

1945. MELESIAS of Oe VI: Tam. 414.

1946. MELESIAS s. of --eles of Phrearrhioi IV: Boul. 371.

1947. MELESIAS s. of Aristoteles of Steiria III (*PA* 9818): Boul. App. VIII.

1948. MELESIPPOS s. of Melesias of Ankyle II (*PA* 9820; *APF* 233): Boul. 341.

1949. MELESIPPOS of Paiania (upper) III (*PA* 9823): Boul. App. VI.

1950. MELETON (MELETOS): Boul. App. IV xxx.

(1950a.) MELETOS (MELETON): Boul. App. IV xxx.

1951. MELETOS (*PA* 9825): Env. 404.

1952. MELETOS s. of Menestratos of Angele III (*PA* 9827): Boul. App. IX.

1953. MELIEUS s. of Ilioneus of Ionidai II (*PA* 10101): Boul.-Hier. 341.

1954. MELOBIOS (*PA* 10102): Thirty 404.

1955. MENAICHMOS of Pambotadai I: Epim. dock. 367.

1956. MENAIOS: Tam. 340.

1957. MENANDROS (*PA* 9856): Tam. 440.

1958. MENANDROS (*PA* 9857): S. 414, 413, 405; Officer 414, 410.

1959. MENANDROS of tribe II/IX: Pol. 370.

1960. MENANDROS s. of Menes of Angele III: Boul. App. VII.

1961. MENEKLES of Anaphlystos x: Gr. 421.

1962. MENEKLES s. of Menestratos of Angele III: Boul. App. VII.

1963. MENEKLES of Hippotomadai VI (*PA* 9922): Ep. Eleusis 408.

1964. MENEKRATES of Oinoe VIII/IX: Tam. 404.

1965. MENELAOS s. of Menelochos of Myrrhinous III (*PA* 9963; *APF* 389): Env. 341.

1966. MENES: Boul. 371 ii.

1967. MENES s. of Menekles of Pelekes IV (*PA* 10028): Gr. Amph. Delos 363.

1968. MENESAICHMOS (*PA* 9983): Fin. administrator 324–322; Kategoros 324.

1969. MENESTHEUS s. of Iphikrates of Rhamnous IX (*PA* 9988; *APF* 249ff.): S. 356, 333.

1970. MENESTRATOS of Aixone VII: Ep. Nomothetai 337 xiv.

1971. MENESTRATOS of Angele III (*PA* 10001): Askl. 350.

1972. MENESTRATOS s. of Straton of Gargettos II (*PA* 10004): Boul. 343.

1973. MENESTRATOS of Kerameis v: Boul. 336.

1974. MENESTRATOS s. of Menekrates of Kolonai IV (*PA* 10010): Boul. App. VII.

1975. MENESTRATOS s. of Oinophilos of Paionidai IV (*PA* 10013): Boul. App. VII.

1976. MENESTRATOS of Phlya VII (*PA* 10019): Boul. App. IX.

1977. MENESTRATOS s. of Menestratos of Phlya VII/Pithos VII (*PA* 10000): Tam. 407.

1978. MENETELES (MENETIMOS *PA* 10026) of Lamptrai I: Gr. Hell. 448.

1979. MENETELES of Phrearrhioi IV (*PA* 10022; *APF* 390): Prop. 412 ii.
1980. MENETIMOS s. of O-- of Hagnous V (*PA* 10025): Boul. 378.
(1978a.) MENETIMOS (MENETELES) of Lamptrai I (*PA* 10026): Gr. Hell. 448.
1981. MENEXENOS (*PA* 9972 = 9971; *APF* 390): Prop. 364 iii, 363 iv.
1982. MENEXENOS s. of Dikaiogenes of Kydathenaion III (*PA* 9976; *APF* 145): Phyl. 430.
1983. MENIOS of Oe VI (*PA* 10031): Epim. dock. 356.
1984. MENIPPOS (*PA* 10033): S. App. IV.
1985. MENIPPOS (*PA* 10034): Prop. 415 xi.
1986. MENIPPOS s. of Xenophantos of Agryle (upper) I: Boul. 367.
1987. MENIPPOS of Phaleron IX: Dem. 402.
1988. MENITES: Prop. App. IV xviii.
1989. MENITES s. of Menon of Kydathenaion III (*PA* 10055): Tax. 349.
1990. MENON (*PA* 10066): A. 473.
1991. MENON of tribe VII (*PA* 10073): Boul. App. VII.
1992. MENON s. of Demophilos of Lamptrai (coast) I: Boul. 367.
1993. MENON of Oe VI (*PA* 10081): Tam. 390.
1994. MENON of Potamos IV (*PA* 10085): S. 362, 357.
1995. MENYLLOS (*PA* 10061): Boul. 455.
1996. METAGENES (*PA* 10086): Gr. 434.
1997. METAGENES of Koile VIII (*PA* 10088): S. 433.
1998. METIOCHOS (*PA* 10131; *APF* 308): S. App. IV.
1999. METROBIOS (*PA* 10133): Gr. App. IV.
2000. MIKON (*PA* 10199): A. 402.
2001. MILTIADES (*PA* 10205; *APF* 299): A. 664.
2002. MILTIADES (*PA* 10205; *APF* 299): A. 659.
2003. MILTIADES s. of Kimon of Lakiadai VI (*PA* 10212; *APF* 301f.): A. 524; S. 490.
2004. MILTIADES s. of Kimon of Lakiadai VI (*PA* 10210; *APF* 309): Oikistes 325.
2005. MISGOLAS of Kollytos II: Gr. Tam. 403.
2006. MISGOLAS s. of Naukrates of Kollytos II (*PA* 10225): ? App. VIII.
2007. MNASILOCHOS (= MNESILOCHOS) (*PA* 10324): A. 411; Thirty 404.
2008. MNASIPPOS (ONASIPPOS *PA* 11439): Gr. App. IV iii.
2009. MNESAGORAS s. of Mnesilochos of Halai II (*PA* 10238; *NPA* 130; *APF* 393): Tam. 349.
2010. MNESARCHIDES s. of Mnesarchos of Halai II (*PA* 10242 = 10245; *APF* 392): Par. A. 340.
2011. MNESARCHIDES of Oinoe VIII: Dem. App. IX.
2012. MNESARCHOS (*PA* 10249): Boul. 356 i.
2013. MNESARCHOS s. of Timostratos of Probalinthos III (*PA* 10255): Boul. App. IX.
2014. MNESIADES of Kothokidai VI (*PA* 10259): Epim. dock. 375.
2015. MNESIBOULOS (*PA* 10264 = 10265; *APF* 225): Gr. 368 i.
2016. MNESIBOULOS s. of Aristoteles of Paiania (lower) III (*PA* 10267): Boul. App. VII.
2017. MNESIERGOS of Athmonon VII (*PA* 10275): Gr. Tam. 398.
2018. MNESIGENES s. of Kalliteles of Kytherros III: Boul. App. VIII.

2019. MNESIKLEIDES s. of Gorgiades of Ikarion II: Boul. App. VII.

2020. MNESIKLES of tribe VI: S. 394.

2021. MNESIKLES of A-- (*PA* 10309): Boul. App. IX v.

2022. MNESIKLES of Kollytos II (*PA* 10314): Boul. 346.

2023. MNESIKLES s. of Pythokles of Poros V: Boul. 338.

2024. MNESIKRATES s. of Lysikrates of tribe VI: Boul. 335.

2025. MNESIKRATES of Thorikos V: Boul. 336.

2026. MNESILOCHOS (*PA* 10323): Hieromn. 343.

2027. MNESILOCHOS s. of Mnesimachos of Konthyle III (*PA* 10327): Tam. 351.

2028. MNESIMACHOS of Hagnous V (*PA* 10336): S. 329.

2029. MNESIMACHOS s. of Nouphrades of Perithoidai VI: Boul. 335.

2030. MNESIPHILOS s. of Mneson of Phaleron IX (*PA* 10378): Gr. 334.

2031. MNESIPHON of Phegous I: Boul. 336.

2032. MNESIPTOLEMOS of Rhamnous IX: Dem. App. IV.

2033. MNESIS s. of Phil--: Amph. Delos 343.

2034. MNESISTRATOS s. of Mnesimachos of Acharnai VI (*PA* 10369): ? App. VIII.

2035. MNESISTRATOS of Kytherros III (*PA* 10372): S. 329.

2036. MNESISTRATOS of Phrearrhioi IV: Boul. App. IX.

2037. MNESITHEIDES (*PA* 10276): A. 457.

2038. MNESITHEIDES (*PA* 10277): Thirty 404.

(820a.) MNESITHEOS (DEXITHEOS): Hier. 558.

2039. MNESITHEOS (*PA* 10281): Gr. 434 i, ii.

2040. MNESITHEOS s. of Proteas of Agryle (lower) I: Boul. 367.

2041. MNESITHEOS of Araphen II: Hell. 418.

2042. MNESITHEOS s. of Nikostratos of Araphen II (*PA* 10288): Boul. 343.

2043. MNESITHEOS s. of Mnesigenes of Kydathenaion III: Boul. App. VII.

2044. MNESON s. of Ariston: Didask. 333.

2045. MNESONIDES of Phrearrhioi IV: Boul. App. IX.

2046. MOIRAGENES of Ikarion II: Phyl. App. IX.

2047. MOIRAGENES of Kydathenaion III (*PA* 10396): Ep. Braur. 350.

2048. MOIROKLES s. of Euthydemos of Eleusis VIII (*PA* 10400 = 10401): Prop. App. VIII xxii; Ass. App. IX.

2049. MOLON (*PA* 10411): A. 362.

2050. MOLOSSOS (= MOLOTTOS) (*PA* 10403 = 10406): S. 348.

2051. MOLOTTOS of Iphistiadai V: Boul. 336.

2052. MOLPIS (*PA* 10407): Arch. Peiraieus 404.

2053. MONIPPIDES (*PA* 10414): Boul.-Prop. App. VI iv, v.

2054. MORMIAS s. of Euboulos of Oinoe VIII (*PA* 10415; *NPA* 131): Tam. 349.

2055. MORYCHIDES of Pallene X (*PA* 10418 = 10419): A. 440.

2056. MORYCHOS of Boutadai VI (*PA* 10422): Gr. Tam. 397.

2057. MOSCHOS of Euonymon I: Boul. 336.

2058. MOSCHOS s. of Kephisodoros of Hybadai IV: Boul. App. IX.

2059. MOSCHOS s. of Thestios of Kydathenaion III (*PA* 10461): Tam. 366; Gr. 368 ii–iv.

2060. MYRONIDES s. of Kallias (*PA* 10509): S. 479, 458, 457, 456; Env. 480.

2061. MYRONIDES s. of Kleon of Araphen II (*PA* 10510; *APF* 229): Boul. 343.

2062. MYRTILOS s. of Lysis of tribe IV (*PA* 10497): Oath 422.
2063. MYRTILOS s. of Chareleides of Steiria III: Boul. 336.
2064. MYSTICHIDES (*PA* 10516): A. 386.

2065. NAUS--: Tam. 441.
2066. NIKE--: Hipp. 368.
2067. NIKI--: Symproedros 333.

(980a.) N . *. . DES (E . . . EDES) of tribe V: Boul. App. IV iii.
2068. NIK-- of tribe IV: Tam. 351.
2069. NAUKLES of Anagyrous I: Boul. 381.
2070. NAUKLES s. of Nauarchos of Halai II: Boul. App. VII.
2071. NAUKLES of Melite VII (*PA* 10523): Tam. o.g. 420.
2072. NAUKRATES of Anaphlystos x (*PA* 10527): Boul. App. VII.
2073. NAUPON s. of Krates of Lamptrai I: Gr. App. V xiv.
2074. NAUSIAS of Atene x: Gr. App. VI xix (cf. App. VII vii).
2075. NAUSIAS s. of Nausikrates of Prospalta V: Boul. 335.
2076. NAUSIGENES (*PA* 10544 + Add.): A. 368.
2077. NAUSIKLES s. of Klearchos of Oe VI (*PA* 10552; *APF* 396ff.): S. 352,
       338, App. IX; Env. 347; Prop. 338 viii, 334 vii.
2078. NAUSIKRATES of Thria VI (*PA* 10562): Boul. 360.
2079. NAUSIKRATES of Thria VI (*PA* 10563): Boul. 360.
2080. NAUSIMENES of Rhamnous IX: Dem. App. IV.
2081. NAUSINIKOS of Kephale V (*PA* 10584): A. 378.
2082. NAUSISTRATOS of tribe III: Tam. 334.
2083. NAUSISTRATOS s. of Megakles of Kollytos II (*PA* 10594): Boul. 343.
2084. NAUSISTRATOS s. of Dipolis of Kropidai IV: Boul. App. IX.
2085. NAUSISTRATOS of Phrearrhioi IV: Boul. 336.
2086. NAUSONIDES s. of Eurrhemon of Euonymon I: Boul. 367.
2087. NAUTES of Boutadai VI (*PA* 10612): Boul. 360.
2088. NEOKLEIDES of tribe III (*PA* 10631): Gr. 424 i–iii; Boul. 424 vii.
2089. NEOKLEIDES s. of Proxenos of tribe VII: Boul. 335.
2090. NEOKLES s. of Neodoros of Ikarion II: Boul. App. VII.
2091. NEON: Env. 424.
2092. NEON of Halai II/VII (*PA* 10660): Gr. 386.
2093. NEOPTOLEMOS s. of Archestratos: App. 356.
2094. NEOPTOLEMOS s. of Antikles of Melite VII (*PA* 10652; *APF* 399f.): Ep.
       App. IX; Hier. 330.
2095. NEOPTOLEMOS of Myrrhinoutte II: Boul. 336.
2096. NIKANDRIDES of tribe VII (*PA* 10676): Boul. App. VII.
2097. NIKANDROS s. of Eunikos of Lamptrai I (*PA* 10688): Tam. 343.
2098. NIKANDROS of Marathon IX: Boul. 328.
2099. NIKANDROS of Myrrhinous III: Boul. 336.
2100. NIKARCHOS s. of Nikoxenos of Cholleidai IV (*PA* 10724): Boul. App.
       VII.
2101. NIKEAS s. of Euthykles of Halimous IV (*PA* 10728): Gr. Tam. 421.
2102. NIKERATOS (*PA* 10731): Tam.-Synegoros App. VIII.
2103. NIKERATOS s. of Nikokrates of Halai II (*PA* 10734; *APF* 411): Boul.
       343.

2104. NIKERATOS s. of Leokrates of Halimous IV (*PA* 10735): Boul. App. VII.

2105. NIKERATOS s. of Nikias of Kydantidai II (*PA* 10742; *APF* 406f.): Tam. strat. 344; Epim. Amphiaraia 329; Hier. 330.

2106. NIKESIAS s. of Telokles of Myrrhinous III: Boul. App. IX.

2107. NIKESIAS s. of Nikesidikos of Phaleron IX (*PA* 10748): Tam. 377.

2108. NIKESION s. of Sosistratos of Sounion IV (*PA* 10752): ? App. VIII.

2109. NIKETES (*PA* 10753): A. 332.

2110. NIKIADES of tribe V (*PA* 10765): Boul. 424 viii.

2111. NIKIADES of Halimous IV: Naop. Delphi 353.

2112. NIKIAS s. of Nikeratos (*APF* 403): Env. 596.

2113. NIKIAS s. of Chaireleides of Angele III (*PA* 10790): Boul. App. IX.

2114. NIKIAS of Erchia II: Boul. 336.

2115. NIKIAS of Kikynna V (*PA* 10805): Boul. App. IX.

2116. NIKIAS s. of Nikeratos of Kydantidai II (*PA* 10808; *APF* 403f.): S. App. IV, 427, 426, 425, 424, 423, 422, 421, 420, 418, 417, 416, 415, 414, 413; Env. 420; Oath 422; Boul. App. IV; Prop. 420 ii; Ass. 425, 420, 416.

2117. NIKIAS s. of Nikeratos of Kydantidai II (*PA* 10809; *APF* 406): Ep. 374.

2118. NIKIAS s. of Diophanes of Paiania III (*PA* 10819): Boul. App. VIII.

2119. NIKIAS s. of Nikides of Sphettos V (*PA* 10825): ? App. VII.

2120. NIKIAS of Themakos I (*PA* 10801): Boul. 333 iv.

2121. NIKOBOULOS of Elaious VIII: Tam. o.g. 421.

2122. NIKOBOULOS s. of Nikodemos of Elaious VIII: Boul. App. VIII.

2123. NIKODEMOS (*PA* 10973): A. 483.

2124. NIKODEMOS (*PA* 10855): Askl. App. VII.

2125. NIKODEMOS s. of Pistonides of Athmonon VII (*PA* 10863; *NPA* 134): Ep. 356–353.

2126. NIKODEMOS s. of Nikeratos of Eupyridai IV: Boul. App. IX.

2127. NIKODEMOS s. of Nikon of Kollytos II: Boul. App. VII.

2128. NIKODEMOS s. of Aristomenes of Oinoe IX: Epim. tribe App. VIII.

2129. NIKODOROS s. of Philotheros of Acharnai VI: Epim. 324.

2130. NIKOKLES of Anaphlystos X: Poletes 367.

2131. NIKOKLES of Rhamnous IX: Boul. 335 v.

2132. NIKOKRATES (*PA* 10910): A. 333.

2133. NIKOKRATES s. of Exekestides of Alopeke X: Par. Bas. App. IX.

2134. NIKOKRATES s. of Nikodemos of Halai II (*APF* 411): Boul. App. VII.

2135. NIKOKRATES of Phlya VII: Boul. 333 vii.

2136. NIKOLAOS s. of Nikoteles (*PA* 10923): Tam. 345.

2137. NIKOLEOS of Thorikos V/Thorai X: Amph. Delos 373.

2138. NIKOMACHIDES (*PA* 10931): Tax. App. VI; Lochagos App. VI.

2139. NIKOMACHOS (*PA* 10933): Prop. App. IV xix.

2140. NIKOMACHOS (*PA* 10934): Anagrapheus 411/10–405, 403–400; Hypogr. App. V.

2141. NIKOMACHOS: Eleusis App. V.

2142. NIKOMACHOS (*PA* 10936): A. 341.

2143. NIKOMACHOS (NIKOMEDES) of tribe VIII: Boul. 426. i.

2144. NIKOMACHOS of Acharnai VI (*PA* 10944): Tam. 385.

2145. NIKOMACHOS s. of Thras . .⁵ . . . of Kydathenaion III (*PA* 10951; *APF* 253): Epim. tribe App. IX.

2146. NIKOMACHOS of Pergase I: Boul. 336.

2147. NIKOMACHOS of Sounion IV (*PA* 10962): Boul. App. VII.

2148. NIKOMACHOS of Steiria III (*PA* 10963): Hier. Eleusis 328.

2149. NIKOMACHOS of Thria VI (*PA* 10947): Boul. 360.

(2143a.) NIKOMEDES (NIKOMACHOS) of tribe VIII: Boul. 426. i.

2150. NIKOMENES (*PA* 10968): Prop. 403 ix.

2151. NIKOMENES s. of Hieron of Halai VII (*PA* 10970): Amph. Delos 375–374.

2152. NIKOMENES of Pallene X (*PA* 10971): Tam. trir. funds 359.

2153. NIKON (*PA* 11093): A. 379.

2154. NIKON of Acharnai VI (*PA* 11107; *APF* 358): Boul. 360.

2155. NIKON s. of Archinos of Alopeke X (*PA* 11104): Boul. 334.

2156. NIKON of Ikarion II (*PA* 11110): Dem. App. VII.

2157. NIKON of Potamos Deiradiotes IV (*PA* 11118): Boul. App. VII.

2158. NIKOPHANES of Marathon IX (*PA* 11065): Gr. 409.

2159. NIKOPHEMOS (*PA* 11067): A. 361.

2160. NIKOPHILOS of Alopeke X (*PA* 11073): Tam. two goddesses 329.

2161. NIKOPHON: Prop. 375 vii.

2162. NIKOPHON of Athmonon VII (*PA* 11078): Boul. 405 iii.

2163. NIKOPHON s. of Timogenes of Themakos I: Boul. 367.

2164. NIKOSTRATOS: Gr. 331.

2165. NIKOSTRATOS of Aithalidai IV: Boul. 336.

2166. NIKOSTRATOS of Halai VII (*PA* 11019; *APF* 410): Dem. App. VII.

2167. NIKOSTRATOS s. of Nikom-- of Halai II (*APF* 410f.): Boul. App. VII.

2168. NIKOSTRATOS s. of Nikiades of Halimous IV (*PA* 11020; *APF* 95): Tam. 340; Boul. 335.

2169. NIKOSTRATOS s. of Nikostratos of Keiriadai VIII (*PA* 11031): Boul. App. VII.

2170. NIKOSTRATOS of Kolonai IV: Boul. 336.

2171. NIKOSTRATOS of Kopros VIII (*PA* 11037): Boul. 332 iii-vi.

2172. NIKOSTRATOS s. of Philostratos of Pallene X (*PA* 11043): Gr. 363.

2173. NIKOSTRATOS of Phegaia II (*PA* 11055; *APF* 412): Boul. App. VII.

2174. NIKOSTRATOS s. of Stratonikos of Potamos Deiradiotes IV: Boul. App. IX.

2175. NIKOSTRATOS s. of Nikeas of Probalinthos III: Boul. 335.

2176. NIKOSTRATOS of Prospalta V (*PA* 11048/11049): Boul. 336.

2177. NIKOSTRATOS s. of Dieitrephes of Skambonidai IV (*PA* 11011): S. 427, 425, 424, 423, 418.

2178. NIKOSTRATOS of Thorai X (*PA* 11029): Env. 384.

2179. NIKOTELES (*PA* 11060): A. 391.

2180. NIKOTELES: App. VII xi.

2181. NIKOTELES: S. App. VII.

2182. NIKOXENOS s. of Nikokles of Cholleidai IV (*PA* 10987): Gr. App. VII viii.

2183. NOMENIOS s. of Kallias of Halai II: Boul. App. VII.

2184. NOTHIPPOS s. of Lysias of Diomeia II (*PA* 11131): Prop. 331 ii.

2185. NOTHIPPOS of Oion IV/VIII: Dem. 402.

2186. NOUMENIOS of Marathon IX (*PA* 11140): Logistes 407.

2187. O . . .⁷ . . . . : Prop. App. VI xvii.

2188. O-- (TH--) of tribe III: Symproedros 328 iv.

2189. OIAX s. of Pedalion of Thorikos V: Boul. 338.

2190. OIKOTELES s. of Geisias of Lamptrai I: Gr. Ep. 421.

2191. OINOBIOS of Dekeleia VIII (*PA* 11357): S. 410; Prop. 404 ii.

2192. OINOPHILOS of tribe II/III (*PA* 11362): Tam. 350.

2193. OINOPHILOS s. of Menestratos of Paionidai IV (*PA* 9999): Boul. App. IX.

2194. OINOSTRATOS of Anagyrous I: Epim. dock. 373.

2195. OLYMPICHOS of Anaphlystos X: Gr. Ep. Braur. 343.

2196. OLYMPIODOROS s. of Lampon (*PA* 11389): Lochagos 479.

2197. OLYMPIODOROS s. of Telesias (*PA* 11391): Amph. Delos 410.

2198. OLYMPIODOROS of tribe IX: Hell. 432.

2199. OLYMPIODOROS s. of Olympiodoros of Eitea X (*PA* 11392; *APF* 516): Boul. App. IX.

2200. OLYMPIODOROS s. of Diotimos of Euonymon I (*PA* 11401; *APF* 164f.): Officer App. IX.

(2008a.) ONASIPPOS (MNASIPPOS) (*PA* 11439): Gr. App. IV iii.

2201. ONASOS of tribe VII (*PA* 11443): Boul. 426 ii.

2202. ONESANDROS s. of Ithaimenes of Eleusis VIII (*APF* 420): Tam. Paralou App. IX.

2203. ONESION of Pelekes IV: Boul. 336.

2204. ONESIPHON: Hell. 404.

2205. ONESIPHON s. of Alki-- of Lousia VI (*PA* 11456): Boul. App. VII.

2206. ONESIPPOS s. of Smikythos of Araphen II (*PA* 11455): Gr. 341.

2207. ONESIPPOS s. of Aitios of Kephisia I: Bas. App. VI.

2208. ONETOR s. of Mene-- of Thorai X: Boul. App. VIII.

2209. ONETORIDES (*APF* 421): A. 527.

2210. ONETORIDES of Acharnai VI (*PA* 11460): Boul. App. VII.

2211. ONOMAKLES (*PA* 11476): S. 412; Thirty 404; Env. 411.

2212. ONOMAKLES of Paionidai IV: Boul. 336.

2213. ONOMAKLES of Perithoidai VI: Tam. o.g. 421.

2214. ONOMAKLES s. of Onomakritos of Potamos (upper) IV: Boul. 335.

2215. OPSIADES of Konthyle III: Boul. App. VII.

2216. OPSIOS of Acharnai VI (*PA* 11508): Boul. 360.

2217. OPSIOS of Lamptrai I: Boul. 336.

2218. OPSIOS of Oe VI (*PA* 11510): Boul. 360.

2219. ORSIMENES s. of Euktimenes of Paiania III (*PA* 11492): Epim. dock. 334

2220. ORTHOBOULOS of Kerameis V (*PA* 11489; *APF* 364f.): Hipp./Phyl. 395; Env. 378.

2221. OULIAS of Steiria III: Boul. 328.

2222. P . . . KRITOS: Prop. 426 ii.

2223. PAT--: Amph. Delos 393–389.

2224. PAUS--: Fin. App. VI.

2225. PH--: Env. App. VII.

2226. PHA--: A. 550.

2227. PHORYS--: Ep. App. V.

2228. POLY--: Hell. 409.

2229. PHILE-- s. of --ektes/--ektos: Gr. Hell. 433.

2230. P-- of tribe VIII: Symproedros 328 iv.

2231. P . . . IOS of tribe V: Tam. App. IX.

2232. PE-- of tribe IV: Tam. 400.

2233. PHILO-- s. of Philo-- of tribe IX: Boul. 335.

2234. PHILOCH-- of tribe III: Tam. 390.

2235. POLY-- of tribe VI: Tam. 400.

2236. PROTO-- of tribe II: Tam. 374.

2237. PACHES s. of Epikouros (*PA* 11746): S. 428.

2238. PAMPHILOS of Acherdous VIII (*PA* 11540): Ass. 361.

2239. PAMPHILOS of Keiriadai VIII (*PA* 11545; *APF* 365): S. 389; Hipp. 395.

2240. PAMPHILOS s. of Euphiletos of Kephisia I/Kikynna V (*PA* 11531; *APF* 206): Prop. 323 ii.

2241. PAMPHILOS of Kydantidai II (*PA* 11548): Boul. App. VII.

2242. PAMPHILOS s. of Chairephilos of Paiania III (*PA* 11555; *APF* 567): Boul. 327 iii.

2243. PAMPHILOS of Phegous I (*PA* 11559): Boul. 328 iv.

2244. PAMPHILOS of Philaidai II: Boul. App. IX i.

2245. PANAITIOS (*PA* 11566): Hipp. 425.

2246. PANDIOS s. of Sokles of Oion VIII (*PA* 11575): Gr. 355 (RHAIDIOS); Boul.-Prop. 369 i, iv; Prop. 368 ii.

2247. PANTAINOS s. of Euthy-- of Melite VII: Boul. App. VIII.

2248. PANTAKLES: Tam. 428.

2249. PANTALEON s. of P-- of Anagyrous I (*PA* 11603): Boul. App. VII.

2250. PANTARETOS (*PA* 11605): Boul. 378 v.

2251. PANTARETOS s. of Antiphilos of Alopeke X (*PA* 11606): Amph. Delos 393–389.

2252. PANTELIDES of Kedoi I: Boul. 408.

2253. PANTENOR s. of Euenor of Skambonidai IV: Boul. App. IX.

2254. PANTIADES s. of Dexixenos of Daidalidai VII: Boul. 335.

2255. PANTOIOS of Anagyrous I: Boul. App. VII.

2256. PARAIBATES (*PA* 11609): Gr. App. III iv, App. IV.

2257. PARALIOS s. of Demodokos of Anagyrous I (*PA* 11611): Tam. 390.

2258. PARAMYTHOS s. of Philinos: App. 355.

2259. PARAMYTHOS s. of Philagros of Erchia II (*PA* 11629): Gr. 387 i.

2260. PARAMYTHOS of Otryne II (*PA* 11631): Gr. 368 iii.

2261. PASIAS of Kydathenaion III: Boul. 336.

2262. PASIMENES of Ptelea/Perithoidai VI (*PA* 11664): Tam. o.g. 418.

2263. PASION: Officer 410.

2264. PASIPHON of Phrearrhioi IV (*PA* 11668): S. 410; Arch. fleet 409; Gr. 413 i.

2265. PATAIKOS (*PA* 11676): Ass. App. IX.

2266. PATAIKOS of Eleusis VIII (*PA* 11677; *APF* 442f.): Askl. 345.

2267. PATAIKOS of Pithos VII (*PA* 11680): Tam. 390.

2268. PATROKLEIDES (*PA* 11685): Prop. 405 iv, App. V iii.

2269. PATROKLES (*PA* 11691): Bas. 404.

2270. PATROKLES (PROKLES *PA* 12208): Kategoros 324.

2271. PATROKLES of tribe II (*PA* 11696): Boul. 422 i.

2272. PATROKLES s. of Pasikles of tribe III/IV/V (*PA* 11695): Tam. 377.

2273. PATROKLES s. of Chairedemos of Alopeke X (*PA* 11697): Athl. 406.

2274. PATROKLES s. of Hierokles of Philaidai II: Hipp. App. IX.

2275. PAUSANIAS s. of Thrasyllos of Anaphlystos X (*PA* 11712): Boul. 334.

2276. PAUSANIAS s. of --es of Angele III: Boul. App. VIII.

2277. PAUSANIAS s. of Pausanias of Oa III (*PA* 11721): Boul. App. VI, App. VII.

2278. PAUSANIAS of Oinoe IX (*PA* 11722): Boul.-Hier. 336 iv.

2279. PAUSIAS s. of Sokrates of Ankyle II (*PA* 11730): Boul. 343.

2280. PEDIEUS (*PA* 11748): A. 449.

2281. PEISANDROS s. of Glauketes of Acharnai VI (*PA* 11770): Ep. 421; Env. 412; Zetetes 415; Boul.-Prop. 415 viii; Prop. 415 v, 412 v, App. V xxx; Ass. 412.

2282. PEISIANAX of Sounion IV (*PA* 11776; *APF* 378): Env. 357.

2283. PEISIAS s. of Aristokrates of Marathon IX (*PA* 11779): Ep. Eleusis 332–329.

2284. PEISISTRATOS (*PA* 11791; *APF* 445): A. 669.

2285. PEISISTRATOS s. of Hippias (*PA* 11792; *APF* 450f.): A. 522.

2286. PEISISTRATOS s. of Hippokrates (*PA* 11793; *APF* 444ff.): S. 562; Tyrant 561, 557, 546.

2287. PEISITHEOS s. of Euxitheos of Phrearrhioi IV: Boul. 371.

2288. PEISON of Kerameis V (*PA* 11791): Thirty 404.

2289. PEITHIADES: Gr. 437.

2290. PEITHIADES s. of Diodoros of Phrearrhioi IV (*PA* 11757): Boul. App. VII.

2291. PEITHON s. of Sosigenes of Ikarion II (*PA* 11765): Boul. 336.

2292. PERIANDROS s. of Polyaratos of Cholargos V (*PA* 11800; *APF* 464): Prop. 362 i, 358 v.

2293. PERIKLES s. of Xanthippos of Cholargos V (*PA* 11811; *APF* 457ff.): S. 465, 455, 451, 448, 447, 446, 445, 443, 442, 441, 440, 439, 438, 437, 436, 435, 434, 433, 432, 431, 430, 429; see 457 S. note; Ep. 438, App. IV; Athl. App. IV; Kategoros 463; Prop. 453, 451 ii, iii, 449 iii, 448 ii, 441, 436, 433 iii, iv, 432 i–iv, App. IV xli–xlv, 431 i–v, 430 ii; Ass. 430.

2294. PERIKLES s. of Perikles of Cholargos V (*PA* 11812; *APF* 458): S. 409, 407, 406; Hell. 410.

2295. PETRAIOS: Tam. 442.

2296. PHAENNOS of Steiria III: Epim. dock. 369.

2297. PHAIAX s. of Erasistratos of Acharnai VI (*PA* 13921; *APF* 521f.): Env. 423.

2298. PHAIAX of Aphidna IX: Eleven 367.

2299. PHAIDON (*PA* 13967): A. 476.

2300. PHAIDRIADES of Hippotomadai VI (*PA* 13932): Boul. 360.

2301. PHAIDRIAS (*PA* 13933): Gr. Hier. 558.

2302. PHAIDRIAS (*PA* 13937): Thirty 404.

2303. PHAIDRIAS s. of Rhodon of Phlya VII (*PA* 13945): Tam. 345.

2304. PHAIDROS (*PA* 13953): Horistes 352.

2305. PHAIDROS s. of Meidon of Cholleidai IV: Gr. 339.

2306. PHAIDROS s. of Kallias of Sphettos V (*PA* 13964; *APF* 525): S. 347, 334, 323.

2307. PHAINIPPIDES (PHAINIPPOS): A. App. II.
(2307a.) PHAINIPPOS (PHAINIPPIDES): A. App. II.
2308. PHAINIPPOS (*PA* 13976; *APF* 269): A. 490.
2309. PHAINIPPOS s. of Kallippos: Hell. 405.
2310. PHAINIPPOS s. of Phrynichos (*PA* 13979): Gr. 424 iv, v, viii.
2311. PHAINIPPOS s. of Sostratos of Aigilia x (*PA* 13981): Boul. 334.
2312. PHAINIPPOS of Azenia VIII (*PA* 13980): Env. 384.
2313. PHAINIPPOS of Paionidai IV (*PA* 13983): Logistes 407.
2314. PHALANTHOS of Alopeke x (*PA* 13995): Hell. 410.
2315. PHALANTHOS of Kerameis v: Boul. 328.
2316. PHANIAS (*PA* 14009): S. 387.
2317. PHANIAS (*PA* 14010): Prop. App. VI xxxv.
2318. PHANIAS of Acharnai VI (*PA* 14011; *NPA* 161): Boul. App. VII.
2319. PHANIAS of Phegaia II (*PA* 14006): Boul. App. VII.
2320. PHANIAS s. of Aganor of Phrearrhioi IV (*PA* 14028): Boul. App. IX.
2321. PHANODEMOS of Phrearrhioi IV (*PA* 14035): Boul. App. VII.
2322. PHANODEMOS s. of Diyllos of Thymaitadai VIII (*PA* 14033): Epim. Amphiaraia 329; Hier. 330; Boul.-Prop. 343 iv; Prop. 332 viii, ix, 329 viii.
2323. PHANOKLES of Oinoe VIII (*PA* 14044): Gr. 364 i, ii.
2324. PHANOKLES of Paiania III: Boul. 336.
2325. PHANOKRITOS of Acharnai VI (*PA* 14062): Tam. 389.
2326. PHANOMACHOS s. of Kallimachos (*PA* 14069): S. 430.
2327. PHANOMACHOS of Acharnai VI (*PA* 14072): Boul. 360.
2328. PHANOMACHOS s. of Charmi(a)des of Sounion IV (*PA* 14077): Amph. Delos 341.
2329. PHANOSTHENES (*PA* 14083): S. 407.
2330. PHANOSTRATOS (*PA* 14095): A. 383.
2331. PHANOSTRATOS of tribe II (*PA* 14096): Epim. dock, 373.
2332. PHANOSTRATOS of Erchia II: Askl. 331.
2333. PHANOSTRATOS s. of Stratios of Oion IV: Boul. 371.
2334. PHANOSTRATOS of Philaidai II (*PA* 14111): Boul. 336, 333 iii.
2335. PHANOSTRATOS of Thorai x (*PA* 14101): Tam. trir. funds 363.
2336. PHANTOKLES (*PA* 14114): Gr, App. V i, ii; Prop. 446 iv.
2337. PHAYLLOS of Acherdous VIII (*PA* 14125; *APF* 53f.): Ten 404.
2338. PHEIDELEIDES: Gr. App. VII xxi.
2339. PHEIDELEIDES of Aphidna IX (*PA* 14134): Tam. 440.
2340. PHEIDESTRATOS s. of Chairestratos of Eupyridai IV (*PA* 14141): Boul. App. VII.
2341. PHEIDESTRATOS s. of Sosikles of Hekale IV (*PA* 14139): Boul. App. VII.
2342. PHEIDIPPOS s. of Pheidon of Paiania III (*PA* 14162; *APF* 567): Epim. tribe App. IX.
2343. PHEIDOLEOS s. of Pheidostratos of Kydantidai II: Boul. 335.
2344. PHEIDON (*PA* 14179): Thirty 404; Ten 404.
2345. PHEIDON of Pelekes IV: Boul. 336.
2346. PHEIDON of Thria VI (*PA* 14178): Hipp. Lemnos App. VIII; Phyl. App. VIII.
2347. PHELLEUS: Gr. 407 iv.

2348. PHEREKLEIDES of Peiraieus VIII (*PA* 14186): Hell. 415.
2349. PHEREKLEIDES s. of Pherekles of Perithoidai VI (*PA* 14187): S. 324, App. IX.
2350. PHEREKLES of Thria/Phyle VI: Boul. App. VI xix.
2351. PHEREKRATES s. of Philokrates of Kollytos II (*PA* 14196): Boul. 341.
2352. PHILAGROS (*PA* 14203): Prop. App. VI i.
2353. PHILAGROS s. of Diokles of Halai II (*PA* 14208; *APF* 534f.): Epim. tribe 340.
2354. PHILAGROS of Phaleron IX (*PA* 14215): Epim. dock. 348.
2355. PHILAIGIDES s. of Leokedes of Anaphlystos X (*PA* 14216): Boul. 334.
2356. PHILAIOS s. of Kallaischros of Kydathenaion III (*PA* 7762): Boul. App. VII.
2357. PHILANTHES of tribe IX (*PA* 12221): Boul. App. IX.
2358. PHILEAS s. of Antiphon: Tam.-Synegoros App. VIII.
2359. PHILEAS s. of Lykos: Gr. App. V vi.
2360. PHILEAS s. of Antigenes of Paionidai IV (*PA* 14242 = 14232): Boul.-Hier. 335; Boul. 336; Prop. 331 i.
2361. PHILEAS s. of Philotheros of Pelekes IV (*PA* 14245): Boul. App. VII.
2362. PHILEAS s. of Philion of Phrearrhioi IV (*PA* 14247): Boul. App. VII.
2363. PHILEMON s. of Lykourgos of Thria VI (*PA* 14282): Tam. 350.
2364. PHILEMONIDES: S. App. IX.
2365. PHILEMONIDES of Alopeke X (*PA* 14265): Boul. App. IX.
2366. PHILEPSIOS of Lamptrai I (*PA* 14256): Ass. App. VI.
2367. PHILERIPHOS s. of Aischeas of Halai VII (*APF* 535, 537f.): Dem. App. IX.
2368. PHILETAIROS of Ikarion II (*PA* 14252): Hell. 432.
2369. PHILEUS s. of Phelleus of Pergase (lower) I: Boul. 367.
2370. PHILINOS of Anagyrous I: Boul. 336.
2371. PHILINOS s. of . .⸴. . nes of Anaphlystos X: Tax./Phyl. 373.
2372. PHILINOS s. of Pyrgion of Marathon IX (*PA* 14330): Tam. 343.
2373. PHILINOS s. of Theodoros of Otryne II (*PA* 14334): Boul. 341.
2374. PHILINOS s. of Gniphon of Phlya VII (*PA* 14339; *APF* 537): Tam. 377.
2375. PHILION: Tam. 407.
2376. PHILION s. of Eua-- of Phyle VI (*PA* 14474): Boul. App. VII.
2377. PHILIPPIDES (*PA* 14351): Prop. App. VIII xxiii, xxiv, 336 viii.
2378. PHILIPPIDES of Acharnai VI (*PA* 14354): Boul. 360.
2379. PHILIPPIDES s. of Kephalion of Kopros VIII (*PA* 14357): Boul. App. VII.
2380. PHILIPPIDES of Paiania (upper) III (*PA* 14360/14361; *APF* 548): Boul. App. VI.
2381. PHILIPPOS (*PA* 14364): A. 588.
2382. PHILIPPOS (*PA* 14365): A. 495.
2383. PHILIPPOS: Gr. 425 ii.
2384. PHILIPPOS (*PA* 14373): Prop. 362 iii.
2385. PHILIPPOS (*PA* 14374): Boul. 356.
2386. PHILIPPOS: Didask. App. IX.
2387. PHILIPPOS s. of Philippos: Prop. App. VII xxvi.
2388. PHILIPPOS of tribe II (*PA* 14370): Tam. 399.
2389. PHILIPPOS s. of Phileas of Deiradiotai IV (*PA* 14407): Gr. 410 ii.

2390. PHILIPPOS of Eiresidai v (*PA* 14390): Boul. 368 i.

2391. PHILIPPOS s. of Antiphemos of Eiresidai v (*PA* 14381): Gr. 338.

2392. PHILIPPOS of Kolonos II: Boul. 336.

2393. PHILIPPOS s. of P-- of Pergase (upper) I (*PA* 14412): Boul. App. VII.

2394. PHILIPPOS s. of Philion of Potamos (lower) IV (*PA* 14414): Boul. App. VII.

2395. PHILIPPOS s. of Philesias of Prospalta v (*PA* 14415): Tam. 407.

2396. PHILIPPOS of Semachidai x: Boul. 367.

2397. PHILISKOS (*PA* 14419): A. 448.

2398. PHILISKOS: Phrourarchos 376.

2399. PHILISTIDES s. of Phil-- (*PA* 14437): ? App. VIII.

2400. PHILISTIDES of tribe VIII (*PA* 14440): Boul. 410 v.

2401. PHILISTIDES of Kephale v: Boul. 336.

2402. PHILISTIDES s. of Philippos of Kephale v: Gr. Naop. Delos 345.

2403. PHILITTIOS of Boutadai VI (*PA* 14465): Boul. 363 iii.

2404. PHILLES of Euonymon I: Boul. 336.

2405. PHILOCHARES s. of Atrometos of Kothokidai VI (*PA* 14775; *APF* 545): S. 345, 344, 343.

2406. PHILOCHARES s. of Philokydes of Paiania III (*PA* 14778; *APF* 544): Boul. App. VIII.

2407. PHILOCHARES of Rhamnous IX (*PA* 14779): S. 357.

2408. PHILODEMOS: Ep. Braur. 342.

2409. PHILODEMOS s. of Autokles of Eroiadai x (*PA* 14488; *APF* 539): Boul. App. VIII; Prop. 340 ii.

2410. PHILODEMOS of Kydathenaion III: Boul. 336.

2411. PHILODEMOS s. of Philokydes of Paiania III (*APF* 544): Boul. 336.

2412. PHILOITIOS of Ionidai II: Tam. App. IX.

2413. PHILOKALOS s. of Exekias of Kerameis v (*PA* 14506): Epim. dock. 349.

2414. PHILOKEDES of Paionidai IV (*PA* 14510): Ep. Braur. 349.

2415. PHILOKEDES s. of Dorotheos of Pallene x (*PA* 4619): Gr. 353.

2416. PHILOKLES (*PA* 14516): A. 459.

2417. PHILOKLES (*PA* 14517): S. 406, 405.

2418. PHILOKLES (*PA* 14519): Tam. 340.

2419. PHILOKLES (*PA* 14524): A. 322.

2420. PHILOKLES s. of. O--/The-- (*PA* 14530): Gr. 375 i.

2421. PHILOKLES of Anaphlystos x (*PA* 14518): A. 392.

2422. PHILOKLES s. of Phormion of Eroiadai VIII (*PA* 14541; *APF* 539ff.): S. 325, App. IX; Hipp. App. IX; Kosmetes 324; Prop. 324 ix.

2423. PHILOKLES of Phaleron IX (*PA* 14564): Epim. dock. 367.

2424. PHILOKLES of Phrearrhioi IV (*PA* 14565): Boul. 336.

2425. PHILOKLES of Sphettos v: Boul. 336.

2426. PHILOKLES s. of Bison of Thorai x (*PA* 14542): Boul. 334.

2427. PHILOKLES of Xypete VII (*PA* 14553): Askl. 326.

2428. PHILOKRATES (*PA* 14568): A. 485.

2429. PHILOKRATES (*PA* 14572): Boul. 415.

2430. PHILOKRATES s. of Demeas (*PA* 14585): S. 416.

2431. PHILOKRATES s. of Ephialtes (*PA* 14586): S. 390.

2432. PHILOKRATES s. of Philon of Aixone VII (*PA* 14600; *APF* 275f.): Boul. 328.

2433. PHILOKRATES of Aphidna IX (*PA* 14603; *NPA* 166): Tam. 398.

2434. PHILOKRATES s. of Pythodoros of Hagnous V (*PA* 14599 = 14576): Env. 347; Prop. App. VII xv, xvi, 352 ii, 348 ii, 347 v, xii, xiii, xvii, App. VIII xiv.

2435. PHILOKRATES s. of Amphitelides of Kettos IV: Boul. 371.

2436. PHILOKRATES of Kolonos II (*PA* 14613): Tam. 390.

2437. PHILOKRATES s. of Philinos of Lamptrai (coast) I: Boul. 367.

2438. PHILOKRATES s. of Sostratos of Phrearrhioi IV (*PA* 14629; *APF* 499): Didask. 332.

2439. PHILOKRATES of Poros V (*PA* 14627; *APF* 547): Boul. 336.

2440. PHILOKYDES: Env. 409.

2441. PHILOKYDES of Acharnai VI (*PA* 14646): Boul. 360.

2442. PHILOKYDES s. of Pantakles of Agryle (lower) I: Boul. 367.

2443. PHILOMBROTOS (*PA* 14655): A. 595.

2444. PHILOMBROTOS s. of Philokles of Anakaia VIII: Boul. 335.

2445. PHILOMELOS: Arch. Salamis App. VI.

2446. PHILOMELOS of Halai II: Boul. 336.

2447. PHILOMELOS of Marathon IX (*PA* 14667; *APF* 548): Hell. 415.

2448. PHILON (*PA* 14805): S. 329.

2449. PHILON s. of . . .l. .̣ . . es of tribe V: Boul. 335.

2450. PHILON s. of Kallippos of Aixone VII (*PA* 14825; *APF* 274f.): S. 361.

2451. PHILON s. of Philaios of Anakaia VIII: Boul. 335.

2452. PHILON of Cholleidai IV: Bas. 370.

2453. PHILON of Epikephisia VI (*PA* 14834): Boul. 360.

2454. PHILON of Koile VIII (*PA* 14847): Env. 403.

2455. PHILON of Kydathenaion III (*PA* 14851): Athl. 410.

2456. PHILON of Phaleron IX (*PA* 14877): Boul. App. IX.

2457. PHILON of Probalinthos III (*PA* 14871): Gr. Ep. App. IV.

2458. PHILON s. of Kleinias of Xypete VII (*PA* 14814): Boul. App. VIII.

2459. PHILONEOS (*PA* 14677): A. 528.

2460. PHILONEOS s. of Idomeneus of Kephisia I (*PA* 14683; *APF* 181): Tam. 444.

2461. PHILONEOS s. of Gnathios of Leukonoion IV: Epim. tribe 357.

2462. PHILONEOS s. of Ameinonikos of Sounion IV: Boul. 371.

2463. PHILONIDES of tribe IX: Boul. App. IX.

2464. PHILONIDES of Acharnai VI (*PA* 14894): Boul. 360.

2465. PHILONIDES s. of D-- of Anagyrous I (*PA* 14890): Boul. App. VII.

2466. PHILONIDES of Anaphlystos X (*PA* 14884): Boul. App. VII.

2467. PHILONIDES of Kephale V: Boul. 336.

2468. PHILONIDES of Pergase (upper) I (*PA* 14914): Boul. App. VII.

2469. PHILONOTHOS s. of L-- of Anagyrous I (*PA* 14687): Boul. App. VII.

2470. PHILOPHRON of Thria VI (*PA* 14757): Tam. 367.

2471. PHILOSTRATOS s. of Philinos of Acharnai VI (*APF* 551): Boul.-Epim. 328.

2472. PHILOSTRATOS of Kydathenaion III (*PA* 14736): Gr. Ep. Eleusis 422–419.

2473. PHILOSTRATOS s. of Philinos of Kydathenaion III: Boul. App. VII.

2474. PHILOSTRATOS of Pallene X (*PA* 14741): Boul. 411/10 ii.

2475. PHILOSTRATOS s. of Nikostratos of Pallene X (*PA* 14742): Boul.-Hier. 335.

2476. PHILOTADES of Dekeleia VIII (*PA* 14923): Tam. 397.

2477. PHILOTADES of Pallene x: Hell. 430.
2478. PHILOTADES s. of Philostratos of Pallene x (*PA* 14927): Boul.-Prop. 354 iii.
2479. PHILOTHEOS s. of Philokles of Sounion IV: Sophr. 333.
2480. PHILOTHEROS of Aixone VII (*PA* 14502): Dem. App. IX.
2481. PHILOTHEROS of Hagnous V (*PA* 14501): ? App. VIII.
2482. PHILOTHEROS s. of Theophrastos of Paionidai IV (*PA* 14504): Boul. App. VII.
2483. PHILOTIMOS s. of Akestothemis (*PA* 14747): Plouton App. IX.
2484. PHILOXENOS: Prop. App. V xix.
2485. PHILOXENOS of tribe III: Hell. 432.
2486. PHILOXENOS s. of Xenophon of Alopeke x (*PA* 14704): Boul. 334.
2487. PHILOXENOS s. of Antiphon of Eleusis VIII (*PA* 14708): ? App. VII.
2488. PHILOXENOS s. of Lysistratos of Potamos (lower) IV: Boul. 371.
2489. PHILOXENOS s.of Demainetos of Thorikos v (*PA* 14696): Gr. 385.
2490. PHILTONIDES of Anaphlystos x: Boul. App. VII.
2491. PHILTONIDES of Anaphlystos x (*PA* 14793): Boul. App. IX.
2492. PHILYLLOS of Eleusis VIII (*PA* 14797): Tam. o.g. 418.
2493. PHILYLLOS of Eleusis VIII (*PA* 14798): Boul. 325 i.
2494. PHOKIADES s. of Polynikos of Eleusis VIII: Boul. 335.
2495. PHOKIADES of Oion IV/VIII (*PA* 15066): Tam. 425.
2496. PHOKION s. of Phokos (*PA* 15076; *APF* 559): S. App. VII, 349, 344, 343, 341, 340, 339, 338, App. VIII, 336, 323, App. IX note; Officer 376; Env. App. VIII, 335, 322; Ass. App. VII, 344, 340, 339, 337, App. VIII, 336, 335, 333, 323, 322.
2497. PHOKION of Potamos IV: Boul. 336.
2498. PHOKOS (*PA* 15082): Boul.-Prop. 366 ii/323 xi.
2499. PHOKOS of Phaleron IX (*PA* 15085): Boul. App. IX.
2500. PHORMION (*PA* 14948): A. 546.
2501. PHORMION (*PA* 14949): A. 396.
2502. PHORMION (*PA* 14950): S. 368.
2503. PHORMION s. of Aristion of Kydathenaion III (*PA* 14956): Gr. Tam. 418.
2504. PHORMION s. of Asopios of Paiania III (*PA* 14958): S. 440, 439, 436, 432, 431, 430, 429.
2505. PHORMION s. of Chairephanes of Thorai x: Boul. App. VIII.
2506. PHORMISIOS (*PA* 14945): Env. 394; Prop. 403 xiii.
2507. PHORYKIDES (PHORYKOS/PHORYS): Fin. App. VI.
(2507a.) PHORYKOS (PHORYKIDES/PHORYS): Fin. App. VI.
(2507b.)PHORYS (PHORYKIDES/PHORYKOS): Fin. App. VI.
2508. PHOXIAS (*PA* 14942): Boul.-Prop. 369 iii.
2509. PHRASIDEMOS: Boul.-Prop. App. V xvii.
2510. PHRASIKLEIDES (PHRASIKLES) (*PA* 14978): A. 460.
2511. PHRASIKLEIDES (*PA* 14979): A. 371.
(2510a.) PHRASIKLES (PHRASIKLEIDES) (*PA* 14978): A. 460.
2512. PHRASIKLES s. of Phrasik-- of Ikarion II: Boul. App. VII.
2513. PHRASITELIDES of Ikarion II (*PA* 14987): Hell. 411/10.
2514. PHRASMON (*PA* 14988): Prop. App. V xxxviii.
2515. PHRYNAIOS: A. 536.

2516. PHRYNAIOS: A. App. III.

2517. PHRYNICHOS (*PA* 15002): A. 337.

2518. PHRYNICHOS of tribe I (*PA* 15009): S. 459.

2519. PHRYNICHOS s. of Stratonides of Deiradiotai IV (*PA* 15011): S. 412; Env. 411.

2520. PHRYNICHOS s. of Aristokleides of Xypete VII (*PA* 1156): Boul. App. VIII.

2521. PHRYNON (*PA* 15029): S. 607.

2522. PHRYNON of Leukonoion IV (*PA* 15030): Gr. App. VII ii.

2523. PHRYNON of Rhamnous IX (*PA* 15032): Env. 347; Ass. 348.

2524. PHYLAKOS of Oinoe VIII/IX (*PA* 15037): Gr. 375 i, iv.

2525. PHYLARCHOS s. of Paramythos of Erchia II (*PA* 15042): Boul. 341.

2526. PHYLEUS s. of Pausanias of Oinoe IX (*PA* 15045): Boul.-Hier. 336 iv; Boul.-Prop. 325 ii.

2527. PHYROMACHOS (*PA* 15053): Bas. App. V.

2528. PHYROMACHOS of tribe VIII (*PA* 15052): Gr. Tam. 441.

2529. PHYSON s. of Pytharchos of Alopeke X (*PA* 15061): Boul. App. IX.

2530. PISTIAS (*PA* 11823): Bas./Pol./Thesm. App. IX.

2531. PISTIDES of tribe VII: Tam. 374.

2532. PISTIDES of Thorai X (*PA* 11825): Gr. Tam. 349.

2533. PISTOKLES of tribe VI: Boul. App. V xxxii.

2534. PISTOKLES s. of Pistogenes of Anaphlystos X (*NPA* 143): Antigrapheus 335.

2535. PISTOXENOS (*PA* 11836): Gr. App. VI xv.

2536. PITHON of Probalinthos III: Boul. App. VII.

2537. PLATON s. of Ant-- of Anagyrous I (*PA* 11851): Boul. App. VII.

2538. PLATON of Anakaia VIII (*PA* 11852): Epim. dock. 373.

2539. PLATON of Aphidna IX: Dem. 402.

2540. PLATON s. of Isotimos of Iphistiadai V (*PA* 11854): Tam. 349.

2541. PLATON s. of Nikochares of Phlya VII (*PA* 11860): Gr. 394 iii.

2542. PLEISTIAS: Env. 426.

2543. PLEISTIAS (*PA* 11864): Gr. 425.

2544. POLEMARCHOS (*PA* 11881): Gr. 426 ii–iv.

2545. POLIAGROS (*PA* 11893): Prop. 387 i.

2546. POLYAINOS s. of Eukrates of Thria VI (*NPA* 144): Tam. 345.

2547. POLYARATOS of Cholargos V (*PA* 11907; *NPA* 144; *APF* 461): Par. Hell. 410; Gr. 405 ii.

2548. POLYARKES of Paiania (upper) III (*PA* 11910): Boul. App. VI.

2549. POLYARKES of Paiania III: Boul. 336.

2550. POLYCHARES (*PA* 12099): Thirty 404.

2551. POLYCHARMICHOS s. of Pataikos of Sounion IV: Boul. 371.

2552. POLYCHARMOS (*PA* 12105): Ass. App. IX.

2553. POLYDAMAS s. of Euthyphron of Kerameis V (*PA* 11915): Tam. o.g. 375.

2554. POLYDAMAS s. of Aristodamas of Myrrhinous III (*PA* 11917); Boul. App. IX.

2555. POLYDOROS s. of Thougenes of tribe V: Boul. 335.

2556. POLYEUCHES s. of Antagoras of Perithoidai VI (*PA* 11956): Ep. Eleusis 332–329.

2557. POLYEUKTOS of Erchia II (*NPA* 144): Tam. 401.

2558. POLYEUKTOS s. of Kallikrates of Hestiaia II (*PA* 11943): Boul.-Prop. 324 iv.

2559. POLYEUKTOS s. of Timokrates of Krioa x (*PA* 11946): Prop. 347 i.

2560. POLYEUKTOS of Kydantidai II (*PA* 11947 = 11928 = 11927): S. App. IX; Prop. 326 iii, App. IX xxix.

2561. POLYEUKTOS of Lamptrai I (*PA* 11948; *APF* 465): Poletes 367.

2562. POLYEUKTOS of Prospalta v: Boul. 336.

2563. POLYEUKTOS s. of Sostratos of Sphettos v (*PA* 11950 = 11925 = 11934): Env. 343, 323; Boul.-Prop. 356 ii; Prop. 335 iii, 332 i, ii.

2564. POLYEUKTOS s. of Harmodios of Themakos I: Hier. 325.

2565. POLYIDOS of Oe vi (*PA* 11967): Boul. 360.

2566. POLYKLEIDES s. of Kallistratos of Erchia II (*PA* 11970; *APF* 362): Boul. 341.

2567. POLYKLES s. of Polykrates of Anagyrous I (*PA* 11988; *APF* 465f.): Boul. 367.

2568. POLYKLES s. of Thrasymachos of Myrrhinous III (*PA* 11997): Boul. App. VIII.

2569. POLYKLES of Philaidai II (*PA* 12001): Gr. App. VI xii.

2570. POLYKLES s. of Heortios of Potamos Deiradiotes IV (*PA* 12000): Boul. App. IX.

2571. POLYKLES of Probalinthos III: Boul. 336.

2572. POLYKRATES s. of Polykrates: Prop. App. VII xx.

2573. POLYKRATES of Aphidna IX (*PA* 12015): Tam. trir. funds 328.

2574. POLYKRATES s. of Lysan-- of Hybadai IV: Boul. 371.

2575. POLYKRATES of Oe vi (*PA* 12023): Boul. 360.

2576. POLYKRATES s. of Polyeuktos of Phegaia II (*PA* 12027): Boul. 343, 336.

2577. POLYKRATES s. of . ˙. . nes of Plotheia II (*PA* 12025): Boul. 343.

2578. POLYKRITOS: Hieromn. 342.

2579. POLYMEDES s. of Kephision of Atene x (*PA* 12036): Gr. Tam. 414.

2580. POLYMEDES s. of Dieitrephes of Phlya VII (*PA* 12038): Ep. Eleusis 332–329.

2581. POLYMNESTOS of Prospalta v (*PA* 12049): Tam. 389.

2582. POLYMNIS of Euonymon I (*PA* 12052): Gr. 405 iii.

2583. POLYPHILOS s. of Polymedes of Oinoe IX: Epim. tribe 342.

2584. POLYSTRATOS (*PA* 12070): S. 394.

2585. POLYSTRATOS of Deiradiotai IV (*PA* 12076; *APF* 467): Officer 411; Arch. Oropos 411; Katalogeus 411; Misc. App. V.

2586. POLYSTROPHOS s. of Th-- of Thymaitadai VIII: Boul. App. VII.

2587. POLYXENIDES of Acharnai VI (*PA* 12057): Tam. 413.

2588. POLYXENOS s. of Smikythos of Kollytos II (*PA* 12063): Boul. 343.

2589. POLYXENOS of Sounion IV: Askl. 339.

2590. POLYXENOS s. of Polykrates of Sounion IV (*PA* 12066): Boul. App. VII.

2591. POLYZELOS (*PA* 11957): S. 490.

2592. POLYZELOS (*PA* 11960): A. 367.

2593. POSEIDIPPOS s. of Kallikrates of Hestiaia II (*PA* 12126; *NPA* 145): Boul.-Tam. tribe.-Hier. 341; Boul. 335.

2594. POSEIDIPPOS of Ikarion II: Boul. 336.

2595. POULYDAMAS of Lamptrai I: Boul. 336.

2596. POULYTION s. of Polykles of Probalinthos III: Boul. 335.

2597. PRAXIAS s. of Anthemion of Paiania III (*PA* 12160): Boul. App. IX.

2598. PRAXIAS of Xypete VII (*NPA* 146): Epim. dock. 368.

2599. PRAXIBOULOS of Paiania III: Hell. 421.

2600. PRAXIERGOS (*PA* 12163): A. 471.

2601. PRAXIKLES s. of Sophortos of Euonymon I (*APF* 469): Boul. 367.

2602. PRAXITELES (*PA* 12166): A. 444.

2603. PRAXITELES s. of Praxiades of Kephale V (*PA* 12170): Tam. 350; Gr. Amph. Delos 364.

2604. PRAXITELES of Melite VII (*PA* 12171): Epim. dock. 369.

2605. PREPIS s. of Eupheros of Xypete VII (*PA* 12184): Gr. 422 i.

2606. PRESBIAS s. of Semias of Phegous I (*PA* 12185; *APF* 66f.): Gr. Tam. 422.

2607. PRESBYCHARES s. of --ochares of Eleusis VIII: Gr. Tam. 409.

2608. PRESBYCHARES s. of Aristion of Halimous IV (*PA* 12186): Boul. App. VII.

2609. PROINAUTES: Boul. App. IV xx.

2610. PROKLEIDES s. of Menekrates of Angele III (*PA* 12192): Boul. App. VIII.

2611. PROKLEIDES s. of Anacharsis of Aphidna IX (*PA* 12191): Gr. 354.

2612. PROKLEIDES s. of Pantaleon of Kerameis V (*PA* 12200): Prop. 328 i.

2613. PROKLEIDES of Lamptrai (coast) I: Boul. 367.

2614. PROKLEIDES s. of Proxenides of Teithras II (*PA* 12204): Boul. 341, 336.

2615. PROKLEIDES of Thorai X: Tax. App. IX.

(2270a.) PROKLES (PATROKLES) (*PA* 12208): Kategoros 324.

2616. PROKLES s. of Theodoros (*PA* 12214): S. 427.

2617. PROKLES of Euonymon/Kephisia I (*PA* 12206): Oath 422.

2618. PROKLES s. of Atarbos of Euonymon I (*PA* 12226): Gr. 421 i, ii.

2619. PROKLES of Gargettos II: Boul. 336.

2620. PROKLES of Kephale V: Boul. 336.

2621. PROKLES of Kephisia I (*PA* 12228): Athl. 406.

2622. PROKLES of Kolonai IV (*PA* 12231 bis; *APF* 470): Epim. dock. 369.

2623. PROKLES s. of Iophon of Kydathenaion III: Gr. A. 394.

2624. PROKLES of Sounion IV (*PA* 12237): Dem. 329.

2625. PROMACHOS: Gr. App. IV xviii.

2626. PRONAPES of Erchia II: Tam. 433.

2627. PRONAPES s. of Pronapides of Prasiai III (*PA* 12250; *APF* 471): Hipp. App. IV.

2628. PROTARCHOS: Hieromn. 339.

2629. PROTARCHOS of Probalinthos III (*PA* 12295): Hell. 407.

2630. PROTEAS s. of Epikles of Aixone VII (*PA* 12298): S. 435, 433, 432, 431.

2631. PROTIAS of Acharnai VI: Boul. 346 ii.

2632. PROTOKLES of Ikarion II (*PA* 12315): Tam. 398.

2633. PROTOKLES of Kephisia I: Boul. 328.

2634. PROTOMACHOS (*PA* 12318): S. 406.

2635. PROTOMACHOS: S. 339.

2636. PROTOMACHOS s. of Herm-- of Keiriadai VIII: Boul. App. VII.

2637. PROTOMACHOS s. of Pytho-- of Kolonai IV: Boul. 371.

2638. PROTOMACHOS s. of Chion of Thorai X: Boul. App. VIII.

2639. PROTONIKOS s. of Epichares of Kerameis v (*PA* 12310): Gr. Hell. 434.
2640. PROXENOS s. of Pylagoras of Acherdous VIII (*PA* 12271): Gr. 335.
2641. PROXENOS s. of Harmodios of Aphidna IX (*PA* 12267; *APF* 476f.): Hell. 410.
2642. PROXENOS s. of Harmodios of Aphidna IX (*PA* 12270; *APF* 478): S. App. VII, 347, 339.
2643. PROXENOS of Cholargos v: Boul. 336.
2644. PROXENOS of Konthyle III: Boul. 336.
2645. PYRGION (*PA* 12485): A. 388.
2646. PYRGION of Otryne II (*PA* 12489): Hypogr. Ep. 408.
2647. PYRGION s. of N-- of Otryne II: Boul. App. VII.
2648. PYRILAMPES s. of Antiphon (*PA* 12493; *APF* 329f.): Env. App. IV (cf. 450).
2649. PYRRHANDROS of Anaphlystos x (*PA* 12496): Env. 378; Prop. 378 v; Ass. 347.
2650. PYRRHOS s. of Pythodoros of Acherdous VIII (*PA* 12514): Plouton App. IX.
2651. PYRRHOS s. of Euthymachos of Potamos Deiradiotes IV (*PA* 12523 = 12522): Boul. App. IX.
2652. PYTHANDRIDES of Acharnai VI (*PA* 12338): Boul. 360.
2653. PYTHARATOS of Kydathenaion III: Boul. 336.
2654. PYTHEAS (*PA* 12340): A. 380.
2655. PYTHEAS (*PA* 12342): Kategoros 324; Ass. 324.
2656. PYTHEAS of Alopeke x (*PA* 12344): Boul. App. IX.
2657. PYTHEAS s. of Sosidemos of Alopeke x (*PA* 12346): Epim. springs 334–331.
2658. PYTHEAS s. of Pythippos of Bate II (*PA* 12348): Boul. 343.
2659. PYTHEAS of Kydathenaion III: Boul. 336.
2660. PYTHIADES of Kedoi I: Boul. 336.
2661. PYTHION s. of Aischronides of Kydantidai II (*PA* 12370): Boul.-Hier. 341.
2662. PYTHODELOS (*PA* 12379): A. 336.
2663. PYTHODELOS s. of Pythodelos of tribe I: Boul. 335.
2664. PYTHODELOS s. of Pythodelos of Hagnous v (*PA* 12380): Gr. 328.
2665. PYTHODOROS (*PA* 12387): A. 432.
2666. PYTHODOROS (*PA* 12389): A. 404.
2667. PYTHODOROS of tribe VIII (*PA* 12405): Phyl. 412.
2668. PYTHODOROS of Acharnai VI (*PA* 12391): Boul. App. VII.
2669. PYTHODOROS s. of Nikostratos of Acharnai VI (*PA* 12413; *APF* 482): Amph. Delos 341.
2670. PYTHODOROS s. of Polyzelos of Anaphlystos x (*PA* 12412): Prop. 412 vi.
2671. PYTHODOROS s. of Epizelos of Halai II (*PA* 12410 = 12402; *APF* 481): S. 414; Hipp. App. V; Tam. 418; Oath 422.
2672. PYTHODOROS s. of Python of Kedoi I (*APF* 486): Naop. Delphi 334, 327, 326.
2673. PYTHODOROS s. of Aristion of Kephisia I (*PA* 12425; *APF* 564): Boul. 367.
2674. PYTHODOROS of Phegaia II (*PA* 12432; *APF* 484): Boul. 336.

2675. PYTHODOROS of Phlya VII (*PA* 12433): Ep. App. IV.
2676. PYTHODOROS s. of Isolochos of Phlya VII (*PA* 12399): S. 426, 425.
2677. PYTHODOROS s. of Antiphilos of Probalinthos III: Boul. App. VII.
2678. PYTHODOROS s. of Pythokles of Skambonidai IV (*PA* 12430): Boul. App. VII.
2679. PYTHODOTOS (*PA* 12386): A. 343.
2680. PYTHOGENES s. of A--: Amph. Delos 360/355.
2681. PYTHOKLES s. of Euthykles of Kedoi I (*PA* 12443; *APF* 486): Tam. o.g. 375.
2682. PYTHOKLES s. of Pythodoros of Kedoi I (*PA* 12444; *APF* 485): Ass. 338.
2683. PYTHOKLES of Lamptrai (lower) I: Boul. 367.
2684. PYTHOKLES of Philaidai II: Boul. 336.
2685. PYTHOKRITOS (*PA* 12451): A. 494.
2686. PYTHON: Tax. 410.
2687. PYTHON of Kedoi I (*PA* 12471): Boul. 403 ii.
2688. PYTHONIKOS (*PA* 12458): Ass. 416.
2689. PYTHONIKOS: Boul.-Prop. App. VI xxi.

2690. RH--: Eleusis App. V.

(2246a.) RHAIDIOS (PANDIOS *PA* 11575) s. of Sokles of Oion VIII: Gr. 355.
2691. RHIKON of Anaphlystos X (*PA* 12530): Boul. App. IX.
2692. RHINON s. of Charikles of Paiania III (*PA* 12532; *APF* 67): S. 403; Par. S. 417; Tam. 402; Ten 404.

2693. S--: Tam. 550.
2694. S--: Gr. 424 vii.
2695. S--: Boul. 340 iii.
2696. S--ON: Paidotribes App. IX.
2697. SIBYRTI--: Hell. 405.
2698. SIMI--: Boul. App. VI xxvii.
2699. STRAT--: Ep. 446.

2700. SI. . ⁶ . . . of tribe X: Boul. App. IV xii.

2701. SALOMINOKLES: Ep. 446.
2702. SATYROS (*PA* 12575): Boul.-Prop. 363 ii.
2703. SATYROS (*PA* 12577): Epim. dock. 357.
2704. SATYROS of Daidalidai VII (*PA* 12593; *APF* 273): Tam. 389.
2705. SATYROS of Kephisia I (*PA* 12598): Eleven 404; Boul. 405.
2706. SATYROS of Leukonoion IV (*PA* 12603): Syngr. Hell. 443, 442.
2707. SAURIAS: Epim. Lemnos App. VIII.
2708. SIBYRTIADES (*PA* 12645): Gr. 410 iv.
2709. SIBYRTIOS of tribe V (*PA* 12646): Boul. 407 iv.
2710. SIMICHOS (STROMBICHIDES *PA* 13016/SYMBICHOS) (*PA* 13030): S. 411/10.
2711. SIMON (*PA* 12685): A. 591.
2712. SIMON (*PA* 12687): Hipp. 425.

2713. SIMON (*PA* 12698): Boul. 378 iii.

2714. SIMON s. of Simondes of Hybadai IV (*PA* 12707): Boul. App. VII.

2715. SIMON s. of Th-- of Phegaia II (*PA* 12708): Boul. App. VII.

2716. SIMON of Phrearrhioi IV: Boul. App. IX.

2717. SIMONIDES (*PA* 12713): S. 426.

2718. SKAMANDRIOS (*PA* 12721): A. 510.

2719. SKAPHON of Philaidai II (*PA* 12725 = 12724): ? App. VIII.

2720. SKIRONIDES (*PA* 12730): S. 412.

2721. SKITON: Prop. App. VIII xvi.

2722. SKOPAS: Gr. 430 i.

2723. SKOPAS: Prop. App. V iii.

2724. SKOPAS of Pithos VII (*PA* 12735): Ep. App. V.

2725. SMIKRIAS of Athmonon VII (*PA* 12741): Boul. 369 iii.

2726. SMIKRIAS s. of Philokedes of Gargettos II (*PA* 12743): Boul. 341.

2727. SMIKRIAS s. of Euripides of Phrearrhioi IV: Boul. 371.

2728. SMIKRON of Sounion IV (*PA* 12761): Boul. App. VII.

2729. SMIKROS: Prop. App. VIII xvii.

2730. SMIKROS of Alopeke X (*PA* 12757): Tam. 389.

2731. SMIKYTHION of Halai II/VII (*PA* 12769): Gr. Ep. Eleusis 407.

2732. SMIKYTHON (SMIKYTHOS *PA* 12773): Gr. Tam. 424.

2733. SMIKYTHOS (*PA* 12775): Boul. App. IV xxiv.

(2732a.) SMIKYTHOS (SMIKYTHON) (*PA* 12773): Gr. Tam. 424.

2734. SMIKYTHOS of tribe V: Boul. 427 ii.

2735. SMIKYTHOS s. of Charinos of Acharnai VI (*PA* 12788; *APF* 542): Gr. App. VI xx.

2736. SMIKYTHOS s. of Hippodamas of Kephisia I: Par. A. App. VIII.

2737. SMIKYTHOS of Kettos IV: Boul. 336.

2738. SMIKYTHOS s. of Epiteles of Thorikos V: Boul. 338.

2739. SMOKORDOS of Aphidna IX (*PA* 12801): Tam. 440.

2740. SMYROS (*PA* 12802): A. 500.

2741. SOKERDES of Halai II/VII (*PA* 13057): Boul. 349 i.

2742. SOKLEIDES of Potamos IV: Boul. 336.

2743. SOKRATES s. of Sophroniskos of Alopeke X (*PA* 13101): Boul. 406.

2744. SOKRATES of Anagyrous I (*PA* 13102; *APF* 497): S. 441, 439.

2745. SOKRATES of Anagyrous I (*PA* 13103; *APF* 497): Boul. App. VII.

2746. SOKRATES s. of Kephisokles of Eitea X: Boul. 335.

2747. SOKRATES s. of Antigenes of Halai II (*PA* 13099): S. 432, 431.

2748. SOKRATES s. of Habron of Halai II (*PA* 13098): Boul. 343.

2749. SOKRATES of Lamptrai I (*PA* 13116): Tam. 399.

2750. SOKRATES s. of Pyr-- of Paionidai IV: Gr. boule 328.

2751. SOKRATIDES (*PA* 13128): A. 374.

2752. SOLON s. of Exekestides (*PA* 12806; *APF* 322ff.): A. 594; Nomothetes 594; S. 600.

2753. SONDRIDES of Euonymon I (*PA* 13142): Epim. dock. 369.

2754. SONDROS of Acharnai VI (*PA* 13143): Boul. 360.

2755. SOPATROS of Alopeke X: S. 329.

2756. SOPHANES s. of Eutychides of Dekeleia VIII (*PA* 13409): S. 465.

2757. SOPHANES of Kedoi I: Boul. 367.

2758. SOPHANES s. of Derketes of Phyle VI: Boul. App. VII.

2759. SOPHIAS of Eleusis VIII (*PA* 12819): Gr. Hell. 443.

2760. SOPHILOS (*PA* 13414): Boul.-Prop. 394 iv, v.

2761. SOPHILOS s. of S-- of Kettos IV: Boul. App. IX.

2762. SOPHILOS s. of Stephanos of Kydathenaion III (*PA* 13417): Boul. App. VIII.

2763. SOPHILOS s. of Aristoteles of Phyle VI (*PA* 13422): S. 334, 333; Epim. Amphiaraia 329.

2764. SOPHOKLES s. of Sostratides (*PA* 12827): S. 426, 425; Thirty 404.

2765. SOPHOKLES s. of Iophon of Kolonos II (*PA* 12833): Tam. 400.

2766. SOPHOKLES s. of Sophillos of Kolonos II (*PA* 12834): S. 441, App. IV, App. V; Hell. 443; Proboulos 412.

2767. SOFOLIS s. of Kephisodoros of Kydathenaion III (*PA* 13155): Boul. App. VII.

2768. SOSIAS (*PA* 13176): Hell. App. IV, App. V.

2769. SOSIAS s. of Pythis (*PA* 13177): 423 note.

2770. SOSIAS s. of D-- of Phrearrhioi IV: Boul. 371.

2771. SOSICHIOS of Hagnous V (*PA* 13301): Tam. o.g. 418.

2772. SOSIGENES (*PA* 13196): A. 342.

2773. SOSIGENES s. of Lykinos of Kydathenaion III: Boul. App. VII.

2774. SOSIGENES s. of Sosigenes of Myrrhinous III (*PA* 13213): Boul. App. IX.

2775. SOSIGENES s. of Sosiades of Xypete VII (*PA* 13214): Amph. Delos 377.

2776. SOSIKEDES s. of Philonides of Pergase (lower) I: Boul. 335.

2777. SOSIMACHOS of Myrrhinous III: Tam. App. IX.

2778. SOSIPPOS of Agryle I: Boul. 336.

2779. SOSISTRATOS (*PA* 13282): A. 455.

(1889a.) SOSISTRATOS (LYSISTRATOS) of Aigilia X (*PA* 13290): Tam. o.g. 421.

2780. SOSISTRATOS s. of Menon of Eleusis VIII: Boul. 335.

2781. SOSISTRATOS of Hybadai IV (*PA* 13297): Gr. Hell. 440.

2782. SOSISTRATOS of Oa III (*PA* 13299): Boul. App. VI.

2783. SOSTHENES of Paiania III: Boul. 336.

2784. SOSTRATIDES s. of Ekphantos/Echphantos of Eupyridai IV (*PA* 13322 = 4657): Gr. 329; Boul. App. IX.

2785. SOSTRATOS of Ankyle II: Boul. 336.

2786. SOSTRATOS s. of Smikythos of Perithoidai VI: Boul. 335.

2787. SOSTRATOS s. of Olympiodoros of Phrearrhioi IV (*PA* 13374 = 13373; *APF* 499): Boul. App. VIII.

2788. SOSTRATOS s. of Mikion of Sypalettos VII: Boul. 335.

2789. SOTADES of Paiania III: Boul. 336.

2790. SOTES of Lamptrai I (*PA* 13399): ? App. VIII.

2791. SOTIADES of Acharnai VI: Tam. boule 328.

2792. SOTIMIDES s. of Aischines of Phegaia II (*PA* 13400): Boul. 343.

2793. SOUNIADES of Acharnai VI (*PA* 12817): A. 397.

2794. SPEUSIAS of Hagnous V: Boul. 336.

2795. SPEUSIKLES s. of Demetrios of Sounion IV (*PA* 12843): Boul. App. VII.

2796. SPEUSIPPOS (*PA* 12845): Boul.-Prop. 415 iii.

2797. SPINTHAROS of Hestiaia II: Boul. 336.

2798. SPINTHON s. of Lamedon of Kydantidai II: Boul. 335.

2799. SPOUDIAS: Gr. 448 i.

2800. SPOUDIAS (*PA* 12861): S. 368.
2801. SPOUDIAS s. of Philistides of Azenia VIII (*PA* 12866): Boul. App. VIII.
2802. SPOUDIAS of Phlya VII (*PA* 12871): Hell. 410.
2803. STEPHANOS: Prop. 378 i.
2804. STEPHANOS (*PA* 12879): Prop. App. IX xxx.
2805. STEPHANOS s. of Thoukydides of Alopeke x (*PA* 12884; *APF* 233): Gr. App. V xli.
2806. STEPHANOS s. of Antidorides of Eroiadai VIII/x (*PA* 12887): Par. Bas. App. VII; Env. 346; Prop. 347 ii, App. VIII xxv.
2807. STEPHANOS of Kephisia I: Boul. 336.
2808. STEPHANOS s. of Demylos of Probalinthos III (*PA* 12892): Boul. App. VIII.
2809. STESILEOS s. of Thrasyleos (*PA* 12906): S. 490.
2810. STHENYLLOS of Eiresidai v (*PA* 12643): S. 329.
2811. STIBON s. of Kletos of tribe IV (*PA* 12908): Boul. App. VIII.
2812. STRATIOS: Boul. App. VI xx.
2813. STRATIPPOS (*PA* 12921): Ep. Braur. 353.
2814. STRATOKLES (*PA* 12926): Ep. App. IV.
2815. STRATOKLES (*PA* 12927): A. 425.
2816. STRATOKLES s. of Euthydemos of Diomeia II (*PA* 12938; *APF* 495): Kategoros 324.
2817. STRATOKLES of Kephale v: Tam. o.g. 421.
2818. STRATOKLES of Lakiadai VI (*PA* 12931 = 12941): S. 338.
2819. STRATOKLES s.of Metalexis of Steiria III: Boul. App. VII.
2820. STRATON of tribe x (*PA* 12971): Boul. App. IV xxii.
2821. STRATON s. of Stratios of Kydathenaion III: Boul. App. VII.
2822. STRATON s. of Kallistratos of Paiania (lower) III: Boul. 335.
2823. STRATON of Poros v: Boul. 336.
2824. STRATONIDES s. of Sosigenes of Paiania III (*PA* 13010): Boul. App. IX.
2825. STRATONIKOS of Potamos Deiradiotes IV (*PA* 12954): Boul. App. VII.
2826. STRATOS s. of Melanopos of Poros v: Boul. 338.
2827. STREPHENEOS of Kydathenaion III: Tam. 354.
2828. STROMBICHIDES of Euonymon I (*PA* 13015): Env. 372.
2829. STROMBICHIDES s. of Diotimos of Euonymon I (*PA* 13016; *APF* 161): S. 413, 412, 411/10 (SIMICHOS *PA* 13030/SYMBICHOS); Tax. 405.
2830. STROMBICHOS of Cholleidai IV (*PA* 13023; *APF* 161): Gr. Hell. 444.
2831. STROSIAS (*PA* 13027): Tam. 440.
2832. SYBARITES of Gargettos II (*PA* 13029): Boul.-Hier. 335.
(2710a.) SYMBICHOS (SIMICHOS *PA* 13030/STROMBICHIDES *PA* 13016): S. 411/10.
2833. SYRAKOSIOS (*PA* 13041): Prop. 414.

2834. T--: Hier. 558.
2835. T . . .⁶. . . /T . . . .⁹. . . . . : Prop. App. V xxv.
2836. TE--: A. 549.
2837. THEODO--: Tam. App. IV.
2838. THEOPH--: Boul./Prop. App. V xxxiii.
2839. TIM--: Tam. o.g. 376.

I: Persons

2840. TIM--: Boul. 363 vii.
2841. TIM--: Boul. 342 i.
2842. TIMO--: Gr. Poletai App. IX.

2843. TA-- of tribe X: Tam. 377.
(2188a.) TH-- (O--) of tribe III: Symproedros 328 iv.
2844. THE-- s. of . ⸢.⸣ . . ylos of tribe V: Boul. 335.
2845. THERS-- of tribe IV: Ep. 375.

2846. TACHYKLES s. of Phormion of Myrrhinous III (*PA* 14957; *NPA* 158): Tam. 349.
2847. TAUREAS (*PA* 13430): Ass. App. IX.
2848. TEISAMENOS s. of Mechanion (*PA* 13443): Anagrapheus 403–400; Hypogr. App. V; Prop. App. V xxxiv, 403 xii.
2849. TEISAMENOS s. of Aleximachos of Koile VIII (*PA* 13444): Tam. o.g. 375.
2850. TEISAMENOS s. of Pythionikos of Kydathenaion III (*PA* 13445): Boul. App. VIII.
2851. TEISAMENOS of Paiania III (*PA* 13447): Tam. 414.
2852. TEISANDROS (*PA* 13455): A. 414.
2853. TEISANDROS of Anagyrous I: Boul. 336.
2854. TEISIADES s. of Teisippos of Sphettos V (*PA* 13468): Gr. Amph. Delos 341.
2855. TEISIADES of Thria VI: Boul. App. VIII.
2856. TEISIAS (*PA* 13471): Gr. App. IV xxxvi.
2857. TEISIAS (*PA* 13470): Boul. 404.
2858. TEISIAS of Kephale V: Askl. 338.
2859. TEISIAS s. of Teisimachos of Kephale V (*PA* 13479; *APF* 501ff.): S. 417, 416.
2860. TEISIAS s. of Dexitheos of Phlya VII (*PA* 13482): Ep. Eleusis 332–329.
2861. TEISIKRATES of Potamos IV: Tam. o.g. 418.
2862. TEISIMACHOS s. of Teisias of Kephale V (*PA* 13487; *APF* 503): Tam. 444.
2863. TEISIMACHOS of Sypalettos VII (*PA* 13490): Boul. App. VII.
2864. TELEAS s. of Telenikos of Pergase I (*PA* 13500): Gr. Tam. 415.
2865. TELEKLEIDES (TELEKLES): A. 596.
(2865a.) TELEKLES (TELEKLEIDES): A. 596.
2866. TELEMACHOS s. of Theangelos of Acharnai VI (*PA* 13562): Boul.-Prop. 339 ii; Prop. 329 ii, iii.
2867. TELEPHANES of Paiania (upper) III (*PA* 13573): Boul. App. VI.
2868. TELEPHONOS: S. 415.
2869. TELEPHONOS of Acharnai VI (*PA* 13578): Boul. App. VII.
2870. TELESARCHIDES of Cholargos V: Boul. 336.
2871. TELESEGOROS of Kollytos II (*PA* 13512): Env. 397.
2872. TELESIAS of Probalinthos III: Ep. 374.
2873. TELESINOS (*PA* 13527): A. 487.
2874. TELESIPPOS s. of Peisias of Kettos IV (*PA* 13539): Boul. App. VII.
2875. TELESKOPOS s. of Aristokritos of Rhamnous IX: Thesm. 328.
2876. TELESTES s. of Theognis of Hagnous V (*PA* 13546; *APF* 220): Gr. Tam. 423.
2877. TELOKLES (*PA* 13580): Naop. Delphi 354.

505

2878. TELOKLES s. of Kle-- of Hekale IV: Boul. App. IX.
2879. TELOPHILOS (*PA* 13585): Antigrapheus Eleusis 329.
2880. THALIARCHOS (*PA* 6572; *APF* 211): Tam. 442.
2881. THALLOS s. of Kineas of Lamptrai I (*PA* 6577; *APF* 492): Officer 349.
2882. THALLOS s. of Phanotheos of Paiania III (*PA* 6581): Tam. App. IX.
2883. THARREX of Lamptrai I: Gr. Ep. App. IV.
2884. THARREX of Lamptrai I (*PA* 6584): Boul. 354 iv.
2885. THARRHIAS s. of Tharrhiades of Erchia II (*PA* 6590): Boul.-Syllogeus 341.
2886. THARRHYNON of Kopros VIII: Hell. 407.
2887. THEAGENES s. of Akesandros of Anaphlystos x (*PA* 6609): Boul. 334.
2888. THEAGENIDES (*PA* 6611): A. 468.
2889. THEAGES of Kolonos II (*PA* 6616): Boul. 341.
2890. THEAIOS (*PA* 6642 + Add.): Gr. App. V xxx; Prop. 422 i.
2891. THEAIOS of Paiania III: Poletes 367.
2892. THEAIOS s. of Hippokles of Potamos (upper) IV: Boul. 371.
2893. THEANGELOS s. of Xenokles of tribe IX: Boul. 335.
2894. THEANGELOS of Cholleidai IV: Boul. 336.
2895. THEANGELOS of Phegaia II: Amph. Delos 411.
2896. THEBAGENES of Eleusis VIII (*PA* 7131): Env. 329.
2897. THEELLOS (*PA* 6641): A. 351.
2898. THEMISTOKLES (*PA* 6650): A. 347.
2899. THEMIST(H)OKLES of Phrearrhioi IV (*PA* 6665; *APF* 219): Boul. App. VII.
2900. THEMISTOKLES of Phrearrhioi IV (*PA* 6666; *APF* 219): ? App. VIII.
2901. THEMISTOKLES s. of Neokles of Phrearrhioi IV (*PA* 6669; *APF* 212ff.): A. 493; S. 490, 483, 481, 480; Epim. revenues App. III; Ep. water supply App. III; Pylag. 478; Env. 479; Prop. 481 i-iii, 479 ii, 477.
2902. THEMITEUS s. of Euthyneus of Pallene x: Boul. 335.
2903. THEOBIOS of Kopros VIII: Epim. dock. 368.
2904. THEODORIDES of Kydathenaion III: Boul. 336.
2905. THEODOROS (*PA* 6823): A. 438.
2906. THEODOROS s. of Antiphanes of Alopeke x (*PA* 6854): Boul. 334; Prop. 335 i.
2907. THEODOROS of Anagyrous I: Hell. 429.
2908. THEODOROS of Paiania III: Boul. 336.
2909. THEODOROS s. of Antidoros of Pallene x: Boul. 335, 328.
2910. THEODOROS s. of Theognis of Phegaia II (*PA* 6908): Boul. 341.
2911. THEODOROS of Plotheia II (*PA* 6896): Boul. 335.
2912. THEODOROS of Prasiai III: Gr. App. IV xii.
2913. THEODOTOS (*PA* 6773): A. 387.
2914. THEODOTOS s. of Neoikos: Amph. Delos 410.
2915. THEODOTOS of Aixone VII (*PA* 6786): Epim. dock. 362.
2916. THEODOTOS of Eupyridai IV: Boul. 336.
2917. THEODOTOS s. of Antiphates of Paiania III (*PA* 6799): Boul. App. IX.
2918. THEODOTOS of Pallene x (*PA* 6800): Boul. 334.
2919. THEODOTOS s. of Pausanias of Steiria III (*PA* 6804): Boul. App. VIII.
2920. THEODOXOS of Anaphlystos x (*PA* 6747): Boul. App. VII.
2921. THEOGENES (*PA* 6688): Env. 409.

2922. THEOGENES (*PA* 6692): Thirty 404.

2923. THEOGENES s. of Pleistos of tribe VI: Boul. 335.

2924. THEOGENES s. of Stibon of tribe IV (*PA* 6695): Boul. App. VIII.

2925. THEOGENES of Acharnai VI (*PA* 6703): Oath 422.

2926. THEOGENES s. of Ergophilos of Angele III (*PA* 6697): Boul. App. IX.

2927. THEOGENES of Erchia II (*PA* 6707): Bas. App. VII.

2928. THEOGENES of Kothokidai VI: Boul. App. VIII.

2929. THEOGENES s. of Theodoros of Paionidai IV (*PA* 6721): Boul. App. VII.

2930. THEOGENES of Peiraieus VIII (*PA* 6703): Kataskopos 425.

2931. THEOGENES s. of Halios of Probalinthos III (*PA* 6724): Boul. App. VIII.

2932. THEOGENES of Thria VI (*PA* 6710): Tam. 403.

2933. THEOGENES of Thria VI (*PA* 6710): Boul. App. VII.

2934. THEOGNETOS of Halimous IV: Boul. 336.

2935. THEOGNIS (THEOMENES of Xypete) (*PA* 6736): Thirty 404.

2936. THEOGNIS of Boutadai VI (*PA* 6741): Epim. dock. 378.

2937. THEOKLES: Symproedros 326 ii.

2938. THEOKRINES of Hybadai IV (*PA* 6946): Tam. tribe App. VIII; Boul. 328.

2939. THEOLLOS s. of Chromades of Phlya VII (*PA* 6952): Gr. Tam. 430.

2940. THEOMENES of Oe VI (*PA* 6957): Amph. Delos 345; Boul.-Prop. App. IX xii, xiii.

(2935a.) THEOMENES of Xypete VII (THEOGNIS *PA* 6736): Thirty 404.

2941. THEOMNESTOS (*PA* 6962): Ass. App. VI.

2942. THEOMNESTOS of tribe IX: Ep. 374.

2943. THEOMNESTOS s. of Theomnestos of Kydantidai II (*PA* 6969): Boul. 343.

2944. THEOMNESTOS s. of Dion of Paiania III (*PA* 6972): Boul. App. IX.

2945. THEOMNESTOS of Phegaia II (*PA* 6978): Boul.-Hier. 341.

2946. THEOPEITHES of Araphen II (*PA* 7002): Boul. App. VII.

2947. THEOPHANES of Acharnai VI (*PA* 7077): Askl. 337.

2948. THEOPHILOS: Askl. App. VII.

2949. THEOPHILOS (*PA* 7106 + Add.): A. 348.

2950. THEOPHILOS s. of Kallimachos of Acharnai VI (*PA* 7132): Ep. Eleusis 336–333.

2951. THEOPHILOS s. of Meliton of Alopeke X (*PA* 7126): Epim. Lemnos App. VIII.

2952. THEOPHILOS s. of Meniskos of Atene X (*PA* 7129): Tam. 345.

2953. THEOPHILOS s. of Charisios of Eiresidai V: Boul. 335.

2954. THEOPHILOS of Halimous IV (*PA* 7125): Boul. 347 i, ii.

2955. THEOPHILOS s. of Euangelos of Hermos V (*PA* 7138): Tax./Phyl. 373.

2956. THEOPHILOS s. of Chaireas of Krioa X (*PA* 7145): Boul. 334.

2957. THEOPHILOS of Kydathenaion III: Boul. 336.

2958. THEOPHILOS s. of Ariston of Kydathenaion III (*PA* 7146): Boul. App. VII.

2959. THEOPHILOS of Myrrhinoutte II (*PA* 7151): Boul.-Hier. 341.

2960. THEOPHILOS of Phegous I (*PA* 7158): Boul. 333 ii.

2961. THEOPHILOS of Probalinthos III: Boul. 336.

2962. THEOPHON (*PA* 7180; *APF* 84): Phyl. App. VII.

2963. THEOPHRASTOS of Halai II/VII (*PA* 7171): A. 340.

2964. THEOPHRON s. of Euthyphron of Lamptrai I (*PA* 7178): Naop. Delphi 326, 324.
2965. THEOPOMPOS (*PA* 7011): A. 411/10.
2966. THEOPOMPOS (*PA* 7016): Env. 378.
2967. THEOPOMPOS: Boul. 326 ii.
2968. THEOPOMPOS of Alopeke x (*PA* 7021): Boul. App. IX.
2969. THEOPOMPOS of Kerameis v: Boul. 336.
2970. THEOPOMPOS of Paiania III: Boul. 336.
2971. THEOPOMPOS of Steiria III: Boul. 336.
2972. THEOPROPOS: Gr. App. VI xvi.
2973. THEOROS (*PA* 7223): Arch. fleet 410; Env. 426.
2974. THEOROS s. of Mnesistratos of Leukonoion IV: Boul. 371.
2975. THEOTIMOS (*PA* 7055): S. 361.
2976. THEOTIMOS of Cholargos v: Ep. App. V.
2977. THEOTIMOS of Lousia VI (*PA* 7066): Boul. 360.
2978. THEOTIMOS of Phrearrhioi IV: Poletes 367.
2979. THEOXENOS of Kephale v (*PA* 6992): Hier. Eleusis 421.
2980. THEOXENOS s. of Theogenes of Potamos Deiradiotes IV: Boul. App. IX.
2981. THEOZOTIDES (*PA* 6913 = 6914; *APF* 222f.): Prop. 403 iv, App. VI iii.
2982. THERAMENES s. of Hagnon of Steiria III (*PA* 7234; *APF* 228): S. 411, 411/10, 410, 409, 408, App. V S. note; Thirty 404; Env. 405; Ass. 406, 405, 404.
2983. THERIKLES (*PA* 7235): A. 533.
2984. THERIKLES s. of Therimachos of Aithalidai IV: Boul. App. IX.
2985. THERSILOCHOS of Oinoe IX (*PA* 7195): Gr. Tam. 400.
2986. THERSIPPOS of Kothokidai VI (*PA* 7201): Tam. 384.
2987. THESPIEUS: A. 547.
2988. THESPIEUS: Prop. App. IV xiii.
2989. THOINILOS of Acharnai VI: Gr. Hell. 435.
2990. THORAX s. of Lykophron of Halimous IV: Boul. 335.
2991. THORYKION (*PA* 7419): Tax. App. V.
2992. THORYKION of tribe IV (*PA* 7420): Tam. 399.
2993. THOUDAITES of Diomeia II (*PA* 7264): Gr. 373 i, ii.
2994. THOUDEMOS (*PA* 7248): A. 353.
2995. THOUDES s. of Thoudiades of Alopeke x (*PA* 7249): Boul. App. IX.
2996. THOUDIPPOS of Araphen II (*PA* 7252 = 7251; *APF* 228f.): Boul.-Prop. 425 i, ii.
2997. THOUDOROS of Gargettos II: Tam. o.g. 421.
2998. THOUDOSIOS of Alopeke x/Epieikidai VII: Amph. Delos 413.
2999. THOUDOSIOS of Phyle VI: Boul. App. IX.
3000. THOUGEITON of Kedoi I: Boul. 367.
3001. THOUGENES (*PA* 6689): Askl. 352.
3002. THOUGENES of Xypete VII: Boul. App. VIII.
3003. THOUKLEIDES of tribe IX: S. 394.
3004. THOUKLEIDES of Agryle (upper) I: Boul. 408.
3005. THOUKLES s. of Theogenes of Paiania III (*PA* 6943): Boul. App. VIII.
3006. THOUKRITIDES s. of Kallias of Thorikos v (*PA* 7257; *APF* 272): Gr. Ep. Eleusis 332–329; Boul. 338.

3007. THOUKRITOS s. of Kephisodoros of Halimous IV (*PA* 7260): Boul. App. VII.

3008. THOUKYDIDES (*PA* 7264): Prop. 424 vii.

3009. THOUKYDIDES (*PA* 7265): Prop. App. VIII xviii.

3010. THOUKYDIDES s. of Kephisodotos: Tam. Delphi 339.

3011. THOUKYDIDES s. of Ariston of Acherdous VIII (*PA* 7271; *APF* 54): S. 440 (s. of Pantainetos of Gargettos *PA* 7272); Tam. 424.

3012. THOUKYDIDES s. of Melesias of Alopeke X (*PA* 7263; *APF* 230ff.): S. 444.

3013. THOUKYDIDES s. of Pantainetos of Gargettos II (*PA* 7272): S. 440 (s. of Ariston of Acherdous *PA* 7271).

3014. THOUKYDIDES of Ikarion II (*PA* 7273): Dem. App. IX.

3015. THOUKYDIDES s. of Theokydes of Lamptrai (lower) I: Boul. 367.

3016. THOUPHANES of Myrrhinous III: Boul. 336.

3017. THOUTIMIDES s. of Phanias of Sounion IV (*PA* 7280): Boul. App. IX.

3018. THRASEAS s. of Polyzelos of Agryle (upper) I: Boul. 367.

3019. THRASIPPOS of Aixone VII (*PA* 7297a): Boul. App. VII.

3020. THRASIPPOS of Gargettos II: Gr. Ep. App. IV.

3021. THRASON s. of Aristokles of Anakaia VIII (*PA* 7380): Boul. App. VII.

3022. THRASON s. of Thrasymedes of Anakaia VIII: Boul. 335.

3023. THRASON of Boutadai VI: Hell. 410.

3024. THRASON of Erchia II (*PA* 7384 = 7377; *APF* 239): Naop. Delphi 353 (THRASON of Kollytos *PA* 7389); Env. App. VI, 356.

3025. THRASON of Kollytos II (*PA* 7389 = 7377): Naop. Delphi 353 (THRASON of Erchia *PA* 7384).

3026. THRASON of Lamptrai I (*PA* 7390): Ep. Braur. 350.

3027. THRASON s. of Nikostratos of Poros V: Boul. 338.

3028. THRASON of Sphettos V: Boul. 336.

3029. THRASONIDES of Eupyridai IV (*PA* 7398): Amph. Delos 363.

3030. THRASYBOULOS s. of Thrason of Erchia II (*PA* 7304; *APF* 239): S. 326; Officer 353.

3031. THRASYBOULOS s. of Thrason of Kollytos II (*PA* 7305; *APF* 238ff.): S. 373; S./Nauarchos 387; Amph. Delos 393–389; Env. 378; Ass. 407.

3032. THRASYBOULOS s. of Diodoros of Oa III: Boul. App. VII.

3033. THRASYBOULOS s. of Lykos of Steiria III (*PA* 7310; *APF* 240f.): S. 411/ 10, 410, 409, 408, 407, 395, 394, 390, 389; Prop. 403 vii, 401; Ass. 396, 395.

3034. THRASYKLES: Hier. 566.

3035. THRASYKLES (*PA* 7317): S. 412; Prop. 421 i.

3036. THRASYKLES of tribe V (*PA* 7317): Oath 422.

3037. THRASYKLES s. of Thrasyllos of Eleusis VIII (*PA* 7322; *APF* 241): Boul. 335.

3038. THRASYKLES of Oion IV/VIII (*PA* 7327): Pylag. 340.

3039. THRASYKLES of Pallene X (*PA* 7328): Env. 384.

3040. THRASYLEON s. of Theophon of Acharnai VI (*PA* 7329): Epim. Amphiaraia 329.

3041. THRASYLEON of Kothokidai VI (*PA* 7330): Boul. 360.

3042. THRASYLLOS (*PA* 7333): S. 411/10, 410, 409, 408, 406.

3043. THRASYLLOS s. of Leonteus of Acharnai VI: Boul. App. IX.
3044. THRASYLLOS s. of Thrasyllos of Dekeleia VIII (*PA* 7341; *APF* 241): Plouton App. IX.
3045. THRASYLLOS s. of Apollodoros of Leukonoion IV (*PA* 7336; *APF* 44f.): Thesm. 356.
3046. THRASYLLOS s. of Gnathios of Leukonoion IV: Gr. Tam. 407.
3047. THRASYLOCHOS of Thorikos V (*PA* 7348): Hell. 407.
3048. THRASYMEDES (*PA* 7359): Boul. App. VI vii.
3049. THRASYMEDES s. of Lysimachos: Poletes 346.
3050. THRASYMEDES s. of Kallistratos of Acharnai VI (*PA* 7365): Tax./Phyl. 373.
3051. THRASYMEDES of Paiania III: Boul. 336.
3052. THUCYDIDES s. of Oloros of Halimous IV (*PA* 7267; *APF* 233ff.): S. 424.
3053. THYMOCHARES s. of Demochares of Leukonoion IV (*APF* 142): Sophr. 324.
3054. THYMOCHARES of Sphettos V (*PA* 7405; *APF* 524): Tam. 440.
3055. THYMOCHARES of Sphettos V (*PA* 7406; *APF* 524f.): S. 411, 411/10.
3056. THYMOCHARES s. of Phaidros of Sphettos V (*PA* 7412 = 7407 = 7409; *APF* 525f.): S. 322; Epim. Amphiaraia 329.
3057. THYMOCHARES of Teithras II (*PA* 7414): Symproedros 333 i.
3058. THYMOTELES of Kedoi I: Boul. 408.
3059. THYON of Phyle VI (*PA* 7416): Boul. 360.
3060. TIMAGORAS (*PA* 13595): Env. 368.
3061. TIMANDROS s. of Timonides of Prasiai III: Boul. App. VII.
3062. TIMANDROS s. of Timandros of Prasiai III: Boul. 336.
3063. TIMARCHIDES (*PA* 13615): A. 447.
3064. TIMARCHOS (*PA* 13623): S. 409.
3065. TIMARCHOS s. of Pe--/of Pe--: Tam. App. IV.
3066. TIMARCHOS of Pallene X (*PA* 13633): Hell. 417.
3067. TIMARCHOS s. of Arizelos of Sphettos V (*PA* 13636): Arch. Andros 363; Logistes 364; Exetastes 348; Env. App. VIII; Boul.-Prop. 347 xix, xx; Boul. 361; Prop. App. VII; Ass. App. VII.
3068. TIMARETOS of Perithoidai VI: Epim. dock. 367.
3069. TIMASITHEOS of Diomeia II: Boul. 336.
3070. TIMASITHEOS s. of Demainetos of Kerameis V (*PA* 13641/13640; *APF* 102f.): ? App. VIII.
3071. TIMIAS of tribe VIII (*PA* 13657): Boul. 421 i.
3072. TIMOCHARES of Prasiai III: Boul. 336.
3073. TIMODEMOS s. of Kephisodotos of Acharnai VI (*PA* 13680): Boul. App. IX.
3074. TIMOGENES of Ikarion II (*PA* 13664): Ep. 437.
3075. TIMOGENES s. of . . .o-- of Ikarion II: Boul. App. VII.
3076. TIMOKEDES s. of Gnathis of Eleusis VIII (*PA* 13718): Tax. 356.
(753a.) TIMOKLEIDES (DEMOKLEIDES) of Aphidna IX: Tam. App. IX.
3077. TIMOKLEIDES of Eupyridai IV: Boul. 336.
3078. TIMOKLES (*PA* 13723): A. 441.
3079. TIMOKLES of Cholargos V: Boul. 336.
3080. TIMOKLES of Eitea V (*PA* 13733): Tam. 423.

3081. TIMOKLES s. of Timok-- of Lamptrai I: Boul. 408.

3082. TIMOKLES of Phlya VII: Boul. App. IX.

3083. TIMOKLES of Sphettos V: Boul. 336.

3084. TIMOKRATES (*PA* 13748): Boul.-Prop. 406 ii.

3085. TIMOKRATES (*PA* 13749): A. 364.

3086. TIMOKRATES of tribe IX (*PA* 13746): Oath 422.

3087. TIMOKRATES s. of T-- of tribe IV/IX: Thesm. App. IX.

3088. TIMOKRATES s. of Nikomachos of Acharnai VI: Hier. Delphi App. IX.

3089. TIMOKRATES of Agryle I: Boul. 336.

3090. TIMOKRATES of Aphidna IX: Epim. tribe 342.

3091. TIMOKRATES s. of Philinos of Eleusis VIII: Hier. 325.

3092. TIMOKRATES s. of Timochares of Halai II: Tax. 356.

3093. TIMOKRATES s. of Teleson of Halimous IV: Boul. 335.

3094. TIMOKRATES s. of Antiphon of Krioa X (*PA* 13772; *APF* 513f.):
    Eispraktor 356; Prop. 354 vii, App. VII xxv.

3095. TIMOKRITOS s. of Timokrates of Ikarion II (*PA* 13790; *APF* 513):
    Boul.-Syllogeus-Hier. 341.

3096. TIMOLAS of Rhamnous IX (*PA* 13792): Epim. dock. 356.

3097. TIMOMACHOS of Acharnai VI (*PA* 13797; *APF* 280): S. 367, 361.

3098. TIMON (*PA* 13837): Askl. App. VIII.

3099. TIMON s. of Timokrates of Kytherros III (*PA* 13846; *APF* 338): Tam.
    376.

3100. TIMONIDES (*PA* 13855): Boul.-Prop. 353 ii.

3101. TIMONIDES of tribe I: Boul. 430 i.

3102. TIMONIDES of Prospalta V: Boul. 336.

3103. TIMONOTHOS (*PA* 13799): Env. 368.

3104. TIMOSTHENES (*PA* 13807): A. 478.

3105. TIMOSTHENES: Hell. 434.

3106. TIMOSTRATOS (*PA* 13816): Boul. 323 iii.

3107. TIMOSTRATOS of Ke--: Ep. 434.

3108. TIMOSTRATOS of Kothokidai VI (*PA* 13820): Boul. 360.

3109. TIMOTELES of Acharnai VI (*PA* 13827): Gr. App. V viii.

3110. TIMOTHEOS (*APF* 507): Gr. Ep. 443.

3111. TIMOTHEOS of Alopeke X (*PA* 13698): Arch. Salamis 329.

3112. TIMOTHEOS s. of Konon of Anaphlystos X (*PA* 13700; *APF* 507ff.): S.
    378, 376, 375, 374, 373, 367, 366, 365, 364, 363, 360, 356; Ass. 357.

3113. TIMOTHEOS of Kerameis V: Boul. 336.

3114. TIMOTHEOS of Marathon IX (*PA* 13709): Epim. dock. 369.

3115. TIMOTHEOS s. of Smikrias of Pallene X (*PA* 13712): Boul. 334.

3116. TIMOTHEOS s. of Hippostratos of Sounion IV: Boul. 371.

3117. TIMOXENOS of tribe V (*PA* 13803): Boul. 433 i, ii.

3118. TLEMPOLEMOS s. of Agathymides of Hamaxanteia VIII: Boul. App.
    VIII.

3119. TLEPOLEMOS (*PA* 13862): A. 463.

3120. TLEPOLEMOS of tribe IX (*PA* 13863): S. 440, 439.

3121. TLESIAS (*PA* 13865): A. 680.

3122. TLETHYMOS s. of Tlempolemos of Kephisia I: Boul. 367.

3123. TOLMAIOS s. of Euthyneides of Probalinthos III (*PA* 13878): Boul. App.
    VIII.

3124. TOLMIDES s. of Tolmaios of Anaphlystos x (*PA* 13879; *APF* 74): S. 457, 456, 455, 452, 451, 448, 447.
3125. TYDEUS s. of Lamachos of Oe VI (*PA* 13884): S. 405.

3126. x-- of tribe VII: Symproedros 324 ii.

3127. XANTHIPPOS (*PA* 11159; *APF* 456): A. 479.
3128. XANTHIPPOS s. of Ariphron of Cholargos v (*PA* 11169; *APF* 455ff.): S. 480, 479; Env. 480, cf. 508.
3129. XANTHIPPOS of G--/E--/P-- (*PA* 11160; *NPA* 167): Tam. trir. funds App. VII.
3130. XANTHIPPOS of Hermos v (*PA* 11162): Boul. 362 i.
3131. XENAINETOS (*PA* 11174): A. 401.
3132. XENODOKOS of Acharnai VI (*PA* 11192): Env. 378.
3133. XENOKLEIDES (*PA* 11197): Ass. 370.
3134. XENOKLEIDES (XENOKLEITOS) of Phrearrhioi IV: Tam. o.g. 421.
3135. XENOKLEIDES of Phrearrhioi IV: Boul. App. IX.
3136. XENOKLEIDES of Thria VI (*PA* 11199): Boul. 360.
(3134a.) XENOKLEITOS (XENOKLEIDES) of Phrearrhioi IV: Tam. o.g. 421.
3137. XENOKLES s. of Kalliades of Erchia II (*PA* 11220): Boul. 341.
3138. XENOKLES of Kydantidai II: Boul. 336.
3139. XENOKLES of Paiania III (*PA* 11230): Boul. 348.
3140. XENOKLES of Perithoidai VI: Peripolarchos App. VIII; Boul. App. VIII.
3141. XENOKLES s. of Xeinis of Sphettos v (*PA* 11234; *APF* 414f.): Fin. administrator 332–329.
3142. XENOKRATES s. of Agathenor of Chalkedon: Env. 322.
3143. XENOPEITHES s. of Xenokles of Halimous IV: Boul. 371.
3144. XENOPHON s. of Euripides of Melite VII (*PA* 11313; *APF* 199f.): S. 441, 439, 430; Hipp. App. IV.
3145. XENOPHON s. of Teisis of Phrearrhioi IV: Boul. 371.
3146. XENOPHON of Rhamnous IX: Tam. o.g. 421.
3147. XENOTIMOS: Boul.-Prop. App. VI xx.
3148. XENOTIMOS s. of Xenokritos of Kopros VIII (*PA* 11271 = 11270): Boul. App. VII.

3149. z--: Ep. App. IV.

3150. ZOPYROS s. of Kratynon of Steiria III (*PA* 6271): Boul. App. IX.

Incomplete

3151. . . . . . .[11] . . . . . s. of Aristippos: Boul. 339 i.
3152. -- s. of --ates: Tam. boule 324.
3153. -- s. of Chaireas: Synegoros 423 note.
3154. . . . . .[9]. . . . . s. of Diom. .o--: Gr. Amph. Delos 342.
3155. -- s. of --eri--: Prop. 324 ii.
3156. -- s. of Eurytimos: Gr. App. V xxxvi.
3157. -- s. of --ilos: Gr. 407 ii.
3158. -- s. of --isio--: Gr. App. VII v.

3159. -- s. of Kleoboulos: Gr. Ep. Eleusis 340–337.
3160. -- s. of . . .l.los: App. 350.
3161. -- s. of Leomedon: App. VII x.
3162. -- s. of --mo--: Prop. App. IX xv.
3163. -- s. of --nes: Boul. 357 ii.
3164. -- s. of --phon: Gr. App. VII iii.
3165. -- s. of Polemonikos: App. 350.
3166. -- s. of Stry--: Poletes App. IX.

3167. -- s. of --os/--es of tribe I: Boul. 335.
3168. -- s. of --os/--es of tribe I: Boul. 335.
3169. -- s. of --os/--es of tribe I: Boul. 335.
3170. -- s. of --onides of tribe III: Tax. App. VII.
3171. -- s. of Amynandros of tribe IV (*PA* 735): Boul. App. IX.
3172. -- s. of Athenotimos of tribe IV (*PA* 284): Boul. App. IX.
3173. -- s. of --chares of tribe IV: Boul. App. VII.
3174. -- s. of --chos of tribe IV: Boul. App. VII.
3175. -- s. of --doros of tribe IV: Boul. App. IX.
3176. -- s. of --es of tribe IV: Boul. App. VII.
3177. -- s. of Kallistratos of tribe IV (*PA* 8151): Boul. App. IX.
3178. -- s. of --okles of tribe IV: Boul. App. IX.
3179. -- s. of --os/--as of tribe IV: Boul. App. VII.
3180. -- s. of --os/--es/--as of tribe IV: Boul. App. IX.
3181. -- s. of . .⁵. . . osios of tribe IV: Boul. 335.
3182. -- s. of Stratonides of tribe IV (*PA* 13005): Boul. App. VII.
3183. -- s. of --telos of tribe IV: Boul. App. VII.
3184. -- s. of Thrason of tribe IV: Boul. App. VII.
3185. -- s. of --os/--es of tribe V: Boul. 335.
3186. -- s. of --ades of tribe VI: Boul. App. IX.
3187. -- s. of Androsthenes of tribe VI (*PA* 903): Boul. App. VIII.
3188. -- s. of --dos/--des of tribe VI: Boul. App. IX.
3189. -- s. of --esippos of tribe VI: Boul. App. IX.
3190. -- s. of --kios of tribe VI: Boul. App. IX.
3191. -- s. of --nides of tribe VI: Boul. App. IX.
3192. -- s. of --oklitos of tribe VI: Boul. App. IX.
3193. -- s. of --omachos of tribe VI: Boul. App. IX.
3194. -- s. of --ophon of tribe VI: Boul. App. IX.
3195. -- s. of --os/--es/--as of tribe VI: Boul. App. IX.
3196. -- s. of --oulos of tribe VI: Boul. App. IX.
3197. -- s. of --los/--les of tribe VII: Boul. 335.
3198. -- s. of --on of tribe X: Boul. App. IX.
3199. -- s. of --sinikos of tribe X: Boul. App. IX.

3200. -- s. of --os/--es/--as of An--: Prop. App. IX vii.
3201. -- s. of Pleistias of Ana-- (*PA* 11866): Ep. App. IX.

3202. . .⁴. . A-- (G--/M--): A. 598.
3203. . .⁵. . . ACHOS s. of Charidemos: App. 356.
3204. . .⁵. . . ADES of tribe X: Boul. 415 i.

3205. --AIK--: Gr. App. V xviii.
3206. . . . AIOS (. . . LIOS) s. of I--: Boul. 358 ii.
3207. --AS: Hier. 429.
3208. --AS (--ON): Env. 378.

3209. . . . ⁶ . . . B . . . S (. . ⁶ . . . R . ⁴ . .): Boul. App. IV x.

3210. . . ⁴ . . CHIDES: Prop. 451 i.
3211. . . . ⁷ . . . . CHOS: Prop. App. IV ix.
3212. . . . ⁷ . . . . CHOS: Prop. App. VI xxii.
3213. . . . ⁶ . . . CHOS s. of Thrasymedes: App. 353.
3214. --CHOS: Boul. 335 ii.

3215. --DEMOS: Tam. 395.
3216. --DOROS: Prop. App. VI xxiii.
3217. --DROKLI--: Gr. App. VI xxv.

3218. .E . ⁴ . . NDROS: Prop. App. IV xxxv.
3219. . . E . . . ANES: Prop. 409.
3220. . . . ⁶ . . . EMOS: Boul. App. VI xxix.
3221. --ENES s. of Demok--: Tam. 430.
3222. --EON s. of Per--: Oath App. VIII.
3223. --EOS of tribe VIII: Boul. App. IX.
3224. . . . ⁷ . . . . ES: Gr. 425 iii.
3225. . . . ⁵ . . ES s. of Krantos: App. 357.
3226. . . . ⁶ . . . ES: Boul.-Prop. 355 iii.
3227. . . . ⁷ . . . . ES: Boul. 355 iv.
3228. . . . . ⁹ . . . . . ES: Prop. 354 iv.
3229. --ES s. of Diopeithes of tribe X: Boul. 335.
3230. --ES s. of Aristarchos of Ph-- (*PA* 1671): Prop. 333 i.
3231. --ES of tribe IV: Boul. App. IX.
3232. --EUS: Hieromn. 331.

(3202a.) . ⁴ . . G-- (A--/M--): A. 598.
3233. . . . . GNETOS s. of Ar--: Boul. 379 ii.

3234. . . ⁴ . . I . . . OS: Gr. 435.
3235. . . . ⁷ . . . . IAS: Prop. App. V xxxv.
3236. . . . ⁵ . . IDES: Gr. 415.
3237. . . . ⁶ . . . IDES: Prop. 355 v.
3238. . . . ⁵ . . IES: Prop. 455.
3239. . . ⁴ . . IGENES s. of Polyeuktos: App. 351.
3240. . . . . IKLES: Prop. App. IV xxiii.
3241. --IKLES: Hipp. 368.
3242. --ILEOS: Prop. App. IV viii.
3243. --ILONIKES: Tam.-Synegoros App. VIII.

3244. . . . IOS s. of T-- of tribe I: Boul. App. VIII.
3245. --IPPOS: Tam. 395.
3246. . .⁴. . IPPOS s. of Agathokles: App. 354.

3247. --KIAS of tribe IX: Boul. App. IX.
3248. .KLE--: Tam.-Synegoros App. VIII.
3249. . .⁵. . . KLEIDES: Gr. App. VI xxix.
3250. . . . KLES: Boul. 413 i.
3251. . . . KLES s. of Kalli . .⁵. . . : Dem. App. VII.
3252. . .⁵. . . KLES s. of Astynomos: App. 352.
3253. --KLES of tribe VIII: Boul. App. IX.
3254. --KLES of tribe VIII: Boul. App. IX.
3255. --KLES of tribe VIII: Boul. App. IX.
3256. --KRATES: Env. 397.
3257. --KRATES of Ko--: Fin. App. VI.
3258. . .⁴. . KRATES s. of Athen--: Prop. 340 v.
3259. --KRATES of tribe IV: Boul. App. VIII.

(362a.) . . LE.AINETOS (ARISTAINETOS): Boul. App. V xxx.
3260. --LES s. of Sopolis: Oath App. VIII.
(3206a.) . . . LIOS (. . . AIOS) s. of I--: Boul. 358 ii.

(3202b.) . .⁴. . M-- (A--/G--): A. 598.
3261. . . . M--: Tam.-Synegoros App. VIII.
3262. . .⁶. . . MOS: Tax. 410.
3263. . . .⁷. . . . MOS: Tax. 410.
3264. . . . MOS: Boul. App. VI v.
3265. . . .⁶. . . MOS s. of Lysippos: App. 354.
3266. --MOS: Askl. 351.

3267. . . .⁷. . . . N: Prop. App. IV xxx.
3268. --NIAS s. of Theopompos: Boul. 324.
3269. . . . NIO--: Gr. Hell. 416.
3270. --NOS: Prop. 363 vii.

3271. . .⁴. . O . . . OIRO--: Epim. dock. 367.
3272. .O--: Tam.-Synegoros App. VIII.
3273. --O-- of tribe I: Tam. App. IX.
3274. --ODOTOS of tribe VIII: S. App. IV.
3275. . . . OI . . . (. . . OK . . .): Prop. 355 iv.
(3275a.) . . . OK . . . (. . . OI . . .): Prop. 355 iv.
3276. . .⁵. . . OKLES s. of Theodoros: App. 357.
3277. --OMA--: Tam.-Synegoros App. VIII.
3278. . .⁶. . . ON: Boul. 448.
3279. . .⁴. . ON: Gr. 425 i.

3323. . . ⁴ . . s: Boul. App. V xiii.
3324. --s: Gr. App. V xxvi.
3325. . . . . ⁸ . . . . s: Gr. 403 iv.
3326. . . . . ⁸ . . . . s: A./Thesm. 402.
3327. . . . .⁷. . . . s: Boul. 399 i.
3328. --s: Boul. App. VI xxv.
3329. . . . .⁷. . . . s s. of Eumelos: App. 353.
3330. --s s. of Charis-- of tribe v: Boul. App. VII.
3331. --s s. of Dikaia--: Oath. App. VIII.
3332. . . . .⁷. . . . s s. of Ar. .aineas of Methone; Didask. 333.
3333. --s of tribe VIII: Boul. App. IX.
3334. --s of tribe IX: Boul. App. IX.
3335. . . ⁴ . . STHEN--: App. 359.
3336. --STRATOS: Gr. Tam. App. IV.
3337. . . . STRATOS: Gr. Tam. o.g. 430.
3338. --STRATOS of A--: Fin. App. VI.

3339. . . . ⁶ . . . T-- of tribe VI: S. 338.
3340. .T--S: Tam.-Synegoros App. VIII.
3341. --TEL--: Oath App. VIII.
3342. . . ⁴ . . THEOS: Prop. 410 iv.
3343. . . ⁴ . . THEOS: Boul.-Prop. 366 i.
3344. --THIPPOS: Boul. App. IV xxiii.
3345. --TIADES of tribe IV: Boul. App. VIII.
3346. . . . . ⁸ . . . . TOS: Gr. 446 iv.
3347. --TOS of tribe VIII: Boul. App. IX.
3348. --YLOS: Gr. Hell. 437.

ACHARNAI (VI)

3349. --: Tam. 407.
3350. --: Tam. 397 (Aixone/Athmonon).
3351. --: Tam. App. VII.
3352. --: Tam. 334.

3353. --DOROS: Tam.-Synegoros App. VIII.
3354. --ES: Tam. App. IX.
3355. --IOS: Gr. Tam. 343.
3356. . . . ODOROS: Gr. 417 (Amphitrope).
3357. --ON: Tam. 354.
3358. --OROS: Env. App. VII.

3359. ARIST--: Boul. App. VII.
3360. DI--: Boul. App. VII.
3361. HEPHAIST--: Boul. App. VII.
3362. NIKO--: Boul. App. VII.

3363. -- s. of --es: Amph. Delos 360/355.
3364. -- s. of --tos: ? App. VIII.
3365. . . . . ⁸ . . . . s. of Ainesistratos: Kosmetes 333.
3366. --OS s. of Diogeiton (*PA* 3793): Gr. Ep. App. V.

3367. --N s. of Lykophron (*PA* 9259): Env. App. VII.
3368. --s s. of Mnesistratos: Tam. o.g. 376.
3369. --ES s. of Oinobios (*PA* 11356): Tam. 351.

ACHERDOUS (VIII)

3370. --: Hell. 430.
3371. --: Hell. 405.

AGRYLE (I)

3372. --: Hell. 421 (Pergase).
3373. . . .⁷. . . . : Dem. 402.
3374. --: Boul. App. VI ix.
3375. --: Tam. 351.

3376. . .⁴. . s: Boul. App. VII.
3377. --SIPPOS: Hell. 434.
3378. . .⁴. . T--: Boul. App. VII.
3379. . .⁴. . YD--: Boul. App. VII.

AIGILIA (X)

3380. --: Tam. 401.
3381. . . . . . .¹¹. . . . . : Tam. 399.
3382. --: Oath App. VIII.

3383. G--: Tax. App. IX.

3384. . . . . . .¹². . . . . s. of --ilos: Gr. Amph. Delos 346.

AITHALIDAI (IV)

3385. PHA-- s. of Smik--: Epim. tribe 357.

AIXONE (VII)

3386. --: Gr. Hell. 436.
3387. --: Hell. 418.
(3350a.) --: Tam. 397 (Acharnai/Athmonon).

3388. --IKRATES: Boul. App. VII.
3389. --IPPOS: ? App. VIII.
3390. --KLES: Tam. 402.
3391. --PHANES: Boul. App. VII.

ALOPEKE (X)

3392. --: Gr. App. IV xxxiv.
3393. --: Amph. Delos 413.
3394. --: Hier. Eleusis App. V.
3395. --: Env. 384.
3396. --: Boul.-Prop. 325 iii.

3397. --IOS: Hell. 409.
3398.. .'.. KLES: Boul. App. IX.
3399.... ODOROS: Tam. App. IX.
3400. --S: Symproedros 324 iii.
3401. --YSI--: Amph. Delos. 408.

3402. KALL...⁷....: Gr. 378 iii.

3403. --ES s. of Glaukon (*PA* 3015): Boul. App. IX.
3404.. .'.. MON s. of Lyson (*PA* 9644): Boul. App. IX.
3405.. .⁵.. DES s. of Nikodromos (*PA* 10875): Boul. App. IX.
3406.. .'.. STRATOS s. of Nikostratos (*PA* 11018): Boul. App. IX.
3407.... YKLES s. of Oinobios (*PA* 11354): Boul. App. IX.
3408. --MON s. of Simonides (*PA* 12718): Epim. dock. 334.

AMPHITROPE (X)

(3356a.).. ODOROS: Gr. 417 (Acharnai).

ANAGYROUS (I)

3409. --: Prop. 323 i.

3410.. .'.. IMACHOS: Boul. 381.
3411.... ISTRATOS: Boul. 381.
3412.. .'.. MACHOS: Boul. 381.
3413...⁶... TON: Tam. o.g. 429.

3414. PERIK--: Sophr. 333.

3415. -- s. of --es: Hell. 416.
3416....⁷.... OS s. of Meixikles (*PA* 9758): Tam. o.g. 376.

ANAKAIA (VIII)

3417. --: Hell. 404.
3418. --: Boul. App. V xviii.
3419. --: Tam. o.g. 374.

ANAPHLYSTOS (X)

3420. --: Ep. 435.
3421. --: Ep. mint App. VII.
3422. --: Oath App. VIII.
3423. --: Symproedros 326 ii.

3424. --ES: Hell. 429.
3425. --XENOS: Tam. 397.

3426. ARCHI--: Tam. trir. funds App. IX.
3427. ATHEN--: Boul. App. VII.
3428. EI--: Boul. App. VII.
3429. PHILO--: Boul. App. VII.

3430. -- s. of --machos: Boul. App. IX.
3431. -- s. of Aristaios (*PA* 1635): Boul. App. IX.
3432. --s s. of Chairephilos (*PA* 15185): Boul. App. IX.
3433. -- s. of Euangelos (*PA* 5223): Boul. App. IX.
3434. --s s. of Leokrates: Boul. App. IX.
3435. --os s. of Lysimachos (*PA* 9494): Boul. App. IX.
3436. --okles s. of Nikokles (*PA* 10894): Boul. App. IX.
3437. --os s. of Philinos (*PA* 14312): Boul. App. IX.
3438. --s s. of Poithikos (*PA* 11877): Boul. App. IX.
3439. --on s. of Theophilos (*PA* 7128): Epim. tribe App. IX.

ANGELE (III)

3440. --pios: Boul. App. VI.
3441. --ratos: Boul. App. VI.
3442. --tes: Boul. App. VI.

ANKYLE (II)

3443. -- s. of --res: ? App. VII.

APHIDNA (IX)

3444. --: ? 429.
3445. . . . .⁷. . . . : Gr. 418.
3446. --: Boul. 363 vi.
3447. --: Boul. 357 ix.

3448. --on: Tam. 354.
3449. --ostratos: Hell. 405.
3450. --res: Gr. Tam. 390.
3451. . . .⁶. . . s: Gr. 407 viii.
3452. --s: Tam.-Synegoros App. VIII.

3453. philo . .⁶. . . : Gr. Tam. 442.
3454. --es s. of Telesarchos (*PA* 13508): Tam. 376.
3455. --emon s. of Theogeiton (*APF* 220): Ep. mint App. VII.

ARAPHEN (II)

3456. . . .⁸. . . . : Boul. 405 ii.
3457. --: ? App. VIII.

ATENE (X)

3458. . . .⁶. . . s. of Glaukippos (*PA* 2985): Gr. App. VII vii.
3459. -- s. of Lysiades (*PA* 9338): Boul. App. IX.
3460. --os s. of Lysiades (*PA* 9339): Boul. App. IX.
3461. --os s. of Menippos (*PA* 10036): Boul. App. IX.

ATHMONON (VII)

(3350b.) --: Tam. 397 (Acharnai/Aixone).

3462. --ON: Tam. App. VII.

3463. PO--: Dem. 325.

3464. -- s. of --on: Boul. App. VIII.
3465. --AS s. of Andron: Boul. App. VIII.
3466. ... OPEITHES s. of Demeas: Boul. App. VIII.
3467. -- s. of Philoktemon (*PA* 14639): Epim. dock. 334.

AURIDAI (VIII)

3468. --OS: Hell. 417.

3469. -- s. of G--: Boul. App. VIII.

AZENIA (VIII)

3470. -- s. of --os/--es: Prop. App. VIII vii.
3471. -- s. of Aischron (*PA* 397): Boul. App. VII.
3472. --S s. of Antikles (*PA* 1061): Boul. App. VII.
3473. -- s. of Epiphanes (*PA* 4970): Ep. App. IX.

BESA (X)

3474. -- s. of Pamphilos (*PA* 11541): Tam. 350.

CHOLARGOS (V)

3475. --: Ep. Braur. App. VII (Cholleidai).

3476. --SIAS: Tam. 367.

CHOLLEIDAI (IV)

(3475a.) --: Ep. Braur. App. VII (Cholargos).
3477. --: Symproedros 328 iv.

3478. P . . . ON: Tam. boule App. IX (Paionidai).

DEIRADIOTAI (IV)

3479. . . . MIAS: Boul. 336.

3480. -- s. of --os: Boul. 171.

DEKELEIA (VIII)

3481. . . . . . .[11]. . . . . s. of Euthoinos (*NPA* 76): Tam. 345.
3482. D . . .[8]. . . . s. of Dorkis (*PA* 4534): Tam. 376.
3483. PYTHA-- s. of --okles: Didask. 324.

EIRESIDAI (V)

3484. --: Tam. 390.

3485. . . . .[7]. . . . IDES: Thesm. 370.
3486. . . . . .[9]. . . . . s: Boul. 345 ii.

EITEA (V/X)

3487. --: Prop. 345 i (Phrearrhioi).

EITEA (X)

3488. -AS s. of Antiphanes (*PA* 1220): Boul. App. IX.

ELEUSIS (VIII)

3489. --: Gr. Tam. o.g. 429.
3490. --: Tam. 407.
3491. --: Tam.-Synegoros App. VIII.
3492. --: ? App. VIII.
3493. --: Symproedros 333 i.

3494. . . . YLOS (*PA* 441): Hell. 440.

3495. MEID--: Prop. 353 vi.

3496. -- s. of --imachos: Gr. Tam. 341.
3497. --POS s. of Aristo. . .os: Epim. dock. 349.
3498. --OS s. of Epikouros: Boul. 335.

ERCHIA (II)

3499. . . . ⁸ . . . . : Boul. 338 ii.

3500. --KLES: Hipp. 375.
3501. . . . ⁶ . . . PHI . . .: Ep. App. IV.

ERIKEIA (II)

3502. . . ⁴ . . x--: Boul. App. VII.

3503. . . . ⁶ . . . ENES s. of Ch--: Boul. App. VII.

EROIADAI (VIII/X)

3504. --: Gr. 388 (Iphistiadai/Keiriadai/Lakiadai).

3505. . . . ⁵ . . . s: Gr. App. VI xviii.

3506. -- s. of --ratos: Tam. 376.

EROIADAI (VIII)

3507. . . . ⁶ . . . OS (*APF* 540 n. 1): S. 326.

EROIADAI (X)

3508. --: Hell. 416.

3509. A--: Boul. App. VII.

3510. --MENES s. of Nausichares (*PA* 10602): Boul. App. IX.

I: Persons

EUONYMON (I)

3511. --: Boul. 384 ii.
3512. --: Env. App. VII.

3513.... [8].... ATOS: Tam. 397.
3514.. [4].. N.S: Amph. Delos 353.
3515... [6]... ON: Boul. 381.
3516.. ROUSELOS: Boul. App. VIII.
3517.... [8].... s: Boul. 381.

3518. CHAIR--: Boul. 408.

3519. -- s. of --nomachos: Boul. 367.
3520. -- s. of Elpines: ? App. VII.
3521. -- s. of Nauphrades: Boul. 367.
3522. -- s. of Pytheides: Boul. 367.

EUPYRIDAI (IV)

3523. --: Hell. 418.

3524. -- s. of Polykles (*PA* 11984): Boul. App. IX.

GARGETTOS (II)

3525. --: Tam. 343.

3526. --ANDROS: Epim. Nikai etc. 334.
3527.... [8].... DES: Boul. 349 iii.
3528. --KLEIDES: Tam. 367.

HAGNOUS (V)

3529. --: Epim. dock. 373.
3530. --: Horistes-Boul. 352.

3531. --MOS: ? App. VIII.

HALAI (II/VII)

3532. --: Gr. Hell. 450.
3533...... [11]..... : Gr. Tam. o.g. 421.
3534. --: Gr. 400.
3535. --: ? App. VIII.

3536. --OKRATES: Tam.-Synegoros App. VIII.
3537. --YDES: Ep. 438.

3538. E... [8].... : Gr. Ep. 446.

HALAI (II)

3539.... [8].... : Symproedros 328 iv.

3540... INIPPOS: Boul. 336.
3541.. [4].. MACHOS: Boul. 336.

3542. --os: Symproedros 324 ii.
3543. . . . ⁶ . . . s: Boul. 336.
3544. . . ⁴ . . stratos: Tam. o.g. 420.

3545. . . . okless. of Charias: Boul. App. VII.
3546. --s. of Nikokrates: Epim. tribe 340.

HALAI (VII)

3547. -- s. of --ares (*PA* 1583): Boul. App. VII.
3548. --os s. of --mos: Boul. App. VII.
3549. -- s. of --on: Boul. App. VIII.
3550. -- s. of --sias: Boul. App. VIII.
3551. -- s. of --thykl--: Boul. App. VII.
3552. -- s. of --ysippos: Boul. App. VIII.
3553. -- s. of Astyphilos: Boul. App. VIII.
3554. -- s s. of Nikodemos: Boul. App. VIII.

HALIMOUS (IV)

3555. --: Tam. 389.

3556. . . . ⁷ . . . . les: Gr. Hell. 451.

HEKALE (IV)

3557. . . . ⁸ . . . . : Symproedros 324 iii.

HERMOS (V)

3558. -- s. of --rhos: Poletes 346.

HESTIAIA (II)

3559. o--: Ep. App. IV.

3560. --nes s. of Philippos (*PA* 14393): Ep. 356–353.

HYBADAI (IV)

3561. --: Thesm. 344.

3562. --des: ? App. IV.

IKARION (II)

3563. . . . . ¹⁰ . . . . . : Dem. App. VIII.

3564. --ates: Gr. App. V xiii.
3565. . . . ⁶ . . . los: Boul. 336.
3566. . . on: Boul. 336.
3567. . . . . . . ¹¹ . . . . . s: Ep. nomothetai 353 vi.

3568. aristoge--: Boul. App. VII.

3569. . . ⁴ . . lykos s. of Ka. . .it. .os: Hier. 325.
3570. --aios s. of Sosigenes: Dem. App. IX.

I: Persons

IONIDAI (II)

3571. --RIDES: Tam. 395.

IPHISTIADAI (V)

(3504a.) --: Gr. 388 (Eroiadai/Keiriadai/Lakiadai).
3572. --: Ep. Braur. App. VII.

3573. --OS: Ep. 443.

KEDOI (I)

3574. --: Prop. App. VIII v (Kerameis/Xypete).

3575. . . .⁴. . OKLES s. of . .⁵ . . . tios: Tax./Phyl. 373.
3576. H--IAS s. of Kephisodoros: Boul. 324.

KEIRIADAI (VIII)

(3504b.) --: Gr. 388 (Eroiadai/Iphistiadai/Lakiadai).

3577. . .⁴. . DOROS s. of Smikythos (*PA* 12789): Boul. App. VII.
3578. --OBIOS s. of Smikythos (*PA* 12790): Tam. o.g. 376.

KEPHALE (V)

3579. --: Hell. 414.

3580. --ARCHIDES: Hell. 421.
3581. --LES: ? App. VIII.
3582. --IPPOS: Tam.-Synegoros App. VIII.
3583. --OS: Symproedros 333 i.
3584. --TES: Tam. 385.

3585. -- s. of --es: Hier. 325.

KEPHISIA (I)

3586. --: Tam. 401.
3587. --: Tam. 374.

3588. --AS: Boul. 367.
3589. --S: Ep. App. IV.

3590. -- s. of --es: Oath App. VIII.

KERAMEIS (V)

3591. --: Tam. 445.
3592. --: Hell. 435.
3593. . . .⁶. . . : Tam. 434.
3594. . . . .⁹. . . . . : Dem. 402.
3595. --: ? App. VIII.
(3574a.) --: Prop. App. VIII v (Kedoi/Xypete).

3596. . . .⁶. . . s: Boul. 362 iii.
3597. . . . .⁸. . . . s: Boul. App. IX ii.

525

I: Persons

KETTOS (IV)

3598. --ON: Ep. App. IV.

3599... THO..O..[5]...: Ep. App. IV.

3600. -- s. of --okles: ? App. VIII.

KOLLYTOS (II)

3601. --: Tam. 334.

3602....[7].... ES: Boul. 336.
3603.... OKLES: Boul. 336.
3604. --ON: Hell. 407.
3605...[6]... OS: Gr. App. VI i.
3606....[7].... S: Boul. 336.

3607. -- s. of --andros: Boul. App. VII.
3608....[7].... s. of Demophantos: Boul. App. VII.
3609...[6]... MOS s. of Leokedes (*PA* 9080): Boul. App. VII.

KOLONAI (IV/X)

3610. -- s. of --ydikos: Amph. Delos 361/356.

KOLONAI (IV)

3611.....[9].....: Tam. o.g. 420.

3612. --OS s. of Arxillas: Boul. 371.

KOLONAI (X)

3613..[4].. MENES: Boul. App. VIII.

KONTHYLE (III)

3614.....[10]..... : Boul. 355 v.

KOPROS (VIII)

3615. LE-- s. of Le--: Boul. App. VIII.

KOTHOKIDAI (VI)

3616. ARISTO--: Boul. App. VIII.

KRIOA (X)

3617. --: Ep. App. IV.

KYDANTIDAI (II)

3618. --E.EOS: Ep. App. IV (Kydathenaion).
3619...[6]... ES: Tam. o.g. 418.
3620.... OTHEOS: Boul. 334 ii (Kydathenaion).

3621. ARISTO--: Boul. App. VII.

KYDATHENAION (III)

3622. . . . ⁸ . . . . : Tam. 442.
3623. --: Hell. App. V.
3624. --: ? App. VII.
3625. . . . ⁷. . . . : Symproedros 333 i.
(3618a.) --E.EOS: Ep. App. IV (Kydantidai).
3626. --E--: Boul. App. VI.
3627. --EOS--: Boul. App. VI.
3628. --ETES: Boul. App. VI.
3629. --MA--: Boul. App. VI.
(3620a.) . . . OTHEOS: Boul. 334 ii (Kydantidai).

3630. A . . ⁵ . . : Amph. Delos 408.
3631. P--ILAS: Boul. App. VI.

3632. -- s. of --dotos: Boul. App. VII.
3633. E-- s. of --ios: Boul. App. VIII.
3634. PHIL--S s. of L--: Boul. App. VI.
3635. L-- s. of Diodotos: Boul. App. VII.
3636. -- s. of Dionysios: Tam. o.g. 374.
3637. . . . ⁷. . . . IOS s. of Kratios: Hier 325.
3638. . . ⁴. . OS s. of Philippos (*PA* 14400 + Add.): Boul. App. VII.

KYTHERROS (III)

3639. A. . . .⁹. . . . . s. of Antisthenes: Epim. tribe App. VII.

LAKIADAI (VI)

3640. . . ⁵ . . : Gr. Tam. 439.
(3504c.) --: Gr. 388 (Eroiadai/Iphistiadai/Keiriadai).
3641. --: Symproedros 324 ii.
3642. --: Boul.-Prop. App. IX ii.

3643. --LOS s. of Mnesitheos: Ep. mint App. VII.

LAMPTRAI (I)

3644. --: Gr. Amph. Delos: 360/355.
3645. --: App. VII iv.
3646. --: ? App. VIII.
3647. --: ? App. VIII.
3648. --: ? App. VIII.
3649. --: ? App. VIII.
3650. --: ? App. VIII.
3651. --: ? App. VIII.

3652. --ES: ? App. VIII.
3653. . . . ESTRATOS: Boul. 353 ii.

3654. . .⁵. . . IOS: Boul. App. VIII.
3655. --MENES: Symproedros 326 ii.
3656. --ODOTOS: Thesm. 370.
3657. . . . OK--: Boul. App. VIII.
3658. --ON: ? App. VIII.
3659. . . .⁷. . . OS: Epim. dock. 368.
3660. --OS: Horistes-Boul. 352.
3661. . . .⁶. . . OS: Boul. 335 iv.
3662. --S: Boul. 408.
3663. --S: Boul. 408.

3664. LAKRAT--: Boul. 336.
3665. XEN--: Boul. 336.

3666. -- s. of --nes: ? App. VIII.
3667. -- s. of --os: ? 328 iii.

LEUKONOION (IV)

3668. --: Ep. 436.
3669. --: Ep. mint App. VII.
3670. --: Hier. 325.

3671. -- s. of Aristodemos: Amph. Delos 342.
3672. -- s. of Smikrion: Ep. mint App. VII.

MARATHON (IX)

3673. --DOROS: Tam. 367.
3674. --LOS: ? App. VIII.

3675. L--: Tax. App. IX.
3676. LYSIPP--: Boul. 357 viii.

3677. . . .⁶. . . s s. of Daippos (*PA* 3101; *APF* 92): Boul. 368 ii.

MELITE (VII)

3678. --: Tam. 433.
3679. --: Hell. 429.
3680. --: Symproedros 328 iv.

3681. --OS: Hell. 405.
3682. . Y--: Boul. App. VII.

3683. EUPHE--: Boul. App. VII.
3684. EXEK--: Boul. App. VII.
3685. HIER--: Boul. App. VII.
3686. M . . . OS: Tam. 442.
3687. PHILE--: Boul. App. VII.

3688. -- s. of --doros: Prop. 323 v.
3689. -- s. of --itheos: Tam. 343.
3690. --ES s. of Antikles (*PA* 1062; *APF* 399): Boul. App. VIII.
3691. -- s. of Demophilos (*PA* 3667): Boul. App. VIII.

MYRRHINOUS (III)

3692. --: Ep. App. IV.
3693. --: Prop. App. IX xiv.

3694. --(ELIESOO): Boul. App. VI.
3695. --ENES: Boul. App. VI.
3696. --LIGES: Boul. App. VI.
3697. . . MOCHARES: Gr. Hell. 432.
3698. --N--: Boul. App. VI.
3699. --ODOROS: Boul. App. VI.
3700. --OIO--: Boul. App. VI.
3701. --OKRATES: Boul. App. VI.

3702. EUDA--: Boul. App. VII.
3703. SE--: Boul. App. VII.

3704. -- s. of --es: Boul. App. VII.
3705. -- s. of --es: Didask. 333.
3706. . .⁴. . AS s. of . .⁵. . . imos: Tax./Phyl. 373.
3707. -- s. of --kles: Boul. App. VII.
3708. --CHIAS s. of Eukleides (*PA* 5961): Boul. App. IX.
3709. . . .⁷. . . . AS s. of Kallisthenes (*PA* 8103): Epim. tribe App. IX.
3710. --OS s. of Lampon: Boul. App. VII.
3711. --OS s. of Polyeuktos: Boul. App. VII.

OA (III)

3712. --: Tam. tribe 348.

3713. --DOROS: Tam. 399.
3714. . . . PPOS: Boul. 329 i.
3715. --THION: Boul. App. VI.

3716. KI-- Boul. 336.
3717. N . .⁶. . . ELOS: Epim. dock. 368.
3718. NIKO--: Boul. 336.

3719. . . EO . . S s. of Ar--: Boul. App. VII.
3720. --ODEMOS s. of Deikiros: Boul. App. IX.

OE (VI)

3721. --: Tam. 401.
3722. --: Symproedros 326 ii.

3723. . . . LON--: Boul. App. IX.
3724. . . O . I--: Boul. App. IX.
3725. --OGENES: Boul. App. IX.
3726. --ON: Phyl. App. IX.

3727. E--: Boul. App. IX.
3728. EUD--: Boul. App. IX.
3729. OINO--: Boul. App. IX.

3730. -- s. of --dos: Amph. Delos 375–374.

OINOE (VIII)
3731. --: Tam. App. IX.

OINOE (IX)
3732. --: Symproedros 328 iv.

OION (IV/VIII)
3733. --: Amph. Delos 372–368.

3734. -- s. of --os/--es/--as: Prop. App. IX vi.

3735. --LEIDES s. of Philotheros (*PA* 14503): Gr. boule and demos App. VI.

OION (IV)
3736. --BOLOS: Eleven 404.

3737. . . . .⁹. . . . . s. of Stephanos: Gr. 384 i.

OION (VIII)
3738. . . . .⁷. . . . : Thesm. 370.

3739. . . .⁵. . . ENOS s. of I . . .⁷. . . . : Gr. 345.

OTRYNE (II)
3740. ARISTOKL--: Boul. App. VII.

PAIANIA (III)
3741. --: Ep. 375.
3742. . . . . .¹⁰. . . . . : Boul. 355 ii.
3743. --: Ep. mint App. VII.
3744. --: Epim. tribe App. VII.
3745. --: Gr. 350.
3746. --: Amph. Delos 342.
3747. --: Didask. 333.
3748. --: Symproedros 326 ii.

3749. . . .⁶. . . LES: Pentekontarchos 405.
3750. -N .⁴. . / -- s. of --n .⁴. . : Prop. 335 v.
3751. . . . .⁷. . . . NES: Boul. 363 i.

3752. DEMOKR . . . S: Boul. 334 i, iii, iv.
3753. PHIL--: Tam. 409.

3754. -- s. of --emos: Epim. dock. 333.
3755. -- s. of --in--: Boul. App. VII.
3756. LYS-- s. of --kles: Boul. App. VII.
3757. -- s. of --nes: Boul. App. VII (upper).

3758. -- s. of --nides: ? App. VIII.

3759. -- s. of --on: Boul. App. VII (upper).

3760. -- s. of --os: Boul. App. VII.

3761. -- s. of --os: Boul. App. VII (upper).

3762. -- s. of --phon: Boul. App. VII.

3763. -- s. of --rhios: Boul. App. VII.

3764. -- s. of --tades: Boul. App. VII (upper).

3765. ANTH-- s. of --s: Boul. App. VIII.

3766. --OS s. of Antikleides: Boul. App. VII.

3767. --OS s. of Demeas (*APF* 105): Boul. App. VIII.

3768. --RATOS s. of Echedamas (*PA* 6164): Boul. 348 (upper).

3769. --IDES s. of Kichonides: Anagrapheus 324.

3770. --OS s. of Leosthenes: Boul. App. VII.

3771. -- s. of Onetides: Boul. App. VII.

3772. --THEOS s. of Phanodemos (*PA* 14034): Boul. 348 (upper).

3773. --DOROS s. of Sostratos (*PA* 13364): Boul. 348 (lower).

3774. --OROS s. of Theodoros: Boul. App. VII.

PAIONIDAI (IV)

3775. --: Gr. App. VI ix.

3776. --: Ep. 356–353.

3777. --OS: App. VII xix.

(3478a.) P . . . ON: Tam. boule App. IX (Cholleidai).

3778. -- s. of --chos: Boul. App. IX.

PALLENE (X)

3779. --: ? App. VIII.

3780. K . . . ⁸ . . . . : Amph. Delos 354.

3781. . . ⁴ . . ANES s. of . . ⁵ . . . thos: Boul. 335.

PAMBOTADAI (I)

3782. --OS: Tam. trir. funds 323.

3783. . . . ⁶ . . . ON s. of Antikrates (*PA* 1086): Boul.-Prop. 343 vi.

PEIRAIEUS (VIII)

3784. --CHOS: Hell. 404.

3785. . . . . ⁷ . . . . s: Gr. App. VI vi.

3786. . . . . . ⁹ . . . . . TOS (*PA* 15171): Ep. Eleusis 408.

3787. -- s. of --etos: Tam. 344.

PELEKES (IV)

3788. --: Gr. Ep. App. IV.

3789. DIO--: Boul. App. IX.

I: Persons

PERGASE (I)

3790. --: Ep. 439.
(3372a.) --: Hell. 421 (Agryle).
3791. --: Hell. 418.

3792. --THEOS: Boul. 367 (upper).

PERITHOIDAI (VI)

3793. CHARM--: Boul. App. VIII.

3794. -- s. of --os/--es: Hier. 325.
3795. --ON s. of Aischines (*PA* 362): Tam. 342.

PHALERON (IX)

3796. --: Athl. 406.

3797. --OS: Pentekontarchos 405.
3798. --TOS: Hell. 407.

PHEGAIA (II)

3799. XENOKL--: Boul. App. VII.

3800. . . . .[10] . . . . . s s. of Demophilos (*PA* 3690): Gr. App. VI xvii
     (Phegous).
3801. -- s. of Diotimos (*PA* 4365): Gr. 432.

PHEGOUS (I)

3800. . . . .[10] . . . . . s s. of Demophilos (*PA* 3690): Gr. App. VI xvii
     (Phegaia).
3802. --OS s. of Lys--: Boul. 367.

PHILAIDAI (II)

3803. --OKLES: Gr. App. IV xxix, App. V.
3804. --RATOS: Tam. App. VII.

PHLYA (VII)

3805. --: Tam. o.g. 418.
3806. --: Env. App. VII.
3807. --: Boul. App. VII xx.
3808. --: Amph. Delos App. VIII.

3809. --ASIPPOS: Hell. 435.
3810. --S: Tam. App. IX.

3811. --LES s. of --dotos: Boul. App. VII.
3812. --SISTRATOS s. of Deinias (*APF* 96): Boul. App. VII.
3813. --S s. of Phaidon: Ep. mint App. VII.

PHREARRHIOI (IV)

3814. --: Ep. 374.
(3487a.) --: Prop. 345 i (Eitea).

3815. --ENES: Tam. App. VII.
3816. --ES: Boul. App. VIII.
3817. . . . PHILOS: Hypogr. Amph. Delos 353.
3818. --S: Env. 384.
3819. --S: Symproedros 324 ii.

3820. ARISTO--: Boul. App. IX.
3821. DIO--: Boul. App. IX.
3822. K--: Boul. App. IX.
3823. XEN--: Boul. App. IX.

3824. -- s. of --ates: Tam. 341.
3825. -- s. of --dikos: Boul. 371.
3826. . . PO.D-- s. of --emos: Boul. 371.
3827. -- s. of --ophiles: Tam. o.g. 376.
3828. -- s. of --os: Prop. 341 ii.
3829. APOLLOD . . OS s. of Kephisokles: Boul. 371.
3830. . . .⁵ . . . OS s. of Meneteles (*NPA* 126): Gr. 397.

PHYLE (VI)

3831. --: Hell. 409.
3832. --: Tam. App. VII.

3833. . . .⁶ . . . S s. of Euphron: Gr. App. VII vi.

PITHOS (VII)

3834. --: Tam. 400.
3835. --: ? App. VIII.

PLOTHEIA (II)

3836. --ATOS/-- s. of --ates: Gr. Poletai 402.

POROS (V)

3837. . . . . .¹⁰ . . . . . : Prop. App. VII vi.

3838. --OSTRATOS: Tam.-Synegoros App. VIII.

POTAMOS (IV)

3839. --: Boul.-Prop. 337 vi.

POTAMOS DEIRADIOTES (IV)

3840. . . . OROS s. of Pan--: Boul. 371.

PRASIAI (III)

3841. --: Tam. 445.
3842. --: Gr. 404.

3843. --KIADES: Boul. App. VI.
3844. --S--: Boul. App. VI.

3845. I--: Boul. App. VII.
3846. ON--: Boul. App. VII.
3847. T--: Boul. App. VII.

3848. --STRATOS s. of E--: Boul. App. VI.

PROBALINTHOS (III)

3849. --: Gr. Ep. 440.
3850. --: Tam. 406.

3851. RH--S: Boul. App. VI.

3852. DE-- s. of . . . ios/ias: Boul. 335.

PROSPALTA (V)

3853. --: ? App. VIII.

3854. -- s. of --nos: Boul. 338.
3855. . . .⁴. . . PEITHES s. of Archinos: Boul. 338.
3856. -- s. of Chairestratos: Boul. 338.
3857. -- s s. of Kallonides: Ep. mint App. VII.
3858. --s s. of Lysanias: Boul. 338.
3859. -- s. of Sostratos: Tam. 345.
3860. -- s. of Theophantos: Boul. 338.

RHAMNOUS (IX)

3861. . . . .⁸. . . . : Gr. 439.
3862. --: Gr. Hell. 438.
3863. . . . . . .¹¹. . . . . : Tam. 400.
3864. . . . .¹⁰. . . .⌐ : Boul. 361 iii.

3865. . . . .⁹. . . . ES (. . .⁸. . . . ON): Tam. 391.
(3865a.). . .⁸. . . . ON (. . . .⁹. . . . ES): Tam. 391.

3866. --s. of --es: ? App. VIII.
3867. -- s. of Oinobios (*PA* 11358): Prop. 344 i.

SEMACHIDAI (X)

3868. -- s. of --ikos: Boul. App. IX.

SKAMBONIDAI (IV)

3869. -- s. of --ktos: Boul.-Prop. 335 xi.
3870. -- s. of --os: Hell. 416.

3871. -- s. of Aitolides: Boul. App. IX.
3872. --: Gr. Tam. App. VII.
3873. --: Horistes 352.

3874. . .⁴. . INOS: Boul. 336.
3875. . .⁴. . LES: Boul. 336.
3876. . .⁴. . MACHOS: Boul. 336.

SPHETTOS (V)

3877. . . . .⁹. . . . . : Dem. 402.
3878. --: Symproedros 326 ii.

3879. --OS: Hell. 429.

3880. -- s. of --es: Prop. App. VIII iv.

STEIRIA (III)

3881. --AS: Boul. App. VI.
3882. --ES: Boul. App. VI.
3883. --ODOROS: Boul. App. VI.

3884. . . . .⁸. . . . S s. of Aristyllos (*PA* 2133): Prop. 351 i.

SYBRIDAI (I)

3885. --: Ep. mint App. VII.

3886. -- s. of --toros/--tores: Prop. 326 ii.

SYPALETTOS (VII)

3887. L. CH-- s. of Kephisodoros (*PA* 8383): Naop. Delos 346.

TEITHRAS (II)

3888. --: Ep. 411.
3889. --: Tam. 402.

3890. . .⁴. . E.OS: Boul. 336.
3891. --ITES: Tam. App. VII.
3892. . . . SIS: Boul. 336.

3893. -INIADES s. of --es/--os: Boul. 331.
3894. --ANES s. of An--: Boul. 331.

THEMAKOS (I)

3895. . . . .⁷. . . . TES: Boul. 375 iv.

THORAI (X)

3896. --: Ep. 434.

3897. --IKOS: Boul. App. IX xvi.

THORIKOS (V)

3898. NIKO . .[4]. . OS (*PA* 10876): Gr. Ep. App. IV.
3899. PH . . . LO . . .: Ep. App. IV.

3900. -- s. of Exekestides (*PA* 4713): Boul. 378.
3901. --LES s. of Ion: Boul. 378.
3902. -- s. of Theodosios (*PA* 6752): Boul. 378.

THRIA (VI)

3903. --: Tam. 374.
3904. --: Prop. 327 iii.

3905. --ES: Horistes-Boul. 352.
3906. --YNEUS: Gr. Ep. App. IV.

THYMAITADAI (VIII)

3907. . . . .[8]. . . . . : Hell. 418.

3908. PHAL . . . OS: Hell. 406.

TRIKORYNTHOS (IX)

3909. --ON: ? App. VIII.

3910. -- s. of --rates: Gr. Tam. 340.

XYPETE (VII)

3911. --: Ep. 440.
3912. --: Hell. 416.
3913. --: Tam. 404.
3914. --: Hier. Eleusis App. V.
(3574b.) --: Prop. App. VIII v (Kedoi/Kerameis).

3915. E--: Boul. App. VIII.

3916. --IOS s. of Androkl--: Boul. App. VIII.
3917. -- s. of Antiphanes (*PA* 1212): Boul. App. VIII.
3918. --ES s. of Aristaios: Boul. App. VIII.
3919. . .[5]. . MACHOS s. of Charidemos: Hell. 434.
3920. . . .[7]. . . . s. of Demainetos (*PA* 3266): Gr. 366 i.
3921. -- s. of Euxitheos: Boul. App. VIII.
3922. --LEOS s. of Hippon: Boul. App. VIII.
3923. --TOS s. of Pausides: Boul. App. VIII.
3924. --ES s. of Philistides: Boul. App. VIII.
3925. --NOS s. of Thrasymedes: Boul. App. VIII.

Index II: Tribes and Demes

Here individuals are listed by tribes in official order and demes within tribes alphabetically. The offices/functions are separated and the index numbers used. Figures in parentheses indicate the total number of individuals represented, when there are more than one.

Tribe I:
Erechtheis (345)
TRIBE ONLY (16)
S. (2): 1413, 2518.
Tam.: 3273.
Sophr.: 26 (/x).
Boul. (12): 25, 27, 143, 440, 983, 1605, 2663, 3101, 3167, 3168, 3169, 3244.

AGRYLE (28)
Tam. (4): 104, 352, 613, 3375.
Hell. (3): 613, 3372 (Pergase I), 3377.
Ep.: 613.
Dem.: 3373.
Env.: 309.
Gr. (2): 1260, 1629.
Decrees: 778.
Boul. (18): 103, 1220, 1424, 1882, 2778, 3089, 3374, 3376, 3378, 3379.
  Upper: 1001, 1518, 1986, 3004, 3018.
  Lower: 1629, 2040, 2442.

ANAGYROUS (46)
S. (3): 88, 747, 2744.
Hipp.: 1921.
Tam. Paralou: 1921.
Sophr.: 3414.
Tam. (3): 948, 1720, 2257.
Tam. o.g. (2): 3413, 3416.
Hell. (3): 747, 2907, 3415.
Epim. dock.: 2194.
Epim. mysteries: 1921.
Hier.: 1921.
Boones: 1921.

Gr. Amph. Delos: 378.
Pylag.: 1921.
Misc.: 747.
?: 305.
Gr.: 445.
Prop. (5): 443, 1103, 1921, 1922, 3409.
Ass.: 1921.
Boul. (26): 345, 528, 719, 787, 940, 1149, 1198, 1242, 1258, 1435, 1458, 1735, 1898, 2069, 2249, 2255, 2370, 2465, 2469, 2537, 2567, 2745, 2853, 3410, 3411, 3412.

EUONYMON (59)
A.: 1092.
S. (6): 265, 515, 926, 927, 1172, 2829.
Tax. (2): 1156, 2829.
Nauarchos: 927 (/S.).
Officer: 2200.
Tam. (3): 1014, 1926, 3513.
Gr. Tam. (2): 1092, 1639.
Tam. o.g.: 235.
Gr. Tam. o.g.: 1548.
Hell. (2): 420, 1508.
Epim. dock. (2): 128, 2753.
Ep.: 1827.
Hier.: 1180 (boul.).
Amph. Delos: 3514.
Env. (4): 515, 927, 2828, 3512.
Oath: 2617 (Kephisia I).
?: 3520.
Gr. (3): 1490, 2582, 2618.
Prop.: 515.
Ass.: 265.
Boul. (32): 76, 132, 162, 228, 237, 264,

537

354, 514, 653, 801, 991, 1015, 1023,
1092, 1180, 1429, 1455, 1460, 1624,
1899, 2057, 2086, 2404, 2601, 3511,
3515, 3516, 3517, 3518, 3519, 3521,
3522.

KEDOI (17)
Tax./Phyl.: 3575.
Tam. o.g. (2): 1873, 2681.
Naop. Delphi: 2672.
Horistes: 576.
Gr.: 1814.
Prop.: 3574 (Kerameis V/Xypete VII).
Ass.: 2682.
Boul. (9): 1244, 1395, 2252, 2660, 2687,
2757, 3000, 3058, 3576.

KEPHISIA (43)
Bas.: 2207.
Par. A.: 2736.
S. (2): 1131 (Sphettos V), 1166.
Hipp.: 1132.
Nauarchos: 1132.
Tam. (4): 1193, 2460, 3586, 3587.
Epim. dock.: 1824.
Ep. (3): 547, 839, 3589.
Ep. Eleusis: 1193.
Athl.: 2621.
Eleven: 2705.
Hier.: 1647.
Amph. Delos: 932.
Env.: 1042.
Oath (2): 2617 (Euonymon I), 3590.
Gr. (2): 583, 1239.
Prop. (3): 914 (boul.), 1194 (Kikynna V),
2240 (Kikynna V).
Boul. (20): 190(a), 229, 238, 532, 625,
680, 913, 914, 1006, 1078, 1209,
1582, 1799, 1891, 2633, 2673, 2705,
2807, 3122, 3588.

LAMPTRAI (87)
Thesm.: 3656.
Ten: 1017.
Officer: 2881.
Tam. (4): 133, 587, 2097, 2749.
Gr. Tam.: 1695.
Tam. o.g.: 670.
Tam. trir. funds: 1266.
Gr. Hell.: 1978(a).
Poletes: 2561.
Epim. dock. (2): 1721, 3659.
Ep.: 114.
Gr. Ep. (2): 2190, 2883.
Ep. Eleusis: 1483.

Ep. Braur.: 3026.
Gr. Amph. Delos: 3644.
Naop. Delphi: 2964.
Plouton: 1712.
Horistai (3): 476, 1122, 3660 (boul.).
Env. (2): 888, 1321.
? (12): 2790, 3645, 3646, 3647, 3648, 3649,
3650, 3651, 3652, 3658, 3666, 3667.
Gr. (4): 571, 639, 1387, 2073.
Prop. (2): 793, 1524 (boul. and other).
Ass. (2): 1269, 2366.
Boul. (43): 335, 341, 410, 476, 518, 671,
845, 1120, 1158, 1262, 1341, 1459,
1524, 1684, 1900, 2217, 2595, 2884,
3081, 3653, 3654, 3655, 3657, 3660,
3661, 3662, 3663, 3664, 3665.
Coastal: 153, 810, 1250, 1511, 1635,
1842, 1992, 2437, 2613.
Lower: 401, 738, 1432, 2683, 3015.

PAMBOTADAI (6)
Tax.: 826.
Tam. trir. funds: 3782.
Epim. dock. (2): 880, 1955.
Prop.: 3783 (boul.).
Boul. (2): 1819, 3783.

PERGASE (25)
A.: 1539.
S.: 1054.
Phyl.: 1252.
Tam.: 1681.
Gr. Tam.: 2864.
Hell. (2): 3372a (Agryle I), 3791.
Epim. Amphiaraia: 1055.
Ep. (2): 375, 3790.
Naop. Delphi: 1055.
Prop. (2): 1055, 1334.
Boul. (15): 171, 422, 442, 1055, 2146.
Upper: 87, 432, 1662, 2393, 2468,
3792.
Lower: 1045, 1734, 2369, 2776.

PHEGOUS (8)
Gr. Tam.: 2606.
Gr.: 3800a (Phegaia II).
Boul. (6): 811, 1171, 2031, 2243, 2960,
3802.

SYBRIDAI (4)
Tam.: 633.
Ep. mint: 3885.
Prop.: 3886.
Boul.: 1255.

538

THEMAKOS (6)

Hier.: 2564.
Boul. (5): 243, 1225, 2120, 2163, 3895.

Tribe II:
Aigeis (337)

TRIBE ONLY (12)

Pol.: 1959 (/IX).
S.: 752.
Tam. (4): 22, 2192 (/III), 2236, 2388.
Epim. dock.: 2331.
Prop. (2): 495 (/VI), 752.
Boul. (5): 246, 495 (/VI), 1324, 2271, 3297.

ANKYLE (10)

Hell.: 65.
Ep.: 1141.
Hier.: 1101 (boul.).
?: 3443.
Prop.: 716 (boul.).
Boul. (7): 716, 887, 1101, 1623(a), 1948,
    2279, 2785.

ARAPHEN (19)

Lochagos: 487.
Tam. (2): 622, 1658.
Hell.: 2041.
Epim. dock.: 135.
Env.: 492.
?: 3457.
Gr.: 2206.
Prop.: 2996 (boul.).
Boul. (11): 649, 993, 1243, 1386, 1535,
    1657, 2042, 2061, 2946, 2996, 3456.

BATE (9)

Gr. Tam.: 1861.
Tam. strat.: 1505.
Hell.: 390.
Prop.: 1725 (boul.).
Boul. (6): 126, 144, 1725, 1796, 1890,
    2658.

DIOMEIA (6)

Kategoros: 2816.
Gr.: 2993.
Prop.: 2184.
Boul. (3): 358, 949, 3069.

ERCHIA (37)

Bas.: 2927.
S. (2): 67, 3030.
Hipp. (2): 1700, 3500.

Tax.: 788.
Officer: 3030.
Tam. (4): 363, 473, 2557, 2626.
Gr. Tam. o.g.: 1110.
Tam. trir. funds: 249.
Poletes: 709.
Epim. dock.: 1285.
Ep.: 3501.
Hier.: 939.
Naop. Delphi: 3024 (/3025).
Askl.: 2332.
Syndikos: 709.
Env.: 3024.
Gr.: 2259.
Prop.: 546 (boul.).
Ass.: 269.
Boul. (17): 472, 529, 546, 557, 731, 866,
    1008, 1226, 1362, 1507, 1741, 2114,
    2525, 2566, 2885 (syllogeus), 3137,
    3499.

ERIKEIA (5)

Boul. (5): 565, 1009, 1441, 3502, 3503.

GARGETTOS (24)

S.: 3013 (/3011).
Hipp.: 1050.
Arch. Arkesine: 159.
Tam. (2): 3525, 3528.
Gr. Tam.: 1855.
Tam. o.g.: 2997.
Epim. Nikai etc.: 3526.
Gr. Ep.: 3020.
Hier.: 2832 (boul.).
Eispraktor: 159.
Env.: 159.
Prop. (2): 156, 159.
Ass.: 159.
Boul. (15): 159, 355, 742, 843 (syllogeus),
    960, 1181, 1649, 1714, 1919, 1929,
    1972, 2619, 2726, 2832, 3527.

HALAI (39)
(See also Halai II/VII at the end)

Par. A.: 2010.
S. (2): 2671, 2747.
Hipp.: 2671.
Tax.: 3092.
Tam. (2): 2009, 2671.
Tam. o.g.: 3544.
Askl.: 1177.
Epim. tribe (3): 145, 2353, 3546.
Dem. (3): 333, 1453, 1738.
Oath: 2671.
Boul. (26): 199, 222, 282, 561, 950, 1041,

1102, 1142, 1162, 1182, 1206, 1542,
1869, 2070, 2103, 2134, 2167, 2183,
2446, 2748, 3539, 3540, 3541, 3542,
3543, 3545.

HESTIAIA (4)
Ep. (2): 3559, 3560.
Hier.: 2593 (boul.).
Tam. tribe: 2593.
Prop.: 2558 (boul.).
Boul. (3): 2558, 2593, 2797.

IKARION (34)
S.: 303.
Phyl.: 2046.
Tam.: 2632.
Tam. o.g.: 1313.
Hell. (3): 951, 2368, 2513.
Epim. dock.: 1062.
Ep.: 3074.
Ep. Eleusis: 258.
Hier. (3): 453 (boul.), 3095 (boul.), 3569.
Tam. tribe: 1312.
Dem. (4): 2156, 3014, 3563, 3570.
Gr.: 3564.
Ep. nomothetai: 3567.
Prop.: 35 (boul.).
Boul. (17): 35, 178, 304, 356, 453, 1062,
1336, 2019, 2090, 2291, 2512, 2594,
3075, 3095 (syllogeus), 3565, 3566,
3568.

IONIDAI (6)
Tam. (2): 2412, 3571.
Hier.: 1953 (boul.).
Gr. (2): 689, 1583.
Boul. (4): 689, 1029, 1076, 1953.

KOLLYTOS (30)
A. 1408 (Cholargos v).
S. (2): 44, 3031.
Nauarchos: 3031 (/S.).
Tam. (2): 1190, 3601.
Gr. Tam.: 2005.
Tam. o.g.: 585.
Hell.: 3604.
Amph. Delos: 3031.
Naop. Delphi: 3025 (/3024).
Kategoros: 1437.
Syndikos: 1437.
Env. (4): 1437, 1581, 2871, 3031.
?: 2006.
Gr. (4): 44, 586, 734, 3605.
Prop. (3): 44, 1437 (boul. and other),
1581.

Ass. (2): 1437, 3031.
Boul. (15): 81, 105, 577, 1437, 2022,
2083, 2127, 2351, 2588, 3602, 3603,
3606, 3607, 3608, 3609.

KOLONOS (10)
S.: 2766.
Tam. (2): 2436, 2765.
Hell.: 2766.
Proboulos: 2766.
Hypogr.?: 1446.
Boul. (6): 163, 167, 735, 1545, 2392, 2889.

KYDANTIDAI (19)
A.: 489.
S. (3): 1157, 2116, 2560.
Tam. o.g.: 3619.
Tam. strat.: 2105.
Epim. Amphiaraia: 2105.
Ep. (2): 2117, 3618 (Kydathenaion III).
Hier. (2): 2105, 2661 (boul.).
Eleven: 863.
Zetetes: 863.
Env.: 2116.
Oath: 2116.
Prop. (2): 2116, 2560.
Ass.: 2116.
Boul. (11): 803, 1572, 2116, 2241, 2343,
2661, 2798, 2943, 3138, 3620
(Kydathenaion III), 3621.

MYRRHINOUTTE (4)
Hier.: 2959 (boul.).
Ep. nomothetai: 412 (Myrrhinous III).
Prop.: 90.
Boul. (2): 2095, 2959.

OTRYNE (7)
Hypogr. Ep.: 2646.
Gr.: 2260.
Boul. (5): 39, 318, 2373, 2647, 3740.

PHEGAIA (20)
Gr. Tam.: 1332 (Prasiai III).
Hier.: 2945 (boul.).
Amph. Delos: 2895.
Gr. (2): 3800 (Phegous I), 3801.
Boul. (16): 69, 70, 201, 232, 261, 383,
1559, 2173, 2319, 2576, 2674, 2715,
2792, 2910, 2945, 3799.

PHILAIDAI (17)
Hipp.: 2274.
Peripolarchos: 437.
Tam.: 3804.

Gr. Tam.: 711.
Hell.: 1339.
?: 2719.
Gr. (2): 2569, 3803.
Boul. (9): 187, 197, 901, 1236, 1245,
1862, 2244, 2334, 2684.

PLOTHEIA (5)
Gr. Poletai: 3836.
Hier.: 594 (boul.).
Boul. (4): 394, 594, 2577, 2911.

TEITHRAS (20)
Tam. (2): 3889, 3891.
Epim. dock.: 536.
Ep. (2): 1356 (Tyrmeidai VI/
Trikorynthos IX), 3888.
Hier.: 1568 (boul.).
Dem.: 1224.
Gr.: 1706.
Gr. demos: 215.
Anagrapheus: 455.
Boul. (12): 536, 785, 796, 1196, 1568,
1908, 2614, 3057, 3890, 3892, 3893,
3894.

Tribe III:
Pandionis (414)
TRIBE ONLY (10)
Tax.: 3170.
Tam. (5): 701, 2082, 2192 (/II), 2234,
2272 (/IV/V).
Hell.: 2485.
Gr.: 2088.
Boul. (3): 217, 2088, 2188(a).

ANGELE (19)
A.: 1503.
S.: 610.
Askl.: 1971.
Env.: 89.
Gr.: 850.
Boul. (14): 214, 1197, 1247, 1370, 1952,
1960, 1962, 2113, 2276, 2610, 2926,
3440, 3441, 3442.

KONTHYLE (7)
Tam.: 2027.
Boul. (6): 559, 782, 1363, 2215, 2644,
3614.

KYDATHENAION (93)
A.: 1168 (Kytherros III)
Thesm.: 1510.

Gr. A.: 2623.
S. (5): 138, 627, 834, 835, 1659.
Phyl. (2): 129, 1982.
Tax.: 1989.
Tam. (7): 139, 211, 481, 1294, 2059,
2827, 3622.
Gr. Tam.: 2503.
Tam. o.g. (2): 1249, 3636.
Tam. dock.: 1593.
Hell. (2): 897, 3623.
Poletes: 1066.
Epim. dock. (2): 251, 626.
Ep.: 3618a (Kydantidai II).
Gr. Ep.: 1080.
Ep. Braur.: 2047.
Gr. Ep. Eleusis: 2472.
Athl.: 2455.
Hier. (2): 1311 (boul.), 3637.
Amph. Delos: 3630.
Kataskopos: 1659.
Epim. tribe: 2145.
Tam.-Synegoros: 151.
Env. (2): 138, 139.
?: 3624.
Gr. (2): 373, 2059.
Tam. boule: 195.
Tam. dedication: 1689.
Prop. (2): 1119, 1659.
Ass. (2): 139, 1659.
Boul. (54): 151, 252, 334, 340, 391, 400,
409, 454, 708, 736, 737, 783, 784,
804, 844, 877, 898, 1084, 1311, 1409,
1447, 1456, 1476, 1659, 1660, 1701,
1786, 2043, 2261, 2356, 2410, 2473,
2653, 2659, 2762, 2767, 2773, 2821,
2850, 2904, 2957, 2958, 3625, 3626,
3627, 3628, 3629, 3620a (Kydantidai
II), 3631, 3632, 3633, 3634, 3635,
3638.

KYTHERROS (13)
A.: 1168 (Kydathenaion III).
S. (2): 259, 2035.
Pentekontarchos: 239.
Tam.: 3099.
Epim. tribe: 3639.
Gr.: 483.
Boul. (6): 368, 770, 851, 878, 1347, 2018.

MYRRHINOUS (50)
A.: 1875.
S.: 1213.
Tax./Phyl.: 3706.
Officer: 920.
Didask.: 3705.

Tam. (3): 86, 2777, 2846.
Tam. trir. funds: 1202.
Gr. Hell.: 3697.
Ep.: 3692.
Gr. Ep.: 1617.
Ep. Eleusis: 596.
Amph. Delos: 1202.
Askl.: 879.
Epim. tribe: 3709.
Env. (3): 920, 1210, 1965.
Gr. (2): 411, 833.
Ep. nomothetai: 412 (Myrrhinoutte II).
Prop. (3): 920 (boul. and other), 1210
    (boul. and other), 3693.
Boul. (31): 58, 230, 654, 714, 920, 1210,
    1251, 1270, 1557, 1876, 1927, 2099,
    2106, 2554, 2568, 2774, 3016, 3694,
    3695, 3696, 3698, 3699, 3700, 3701,
    3702, 3703, 3704, 3707, 3708, 3710,
    3711.

OA (27)

Tam.: 3713.
Gr. Tam.: 1944.
Tam. o.g.: 209.
Epim. dock. (2): 1513, 3717.
Tam. tribe: 3712.
Boul. (21): 121, 147, 179, 231, 748, 762,
    889, 1203, 1204, 1227, 1512, 1632,
    2277, 2782, 3032, 3714, 3715, 3716,
    3718, 3719, 3720.

PAIANIA (113)

S. (4): 174, 1516, 1613, 3745.
Par. S.: 2692.
Hipp.: 744.
Phyl. (4): 720, 725, 794, 1327.
Didask. (2): 1480, 3747.
Pentekontarchos: 3749.
Theorikon: 795.
Tam. (7): 85, 668, 1613, 2692, 2851,
    2882, 3753.
Gr. Tam.: 1332 (Phegaia II).
Tam. strat.: 717.
Hell.: 2599.
Poletes: 2891.
Fin.: 1614.
Epim. dock. (2): 2219, 3754.
Epim. Amphiaraia (2): 717, 1019.
Ep.: 3741.
Ep. navy: 795.
Ep. mint: 3743.
Ten: 2692.
Sitones: 795.
Teichopoios: 795.

Hier. (2): 717, 795.
Amph. Delos: 3746.
Pylag.: 795.
Askl.: 768.
Kategoros: 795.
Env. (4): 717, 795, 1200, 1613.
?: 3758.
Gr. (4): 174, 1516, 1613, 3745.
Anagrapheus: 3769.
Prop. (10): 717, 724, 767, 768, 795 (boul.
    and other), 1128, 1550, 1613 (boul.),
    1614 (boul. and other), 3750.
Ass. (4): 717, 724, 795, 1614.
Boul. (74): 92, 186, 336, 338, 519, 533,
    589, 611, 650, 686, 717, 757, 795,
    933, 941, 987, 1079, 1376, 1613,
    1614, 1883, 2118, 2242, 2324, 2406,
    2411, 2549, 2597, 2783, 2789, 2824,
    2908, 2917, 2944, 2970, 3005, 3051,
    3139, 3742, 3748, 3751, 3752, 3755,
    3756, 3760, 3762, 3763, 3765, 3766,
    3767, 3770, 3771, 3774.
Upper: 91, 291, 616, 662, 749, 852,
    1396, 1949, 2380, 2548, 2867, 3757,
    3759, 3761, 3764, 3768, 3772.
Lower: 846, 2016, 2822, 3773.

PRASIAI (22)

Hipp.: 2627.
Tam. (2): 1826, 3841.
Tam. o.g.: 1736.
Env.: 125.
Gr. (2): 2912, 3842.
Boul. (15): 415, 629, 1118, 1121, 1215,
    1322, 3061, 3062, 3072, 3843, 3844,
    3845, 3846, 3847, 3848.

PROBALINTHOS (33)

Thesm. (2): 202, 1113.
S.: 1358.
Theorikon: 1113.
Tam.: 3850.
Hell.: 2629.
Ep.: 2872.
Gr. Ep. (2): 2457, 3849.
Epim. tribe: 1924.
?: 992.
Prop.: 1113.
Ass.: 1113.
Boul. (23): 306, 324, 663, 999, 1000,
    1233, 1519, 1653, 1808, 1844, 1923,
    2013, 2175, 2536, 2571, 2596, 2677,
    2808, 2931, 2961, 3123, 3851,
    3852.

STEIRIA (27)

S. (3): 1333, 2982, 3033.
Epim. dock.: 2296.
Epim. mysteries: 1529.
Ep. Braur.: 1530.
Hier. Eleusis: 2148.
Thirty: 2982.
Proboulos: 1333.
Env.: 2982.
Oath: 1333.
?: 1530.
Anagrapheus: 1530.
Prop. (3): 1333, 3033, 3884.
Ass. (2): 2982, 3033.
Boul. (19): 53, 465, 632, 641, 712, 1366,
    1540, 1585, 1607, 1947, 2063, 2221,
    2819, 2919, 2971, 3150, 3881, 3882,
    3883.

Tribe IV:
Leontis (392)

TRIBE ONLY (33)

Thesm.: 3087 (/IX).
S.: 555.
Tam. (4): 2068, 2232, 2272 (/III/V), 2992.
Hell.: 1398.
Ep.: 2845.
Oath: 2062.
Prop.: 1304 (boul.).
Boul. (24): 496, 598, 984, 1304, 2811,
    2924, 3171, 3172, 3173, 3174, 3175,
    3176, 3177, 3178, 3179, 3180, 3181,
    3182, 3183, 3184, 3231, 3259, 3313,
    3345.

AITHALIDAI (10)

Tam.: 1100.
Hell.: 460.
Ep. Eleusis: 1100.
Plouton: 1082.
Epim. tribe: 3385.
Boul. (6): 1140, 1330, 1533, 1733, 2165,
    2984.

CHOLLEIDAI (16)

Bas.: 2452.
Tam. Paralou: 1930.
Tam.: 1544.
Gr. Hell.: 2830.
Ep. Braur.: 3475a (Cholargos v).
Gr. (2): 2182, 2305.
Tam. boule: 3478 (Paionidai IV).
Boul. (8): 95, 475, 638, 1040, 1235, 2100,
    2894, 3477.

DEIRADIOTAI (11)

S.: 2519.
Officer: 2585.
Arch. Oropos: 2585.
Epim. dock.: 346.
Epim. tribe: 599.
Katalogeus: 2585.
Env.: 2519.
Misc.: 2585.
Gr.: 2389.
Boul. (6): 42, 575, 1331, 1373, 3479, 3480.

EUPYRIDAI (13)

Tam.: 1479.
Hell.: 3523.
Amph. Delos: 3029.
Gr.: 2784.
Boul. (10): 256, 1005, 1727, 1840, 2126,
    2340, 2784, 2916, 3077, 3524.

HALIMOUS (22)

S.: 3052.
Tam. (2): 2168, 3555.
Gr. Tam.: 2101.
Gr. Hell.: 3556.
Naop. Delphi: 2111.
Dem. (3): 242, 1106, 1275.
Par. Dem.: 661.
Prop.: 1106 (boul.).
Boul. (14): 273, 497, 660, 1099, 1106,
    2104, 2168, 2608, 2934, 2954, 2990,
    3007, 3093, 3143.

HEKALE (4)

Boul. (4): 994, 2341, 2878, 3557.

HYBADAI (12)

Thesm.: 3561.
Gr. Hell.: 2781.
Tam. tribe: 2938.
?: 3562.
Boul. (9): 602, 645, 1439, 1762, 1841,
    2058, 2574, 2714, 2938.

KETTOS (17)

Gr. Tam.: 1218.
Ep. (2): 3598, 3599.
? (2): 1337, 3600.
Boul. (12): 109, 124, 191, 584, 781, 1111,
    1931, 1932, 2435, 2737, 2761, 2874.

KOLONAI (10)
(See also Kolonai IV/X at the end)

Tam. o.g.: 3611.
Epim. dock.: 2622.

Boul. (8): 184, 463, 1175, 1374, 1974, 2170, 2637, 3612.

KROPIDAI (4)
Tam. trir. funds: 1807.
Boul. (3): 938, 998, 2084.

LEUKONOION (24)
Thesm.: 3045.
Sophr.: 3053.
Tam.: 1915.
Gr. Tam.: 3046.
Syngr. Hell.: 2706.
Ep.: 3668.
Ep. mint (2): 3669, 3672.
Hier.: 3670.
Amph. Delos: 3671.
Epim. tribe: 2461.
Gr. (2): 1914, 2522.
Ass.: 743.
Boul. (10): 73, 435, 614, 646, 706, 864, 1525, 1538, 1835, 2974.

OION (10)
(See also Oion IV/VIII at the end)
Bas.: 1170.
Eleven: 3736.
Hier.: 1293.
Env.: 1323.
Gr.: 3737.
Boul. (5): 588, 685, 1305, 1631, 2333.

PAIONIDAI (20)
Gr. Hell.: 840.
Logistai (2): 298, 2313.
Ep.: 3776.
Ep. Eleusis: 116
Ep. Braur.: 2414.
Hier.: 2360 (boul.).
?: 3777.
Gr.: 3775.
Gr. boule and demos: 535.
Gr. boule: 2750.
Tam. boule: 3478a (Cholleidai IV).
Prop. (3): 299 (boul.), 535, 2360.
Boul. (9): 299, 1894, 1975, 2193, 2212, 2360, 2482, 2929, 3778.

PELEKES (13)
Tax./Phyl.: 210.
Tam. (2): 628, 655.
Logistes: 300.
Gr. Ep.: 3788.
Gr. Amph. Delos: 1967.
Env.: 300.

Prop.: 78.
Boul. (7): 79, 666, 1388, 2203, 2345, 2361, 3789.

PHREARRHIOI (74)
A.: 2901.
Par. A.: 500.
S. (3): 321, 2264, 2901.
Didask.: 2438.
Arch. fleet: 2264.
Tam. (2): 3815, 3824.
Gr. Tam.: 505.
Tam. o.g. (2): 3134 (a), 3827.
Poletes: 2978.
Epim. dock.: 1596(a).
Epim. revenues: 2901.
Ep.: 3814.
Ep. water supply: 2901.
Hypogr. Amph. Delos: 3817.
Gr. Naop. Delos: 1081.
Pylag.: 2901.
Askl.: 1813.
Env. (2): 2901, 3818.
?: 2900.
Gr. (4): 832, 865, 2264, 3830.
Prop. (4): 1979, 2901, 3487a (Eitea v), 3828.
Boul. (51): 154, 170, 233, 286, 322, 323, 424, 427, 723, 828, 868, 908, 1095, 1096, 1112, 1348, 1481, 1491, 1514, 1567, 1578, 1813, 1820, 1825, 1843, 1946, 2036, 2045, 2085, 2287, 2290, 2320, 2321, 2362, 2424, 2716, 2727, 2770, 2787, 2899, 3135, 3145, 3816, 3819, 3820, 3821, 3822, 3823, 3825, 3826, 3829.

POTAMOS (20)
S.: 1994.
Tam.: 746.
Tam. o.g.: 2861.
Gr. Ep. Eleusis: 122.
Prop.: 3839 (boul.).
Boul. (16): 234, 414, 909, 2497, 2742, 3839.
    Upper: 1365, 1661, 1763, 2214, 2892.
    Lower: 656, 758, 1056, 2394, 2488.

POTAMOS DEIRADIOTES (7)
Boul. (7): 2157, 2174, 2570, 2651, 2825, 2980, 3840.

SKAMBONIDAI (28)
A. (2): 255, 1515.
S. (7): 31, 84, 830, 1676 (Thria VI), 1705, 2177, 2678.

Hipp.: 830.
Phyl.: 830.
Hell. (2): 676, 3870.
Taktes: 84.
Gr. Amph. Delos: 847.
Dem.: 301.
Env.: 84.
Prop. (6): 83, 84, 525 (boul.), 830 (boul.),
    1636, 3869 (boul.).
Ass. (2): 31, 84.
Boul. (14): 203, 325, 326, 376, 525, 830,
    952, 1433, 1492, 1788, 1829, 2253,
    3869, 3871.

SOUNION (41)
S.: 910.
Sophr.: 2479.
Tam. Paralou: 1845.
Tam. (3): 620, 1350, 1355.
Gr. Tam. (2): 403, 3872.
Amph. Delos (2): 679, 2328.
Askl.: 2589.
Plouton: 1047.
Dem.: 2624.
Horistes: 3873.
Kleroucharchos: 1219.
Env. (3): 1214, 1360, 2282.
?: 2108.
Prop. (4): 911, 937, 1350, 1360.
Ass. (3): 1214, 1350, 1360.
Boul. (20): 80, 155, 517, 631, 903, 915,
    1020, 1675, 1715, 2147, 2462, 2551,
    2590, 2728, 2795, 3017, 3116, 3874,
    3875, 3876.

Tribe v:
Akamantis (260)
TRIBE ONLY (22)
Phyl.: 226.
Tax.: 28.
Tam. (3): 886 (/VI), 2231, 2272 (/III/IV).
Hier. (2): 538 (/X), 1418 (/X).
Oath: 3036.
Boul. (14): 24, 198, 980(a), 1234, 2110,
    2449, 2555, 2709, 2734, 2844, 3117,
    3185, 3306, 3330.

CHOLARGOS (16)
A.: 1408 (Kollytos II).
S. (4): 1419, 2293, 2294, 3128.
Tam.: 3476.
Hell.: 2294.
Par. Hell.: 2547.
Epim. Amphiaraia: 1611.

Ep. (2): 2293, 2976.
Ep. Braur.: 3475 (Cholleidai IV).
Athl.: 2293.
Kategoros: 2293.
Env.: 3128.
Gr.: 2547.
Prop. (4): 1419, 1611, 2292, 2293.
Ass.: 2293.
Boul. (5): 332, 1880, 2643, 2870, 3079.

EIRESIDAI (8)
Thesm.: 3485.
S.: 2810.
Tam.: 3484.
Gr.: 2391.
Boul. (4): 1506, 2390, 2953, 3486.

EITEA (4)
(See also Eitea V/X at the end)
Tam.: 3080.
Tam. trir. funds: 761.
Ep. Eleusis: 754.
Boul. (2): 754, 1646.

HAGNOUS (26)
S. (2): 1868, 2028.
Gr. Tam.: 2876.
Tam. o.g.: 2771.
Hell.: 1537.
Epim. springs: 1592.
Epim. dock.: 3529.
Ep.: 558.
Askl.: 1726.
Horistes: 3530 (boul.).
Env. (2): 813, 2434.
? (2): 2481, 3531.
Gr.: 2664.
Tam. boule: 959.
Prop.: 2434.
Ass.: 813.
Boul. (11): 381, 566, 1016, 1051, 1451,
    1547, 1767, 1878, 1980, 2794, 3530.

HERMOS (12)
Par. S.: 207.
Hipp.: 200.
Tax./Phyl.: 2955.
Gr. Tam.: 1612.
Hell.: 257.
Poletes: 3558.
Epim. dock.: 364.
Boul. (5): 624, 1094, 1117, 1522, 3130.

IPHISTIADAI (8)
Tam.: 2540.

Poletes: 399.
Ep. (2): 274, 3573.
Ep. Braur.: 3572.
Gr.: 3504a (Eroiadai VIII/X/Keiriadai
    VIII/Lakiadai VI).
Boul. (2): 928, 2051.

KEPHALE (30)

A.: 2081.
Thesm.: 430.
S. (3): 1801, 1802, 2859.
Tam. (4): 756, 2603, 2862, 3584.
Tam. o.g.: 2817.
Hell. (2): 3579, 3580.
Hier.: 3585.
Hier. Eleusis: 2979.
Gr. Amph. Delos: 2603.
Gr. Naop. Delos: 2402.
Askl.: 2858.
Tam.-Synegoros: 3582.
?: 3581.
Gr. (2): 421, 780.
Ass.: 1802.
Boul. (10): 37, 807, 1003, 1071, 1403,
    1407, 2401, 2467, 2620, 3583.

KERAMEIS (34)

A.: 802.
S. (2): 1300, 1776.
Hipp./Phyl.: 2220.
Phrourarchos: 1314.
Tam. (4): 1098, 1399, 3591, 3593.
Tam. o.g.: 2553.
Hell.: 3592.
Gr. Hell.: 2639.
Thirty: 2288.
Epim. dock.: 2413.
Ep.: 408.
Amph. Delos: 876.
Askl.: 146.
Dem.: 3594.
Horistes: 1420.
Syndikos: 1603.
Env. (3): 157, 1603, 2220.
? (2): 3070, 3595.
Prop. (3): 1603, 2612, 3574a (Kedoi I/
    Xypete VII).
Ass.: 1603.
Boul. (9): 1148, 1167, 1509, 1973, 2315,
    2969, 3113, 3596, 3597.

KIKYNNA (6)

Prop. (2): 1194 (Kephisia I), 2240
    (Kephisia I).
Boul. (4): 827, 1195, 1523, 2115.

POROS (10)

Tam.: 814.
Tam.-Synegoros: 3838.
Env.: 1371.
Prop.: 3837.
Boul. (6): 1454, 2023, 2439, 2823, 2826,
    3027.

PROSPALTA (24)

Tam. (3): 2395, 2581, 3859.
Gr. Tam.: 1271.
Tam. o.g.: 687.
Ep. mint: 3857.
Amph. Delos: 307.
Askl.: 123.
?: 3853.
Boul. (15): 158, 284, 836, 1046, 1176,
    1404, 2075, 2176, 2562, 3102, 3854,
    3855, 3856, 3858, 3860.

SPHETTOS (28)

S. (4): 1131 (Kephisia I), 2306, 3055,
    3056.
Arch. Andros: 3067.
Fin. administrator: 3141.
Theorikon: 921.
Tam.: 3054.
Hell. (2): 130, 3879.
Logistes: 3067.
Exetastes: 3067.
Thirty: 130.
Epim. Amphiaraia: 3056.
Hier.: 573 (boul.).
Gr. Amph. Delos: 2854.
Dem. (2): 223, 3877.
Env. (3): 1702, 2563, 3067.
?: 2119.
Gr.: 106.
Prop. (7): 726 (boul.), 911, 921 (boul. and
    other), 1133 (boul.), 2563 (boul. and
    other), 3067 (boul. and other), 3880.
Ass.: 3067.
Boul. (12): 507, 573, 726, 921, 1133,
    1254, 2425, 2563, 3028, 3067, 3083,
    3878.

THORIKOS (32)

Bas./Pol./Thesm.: 520.
Par. A.: 425.
S. (3): 1279, 1576, 1907.
Tax.: 1911.
Kosmetes: 521.
Tam.: 111.
Tam. dock.: 1907.

Hell.: 3047.
Epim. dock.: 1729.
Ep.: 3899.
Gr. Ep. (2): 1032, 3898.
Gr. Ep. Eleusis: 3006.
Ep. Braur.: 1569.
Amph. Delos: 2137 (Thorai x).
Dem. 1881.
Env.: 520.
?: 1846.
Gr.: 2489.
Prop. (2): 1279, 1569 (boul.).
Ass. (2): 520, 1910.
Boul. (14): 188, 456, 902, 1143, 1328,
    1546, 1569, 2025, 2189, 2738, 3006,
    3900, 3901, 3902.

Tribe VI:
Oineis (278)
TRIBE ONLY (28)
S. (3): 644, 2020, 3339.
Tax.: 1698.
Tam. (2): 886 (/v), 2235.
Thirty: 644.
Zetetes: 644.
Prop.: 495 (/II).
Boul. (22): 23, 495 (/II), 621, 1178, 1288,
    1329, 1756, 2024, 2533, 2923, 3186,
    3187, 3188, 3189, 3190, 3191, 3192,
    3193, 3194, 3195, 3196, 3298.

ACHARNAI (109)
A. (2): 1867, 2793.
S. (9): 637, 713, 1060, 1562, 1601, 1638,
    1645, 1672, 3097.
Tax./Phyl.: 3050.
Kosmetes: 3365.
Tam. (14): 665, 715, 855, 1174, 2144,
    2325, 2587, 3349, 3350 (Aixone VII/
    Athmonon VII), 3351, 3352, 3354,
    3357, 3369.
Gr. Tam. (2): 1109, 3355.
Tam. o.g.: 3368.
Hell. (2): 896, 1065.
Gr. Hell.: 2989.
Epim. (2): 2129, 2471 (boul.).
Epim. dock. (2): 815, 855.
Epim. Amphiaraia: 3040.
Ep.: 2281.
Gr. Ep. (2): 1562, 3366.
Ep. Eleusis: 2950.
Ep. Braur.: 1852.
Hier. Eleusis: 777.
Hier. Delphi: 3088.

Amph. Delos (3): 1444, 2669, 3363.
Askl.: 2947.
Tam.-Synegoros: 3353.
Zetetes: 2281.
Syndikos: 1781.
Oath: 2925.
Env. (5): 1781, 2297, 3132, 3358, 3367.
? (2): 2034, 3364.
Gr. (7): 466, 510, 580, 1872, 2735, 3109,
    3356 (Amphitrope x).
Tam. boule: 2791.
Prop. (6): 279 (boul.), 777, 1602 (boul.),
    1672, 2281 (boul. and other), 2866
    (boul. and other).
Ass. (2): 1672, 2281.
Boul. (47): 173, 279, 316, 490, 501, 509,
    530, 612, 684, 759, 790, 873, 946,
    1052, 1053, 1127, 1139, 1191, 1201,
    1299, 1563, 1570, 1602, 1609, 1823,
    2154, 2210, 2216, 2281, 2318, 2327,
    2378, 2441, 2464, 2471, 2631, 2652,
    2668, 2754, 2866, 2869, 3043, 3073,
    3359, 3360, 3361, 3362.

BOUTADAI (7)
S.: 1831.
Fin. administrator: 1832.
Gr. Tam.: 2056.
Hell.: 3023.
Epim. dock.: 2936.
Epim. Amphiaraia: 1832.
Hier.: 1832.
Kategoros: 1832.
Env.: 1832.
Various: 1832.
Prop.: 1832 (boul. and other).
Ass.: 1832.
Boul. (3): 1832, 2087, 2403.

EPIKEPHISIA (4)
?: 1155.
Boul. (3): 1536, 1650, 2453.

HIPPOTOMADAI (2)
Ep. Eleusis: 1963.
Boul.: 2300.

KOTHOKIDAI (14)
S.: 2405.
Theorikon: 271.
Tam.: 2986.
Tam. o.g.: 1892.
Gr. Poletai: 1286.
Epim. dock.: 2014.
Ep.: 1277.

Pylag.: 51.
Askl.: 367.
Env. (2): 51, 271.
Gr. (2): 51, 271.
Hypogr. (2): 51, 271.
Ass.: 51.
Boul. (5): 1083, 2928, 3041, 3108, 3616.

LAKIADAI (17)
A.: 2003.
S. (4): 1619, 1766, 2003, 2818.
Hipp.: 1766.
Sophr.: 681.
Tam.: 464.
Gr. Tam.: 3640.
Poletes: 1301.
Ep. mint: 3643.
Oikistes: 2004.
Env. (2): 1618, 1619.
Gr.: 3504c (Eroiadai VIII/X/Iphistiadai V/
    Keiriadai VIII).
Prop. (3): 1310, 1619, 3642 (boul.).
Boul. (4): 448, 771, 3641, 3642.

LOUSIA (3)
Naop. Delphi: 1169.
Kleroucharchos: 1169.
Boul. (2): 2205, 2977.

OE (30)
S. (4): 1566, 1770, 2077, 3125.
Hipp.: 1566.
Phyl.: 3726.
Tam. (3): 1945, 1993, 3721.
Epim. dock.: 1983.
Amph. Delos (2): 2940, 3730.
Plouton: 185.
Horistes: 374.
Oath: 1770.
Env. (3): 996, 1770, 2077.
Gr. (2): 38, 1566.
Prop. (2): 2077, 2940 (boul.).
Boul. (16): 275, 615, 997, 1199, 1732,
    2218, 2565, 2575, 2940, 3722, 3723,
    3724, 3725, 3727, 3728, 3729.

PERITHOIDAI (21)
S. (2): 1436, 2349.
Peripolarchos: 3140.
Tam.: 3795.
Tam. o.g. (2): 2213, 2262.
Hell.: 52.
Epim. dock. (2): 164, 3068.
Ep. Eleusis: 2556.
Hier.: 3794.

Hieromn.: 1436.
Horistes: 1302.
Prop. (2): 1342 (boul.), 1436 (boul. and
    other).
Boul. (11): 253, 763, 1070, 1320, 1342,
    1436, 1526, 2029, 2786, 3140, 3793.

PHYLE (14)
Thesm.: 1253.
S.: 2763.
Tam.: 3832.
Hell.: 3831.
Gr. Hell.: 707.
Epim. Amphiaraia: 2763.
?: 1896.
Gr.: 3833.
Boul. (7): 1129, 1130, 2350 (Thria VI),
    2376, 2758, 2999, 3059.

PTELEA (3)
Tam. o.g.: 2262 (Perithoidai VI).
Hier.: 285 (boul.).
Boul. (2): 285, 882.

THRIA (25)
S.: 1676 (Skambonidai IV).
Hipp.: 175.
Hipp. Lemnos: 2346.
Phyl.: 2346.
Tam. (6): 825 (Phyla VII), 2363, 2470,
    2546, 2932, 3903.
Gr. Ep.: 3906.
Horistes: 3905 (boul.).
Prop.: 3904.
Boul. (14): 181, 343, 1186, 1673, 1677,
    1920, 2078, 2079, 2149, 2350 (Phyle
    VI), 2855, 2934, 3136, 3905.

TYRMEIDAI (1)
Ep.: 1356 (Teithras II/Trikorynthos IX).

Tribe VII:
Kekropis (216)
TRIBE ONLY (14)
Tax.: 3311.
Tam. (3): 702 (a), 849 (/VIII), 2531.
Boul. (10): 1183, 1384, 1431, 1744, 1991,
    2089, 2096, 2201, 3126, 3197.

AIXONE (28)
S. (7): 556, 936, 1760, 1761, 1933, 2450,
    2630.
Tax.: 1759.
Officer: 1761.

Ship commander: 1549.
Tam. (3): 511, 3350a (Acharnai VI/
  Athmonon VI), 3390.
Hell.: 3387.
Gr. Hell.: 3386.
Epim. dock.: 2915.
Ep. Braur.: 1281.
Dem. (3): 791, 947, 2480.
Oath: 1761.
Env.: 1933.
?: 3389.
Ep. nomothetai: 1970.
Prop. (2): 1761, 1933 (boul.).
Ass. (2): 936, 1933.
Boul.(8): 292, 595, 1777, 1933, 2432,
  3019, 3388, 3391.

ATHMONON (23)
Sophr.: 32.
Tam. Paralou (2): 1346, 1688.
Tam. (2): 3350b (Acharnai VI/Aixone
  VII), 3462.
Gr. Tam. (2): 1283, 2017.
Tam. o.g.: 461.
Par. Hell.: 1391.
Epim. dock. (2): 1237, 3467.
Ep.: 2125.
Dem.: 3463.
Laws: 986.
Boul. (9): 317, 652, 1504, 1928, 2162,
  2725, 3464, 3465, 3466.

DAIDALIDAI (3)
Tam.: 2704.
Hell.: 623.
Boul.: 2254.

EPIEIKIDAI (2)
Thesm.: 1668.
Amph. Delos: 2998 (Alopeke x).

HALAI (16)
(See also Halai II/VII at the end)
Tam.: 1943.
Poletes: 1207.
Epim. dock.: 1067.
Amph. Delos: 2151.
Dem. (2): 2166, 2367.
Boul. (10): 488, 1797, 3547, 3548, 3549,
  3550, 3551, 3552, 3553, 3554.

MELITE (32)
S. (3): 196, 1159, 3144.
Hipp.: 3144.
Tam. (3): 3678, 3686, 3689.

Tam. o.g.: 2071.
Tam. rigging: 402.
Hell. (3): 498, 3679, 3681.
Gr. Hell.: 607.
Epim. dock. (2): 1359, 2604.
Ep. (2): 474, 2094.
Hier.: 2094.
? (2): 1238, 1893.
Gr. boule and demos: 942.
Tam. boule: 858.
Prop. (2): 196, 3688.
Boul. (11): 499, 1833, 2247, 3680, 3682,
  3683, 3684, 3685, 3687, 3690,
  3691.

PHLYA (44)
A.: 964.
S. (4): 320, 560, 1652, 2676.
Tax.: 541.
Tam. (11): 148, 262, 319, 825 (Thria VI),
  883, 891, 1775, 1977 (Pithos VII),
  2303, 2374, 3810.
Gr. Tam.: 2939.
Tam. o.g.: 3805.
Tam. two goddesses: 1616.
Hell. (2): 2802, 3809.
Epim. dock.: 268.
Ep.: 2675.
Ep. Eleusis (2): 2580, 2860.
Ep. mint: 3813.
Amph. Delos: 3808.
Plouton: 541.
Env.: 3806.
?: 384.
Gr. (2): 1595, 2541.
Prop. (2): 320, 604.
Boul. (11): 149, 360, 438, 745, 1093,
  1976, 2135, 3082, 3807, 3811, 3812.

PITHOS (12)
Tam. (4): 270, 1977 (Phlya VII), 2267,
  3834.
Ep. (2): 881, 2724.
Theoros: 150.
?: 3835.
Gr.: 1853.
Boul. (3): 593, 605, 1087.

SYPALETTOS (10)
Ep. Eleusis: 1773.
Gr. Ep. Eleusis: 1737.
Naop. Delos: 3887.
Prop.: 180 (boul.).
Boul. (7): 180, 503, 853, 859, 1877, 2788,
  2863.

TRINEMEIA (3)

S.: 426.
Tax.: 426.
Oath: 426.
Prop.: 1558 (boul.).
Boul. (2): 674, 1558.

XYPETE (29)

Tam. (2): 1280, 3913.
Gr. Tam.: 805.
Hell. (2): 3912, 3919.
Poletes: 189.
Epim. dock.: 2598.
Ep.: 3911.
Hier.: 524 (boul.).
Hier. Eleusis: 3914.
Amph. Delos: 2775.
Askl.: 2427.
Thirty: 2935a.
Gr. (2): 2605, 3920.
Prop.: 3574b (Kedoi I/Kerameis v).
Boul. (14): 54, 524, 2458, 2520, 3002,
    3915, 3916, 3917, 3918, 3921, 3922,
    3923, 3924, 3925.

Tribe VIII:
Hippothontis (190/191)

TRIBE ONLY (21)

S.: 3274.
Phyl.: 2667.
Tax./Phyl.: 636.
Tam. (4): 227, 823, 849 (/VII), 1037.
Gr. Tam.: 2528.
Hell.: 982.
Oath: 1445.
Boul. (11): 1591, 2143(a), 2230, 2400,
    3071, 3223, 3253, 3254, 3255, 3333,
    3347.

ACHERDOUS (8)

S.: 3011 (/3013).
Tam.: 3011.
Hell. (2): 3370, 3371.
Plouton: 2650.
Ten: 2337.
Gr. (2): 1126, 2640.
Ass.: 2238.

ANAKAIA (16)

Tam.: 1489.
Tam. o.g.: 3419.
Hell.: 3417.
Epim. dock.: 2538.

?: 1282.
Boul. (12): 59, 141, 372, 406, 1282, 1287,
    1517, 2444, 2451, 3021, 3022, 3418.

AURIDAI (4)

Hell.: 3468.
Hier.: 113 (boul.).
Boul. (3): 113, 1839, 3469.

AZENIA (14)

Par. A.: 462.
S.: 462.
Tam.: 433.
Ep.: 3473.
Syndikos: 462.
Env.(3): 462, 800, 2312.
Gr.: 1284.
Prop. (2): 462, 3470.
Ass.: 462.
Boul. (7): 55, 434, 452, 1325, 2801, 3471,
    3472.

DEKELEIA (14)

S. (3): 366, 2191, 2756.
Didask.: 3483.
Tam. (4): 1326, 2476, 3481, 3482.
Plouton: 3044.
?: 677.
Prop.: 2191.
Boul. (4): 194, 1477, 1556, 1925.

ELAIOUS (4)

Tam. o.g.: 2121.
Epim. dock.: 359.
Boul. (2): 1571, 2122.

ELEUSIS (36)

A.: 1105.
Par. A.: 837.
S.: 1746.
Tax.: 3076.
Tam. Paralou: 2202.
Tam. (2): 818, 3490.
Gr. Tam. (3): 601, 2607, 3496.
Tam. o.g.: 2492.
Gr. Tam. o.g.: 3489.
Hell.: 3494.
Gr. Hell.: 2759.
Epim. dock. (2): 1757, 3497.
Hier.: 3091.
Askl. (2): 1232, 2266.
Dem.: 1309.
Tam.-Synegoros: 3491.
Env. (2): 1105, 2896.
? (2): 2487, 3492.

Gr. (2): 248, 1074.
Prop. (2): 2048, 3495.
Ass.: 2048.
Boul. (8): 905, 1268, 2493, 2494, 2780,
    3037, 3493, 3498.

EROIADAI (4)
(See also Eroiadai VIII/X at the end)
S. (2): 2422, 3507.
Hipp.: 2422.
Kosmetes: 2422.
Prop.: 2422.
Boul. (2): 659, 1028.

HAMAXANTEIA (5)
Tam.: 407.
Logistes: 732 (732a).
Boul. (3): 47, 824, 3118.

KEIRIADAI (9)
Pol.: 45.
S.: 2239.
Hipp.: 2239.
Tam. o.g.: 3578.
Gr.: 3504b (Eroiadai VIII/X/Iphistiadai V/
    Lakiadai VI).
Boul. (5): 1150, 1377, 2169, 2636,
    3577.

KOILE (14)
S. (4): 347, 733, 1765, 1997.
Tam.: 1830.
Tam. o.g.: 2849.
Fin.: 1810.
Ep.: 838.
Ep. Eleusis: 77.
Amph. Delos: 1030.
Askl.: 351.
Syndikos: 1810.
Horistes: 995.
Env. (2): 1765, 2454.
Prop. (3): 347, 995, 1810.
Ass. (2): 347, 1810.
Boul. (2): 995, 1393.

KOPROS (9)
Hell. (2): 1033, 2886.
Epim. dock.: 2903.
Boul. (6): 1107, 1125, 2171, 2379, 3148,
    3615.

OINOE (6)
(See also Oinoe VIII/IX at the end)
Tam. (2): 2054, 3731.
Epim. dock. (2): 393, 413.

Dem.: 2011.
Gr.: 2323.

OION (3/4)
(See also Oion IV/VIII at the end)
Thesm.: 3738.
Gr. (2): 2246(a), 3739.
Prop.: 2246 (boul. and other).
Boul.: 2246.

PEIRAIEUS (15)
S.: 1771.
Tam. (3): 899, 1774, 3787.
Gr. Tam.: 867.
Hell. (2): 2348, 3784.
Poletes: 1606.
Ep.: 516.
Ep. Eleusis: 3786.
Kataskopos: 2930.
Gr. (2): 1025, 3785.
Prop. (2): 471, 1160.

THYMAITADAI (8)
Gr. Tam.: 43.
Hell. (3): 1901, 3907, 3908.
Epim. Amphiaraia: 2322.
Hier.: 2322.
Prop.: 2322 (boul. and other).
Boul. (4): 107, 985, 2322, 2586.

Tribe IX:
Aiantis (167)
TRIBE ONLY (27)
Pol.: 1959 (/II).
Thesm.: 3087 (/IV).
S. (2): 3033, 3120.
Tax.: 1138.
Toxarchos: 1457.
Tam.: 1474 (/X).
Hell.: 2198.
Epim. dock.: 700.
Ep.: 2942.
Epim. tribe (3): 115, 117, 1089(a).
Oath: 3086.
?: 895.
Boul. (12): 388, 537, 981, 1574, 1691,
    2233, 2357, 2463, 2893, 3247, 3309,
    3334.

APHIDNA (44)
Pol.: 1534.
Thesm.: 1115.
S. (4): 792, 1564, 1610, 2642.
Theorikon: 1610.

Tam. (7): 567, 753(a), 2339, 2433, 2739,
   3448, 3454.
Gr. Tam. (4): 281, 1811, 3450, 3453.
Tam. o.g.: 919.
Tam. trir. funds: 2573.
Tam. two goddesses: 1478.
Hell. (3): 1205, 2641, 3449.
Epim.: 1248 (boul.).
Epim. mysteries: 1248.
Ep. (2): 119, 1564.
Gr. Ep.: 1115.
Ep. mint: 3455.
Eleven: 2298.
Thirty: 955.
Hier. (2): 1039 (boul.), 1630.
Amph. Delos: 441.
Naop. Delos: 350.
Epim. tribe: 3090.
Dem.: 2539.
Tam.-Synegoros: 3452.
Oath: 792.
Env. (2): 963, 1564.
?: 3444.
Gr. (3): 2611, 3445, 3451.
Prop. (4): 730 (boul.), 955, 1564, 1610.
Ass. (2): 760, 1564.
Boul. (5): 730, 1039, 1248, 3446, 3447.

MARATHON (26)
Hipp.: 1594.
Tax./Phyl.: 1669.
Tax.: 3675.
Tam. (4): 831, 1565, 2372, 3673.
Tam. o.g.: 544.
Hell. (2): 56, 2447.
Logistai (2): 297, 2186.
Epim. dock.: 3114.
Ep. Eleusis: 2283.
Amph. Delos: 208.
Env.: 467.
? (3): 545, 721, 3674.
Gr.: 2158.
Decrees: 1713.
Prop. (2): 444, 467.
Boul. (4): 1354, 2098, 3676, 3677.

OINOE (8)
(See also Oinoe VIII/IX at the end)
Sophr.: 1018.
Gr. Tam.: 2985.
Hier. (3): 640 (boul.), 2278 (boul.), 2526
   (boul.).
Epim. tribe (2): 2128, 2583.
Prop.: 2526 (boul.).
Boul. (4): 640, 2278, 2526, 2732.

PHALERON (26)
S.: 740.
Hipp.: 740.
Pentekontarchos: 3797.
Tam. (2): 816, 2107.
Tam. rigging: 260.
Hell. (2): 423, 3798.
Epim. dock.(2): 2354, 2423.
Athl.: 3796.
Thirty: 1173.
Epim. tribe: 890.
Dem.: 1987.
Kategoros: 1406.
Env.: 740.
Gr. (2): 603, 2030.
Boul. (11): 365, 502, 539, 739, 900, 1090,
   1161, 1527, 1528, 2456, 2499.

RHAMNOUS (30)
Thesm.: 2875.
S. (3): 1449, 1969, 2407.
Tam. (4): 678, 764, 3863, 3865(a).
Tam. o.g. (2): 254, 3146.
Hell.: 491.
Gr. Hell.: 3862.
Epim.: 592 (boul.).
Epim. dock. (2): 1879, 3096.
Dem. (5): 506, 772, 1088, 2032, 2080.
Env. (2): 1448, 2523.
?: 3866.
Gr. (2): 1185, 3861.
Gr. demos: 657.
Prop. (2): 1400 (boul.), 3867.
Ass.: 2523.
Boul. (4): 592, 1400, 2131, 3864.

TRIKORYNTHOS (6)
Gr. Tam.: 3910.
Ep.: 1356 (Teithras II/Tyrmeidai VI).
Ep. Eleusis: 931.
Askl.: 1902.
?: 3909.
Boul.: 266.

Tribe x:
Antiochis (284)
TRIBE ONLY (17)
Sophr.: 26 (/I).
Tam. (3): 1021, 1474 (/IX), 2843.
Hier. (2): 538 (/V), 1418 (/V).
Oath: 1795.
?: 63.
Boul. (9): 1389, 1475, 1555, 2700, 2820,
   3198, 3199, 3204, 3229.

AIGILIA (16)

S.: 817.
Tax.: 3383.
Tam. (2): 3380, 3381.
Gr. Tam.: 1027.
Tam. o.g.: 1889(a).
Gr. Amph. Delos: 3384.
Hypogr. Amph. Delos: 1860.
Oath: 3382.
Gr.: 1678.
Boul. (6): 296, 389, 1272, 1699, 1703,
2311.

ALOPEKE (78)

A.: 371.
Par. Bas.: 2133.
S. (6): 371, 874, 1426, 1502, 2755, 3012.
Phyl.: 727.
Officer: 1426.
Tam. (5): 1340, 1382, 1779, 2730,
3399.
Gr. Tam.: 1918.
Tam. o.g.: 512.
Tam. two goddesses: 2160.
Hell. (2): 2314, 3397.
Logistes: 218.
Epim. dock.(2): 1805, 3408.
Epim. revenues: 371.
Epim. springs: 2657.
Epim. Lemnos: 2951.
Gr. Ep. Eleusis: 1335.
Athl.: 2273.
Hier. Eleusis (2): 766, 3394.
Amph. Delos (4): 2251, 2298 (Epieikidai
VII), 3393, 3401.
Arch. Salamis: 3111.
Env. (7): 371, 1501, 1502, 1917, 1918,
1941, 3395.
Gr. (7): 331, 769, 1426, 1739, 2805, 3392,
3402.
Gr. boule: 213.
Prop. (5): 371, 1385 (boul.), 1411 (boul.),
2906, 3396 (boul.).
Boul. (35): 140, 206, 247, 272, 522, 564,
581, 779, 857, 912, 1061, 1385, 1411,
1427, 1656, 1722, 1815, 1940, 2155,
2365, 2486, 2529, 2656, 2743, 2906,
2968, 2995, 3396, 3398, 3400, 3403,
3404, 3405, 3406, 3407.

AMPHITROPE (6)

Ep.: 1022.
Naop. Delphi: 1246.
Gr.: 3356a (Acharnai VI).

Boul. (3): 64, 349, 875.

ANAPHLYSTOS (69)

A.: 2421.
S. (5): 513, 1686, 1687, 3112, 3124.
S./Nauarchos: 1686.
Tax./Phyl.: 2371.
Tam. (3): 161, 241, 3425.
Gr. Tam.: 1217.
Tam. o.g.: 93.
Tam. trir. funds: 3426.
Hell.: 3424.
Gr. Hell.: 1073.
Poletes: 2130.
Ep.: 3420.
Ep. mint: 3421.
Ep. Eleusis: 1086.
Gr. Ep. Braur.: 2195.
Amph. Delos: 569(a).
Hieromn.: 862.
Epim. tribe: 3439.
Oath: 3422.
Env. (2): 1686, 2649.
Gr.: 1961.
Antigrapheus: 2534.
Prop. (2): 2649, 2670.
Ass. (2): 2649, 3112.
Boul. (41): 41, 280, 477, 504, 582, 728,
729, 842, 953, 1038, 1064, 1077,
1154, 1390, 1620, 1654, 1743, 1745,
1764, 2072, 2275, 2355, 2466, 2490,
2491, 2691, 2887, 2920, 3423, 3427,
3428, 3429, 3430, 3431, 3432, 3433,
3434, 3435, 3436, 3437, 3438.

ATENE (12)

Tam. (2): 1208, 2952.
Gr. Tam.: 2579.
Ep. Braur.: 1679.
Gr. (2): 2074, 3458.
Boul. (6): 385, 1192, 1308, 3459, 3460,
3461.

BESA (6)

Thesm.: 1719.
Tam. (2): 1392, 3474.
Hell.: 1069.
Boul. (2): 377, 1615.

EITEA (5)
(See also Eitea V/X at the end)
Boul. (5): 66, 1405, 2199, 2746, 3488.

EROIADAI (5)
(See also Eroiadai VIII/X at the end)

Hell.: 3508.
Prop.: 2409.
Boul. (4): 166, 2409, 3509, 3510.

KOLONAI (10)
(See also Kolonai IV/X at the end)
Boul. (6): 219, 1024, 1163, 1184, 1440, 3613.

KRIOA (5)
Tam.: 250.
Ep.: 3617.
Eispraktor: 3094.
Prop. (2): 2559, 3094.
Boul.: 2956.

PALLENE (36)
A.: 2055.
Didask. (2): 590, 1787.
Ship commander: 1818.
Gr. Tam.: 1895.
Tam. o.g.: 597.
Tam. trir. funds: 2152.
Hell. (2): 2477, 3066.
Ep.: 1780.
Hier.: 2475 (boul.).
Amph. Delos (2): 1044, 3780.
Epim. tribe: 1670.
Env. (2): 1278, 3039.
? (2): 1223, 3779.
Gr. (3): 302, 2172, 2415.
Antigrapheus: 382.
Prop. (5): 1043, 1044 (boul.), 1278, 1428, 2478 (boul.).
Boul. (16): 293, 591, 1043, 1044, 1357, 1584, 1670, 1854, 2474, 2475, 2478, 2902, 2909, 2918, 3115, 3781.

SEMACHIDAI (3)
Boul. (3): 1682, 2396, 3868.

THORAI (20)
S. (3): 469, 956, 1644.
Tax.: 2615.
Nauarchos: 469.
Gr. Tam.: 2532.
Tam. trir. funds: 2335.
Hell.: 468.
Ep.: 3896.
Amph. Delos: 2137 (Thorikos V).
Thirty: 469.
Env.: 2178.

Prop.: 956.
Boul. (11): 543, 647, 648, 956, 1520, 1626, 2208, 2426, 2505, 2638, 3897.

Homonymous Demes
In Two Tribes

EITEA V/X (1)
Prop.: 3487 (Phrearrhioi IV).

EROIADAI VIII/X (5)
Par. Bas.: 2806.
Tam.: 3506.
Env.: 2806.
Gr. (2): 3504 (Iphistiadai V/Keiriadai VIII/Lakiadai VI), 3505.
Prop.: 2806.
Boul.: 1031.

HALAI II/VII (16)
A.: 2963.
Pol.: 806.
Gr. Tam. o.g.: 3533.
Gr. Hell.: 3532.
Ep.: 3537.
Gr. Ep.: 3538.
Gr. Ep. Eleusis: 2731.
Tam.-Synegoros: 3536.
?: 3535.
Gr. (4): 339, 1634, 2092, 3534.
Boul. (3): 1579, 1942, 2741.

KOLONAI IV/X (3)
Hier. Eleusis: 1711.
Amph. Delos: 3610.
Gr.: 1874.

OINOE VIII/IX (4)
Tam.: 1964.
Env.: 1865.
Gr.: 2524.
Boul.: 929.

OION IV/VIII (9)
Tam. (2): 1104, 2495.
Amph. Delos: 3733.
Pylag.: 3038.
Naop. Delphi: 1637.
Dem.: 2185.
Gr. boule and demos: 3735.
Prop.: 3734.
Boul.: 431.

Index III: Problematic Documents

Here I include inscriptional documents the date of which is dubious or debatable, where dates have been removed or assigned. There are two categories, decrees and documents used for placing officials, each indicating the inscription and the year or Appendix in which it will be found. I exclude those inscriptions which relate to priests of Asklepios and to Delphi, and those dealt with by Linders, *Artemis*, and Reinmuth.

A. 684–404

DECREES

IG i³ 9: 457.
    10: App. IV iii.
    11: 458.
    14: App. IV v.
    17: 451.
    21: 450.
    27: App. IV ix.
    28: App. IV x.
    31: App. IV xii.
    32: App. IV Tam. and xiii.
    34: 448.
    37: 447.
    39: 446.
    40: 446.
    41: 446.
    46: 444.
    52: 434.
    59: App. V i, ii.
    61: 430.
    62: 428.
    72: App. V vi, vii.
    89: App. V ix, x.
    91: App. V xi.
    93: 416.
    98: App. V xiii.
    100: 410.
    106: App. V xiv.
    112: 408.
    113: App. V xvii.
    114: 407.

    117: 407.
    123: 407.
    136: 413.
    177: App. V xxxii.
    179: App. V xxxiii.
    227: 424.
    1453: 449.

OTHER

IG i³ 265: 447.
    281: 430.
    282: 429.
    287: 418.
    376: 409.
    377: 407.
    411: 430 and App. V Misc.
    454: 445.
    455: 444.
    477: 406.
    507: 566.
    508: 558.
    509: 558.
    510: 550.
    511: App. IV Hipp.
    590: 550.
    1032: 405.
    1162: 448.
SEG 19.42: 413.
Insc. Délos 91: 413.
    92: 413.
Agora XVII.23: 410.

B. 403–322

DECREES

IG ii² 2: App. VI i.
 10: 401.
 16: 394.
 20: 394.
 21: 390.
 22: 390.
 36: 384.
 47: 355.
 61: App. VI xiii.
 85: App. VI xxv.
 97: 375.
 98: 375.
 102: 375.
 113: 362.
 118: 361.
 119: 364.
 120: 358, 353.
 124: 357.
 140: App. VI xxxviii.
 141: 364.
 145: App. VI xxvii.
 145.11ff.: 364, 359.
 147: 357.
 148: 356.
 149: App. VII i.
 150: 355.
 173: 376.
 179: App. VII xiv.
 190: 371.
 207: App. VII S. and xx.
 211: 348.
 214: 356.
 216 + 261 = 217: 365.
 222: 335.
 227: 342.
 230: 341.

 244: 337.
 248: 358.
 249: 350.
 263: App. VIII v.
 276: 337.
 332: 353.
 334: 336.
 341: see 333.
 360.28ff.: 329.
 363: 335.
 410: 335.
 420: 332.
SEG 16.45: 374.
 21.246: 359.
 21.288: 327.
 21.340: 323.
 32.86: 329.
Hesperia 1944, 229ff. (3): 357.
AE 1923, 36ff. (123): 369.

OTHER

IG ii² 175: App. VII Env.
 1442: 354.
 1544.30: 332.
 1604: 378.
 1609: 370.
 1673 + : 333.
 2824: 340.
IG xii 5, 714: 356.
 7, 5: 358, 357.
SEG 32.161: 402.
 32.239: App. VI Bas.
Hesperia 1935, 167 (28): 374.
 1938, 95 (15): 328.
 1940, 324f. (34): App. VII Tam.
 1946, 178 (25): App. IX Tam.
Agora xv.13: App. VII.
 xv. 39: 338.